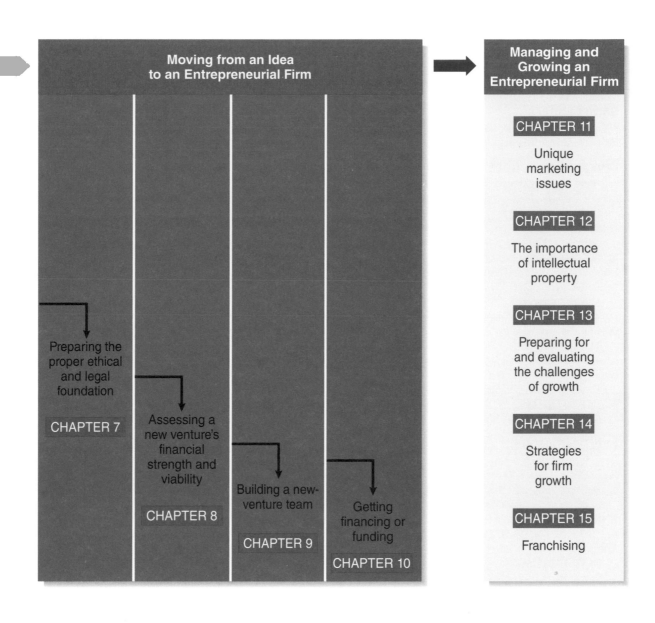

Moving from an Idea to an Entrepreneurial Firm

Preparing the proper ethical and legal foundation

CHAPTER 7

Assessing a new venture's financial strength and viability

CHAPTER 8

Building a new-venture team

CHAPTER 9

Getting financing or funding

CHAPTER 10

Managing and Growing an Entrepreneurial Firm

CHAPTER 11

Unique marketing issues

CHAPTER 12

The importance of intellectual property

CHAPTER 13

Preparing for and evaluating the challenges of growth

CHAPTER 14

Strategies for firm growth

CHAPTER 15

Franchising

Where a great idea meets a great process

Introducing the
Prentice Hall Entrepreneurship Series…

The Entrepreneurship Series by Prentice Hall is a compilation of brief, practical, and engaging titles that focus on the latest research findings, issues, and trends that guide successful entrepreneurs today. Written by experts of selected areas of entrepreneurship, each title is perfect for covering a special topic or to enhance your textbook material.

Series Editors

R. Duane Ireland, Mays Business School, Texas A&M University

Michael H. Morris, Department of Entrepreneurship, Spears School of Business, Oklahoma State University

Current Series Titles

Kathleen Allen, *Entrepreneurship for Scientists and Engineers*, ISBN 0-13-235727-5

Bruce R. Barringer, *Preparing Effective Business Plans: An Entrepreneurial Approach*,
    ISBN 0-13-231832-6

Arthur C. Brooks, *Social Entrepreneurship: A Modern Approach to Social Value Creation*,
    ISBN 0-13-233076-8

Jeffrey Cornwall, *Bootstrapping*, ISBN 0-13-604425-5

Daniel Davidson and Lynn Forsythe, *The Entrepreneur's Legal Companion*, ISBN 0-13-607723-4

Gerard George and Adam J. Bock, *Inventing Entrepreneurs: Technology Innovators and
    Their Entrepreneurial Journey*, ISBN 0-13-157470-1

Frank Hoy and Pramodita Sharma, *Entrepreneurial Family Firms*, ISBN 0-13-157711-5

Donald F. Kuratko and Jeffrey S. Hornsby, *New Venture Management: The Entrepreneur's Roadmap*,
    ISBN 0-13-613032-1

Jeffrey J. Reuer, Africa Ariño, and Paul M. Olk, *Entrepreneurial Alliances*, ISBN 0-13-615636-3

Minet Schindehutte, Michael H. Morris, and Leyland F. Pitt, *Rethinking Marketing*:
The Entrepreneurial Imperative, ISBN 0-13-239389-1

Donald F. Kuratko, Michael G. Goldsby, and Jeffrey S. Hornsby, *Innovation Acceleration: Transforming
    Organizational Thinking*, ISBN 0-13-602148-4

Future Titles in the Series*

James Davis, *Go to Market: What to do After the Business Plan is Written*, ISBN 0-13-606016-1

Thomas Dean, *Sustainable Venturing*, ISBN 0-13-604489-1

Alex DeNoble, Sanford B. Ehrlich, and Craig Galbraith, *Managing New Venture Growth
    in a Globally Connected World*, ISBN 0-13-800249-5

Jeff Shay and Siri Terjesen, *International Entrepreneurship*, ISBN 0-13-611964-6

Ray Smilor and John Eggers, *Entrepreneurial Leadership*, ISBN 0-13-603237-0

Jeffrey A. Stamp, *Bold Thinking for Entrepreneurs: Creating and Managing Ideas That Matter*,
    ISBN 0-13-611969-7

*We will be publishing new titles every year. Please visit www.pearsonhighered.com/ entrepreneurship for an up-to-date list.

Interested?
For more information on these titles or to request an examination copy for adoption consideration, please contact your local Pearson sales representative.

The Entrepreneurial Process

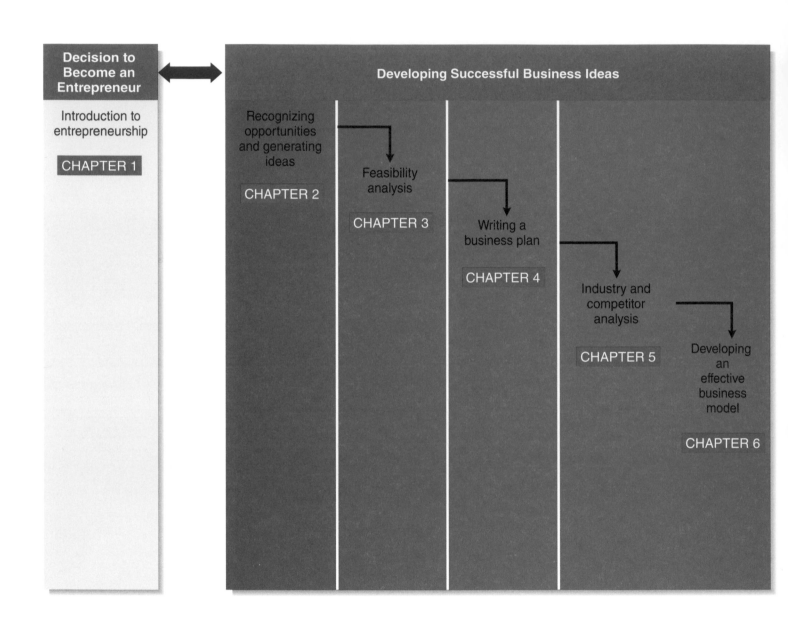

Decision to Become an Entrepreneur	Developing Successful Business Ideas
Introduction to entrepreneurship CHAPTER 1	Recognizing opportunities and generating ideas — CHAPTER 2 → Feasibility analysis — CHAPTER 3 → Writing a business plan — CHAPTER 4 → Industry and competitor analysis — CHAPTER 5 → Developing an effective business model — CHAPTER 6

Passion plus

Entrepreneurship

Successfully Launching New Ventures

Global Edition

Entrepreneurship

Success ... ntures

R. Duane Ireland
Texas A&M University

PEARSON

Boston   Columbus   Indianapolis   New York   San Francisco   Upper Saddle River
Amsterdam   Cape Town   Dubai   London   Madrid   Milan   Munich   Paris   Montreal   Toronto
Delhi   Mexico City   Sao Paulo   Sydney   Hong Kong   Seoul   Singapore   Taipei   Tokyo

Editorial Director: Sally Yagan
Senior Acquisitions Editor: Kim Norbuta
Senior Acquisitions Editor, Global Edition:
    Steven Jackson
Director of Editorial Services: Ashley Santora
Editorial Project Manager: Claudia Fernandes
Director of Marketing: Patrice Lumumba
    Jones
Executive Marketing Manager:
    Maggie Moylan
Assistant Marketing Manager: Ian Gold
Marketing Manager, International: Dean
    Erasmus
Senior Managing Editor: Judy Leale
Production Project Manager: Ann Pulido

Senior Operations Supervisor: Arnold Vila
Operations Specialist: Cathleen Petersen
Director of Design: Christy Mahon
Creative Art Director: Blair Brown
Senior Art Director: Kenny Beck
Interior Designer: LCI Design
Cover Designer: Jodi Notowitz
Cover Image: © Orlando Florin Rosu-
    Fotolia.com
Lead Media Project Manager: Lisa Rinaldi
Editorial Media Project Manager:
    Denise Vaughn
Full-Service Project Management:
    Sharon Anderson/Bookmasters, Inc.
Cover Printer: Courier/Kendallville

Pearson Education Limited
Edinburgh Gate
Harlow
Essex CM20 2JE
England

and Associated Companies throughout the world

Visit us on the World Wide Web at:
www.pearson.com/uk

© Pearson Education Limited 2012

ISBN–13: 978-0-27-376140-2
ISBN–10: 0-273-76140-4

British Library Cataloguing-in-Publication Data
A catalogue record for this book is available from the British Library

10 9 8 7 6 5 4 3 2 1
15 14 13 12 11

Typeset in 10.5/12, Times New Roman by Bookmasters
Printed and bound by Courier/Kendallville in The United States of America

The publisher's policy is to use paper manufactured from sustainable forests.

DEDICATION

To my wife Jan. Thanks for your never-ending encouragement and support. Without you, this book would have never been possible. Also, thanks to all the student entrepreneurs who contributed to the chapter opening features in the book. Your stories are both insightful and inspiring.

—Bruce R. Barringer

To my family: I am so proud of each of you and so blessed by your perseverance and never-ending love and support. I know that sometimes it seems as though "we lose ourselves in work to do and bills to pay and that it's a ride, ride, ride without much cover." But you are always in my heart, a gift for which I remain deeply grateful.

—R. Duane Ireland

BRIEF CONTENTS

CONTENTS

PART 4 Managing and Growing an Entrepreneurial Firm   381

PREFACE

INTRODUCTION

We are truly excited about the fourth edition of our book and the promise it brings to you. A key reason for this is that in many parts of the world, studying and practicing entrepreneurship are very exciting and potentially highly rewarding activities for entrepreneurs and the nations in which they launch their ventures and conduct their operations. In this sense then, across the world, even during what are challenging economic conditions on a global basis, entrepreneurial ventures are creating and bringing to market new products and services that make our lives easier, enhance our productivity at work, improve our health, and entertain us in new and fascinating ways. As you will see from reading this book, entrepreneurs are some of the most passionate and inspiring people you'll ever meet. This is why successful firms have been launched in a variety of unexpected places such as garages and an array of coffeehouses with wireless hot spots. Indeed, we never know the amount of success the person sitting next to us drinking coffee might achieve after launching an entrepreneurial venture!

As you might anticipate, the passion an entrepreneur has about a business idea, rather than fancy offices or other material things, is typically the number one predictor of a new venture's success. Conversely, a lack of passion often leads to entrepreneurial failure.

The purpose of this book is to introduce you, our readers and students of entrepreneurship, to the entrepreneurial process. We do this because evidence suggests that the likelihood entrepreneurs will be successful increases when they thoroughly understand the parts of the entrepreneurial process as well as how to effectively use those parts. The fact that in the United States alone roughly one-third of new firms fail within the first two years while another 20 percent fail within four years of their launching is the type of evidence we have in mind. These failure rates show that while many people are motivated to start new firms, motivation alone is not enough; indeed, motivation must be coupled with accurate and timely information, a solid business idea, an effective business plan, and sound execution to maximize chances for success. In this book, we discuss many examples of entrepreneurial ventures and the actions separating successful firms from unsuccessful ones.

This book provides a thoughtful, practical guide to the process of successfully launching and growing an entrepreneurial venture. To do this, we provide you with a thorough analysis of the entrepreneurial process. We model this process for you in the first chapter and then use the model's components to frame the book's remaining parts. Because of its importance, we place a special emphasis on the beginnings of the entrepreneurial process—particularly opportunity recognition and feasibility analysis. We do this because history shows that many entrepreneurial ventures struggle or fail not because the business owners weren't committed or didn't work hard, but because the idea they were pushing to bring to the marketplace wasn't the foundation for a vibrant, successful business.

WHAT IS NEW TO THIS EDITION?

We are committed to presenting you with the most up-to-date and applicable treatment of the entrepreneurial process available in the marketplace. While serving your educational interests, we want to simultaneously increase the likelihood that you will become excited by entrepreneurship's promise as you read and study current experiences of entrepreneurs and their ventures as well as the findings springing from academic research.

To verify currency, thoroughness, and reader interest, we have made several important changes, as presented next, while preparing this fourth edition of our book:

Opening Profile   Each chapter opens with a profile of an entrepreneurial venture. All 15 Opening Profiles (one for each chapter) are new to this edition. Each profile is specific to a chapter's topic. While reading each profile, imagine yourself in the role of one or more of the entrepreneurs who launched a venture.

Entrepreneurs' Insights   At the side of each Opening Profile, we present entrepreneurs' answers to a series of questions. In providing answers to these questions, the entrepreneurs who launched their venture express their perspectives about various issues. An important benefit associated with thinking about these responses is that those reading this book today have opportunities to see that they, too, may indeed have the potential to launch an entrepreneurial venture quicker than originally thought.

Updated Features   Almost every one of the "What Went Wrong?," "Savvy Entrepreneurial Firm," "Partnering for Success," and "You Be the VC" features are new to this edition. The very few features we did retain have been thoroughly updated. These features present you with contemporary issues facing today's entrepreneurial ventures. The "You Be the VC" features, for example, allow readers to decide if the potential of a proposed entrepreneurial venture is sufficient to warrant funding.

New and Updated Cases   Virtually all of the pairs of end-of-chapter cases are new to this edition. Those retained have been completely updated. Comprehensive in nature, we wrote these cases with the purpose of presenting readers with opportunities to use chapter-specific concepts to identify problems and propose solutions to situations facing actual entrepreneurial ventures. Questions appearing at the end of each case can be used to stimulate classroom discussions.

Updated References   The amount of academic research examining entrepreneurship topics continues to grow. To provide you, our readers, with the most recent insights from the academic literature, we draw from newly published articles in important journals such as *Strategic Entrepreneurship Journal*, *Entrepreneurship Theory and Practice*, *Journal of Business Venturing*, and *Academy of Management Journal*. Similarly, we relied on the most current articles appearing in business publications such as *The Wall Street Journal* and *Entrepreneur* among others, to present you with examples of the actions being taken by today's entrepreneurial ventures.

HOW IS THIS BOOK ORGANIZED?

To explain the entrepreneurial process and the way it typically unfolds, we divide our book into four parts and 15 chapters. The four parts of the entrepreneurial process model are:

    Part 1: Decision to Become an Entrepreneur
    Part 2: Developing Successful Business Ideas
    Part 3: Moving from an Idea to an Entrepreneurial Firm
    Part 4: Managing and Growing an Entrepreneurial Firm

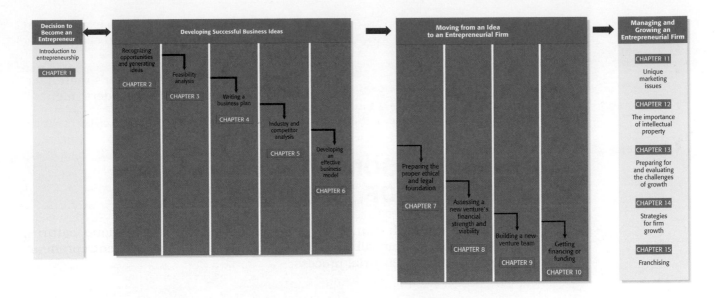

We believe that this sequence will make your journey toward understanding the entrepreneurial process both enjoyable and productive. The model is shown above. The step in the model that corresponds to the chapter being introduced is highlighted to help you form a picture of where each chapter fits in the entrepreneurial process.

WHAT ARE THE BOOK'S BENEFICIAL FEATURES?

To provide as thorough and meaningful an introduction to the entrepreneurial process as possible, we include several features, as follows, in each chapter of the book:

FEATURE INCLUDED IN EACH CHAPTER	BENEFIT
Learning objectives	Help focus the reader's attention on the major topics in the chapter
Chapter opening profile	Introduces the chapter's topic by focusing on a company that was started while its founder or founders were still in college, showing that you do not have to wait until you have years and years of experience to launch your entrepreneurial venture
Boldfaced key terms	Draw the reader's attention to key concepts
Examples and anecdotes	Liven up the text and provide descriptions of both successful and unsuccessful approaches to confronting the challenges discussed in each chapter
End-of-chapter summary	Integrates the key topics and concepts included in each chapter
Review questions	Allow readers to test their recall of chapter material
Application questions	Allow readers to apply what they learned from the chapter material

| Case discussion questions | Provide opportunities to use concepts examined following each case in each chapter to evaluate situations faced by entrepreneurs |
| Case application questions | Provide opportunities to use a chapter's materials following each case for situations readers might face as entrepreneurs |

WHAT ARE SOME OTHER UNIQUE FEATURES OF THIS BOOK?

While looking through your book, we think you'll find several unique features, as presented next, that will work to your benefit as a student of entrepreneurship and the entrepreneurial process.

UNIQUE FEATURE OF THE BOOK	EXPLANATION
Focus on opportunity recognition and feasibility analysis	We open your book with strong chapters on opportunity recognition and feasibility analysis. This is important, because opportunity recognition and feasibility analysis are key activities that must be completed early when investigating a new business idea.
What Went Wrong? boxed feature	Each chapter contains a boxed feature titled "What Went Wrong?" We use these features to explain the missteps of seemingly promising entrepreneurial firms. The purpose of these features, as you have no doubt already guessed, is to highlight the reality that things can go wrong when the fundamental concepts in the chapters aren't carefully followed.
Partnering for Success boxed feature	Each chapter contains a boxed feature titled "Partnering for Success." The ability to partner effectively with other firms is becoming an increasingly important attribute for successful entrepreneurial ventures.
Savvy Entrepreneurial Firm boxed feature	Each chapter contains a boxed feature titled "Savvy Entrepreneurial Firm." These features illustrate the types of business practices that facilitate the success of entrepreneurial ventures. As such, these are practices you should strongly consider putting into play when you are using the entrepreneurial process.
You Be the VC end-of-chapter features	Two features, titled "You Be the VC," are provided at the end of each chapter. These features present a "pitch" for funding from an emerging entrepreneurial venture. The features are designed to stimulate classroom discussion by sparking debate on whether a particular venture should or shouldn't receive funding. All the firms featured are real-life entrepreneurial start-ups. Thus, you'll be talking about real—not hypothetical or fictitious—entrepreneurial ventures.
A total of 30 original end-of-chapter cases	Two medium-length cases, are featured at the end of each chapter. The cases are designed to stimulate classroom discussion between you and your professor and with your follow students for the purpose of illustrating the issues discussed in the chapter.

Student Resources

■ **Companion Website: www.pearsonglobaleditions.com/barringer**—contains free access to a student version of the PowerPoint package, chapter quizzes, and links to featured Web sites.
■ **Business Feasibility Analysis Pro**—This wizard-based software is a step-by-step guide and an easy-to-use tool for completing a feasibility analysis of a business idea. The program allows instructors the flexibility to assign each step in the feasibility analysis separately or to assign the entire feasibility analysis as a semester-long project. It can be packaged with the textbook at a nominal cost.

FEEDBACK

If you have questions related to this book about entrepreneurship, please contact our customer service department online at http://247.pearsoned.com.

ACKNOWLEDGMENTS

We are pleased to express our sincere appreciation to four groups of people for helping bring both editions of our book to life.

Prentice Hall Professionals A number of individuals at Prentice Hall have worked with us conscientiously and have fully supported our efforts to create a book that will work for those both studying and teaching the entrepreneurial process. From Prentice Hall, we want to extend our sincere appreciation to our senior acquisitions editor, Kim Norbuta; our director of marketing, Patrice Lumumba Jones; and our editorial project manager, Claudia Fernandes. Each individual provided us invaluable guidance and support, and we are grateful for their contribution.

Student Entrepreneurs We want to extend a heartfelt "thank you" to the student entrepreneurs who contributed to the opening features in our book. Our conversations with these individuals were both informative and inspiring. We enjoyed getting to know these bright young entrepreneurs, and wish them nothing but total success as they continue to build their ventures.

Academic Reviewers We want to thank our colleagues who participated in reviewing individual chapters of the book while they were being written. We gained keen insight from these individuals (each of whom teaches courses in entrepreneurship) and incorporated many of the suggestions of our reviewers into the final version of the book.

Thank you to these professors who participated in reviews:

Dr. Richard Bartlett, *Columbus State Community College*

Greg Berezewski, *Robert Morris College*

Jeff Brice, Jr., *Texas Southern University*

Ralph Jagodka, *Mt. San Antonio College*

Christina Roeder, *James Madison University*

Aron S. Spencer, *New Jersey Institute of Technology*

Vincent Weaver, *Greenville Technical College*

Lisa Zidek, *Florida Gulf Coast University*

Academic Colleagues We thank this large group of professors whose thoughts about entrepreneurial education have helped shape our book's contents and presentation structure:

David C. Adams, *Manhattanville College*

Sol Ahiarah, *SUNY—Buffalo State College*

Frederic Aiello, *University of Southern Maine*

James J. Alling Sr., *Augusta Technical College*

Jeffrey Alstete, *Iona College*

Jeffrey Alves, *Wilkes University*

Joe Aniello, *Francis Marion University*

Mary Avery, *Ripon College*

Jay Azriel, *Illinois State University*

Richard Barker, *Upper Iowa University*

Jim Bell, *Texas State University*

Robert J. Berger, *SUNY Potsdam*

James Bloodgood, *Kansas State University*

Jenell Bramlage, *University of Northwestern Ohio*

Michael Brizek, *South Carolina State University*

Barb Brown, *Southwestern Community College*

James Burke, *Loyola University—Chicago*

Lowell Busenitz, *University of Oklahoma*

John Butler, *University of Texas—Austin*

Jane Byrd, *University of Mobile*

Art Camburn, *Buena Vista University*

Carol Carter, *Louisiana State University*

Gaylen Chandler, *Utah State University*

James Chrisman, *Mississippi State University*

Delena Clark, *Plattsburgh State University*

Dee Cole, *Middle Tennessee State University*

Roy Cook, *Fort Lewis College*

Andrew Corbett, *Babson College*

Simone Cummings, *Washington University School of Medicine*

Suzanne D'Agnes, *Queensborough Community College*

Douglas Dayhoff, *Indiana University*

Frank Demmler, *Carnegie Mellon University*

David Desplaces, *University of Hartford/Barney*

Vern Disney, *University of South Carolina—Sumter*

Dale Eesley, *University of Toledo*

Alan Eisner, *Pace University*

Susan Everett, *Clark State Community College*

Henry Fernandez, *North Carolina Central University*

Charles Fishel, *San Jose State University*

Dana Fladhammer, *Phoenix College*

Brenda Flannery, *Minnesota State University*

John Friar, *Northeastern University*

Barbara Fuller, *Winthrop University*

Barry Gilmore, *University of Memphis*

Caroline Glackin, *Delaware State University*

Cheryl Gracie, *Washtenaw Community College*

Frederick Greene, *Manhattan College*

Lee Grubb, *East Carolina University*

Brad Handy, *Springfield Technical Community College*

Carnella Hardin, *Glendale College*

Ashley Harmon, *Southeastern Technical College*

Steve Harper, *University of North Carolina at Wilmington*

Alan Hauff, *University of Missouri—St. Louis*

Gordon Haym, *Lyndon State College*

Andrea Hershatter, *Emory University*

Richard Hilliard, *Nichols College*

Jo Hinton, *Copiah Lincoln Community College*

Dennis Hoagland, *LDS Business College*

Kathie Holland, *University of Central Florida*

Frank Hoy, *University of Texas at El Paso*

Jeffrey Jackson, *Manhattanville College*

Grant Jacobsen, *Northern Virginia Community College-Woodbridge*

Susan Jensen, *University of Nebraska—Kearney*

Alec Johnson, *University of St. Thomas*

James M. Jones, *University of the Incarnate Word, ERAU, Del Mar College*

Jane Jones, *Mountain Empire Community College*

Joy Jones, *Ohio Valley College*

Tom Kaplan, *Fairleigh Dickinson University—Madison*

Elizabeth Kisenwether, *Penn State University*

James Klingler, *Villanova University*

Edward Kuljian, *Saint Joseph's University*

James Lang, *Virginia Tech University*

Allon Lefever, *Eastern Mennonite University*

Anita Leffel, *University of Texas—San Antonio*

Gary Levanti, *Polytechnic University—LI Campus*

Benyamin Lichtenstein, *University of Massachusetts, Boston*

Bruce Lynskey, *Vanderbilt University*

Janice Mabry, *Mississippi Gulf Coast Community College*

Jeffrey Martin, *University of Alabama*

Greg McCann, *Stetson University*

Elizabeth McCrea, *Pennsylvania State—Great Valley*

Brian McKenzie, *California State University—Hayward*

Chris McKinney, *Vanderbilt University*

Dale Meyer, *University of Colorado*

Steven C. Michael, *University of Illinois Urbana—Champaign*

Angela Mitchell, *Wilmington College*

Bryant Mitchell, *University of Maryland—Eastern Shore*

Rob Mitchell, *University Western Ontario*

Patrick Murphy, *DePaul University*

Charlie Nagelschmidt, *Champlain College*

William Naumes, *University of New Hampshire*

Connie Nichols, *Odessa College*

Gary Nothnagle, *Nazareth College*

Edward O'Brien, *Scottsdale Community College*

David Orozco, *Florida State University*

Haesun Park, *Louisiana State University*

John Pfaff, *University of the Pacific*

Joseph Picken, *University of Texas at Dallas*

Emmeline de Pillis, *University of Hawaii—Hilo*

Carol Reeves, *University of Arkansas*

John Richards, *Brigham Young University*

Christo Roberts, *University of Minnesota—Twin Cities*

George Roorbach, *Lyndon State College*

Michael Rubach, *University of Central Arkansas*

Janice Rustia, *University of Nebraska Medical Center*

James Saya, *The College of Santa Fe*

William Scheela, *Bemidji State University*

Gerry Scheffelmaier, *Middle Tennessee State University*

Gerald Segal, *Florida Gulf Coast University*

Cynthia Sheridan, *St. Edward's University*

Donald Shifter, *Fontbonne University*

C. L. J. Spencer, *Kapi'olani Community College*

Joseph Stasio, *Merrimack College*

Deborah Streeter, *Cornell University*

Dara Szyliowicz, *University of Denver*

Clint B. Tankersley, *Syracuse University*

Craig Tunwall, *Empire State College*

Barry Van Hook, *Arizona State University*

George Vozikis, *University of Tulsa*

David Wilemon, *Syracuse University*

Charlene Williams, *Brewton Parker College*

Doug Wilson, *University of Oregon*

Diana Wong, *Eastern Michigan University*

Finally, we want to express our appreciation to our home institutions (Oklahoma State University and Texas A&M University) for creating environments in which ideas are encouraged and supported.

We wish each of you—our readers—all the best in your study of the entrepreneurial process. And, of course, we hope that each of you will be highly successful entrepreneurs as you pursue the ideas you'll develop at different points in your careers.

Global Edition Contributors and Reviewers Pearson wishes to acknowledge and thank the following people for their involvement in the Global Edition:

Britta Boyd, Department of Border Region Studies, University of Southern Denmark, Denmark

Anushia Chelvarayan, Multimedia University, Malaysia

Massimo Garbuio, Discipline of International Business, The University of Sydney Business School, Australia

Dr. Hussin Jose Hejase, Dean, Faculty of Business and Economics, American University of Science and Technology, Lebanon

Lim Chin Hock, Marketing Division/School of Business Studies, TAR College, Malaysia

Stephen Ko, Department of Management and Marketing, The Hong Kong

Polytechnic University, Hong Kong

Eric Lam, The Hong Kong Polytechnic University, Hong Kong

Teena Lyons

Prof. Dr. Abdul Rahim Said, HELP University College, Malaysia

Thevendran Renganathan, Multimedia University, Malaysia

Iman Seoudi, Assistant Professor of Strategy and Entrepreneurship, Department of Management, American University in Cairo, Egypt

Dr. Pei-Lee Teh, School of Business, Monash University, Malaysia

Bruce R. Barringer

Bruce R. Barringer holds the Johnny D. Pope Entrepreneurship Chair in the Department of Entrepreneurship at Oklahoma State University. He earned his PhD from the University of Missouri and his MBA from Iowa State University. His research interests include feasibility analysis, firm growth, corporate entrepreneurship, and the impact of interorganizational relationships on business organizations. Over the years, he has worked with a number of technology-based incubators and student-led entrepreneurship activities and clubs.

He serves on the editorial review board of *Entrepreneurship Theory and Practice* and *Journal of Small Business Management*. His work has been published in *Strategic Management Journal*, *Journal of Management*, *Journal of Business Venturing*, *Journal of Small Business Management*, *Journal of Developmental Entrepreneurship*, and *Quality Management Journal*.

Bruce's outside interests include running, trail biking, and swimming.

R. Duane Ireland

R. Duane Ireland is a University Distinguished Professor and holds the Conn Chair in New Ventures Leadership in the Mays Business School, Texas A&M University. Previously, he served on the faculties at University of Richmond, Baylor University, and Oklahoma State University. His research interests include strategic entrepreneurship, corporate entrepreneurship, strategic alliances, and effectively managing organizational resources.

Duane's research has been published in journals such as *Academy of Management Journal*, *Academy of Management Review*, *Academy of Management Executive*, *Strategic Management Journal*, *Administrative Science Quarterly*, *Journal of Management*, *Journal of Business Venturing*, *Entrepreneurship Theory and Practice*, and *Strategic Entrepreneurship Journal* among others. He is a co-author of both scholarly books and textbooks, including best-selling strategic management texts. Along with Dr. Mike Morris (Syracuse University), Duane serves as a co-editor for the Prentice Hall Entrepreneurship Series. These books offer in-depth treatments of specific entrepreneurship topics, such as *Business Plans for Entrepreneurs* (authored by Bruce Barringer).

Duane has served or is serving on the editorial review boards for a number of journals, including *AMJ*, *AMR*, *AME*, *JOM*, *JBV*, and *ETP*. He just completed a term as Editor for *AMJ*. He has completed terms as an associate editor for *AME* and as a consulting editor for *ETP* and has served as a guest co-editor for special issues of a number of journals including *AMR*, *AME*, and *SMJ*. He is a Fellow of the Academy of Management and a Fellow of the Strategic Management Society. He is the current Vice President and Program Chair for the Academy of Management. He is the recipient of both teaching and research awards.

Duane's outside interests include running, reading, listening to a variety of music, and playing with his grandson.

PART 1

Decision to Become an Entrepreneur

CHAPTER 1
Introduction to *Entrepreneurship*

Founder:

FRASER DOHERTY

Dialogue *with*
Fraser Doherty

MY BIGGEST WORRY AS AN ENTREPRENEUR
That we're not innovating fast enough to keep ahead of the competition

WHAT I DO WHEN I'M NOT WORKING
Drive my 40-year-old VW camper van round the countryside!

MY FAVORITE SMARTPHONE APP
SuperJam's Recipe App

MY FIRST ENTREPRENEURIAL EXPERIENCE
Hatching chickens on top of the TV, age 10, and selling their eggs

FAVORITE PERSON I FOLLOW ON TWITTER
Has to be Stephen Fry.

Super Jam™

©SuperJam

Introduction to *Entrepreneurship*

OPENING PROFILE

SUPERJAM
The Classic Entrepreneurial Story

Web: http://www.superjam.co.uk
Facebook: SuperJam 100% Fruit Spread

Growing up in Scotland, Fraser Doherty spent his childhood coming up with ideas for new products. Not all his money-making ideas were a success—indeed his fledgling egg-selling enterprise ended abruptly when a fox ate all his chickens—but he had a hunger to set up a business.

At the age of 14, Doherty gave jam-making a try. He had always enjoyed the jam his grandmother made and thought there might be an opportunity here. After making a batch and selling it door-to-door, he discovered people really liked it, and Doherty's jam enterprise gradually spread into local shops and farmers' markets. A feature in the Edinburgh Evening News brought in even more orders from further afield.

After resolving to expand the business, Doherty did some research and found that sales of jam had been in decline for the past few decades. Jam had acquired an old-fashioned image and people preferred healthier alternatives on their toast.

The solution the young Scottish entrepreneur came up with was a jam for the modern world. Doherty's SuperJam would be made using traditional recipes, completely from fruit juice. The jars would contain no sugar and no artificial flavorings. He also boldly resolved to target supermarkets to sell his products.

Fraser faced a number of challenges. At this point, he was making hundreds of jars of jam every week in his parents' kitchen. Apart from the fact his parents were struggling to get in there to cook their dinner, the business clearly couldn't grow any further.

At the age of 17, he was in no position to start a factory and he did not have any money to pay a design agency to create a brand either. He also did not have a clue how to approach supermarkets. In fact, all he had was a passion about his product and a great recipe.

The first supermarket Fraser approached was Waitrose on a "meet the buyer" day. Fraser pitched his idea to the senior jam buyer who liked it, but said it had a long way to go. He advised Fraser that he had to set up a production facility and create a brand before coming back with a well-priced product.

LEARNING OBJECTIVES

After studying this chapter you should be ready to:

1. Explain entrepreneurship and discuss its importance.
2. Describe corporate entrepreneurship and its use in established firms.
3. Discuss three main reasons people decide to become entrepreneurs.
4. Identify four main characteristics of successful entrepreneurs.
5. Explain the five common myths regarding entrepreneurship.
6. Explain how entrepreneurial firms differ from salary-substitute and lifestyle firms.
7. Discuss the changing demographics of entrepreneurs in the United States.
8. Discuss the impact of entrepreneurial firms on economies and societies.
9. Identify ways in which large firms benefit from the presence of smaller entrepreneurial firms.
10. Explain the entrepreneurial process.

Fraser set off around the United Kingdom trying to convince food manufacturers to believe in his 100 percent fruit jam. He told them that he didn't have any money to invest, but if they took the long-term view, then they too would reap the benefit. He did the same with a string of advertising agencies to persuade them to help him create a brand. Eventually, after two years of persistence, Doherty finally convinced a factory and an advertising agency to work with him.

The Waitrose buyer stood by his word and stocked SuperJam for a trial in March 2007. The story of the persistent entrepreneur got massive media coverage in the United Kingdom and abroad. Doherty even earned a slot on China's TV news. Best of all, consumers loved SuperJam. On day one, Waitrose's Edinburgh store sold 1,500 jars, which is more jam than it traditionally sold in a month. Tesco, the United Kingdom's largest supermarket, then phoned Doherty out of the blue and agreed to stock it. Before long, the rest of the major chains followed suit.

Doherty has kept close to his customers throughout SuperJam's meteoric rise and is conscious of the part technology and in particular social networks play in his business and in retaining a meaningful conversation with his customers.

SuperJam's Web site has a page where consumers can suggest a store that they think the brand should supply and gets hundreds of suggestions each month. The company then sends a postcard to the nominated stores saying that one of their customers thinks they should stock SuperJam and offering them a discount code when they place their first order. When the store places that order—and most do—the person who suggested the store is sent a free jar of jam as a thank-you.

From humble beginnings working at his kitchen table to grow his entrepreneurial venture, Fraser now supplies all the major UK supermarkets with SuperJam and has won a variety of awards for the range. The jam has become so well known that it has even been included in a museum exhibit as an example of an "iconic Scottish Food Brand."[1]

In this first chapter of your book about the successful launching of an entrepreneurial firm, we define entrepreneurship and discuss why some people decide to become entrepreneurs. We then look at successful entrepreneurs' characteristics, the common myths surrounding entrepreneurship, the different types of start-up firms, and the changing demographics of entrepreneurs in the United States and in nations throughout the world. We then examine entrepreneurship's importance, including the economic and social impact of new firms as well as the importance of entrepreneurial firms to larger businesses. To close this chapter, we introduce you to the entrepreneurial process. This process, which we believe is the foundation for successfully launching a start-up firm, is the framework we use to present the book's materials to you.

INTRODUCTION TO ENTREPRENEURSHIP

There is tremendous interest in entrepreneurship around the world. Although this statement may seem bold, there is evidence supporting it, some of which is provided by the Global Entrepreneurship Monitor (GEM). GEM, which is a joint research effort by Babson College, London Business School, and Universidad del Desarrollo, Santiago, Chile, tracks entrepreneurship in 59 countries, including the United States. Of particular interest to GEM is early stage entrepreneurial activity, which consists of businesses that are just being started and businesses that have been in existence for less than three and one-half years. The 2010 survey shows, in the countries analyzed, some 110 million people between 18 and 64 years old just starting businesses, and another 140 million running businesses they started less than three and one-half years ago. Taken together, some 250 million people were involved in early entrepreneurial activity in the 59 countries included in the study. A sample of the rate of early-stage entrepreneurial activity in countries included in the GEM study is shown in Table 1.1. While the highest rates of entrepreneurial start-up activities occur in low-income countries, where good jobs are not plentiful, the rates are also impressive in high-income countries like France (5.8 percent), United Kingdom (6.4 percent), and the United States (7.6 percent). What the 7.6 percent means for the United States is that almost 1 out of every 13 American adults is actively engaged in starting a business or is the owner/manager of a business that is less than three and one-half years old.[2]

The GEM study also identifies whether its respondents are starting a new business to take advantage of an attractive opportunity or because of necessity to earn an income. The majority of people in high-income countries are drawn to entrepreneurship to take advantage of attractive opportunities. The reverse is true of people in low-income countries, who tend to be drawn to entrepreneurship primarily because of necessity (resulting from a lack of career prospects).[3]

One criticism of entrepreneurship, which is often repeated in the press, is that the majority of new businesses fail. It simply isn't true. The often used statistic that 9 out of 10 businesses fail in their first few years is an exaggeration. According to Brian Headd, an economist for the U.S. Small Business Administration, after four years 50 percent of new businesses are still open, 33 percent have failed, and 17 percent are closed but were considered to be successful by their owners.[4] While overall these figures are heartening, the 33 percent of start-ups that fail show that a motivation to start and run a business isn't enough; it must be coupled with a solid business idea, good financial management, and effective execution to maximize chances for success. In this book, we'll discuss many examples of entrepreneurial firms and the factors separating successful new ventures from unsuccessful ones.

TABLE 1.1   RATES OF EARLY-STAGE ENTREPRENEURIAL ACTIVITY (AGES 18 TO 64)

Country	Percent of Population Starting a New Business
Argentina	14.2%
Brazil	17.5%
China	14.4%
France	5.8%
Germany	4.2%
Peru	27.2%
Russia	3.9%
Turkey	8.6%
United Kingdom	6.4%
United States	7.6%

Source: Based on D. Kelley, N. Bosma, and J. E. Amoros, *Global Entrepreneurship Monitor 2010 Global Report* (Babson College and Universidad del Desarrollo, 2010).

Many people see entrepreneurship as an attractive career path. Think about your friends and others you know. In all probability, you are acquainted with at least one or two people who want to become an entrepreneur—either now or at some point in the future. The number of books dealing with starting one's own business is another indication entrepreneurship is growing in popularity. Amazon.com, for example, currently lists over 35,600 books and other items dealing with entrepreneurship and over 62,700 books concerned with small businesses.

What Is Entrepreneurship?

The word *entrepreneur* derives from the French words *entre*, meaning "between," and *prendre*, meaning "to take." The word was originally used to describe people who "take on the risk" between buyers and sellers or who "undertake" a task such as starting a new venture.[5] Inventors and entrepreneurs differ from each other. An inventor creates something new. An entrepreneur assembles and then integrates all the resources needed—the money, the people, the business model, the strategy, and the risk-bearing ability—to transform the invention into a viable business.[6]

LEARNING OBJECTIVE
1. Explain entrepreneurship and discuss its importance.

Entrepreneurship is defined as the process by which individuals pursue opportunities without regard to resources they currently control.[7] Others such as venture capitalist Fred Wilson define it more simply, seeing entrepreneurship as the art of turning an idea into a business. In essence, an entrepreneur's behavior finds him or her trying to identify opportunities and putting useful ideas into practice.[8] The tasks called for by this behavior can be accomplished by either an individual or a group and typically require creativity, drive, and a willingness to take risks. Fraser Doherty, the founder of SuperJam, exemplifies all these qualities. Doherty saw an *opportunity* to create a modern, 100 percent fruit jam, to appeal to more health-conscious consumers, he *risked* his career prospects by dedicating two years to searching for factories and designers to help him, and he is now *working hard* to offer a *useful* service to SuperJam's customers.

In this book, we focus on entrepreneurship in the context of an entrepreneur or team of entrepreneurs launching a new business. However, ongoing firms can also behave entrepreneurially. Typically, established firms with an entrepreneurial emphasis are proactive, innovative, and risk-taking. For example, Apple Inc. is widely recognized as a firm in which entrepreneurial behaviors are clearly evident. Steve Jobs is at the heart of Apple's entrepreneurial culture. With his ability to persuade and motivate others' imaginations, Jobs continues to inspire Apple's employees as they develop innovative product after innovative product. To consider the penetration Apple has with some of its innovations, think of how many of your friends own an iPhone, iPad, or Macintosh computer. Similarly, studying Facebook or Zynga's ability to grow and succeed reveals a history of entrepreneurial behavior at multiple levels within the firms.[9] In addition, many of the firms traded on the NASDAQ, such as Intuit, Amazon.com, Google, and Research In Motion are commonly thought of as entrepreneurial firms. The NASDAQ is the largest U.S. electronic stock market, with over 2,850 companies listed on the exchange.

LEARNING OBJECTIVE
2. Describe corporate entrepreneurship and its use in established firms.

We want to note here that established firms with an orientation to acting entrepreneurially practice **corporate entrepreneurship**.[10] All firms fall along a conceptual continuum that ranges from highly conservative to highly entrepreneurial. The position of a firm on this continuum is referred to as its **entrepreneurial intensity**.[11] As we mentioned previously, entrepreneurial firms are typically proactive innovators and are not averse to taking calculated risks. In contrast, conservative firms take a more "wait and see" posture, are less innovative, and are risk averse.

One of the most persuasive indications of entrepreneurship's importance to an individual or to a firm is the degree of effort undertaken to behave in an entrepreneurial manner. Firms with higher entrepreneurial intensity regularly look for ways to cut bureaucracy. For example, Virgin Group, the large British conglomerate, works hard to keep its units small and instill in them an entrepreneurial spirit. Virgin is one of the most recognized brands in Britain and is involved in businesses as diverse as airlines and music. In the following quote, Sir Richard Branson, the founder and CEO of Virgin, describes how his company operates in an entrepreneurial manner:

> Convention . . . dictates that "big is beautiful," but every time one of our ventures gets too big we divide it up into smaller units. I go to the deputy managing director, the deputy sales director, and the deputy marketing director and say, "Congratulations. You're now MD [managing director], sales director and marketing director—of a new company." Each time we've done this, the people involved haven't had much more work to do, but necessarily they have a greater incentive to perform and a greater zeal for their work. The results for us have been terrific. By the time we sold Virgin Music, we had as many as 50 subsidiary record companies, and not one of them had more than 60 employees.[12]

Why Become an Entrepreneur?

The three primary reasons that people become entrepreneurs and start their own firms are to be their own boss, pursue their own ideas, and realize financial rewards.

Be Their Own Boss The first of these reasons—being one's own boss—is given most commonly. This doesn't mean, however, that entrepreneurs are difficult to work with or that they have trouble accepting authority. Instead, many entrepreneurs want to be their own boss because either they have had a long-time ambition to own their own firm or because they have become frustrated working in traditional jobs. The type of frustration that some entrepreneurs feel working in conventional jobs is exemplified by Wendy DeFeudis, the founder of VeryWendy, a company that makes customized social invitations. Commenting on how her experiences working for herself have been more satisfying than working for a large firm, DeFeudis remarked:

> I always wanted to be my own boss. I felt confined by the corporate structure. I found it frustrating and a complete waste of time—a waste to have to sell my ideas to multiple people and attend all kinds of internal meetings before moving forward with a concept.[13]

Sometimes the desire to be their own boss results from a realization that the only way they'll achieve an important personal or professional goal is to start their own business. Christopher Jones, David LaBat, and Mary McGrath started a business for this reason. The three, who are educational psychologists, had secure jobs at a public school in the Santa Clarita Valley, north of Los Angeles. Over time, they felt inhibited by the limited range of services they were able to provide students in a school setting, so they left their jobs to start Dynamic Interventions, a more full-service educational psychology and counseling center. Recalling why it was necessary for him and his colleagues to leave their jobs to become their own bosses Jones said:

> The idea came from some general frustrations with not being able to practice the breadth of service that [we wanted to]. And instead of going to work and being angry about it for the next 30 years, we decided to do something about it. With Dynamic Interventions, our service doesn't stop at the end of the school day. We can go more in-depth and be more beneficial to the whole family."[14]

<aside>
LEARNING OBJECTIVE

3. Discuss three main reasons people decide to become entrepreneurs.
</aside>

Steve Jobs is perhaps America's best-known entrepreneur. He cofounded Apple Inc. in 1976, and has since built the company into a premier entrepreneurial firm. Apple's lastest innovations include the widely popular iPhone, iPad, iPod, and Apple's App Store and its iTunes music store.

Ryan Anson/AFP/Getty Images/Newscom

Pursue Their Own Ideas The second reason people start their own firms is to pursue their own ideas.[15] Some people are naturally alert, and when they recognize ideas for new products or services, they have a desire to see those ideas realized. Corporate entrepreneurs who innovate within the context of an existing firm typically have a mechanism for their ideas to become known. Established firms, however, often resist innovation. When this happens, employees are left with good ideas that go unfulfilled.[16] Because of their passion and commitment, some employees choose to leave the firm employing them in order to start their own business as the means to develop their own ideas.

This chain of events can take place in noncorporate settings, too. For example, some people, through a hobby, leisure activity, or just everyday life, recognize the need for a product or service that is not available in the marketplace. If the idea is viable enough to support a business, they commit tremendous time and energy to convert the idea into a part-time or full-time firm. In Chapters 2 and 3, we focus on how entrepreneurs spot ideas and determine if their ideas represent viable business opportunities.

An example of a person who left a job to pursue an idea is Kevin Mann, the founder of Graphic.ly, a social digital distribution platform for comic book publishers and fans. Mann became discouraged when he couldn't find a comic book in which he was interested. He even took a 100 mile train ride to search for it in a neighboring city. His frustration boiled over on the train ride home:

> I kept thinking that there had to be a better way of buying comics; and then it dawned on me. That morning I had purchased a movie from iTunes, which I was watching right there on the train. Why shouldn't buying comics be just as easy? Why did I have to travel over a 100 miles and waste the better part of day, all for nothing? I realized I had two options. I could quit buying comics or I could quit my job and build the iTunes of comics.[17]

This revelation led to the launch of Graphic.ly in the fall of 2009. Today, Graphic.ly is both a robust platform for the sale of digital comics and a social network for people who enjoy discussing the comics they're reading. Following up on the story about the train ride, Mann went on to say:

> That's how Graphic.ly started and my enthusiasm for comics has now transferred to a business I love being part of. Every single day I am excited to go to work. I get to create and innovate in a sector I love. Ultimately, I'll solve a problem that was ruining something very special to me.[18]

Pursue Financial Rewards Finally, people start their own firms to pursue financial rewards. This motivation, however, is typically secondary to the first two and often fails to live up to its hype. The average entrepreneur does not make more money than someone with a similar amount of responsibility in a traditional job. The financial lure of entrepreneurship is its upside potential. People such as Jeff Bezos of Amazon.com, Mark Zuckerberg of Facebook, and Larry Page and Sergey Brin of Google made hundreds of millions of dollars building their firms. Money is also a unifier. Making a profit and increasing the value of a company is a solidifying goal that people can rally around. But money is rarely the primary motivation behind the launch of an entrepreneurial firm. Some entrepreneurs even report that the financial rewards associated with entrepreneurship can be bittersweet if they are accompanied by losing control of their firm. For example, Sir Richard Branson, after selling Virgin Records, wrote, "I remember walking down the street [after the sale was completed]. I was crying. Tears . . . [were] streaming down my face. And there I was holding a check for a billion dollars. . . . If you'd have seen me, you would have thought I was loony. A billion dollars."[19] For Branson, it wasn't just the money—it was the thrill of building the business and of seeing the success of his initial idea.

Characteristics of Successful Entrepreneurs

LEARNING OBJECTIVE
4. Identify four main characteristics of successful entrepreneurs.

Although many behaviors have been ascribed to entrepreneurs, several are common to those who are successful. Those in new ventures and those who are already part of an entrepreneurial firm share these qualities, which are shown in Figure 1.1 and described in the following section.

Passion for the Business The number one characteristic shared by successful entrepreneurs is a **passion for their business**, whether it is in the context of a new firm or an existing business. This passion typically stems from the entrepreneur's belief that the business will positively influence people's lives. This is the case with Aquaflow, the subject of Case 1.2, which is a company that transforms algae grown on sewage into a substitute for crude oil. It's founder, Nick Gerritsen, hopes to encourage governmental urgency on climate change issues. Making a difference in people's lives is also the primary motivator behind many social enterprises, which are often started by people who set aside promising careers to pursue a social goal. This was the case with John Wood, who founded Room to Read, and is the author of the book *Leaving Microsoft to Change the World*. Wood's deep passion to help children in the developing world caused him to start cashing in small amounts of Microsoft stock to buy books and build schools, even before he left the company. In excerpts from a 2007 interview published by *Forbes* magazine, Wood said:

> During my travels, I met so many children in the poorest parts of the world, lacking access to school, books, and libraries, that I began cashing in small amounts of stocks to help them. Two hundred shares of Microsoft stock was enough to build an entire school in rural Napal.[20]

FIGURE 1.1
Four Primary
Characteristics
of Successful
Entrepreneurs

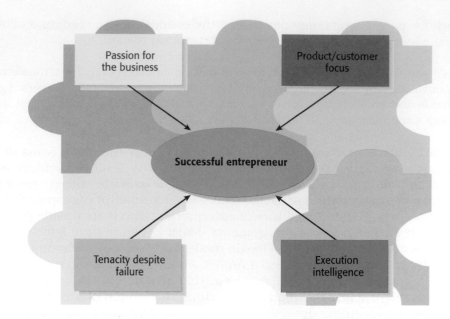

Wood eventually left Microsoft to work on Room to Read full-time. As of May 2011, Room to Read had built over 1,440 schools and distributed over 9.4 million books in developing parts of the world.

Passion is particularly important for both for-profit and not-for-profit entrepreneurial organizations because, although rewarding, the process of starting a firm or building a social enterprise is demanding. There are five primary reasons passion is important, as reflected in Table 1.2. Each of these reasons reflects a personal attribute that passion engenders. Removing just one of these qualities would make it much more difficult to launch and sustain a successful entrepreneurial organization.

TABLE 1.2　FIVE PRIMARY REASONS PASSION IS IMPORTANT FOR THE LAUNCH OF A SUCCESSFUL ENTREPRENEURIAL ORGANIZATION

Reason Passion Is Important	Explanation
1. The ability to learn and iterate	Founders don't have all the answers. It takes passion and drive to solicit feedback, make necessary changes, and move forward. The changes won't always be obvious. Passion makes the search for the right answers invigorating and fun.
2. A willingness to work hard for an extended period of time	Commonly, entrepreneurs work longer hours than people with traditional jobs. You can only do that, on a sustained basis, if you're passionate about what you're doing.
3. Ability to overcome setbacks and "no's"	It's rare that an entrepreneur doesn't experience setbacks and hear many "no's" from potential customers, investors, and others while building an entrepreneurial business or social enterprise. The energy to continue comes from passion for an idea.
4. The ability to listen to feedback on the limitations of your organization and yourself	You'll meet plenty of people along the way—some with good intentions and some without—who will tell you how to improve your organization and how to improve yourself. You have to be willing to listen to the people with good intentions and make changes if it helps. You have to be able to brush aside feedback from people with bad intentions without letting them get you down.
5. Perseverance and persistence when the going gets tough	Perseverance and persistence come from passion. As an entrepreneur, you'll have down days. Building an entrepreneurial organization is fraught with challenges. Passion is what provides an entrepreneur the motivation to get through tough times.

Source: Adapted from A. Sack, "Why Is Passion so Important to a Startup," A Sack of Seattle blog, http://asack.typepad.com/a_sack_of_seattle/2010/03/why-is-passion-so-important-to-a-startup.html (accessed May 22, 2011, originally posted on March 16, 2010).

A note of caution is in order here: While entrepreneurs should have passion, they should not wear rose-colored glasses. It would be a mistake to believe that all one needs is passion and anything is possible. It is important to be enthusiastic about a business idea, but it is also important to understand its potential flaws and risks. In addition, entrepreneurs should understand that the most effective business ideas take hold when their passion is consistent with their skills and is in an area that represents a legitimate business opportunity.

To illustrate the importance of passion, as well as other factors that are critical in determining a firm's success or failure, we include a boxed feature titled "What Went Wrong?" in each chapter. The feature for this chapter shows how YouCastr, an online platform that people used to provide live commentary for sporting events, ultimately failed in part because its founders were not able to remain passionate about their business idea.

Product/Customer Focus   A second defining characteristic of successful entrepreneurs is a **product/customer focus**. This quality is exemplified by Steven Jobs, the cofounder of Apple Inc., who wrote, "The computer is the most remarkable tool we've ever built . . . but the most important thing is to get them in the hands of as many people as possible."[21] This sentiment underscores an understanding of the two most important elements in any business—products and customers. While it's important to think about management, marketing, finance, and the like, none of those functions makes any difference if a firm does not have good products with the capability to satisfy customers.

It's also important to focus on the right things. For example, JibJab is a digital entertainment company, which was founded in 1999 by Evan and Gregg Spiridellis. It gained attention during the 2004 presidential election when its animated video of George W. Bush and John Kerry singing "This Land Is Your Land" became a hit. (It's been viewed on YouTube over 2.1 million times.) The goal of the company, from the start, was to build a scalable platform for creating and distributing digital entertainment products. A problem the founders had was they were really good animated content creators, so would get offers to do side jobs while working on their core business. They learned they needed to be disciplined and quit doing this because it took time away from their real passion:

> You need to be disciplined. You need to turn down jobs. You need to say, 'I could really use that $50,000 gig, but if we do that, we're going to be locked down for three months and we're not going to be able to do these other projects.' So it does require discipline and passing on opportunities. Knowing what to pass on is a really important skill we developed.[22]

A product/customer focus also involves the diligence to spot product opportunities and to see them through to completion. The idea for the Apple Macintosh, for example, originated in the early 1980s when Steven Jobs and several other Apple employees took a tour of a Xerox research facility. They were astounded to see computers that displayed graphical icons and pull-down menus. The computers also allowed users to navigate desktops using a small, wheeled device called a mouse. Jobs decided to use these innovations to create the Macintosh, the first user-friendly computer. Throughout the two and one-half years the Macintosh team developed this new product, it maintained an intense product/customer focus, creating a high-quality computer that is easy to learn, is fun to use, and meets the needs of a wide audience of potential users.[23]

Tenacity Despite Failure   Because entrepreneurs are typically trying something new, the failure rate associated with their efforts is naturally high. In addition, the process of developing a new business is somewhat similar to what

WHAT WENT WRONG?

How a Lack of Passion and Too Few Customers Can Kill a Business

The idea for YouCastr was hatched in mid-2006, during a road trip involving Ariel Diaz, Jay Peak, and Jeff Dwyer. Throughout the ride, the friends bounced business ideas off each other. One idea stuck. How about creating a platform that people could use to provide live commentary for sporting events? It would be fun, the friends thought, for people to watch a sporting event, like a high school football game, and stream their own live commentary across the Web.

Diaz shared the idea with Jeff Hebert, a friend, and within a couple of months he, Hebert, Peak, and Dwyer started building an alpha version of the site. Initially, each member of the group kept his day job, working on the idea, which they dubbed YouCastr, on nights and weekends. Eventually, each quit his job, and the four spent the next three years raising money, opening an office, hiring people, getting YouCastr up and running and pivoting the business. (A pivot is when a business changes course.) Often, start-ups iterate or pivot based on user feedback. YouCastr started as a virtual sports bar where people could chime in audio commentary on televised sporting events. That approach didn't stick. It then pivoted to focusing on enabling people to provide commentary on sporting events that weren't televised, like high school football games. Its final pivot was to expand beyond sports, mainly by de-emphasizing the sports branding on its Web site, by adding a few features geared more toward video producers than ordinary sports enthusiasts. All this time, YouCastr's revenue model called for the firm to take a commission on the sales its site generated. Each person who used the site to provide live commentary of a sporting event would sign up listeners who would pay a small fee to listen to the event.

Ultimately, YouCastr didn't work. In a blog post about YouCastr's failure, Diaz provided five reasons that YouCastr failed, three of which involved either a lack of passion or an absence of customers.

First, the company ran out of money. Despite operating in a very lean manner, toward the end there simply wasn't enough money to continue operating. Second, the market was not there. The underlying assumption of YouCastr's business model is that people would pay for audio and video commentary of sporting events that weren't covered on radio or TV. As it turned out, not enough people wanted it. YouCastr did find some narrow markets where people would pay, such as high school sports, some boxing matches, and some mixed martial arts events. But these markets weren't large enough to build a sustainable company. Third, the team was ready to move on. The four cofounders started YouCastr because they wanted to do something entrepreneurial—not because they loved broadcasting or loved sports. They weren't the core users of their own product. This made it hard to sustain effort when things got tough. Fourth, they saw no light at the end of the tunnel. They'd guessed wrong about people's willingness to pay to listen to live broadcasts of sporting events, and didn't see any prospects that would change. Finally, three and a half years after that car ride, it was time to call it quits. Although the founders considered themselves to be survivors, they made the tough decision to shut things down and move on.

Questions for Critical Thinking

1. Why do you think Ariel Diaz and his cofounders didn't realize that they were starting a business that they weren't really passionate about? Should that have been a warning sign to them? Describe what you believe are the keys to ensuring that a person is truly passionate about a business idea before moving forward with the idea.
2. Why is passion such a critical component of entrepreneurial success? If people are willing to work hard and dedicate themselves, do you think they can build a successful business without being passionate about their business idea?
3. How could YouCastr's cofounders have better anticipated that people would be reluctant to pay to listen to or watch sporting events that weren't being covered on radio or TV?
4. Do you think YouCastr could have been saved? If so, how?

Source: A. Diaz, "YouCastr—A Post-Mortem," The Ambitious Life Blog, http://theambitiouslife.com/youcastr-a-post-mortem, June 3, 2010 (accessed February 28, 2011).

a scientist experiences in the laboratory. A chemist, for example, typically has to try multiple combinations of chemicals before finding an optimal combination that can accomplish a certain objective. In a similar fashion, developing a new business idea may require a certain degree of experimentation before a success is attained. Setbacks and failures inevitably occur during this process. The litmus test for entrepreneurs is their ability to persevere through setbacks and failures.

An example of the degree of tenacity it sometimes takes to launch a successful firm is provided by Kyle Smitley, the founder of barley & birch, a business that sells organic children's clothing. Smitley launched barley & birch in January 2009, at age 22, with the goal of giving parents and children the most environmentally friendly clothing possible. Despite having flawless credit, she was turned down at every bank she approached. She finally received a $10,000 loan from ACCION, a microfinance organization. She next embarked on a major marketing campaign, sending 500 hand-signed letters with literature about her products to environmentally friendly stores. That effort fell flat. She finally reached out to mom bloggers, who spread the word about her company, and motivated their readers to start asking about barley & birch products at children's clothing stores. By the end of 2009, Smitley's products were in 30 stores.[24] Only sheer tenacity and will prevented Smitley from giving up before she reached this critical milestone.

Two additional examples of tenacity are provided in the boxed feature titled "Savvy Entrepreneurial Firm." In each chapter, this feature will provide an illustration of the exemplary behavior of one or more entrepreneurial firms or will provide an example of a tool or technique that well-managed entrepreneurial firms use to improve their performance.

Execution Intelligence   The ability to fashion a solid idea into a viable business is a key characteristic of successful entrepreneurs. Commonly, this ability is thought of as **execution intelligence**.[25] In many cases, execution intelligence is the factor that determines whether a start-up is successful or fails. An ancient Chinese saying warns, "To open a business is very easy; to keep it open is very difficult."

The ability to effectively execute a business idea means developing a business model, putting together a new venture team, raising money, establishing partnerships, managing finances, leading and motivating employees, and so on. It also demands the ability to translate thought, creativity, and imagination into action and measurable results. As Jeff Bezos, the founder of Amazon.com once said, "Ideas are easy. It's execution that's hard."[26] For many entrepreneurs, the hardest time is shortly after they launch their firm. This reality was expressed by Jodi Gallaer, the founder of a lingerie company, who said, "The most challenging part of my job is doing everything for the first time."[27]

To illustrate solid execution, let's look at Starbucks. Although Starbucks is not growing as fast and profitably as it once did, it is still a remarkable success story. The business idea of Howard Schultz, the entrepreneur who purchased Starbucks in 1987, was his recognition of the fact that most Americans didn't have a place to enjoy coffee in a comfortable, quiet setting. Seeing a great opportunity to satisfy customers' needs, Schultz attacked the marketplace aggressively to make Starbucks the industry leader and to establish a national brand. First, he hired a seasoned management team, constructed a world-class roasting facility to supply his outlets with premium coffee beans, and focused on building an effective organizational infrastructure. Then Schultz recruited a management information systems expert from McDonald's to design a point-of-sale system capable of tracking consumer purchases across 300 outlets. This decision was crucial to the firm's ability to sustain rapid growth over the next several years. Starbucks succeeded because Howard Schultz knew how to execute a business idea.[28] He built a seasoned management team, implemented an effective strategy, and used information technology wisely to make his business thrive.[29] These fundamental aspects of execution excellence should serve Schultz and Starbucks when it comes to dealing with the competitive challenges facing the firm in 2011 and beyond. In contrast to what Schultz has accomplished at Starbucks, the cost of ignoring execution is high, as explained by Bob Young, the founder of several entrepreneurial firms. When asked "What was your hardest lesson

SAVVY ENTREPRENEURIAL FIRM

Angry Birds and Zeo

Rovio Mobile (maker of Angry Birds) Web: http://rovio.com; Twitter: RovioMobile; Facebook: Rovio Mobile Zeo Web: www.myzeo.com; Twitter: zeo; Facebook: Zeo

Most everyone is familiar with Angry Birds, the video game in which players use a slingshot to launch birds at pigs stationed on or within various structures. The goal is to destroy all the pigs on the playfield. Inspired by a sketch of stylized wingless birds, the game was first released for the Apple iPhone in December 2009. Since then it has been widely popular and its creator, Finland-based Rovio Mobile, has created versions of Angry Birds for the Android operating system and other platforms. While it's hard to know for sure why Angry Birds has been such a success, it's been praised for its successful combination of addictive game play, comical style, and low price (99 cents per download). Across all platforms, Angry Birds has been downloaded more than 100 million times, making it one of the most successful electronic games in history. In fact, the birds in the game, outfitted with different colors and destructive capability, have become cultural icons. They have been made into plush toys, which sell for $12 to $15 each, and Rovio Mobile is thinking about creating a children's cartoon series focused on the birds.

Impressive, isn't it? The company behind Angry Birds, Rovio Mobile, was started in 2003 by three students, Niklas Hed, Jarno Vakevainen, and Kim Dikert, from Helsinki University of Technology (now called Aalto University School of Science and Technology) in Finland. While still in school, the three entered a mobile game development contest sponsored by Nokia and HP. Their entry, a multiplayer game named "King of the Cabbage World," won the contest, which prompted the three to start a company to make mobile games. Incredibly, from 2003 until 2009, Rovio Mobile produced 51 electronic games, none of which were a hit. Angry Birds was its 52nd release. To say that the three entrepreneurs were persistent is a true understatement!

The same year Rovio Mobile started, Jason Donahue and Ben Rubin, two students at Brown University, launched Zeo, formerly known as Axon Labs. Looking for ways to fight grogginess and help people feel more alert, Donahue and Rubin found that the stage of sleep from which a person awakens has a major effect on how that person feels during the day. So Zeo was launched to help people track the quality of their sleep and awaken at the ideal time. To do this, Zeo created an alarm clock and related accessories that monitor sleep states. The state of sleep is detected by a headband that the user wears while sleeping. A bedside base unit monitors the state of sleep and awakens the sleeper during the last light sleep before the desired waking time. A complementary personal sleep coaching service, in the form of a Web-based platform, helps users measure and analyze their sleep patterns, and makes recommendations for how to improve the quality of their sleep.

The Zeo system is dependent on both software and hardware, both of which were built from scratch by Donahue and Rubin. An initial prototype was built, and the two then started cold-calling entrepreneurs in their area who had built a physical product to get their advice on how to proceed. One person they targeted was Colin Angle, the CEO of iRobot, the maker of the popular Roomba robotic vacuum cleaner. Getting Angle on the phone wasn't easy. Donahue and Rubin called a number of times and got to know Angle's secretary. They were repeatedly told he wasn't available, but were polite, and always asked if it was okay to call again. One day, while driving home from a meeting, they tried again and boom— their call was put through. They got five minutes of Angle's attention and convinced him to meet with them. Angle eventually became a Zeo adviser and then a board member, and was instrumental in introducing Donahue and Rubin to Chinese manufacturers who now produce the hardware portion of Zeo's products. Donahue and Rubin have publicly commented that Zeo wouldn't have been possible without Angle's involvement and advice.

Questions for Critical Thinking

1. Contrast Rovio Mobile with YouCastr, the company featured in this chapter's "What Went Wrong" feature. Why do you think Rovio Mobile survived and is now thriving while YouCastr failed?
2. Why do you think Angry Birds has been so successful?
3. Do you think you'd be able to "hang in there" as long as the founders of Rovio Mobile did? Would you have been able to keep picking up the phone and calling Colin Angle's office, even after being repeatedly told he wasn't available? What are the keys to remaining "tenacious" when things take longer than planned?
4. Although the case doesn't provide specific information to help you answer these questions, give them a stab anyway. Why do you think the founders of Rovio Mobile stuck with their company as long as they did? Wouldn't it have made perfect sense for them to throw in the towel before they got to release number 52, which turned out to be Angry Birds? Similarly, why do you think Donahue and Rubin kept calling Colin Angle?

Sources: A. Warner and B. Rubin, "Benjamin Rubin (Zeo)," Mixergy Podcast, www.mixergy.com, January, 3, 2011 (accessed March 11, 2011); A. Moen and N. Wingfield, "Angry Birds Raises $42 Million," *Wall Street Journal*, March 3, 2011, B1.

or biggest mistake?" Young replied, "In my first two businesses, my interest was always in 'the new thing,' so I wasn't paying attention to details. As a result of my lack of interest in getting the repetitive stuff right, we never achieved the profitability we should have."[30]

Common Myths About Entrepreneurs

LEARNING OBJECTIVE
5. Explain the five common myths regarding entrepreneurship.

There are many misconceptions about who entrepreneurs are and what motivates them to launch firms to develop their ideas. Some misconceptions are because of the media covering atypical entrepreneurs, such as a couple of college students who obtain venture capital to fund a small business that they grow into a multimillion-dollar company. Such articles rarely state that these entrepreneurs are the exception rather than the norm and that their success is a result of carefully executing an appropriate plan to commercialize what inherently is a solid business idea. Indeed, the success of many of the entrepreneurs we study in each chapter's Opening Profile is a result of carefully executing the different aspects of the entrepreneurial process. Let's look at the most common myths and the realities about entrepreneurs.

Myth 1: Entrepreneurs are born, not made.   This myth is based on the mistaken belief that some people are genetically predisposed to be entrepreneurs. The consensus of many hundreds of studies on the psychological and sociological makeup of entrepreneurs is that entrepreneurs are not genetically different from other people. This evidence can be interpreted as meaning that no one is "born" to be an entrepreneur and that everyone has the potential to become one. Whether someone does or doesn't is a function of environment, life experiences, and personal choices.[31] However, there are personality traits and characteristics commonly associated with entrepreneurs; these are listed in Table 1.3. These traits are developed over time and evolve from an individual's social context. For example, studies show that people with parents who were

You might describe an entrepreneur as an independent thinker, an innovator, or perhaps a risk taker. These young entrepreneurs are passionate enough to work at a hectic pace if that's what it takes to get their company up and running. Consider Mark Zuckerberg, who was so enthused about the future of Facebook that he dropped out of Harvard University to pursue his vision.

Eric Audras/Altopress/Newscom

TABLE 1.3   COMMON TRAITS AND CHARACTERISTICS OF ENTREPRENEURS

A moderate risk taker	Optimistic disposition
A networker	Persuasive
Achievement motivated	Promoter
Alert to opportunities	Resource assembler/leverager
Creative	Self-confident
Decisive	Self-starter
Energetic	Tenacious
A strong work ethic	Tolerant of ambiguity
Lengthy attention span	Visionary

self-employed are more likely to become entrepreneurs.[32] After witnessing a father's or mother's independence in the workplace, an individual is more likely to find independence appealing.[33] Similarly, people who personally know an entrepreneur are more than twice as likely to be involved in starting a new firm as those with no entrepreneur acquaintances or role models.[34] The positive impact of knowing an entrepreneur is explained by the fact that direct observation of other entrepreneurs reduces the ambiguity and uncertainty associated with the entrepreneurial process.

Myth 2: Entrepreneurs are gamblers.   A second myth about entrepreneurs is that they are gamblers and take big risks. The truth is, entrepreneurs are usually **moderate risk takers**, as are most people.[35] The idea that entrepreneurs are gamblers originates from two sources. First, entrepreneurs typically have jobs that are less structured, and so they face a more uncertain set of possibilities than managers or rank-and-file employees.[36] For example, an entrepreneur who starts a social network consulting service has a less stable job than one working for a state governmental agency. Second, many entrepreneurs have a strong need to achieve and often set challenging goals, a behavior that is sometimes equated with risk taking.

Myth 3: Entrepreneurs are motivated primarily by money.   It is naïve to think that entrepreneurs don't seek financial rewards. As discussed previously, however, money is rarely the primary reason entrepreneurs start new firms and persevere. The importance and role of money in a start-up is put in perspective by Colin Angle, the founder and CEO of iRobot, the maker of the popular Roomba robotic vacuum cleaner. Commenting on his company's mission statement Angle said:

> Our, "Build Cool Stuff, Deliver Great Products, Have Fun, Make Money, Change the World" (mission statement) kept us (in the early days of the Company) unified with a common purpose while gut-wrenching change surrounded us. It reminded us that our goal was to have fun and make money. Most importantly, it reminded us that our mission was not only to make money, but to change the world in the process.[37]

Some entrepreneurs warn that the pursuit of money can be distracting. Media mogul Ted Turner said, "If you think money is a real big deal . . .

you'll be too scared of losing it to get it."[38] Similarly, Sam Walton, commenting on all the media attention that surrounded him after he was named the richest man in America by *Forbes* magazine in 1985, said:

> Here's the thing: money never has meant that much to me, not even in the sense of keeping score. . . . We're not ashamed of having money, but I just don't believe a big showy lifestyle is appropriate for anywhere, least of all here in Bentonville where folks work hard for their money. We all know that everyone puts on their trousers one leg at a time. . . . I still can't believe it was news that I get my hair cut at the barbershop. Where else would I get it cut? Why do I drive a pickup truck? What am I supposed to haul my dogs around in, a Rolls-Royce?[39]

Myth 4: Entrepreneurs should be young and energetic.   Entrepreneurial activity is fairly evenly spread out over age ranges. According to an Index of Entrepreneurial Activity maintained by the Kauffman Foundation, 26 percent of entrepreneurs are ages 20 to 34, 25 percent are ages 35 to 44, 25 percent are ages 45 to 54, and 23 percent are ages 55 to 64. The biggest jump, by far, from 1996 to 2010, which is the period the Kauffman date covers, is the 55 to 64 age bracket. A total of 14 percent of entrepreneurs were 55 to 64 years old in 1996, compared to 23 percent in 2010. The increasing number of older-aged entrepreneurs is a big change in the entrepreneurial landscape in the United States.[40]

Although it is important to be energetic, investors often cite the strength of the entrepreneur (or team of entrepreneurs) as their most important criterion in the decision to fund new ventures.[41] In fact, a sentiment that venture capitalists often express is that they would rather fund a strong entrepreneur with a mediocre business idea than fund a strong business idea and a mediocre entrepreneur. What makes an entrepreneur "strong" in the eyes of an investor is experience in the area of the proposed business, skills and abilities that will help the business, a solid reputation, a track record of success, and passion about the business idea. The first four of these five qualities favor older rather than younger entrepreneurs.

Myth 5: Entrepreneurs love the spotlight.   Indeed, some entrepreneurs are flamboyant; however, the vast majority of them do not attract public attention. In fact, many entrepreneurs, because they are working on proprietary products or services, avoid public notice. Consider that entrepreneurs are the source of the launch of many of the 2,850 companies listed on the NASDAQ, and many of these entrepreneurs are still actively involved with their firms. But how many of these entrepreneurs can you name? Perhaps a half dozen? Most of us could come up with Bill Gates of Microsoft, Jeff Bezos of Amazon.com, Steve Jobs of Apple Inc., Mark Zuckerberg of Facebook and maybe Larry Page and Sergey Brin of Google. Whether or not they sought attention, these are the entrepreneurs who are often in the news. But few of us could name the founders of Netflix, Twitter, or GAP even though we frequently use these firms' products and services. These entrepreneurs, like most, have either avoided attention or been passed over by the popular press. They defy the myth that entrepreneurs, more so than other groups in our society, love the spotlight.

Types of Start-Up Firms

As shown in Figure 1.2, there are three types of start-up firms: salary-substitute firms, lifestyle firms, and entrepreneurial firms.

FIGURE 1.2
Types of Start-Up Firms

Salary-Substitute Firms	Lifestyle Firms	Entrepreneurial Firms
Firms that basically provide their owner or owners a similar level of income to what they would be able to earn in a conventional job	Firms that provide their owner or owners the opportunity to pursue a particular lifestyle, and make a living at it	Firms that bring new products and services to the market by creating and seizing opportunities regardless of the resources they currently control

LEARNING OBJECTIVE
6. Explain how entrepreneurial firms differ from salary-substitute and lifestyle firms.

Salary-substitute firms are small firms that yield a level of income for their owner or owners that is similar to what they would earn when working for an employer. Dry cleaners, convenience stores, restaurants, accounting firms, retail stores, and hairstyling salons are examples of salary-substitute firms. The vast majority of small businesses fit into this category. Salary-substitute firms offer common, easily available products or services to customers that are not particularly innovative.

Lifestyle firms provide their owner or owners the opportunity to pursue a particular lifestyle and earn a living while doing so. Lifestyle firms include ski instructors, golf and tennis pros, wine bars, and tour guides. These firms are not innovative, nor do they grow quickly. Commonly, lifestyle companies promote a particular sport, hobby, or pastime and may employ only the owner or just a handful of people. Tahoe Trips & Trails, owned by Hanna Sullivan, is an example of a lifestyle firm. The company leads multiday outdoor adventure trips for private groups and corporate clients to Lake Tahoe, Yosemite, Death Valley, Jackson Hole, and similar locations. Sullivan left a prestigious job with Freemont Ventures, a private investment company, to start Tahoe Trips & Trails because it better accommodates her preferred lifestyle.

Entrepreneurial firms bring new products and services to market. As we noted earlier in this chapter, the essence of entrepreneurship is creating value and then disseminating that value to customers. In this context, **value** refers to worth, importance, or utility. Entrepreneurial firms bring new products and services to market by creating and then seizing opportunities. Google, Facebook, and Zynga are well-known, highly successful examples of entrepreneurial firms. Having recognized an opportunity, the entrepreneurs leading companies of this type create products and services that have worth, that are important to their customers, and that provide a measure of usefulness to their customers that they wouldn't have otherwise.

Next, we describe the newly emerging characteristics of today's entrepreneurs. You may be surprised to learn about the types of individuals who are choosing to become entrepreneurs! While reading these characteristics, think about people you know who are accurately described by these characteristics. Do you think any of these people will choose to become entrepreneurs?

LEARNING OBJECTIVE
7. Discuss the changing demographics of entrepreneurs in the United States.

CHANGING DEMOGRAPHICS OF ENTREPRENEURS

Over the past 10 years, the demographic makeup of entrepreneurial firms has changed in the United States and around the world. Of the 27.5 million businesses in the United States,[42] women, minorities, seniors, and young people own an increasingly larger number of them. This is an exciting development for the entrepreneurial sector of the U.S economy.

Women Entrepreneurs While men are still more likely to start businesses than women, the number of women-owned businesses is increasing. According to the U.S. Census Bureau, there were 6.5 million privately held women-owned firms in the United States in 2002, the most recent year the U.S. Census Bureau collected ownership data. These firms generated an estimated $940 billion in sales and employed 7.1 million people. The number of women-owned firms increased by 19.8 percent from 1997 to 2002, compared with a growth rate of 10.3 percent for United States firms overall.[43]

According to a survey of both women-owned and men-owned businesses in the United States, the average age of the individuals who lead women-owned firms is 44.7 years old. A total of 52.7 percent of women-owned firms are home-based, 31.9 percent are multi-owner firms, and 19.5 percent were started for less than $2,000. The top industry for women-owned business is retail (19 percent) followed by professional, management, and educational services (16.3 percent).[44] Women-owned firms still trail male-owned businesses in terms of sales and profits. The average women-owned firm has annual sales of $60,264 and annual profits of $14,549, compared to annual sales of $118,987 and profits of $30,373 for male-owned businesses.[45]

There are a growing number of groups that support and advocate for women-owned businesses. An example is Count Me In (www.makeminea-million.org), which is the leading national not-for-profit provider of resources, business education, and community support for women entrepreneurs.[46]

Minority Entrepreneurs There has been a substantial increase in minority entrepreneurs in the United States from 1996 to 2010. The biggest jump has come in Latino entrepreneurs, which increased from 11 percent to 23 percent from 1996 to 2010, followed by Asian entrepreneurs, which jumped from 4 percent to 6 percent during the same period. While these numbers are encouraging, in general the firms created by minority entrepreneurs lag behind averages for all firms in terms of economic indicators. The Kauffman Foundation is one group that is actively engaged in research to not only track the growth in minority entrepreneurs, but to better understand how to

These are the faces of the entrepreneurs of the future. Collectively they will be older, more ethnically diverse, and will include more women than any time in the past.

strengthen the infrastructures and networks to enable minority entrepreneurs to reach higher levels of financial success.[47]

Similar to women entrepreneurs, an important factor facilitating the growth of minority entrepreneurs is the number of organizations that promote and provide assistance. Examples include the Latin Business Association, Black Business Association, National Indian Business Association, The National Council of Asian American Business Associations, and the Minority Business Development Agency, which is part of the United States Department of Commerce.

Senior Entrepreneurs The increase in entrepreneurial activity among senior entrepreneurs, consisting of people 55 years and older, between 1996 and 2010 is substantial (from 14 percent to 23 percent). This increase is attributed to a number of factors, including corporate downsizing, an increasing desire among older workers for more personal fulfillment in their lives, and growing worries among seniors that they need to earn additional income to pay for future health care services and other expenses. Many people in the 55 and older age range have substantial business experience, financial resources that they can draw upon, and excellent vigor and health.

There are a number of interesting statistics associated with the increasing incidence of senior entrepreneurs. For example, 39 is now the average age of the founders of technology companies in the United States, with twice as many over age 50 as under age 25. Similarly, the steady increase in life expectancy means that Americans are not only living longer, but are living healthier longer, and are likely to remain engaged in either a job or an entrepreneurial venture longer in their lives than earlier generations.[48]

Young Entrepreneurs Interestingly, a drop in new entrepreneurial activity for people in the 20 to 34 age range occurred between 1996 and 2010 (from 35 percent in 1996 to 26 percent in 2010); nonetheless, the number of young people interested in entrepreneurship remains strong. At the high school and younger level, according to a Harris Interactive survey of 2,438 individual ages 8 to 21, 40 percent said they'd like to start their own business someday. A total of 59 percent of the 8- to 21-year-olds said they know someone who has started his or her own business.[49] The teaching of entrepreneurship courses is becoming increasingly common in both public and private high schools. Not-for-profit agencies are involved in these efforts too. The Network for Teaching Entrepreneurship (NFTE), for example, provides entrepreneurship education programs to young people from low-income communities. The organization's largest annual event is called "Lemonade Day" and is held each May. In 2011, over 120,000 kids attended one-day entrepreneurial training sessions in 31 cities. The program teaches children and teens how to borrow money and repay investors who help start their stands, and what to do with the profit, including donating some to nonprofit causes.[50] Since its founding, the NFTE has reached more than 300,000 young people, and currently has programs in 21 states and 10 foreign countries.[51]

In addition to the NFTE, a growing number of colleges and universities are offering entrepreneurship-focused programs for high school students. Babson College, for example, offers three Summer Study Programs for high school students. The first two programs, Babson Entrepreneur Development Experience and Babson Idea Generation Program, are resident programs for high school students entering their junior or senior year. Members of the Babson faculty teach in these programs; each program last seven weeks. The third program, Service Learning Experience, is a nonresident program for high school sophomores who are passionate about social outreach.[52]

On college campuses, interest in entrepreneurship education is at an all-time high, as will be described throughout this book. More than 2,000 colleges and universities in the United States, which is about two-thirds of the total, offer at least one course in entrepreneurship. Although the bulk of entrepreneurship education takes place within business schools, many other colleges and departments are offering entrepreneurship courses as well—including engineering, agriculture, theater, dance, education, law, and nursing.

ENTREPRENEURSHIP'S IMPORTANCE

LEARNING OBJECTIVE
8. Discuss the impact of entrepreneurial firms on economics and societies.

Entrepreneurship's importance to an economy and the society in which it resides was first articulated in 1934 by Joseph Schumpeter, an Austrian economist who did the majority of his work at Harvard University. In his book *The Theory of Economic Development*, Schumpeter argued that entrepreneurs develop new products and technologies that over time make current products and technologies obsolete. Schumpeter called this process **creative destruction**. Because new products and technologies are typically better than those they replace and the availability of improved products and technologies increases consumer demand, creative destruction stimulates economic activity. The new products and technologies may also increase the productivity of all elements of a society.[53]

The creative destruction process is initiated most effectively by start-up ventures that improve on what is currently available. Small firms that practice this art are often called "innovators" or "agents of change." The process of creative destruction is not limited to new products and technologies; it can include new pricing strategies (e.g., Netflix in DVDs), new distribution channels (such as e-books for books), or new retail formats (such as IKEA in furniture and Whole Foods Market in groceries).

Now let's look more closely at entrepreneurship's importance.

Economic Impact of Entrepreneurial Firms

For two reasons, entrepreneurial behavior has a strong impact on an economy's strength and stability.

Innovation **Innovation** is the process of creating something new, which is central to the entrepreneurial process.[54] According to a 2010 Small Business Administration report, small firms (fewer than 500 employees) are providers of a significant share of the innovations that take place in the United States. In addition, several studies funded by the Office of Advocacy for the Small Business Administration have found that small businesses outperform their larger counterparts in terms of patent activity (issuance).[55]

Job Creation Small businesses are the creators of most new jobs in the United States, and employ more than half of all private sector employees.[56] Small business is held in high regard in this area. According to a Kauffman Foundation survey, 92 percent of Americans say entrepreneurs are critically important to job creation. A total of 75 percent believe that the United States cannot have a sustained economic recovery without another burst of entrepreneurial activity.[57]

The statistics are persuasive regarding the importance of small business to job growth. From 1980 to 2005, firms less than five years old accounted for all net job growth in the United States.[58] Collectively, new firms add an average of 3 million jobs to the U.S. economy during their first year, while older companies lose 1 million jobs annually.[59]

Entrepreneurial Firms' Impact on Society

The innovations of entrepreneurial firms have a dramatic impact on a society. Think of all the new products and services that make our lives easier, enhance our productivity at work, improve our health, and entertain us. For example, Amgen, an entrepreneurial firm that helped pioneer the biotechnology industry, has produced a number of drugs that have dramatically improved people's lives. An example is NEUPOGEN, a drug that decreases the incidence of infection in cancer patients who are undergoing chemotherapy treatment. In addition to improved health care, consider smartphones, social networks, Internet shopping, overnight package delivery, and digital photography. All these products are new to this generation, yet it's hard to imagine our world without them.

However, innovations do create moral and ethical issues with which societies are forced to grapple. For example, bar-code scanner technology and the Internet have made it easier for companies to track the purchasing behavior of their customers, but this raises privacy concerns. Similarly, bioengineering has made it easier to extend the shelf life of many food products, but some researchers and consumers question the long-term health implications of bioengineered foods.

Entrepreneurial Firms' Impact on Larger Firms

LEARNING OBJECTIVE

9. Identify ways in which large firms benefit from the presence of smaller entrepreneurial firms.

In addition to the impact that entrepreneurial firms have on the economy and society, they also have a positive impact on the effectiveness of larger firms. For example, some entrepreneurial firms are original equipment manufacturers, producing parts that go into products that larger firms manufacture and sell. Thus, many exciting new products, such as smartphones, digital cameras, and improved prescription drugs, are not solely the result of the efforts of larger companies with strong brand names, such as Samsung, Canon, and Johnson & Johnson. They were produced with the cutting-edge component parts or research and development efforts provided by entrepreneurial firms.

The evidence shows that many entrepreneurial firms have built their entire business models around producing products and services that help larger firms be more efficient or effective. For example, an increasing number of U.S. firms are competing in foreign markets. These initiatives often require firms to employ translators to help them communicate with their foreign counterparts. SpeakLike, a 2008 start-up, has created an online service that provides real-time translation services for two or more people who speak different languages, at a cost considerably below what it costs to employ human translators. Similarly, CADI Scientific, the focus of the "You Be the VC 3.2" feature, sells a wireless patient monitoring system which regularly checks hospital patients' vital medical data including temperature and blood pressure. The system, which is primarily used in hospitals in the Middle East and Asia, decreases the risk of human error and reduces nurses' workload.

In many instances, entrepreneurial firms partner with larger companies to reach mutually beneficial goals. Participation in business partnerships accelerates a firm's growth by giving it access to some of its partner's resources, managerial talent, and intellectual capacities. We examine the idea of partnering throughout this book. In each chapter, look for the boxed feature titled "Partnering for Success," which illustrates how entrepreneurial firms use business partnerships to boost their chances for success. The feature in this chapter discusses how small biotechnology firms and large drug companies partner with one another to bring pharmaceutical products to market.

PARTNERING FOR SUCCESS

Working Together: How Biotech Firms and Large Drug Companies Bring Pharmaceutical Products to Market

Large firms and smaller entrepreneurial firms play different roles in business and society and can often produce the best results by partnering with each other rather than acting as adversaries. The pharmaceutical industry is an excellent example of how this works.

It is well-known that barriers to entry in the pharmaceutical industry are high. The average new product takes between 10 and 15 years from discovery to commercial sale. The process of discovering, testing, obtaining approval, manufacturing, and marketing a new drug is long and expensive. How, then, do biotech start-ups make it? The answer is that few biotech firms actually take their products to market. Here's how it works.

Biotech firms specialize in discovering and patenting new drugs—it's what they're good at. In most cases, however, they have neither the money nor the know-how to bring the products to market. In contrast, the large drug companies, such as Johnson & Johnson, Pfizer, and Merck, specialize in developing and marketing drugs and providing information to doctors about them. It's what they are good at. But these companies typically don't have the depth of scientific talent and the entrepreneurial zeal that the small biotech firms do. These two types of firms need one another to be as successful as possible. Often, but not always, what happens is this. The biotech firms discover and patent new drugs, and the larger drug companies develop them and bring them to market.

Biotech firms earn money through this arrangement by licensing or selling their patent-protected discoveries to the larger companies or by partnering with them in some revenue-sharing way. The large drug companies make money by selling the products to consumers.

The most compelling partnership arrangements are those that help entrepreneurial firms focus on what they do best, which is typically innovation, and that allow them to tap into their partners' complementary strengths and resources.

Questions for Critical Thinking

1. In your opinion, what factors in the business environment encourage firms to partner to compete?
2. What risks do small firms face when partnering with large, successful companies? What risks do large companies take when they rely on small firms as a source of innovation?
3. How might government policies affect partnering actions between small and large firms in the pharmaceutical industry?
4. If you worked for an entrepreneurial venture, what would you want to know about a large firm before recommending that your firm form a partnership with that large, established company?

THE ENTREPRENEURIAL PROCESS

LEARNING OBJECTIVE
10. Explain the entrepreneurial process.

The entrepreneurial process we discuss in this book consists of four steps:

Step 1 Deciding to become an entrepreneur

Step 2 Developing successful business ideas

Step 3 Moving from an idea to an entrepreneurial firm

Step 4 Managing and growing the entrepreneurial firm

Figure 1.3 models the entrepreneurial process you will study while reading this text. This process is the guide or framework around which we develop this book's contents. The double-headed arrow between the decision to become an entrepreneur and the development of successful business ideas indicates that sometimes the opportunity to develop an idea prompts a person to become an entrepreneur. Each section of Figure 1.3 is explained in the following sections.

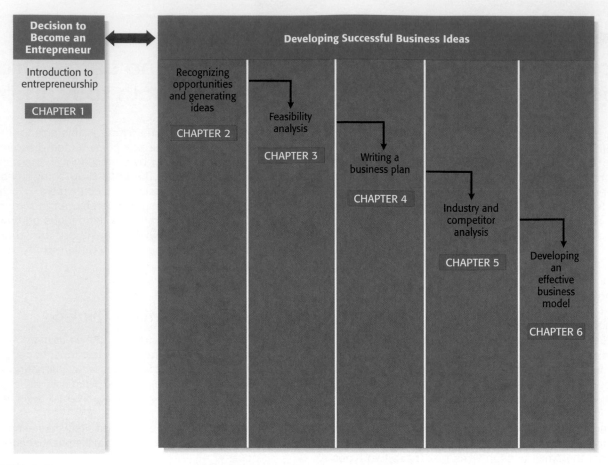

FIGURE 1.3
Basic Model of the
Entrepreneurial Process

Decision to Become an Entrepreneur (Chapter 1)

As discussed earlier, people become entrepreneurs to be their own bosses, to pursue their own ideas, and to realize financial rewards. Usually, a **triggering event** prompts an individual to become an entrepreneur.[60] For example, an individual may lose her job and decide that the time is right to start her own business. Or a person might receive an inheritance and for the first time in his life have the money to start his own company. Lifestyle issues may also trigger entrepreneurial careers. For example, a woman may wait until her youngest child is in school before she decides to launch her own entrepreneurial venture.

Developing Successful Business Ideas (Chapters 2–6)

Many new businesses fail not because the entrepreneur didn't work hard but because there was no real opportunity to begin with. Developing a successful business idea includes opportunity recognition, feasibility analysis, writing a business plan, industry analysis, and the development of an effective business model. Chapter 2 takes a scientific look at how entrepreneurs recognize opportunities and describes how the opportunity recognition process typically unfolds. Chapter 3 focuses on feasibility analysis: the way to determine whether

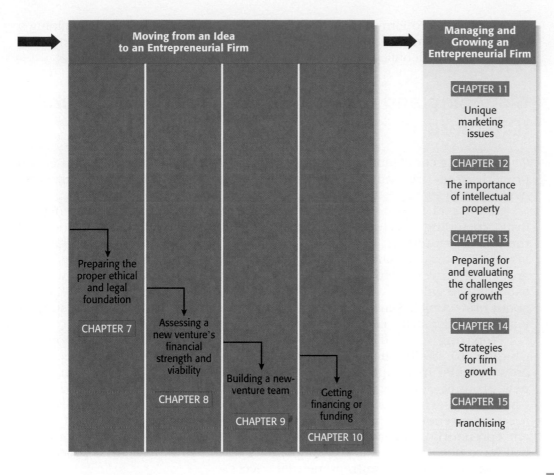

FIGURE 1.3
Continued

an idea represents a viable business opportunity. Chapter 4 describes how to write a business plan. A **business plan** is a written document that describes all the aspects of a business venture in a concise manner. It is usually necessary to have a written business plan to raise money and attract high-quality business partners. Some entrepreneurs are impatient and don't want to spend the time it takes to write a business plan.[61] This approach is usually a mistake. Writing a business plan forces an entrepreneur to think carefully through all the aspects of a business venture. It also helps a new venture establish a set of milestones that can be used to guide the early phases of the business rollout. Industry and competitor analysis is our concern in Chapter 5. Knowing the industry in which a firm will choose to compete is crucial to an entrepreneur's success. Chapter 6 focuses on the important topic of developing an effective business model. A firm's **business model** is its plan for how it competes, uses its resources, structures its relationships, interfaces with customers, and creates value to sustain itself on the basis of the profits it generates.

Moving from an Idea to an Entrepreneurial Firm (Chapters 7–10)

The first step in turning an idea into reality is to prepare a proper ethical and legal foundation for a firm, including selecting an appropriate form of business ownership. These issues are discussed in Chapter 7. Chapter 8 deals with the important topic of assessing a new venture's financial strength and viability. Important information is contained in this chapter about completing and analyzing both historical and pro forma financial statements. Chapter 9 focuses on building a new-venture team. Chapter 10 highlights the important task of getting financing or funding and identifies the options that a firm has for raising money.

Managing and Growing an Entrepreneurial Firm (Chapters 11–15)

Given today's competitive environment, all firms must be managed and grown properly to ensure their ongoing success. This is the final stage of the entrepreneurial process.

Chapter 11 focuses on the unique marketing issues facing entrepreneurial firms, including selecting an appropriate target market, building a brand, and the four Ps—product, price, promotion, and place (or distribution)—for new firms. Chapter 12 examines the important role of intellectual property in the growth of entrepreneurial firms. More and more, the value of "know-how" exceeds the value of a company's physical assets. In addition, we will talk about protecting business ideas through intellectual property statutes, such as patents, trademarks, copyrights, and trade secrets.

Preparing for and evaluating the challenges of growth is the topic of Chapter 13. We'll look at the characteristics and behaviors of successful growth firms. In Chapter 14, we'll study strategies for growth, ranging from new product development to mergers and acquisitions. We conclude with Chapter 15, which focuses on franchising. Not all franchise organizations are entrepreneurial firms, but franchising is a growing component of the entrepreneurial landscape. When you finish studying these 15 chapters, you will have been exposed to all components of the entrepreneurial process—a process that is vital to entrepreneurial success.

CHAPTER SUMMARY

1. Entrepreneurship is the process by which individuals pursue opportunities without regard to resources they currently control.

2. Corporate entrepreneurship is the conceptualization of entrepreneurship at the organizational level. Entrepreneurial firms are proactive, innovative, and risk taking. In contrast, conservative firms take a more "wait and see" posture, are less innovative, and are risk averse.

3. The three primary reasons that people decide to become entrepreneurs and start their own firms are as follows: to be their own boss, to pursue their own ideas, and to realize financial rewards.

4. Passion for the business, product/customer focus, tenacity despite failure, and execution intelligence are the four primary characteristics of successful entrepreneurs.

5. The five most common myths regarding entrepreneurship are that entrepreneurs are born, not made; that entrepreneurs are gamblers; that entrepreneurs are motivated primarily by money; that entrepreneurs should be young and energetic; and that entrepreneurs love the spotlight.

6. Entrepreneurial firms are the firms that bring new products and services to market by recognizing and seizing opportunities regardless of the resources they currently control. Entrepreneurial firms stress innovation, which is not the case for salary-substitute and lifestyle firms.

7. The demographic makeup of those launching entrepreneurial firms is changing in the United States and around the world. There is growing evidence that an increasing number of women, minorities, seniors, and young people are becoming actively involved in the entrepreneurial process.

8. There is strong evidence that entrepreneurial behavior has a significant impact on economic

stability and strength. The areas in which entrepreneurial firms contribute the most are innovation and job creation. Entrepreneurial behavior also has a dramatic impact on society. It's easy to think of new products and services that have helped make our lives easier, that have made us more productive at work, that have improved our health, and that have entertained us in new ways.

9. In addition to the impact that entrepreneurial firms have on an economy and society, entrepreneurial firms have a positive impact on the effectiveness of larger firms. There are many entrepreneurial firms that have built their entire business models around producing products and services that help larger firms increase their efficiency and effectiveness.

10. The four distinct elements of the entrepreneurial process, pictured in Figure 1.3, are deciding to become an entrepreneur, developing successful business ideas, moving from an idea to establishing an entrepreneurial firm, and managing and growing an entrepreneurial firm.

KEY TERMS

business model, **51**
business plan, **51**
corporate entrepreneurship, **32**
creative destruction, **47**
entrepreneurial firms, **44**
entrepreneurial intensity, **32**

entrepreneurship, **32**
execution intelligence, **39**
innovation, **47**
lifestyle firms, **44**
moderate risk takers, **42**
passion for their business, **35**

product/customer focus, **37**
salary-substitute firms, **44**
triggering event, **50**
value, **44**

REVIEW QUESTIONS

1. Increasingly, entrepreneurship is being practiced in countries throughout the world. Why do you think this is the case? Do you expect entrepreneurship to continue to spread throughout the world, or do you think its appeal will subside over time?
2. What key insights does the GEMS study provide us about entrepreneurship?
3. What evidence is available suggesting that the often reported statistic that 9 out of 10 new businesses fail is an exaggeration? What is a more realistic failure rate for new firms?
4. What is entrepreneurship? How can one differentiate an entrepreneurial firm from any other type of firm? In what ways is an entrepreneur who just launched a restaurant different from someone who just took a job as the general manager of a restaurant owned by a major restaurant chain?
5. What are the three main attributes of firms that pursue high levels of corporate entrepreneurship? Would these firms score high or low on an entrepreneurial intensity scale?
6. What are the three primary reasons people become entrepreneurs? Which reason is given most commonly? Which reason best describes why you may choose to become an entrepreneur?
7. Some people start their own firms to pursue financial rewards. However, these rewards are often far fewer than imagined and/or expected. Why is this so?
8. What are the four primary traits and characteristics of successful entrepreneurs?
9. Why is passion such an important characteristic of successful entrepreneurs? What is it about passion that makes it particularly compatible with the entrepreneurial process?
10. Why is a product/customer focus an important characteristic of successful entrepreneurs?
11. What is it about "tenacity" that makes it such an important characteristic for entrepreneurs?
12. What are the five common myths of entrepreneurship?
13. What evidence do we have that debunks the myth that entrepreneurs are born, not made?

14. What are the four distinctive parts of the entrepreneurial process and what is the relationship among the parts?

15. How would you characterize the risk-taking propensity of most entrepreneurs?

16. What factors favor older entrepreneurs as opposed to younger entrepreneurs?

17. What did Joseph Schumpeter mean by the term *creative destruction*?

18. In general, what effects does entrepreneurship have on economies around the world?

19. How is the demographic makeup of entrepreneurs changing in the United States? What do you believe is accounting for these changes?

20. Describe several examples of the impact that entrepreneurial firms have on a society.

APPLICATION QUESTIONS

1. Reread the opening case, and then list all the smart or effective moves Fraser Doherty made in the early days of building SuperJam. Which three moves were most instrumental in SuperJam's early success? Be prepared to justify your selections.

2. Imagine that you're the dean of your college and you've suggested that more entrepreneurship courses be taught throughout your college's curriculum. You're getting resistance from some professors who think that entrepreneurship is a fad. Make the argument that entrepreneurship isn't a fad and is an extremely important topic.

3. Select one of the following large firms: Cessna Aircraft Company, Tempur-Pedic, or Corning Incorporated. Familiarize yourself with the company. Assess how entrepreneurial the firm is, based on the definitions of corporate entrepreneurship and entrepreneurial intensity provided in the chapter.

4. Karen Jenkins has a good job working for the city of Rapid City, South Dakota, but is weary of 2 percent (or less) per year pay raises. Because she has read magazine articles about young entrepreneurs becoming extremely wealthy, she decides to start her own firm. Do you think Karen is starting a firm for the right reason? Do you think the money she likely will earn will disappoint her? Do you think Karen's reason for starting a firm will contribute in a positive manner or a negative manner to the tenacity that is required to successfully launch and run an entrepreneurial venture?

5. Mark, a friend of yours, has always had a nagging desire to be his own boss. He has a good job with AT&T but has several ideas for new products that he can't get

AT&T interested in. Mark has done a good job saving money over the years and has over $100,000 in the bank. He asks you, "Am I crazy for wanting to leave AT&T to start my own businesses? How do I know that I have what it takes to be a successful entrepreneur?" What would you tell him?

6. Make a list of 10 prominent entrepreneurs who are women, minorities, or seniors (55 years or older when their firms were started). Single out one of these entrepreneurs and provide a brief overview of her or his entrepreneurial story. What did you learn about entrepreneurship by familiarizing yourself with this person's story?

7. People are sometimes puzzled by the fact that entrepreneurs who have made millions of dollars still put in 60- to 80-hour weeks helping their companies innovate and grow. After reading the chapter, why do you think millionaire and multimillionaire entrepreneurs still get up and go to work every day? If you were one of these entrepreneurs, do you think you would feel the same way? Why or why not?

8. Identify a successful entrepreneur that you admire and respect. (It can be someone that is nationally prominent or someone you know personally, such as a family member or a friend.) Briefly describe the person you identified, the company that he or she started, and the manner in which the individual exemplifies one or more of the four characteristics of a successful entrepreneur.

9. You just made a trip home and are visiting with your dad. He is 59 years old and has spent the past 12 years working in various management positions for Target. Prior to that, he served 20 years in the U.S. Marine Corps. Your father has always loved to fish and has several ideas for new fishing tackle and gear. He's made several prototypes of his ideas and has received positive feedback from other fishermen. He wonders if he is too old to start a firm and if his management experience and his military background will help him or hurt him in a new-venture context. If your dad asked you for your advice, what would you tell him?

10. Make a list of 10 prominent entrepreneurs who post frequently on Twitter. Also, make a list of five prominent entrepreneurship-related blogs. Is it a good use of a student entrepreneur's time to follow prominent entrepreneurs on Twitter and/or read entrepreneurship-related blogs?

11. Jacob Lacy is an undergraduate student at a Big 12 school. He has an idea to start an Internet-based firm that will help high school students prepare for college entrance exams. Jacob just talked to a trusted family friend, who told him that college is a poor time and place to launch a firm. The family friend told Jacob, "Try to distance yourself from the college atmosphere before you start your firm." Do you think Jacob is getting good advice? Why or why not?

12. The "You Be the VC 1.2" feature focuses on Songkick, a company that has created a single place for music lovers to track or keep up with their favorite bands, so they'll always know where and when the bands will be performing in their area.

Do some research on Songkick and write a short summary of where the firm is today in regard to its early success (or failure) and how effectively it has executed its business plan.

13. A friend of yours just bought a Samsung smartphone equipped with the Android operating system. While showing it to you, he said, "You think entrepreneurial firms are so smart, look at what Samsung has done. It has produced a smartphone that allows me to make calls, take pictures, run apps, surf the Internet, and perform dozens of other tasks. Samsung's a big company, not a small entrepreneurial firm. What do you have to say to that?" If you were to defend the role of entrepreneurial firms in developing new technologies, how would you respond?

14. Read Case 1.1, which focuses on RunKeeper. What similarities, if any, do you see between RunKeeper's start-up story and the start-up stories of Rovio Mobile (the company behind Angry Birds) and Zeo, the two firms featured in the "Savvy Entrepreneurial Firm" boxed feature in the chapter?

15. Spend some time familiarizing yourself with the following student-founded firms: Morphology (www.morphologygames.com), and XploSafe (www.xplosafe.com). Classify each firm as a salary-substitute, lifestyle, or entrepreneurial firm. Justify your classifications.

YOU BE THE VC 1.1

Company: Windspire Energy

Web: www.windspire.com
Twitter: WindspireEnergy
Facebook: Windspire

Business Idea: Manufacture an efficient, quiet, and sleek wind power turbine that both businesses and home owners can use to harness the power of the wind to produce electricity.

Pitch: Although wind power is clean and increasingly cost-competitive, it is largely confined to large wind farms in rural areas. The primary obstacle to building windmills in more densely populated areas is the

"not-in-my-backyard" sentiment. This sentiment arises from the large scale of most wind-powered devices, the noise and shadows that are created, and the height of traditional windmills, which normally exceed local zoning requirements.

Windspire's mission is to make wind power available to businesses and home owners by avoiding these complications. The company has invented and is selling a low-cost, attractive, plug-n-produce wind power appliance that can fit within the aesthetic schemes of many business and residential environments. The appliance, called the Windspire, doesn't look like a traditional windmill or wind generator. It is 30 feet tall by 4 feet wide, ultra quiet, and is distinguished by its sleek propeller-free design. The sleek profile allows customers to easily scale up the number of turbines to meet higher energy needs. An individual unit is priced at $9,000 to $12,000 fully installed. After tax credits, the cost can be as low as $3,800, much lower than comparable wind turbines and other alternative energy options.

To make the Windspire more palatable for business and residential environments, it is manufactured with a corrosion-resistant soft silver paint that can be repainted in any color. At 30 feet (which is equivalent to a three-story building), it is below typical residential and urban zoning requirements and its uniquely slender vertical axis design allows it to operate with a low speed ratio, which makes it quiet and more visible to birds. In a business setting, several Windspires clustered together can be visually appealing and can display a company's commitment to environmental stewardship. Like other sources of wind power, a Windspire generates clean, renewable energy that doesn't require the burning of fossil fuels.

Windspire is sold in a "kit" form and includes everything that is needed except the concrete foundation. Maintenance is limited to oiling the bearings, which are 9 feet off the ground, once a year. The 1.2 kilowatt (or 1,200 watts) Windspire will produce approximately 2,000 kilowatt hours per year in 12 mile per hour average wind. This amount of electricity is sufficient to supply roughly 25 to 30 percent of the power needed for an average house. A household that spends $3,600 a year on electricity could recoup its investment in Windspire in just over five years.

Windspire turbine units are sold through local authorized dealers and siting experts.

Q&A: Based on the material covered in this chapter, what questions would you ask the firm's founders before making your funding decision? What answers would satisfy you?

Decision: If you had to make your decision on just the information provided in the pitch and on the company's Web site, would you fund this company? Why or why not?

YOU BE THE VC 1.2

Company: Songkick

Web: www.songkick.com
Twitter: Songkick
Facebook: Songkick

Business Idea: Create a single place for music lovers to track or keep up with their favorite bands, so they'll always know where and when the bands will be performing in their area. In addition, create an online platform for concert attendees to record memories of the concerts they've seen by sharing anecdotes, posting photos, and discussing the events with other people who were there.

Pitch: Songkick's founders believe that an amazing concert can change a person's life. Too often, however, people miss seeing their favorite bands because they didn't realize the bands would be in their area. Concert goers try to avoid this problem by subscribing to venue mailing lists, checking band Web sites, and sifting through generic concert newsletters. This is a clumsy process and doesn't assure music fans that they won't miss a concert they'd like to see.

Songkick offers a solution to this problem. Songkick indexes 132 different ticket vendors, venue Web sites, and local newspapers to create the most comprehensive database of upcoming concerts available. Its mission is to know about every concert that's happening in every location—from an indie band playing at a local bar to Coldplay playing Madison Square Garden. Songkick then pushes this information to its users. Users can track the performers they like, and Songkick will send them a personalized concert alert when those performers announce a tour date in their area. If a user has lots of bands he or she wants to track, artists can be tracked in bulk via Songkick's iTunes application, Last.fm import, or by importing their Facebook likes.

It doesn't stop here. Songkick's Web site is a destination for music lovers, with lots of useful and fun information. Users can check out the popular artists that are on tour. Songkick develops a profile for each member, based on their musical tastes, and recommends local concerts that align with their preferences. A particularly novel thing that Songkick has done, which took a full year to accomplish, is to assemble a list of over 1 million concerts stretching back to the 1960s, and set up a discussion forum for each concert. Now people who saw the Beatles on August 15, 1965, for example, at their famous concert at Shea Stadium in New York City can reminisce and share memories about that event.

Songkick is completely free to the user. The firm earns money via commissions on concert tickets that are purchased through its site.

Q&A: Based on the material covered in this chapter, what questions would you ask the firm's founders before making your funding decision? What answers would satisfy you?

Decision: If you had to make your decision on just the information provided in the pitch and on the company's Web site, would you fund this company? Why or why not?

CASE 1.1

RunKeeper: Combining a Passion for Running and Technology to Build an Incredibly Successful Business

Web: www.runkeeper.com
Twitter: runkeeper
Facebook: RunKeeper

Bruce R. Barringer, *Oklahoma State University*
R. Duane Ireland, *Texas A&M University*

Introduction

In early 2008, Jason Jacobs was actively looking for a business idea to pursue. He knew he wanted to start his own business—he just didn't know what that business would be. Anticipating the need for start-up funds, he lived like a bootstrap entrepreneur, even though he had a good job. He was trying to save at least two years of living expenses to support himself when he settled on a business to start.

Trying to settle on a business idea was frustrating for Jacobs. He looked at clean tech, enterprise software, and several other alternatives, but nothing resonated. He got so frustrated that he started training for a marathon as a way to clear his head. While training for the marathon he tried several of the devices that were available at the time to time and track practice runs, including GPS-enabled watches and the Nike+iPod device. Although the devices worked, he found preparing for the marathon to be a fragmented experience. Different devices offered different features, but none tied the whole experience of training and running together. Jacobs had his business idea. He would create a company that would combine his passions for running and technology, and build a Web-based platform that would allow runners to integrate the hardware devices they were running with a Web-based platform that would provide them analytics, coaching, running-related tips, and social support. In this sense, Jacobs's business idea created a "turnkey" operation for runners interested in tracking their progress.

Getting Started

After a brief period of indecision, Jacobs quit his job to focus on his business idea full-time. He remembers thinking, "Now you've got your idea and you're going to work on it nights and weekends in a coffee shop—are you kidding me?" He started asking around about people who might help him get started. He was introduced to some traditional Web site developers, who wanted $50,000 to $75,000 to build the site and functionality he envisioned. Although Jacobs had a tidy sum of money tucked away, these suggested fees were just too high. He met three guys who were willing to moonlight to help him get his project off the ground at a much lower cost. He didn't bite, thinking that if he was going to commit full-time he didn't want to hitch his wagon to people who were only in it part-time. He then became acquainted with a two-man development shop that listened to his idea and asked him if he'd thought about building an iPhone app. That thought had never occurred to Jacobs, but sounded like a great idea. The iPhone app store was set to debut on July 12, 2008, in just a few months, and the two developers had just received a development license from Apple. They hadn't built an app yet but were eager to try, and offered Jacobs a deal if he could pay for their first development effort. Jacobs knew he could go back to the three moonlighters to get the Web site side of the business built. So in Jacobs's mind, the business that was taking shape was to build an iPhone app, with the help of the

(continued)

two developers, that would time and track a runner's runs, along with a Web-based platform, built by the three moonlighters, that would take data from the app and provide runners analytics, coaching, social support, etc., regarding their most recent runs and their entire running programs.

Jacobs now had a six-person team—himself, the two-man development shop, and the three moonlighters working on his business idea. The six held weekly meetings during the development process, and as unorthodox of a structure as it was, it worked well. Both sides delivered on time, and the system was put together and was ready to go for the launch of the iPhone app store.

Doubters, Good Press, and Execution Intelligence

When Jacobs talked to others about what his team was building, there were plenty of doubters. The biggest source of skepticism focused on whether people would actually run with their iPhone. To Jacobs this was a no brainer. The iPod was a perfect analog. Just two versions earlier, the iPod was nearly as big as the iPhone, and people ran with their iPods. Still, the doubters remained unconvinced. Another source of skepticism was Jacobs's team. He was literally his company's only full-time employee, yet he was about to debut a high-profile app in the new iPhone app store. Generally, the problem with using contract employees rather than hiring people full-time is that a company runs the risk of the contract employees getting distracted or not delivering on time—whatever the excuse might be. Jacobs gambled in this regard and it worked. The two-man development shop and the moonlighters came through in an exemplary manner.

In the midst of the skepticism, one thing that worked in Jacobs's favor was perfect timing. The opening of the iPhone app store created lots of press, and news outlets were eager to profile apps that would soon be available for the iPhone. Jacobs worked this angle to his favor and RunKeeper, the name he gave the app, got lots of prelaunch press. The launch of RunKeeper also aligned nicely with the emergence of Twitter and with the growth of interest in Facebook. RunKeeper engaged its users from the beginning via both Twitter and Facebook, and created a "community" of users around the RunKeeper experience. A little guerilla marketing also helped. For example, Jacobs ran the 2008 Boston Marathon dressed as an iPhone, and periodically posted on Twitter as he ran. The idea was to draw attention to RunKeeper and the iPhone app store in general. The payoff was a front page story in the *New York Times*.

Although Jacobs promoted RunKeeper when he could, he remained laser focused on execution, and turned down many promotional opportunities. In his mind, the best way to build RunKeeper was through creating an exemplary user experience. Jacobs's success in this regard can be seen in the numbers. RunKeeper has a freemium business model, meaning that the basic download is free and users can pay $10 for the premium service. As of mid-2010, 54 percent of

the people who bought the premium service from mid-2008 until the present day are still active RunKeeper users. That's an extremely high retention rate for a smartphone application.

A photo of the RunKeeper app in action is shown next. Along with timing a runner's run, the app shows how fast a runner is running (in mph), the number of miles run, the calories burned during a workout, and the pace of the run (in minutes per mile). The bars in the middle of the screen show how the pace has varied during the run. All this data can be automatically uploaded to the RunKeeper Web site, where a user can keep a history of his or her runs and run a variety of analytics on past and present workouts. An especially enjoyable feature is that the RunKeeper app allows users to stream their runs in real time, allowing others to follow them. The results of RunKeeper runs can also be automatically posted to a user's Twitter or Facebook account, providing the runner extra incentive to do well because the results will be immediately available for friends, family members, and other followers to see.

What Does the Future Hold for RunKeeper?

Currently, RunKeeper is primarily a smartphone app. The company has more than 2 million downloads on the Apple iPhone, and has launched an Android version that's taking off. RunKeeper has been cash flow positive since day one. Jacobs now has about a dozen employees. The company has never raised a dime of investment capital. Instead, its users have basically provided the seed funding for the company through downloads of the premium version of the product. RunKeeper sells a Web-subscription service for people who don't have a

The RunnKeeper App.

Andre J. Jackson/MCT/Newscom

smartphone. The RunKeeper app is consistently one of the top selling apps in the iTunes store.

Jacobs's long-term goals may surprise you. Technically, the name of his company is FitnessKeeper rather than RunKeeper, which gives the company room to expand. Although he envisions eventually building iPhone and Android apps for other sports, such as cycling, swimming, and skiing, he doesn't see that happening anytime soon. He believes RunKeeper has only scratched the surface of running, which Jacobs sees as a strong and vibrant industry. The company also does very little in the area of paid advertising or marketing, instead relying on the quality of its product to generate buzz and stimulate additional downloads.

Even though Jacobs says that he doesn't see RunKeeper expanding beyond running anytime soon, his ultimate goal is to build a billion-dollar company and change the way people interact with their health. How that will be achieved remains unclear. Jacobs readily admits that selling smartphone apps is not the route to building a billion-dollar company. The top smartphone app, Bejeweled 2, a puzzle game, has sold around 3 million downloads at $2.99 a piece. While impressive, that's just $9 million in one-time download fees—which is a far cry from $1 billion. Jacobs sees apps as a way of engaging users and funneling them to his Web site. The Web site will presumably offer additional products and services for sale over time.

Discussion Questions

1. Which of the characteristics of successful entrepreneurs, discussed in this chapter, do you see in Jason Jacobs? To what degree do you think these characteristics have contributed to RunKeeper's success?
2. To what extent do you think RunKeeper's basic business idea "adds value" to the lives of its customers? Who is the ideal candidate to be a RunKeeper customer?
3. To what degree do you think it would be easy or difficult for another company to imitate what RunKeeper is doing?
4. Spend some time studying the RunKeeper app. What functionality do you think the app should have that it currently doesn't have?

Application Questions

1. Make a list of three things that you are passionate about. Don't worry if they don't seem like logical choices for business ideas. Many people have built businesses around things that didn't seem like logical choices for business ideas like art, music, fitness, and spending time with family. Now brainstorm business ideas that might align with each of your passions.
2. Do you think Jacobs will achieve his dream of building a billion-dollar company? If so, write a brief scenario that describes your view of how Jacobs will achieve this objective. If you don't think Jacobs will achieve his dream, explain why.

Sources: A. Warner and J. Jacobs, "Jason Jacobs (RunKeeper)," *Mixergy*, www.mixergy.com (accessed March 28, 2011, originally posted on August 27, 2010); Runkeeper Web site, www.runkeeper.com (accessed March 28, 2011).

CASE 1.2

Aquaflow Bionomic Corporation: Passion Has Helped Turn Green Slime into Black Gold—Its Success Now Hinges on Execution Intelligence

Web: www.aquaflowgroup.com

Introduction

Ask most gardeners, fish keepers, or pool owners about algae and it is doubtful there will be a positive response. However, you will get an altogether different reaction from a group of antipodean entrepreneurs, who believe that far from being smelly, slimy, and revolting, algae is actually beautiful stuff. Their innovation, which transforms algae grown on sewage into a substitute for crude oil, is now being hailed as the answer to finding a fuel supply that doesn't exacerbate global warming.

Nick Gerritsen's Passion for Clean Technology

New Zealand–born entrepreneur Nick Gerritsen has two main passions: protecting the environment and making the seemingly impossible happen. His attention was drawn to the lack of communication between innovators and investors while he worked as an intellectual property consultant following his graduation. It was a gap in the market that he could see was preventing some vital environmental technologies from getting off the ground. Setting himself up as "an enabler," his goal was to

(continued)

specialize in discovering start-up technology companies and developing them by bringing in other people, often financiers, to help them grow. He told New Zealand's *Listener* magazine that he often reduces hard-working scientists to tears by asking them about their real dreams and ambitions. It seems that no one ever bothered to ask them about what it is they really want to achieve, and their talents get ignored.

Developments in "clean technology" particularly interested Gerritsen, and that led him to a group that was attempting to convert wood into biofuel. Although this technology was unsuccessful, Gerritsen was hooked. He then read a U.S. Energy Office report naming algae as the best land-based solution for sustainable resources for biofuel. The reasons are threefold: Algae grow continuously and don't require extensive land cropping or intensive chemical input, algae don't compete with other agricultural or horticultural uses of land, and the process produces a sustainable net energy gain by capturing free solar energy from the sun.

From that report, the idea for a company that brings algae-based biofuel to the world was born. In October 2008, three years after the company was set up, Aquaflow Bionomic Corporation announced it had produced the world's first sample of green-crude oil from wild algae using a proprietary process. Just three months later, Gerritsen announced another major breakthrough and predicted that the world's first test flight using wild-algae-based jet fuel was possibly just months away. The company had produced the world's first sample of synthetic paraffinic kerosene (SPK) converted from compounds derived from wild algae. The SPK meets Jet A-1 industry specifications for commercial aircraft fuel, which include density, flash point, and freeze point and are vital in persuading a highly safety-conscious industry that this is a viable product for the $48 billion world airline fuel market.

Balanced Expertise

Aquaflow's entry into the biofuel market coincided with the heightened international debate over the future of the technology. Questions are being increasingly raised about the carbon footprint of the first generation of biofuel production from crops like corn, maize, and rapeseed, while serious food shortages and price hikes have been blamed on rising demand for food crops for fuel.

Faith in algae to provide energy is growing. In January 2008, fuel-giant Shell announced a joint venture with HR Biopetroleum to construct a demonstration plant to harvest algae. Meanwhile, the Commercial Aviation Alternative Fuels Initiative, an alliance of aircraft manufacturers, industry organizations, and entrepreneurs, is seeking a biojet fuel that could come from algae; and a recent San Francisco "algae summit" drew more than 300 delegates.

To make the Aquaflow business model work, and take its place in the market for biofuel, it was important to combine strong skills across-the-board with strengths in scientific, business, political, and entrepreneurial disciplines.

Cofounders Vicki Buck, the former mayor of Christchurch, and Barrie Leay, the former executive director of New Zealand's Electricity Supply Association, had both worked with Gerritsen before and were inspired to join him in pursuing algae's role as an intelligent alternative in the contentious biofuel debate. Leay, a British-educated geologist, began investigating biofuels 20 years earlier. He says the difference between refining oil from algae and that pumped from beneath the earth's surface is that Aquaflow is just taking a few million years out of the process. Harvesting algae is creating energy from "new sunlight," whereas oil and gas taken from the ground is the product of "old sunlight." For Buck, who as well as her corporate and mayoral experience has served on the Government's Science and Innovation Advisory Council, the attraction of the venture was taking something that's a waste product and turning it into something useful. To complete the team, technical advisers including organic chemist Dr. Ian Miller and fuel expert Dr. Chris Bumby were brought in, along with a number of biochemists and aquaculturists.

Initial trials began at the Blenheim sewage treatment plant on New Zealand's South Island, and the resultant 5 percent algae-based component, extracted from the algae's natural oils, produced 90 percent less emissions than regular diesel. The process also produced millions of gallons of clean water along the way, which can be released back into the community for irrigation, industrial washing, or cooling. It has an impressive oil yield of 16,500 pounds per acre, which compares with palm oil's 5,500 and soybean's 1,000 pounds. In 2006, just one year after launching the company, Aquaflow staged the world's first wild algae biodiesel test drive in Wellington.

Aquaflow's Three-Part Plan

Gerritsen, Buck, and Leay's goal is that algae from waste will address the worldwide problem of the increasing volatility in crude oil supplies and pricing, increasing demand and stresses on water supplies, and instability of the global markets due to fears over climate change and the nonsustainability of fossil fuels. It is backed by the knowledge that if something as ubiquitous as sewage can be used to make a valuable transport fuel and if the process of removing the algae makes water reusable at the same time, it is an exciting proposition with global implications. The trio's plan to make algae-based biofuels a competitive player in the world market is summarized in the following table.

First, following the successful trials, Aquaflow must show that algae harvesting and conversion can work on a commercial scale in a world that urgently needs renewable fuel and clean water. This will entail working on the conversion process to give a better energy balance and developing lower-cost algae harvesting technologies. Put simply, the technology has to be cheap enough to be adopted anywhere. To fund these aims, the company embarked on an investment round to raise $20 million in funding in late 2008.

Aquaflow's Three-Part Plan to Drive Down the Cost of Biodiesel

Step 1	Increase the commercial scale of Aquaflow and implement process efficiencies.
Step 2	Increase the production of algae-based biofuels by licensing the technology worldwide.
Step 3	Support any legislative moves to encourage the switch to sustainable biofuels.

Second, in order to encourage increased production of algae-based biofuel and get the product to market as fast as possible, the company plans to license the technology to various parties worldwide and link into established companies that have the capacity to establish, service, and maintain the technology in their own territories. The company has already joined forces with a division of U.S. conglomerate Honeywell, UOP. Processes developed by UOP will be used to convert algae into fuel products that meet international standards. UOP, which is already involved with aviation biofuel research with Airbus and Boeing, will be involved in the secondary processing stage, refining the crude oil into products ready for industrial use.

Finally, Aquaflow is committed to encouraging more governmental urgency on climate-change issues, increased commitment to carbon neutrality, and any legislative moves that will encourage the switch to sustainable biofuels.

The Ultimate Importance of Execution Intelligence

The future of Aquaflow hinges on the ability of Gerritsen, Buck, and Leay to execute this carefully conceived plan. While passion is important, the entrepreneurs know that a process featuring sharp planning and execution must be in place and used to help a venture grow. There is still a great deal of ongoing research and development to do in the field, but at stake is a massive worldwide market in a number of different disciplines. Aquaflow has already been approached from interested parties involved in wastewater treatment, biopharmaceutical development, and jet fuel production.

Discussion Questions

1. What degree of confidence do you have that Gerritsen, Buck, and Leay will be able to execute their three-point plan? What factors have to come together for the plan to work? What advantages does Aquaflow have in its efforts to execute the plan and continue to grow?
2. To what extent did passion play a role in the founding of Aquaflow and its early success? Do you think that someone without passion for alternative fuels could have successfully founded the firm? Why or why not?
3. Which of the myths of entrepreneurs are dispelled by Nick Gerritsen's involvement in Aquaflow?
4. To what extent does Aquaflow have the potential to (1) make an economic impact on New Zealand, (2) make an impact on society, and (3) make an impact on larger firms?

Application Questions

1. To what extent is Aquaflow creating a network of stakeholders that have a vested interest in seeing the company succeed? Make a list of these people or groups. Comment on how each group's success is linked to Aquaflow's ultimate success.
2. Make a list of 10 people you know who might help you if you decided to start a firm. Briefly comment on the ways that each individual could offer you assistance. In each case, make a note of what you are doing, or should be doing, to solidify and nurture these relationships.

Sources: www.aquaflowgroup.com; *Listener*, May 24, 2008; "Black Gold," *IBM Business Insight* (accessed November 17, 2008); Good: *New Zealand's Guide to Sustainable Living*; "Boeing Planes Successfully Fly with Biofuels," *Biodiesel Magazine*, February 2009.

ENDNOTES

1. SuperJam homepage, www.superjam.co.uk; "Fraser Doherty: 'How I Set Up SuperJam,'" *Newbusiness.co.uk*, www.newbusiness.co.uk/articles/entrepreneurs/fraser-doherty-how-i-set-superjam (accessed September 5, 2011, originally posted December 21, 2009); "Q&A: Fraser Doherty—SuperJam," *Inspiresme.co.uk*, www.inspiresme.co.uk/interviews/q-a--fraser-doherty---superjam (accessed September 5, 2011, originally posted May 31, 2011).

2. D. Kelley, N. Bosma, and J. E. Amoros, *Global Entrepreneurship Monitor 2010 Global Report* (Babson College and Universidad del Desarrollo, 2010).

3. G. Kistruck, J. W. Webb, C. Sutter, and R. D. Ireland, "Microfranchising in Base-of-the-Pyramid Markets: Institutional Challenges and Adaptations to the Franchise Model," *Entrepreneurship Theory and Practice* 35, no. 3 (2011): 503–31.

4. B. Headd, "Redefining Business Success: Distinguishing Between Closure and Failure," *Small Business Economics* 21 (2003): 51–61.

5. T. Tyszka, J. Cieslie, A. Domurat, and A. Macko, "Motivation, Self-Efficacy, and Risk Attitudes Among Entrepreneurs During Transition to a Market Economy," *Journal of Socio-Economics* 40, no. 2 (2011): 124–31.

6. T. Astebro and P. Thompson, "Entrepreneurs, Jacks of all Trades or Hobos," *Research Policy* 40, no. 5 (2011): 637–49.

7. H. H. Stevenson and J. C. Jarillo, "A Paradigm for Entrepreneurship: Entrepreneurial Management," *Strategic Management Journal* 11 (1990): 17–27.

8. Z. J. Acs, "High-Impact Entrepreneurship," *International Handbook Series on Entrepreneurship* 5, part 2 (2010): 165–82; R. D. Ireland and J. W. Webb, "A Cross-Disciplinary Exploration of Entrepreneurship Research," *Journal of Management* 33 (2007): 891–927.

9. R. Bodle, "Regimes of Sharing Open APIs, Interoperability, and Facebook," *Information, Communication & Society* 14, no. 3 (2011): 320–37.

10. S. C. Parker, "Intrapreneurship or Entrepreneurship?" *Journal of Business Venturing* 26, no. 1 (2011): 19–34; R. D. Ireland, J. G. Covin, and D. F. Kuratko, "Conceptualizing Corporate Entrepreneurship Strategy," *Entrepreneurship Theory and Practice* 33, no. 1 (2009): 19–46.

11. V. Bouchard and O. Basso, "Exploring the Links Between Entrepreneurial Orientation and Intrapreneurship in SMEs," *Journal of Small Business and Enterprise Development* 18, no. 2 (2011): 219–31.

12. R. Branson, *Losing My Virginity* (New York: Time Warner, 1999).

13. Ladies Who Launch homepage, www.ladieswholaunch.com (accessed April 12, 2006).

14. A. Clark, "A Risk Worth Taking," *The Signal*, October 26, 2006.

15. A. Chwolka ad M. G. Raith, "The Value of Business Planning Before Start-Up—A Decision-Theoretical Perspective," *Journal of Business Venturing* (2011): in press.

16. C. Williams and S. H. Lee, "Political Heterarchy and Dispersed Entrepreneurship in the MNC," *Journal of Management Studies* (2011): in press.

17. K. Mann, "Start with Your Passion." In eds. D. Cohen and B. Feld, *Do More Faster* (Hoboken, NJ: John Wiley & Sons 2011), p. 8.

18. Mann, "Start With Your Passion."

19. D. Carnoy, "Richard Branson," *Success*, April 1998, 62–63.

20. J. Wood, "John Wood, 43, Founder of Room to Read and Author of Leaving Microsoft to Change the World," In K. Finneran's *Forbes* magazine article "In Pictures: The Greatest Risk They Ever Took," *Forbes*, January 20, 2010.

21. K. Farrell and L.C. Farrell, *Entrepreneurial Age* (New York, Allworth Press, 2001).

22. G. Spiridellis and A. Warner, "The JibJab Story. Maybe the Most Inspiring Mixergy Interview Ever!—With Gregg Spiridellis." Mixergy Podcast, www.mixergy.com (accessed May 21, 2011, originally posted on July 29, 2009).

23. R. D. Jager and R. Ortiz, *In the Company of Giants* (New York, McGraw-Hill, 2007).

24. Ladies Who Launch Home Page, www.ladieswholaunch.com (accessed May 22, 2011).

25. N. Evers, "Exploring Market Orientation in New Export Ventures," *International Journal of Entrepreneurship and Innovation Management* 13, nos. 3–4 (2011): 357–76.

26. L. Hazleton, "Profile: Jeff Bezos," *Success*, July 1998: 60.

27. Ladies Who Launch homepage, www.ladieswholaunch. com (accessed April 16, 2006).

28. N. Koehn, *Brand New: How Entrepreneurs Earned Consumers' Trust from Wedgwood to Dell* (Boston: Harvard Business School Press, 2001).

29. Koehn, *Brand New.*

30. S. Baillie, "High Tech Heroes," *Profit*, December 2000/January 2001.

31. T. Kautonen, E. T. Tomikoski, and E. Kibler, "Entrepreneurial Intentions in the Third Age: The Impact of Perceived Age Norms," *Small Business Economics* (2011): in press.

32. S. C. Parker and C. M. van Praag, "The Entrepreneur's Mode of Entry: Business Takeover or New Venture Start?" *Journal of Business Venturing* (2011): in press.

33. H. A. Ndofor and R. L. Priem, "Immigrant Entrepreneurs, the Ethnic Enclave Strategy, and Venture Performance," *Journal of Management* 37, no. 3 (2011): 790–818.

34. P. D. Reynolds, W. D. Bygrave, E. Autio, L. Cox, and M. Hay, *Global Entrepreneurship Monitor 2002 Executive Report* (Kansas City, MO: Kauffman

Foundation Center for Entrepreneurship Leadership, 2002).

35. R. A. Baron and J. Tang, "The Role of Entrepreneurs in Firm-Level Innovation: Joint Effects of Positive Affect, Creativity, and Environmental Dynamism," *Journal of Business Venturing* 26, no. 1 (2011): 49–60.

36. H. M. Neck and P. G. Greene, "Entrepreneurship Education: Known Worlds and New Frontiers," *Journal of Small Business Management* 49, no. 1 (2011): 55–70.

37. C. Angle, "Iterate Again," In eds. D. Cohen and B. Feld, *Do More Faster* (Hoboken, NJ: John Wiley & Sons, Inc., 2011), p. 50.

38. C. Williams, *Lead, Follow, or Get Out of the Way* (New York: Times Books, 1981), 111.

39. S. Walton, *Made in America: My Story* (New York: Doubleday, 1992).

40. R. W. Fairlie, *Kauffman Index of Entrepreneurial Activity 1996–2010* (Kansas City, MO: Kauffman Foundation, March 2011).

41. J. Zhang, "The Advantage of Experienced Start-Up Founders in Venture Capital Acquisition: Evidence from Serial Entrepreneurs," *Small Business Economics* 36, no. 2 (2010): 187–208.

42. U.S. Small Business Administration, http://web.sba.gov/faqs/faqindex.cfm?areaID=24 (accessed May 21, 2011).

43. A. M. Robb and S. Coleman, "Characteristics of New Firms: A Comparison by Gender," Kauffman Foundation, January 2009. A number of the remaining statistics in this section of material are drawn from this source.

44. Robb and Coleman, "Characteristics of New Firms: A Comparison by Gender."

45. Robb and Coleman, "Characteristics of New Firms: A Comparison by Gender."

46. Count Me In homepage, www.makemineamillion.org (accessed May 21, 2011).

47. "Minority Entrepreneurship," Kauffman Foundation, www.kauffman.org/entrepreneurship/minority-entrepreneurship.aspx (accessed May 21, 2011).

48. V. Wadhwa, R. Freeman, and B. Rissing, "Education and Tech Entrepreneurship," Kauffman Foundation, http://sites.kauffman.org/pdf/ Education_Tech_Ent_042908.pdf, May 2008 (accessed May 21, 2011).

49. "Young People Want to Be Their Own Boss to Realize Their Own Ideas," Kauffman Foundation, www.kauffman.org/uploadedFiles/KF_Harris_Poll_Fact%20Sheet.pdf (accessed May 21, 2011).

50. A. V. Smith, "Who's the Boss? When Jobs Are Scarce, the Kids Are." *Wall Street Journal*, http://online.wsj.com/article/SB10001424052748704662604576202473412495838.html (accessed May 21, 2011, originally posted on March 16, 2011).

51. Network for Teaching Entrepreneurship Web site, www.nfte.com (accessed May 21, 2011).

52. Babson College homepage, www.babson.edu (accessed May 21, 2011).

53. J. A. Schumpeter, *The Theory of Economic Development* (Cambridge, MA: Harvard University Press, 1994).

54. W. J. Baumol, "Formal Microeconomic Structure for Innovative Entrepreneurship Theory," *Entrepreneurship Research Journal* 1, no. 1 (2011): 1–3.

55. *The Small Business Economy*, www.sba.gov/sites/default/files/sb_econ2010.pdf, Small Business Administration, 2010.

56. *The Small Business Economy*.

57. Kauffman Foundation, "Kauffman Foundation Survey of Entrepreneurs," www.kauffman.org/uploadedFiles/entrepreneurs_survey_results_9-22-09.pdf, 2009.

58. J. Haltiwanger, R. Jarmin, and J. Miranda, "Business Dynamics Statistics Briefing: High Growth and Failure of Young Firms," Kauffman Foundation, www.kauffman.org/uploadedFiles/entrepreneurs_survey_results_9-22-09.pdf, March 2009.

59. "The Importance of Startups in Job Creation and Job Destruction," Kauffman Foundation, www.kauffman.org/uploadedFiles/firm_formation_importance_of_startups.pdf, July 2010.

60. J.-M. Degeorge and A. Fayolle, "The Entrepreneurial Process Trigger: A Modelling Attempt in the French Context," *Journal of Small Business and Enterprise Development* 18, no. 2 (2011): 251–77.

61. B. Barringer, *Preparing Effective Business Plans* (Upper Saddle River, NJ: Prentice Hall), 2009.

PART 2

Developing Successful Business Ideas

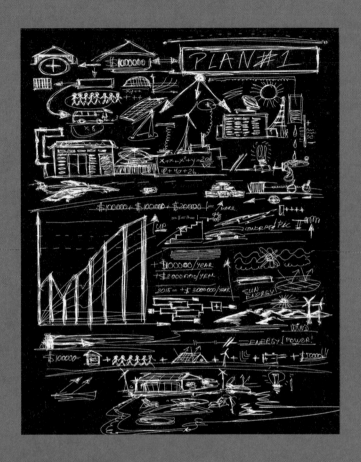

CHAPTER **2**
Recognizing *Opportunities* and Generating Ideas

CHAPTER **3**
Feasibility *Analysis*

CHAPTER **4**
Writing a *Business* Plan

CHAPTER **5**
Industry and Competitor *Analysis*

CHAPTER **6**
Developing an *Effective* Business Model

Getting Personal *with* BENCHPREP EXPRESS

Cofounders:

ASHISH RANGNEKAR
MBA, University of Chicago,
expected 2011

UJJWAL GUPTA
PhD, Penn State University,
expected 2012

Dialogue *with*
Ashish Rangnekar

MY BIGGEST WORRY AS AN ENTREPRENEUR
How to build the company culture—the human element of the business

BEST ADVICE I'VE RECEIVED
Don't wait, just do it. And talk to as many people (customers, entrepreneurs, mentors, advisors, VCs) as possible.

FIRST ENTREPRENEURIAL EXPERIENCE
In 1999, as an undergraduate student in India, I built Web apps for small businesses in (the) US. This was during the first wave of outsourcing.

MY FAVORITE SMARTPHONE APP
Pandora

FAVORITE PERSON I FOLLOW ON TWITTER
Jasonfried and vkhosla (Vinond Khosla)

BEST PART OF BEING A STUDENT
Freedom to experiment in a risk-free environment and access to the intellectual community

CHAPTER 2

Recognizing *Opportunities* and Generating Ideas

OPENING PROFILE

BENCHPREP

Solving a Problem by Merging a Customer Pain with an Emerging Technology

Web: http://benchprep.com
Twitter: benchprep
Facebook: BenchPrep

In 2008, Ashish Rangnekar was working full time and trying to prepare for the GMAT exam. He did all the normal things in preparing for the GMAT, like buying the study books and taking the practice exams. Lugging the big study books around and trying to find time to take the practice exams was a frustrating experience. It seemed as though when he had the books he didn't have time to study, and when he had time to study he didn't have the books. He thought, "There has to be a better way to manage this process."

At the same time Rangnekar was preparing for the GMAT, the iPhone came out, and Rangnekar was one of those people who waited in line to get one. He found himself spending a disproportionate amount of time messing with his phone—whether it was checking e-mail, surfing the Web, or playing a game. Thinking about the GMAT and the iPhone, a thought occurred to Rangnekar. If people could use their iPhones to study for the GMAT, they could solve two problems at the same time. First, they wouldn't have to carry the heavy study books around. And second, because people normally carry their phones with them, they could maximize their study time by catching a few minutes of study between meetings and on similar occasions.

Excited about the prospect, Rangnekar contacted a friend, Ujjwal Gupta, to discuss the idea. Gupta was a PhD student at Penn State University, and Rangnekar and Gupta had known each other since they were undergraduates in India. Both were fascinated by the idea. It merged a pain, the hassle of carrying around big study books to prepare for the GMAT, with a technology, the iPhone, in a manner that could potentially improve the way people prepare for the GMAT. The obvious thing to do was to create an iPhone app. Neither Rangnekar nor Gupta were programmers, so

LEARNING OBJECTIVES

After studying this chapter you should be ready to:

1. Explain why it's important to start a new firm when its "window of opportunity" is open.

2. Explain the difference between an opportunity and an idea.

3. Describe the three general approaches entrepreneurs use to identify opportunities.

4. Identify the four environmental trends that are most instrumental in creating business opportunities.

5. List the personal characteristics that make some people better at recognizing business opportunities than others.

6. Identify the five steps in the creative process.

7. Describe the purpose of brainstorming and its use as an idea generator.

8. Describe how to use library and Internet research to generate new business ideas.

9. Explain the purpose of maintaining an idea bank.

10. Describe three steps for protecting ideas from being lost or stolen.

they didn't have the background to create an app themselves. Fortunately, they found an undergraduate at Penn State who was a great programmer and was interested in the project. By the end of 2008, they had the first version of their app. In the photo, Rangnekar is on the left and Gupta is on the right.

Rangnekar kept his job, working for Capital One through most of 2009 but focused intently on the app. It was more than just a GMAT study guide and catalog of practice questions. The app could do many things, like compare a student's practice scores with others who were using the app and project a student's score on the GMAT based on his or her practice exams. Once available in the iTunes store, the app immediately started being downloaded. Incredibly, in just two months after the app was launched, they had more than 1,000 customers in seven countries, all of whom had paid a one-time fee of $10 to download the app. This level of interest was validation for Rangnekar and Gupta that they were onto something. At that time, the majority of iPhone apps were either free or cost 99 cents. To have 1,000 people pay $10 a piece to download the app was evidence of the value of the product. One thing that really helped Rangnekar and Gupta, which was more a fortunate turn of fate than anything they planned, is that their timing was perfect. Their app came out just at the time when apps were becoming popular—not too early and not too late. They were also the first GMAT prep app in the iTunes store. The first group of practice questions was written by Rangnekar and Gupta, but they quickly learned that that method didn't scale. Their approach shifted to a model where their app, named BenchPrep, became a platform, and they then entered into partnerships with companies like McGraw-Hill to place their test prep guides on smartphones.

Rangnekar quit his job and entered the Booth School of Business at the University of Chicago in August 2009. Buoyed by BenchPrep's early success, Rangnekar was determined to make his business school experience as useful as possible, so he took classes, joined clubs, and attended conferences sponsored by the Polsky Center for Entrepreneurship to boost his entrepreneurship-related knowledge and network. In May 2010, BenchPrep's won the New Venture Challenge at the Booth School of Business, which was further validation of the company's potential as an ongoing business.

BenchPrep has continued to mature and grow. The company now provides cross-platform apps to help students prepare for a number of standardized tests including the GMAT, GRE, SAT, LSAT, and MCAT. The functionality of the app has also expanded. For example, the app gives students progress reports to show where they are excelling and where performance needs to be improved. The app can also be synced across mobile, desktop, and Web platforms. So you can access the GMAT app, for example, on your iPhone, and access the same place you left off in the app on the Web when you get home. As of late 2010, BenchPrep's apps had been used by 75,000 people in 20 countries. Some apps cost upward of $30 to download.

BenchPrep obtained Series A funding from Lightbank, the fund operated by Groupon cofounders Eric Lefkofsky and Brad Keywell, in July 2010. The company now has about 15 apps available and another 15 in the pipeline, and around 10 employees.

In this chapter, we discuss the importance of understanding the difference between ideas and opportunities. While ideas are interesting and can intrigue us as possibilities, not every idea is in fact the source of an opportunity for an entrepreneur to pursue. In addition to describing the differences between ideas and opportunities, this chapter also discusses approaches entrepreneurs use to spot opportunities as well as factors or conditions in the external environment that may result in opportunities. As you will see too, certain characteristics seem to be associated with individuals who are adept at spotting viable business opportunities.

IDENTIFYING AND RECOGNIZING OPPORTUNITIES

Essentially, entrepreneurs recognize an opportunity and turn it into a successful business.[1] An **opportunity** is a favorable set of circumstances that creates a need for a new product, service, or business. Most entrepreneurial ventures are started in one of two ways. Some ventures are externally stimulated. In this instance, an entrepreneur decides to launch a firm, searches for and recognizes an opportunity, and then starts a business, as Jeff Bezos did when he created Amazon.com. In 1994, Bezos quit his lucrative job at a New York City investment firm and headed for Seattle with a plan to find an attractive opportunity and launch an e-commerce company.[2] Other firms are internally stimulated, like BenchPrep. An entrepreneur recognizes a problem or an **opportunity gap** and creates a business to fill it.

Regardless of which of these two ways an entrepreneur starts a new business, opportunities are tough to spot. Identifying a product, service, or business opportunity that isn't merely a different version of something already available is difficult. A common mistake entrepreneurs make in the opportunity recognition process is picking a currently available product or service that they like or are passionate about and then trying to build a business around a slightly better version of it. Although this approach seems sensible, such is usually not the case. The key to opportunity recognition is to identify a product or service that people need and are willing to buy, not one that an entrepreneur wants to make and sell.[3]

As shown in Figure 2.1, an opportunity has four essential qualities: It is (1) attractive, (2) durable, (3) timely, and (4) anchored in a product, service, or business that creates or adds value for its buyer or end user.[4] For an entrepreneur to capitalize on an opportunity, its **window of opportunity** must be open.[5] The term *window of opportunity* is a metaphor describing the time period in which a firm can realistically enter a new market. Once the market for a new product is established, its window of opportunity opens. As the market grows, firms enter and try to establish a profitable position. At some point, the market matures, and the window of opportunity closes. This is the case with Internet search engines. Yahoo!, the first search engine, appeared

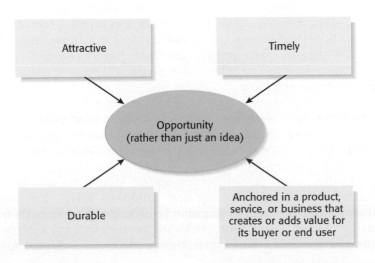

FIGURE 2.1
Four Essential Qualities of an Opportunity

FIGURE 2.2
Three Ways to Identify
an Opportunity

Observing Trends	Solving a Problem	Finding Gaps in the Marketplace

in 1995, and the market grew quickly, with the addition of Lycos, Excite, AltaVista, and others. Google entered the market in 1998, sporting advanced search technology. Since then, the search engine market has matured, and the window of opportunity is less prominent. Today, it would be very difficult for a new start-up search engine firm to be successful unless it offered compelling advantages over already established competitors or targeted a niche market in an exemplary manner. Bing, Microsoft's search engine, is enjoying success with approximately 27 percent market share (compared to 68 percent for Google), but only after Microsoft has exerted an enormous amount of effort in head-to-head competition with Google.

It is important to understand that there is a difference between an opportunity and an idea. An **idea** is a thought, an impression, or a notion.[6] An idea may or may not meet the criteria of an opportunity. This is a critical point because many entrepreneurial ventures fail not because the entrepreneurs that launched them didn't work hard, but rather because there was no real opportunity to begin with. Before getting excited about a business idea, it is crucial to understand whether the idea fills a need and meets the criteria for an opportunity.

Now let's look at the three approaches entrepreneurs can use to identify an opportunity, as depicted in Figure 2.2. Once you understand the importance of each approach, you'll be much more likely to look for opportunities and ideas that fit each profile.

LEARNING OBJECTIVE

2. Explain the difference between an opportunity and an idea.

LEARNING OBJECTIVE

3. Describe the three general approaches entrepreneurs use to identify opportunities.

Observing Trends

The first approach to identifying opportunities is to observe trends and study how they create opportunities for entrepreneurs to pursue. The most important trends to follow are economic trends, social trends, technological advances, and political action and regulatory changes. As an entrepreneur or potential entrepreneur, it's important to remain aware of changes in these areas. This sentiment is affirmed by Michael Yang, the founder of Become.com, a comparison shopping site, who believes that keen observation skills and a willingness to stay on top of changing environmental trends are key attributes of successful entrepreneurs:

> One of the most important attributes of a good entrepreneur is having a keen observation ability. Basically seeing what's needed in people's everyday lives and coming up with innovative new ideas and services that meet those needs . . . I always believe the entrepreneurs that anticipate trends and maintain observations of what's needed . . . to solve those needs will have a higher chance of succeeding in the marketplace.[7]

When looking at environmental trends to discern new business ideas, there are two caveats to keep in mind. First, it's important to distinguish between trends and fads. New businesses typically do not have the resources to ramp up fast enough to take advantage of a fad. Second, even though we discuss each trend individually, they are interconnected and should be considered simultaneously when brainstorming new business ideas. For example, one reason that smartphones are so popular is because they benefit from several trends converging at the same time, including an increasingly mobile population (social trend), the continual miniaturization of electronics (technological trend),

As baby boomers age, opportunities will grow for firms that provide unique products and services to the age group. Look for the resulting expansion in organic foods, health care, insurance, travel, and entertainment.

and their ability to help users better manage their money via online banking and comparison shopping (economic trend). If any of these trends weren't present, smartphones wouldn't be as successful as they are and wouldn't hold as much continuing promise to be even more successful as is the case.

Figure 2.3 provides a summary of the relationship between the environmental factors just mentioned and identifying opportunity gaps. Next, let's look at how entrepreneurs can study each of these factors to help them spot business, product, and service opportunity gaps.

Economic Forces   Understanding economic trends is helpful in determining areas that are ripe for new business ideas as well as areas to avoid.[8] When the economy is strong, people have more money to spend and are willing to buy discretionary products and services that enhance their lives. In contrast, when

> **LEARNING OBJECTIVE**
>
> **4.** Identify the four environmental trends that are most instrumental in creating business opportunities.

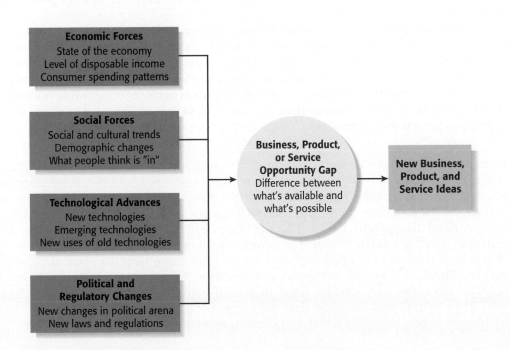

FIGURE 2.3
Environmental Trends Suggesting Business or Product Opportunity Gaps

the economy is weak, not only do people have less money to spend, they are typically more reluctant to spend the money they have, fearing the economy may become even worse—and that in turn, they might lose their jobs because of a weakening economy. Paradoxically, a weak economy provides business opportunities for start-ups that help consumers save money. Examples include GasBuddy and GasPriceWatch.com, two companies started to help consumers save money on gasoline. A similar example is e.l.f., a discount retailer of women's cosmetics. The company (which stands for Eyes Lips Face) sells cosmetics products for as little as $1.00.

A poor or weak economy also provides opportunities for firms to sell upscale and everyday items at a "discount." For example, daily deal sites like Groupon and LivingSocial have experienced rapid growth by providing consumers' access to local providers of massages, trips to museums, high-end restaurants, and similar products or services at deep discounts. A similar example is Gilt Groupe, which sells luxury goods at a discount in time-limited sales. Brick-and-mortar retailers are affected by the search for discounts too. For example, in 2009, Neiman Marcus reported a 14.8 percent drop in sales while Family Dollar experienced a 25 percent increase in revenues.[9] The same mind-set is contributing to people wanting the most value for their money, across the spectrum. For example, the recession has caused an upswing in the number of people frequenting local farmers markets, where people can buy locally grown produce, meats, and other food products that are fresher and often cheaper than similar products at the grocery store.[10]

It's also important to evaluate how economic forces affect people's behaviors—beyond looking for discounts and the most value for their money. For example, when the economy is weak, more people go back to school, largely as a result of poor employment prospects. This trend provides opportunities for not only traditional and online colleges and universities but for businesses that develop products to assist them. An example is BenchPrep, the student-initiated business profiled in the opening feature. BenchPrep, which sells Apple iPhone and Android apps that help people prepare for college admission tests, is benefiting from an increase in college enrollments. Similarly, when the economy is poor, more people start businesses. Web-based businesses like Etsy, which provides a platform for people to sell handmade items, thrive when an increasing number of people are looking to open full-time or part-time businesses.

An understanding of economic trends can also help identify areas to avoid. For example, this is not a good time to start a company that relies on fossil fuels, such as airlines or trucking or perhaps even local transportation-related businesses such as a taxicab company, because of high fuel prices. There are also certain product categories that suffer as result of economic circumstances. This is not a good time to open a store or franchise that sells premium-priced food products like cookies or ice cream.

Social Forces An understanding of the impact of social forces on trends and how they affect new product, service, and business ideas is a fundamental piece of the opportunity recognition puzzle. Often, the reason that a product or service exists has more to do with satisfying a social need than the more transparent need the product fills. The proliferation of fast-food restaurants, for example, isn't primarily because of people's love of fast food but rather because of the fact that people are busy and often don't have time to cook their own meals. Similarly, social networking sites like Facebook and Twitter aren't popular because they can be used to post information and photos on a Web site. They're popular because they allow people to connect and communicate with each other, which is a natural human tendency.

Changes in social trends alter how people and businesses behave and how they set their priorities. These changes affect how products and services are built and sold. Here is a sample of the social trends that are currently affecting how individuals behave and set their priorities:

■ Aging of baby boomers

■ The increasing diversity of the workforce

■ Increasing interest in social networks such as Facebook and Twitter

■ Proliferation of mobile phones and mobile phone apps

■ An increasing focus on health and wellness

■ Emphasis on clean forms of energy including wind, solar, biofuels, and others

■ Increasing number of people going back to school and/or retraining for new jobs

■ Increasing interest in healthy foods and "green" products

Each of these trends is providing the impetus for new business ideas. An increasing emphasis on alternative forms of energy is spawning business ideas ranging from solar power to biofuels. The aging of the baby boomers is creating business opportunities from vision care to tech assistance to senior dating sites. An example is Glaukos, a company that's developing new approaches for treating glaucoma, which is an age-related eye disorder.[11] There are now 76 million baby boomers (people born between 1946 and 1964) in the United States. Many baby boomers will develop glaucoma and similar age-related ailments. The fact that roughly 10,000 baby boomers in the United States are now retiring on a daily basis also creates entrepreneurial opportunities related to social trends associated with this population of senior citizens.

The proliferation of mobile phones and mobile phone apps is a social trend that's opening business opportunities for entrepreneurs across the globe. For example, Runkeeper, the focus of Case 1.1 is a mobile phone app. In the past 10 years, the worldwide penetration of mobile phones has grown from 1 billion to 4 billion active users. One company, PharmaSecure, is leveraging this trend to save lives in developing countries. It's estimated that 10 percent of medications sold worldwide are counterfeit. In India alone, 1 million people a year die from ingesting counterfeit drugs. PharmaSecure provides drug companies the ability to place a nine-digit alphanumeric code directly on the blister pack, medicine bottle or vial, or on the product's label, along with a phone number. Consumers can verify the code—and by extension make sure the drug they have purchased isn't counterfeit—by texting it to the accompanying phone number. In India, PharmaSecure's initial market, 55 percent of the population has a mobile phone, and it's the fastest-growing market for mobile phones in the world. If it weren't for the proliferation of mobile phones in India and elsewhere, PharmaSecure's business wouldn't be possible.

The booming interest in social networking sites such as Facebook and Twitter is a highly visible social trend. Nearly half of all Americans are now members of at least one social network, double from just two years ago. Social networks not only provide people new ways to communicate and interact with each other, but they act as platforms for other businesses to build on. Zynga, for example, the maker of popular online games like FarmVille and Scramble, became popular by making browser-based games that worked as application widgets on Facebook and MySpace. Similarly, entrepreneurs have launched businesses for the purpose of starting social networks that cater to specific niches. An example is PatientsLikeMe, which is a social networking site for people with serious diseases.

Technological Advances   Advances in technology frequently dovetail with economic and social changes to create opportunities.[12] For example, there are many overlaps between an increased focus on health and wellness and technology. Airstrip Technologies, a recent start-up, enables doctors to monitor critical patient information remotely on a smartphone or computer. The company's founding was motivated by a desire on the part of doctors to stay in closer contact with their critical care patients while away from the hospital and while those patients are receiving treatment in locations outside a hospital. Advances in wireless technologies made the system possible. In most cases the technology isn't the key to recognizing business opportunities. Instead, the key is to recognize how technologies can be used and harnessed to help satisfy basic or changing needs. It's always been difficult for doctors to leave the bedsides of critically ill patients, for example. Now, as a result of the advent of smartphones and wireless networks, a company like Airstrip Technologies can develop products to help doctors remotely monitor their patients' conditions.

Technological advances also provide opportunities to help people perform everyday tasks in better or more convenient ways. For example, OpenTable.com is a Web site that allows users to make restaurant reservations online and now covers most of the United States. If you're planning a trip to San Diego, for example, you can access OpenTable.com, select the area of the city you'll be visiting, and view descriptions, reviews, customer ratings, and in most cases the menus of the restaurants in the area. You can then make a reservation at the restaurant and print a map and the directions to it. The basic tasks that OpenTable.com helps people perform have always been done—looking for a restaurant, comparing prices and menus, soliciting advice from people who are familiar with competing restaurants, and getting directions. What OpenTable.com does is help people perform these tasks in a more convenient and expedient manner.

Another aspect of technological advances is that once a technology is created, products often emerge to advance it. For example, the creation of the Apple iPod, iPhone, iPad and similar devices has in turned spawned entire industries that produce compatible devices. An example is H2OAudio, a company that was started by four former San Diego State University students, which makes waterproof housings for the Apple iPhone and iPod. The waterproof housings permit iPhone and iPod users to listen to their devices while swimming, surfing, snowboarding, or engaging in any activity where the device is likely to get wet. A similar industry is the one dealing with smartphone apps. As of May 2011 there were over 381,000 third-party apps available in Apple's App Store and over 294,000 in the Android Market (Google's app store).[13] The app market is large and growing, all because of the advent of wireless networks and smart devices like the iPhone and iPad. To provide perspective on how big the app market is, at 10:26 A.M. GMT on Saturday, January 22, 2011, the 10 billionth app was downloaded from the Apple App Store.[14]

Political Action and Regulatory Changes   Political and regulatory changes also provide the basis for opportunities.[15] For example, new laws create opportunities for entrepreneurs to start firms to help companies, individuals, and governmental agencies comply with these laws. For example, the No Child Left Behind Act of 2002, which is based on the notion of outcome-based education, requires states to develop criterion-based assessments in basic skills to be periodically given to all students in certain grades. Shortly after the act was passed, Kim and Jay Kleeman, two high school teachers, started Shakespeare Squared, a company that produces materials to help schools comply with the act.

On some occasions, changes in government regulations motivate business owners to start firms that differentiate themselves by "exceeding" the regulations. For example, several years ago, the Federal Trade Commission changed the regulation about how far apart the wood or metal bars in an infant crib can be. If the bars are too far apart, a baby can get an arm or leg caught between the bars, causing an injury. An obvious business idea that might be spawned by this type of change is to produce a crib that is advertised and positioned as "exceeding" the new standard for width between bars and is "extra safe" for babies and young children. The change in regulation brings attention to the issue and provides ideal timing for a new company to reassure parents by providing a product that not only meets but exceeds the new regulation.

Some businesses and industries are so dependent on favorable government regulations that their literal survival is threatened if a regulation changes. An example of a business that fits this profile is Almost Family, a company that provides home health nursing services. Almost Family receives the majority of its income via fixed payments from Medicare based on the level of care that it provides its clients. As a result, the company's profitability is highly sensitive to any changes in Medicare reimbursement policies.[16]

Political change also engenders new business and product opportunities. For example, global political instability and the threat of terrorism have resulted in many firms becoming more security conscious. These companies need new products and services to protect their physical assets and intellectual property as well as to protect their customers and employees. The backup data storage industry, for example, is expanding because of this new trend in the tendency to feel the need for data to be more protected than in the past. An example of a start-up in this area is Box.net, which was funded by Mark Cuban, the owner of the Dallas Mavericks. Box.net allows its customers to store data "offsite" on Box.net servers, and access it via any Internet connection."[17]

Table 2.1 offers additional examples of changes in environmental trends that provided fertile soil for opportunities and subsequent concepts to take advantage of them.

TABLE 2.1 **EXAMPLES OF HOW CHANGES IN ENVIRONMENTAL TRENDS PROVIDE OPENINGS FOR NEW BUSINESS AND PRODUCT OPPORTUNITIES**

Changing Environmental Trend	Resulting New Business, Product, and Service Opportunities	Companies That Resulted
Economic Trends		
Search for alternatives to traditional fossil fuels like gasoline	Ethanol, biodiesel, solar power, wind-generated power	Windspire Energy, Solix Biofuels, eSolar
Sales of upscale items at a discount	Deal of the day sites, discount stores, niche sites that sell specialized items at a discount	Groupon, LivingSocial, Gilt Groupe, e.l.f.
Social Trends		
Increased interest in different, tastier, and healthier food	Healthy-fare restaurants, organic foods, healthy-focused grocery stores	Chipotle, Great Wraps, White Wave, Whole Foods
Increased interest in fitness as the result of new medical information warning of the hazards of being overweight	Fitness centers, in-house exercise equipment, weight-loss centers, fitness-focused smartphone apps	Fitbit, Cool Palms, Runkeeper, Shapes for Women

(Continued)

TABLE 2.1 CONTINUED

Changing Environmental Trend	Resulting New Business, Product, and Service Opportunities	Companies That Resulted
Technological Advances		
Development of wireless networks	Smartphones, smartphone apps, Wi-Fi networks, GPS devices	Airstrip Technologies, ScriptPad, TomTom, DLO
Miniaturization of electronics	Laptop computers, MP3 players, patient monitoring devices	ASUS Eee PC, Research In Motion, MiLife
Political and Regulatory Changes		
Increased EPA and OSHA standards	Consulting companies, software to monitor compliance	ESS, PrimaTech, Compliance Consulting Services, Inc.
Threat of terrorism	Security consulting, explosives detection devices, secure computer networks	BJ Smith Consulting, Xplosafe

Solving a Problem

The second approach to identifying opportunities is to recognize problems and find ways to solve them.[18] These problems can be recognized by observing the challenges that people encounter in their daily lives and through more simple means, such as intuition, serendipity, or chance. There are many problems that have yet to be solved. Commenting on this issue and how noticing problems can lead to the recognition of business ideas, Philip Kotler, a marketing expert, said:

> Look for problems. People complain about it being hard to sleep through the night, get rid of clutter in their homes, find an affordable vacation, trace their family origins, get rid of garden weeds, and so on. As the late John Gardner, founder of Common Cause, observed: "Every problem is a brilliantly disguised opportunity."[19]

Consistent with this observation, many companies have been started by people who have experienced a problem in their own lives, and then realized that the solution to the problem represented a business opportunity. For example, in 1991, Jay Sorensen dropped a cup of coffee in his lap because the paper cup was too hot. This experience led Sorensen to invent an insulating cup sleeve and to start a company to sell it. Since launching his venture, the company, Java Jacket, has sold over 1 billion cup sleeves. Sometimes there is more than one way to solve a specific problem, as illustrated in the "Savvy Entrepreneurial Firm" feature.

Advances in technology often result in problems for people who can't use the technology in the way it is sold to the masses. For example, some older people find traditional cell phones hard to use—the buttons are small, the text is hard to read, and it's often difficult to hear someone on a cell phone in a noisy room. To solve these problems, GreatCall Inc. is producing a cell phone called the Jitterbug, which is designed specifically for older users. The Jitterbug features a large keypad that makes dialing easy, powerful speakers that deliver clear sound, easy to read text, and simple text messaging capability. Another company, Firefly Mobile, has created a cell phone designed specifically for kids and tweens. The phone only weighs 2 ounces and is designed to fit in a kid's hand. The phone includes a full color screen, built-in games, built-in parental controls that allow parents to restrict incoming and outgoing calls as well as limit or restrict texting, and special speed dials for mom and dad.

One of the most pressing problems facing the United States and other countries is finding alternatives for fossil fuels. A large number of entrepreneurial firms are being launched to take on this challenge. Among the potential solutions is solar-generated power.

©Jakub Jirsák/Dreamstime.com

Some problems are solved by entrepreneurs who frame a problem differently than it's been thought of before, and then propose an appropriate solution. The solution is often easier and less expensive than traditional fixes. An example of a problem that was solved in this manner is illustrated through a story told by Matt Linderman, an employee of 37 signals, on the company's blog. The story's about a multistory building in New York City where tenants were complaining about long elevator wait times. Several of the tenants threatened to break their leases and move out of the building unless something was done. A study found that because of the age of the building, nothing could be done to speed up the elevators. The tenants would just have to live with the problem. The desperate manager of the building called a meeting of his staff, which included a young, recently hired graduate in personnel psychology. Instead of focusing on the speed of the elevators, the young new-hire wondered why people complained about waiting for only a few minutes. He concluded that the complaints were a consequence of boredom, rather than the few minutes that people waited, and the solution was to give people something to do while waiting for an elevator. He suggested installing mirrors in elevator boarding areas so that those waiting could look at each other or themselves (without appearing to do so) while waiting for an elevator. The manager accepted his suggestion. Mirrors were installed quickly and relatively inexpensively. Remarkably, the complaints about waiting stopped. Today, mirrors in elevator lobbies and even on elevators are commonplace.[20]

Some business ideas are gleaned by recognizing problems that are associated with emerging trends. For example, SafetyWeb, a 2009 start-up, has created a Web-based service that helps parents protect their children's online reputation, privacy, and safety. The social trend toward more online activity by children resulted in the need for this service. Similarly, the proliferation of smartphones enables people to stay better connected, but results in problems when people aren't able to access electricity to recharge their phones for a period of time. Several companies, including Iogear and Solio, now make solar rechargers for smartphones.

Additional examples of people who launched businesses to solve problems are included in Table 2.2.

SAVVY ENTREPRENEURIAL FIRM

Xhale and Vestagen: Solving the Same Problem in Different Ways

Xhale: Web: www.xhale.com; Twitter: GoHyGreen; Facebook: HyGreen
Vestagen: Web: www.vestagen.com; Twitter: cleancooldry; Facebook: Vestex High Tech Medical Apparel

When trying to solve a problem, one thing to be mindful of is that there is typically more than one way to tackle it. A vivid example of this is the problem that hospitals and clinics have with health care–associated infections. About 1.7 million people each year contract health care–associated infections. These are infections that patients acquire during the course of receiving treatment. You might be surprised to learn that health care–associated infections are the most common complication of hospital care and are one of the 10 leading causes of death in the United States. According to a recent study by the Centers for Disease Control and Prevention, the total cost of health care–associated infections is between $28 billion and $34 billion per year. That figure includes direct medical costs, the indirect costs related to lost productivity, and the intangible costs related to diminished quality of life. The most direct financial burden is felt by health care providers themselves. Of the $28 billion to $34 billion determined by the Centers for Disease Control and Prevention study, approximately $6.65 billion is borne by the U.S. health care industry.

Obviously, health care–associated infections are a problem. The question is how to best solve the problem. It turns out there is no single answer. Health care–associated infections are caused by a wide range of common and unusual bacteria, fungi, and viruses that are brought into a health care setting through improper sterilization of medical equipment, improper hygiene on the part of health care workers, bacteria brought in by guests visiting patients, and for many other reasons. Because there is no silver bullet to simultaneously eliminate all health care–associated inflections, it's a wide open field for entrepreneurs, and health care providers are typically eager to vet solutions with the potential to reduce the number of infections that patients contract while in their care.

Two recent start-ups are tackling the challenge of health care–associated infections in innovative, yet very different ways. The first is Xhale, which was started in 2008, and makes HyGreen, a hand washing compliance system. According to the company, of all the high-tech machines in a modern hospital, the simple hand soap dispenser may be the best defense against health care–associated infections. The problem is that despite all the education and warnings, according to recent studies, health care workers still wash their hands less than half the time after direct contact with patients. The excuses are many—too little time, rushing to an emergency, or simply forgetfulness. Here's how HyGreen works. After cleaning their hands with an alcohol-based

sanitizer (soap or gel), a health care worker places his or her hands under a HyGreen sensor that sniffs for alcohol. When sufficient alcohol is present, indicating that the worker's hands are clean, the device sends a wireless "all clear" message to a badge worn by the worker. A wireless monitor mounted above each patient's bed is able to tell if an approaching worker has received an "all clear" message recently. If the worker hasn't, his or her badge vibrates, reminding the worker to wash his or her hands. All interactions are recorded in real time, showing who is and who isn't washing their hands. This data allows hospital administrators to analyze who is washing their hands and who isn't, and provides them the information they need to distribute rewards or take corrective action as they see fit.

The second start-up tackling health care–associated infections is Vestagen, albeit in a very different manner. Launched in 2009, this company hopes to reduce the number of infections with a new type of fabric for hospital scrubs, lab coats, and isolation gowns. The nanotechnology-based material, which is called Vestex, repels blood and body fluids, resists stains, contains an antimicrobial to prevent degradation from micro organisms, and reduces perspiration odor. The idea is that health care workers' uniforms can harbor high levels of microorganisms—just the type of microorganisms that lead to health care–associated infections. By keeping health care workers' uniforms cleaner and more bacteria free, the spread of containments from health care worker to patent is greatly reduced. The product also provides health care workers increased peace of mind when they leave the hospital or clinic and return home in that these individuals can transmit bacteria, fungi, and viruses from their uniforms to their families just as easily as they can to patients at work.

The technology behind the Vestex fabric is licensed from Schoeller, a large Swiss textiles company. As Vestagan expands its offerings, it hopes to incorporate its technology into patient gowns, bed linens, and clinical privacy curtains.

Questions for Critical Thinking

1. Evaluate Xhale's idea and Vestagen's idea on all four dimensions of an opportunity. Rank each idea on a scale of 1 to 5 (5 is high) regarding how strongly it satisfies the four dimensions.
2. Along with "solving a problem," are the strengths of Xhale and Vestagen's business ideas bolstered by

environmental trends? If so, how powerful are these trends and how much do they strengthen Xhale's and Vestagen's business concepts?

3. Do some brainstorming and come up with an additional idea for helping reduce health care–associated infections. How would you go about vetting your idea to see if it is realistic?

4. Do some Internet research to learn about the founders of both Xhale and Vestagen. To what degree does each founder reflect the personal characteristics that tend to make some people better at recognizing opportunities than others?

Sources: Xhale Web site, www.xhale.com (accessed March 20, 2011); Vestagen Web site, www.vestagen.com (accessed March 20, 2011); R. Douglas Scott II, "The Direct Medical Costs of Healthcare–Associated Infections in the U.S. Hospitals and the Benefits of Prevention," *Centers for Disease Control and Prevention*, March 2009.

TABLE 2.2   BUSINESSES CREATED TO SOLVE A PROBLEM

Entrepreneur(s)	Year	Problem	Solution	Name of Business That Resulted
Arlene Harris	2006	Many cell phones are too complicated and the buttons are too small for older people.	Design cell phones that are easy to use and have large buttons.	GreatCall
Sam Goldman and Ned Tozen	2008	Hundreds of millions of "base of the pyramid" consumers in developing countries lack access to reliable electricity.	Create affordable and durable portable solar-powered lanterns.	d.light
Roger Marsh	2009	Concrete block construction takes time, requires water; and, a building built with concrete blocks cannot be occupied immediately because the building's mortar needs time to cure.	Alter traditional methods of concrete block construction to enable the assembly of the block to be completed in a manner that requires no water, has immediate occupancy, and is faster than current procedures.	Bolt-A-Blok Systems
Peter Chen, Yancey Strickler, and Charles Adler	2009	No easy-to-access platform for funding creative projects, like indie films, record albums, or food-related projects.	Create a Web-based "crowdfunding" platform that helps artists, musicians, and people involved in other creative projects raise money from the public.	Kickstarter
Tommy Patterson	2008	Men's undershirts don't fit well and don't stay tucked in.	Create long-tailored undershirts that fit well and stay tucked in.	Tommy John

FINDING GAPS IN THE MARKETPLACE

Gaps in the marketplace are the third source of business ideas. There are many examples of products that consumers need or want that aren't available in a particular location or aren't available at all. Part of the problem is created by large retailers, like Walmart and Costco, which compete primarily on price and offer the most popular items targeted toward mainstream consumers. While this approach allows the large retailers to achieve economies of scale, it leaves gaps in the marketplace. This is the reason that clothing boutiques and specialty shops exist. These businesses are willing to carry merchandise that doesn't sell in large enough quantities for Walmart and Costco to carry.

TABLE 2.3 BUSINESSES CREATED TO FILL A GAP IN THE MARKETPLACE

Gap in the Marketplace	Resulting New Business Opportunity	Name of Businesses That Resulted
No fitness centers that are open 24 hours a day	24-hour fitness centers to accommodate people who work odd hours	Snap Fitness, 24 Hour Fitness
Lack of toys and toy stores that focus on a child's intellectual development	Toy stores, toy manufacturers, and Web sites that sell educational toys	Discovery Toys, Sprig Toys, Kazoo & Company
Restaurants that are both fast and serve good food	Fast-casual restaurants that combine the advantages of fast-food (fast service) and casual dining (good food)	Panera Bread, Chipotle, Cosi, Bruegger's
Shortage of clothing stores that sell fashionable clothing for hard-to-fit people	Boutiques and retail chains that sell fashionable clothing for hard-to-fit people, including plus size clothing and clothing for tall or short people	Casual Male, Ashley Stewart, iGigi, RealKidz

Product gaps in the marketplace represent potentially viable business opportunities. For example, in 2000, Tish Cirovolo realized that there were no guitars on the market made specifically for women. To fill this gap, she started Daisy Rock guitars, a company that makes guitars just for women. Daisy Rock guitars are stylish, come in feminine colors, and incorporate design features that accommodate a woman's smaller hand and build. In a related manner, Southpaw Guitars located in Houston, Texas, carries only guitars that are designed and produced for left-handed players. Another company that is filling a gap in the marketplace is ModCloth, the subject of Case 11.1. ModCloth sells vintage and vintage-inspired clothing for 18- to 32-year-old women, which is a surprisingly large market. The company just raised $19.8 million in Series B funding. A start-up in a completely different industry is GreenJob Spider. GreenJob Spider fills a gap in the online recruiting industry by supporting a job site for employers and prospective employees in "green" industries such as solar, wind, recycling, green buildings, and LED lighting.

Additional examples of companies started to fill gaps in the marketplace are provided in Table 2.3.

A common way that gaps in the marketplace are recognized is when people become frustrated because they can't find a product or service that they need and recognize that other people feel the same way. This scenario played out for Lorna Ketler and Barb Wilkins, who became frustrated when they couldn't find stylish "plus-sized" clothing that fit. In response to their frustration, they started Bodacious, a store that sells fun and stylish "plus size" clothing that fits. Ketler and Wilkins's experience illustrates how compelling a business idea can be when it strikes just the right chord by filling a gap that deeply resonates with a specific clientele. Reflecting on the success of Bodacious, Wilkins said:

> It's so rewarding when you take a risk and it pays off for you and people are telling you every single day, "I am so glad you are here." We've had people cry in our store. It happens a lot. They're crying because they're so happy (that they're finding clothes that fit). One woman put on a pair of jeans that fit her, and she called me an hour later and said, "They still look good, even at home!" Sometimes people have a body change that happens, whether they have been ill or had a baby, and there's lots of emotion involved in it. If you can go and buy clothes that fit, that helps people feel good about themselves.[21]

A related technique for generating new business ideas is to take an existing product or service and create a new category by targeting a completely different target market. This approach essentially involves creating a gap and filling it. An example is PopCap games, a company that was started to create a new category in the electronic games industry called "casual games." The games are casual and relaxing rather than flashy and action-packed and are made for people who want to wind down after a busy day.

New start-up ventures will try to bridge a gap they see in a marketplace or fill a niche in a new trend. The quickest way for it to lose its prospective customers is for it to fail to deliver promised products or services. This scenario played out with My Favourite Booking, as illustrated in the "What Went Wrong?" boxed feature.

Personal Characteristics of the Entrepreneur

How did Michael Dell come up with the idea of a "build it yourself" computer company? How did Dave Roberts, the founder of PopCap Games, figure out that there is a large and growing market for "casual" electronic games?

Researchers have identified several characteristics that tend to make some people better at recognizing opportunities than others. Before we talk about them, there is an important yet subtle difference between two key terms pertaining to this topic. We've already defined an opportunity as a favorable set of circumstances that create the need for a new product, service, or business. But, the term **opportunity recognition** refers to the process of *perceiving* the possibility of a profitable new business or a new product or service. That is, an opportunity cannot be pursued until it's *recognized*.[22] Now let's look at some specific characteristics shared by those who excel at recognizing an opportunity.

Prior Experience   Several studies show that prior experience in an industry helps entrepreneurs recognize business opportunities.[23] For example, evidence over time about the founders of firms appearing on the *Inc.* 500 list shows that well over 40 percent of those studied got the idea for their new businesses while working as employees for companies in the same industries.[24] This finding is consistent with the findings of research studies the National Federation of Independent Businesses' group has completed over time.[25] There are several explanations for these findings. By working in an industry, an individual may spot a market niche that is underserved. It is also possible that while working in a particular area, an individual builds a network of social contacts in that industry that may provide insights that lead to opportunities.[26]

Once an entrepreneur starts a firm, new venture opportunities become apparent. This is called the **corridor principle**, which states that once an entrepreneur starts a firm, he or she begins a journey down a path where "corridors" leading to new venture opportunities become apparent.[27] The insight provided by this principle is simply that once someone starts a firm and becomes immersed in an industry, it's much easier for that person to see new opportunities in the industry than it is for someone looking in from the outside.

Cognitive Factors   Opportunity recognition may be an innate skill or a cognitive process.[28] There are some who think that entrepreneurs have a "sixth sense" that allows them to see opportunities that others miss. This sixth sense is called **entrepreneurial alertness**, which is formally defined as the ability to notice things without engaging in deliberate search.[29] Most entrepreneurs see

LEARNING OBJECTIVE

5. List the personal characteristics that make some people better at recognizing business opportunities than others.

WHAT WENT WRONG?

My Favourite Booking: What Happens When You Don't Deliver on Your Promises

Web: www.myfavouritebooking.com
Twitter: myfavebooking
Facebook: My Favourite Booking

One of the worst crises faced by any company is the failure of one of its products or services to fulfill the promises set out in the company's publicity brochures and advertisements. This is what happened to My Favourite Booking (MFB), one of the first online reservation Web sites in Malaysia, which has sought to position itself in the Internet restaurant booking service category.

At peak hours, restaurants lose customers because of unanswered calls and miscommunication of reservation information. The founder of MFB, John Ng, 30, started the Web site to offer diners online access to restaurant reservations, menus, promotions, prices, and cash point rewards. For the restaurateurs, MFB offers online marketing services through the restaurant's microsite by providing diners with information such as opening hours, type of cuisine, sample menus, photos of the restaurant's interiors, and improved booking management. A bi-yearly evaluation report based on feedback from customers on individual restaurant performance (e.g., food and service quality, etc.) is also sent to participating restaurants.

So, what went wrong? The participating restaurants expected a substantial number of bookings as a result of signing up to the MFB service. However, MFB was not able to provide enough bookings for the participating restaurants on a monthly basis and therefore MFB failed to fulfill the expectations of the participating restaurants. An analysis of the failure suggests that the Malaysian dining culture played a large part in this lack of bookings. Malaysian diners often make dinner plans on the spur of the moment because there are a large number of diverse restaurants in every town and city. This therefore cut out the need for an advanced online reservation system. Eating out is widespread in Malaysia due to the relatively low costs involved and ubiquitous availability of eateries at all hours of the day and night.

Eventually, some participating restaurants lost confidence in MFB and joined other local alternatives such as Groupon Malaysia and StreetDeal.my. MFB has since reformulated its business model. It still offers an online reservation service but to attract more customers it now collaborates with banks and social media Web sites to offer discounts and vouchers. MFB reservation holders can enjoy certain discounts if they pay with a partner bank's credit card. However, MFB has yet to gain much traction in the restaurant industry.

The message from MFB's experience is very clear—a company must fulfill its commitments to its customers (in this case its commitment to the participating restaurants), and must carry out appropriate market research before undertaking a new business venture.

Questions for Critical Thinking

1. Evaluate MFB's online restaurant booking Web site on all "four essential qualities of an opportunity."
2. When you choose a restaurant booking, do you read the review in the system to see if the restaurant is offering attractive dining deals compared with other alternatives? If your dining experience does not meet your expectations, do you feel deceived by the marketing?
3. How can a promising start-up ensure that its service meets the need that it was designed for?
4. How does MFB's online reservation system compare with other online restaurant booking services?

Source: MyFavouriteBooking.com homepage, www.myfavouritebooking.com (accessed August 2011). Written with the permission of MFB.

---

themselves in this light, believing they are more "alert" than others.[30] Alertness is largely a learned skill, and people who have more knowledge of an area tend to be more alert to opportunities in that area than others. A computer engineer, for example, would be more alert to needs and opportunities within the computer industry than a lawyer would be.

The research findings on entrepreneurial alertness are mixed. Some researchers conclude that alertness goes beyond noticing things and involves a more purposeful effort.[31] For example, one scholar believes that the crucial difference between opportunity finders (i.e., entrepreneurs) and nonfinders is their relative assessments of the marketplace.[32] In other words, entrepreneurs may be better than others at sizing up the marketplace and inferring the likely implications.

Social Networks　The extent and depth of an individual's social network affects opportunity recognition.[33] People who build a substantial network of social and professional contacts will be exposed to more opportunities and ideas than people with sparse networks. [34] This exposure can lead to new business starts.[35] Research results over time consistently suggest that somewhere between 40 percent and 50 percent of those who start businesses got their ideas through social contacts.[36] In a related study, the differences between **solo entrepreneurs** (those who identified their business ideas on their own) and **network entrepreneurs** (those who identified their ideas through social contacts) were examined. The researchers found that network entrepreneurs identified significantly more opportunities than solo entrepreneurs but were less likely to describe themselves as being particularly alert or creative.[37]

An important concept that sheds light on the importance of social networks to opportunity recognition is the differential impact of strong-tie versus weak-tie relationships. Relationships with other people are called "ties." We all have ties. **Strong-tie relationships** are characterized by frequent interaction and ties between coworkers, friends, and spouses. **Weak-tie relationships** are characterized by infrequent interaction and ties between casual acquaintances. According to research in this area, it is more likely that an entrepreneur will get a new business idea through a weak-tie than a strong-tie relationship[38] because strong-tie relationships, which typically form between like-minded individuals, tend to reinforce insights and ideas the individuals already have. Weak-tie relationships, on the other hand, which form between casual acquaintances, are not as apt to be between like-minded individuals, so one person may say something to another that sparks a completely new idea.[39] An example might be an electrician explaining to a restaurant owner how he solved a business problem. After hearing the solution, the restaurant owner might say, "I would never have heard that solution from someone in my company or industry. That insight is completely new to me and just might help me solve my problem."

Creativity　**Creativity** is the process of generating a novel or useful idea. Opportunity recognition may be, at least in part, a creative process.[40] On an anecdotal basis, it is easy to see the creativity involved in forming many products, services, and businesses. Increasingly, teams of entrepreneurs working within a company are sources of creativity for their firm.[41]

For an individual, the creative process can be broken into five stages, as shown in Figure 2.4.[42] Let's examine how these stages relate to the opportunity recognition process.[43] In the figure, the horizontal arrows that point from box to box suggest that the creative process progresses through five stages. The vertical arrows suggest that if at any stage an individual (such as an entrepreneur) gets "stuck" or doesn't have enough information or insight to continue, the best choice is to return to the preparation stage—to obtain more knowledge or experience before continuing to move forward.

> **Preparation.**　Preparation is the background, experience, and knowledge that an entrepreneur brings to the opportunity recognition process. Just as an athlete must practice to excel, an entrepreneur needs experience to spot opportunities. Over time, the results of research suggest that as much as 50 to 90 percent of start-up ideas emerge from a person's prior work experience.[44]

LEARNING OBJECTIVE

6. Identify the five steps in the creative process.

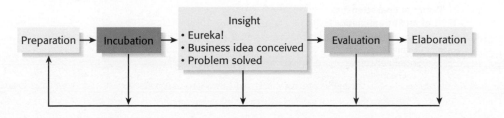

FIGURE 2.4
Five Steps to Generating Creative Ideas

Incubation. Incubation is the stage during which a person considers an idea or thinks about a problem; it is the "mulling things over" phase. Sometimes incubation is a conscious activity, and sometimes it is unconscious and occurs while a person is engaged in another activity. One writer characterized this phenomenon by saying that "ideas churn around below the threshold of consciousness."[45]

Insight. Insight is the flash of recognition—when the solution to a problem is seen or an idea is born. It is sometimes called the "eureka" experience. In a business context, this is the moment an entrepreneur recognizes an opportunity. Sometimes this experience pushes the process forward, and sometimes it prompts an individual to return to the preparation stage. For example, an entrepreneur may recognize the potential for an opportunity but may feel that more knowledge and thought is required before pursuing it.

Evaluation. Evaluation is the stage of the creative process during which an idea is subjected to scrutiny and analyzed for its viability. Many entrepreneurs mistakenly skip this step and try to implement an idea before they've made sure it is viable. Evaluation is a particularly challenging stage of the creative process because it requires an entrepreneur to take a candid look at the viability of an idea.[46] The process of evaluating the feasibility of new business ideas is discussed in Chapter 3.

Elaboration. Elaboration is the stage during which the creative idea is put into a final form: The details are worked out and the idea is transformed into something of value, such as a new product, service, or business concept. In the case of a new business, this is the point at which a business plan is written.

Figure 2.5 illustrates the opportunity recognition process. As shown in the figure, there is a connection between an awareness of emerging trends and the personal characteristics of the entrepreneur because the two facets of opportunity recognition are interdependent. For example, an entrepreneur with a well-established social network may be in a better position to recognize emerging technological trends than an entrepreneur with a poorly established social network. Or the awareness of an emerging technology trend, such as digitization, may prompt an entrepreneur to attend conferences or workshops to learn more about the topic, expanding the social network.

FIGURE 2.5
The Opportunity
Recognition Process

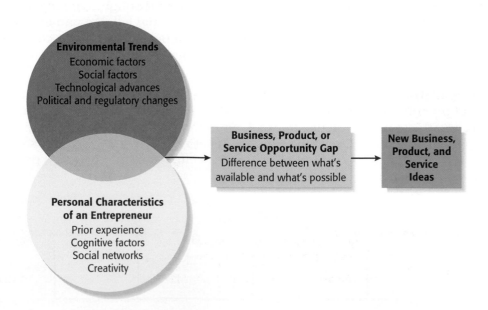

TECHNIQUES FOR GENERATING IDEAS

In general, entrepreneurs identify more ideas than opportunities[47] because many ideas are typically generated to find the best way to capitalize on an opportunity. Several techniques can be used to stimulate and facilitate the generation of new ideas for products, services, and businesses. Let's take a look at some of them.

Brainstorming

A common way to generate new business ideas is through **brainstorming**. In general, brainstorming is simply the process of generating several ideas about a specific topic. The approaches range from a person sitting down with a yellow legal pad and jotting down interesting business ideas to formal "brainstorming sessions" led by moderators that involve a group of people.

In a formal brainstorming session, the leader of the group asks the participants to share their ideas. One person shares an idea, another person reacts to it, another person reacts to the reaction, and so on. A flip chart or an electronic whiteboard is typically used to record all the ideas. A productive session is freewheeling and lively. The session is not used for analysis or decision making—the ideas generated during a brainstorming session need to be filtered and analyzed, but this is done later. We show the four strict rules for conducting a formal brainstorming session in Table 2.4. As you'll see, the number one rule for a brainstorming session is that no criticism is allowed, including chuckles, raised eyebrows, or facial expressions that express skepticism or doubt. Criticism stymies creativity and inhibits the free flow of ideas.

Brainstorming sessions dedicated to generating new business ideas are often less formal. For example, as described in more detail in Case 11.2, during the creation of Proactiv, a popular acne treatment product, Dr. Katie Rodan, one of the company's founders, hosted dinner parties at her house and conducted brainstorming sessions with guests. The guests included business executives, market researchers, marketing consultants, an FDA regulatory attorney, and others. Rodan credits this group with helping her and her cofounder brainstorm a number of ideas that helped shape Proactiv and move the process of starting the company forward.[48] Similarly, Sharelle Klause, the founder of Dry Soda, a company that makes an all-natural soda that's paired with food the way wine is in upscale restaurants, tested her idea by first talking to her husband's colleagues, who were in the food industry, and then tapped into the professional

> **LEARNING OBJECTIVE**
> **7.** Describe the purpose of brainstorming and its use as an idea generator.

TABLE 2.4   RULES FOR A FORMAL BRAINSTORMING SESSION

Rule	Explanation
1	No criticism is allowed, including chuckles, raised eyebrows, or facial expressions that express skepticism or doubt. Criticism stymies creativity and inhibits the free flow of ideas.
2	Freewheeling, which is the carefree expression of ideas free from rules or restraints, is encouraged; the more ideas, the better. Even crazy or outlandish ideas may lead to a good idea or a solution to a problem.
3	The session moves quickly, and nothing is permitted to slow down its pace. For example, it is more important to capture the essence of an idea than to take the time to write it down neatly.
4	Leapfrogging is encouraged. This means using one idea as a means of jumping forward quickly to other ideas.

network of a friend who owned a bottled water company. Through the process, she met a chemist, who was instrumental in helping her develop the initial recipes for her beverage. Klause also went directly to restaurant owners and chefs to ask them to sample early versions of her product.[49] While this approach only loosely fits the definition of brainstorming, the spirit is the same. Klause was bouncing ideas and early prototypes of her product off others to get their reactions and generate additional ideas. DRY Soda is the subject of Case 9.1.

Approaches to brainstorming are only limited by a person's imagination. For example, to teach her students an approach to utilizing brainstorming to generate business ideas, Professor Marcene Sonneborn, an adjunct professor at the Whitman School of Management Syracuse University, uses a tool she developed called the *"bug report"* to help students brainstorm business ideas. She instructs her students to list 75 things that "bug" them in their everyday lives. The number 75 was chosen because it forces students to go beyond thinking about obvious things that bug them (campus parking, roommates, scraping snow off their windshields in the winter), and think more deeply. On occasions, students actually hold focus groups with their friends to brainstorm ideas and fill out their lists.

Focus Groups

A **focus group** is a gathering of 5 to 10 people who are selected because of their relationship to the issue being discussed. Although focus groups are used for a variety of purposes, they can be used to help generate new business ideas.

Focus groups typically involve a group of people who are familiar with a topic, are brought together to respond to questions, and shed light on an issue through the give-and-take nature of a group discussion. Focus groups usually work best as a follow-up to brainstorming, when the general idea for a business has been formulated, such as casual electronic games for adults, but further refinement of the idea is needed. Usually, focus groups are conducted by trained moderators. The moderator's primary goals are to keep the group "focused" and to generate lively discussion. Much of the effectiveness of a focus group session depends on the moderator's ability to ask questions and keep the discussion on track. For example, a retail establishment in which coffee is sold, such as Starbucks, might conduct a focus group consisting of 7 to 10 frequent customers and ask the group, "What is it that you *don't* like about our coffee shop?" A customer may say, "You sell 1-pound bags of your specialty ground coffees for people to brew at home. That's okay, but I often run out of the coffee in just a few days. Sometimes it's a week before I get back to the shop to buy another bag. If you sold 3-pound or 5-pound bags, I'd actually use more coffee because I wouldn't run out so often. I guess I could buy two or three 1-pound bags at the same time, but that gets a little pricey. I'd buy a 3- or 5-pound bag, however, if you'd discount your price a little for larger quantities." The moderator may then ask the group, "How many people here would buy 3-pound or 5-pound bags of our coffee if they were available?" If five hands shoot up, the coffee shop may have just uncovered an idea for a new product line.

Some companies utilize hybrid focus group methodologies to achieve specific insights and goals. An example is "college drop-ins." This approach involves paying college students to host a party at their campus and providing them a budget to buy food and snacks. During the party, the hosts interview and videotape other students about specific market issues. Everything is up-front—the partygoers are told that the information is being collected for a market research firm (on behalf of a client).[50]

Library and Internet Research

A third approach to generate new business ideas is to conduct library and Internet research. A natural tendency is to think that an idea should be chosen, and the process of researching the idea should then begin. This approach is too linear. Often, the best ideas emerge when the general notion of an idea, like creating casual electronic games for adults, is merged with extensive library and Internet research, which might provide insights into the best type of casual games to create.

Libraries are often an underutilized source of information for generating business ideas. The best approach to utilizing a library is to discuss your general area of interest with a reference librarian, who can point out useful resources, such as industry-specific magazines, trade journals, and industry reports. Simply browsing through several issues of a trade journal on a topic can spark new ideas. Very powerful search engines and databases are also available through university and large public libraries, which would cost hundreds or thousands of dollars to access on your own. An example is IBIS World (www.ibisworld.com), a company that publishes market research on all major industries and subcategories within industries. IBIS World published a 30-page report on the solar power industry, for example, in March 2011, which includes key statistics (about industry growth and profitability), a complete industry analysis, and an outlook for the future. Spending time reading this report could spark new ideas for solar powered devices or help affirm an existing idea.

Internet research is also important. If you are starting from scratch, simply typing "new business ideas" into Google or Yahoo! will produce links to newspaper and magazine articles about the "hottest" and "latest" new business ideas. Although these types of articles are general in nature, they represent a starting point if you're trying to generate new business ideas from scratch. If you have a specific idea in mind, a useful technique is to set up a Google or Yahoo! "e-mail alert" using keywords that pertain to your topic of interest. Google and Yahoo! alerts are e-mail updates of the latest Google or Yahoo! results including press releases, news articles, and blog posts based on your topic. This technique, which is available for free, will feed you a daily stream of news articles and blog postings about specific topics. Another approach is to follow business leaders and experts in the industries you're interested in on Twitter. The best way to locate people on Twitter you might be interested in following is by typing into the search bar labeled "Who to Follow" relevant keywords preceded by the "#" sign. For example, if you're interested in solar power, type "#solarpower" into the search bar. All the results will be people or companies who tweet about solar power topics.

Once an entrepreneur has an idea, it often needs to be shaped and fine-tuned. One way to do this, in conjunction with the suggestions made previously, is to enlist a mentor to help. An explanation of how to use a mentor in this regard, and where mentors can be found, is described in the "Partnering for Success" feature.

Other Techniques

Firms use a variety of other techniques to generate ideas. Some companies set up **customer advisory boards** that meet regularly to discuss needs, wants, and problems that may lead to new ideas. Other companies conduct varying forms of anthropological research, such as **day-in-the-life research**. Intuit, the maker of Quicken, Quickbooks, and TurboTax, practices day-in-the life research. The company routinely sends teams of testers to the homes and businesses of its users to see how its products are working and to seek insights for new product ideas.

PARTNERING FOR SUCCESS

Want Help Fine-Tuning a Business Idea?
Find a Mentor

Fine-tuning a business idea isn't easy. While fairly course-grained ideas are rather easy to develop, like creating a cell-phone that's designed specifically for elderly people, fleshing out the details is where experience helps. This reality puts first-time entrepreneurs at a disadvantage. While there are many books and Web sites about new business ideas, what many first-time entrepreneurs find most helpful in the idea generation and perfecting stage is to find a mentor to guide them through the process.

A mentor is someone who is more experienced than you and is willing to be your counselor, confidant, and go-to person for advice. There are two ways to find a mentor. First, you can work with your network of acquaintances—professors, business owners, coaches—to determine if there is someone available that you trust, has experience helping first-time entrepreneurs, and is willing to become your mentor. Many first-time entrepreneurs are surprised by the number of talented and experienced people who are eager to share their expertise and enter into a mentoring relationship. The second way is to utilize one of the growing numbers of Web sites and organizations that help match business founders with people who are willing to become mentors. One Web site is MicroMentor.org, which is a nonprofit that matches business founders with mentors. You can go to the site and fill out a profile about yourself and your goals, and then search profiles of potential mentors who match your needs. Once a match is made, the mentoring can take place through e-mail, via Web conferencing, over the phone, or in person. There is a tab on MicroMentor's Web site that provides access to "success stories" of business founders who have had excellent results using its service. A number of organizations provide a similar service. For example, the National Association for Women Business Owners has over 7,000 members in 70 chapters across the United States. Some chapters sponsor mentorship programs.

There are also Web sites and organizations that do not provide mentorship services per se, but provide entrepreneurship-related services and advice that can help entrepreneurs fine-tune business ideas. An example is PartnerUp, a site that matches entrepreneurs with associates and business services. A particularly useful Web site is Buzgate.org, where you can hunt for reputable organizations based on your specific needs and location. This aggregator site provides explanations and links to associations such as local SCORE chapters, Small Business Development Centers, small business incubators, and so forth.

The ideal situation is to find a mentor in your own community so you can meet face-to-face. Still, the online options provide a wide range of mentors to choose from, which may result in a better match. Online mentoring and counseling relationships are becoming increasingly common. For example, nearly 40 percent of all the counseling and mentoring done by SCORE counselors is now done online.

Similar to any relationship, a business founder should be careful and only share private information with a mentor once a trusting relationship has been established.

Questions for Critical Thinking

1. If you were working on fine-tuning a business idea, would you check out one of these online mentoring sites or an association in your area that provides mentoring and advice for business founders? Why or why not?

2. To what degree do you believe that having a mentor can make the difference between an entrepreneur succeeding or failing? In what areas of the entrepreneurial process do you believe that mentors are called on the most?

3. Make a list of the organizations in your area that provide mentorship and advice for business founders. Which organizations make the most sense to reach out to for someone who is still in the opportunity recognition stage of the start-up process?

4. How do you know what to do with a mentor's advice? If you get advice from several mentors or counselors at organizations like SCORE and local Small Business Development Centers, how can you best sort through the advice and know which advice to take and which advice to set aside?

Source: Pamela Ryckman, "How to Choose and Work with a Mentor," *New York Times,* www.nytimes.com/2010/09/02/business/smallbusiness/02sbiz.html?_r=2&emc=eta1 (accessed April 2, 2011, originally posted on September 1, 2010).

ENCOURAGING AND PROTECTING NEW IDEAS

In many firms, idea generation is a haphazard process. However, entrepreneurial ventures can take certain concrete steps to build an organization that encourages and protects new ideas. Let's see what these steps are.

Establishing a Focal Point for Ideas

Some firms meet the challenge of encouraging, collecting, and evaluating ideas by designating a specific person to screen and track them—for if it's everybody's job, it may be no one's responsibility.[51] Another approach is to establish an **idea bank** (or vault), which is a physical or digital repository for storing ideas. An example of an idea bank would be a password-protected location on a firm's **intranet** that is available only to qualified employees. It may have a file for ideas that are being actively contemplated and a file for inactive ideas. Other firms do not have idea banks but instead encourage employees to keep journals of their ideas.

LEARNING OBJECTIVE

9. Explain the purpose of maintaining an idea bank.

Encouraging Creativity at the Firm Level

There is an important distinction between creativity and innovation. As indicated in Chapter 1, innovation refers to the successful introduction of new outcomes by a firm. In contrast, creativity is the process of generating a novel or useful idea but does not require implementation. In other words, creativity is the raw material that goes into innovation. A team of employees may come up with a hundred legitimate creative ideas for a new product or service, but only one may eventually be implemented. Of course, it may take a hundred creative ideas to discover the one that ideally satisfies an opportunity.

An employee may exhibit creativity in a number of ways, including solving a problem or taking an opportunity and using it to develop a new product or service idea. Although creativity is typically thought of as an individual attribute, it can be encouraged or discouraged at the firm level.[52] The extent to which an organization encourages and rewards creativity affects the creative output of its employees.[53] Table 2.5 provides a list of actions and behaviors that encourage and discourage creativity at both the organizational level and the individual supervisor level.

TABLE 2.5 ACTIONS AND BEHAVIORS THAT ENCOURAGE AND DISCOURAGE CREATIVITY

Organizational Level	*Inhibitors of Creativity*	■ Failing to hire creative people ■ Maintaining an organizational culture that stifles people ■ Retaining people in the same job for years, preventing them from broad and deep experiences ■ Promoting a mentality suggesting that the best solutions to all problems are known
	Facilitators of Creativity	■ Supporting and highlighting creativity's importance in all parts of the firm ■ Overtly rewarding those demonstrating creativity in their work ■ Investing in resources for the purpose of helping employees become more creative ■ Hiring people with different skills and viewpoints compared to current employees
Individual Supervisory Level	*Inhibitors of Creativity*	■ Being pessimistic, judgmental, and critical ■ Punishing people for failed ideas ■ Insisting on precision and certainty early in the creative process ■ Being inattentive, acting distant, and remaining silent when employees want to discuss new ideas
	Facilitators of Creativity	■ Listening attentively for the purpose of openly acknowledging and supporting ideas early in their development ■ Treating employees as equals for the purpose of demonstrating that status isn't important ■ Speculating, being open, and building on others' ideas ■ Protecting people who make honest mistakes and commit to learning from them

Protecting Ideas from Being Lost or Stolen

LEARNING OBJECTIVE

10. Describe three steps for protecting ideas from being lost or stolen.

Intellectual property is any product of human intellect that is intangible but has value in the marketplace. It can be protected through tools such as patents, trademarks, copyrights, and trade secrets, which we'll discuss in depth in Chapter 12. As a rule, a mere idea or concept does not qualify for intellectual property protection; that protection comes later when the idea is translated into a more concrete form. At the opportunity recognition stage, however, there are three steps that should be taken when a potentially valuable idea is generated:

Step 1 The idea should be put into a tangible form—either entered into a physical idea logbook or saved on a computer disk—and dated. When using a physical logbook, be sure that it is bound so that it cannot be alleged that a page was added. Make all entries in ink and have them witnessed. If an idea has significant potential, the signature of the person who entered the idea into the logbook and the witness should be notarized.

Putting the idea into tangible form is important for two reasons. First, if the idea is in concrete form, is original and useful, and is kept secret or is disclosed only in a situation where compensation for its use is contemplated, the idea may qualify as a "property right" or "trade secret" and be legally protected under a variety of statutes.

Second, in the case of an invention, if two inventors independently come up with essentially the same invention, the right to apply for the patent belongs to the first person who invented the product. A properly maintained idea log provides evidence of the date that the idea for the invention was first contemplated.

Step 2 The idea, whether it is recorded in a physical idea logbook or saved in a computer file, should be secured. This may seem like an obvious step, but it is one that is often overlooked. The extent to which an idea should be secured depends on the circumstances. On the one hand, a firm wants new ideas to be discussed, so a certain amount of openness in the early stages of refining a business idea may be appropriate. On the other hand, if an idea has considerable potential and may be eligible for patent protection, access to the idea should be restricted. In the case of ideas stored on a computer network, access to the ideas should be at a minimum password protected.

Step 3 Avoid making an inadvertent or voluntary disclosure of an idea in a way that forfeits your claim to its exclusive rights. In general, the intellectual property laws seek to protect and reward the originators of ideas as long as they are prudent and try to protect the ideas. For example, if two coworkers are chatting about an idea in an elevator in a public building and a competitor overhears the conversation, the exclusive rights to the idea are probably lost.

In summary, opportunity recognition is a key part of the entrepreneurial process. As mentioned, many firms fail not because the entrepreneurs didn't work hard, but because there was no real opportunity to begin with.

CHAPTER SUMMARY

1. Once an opportunity is recognized, a window opens, and the market to fill the opportunity grows. At some point, the market matures and becomes saturated with competitors, and the window of opportunity closes.

2. An idea is a thought, an impression, or a notion. An opportunity is an idea that has the qualities of being attractive, durable, and timely and is anchored in a product or service that creates value for its buyers or end users. Not all ideas are opportunities.

3. Observing trends, solving a problem, and finding gaps in the marketplace are the three general approaches entrepreneurs use to identify an opportunity.

4. Economic forces, social forces, technological advances, and political action and regulatory changes are the four environmental trends that are most instrumental in creating opportunities.

5. Prior experience, cognitive factors, social networks, and creativity are the personal characteristics researchers have identified that tend to make some people better at recognizing business opportunities than others.

6. For an individual, the five steps in the creative process are preparation, incubation, insight, evaluation, and elaboration.

7. Brainstorming is a technique used to quickly generate a large number of ideas and solutions to problems. One reason to conduct a brainstorming session is to generate ideas that might represent product, service, or business opportunities.

8. A focus group is a gathering of 5 to 10 people who have been selected on the basis of their common characteristics relative to the issue being discussed. One reason to conduct a focus group is to generate ideas that might represent product or business opportunities.

9. An idea bank is a physical or digital repository for storing ideas.

10. The three main steps that can be taken to protect ideas from being lost or stolen are putting the idea into tangible form by such means as entering it in a logbook or saving it in a computer file, securing the idea, and avoiding making an inadvertent or voluntary disclosure of an idea in a manner that forfeits the right to claim exclusive rights to it if it falls into someone else's hands.

KEY TERMS

brainstorming, **85**
corridor principle, **81**
creativity, **83**
customer advisory boards, **87**
day-in-the-life research, **87**
entrepreneurial alertness, **81**
focus group, **86**

idea, **70**
idea bank, **89**
intellectual property, **90**
intranet, **89**
network entrepreneurs, **83**
opportunity, **69**
opportunity gap, **69**

opportunity recognition, **81**
solo entrepreneurs, **83**
strong-tie relationships, **83**
weak-tie relationships, **83**
window of opportunity, **69**

REVIEW QUESTIONS

1. What is a product opportunity gap? How can an entrepreneur tell if a product opportunity gap exists?

2. What is an opportunity? What are the qualities of an opportunity, and why is each quality important?

3. What four environmental trends are most instrumental in creating business opportunities? Provide an example of each environmental trend and the type of business opportunity that it might help create.

4. Explain how "solving a problem" can create a business opportunity. Provide an example that was not mentioned in the chapter of a business opportunity that was created in this way.

5. Explain how finding a gap in the marketplace can create a business opportunity.

6. What is meant by opportunity recognition?

7. In what ways does prior industry experience provide an entrepreneur an advantage in recognizing business opportunities?

8. What is the corridor principle? How does this corridor principle explain why the majority of business ideas are conceived at work?

9. What is entrepreneurial alertness? Why is it important?

10. In what ways does an extensive social network provide an entrepreneur an advantage in recognizing business opportunities?

11. Describe the difference between strong-tie relationships and weak-tie relationships. Is an entrepreneur more likely to get new business ideas through strong-tie or weak-tie relationships? Why?

12. Define creativity. How does creativity contribute to the opportunity recognition process?

13. Briefly describe the five stages of the creative process for an individual.

14. Explain the difference between an opportunity and an idea.

15. Describe the brainstorming process. Why is "no criticism" the number one rule for brainstorming?

16. Describe how a focus group is set up and how it is used to generate new business ideas.

17. Describe how library and Internet research can be used to generate new business ideas.

18. What is the purpose of day-in-the-life research?

19. What is the purpose of an idea bank? Describe how an idea bank can be set up in a firm.

20. What are the three main steps to protect ideas from being lost or stolen?

APPLICATION QUESTIONS

1. Justin, a product development specialist at DuPont, plans to write an e-mail message to his dad asking for a loan. The purpose of the loan will be to start a company to sell an environmentally friendly line of cleaning supplies that are suitable for light manufacturing facilities. Justin has spent the past two years developing the products in his spare time, and wants to convince his dad that the idea represents an attractive business opportunity. In your opinion, what information and insights about the company he wants to start should Justin include in the e-mail message?

2. Spend some time studying Yammer (www.yammer.com), which is an enterprise social network. What is the basis of Yammer's business opportunity? Evaluate Yammer on the four essential qualities of an opportunity. On a scale of 1 to 10 (10 is high), rate Yammer in terms of the strength of its opportunity?

3. Go to DEMO's Web site at www.demo.com. Watch several videos from the most current DEMO conference. The videos are start-ups pitching their product ideas to investors and other DEMO participants. Identify a start-up that is pitching a business idea that "solves a problem." Write a short description of the idea and your assessment of its potential.

4. The "You Be the VC 2.2" feature focuses on ecoATM, a company that is deploying a network of self-service kiosks that enables shoppers to recycle unwanted electronic gear. Imagine you're in a class where the instructor has set up a debate-type format to discuss the strength of ecoATM's business opportunity. A classmate of yours has been assigned to argue that ecoATM has a strong opportunity, and you've been assigned to argue that ecoATM has a weak opportunity. Briefly summarize what your arguments will be.

5. Identify three start-ups, other than those discussed in the chapter or listed in Table 2.1, which were started to satisfy a changing environmental trend. Briefly describe the start-up and the environmental trend that it was started to satisfy.

6. Marshall Hanson, the founder of Santa Fe Hitching Rail, a chain of nine steak restaurants in New Mexico, is considering expanding his menu, which is currently restricted to steak, hamburger, potatoes, and fries. He has just read a book about entrepreneurship and learned that entrepreneurs should study social trends to help identify new product opportunities. List the social trends that might help Marshall choose items to add to his menu.

Given the trends you list, what items do you suggest Marshall add?

7. One of the social trends identified in the chapter is the increasing number of people going back to school or retraining for new jobs. Propose a business idea, which isn't a near duplicate of an idea you're already familiar with, that takes advantage of this social trend.

8. The "You be the VC features" included in Chapters 1 and 2 focus on Pie Face, Songkick, Freedirectoryenquiries, and ecoATM. Which of these four companies do you think is pursuing the strongest business opportunity? Justify your answer.

9. Go to Vator.tv's Web site at www.vator.tv. Search the Web site and find an example of an entrepreneur talking about his or her business idea. Describe the idea, and the extent to which it satisfies a changing environmental trend, solves a problem, or fills a gap in the marketplace. Evaluate the entrepreneur's ability to clearly explain his or her own idea.

10. Tiffany Jones owns a small chain of fast-casual restaurants in Denver, which sell sandwiches, soups, wraps, and desserts. In general, her restaurants are successful, but she feels they are getting "stale" and could benefit from new ideas. Suggest to Tiffany some ways she could generate new ideas for her restaurants.

11. As mentioned in the chapter, "prior experience" in an industry helps entrepreneurs recognize business opportunities. This concept extends to prior experience in any aspect of life—whether it is in sports, music, or a volunteer activity. In what area or areas do you have a good amount of "prior experience"? How could this position you to start a business drawing on your experiences?

12. Make a list of your strong-tie and weak-tie relationships. (Include at least five names on each list.) Select two names from your list of weak-tie relationships and speculate on the types of new business ideas that you think these individuals would be uniquely qualified to assist you with.

13. Imagine that you've been hired by Foursquare, the local-based social network, to conduct focus groups on your campus to get a better sense of how Foursquare can be as relevant and useful to college students as possible. How would you go about setting up the focus groups? What are the primary issues that you'd zero in on?

14. How could the founders of Songkick, the subject of the "You Be the VC 1.2" feature at the end of Chapter 1, have utilized library and Internet research to flesh out their business idea? What information would have been most helpful to them?

15. Freedom Electronics is a start-up with about 20 sales representatives. The company has a solid product line but knows that to remain competitive it must continue recognizing opportunities for new products and services. The firm has not developed a systematic way for its sales staff to report new ideas. Suggest some ways that Freedom can record and protect the ideas of its sales representatives.

YOU BE THE VC 2.1

Company: Freedirectoryenquiries

Web: www.freedirectoryenquiries.com

Business Idea Launch the first free national directory enquiry service.

Pitch: Since the U.K. directory enquiry market was deregulated in 2003, call numbers have fallen by more than half. In surveys, consumers say they are put off by the wide diversity of 118 (directory enquiry) suppliers and high charges. Most companies charge a fixed price per call, plus the caller searching for the number is charged per second throughout the call. So, for example, Yellow Pages charges a fixed charge of $1.20 per call and then 21 cents per minute, while the most frequently used service, The Number, costs $1.05 to call, plus 29 cents per minute.

Freedirectoryenquiries, launched in February 2008, aims to get a slice of the 76 million calls made to 118 numbers each year. Callers pay nothing for the service, but must listen to an advertisement for 20 seconds before their requested number is read out. Advertisers already signed up with the 0800 100 100 service include EDF Energy, NatWest, Simply Switch, ASDA, and Eurostar.

The advertisement being played often relates to the number being requested (i.e., a query about a restaurant might prompt an ad for a pizza delivery firm). The caller is able to connect with the advertiser for free at the end of the call.

Freedirectoryenquiries was founded by business partners Isabel Megan-Campbell and Murray McPherson, who were previously involved with the launch of a paid directory enquiry service. Their research into callers' reactions to advertisements being played has had a positive response. Consumers felt that 20 seconds was not an intrusion given that they were getting the number for free. The business model is expected to appeal to the corporate market too. Of the $450 million spent a year on

directory enquiry calls, an estimated 20 percent are made from workplace phones.

Regular users of directory enquiry services are typically young and affluent and want to get the number of a taxi or restaurant, so it is little wonder that advertisers are keen to get involved with this new way of targeting them. The number is also free for mobile phone callers who will then receive a text message with the requested number, along with an offer from one of the advertising companies.

Q&A: Based on the material covered in this chapter, what questions would you ask the firm's founders before making your funding decision? What answers would satisfy you?

Decision: If you had to make your decision on just the information provided in the pitch and on the company's Web site, would you fund this firm? Why, or why not?

YOU BE THE VC 2.2

Company: ecoATM

Web: www.ecoatm.com
Twitter: ecoATM
Facebook: ecoATM

Business Idea: Deploy a network of self-service kiosks that enables shoppers to recycle unwanted electronic gear safely, starting with cell phones, and offering shoppers cash, gift cards, or the ability to donate the value of their cell phones to charity in exchange for the phone.

Pitch: The average household has five to six outdated cell phones tucked away, worth an estimated $12.2 billion in secondary markets or in recyclable material. While many phones are eventually sold or recycled (ReCellular processes 400,000 used cell phones per month), many are not, which results in an environmental hazard. Many discarded phones go into landfills, and pose a danger due to the presence of high levels of lead, cadmium,

copper, and other hazardous material. With the average life span of cell phones shrinking to about 18 months, this problem is expected to quickly become worse.

ecoATM has devised a solution that not only allows the owners of used cell phones to get a fair price for their phones, but has the potential to make a meaningful impact on the number of cell phones that enter landfills. The company has devised a kiosk that can quickly assess the value of a used cell phone, and pay the owner of the phone on the spot the value of the phone. It works like this. A cell phone owner approaches the machine, which looks like an ATM machine, and follows a set of visual prompts. The cell phone is placed in a tray, and is plugged in to a universal adapter. The machine, following sophisticated computer algorithms developed by ecoATM, inspects the exterior of the phone for flaws and damage, and the interior of the phone for the condition of the software. A price is then offered, which the owner of the phone has the discretion to accept or reject. If the price is accepted, the phone falls into a lower bin in the machine and the user is paid the offer price in cash, a store gift card, or can elect to donate the value of the phone to charity. Once in ecoATM's possession, about half the phones are sold into secondary markets (both in the United States and in other countries) and half are sold to material reclamation companies that are carefully screened by ecoATM. Offshore markets include emerging markets such as Brazil, Russia, India, China, Africa, and the Caribbean. Cell phone usage is booming in emerging markets and demand for used phones is high. Any private data that remains on phones is erased before they're sold.

ecoATM is working with retailers to secure high-traffic locations for its machines. A benefit to retailers is increased traffic in their locations (due to the draw of the ecoATM machine) and the ability to dispense gift cards for their store through the machines. ecoATM sees cell phones as its point of market entry. It is working on similar automated processes to purchase used computers, iPods, and other electronic devices.

Q&A: Based on the material covered in this chapter, what questions would you ask the firm's founders before making your funding decision? What answers would satisfy you?

Decision: If you had to make your decision on just the information provided in the pitch and on the company's Web site, would you fund this company? Why or why not?

CASE 2.1

ScriptPad: Interesting Idea—But Will Doctors and Pharmacies Sign On?

Web: http://scriptpad.net
Twitter: ScriptPad
Facebook: ScriptPad

Bruce R. Barringer, *Oklahoma State University*

R. Duane Ireland, *Texas A&M University*

Introduction

To ScriptPad founder and CEO Shane Taylor, the problem his company solves is personal. Taylor's father, who is fighting both heart disease and cancer, takes 26 different medications to fight his illnesses. Any mix-up or error associated with taking his medications could cause Taylor's father severe health complications or even his life. A related complication associated with taking multiple medications is finding it necessary to essentially start over every time a person sees a new specialist. The specialist will want a list of the medications that are currently being taken. If the patient or the patient's caregiver forgets a medication or gets confused, it can hinder the new doctor's diagnosis and treatment plan.

Observing this set of circumstances motivated Taylor to start ScriptPad. ScriptPad is a software platform that transforms an Apple iPhone, iPad, or iPod Touch into a digital prescription pad, which stores a patient's medication history and enables a doctor to write a prescription faster and safer than using a traditional prescription pad. Once the doctor enters a prescription and approves it, it is sent electronically to the pharmacy.

Scope of the Problem

Taylor's fears about his father and the possibility of a prescription mix-up aren't unwarranted. Although this may surprise you, evidence suggests that a total of 40 percent of handwritten prescriptions contain some type of medication error, whether it's improper dosage, potential drug interactions with other medications the patient is taking, or simple handwriting errors including handwriting that's hard to read. In most cases the errors are caught, with the only harm being the inconvenience caused by correcting the error. But sometimes the errors aren't caught, and real damage occurs. In fact, according to ScriptPad's Web site, 7,000 deaths occur each year in the United States as the result of prescription writing mistakes.

(continued)

How ScriptPad Works

ScriptPad is an app that resides on the Apple iPhone, iPad, and iPad Touch and will soon be available for Android-platform devices. To write a prescription, a doctor clicks on the ScriptPad icon and pulls up a list of his or her patients. Once the correct patient is selected, the doctor searches for a drug based on a catalog of all prescription medications. The desired medication is selected, and the available dosages for that medication are shown. The doctor then selects the desired dosage, decides how often the medication should be taken—say one pill twice per day—and then determines how large of a bottle of the medicine to prescribe—say enough pills for two weeks. This is all done by moving from screen to screen on the iPhone or similar device, in the same sequence that a doctor would mentally think through when writing a handwritten prescription. A display is shown where the doctor confirms that the prescription is correct. Then a list of pharmacies appears, along with the cost of the medication at each pharmacy and whether generic equivalents are available. After conferring with the patient, a pharmacy and the specific drug are chosen and the prescription is electronically sent.

In a true win-win scenario, this approach has advantages for the doctor, the patient, and the pharmacy. For the doctor and the patient, it dramatically lessens the possibility of a medication error. The app is "smart" in that it knows the patient's medical history and alerts the doctor if a prescription is attempted that has known negative interactions with a medication the patient is currently taking or the patient's medical profile. It also eliminates a mistake being made through a simple handwriting error. For the pharmacy, the ScriptPad app only shows the dosages of a medication that are available. When writing a handwritten prescription, if a doctor prescribes a dosage that isn't available, the pharmacy will have to call the doctor to get the right dosage. This process is called "call back." Pharmacies like to avoid call backs because it consumes staff time and frustrates patients, who are often at the pharmacy waiting for their prescription to be filled. Few things are more frustrating to patients than waiting for a prescription and being told that they'll have to come back the next day because the pharmacy needs to verify the dosage with the doctor. The doctor is often

unavailable when the pharmacy makes the first call, so it can take several hours or even until the next day before the doctor calls back and the correct dosage is set.

Business Model and Positioning

ScriptPad will make money in two ways. First, a free version of the app will be available. In addition, a premium subscription-based service will be available for $49 per month. The timing is good for a doctor that selects the premium service. There are federal financial incentives available to doctors for switching to medical recording technologies, which will more than offset the cost of the service. The second way the company will make money is via pharmacies. A transaction fee will be charged to pharmacies for each ScriptPad initiated prescription that it fills.

In regard to competitive positioning, ScriptPad believes it has found a sweet spot in the market. There are companies that provide comprehensive electronic medical records platforms, which not only provide electronic prescription capabilities but help a doctor's office improve its entire record keeping system and office workflow. The challenge with these systems is that they're expensive, require considerable training to implement, and no single component of the system is developed to perfection. In comparison, a doctor can start using ScriptPad for the cost of an Apple iPhone, iPad, or iPod Touch, and the interface is intuitive. It doesn't require any special training. ScriptPad is also singularly focused on one function—electronic prescriptions. Taylor and his team believe that this singular focus allows ScriptPad to maintain usability and a cost advantage over its competitors for electronic prescriptions.

ScriptPad's target market is smaller physician practice groups with one to five physicians. A single physician can download the ScriptPad app from the Apple app store and start using it without having to convert the entire practice.

The Challenge—User Adoption

ScriptPad believes that its major challenge will be user adoption. For ScriptPad to be successful, it needs adoption on both the physician and the pharmacy sides. The medical industry is known to be tough to change. Despite the advantages of electronic prescriptions, currently only about 10 percent of prescriptions are handled electronically. Government incentives are helping spur adoption of electronic prescriptions and electronic medical records, as mentioned earlier. In 2009, the U.S. Congress authorized funding to promote electronic health records as part of the economic stimulus package.

Still, there are reasons to be optimistic that ScriptPad will be a success. ScriptPad is a company that can literally save lives, which is a claim that not many companies can make. It is also very intuitive, easy to learn, and reduces pharmacy call backs. The crucial question is whether ScriptPad will be able to gain a large enough critical mass of adopters to prove its concept, capture the attention of investors, expand to additional platforms, and grow the business.

ScriptPad screen showing the dosage selections for a particular medication.

ScriptPad Inc. (www.scriptpad.net)

Discussion Questions

1. In this chapter, an opportunity is defined as being (1) attractive, (2) durable, (3) timely, and (4) anchored in a product or service that creates value for its buyer or end user. To what extent does ScriptPad meet each of these tests of an opportunity?
2. What environmental trends are working in ScriptPad's favor? If ScriptPad has uncovered a promising business opportunity, what environmental trends have made ScriptPad possible?
3. Put yourself in the shoes of a family physician that's part of a small practice (containing five doctors). If you were that doctor and were being pitched on ScriptPad's method for writing prescriptions, how would you react? What would you see as the pluses and minuses of adopting the service? Ultimately, based on the information in the case and ScriptPad's Web site, what would your decision be?

4. On what side do you think ScriptPad faces the biggest adoption challenge—the physician side or the pharmacy side? Explain your answer.

Application Questions

1. ScriptPad's basic premise is that it solves the problem of prescription mistakes. Is this true? Can you think of scenarios in which a mistake could be made even when using ScriptPad's service? If so, how could ScriptPad correct for these possibilities?
2. If you were ScriptPad's founder, and you now have a working prototype of your device, how would you proceed? Are you ready to go to market or are there additional steps that need to be completed before ScriptPad is available for sale?

Sources: ScriptPad homepage, http://scriptedpad.com (accessed January 10, 2011); Shane Taylor, "Making Getting a Prescription Safer: ScriptPad," YouTube (accessed January 10, 2011).

CASE 2.2

Creative Conversion Factory: Turning Promising Ideas into Brilliant Products

Web: www.designconnectionbrainport.nl

Introduction

For many entrepreneurs, the idea of sharing ideas and innovation between companies and competitors, or indeed any "outsider," may seem a complete anathema. Imagine though, that you have a product or design idea but don't have the time, the money, or the know-how to turn the idea into reality. There may now be a solution to your problem—Creative Conversion Factory (CCF) in Eindhoven, the Netherlands, is one of many emerging collaborative projects which brings together inventors, manufacturers, and investors in order to transform promising ideas into viable products. It uses industry collaboration, or open development, where you use the collaborative brainpower of experts to come up with the optimal solution to get your product to market. It turns on its head the common idea of R&D which has always been a very guarded part of business because any innovation must be protected in order to provide the inventor with the opportunity to make back (and hopefully exceed) his or her investment. The concept of open innovation is becoming increasingly prominent and has helped start hundreds of businesses around the globe, which may never have seen the light of day without a little help.

To understand a little more about the thinking behind the CFF, you have to know a little bit about Hans Robertus, who was on the team that started the project.

Hans Robertus

Hans Robertus graduated from the Academy for Industrial Design in Eindhoven in 1978 and started his career at a small consultancy. He joined the Dutch consumer electronics giant Philips in 1990, where he initially specialized in professional broadcasting products, but he gradually expanded his role to become senior director of business development for the product and communication teams at Philips Design.

Philips Design is one of the largest design organizations of its kind in the world, boasting a creative team of some 500 professionals, representing more than 35 different nationalities. However, Robertus was finding that sometimes, many of the brilliant ideas that were emerging from this impressive team were falling by the

(continued)

wayside. Sometimes it was a case of wrong place or wrong time; on other occasions it was simply that the idea didn't fit in with the corporate strategy of the day. Robertus, who is a champion of Dutch design and a director of Dutch Design Week, could see that this would be the experience elsewhere too. Smart ideas from all over the Netherlands were simply not able to progress beyond the stage of being an idea or drawing. The challenge he saw was to give some of these concepts a tangible form and prevent any good ideas from going to waste.

A Match Made in Heaven

Eindhoven has had strong links with design for many years. It was the birthplace to Philips, indeed the industrial city was practically built around the consumer electronics firm, and it is home to one of Europe's best design academies. However, over the past few years, there has been a trend for many of the talented graduates to be lured away by the attractions of other European centers such as Amsterdam, Berlin, and London.

The authorities and corporations of Eindhoven wanted to reverse this decline and have been on a mission to keep and attract an entrepreneurial crowd and the traditional culture of design. This has required renewed dedication to the creative industries that had sustained the area in the past.

Initiatives to promote Eindhoven as a laboratory of creativity include a design city, called Strijp S. The site, an old industrial estate, has housing, studio space, and facilities for thousands of designers, artists, and creative professionals.

There are also a growing number of opportunities and initiatives for corporate partners and educational establishments to get involved in encouraging new, innovative ideas.

Design Cooperation Is Child's Play

To promote Eindhoven's design credentials and capitalize on all the smart ideas that were failing to find a market, Robertus, together with Emile Aarts, the scientific program manager of Philips Research, set up CCF in 2007, with $1.3 million in public funding. The venture is a partnership between Philips Design, Philips Research, the Eindhoven University of Technology, and a number of other research, design, and business partners. The basic concept is that, through CCF, ideas from virtually any source can be examined for potential and then put through the process of business development. Successful ideas are then matched to likely business partners who will help bring the concept to market.

One of the earliest successes was the Intelligent Playground, which was the brainchild of two students at Eindhoven University of Technology. The pair came up with a concept of interactive, large-scale games for young children, to get kids to play in the physical world, rather than being constantly glued to their computers.

Remarkably, the idea from the two entrepreneurs neatly dovetailed with some earlier concepts that had been floated around, and rejected by, Philips. Philips had not taken that idea further at the time because the firm had not felt that the timing was right, or that it was the company to take the idea to the next stage. Now, the consumer electronics giant was more than happy to share its ideas and make it into a business.

Once the idea was converted into a viable product, the other partners in CCF helped the students make contact with Korein, a company that runs 80 day-care centers around the southern Netherlands and a group of businessmen who were keen to market the interactive games through the NYON (pronounced "Enjoy'en") company. The beauty of it is that this idea could easily have been left gathering dust. But, by putting the entrepreneurs and Philips together, and then adding the expertise and advice of industry experts, both parties could see the potential of the product.

Another successful idea developed by entrepreneurs through CCF was for a navigation system for large buildings such as hotels, hospitals, and universities, based, in part, on the popular sat-nav units for vehicles. Collaborators from the various teams involved in the venture helped to find a way to navigate inside a building without a link to satellites and came up with an "ambient wayfinding system" which guides people to the right rooms by means of light, sound, and even smell.

The Creative Conversion Factory

The basic concept of CCF is to provide inventors and designers with a platform to vet and improve their product ideas, and then take the best ideas to market. Each idea put forward must satisfy a number of criteria such as demand, feasibility, and originality. The aim is to align the following disciplines at a very early stage of development:

- Design
- Business intelligence
- Financing
- Legal
- Marketing communication

Here is how it works:

Step 1 Ideas and technological innovations are submitted to CCF. You can include sketches, drawings, videos—anything that you think will help illustrate your idea.

Step 2 The CCF community—that is the team at Philips Design, Philips Research, the Eindhoven University of Technology, and the other research, design, and business partners—will provide feedback on the idea. Submissions are evaluated on the basis of a number of criteria, including the extent to which they may be viable ideas for any of these organizations or add anything to any of their existing products. Projects are also evaluated as to whether there may be other markets elsewhere.

Step 3 If the concept meets the previously mentioned criteria, CCF will investigate whether the project is technically feasible and an analysis will be done of the legal, financial, and marketing position. Products are then selected for development.

Step 4 CCF's team then assists in creating prototypes of ideas that are selected to move on to the next stage. It will also issue guidance to the designer on business development, partner search, and matchmaking potential partners to bring the project to market and provide finance.

Step 5 Once the project has been completed, ownership of the final product is transferred to the external interested party, which was identified at the earlier matchmaking stage, or will become part of the CCF alliance.

CCF is so effective because it allows several parties with differing expertise to look in on the process at an early stage. Working together with companies in the fields of product development, marketing, finance, and law can be complex, and this simplifies it for entrepreneurs by providing experts in each field in one place.

The team at CCF is in tune with the importance of understanding each entrepreneur's starting positions and objectives, as well as getting the right people onboard to cover the legal, financial, and marketing communication issues.

CCF is currently home to dozens of new ideas, predominantly in the high-tech arena, all at various stages of development.

Discussion Questions

1. It what ways was Hans Robertus the ideal person to be one of the founders of CCF? If you were an investor in CCF, would you have any concerns about his qualifications moving forward?

2. Do you think CCF's basic business model, described in the five steps shown previously, is sound and fair? If you could suggest any changes, what would they be?

3. Do you think there should be any concerns that CCF will systematically attract novice inventors, who are likely to submit the least promising ideas, rather than experienced inventors and product designers, who are likely to submit the most promising ideas? Should CCF vary its approach in order to attract mainly experienced inventors and product designers, or leave things the way they are and live with the consequences.

4. Do you think CCF is a real opportunity or just a feel good idea for large corporations who want to be seen promoting innovation? Justify your answer.

Application Questions

1. Do some research into CCF and the products it has successfully brought to market. Provide feedback on two separate products. Briefly relate your views on those products and comment on the quality and innovation of the products that you evaluated.

2. Think of the challenges in your own life that might represent a product idea for CCF. If you don't think of something right away, don't give up. All of us encounter problems and challenges in our everyday lives that might represent the basis of a promising business opportunity. Be prepared to describe to others one of the challenges or problems you encounter and how a solution to the problem could be fashioned into a product idea to submit to CCF.

Sources: "Interview with Hans Robertus," *Designed.rs*, www.designed.rs/intervju/hans_robertus (accessed September 5, 2011, originally posted October 30, 2009); Experienta homepage, www.experienta.com/blog/creative-conversion-factory/ (accessed September 5, 2011); Design Connect Brainport homepage, www.designconnectionbrainport.nl (accessed September 5, 2011).

ENDNOTES

1. J. C. Short, C. L. Shook, D. J. Ketchen, Jr., and R. D. Ireland, "The Concept of 'Opportunity' in Entrepreneurship Research: Past Accomplishments and Future Challenges," *Journal of Management* 36, no. 4 (2010): 40–65. C. Hsieh, J. A. Nickerson, and T. R. Zenger, "Opportunity Discovery, Problem Solving and a Theory of the Entrepreneurial Firm," *Journal of Management Studies* 44, no. 72008: 1253–77.

2. Amazon.Com Company Report, *Standard and Poor's Stock Report*, May 16, 2011; *Time*, "Amazing Person.com," December 27, 1999.

3. J. W. Webb, R. D. Ireland, G. Kistruck, L. Tihanyi, and M. A. Hitt, "Where Is the Opportunity Without the Customer? An Integration of Marketing Entrepreneurship Process and Institutional Theory," *Journal of the Academy of Marketing Science* (2011): in press.

4. J. Hayton, G. N. Chandler, and D. R. DeTienne, "Entrepreneurial Opportunity Identification and New Firm Development Processes: A Comparison of Family and Non-Family New Ventures," *International Journal of Entrepreneurship and Innovation Management* 13, no. 1 (2011): 12–31.

5. M.-S. Cha and Z.-T. Bae, "The Entrepreneurial Journey: From Entrepreneurial Intent to Opportunity Realization," *Journal of High Technology Management Research* 21, no. 1 (2010): 31–42.

6. M. A. Hitt, R. D. Ireland, D. G. Sirmon, and C. Trhams, "Strategic Entrepreneurship: Creating Value for Individuals, Organizations and Society,"

Academy of Management Perspectives 25, no. 2 (2011): 57–75.

7. M. Yang, nPost homepage, www.npost.com (accessed November 6, 2008, originally posted on April 24, 2006).

8. H. S. Alhorr, C. B. Moore, and G. T. Payne, "The Impact of Economic Integration on Cross-Border Venture Capital Investments: Evidence from the European Union," *Entrepreneurship Theory and Practice*, 32, no. 5 (2008): 897–917.

9. *Entrepreneur*, "2010 Trends: 10 [and 1.2] Trends," http://entrepreneur.com/trends/index.html (accessed May 16, 2011, originally posted on December 2, 2010).

10. *Entrepreneur*, "2010 Trends: 10 [and 1.2] Trends."

11. Glaukes homepage, www.glaukes.com (accessed May 16, 2011).

12. B. Clarysse, M. Wright, and E. Van de Velde, "Entrepreneurial Origin Technological Knowledge, and the Growth of Spin-Off Companies," *Journal of Management Studies* (2011): in press.

13. R. Wauters, "Android to Surpass Apple's App Store in Size by August 2011: Report (Exclusive)," *TechCrunch*, http://techcrunch.com/2011/05/05/android-to-surpass-apples-app-store-in-size-in-august-2011-report-exclusive/?utm_source=feedburner&utm_medium=feed&utm_campaign=Feed%3A+Techcrunch+%28TechCrunch%29 (accessed May 16, 2011, originally posted on May 5, 2011).

14. Apple Web site, "Thank You. Ten Billion Times," www.apple.com/itunes/10-billion-app-count-down/ (accessed May 16, 2011, originally posted on January 22, 2011).

15. G. Kistruck, J. W. Webb, C. Stutter, and R. D. Ireland, "Microfranchising in Base-of-the-Pyramid Markets: Institutional Challenges and Adaptations to the Franchise Model," *Entrepreneurship Theory and Practice* 35, no. 3 (2011): 503–31; M. Minniti, "The Role of Government Policy on Entrepreneurial Activity: Productive, Unproductive, or Destructive?" *Entrepreneurship Theory and Practice*, 32, no. 5 (2008): 779–90.

16. Almost Family Inc. 10-K Annual Report filed with the Securities and Exchange Commission, February 28, 2011.

17. Box.net homepage, www.box.net.com (accessed May 17, 2011).

18. M. Rollins, D. N. Bellenger, and W. J. Johnston, "Customer Information Utilization in Business-to-Business Markets: Muddling Through Process?" *Journal of Business Research* (2011): in press.

19. P. Kotler, *Marketing Insights from A to Z* (New York: John Wiley & Sons, 2003), 128.

20. M. Linderman, Signals Vs. Noise Blog, www.37signals.com/svn/posts/1244-definiing-the-problem-of-elevator-waiting-times (accessed September 17, 2008).

21. Ladies Who Launch homepage, www.ladieswholaunch.com (accessed October 4, 2007).

22. D. A. Shepherd, "Multilevel Entrepreneurship Research: Opportunities for Studying Entrepreneurial Decision Making," *Journal of Management* 37, no. 2 (2010): 395–403; V. Mahnke, M. Venzin, and S. A. Zahra, "Governing Entrepreneurial Opportunity Recognition in MNEs: Aligning Interest and Cognition Under Uncertainty," *Journal of Management Studies*, 44, no. 7 (2007): 1278–98.

23. S. M. Farmer, X. Yao, and K. Kung-Mcintyre, "The Behavioral Impact of Entrepreneur Identity Aspiration and Prior Entrepreneurial Experience," *Entrepreneurship Theory and Practice* 35, no. 2 (2010): 245–73; J. Wiklund and D. A. Shepherd, "Portfolio Entrepreneurship: Habitual and Novice Founders, New Entry, and Mode of Organizing," *Entrepreneurship Theory and Practice*, 32, no. 4 (2008): 701–25.

24. A. G. Lafley and R. Charan, "Innovation: Making Inspiration Routine," *Inc.*, www.inc.com, June 1, 2008; J. Case, "The Origins of Entrepreneurship," *Inc.*, June 1989.

25. A. C. Cooper, W. Dunkelberg, C. Woo, and W. Dennis, *New Business in America: The Firms and Their Owners* (Washington, DC: National Federation of Independent Business, 1990).

26. J. Aarstad, S. A. Haugland, and A. Greve, "Performance Spillover Effects in Entrepreneurial Networks: Assessing a Dyadic Theory of Social Capital," *Entrepreneurship Theory and Practice* 34, no. 5 (2010): 1003–1019; R. L. Sorenson, C. A. Folker, and K. H. Brigham, "The Collaborative Network Orientation: Achieving Business Success Through Collaborative Relationships," *Entrepreneurship Theory and Practice* 32, no. 4 (2008): 615–34.

27. K. Thoren and T. E. Brown, "The Sarimner Effect and Three Types of Ever-Abundant Business Opportunities," *International Journal of Entrepreneurial Venturing* 2, no. 2 (2010): 114–28; E. Stam, D. Audretsch, and J. Meijaard, "Renascent Entrepreneurship," *Journal of Evolutionary Economics*, 18, no. 3 (2008): 493–507.

28. I. P. Vaghely and P.-A. Julien, "Are Opportunities Recognized or Constructed? An Information Perspective on Entrepreneurial Opportunity Identification," *Journal of Business Venturing* 25, no. 1 (2010): 73–86.

29. D. J. Hansen, R. Shrader, and J. Monillor, "Defragmenting Definitions of Entrepreneurial Opportunity," *Journal of Small Business Management* 49, no. 2 (2011): 283–304; I. M. Kirzner, *Perception, Opportunity, and Profit: Studies in the Theory of Entrepreneurship* (Chicago: University of Chicago Press, 1979).

30. G. E. Shockley and P. M. Frank, "Schumpeter, Kirzner, and the Field of Social Entrepreneurship," *Journal of Social Entrepreneurship* 2, no. 1 (2011): 6–26; S. A. Alvarez and J. B. Barney, "Entrepreneurial Alertness," in *The Blackwell Encyclopedia of Management—Entrepreneurship,*

eds. M. A. Hitt and R. D. Ireland, (Malden, MA: Blackwell Publishing, 2005), 63–64.

31. P. J. Murphy, "A 2X2 Conceptual Foundation for Entrepreneurial Discovery Theory," *Entrepreneurship Theory and Practice* 35, no. 1 (2010): 1–16.

32. I. M. Kirzner, "The Primacy of Entrepreneurial Discovery," in *The Prime Mover of Progress*, ed. A. Seldon (London: Institute of Economic Affairs, 1980), 5–30.

33. J. M. Haynie, D. Shepherd, E. Mosakowski, and P. C. Earley, "A Situated Metacognitive Model of the Entrepreneurial Mindset," *Journal of Business Venturing* 25, no. 2 (2010): 217–29; S. C. Parker, "The Economics of Formal Business Networks," *Journal of Business Venturing* 23, no. 6 (2008): 627–40.

34. S. L. Jack, "Approaches to Studying Networks: Implications and Outcomes," *Journal of Business Venturing* 25, no. 1 (2010): 120–37; A. C. Cooper and X. Yin, "Entrepreneurial Networks," in *The Blackwell Encyclopedia of Management— Entrepreneurship*, eds. M. A. Hitt and R. D. Ireland (Malden, MA: Blackwell Publishing, 2005), 98–100.

35. J. R. Mitchell and D. A. Shepherd, "To Thine Own Self Be True: Images of Self, Images of Opportunity, and Entrepreneurial Action," *Journal of Business Venturing* 25, no. 1 (2010): 138–54; D. B. Audretsch, W. Bonte, and M. Keilbach, "Entrepreneurship Capital and Its Impact on Knowledge Diffusion and Economic Performance," *Journal of Business Venturing* 23, no. 6 (2008): 687–98.

36. L. Harris and A. Rae, "The Online Connection: Transforming Marketing Strategy for Small Businesses," *Journal of Business Strategy* 31, no. 2 (2010): 4–12.

37. G. E. Hills, C. M. Hultman, S. Kraus, and R. Schulte, "History, Theory and Evidence of Entrepreneurial Marketing—An Overview," *International Journal of Entrepreneurship and Innovation Management* 11, no. 1 (2010): 3–18.

38. S.-W. Kwon and P. Arenius, "Nations of Entrepreneurs: A Social Capital Perspective," *Journal of Business Venturing* 25, no. 3 (2010): 315–30; R. Braun, "In the Eye of the Beholder: How Construing Situations Affects Opportunity Recognition," *Social Science Research Network*, 2008, http://papers.ssrn.com.

39. J. Zhang, P.-H. Soh and P.-K. Wong, "Entrepreneurial Resource Acquisition Through Indirect Ties: Compensatory Effects of Prior Knowledge," *Journal of Management* 36, no. 2 (2010): 511–36; M. Granovetter, "The Strength of Weak Ties," *American Journal of Sociology* 78, no. 6 (1973): 1360–80.

40. D. Dimov, "Nascent Entrepreneurs and Venture Emergence: Opportunity Confidence, Human Capital and Early Planning," *Journal of Management Studies* 47, no. 6 (2010): 1123–53.

41. J. Brinckmann S. Salomo, and H. G. Gemuenden, "Financial Management Competence of Founding Teams and Growth of New Technology-Based Firms," *Entrepreneurship Theory and Practice* 35, no. 2 (2011): 217–43; D. A. Harper, "Towards a Theory of Entrepreneurial Teams," *Journal of Business Venturing* 23, no. 6 (2008): 613–26.

42. C.-Y. Chiu and L. Y.-Y. Kwan, "Culture and Creativity: A Process Model," *Management and Organization Review* 6, no. 3 (2010): 447–61; J. J. Kao, *Entrepreneurship, Creativity, and Organization* (Upper Saddle River, NJ: Prentice Hall, 1989).

43. R. A. Baro and J. Tang, "The Role of Entrepreneurs in Firm-Level Innovation: Joint Effects of Positive Affect, Creativity and Environmental Dynamism," *Journal of Business Venturing* 26, no. 1 (2011): 49–60.

44. S. C. Parker and C. M van Praag, "The Entrepreneur's Mode of Entry: Business Takeover or New Venture Start?" *Journal of Business Venturing* (2011): in press.

45. M. Csikszentmihalyi, *Creativity* (New York: HarperCollins, 1996).

46. M.-D. Foo, "Member Experience, Use of External Assistance and Evaluation of Business Ideas," *Journal of Small Business Management* 48, no. 1 (2010): 32–43.

47. M.-D. Foo, "Teams Developing Business Ideas: How Member Characteristics and Conflict Affect Member-Rated Team Effectiveness," *Small Business Economics* 36, no. 1 (2010): 33–46; J. S. Park, "Opportunity Recognition and Product Innovation in Entrepreneurial High-Tech Start-Ups: A New Perspective and Supporting Case Study," *Technovation* 2, no. 7 (2005): 739–52.

48. K. Rodan, Entrepreneurial Thought Leaders Podcast, Stanford Technology Ventures Program, http://stvp.stanford.edu (accessed May 16, 2011).

49. Greg Galant and Sharelle Klause, "VV Show #35," *Venture Voice Podcast*, www.venturevoice.com/ 2006/06/vv_show_35_sharelle_klaus_of_d.html (accessed March 20, 2011, originally posted on June 14, 2006).

50. College Drop-Ins homepage, http://collegedropins .com (accessed May 18, 2011).

51. L. Ronning, "Social Capital and New Business Start-Ups: The Moderating Effect of Human Capital," *International Journal of Entrepreneurship and Small Business* 12, no. 2 (2011): 207–26.

52. L. K. Williams and S. J. McGuire, "Economic Creativity and Innovation Implementation: The Entrepreneurial Drivers of Growth? Evidence from 63 Countries," *Small Business Economics* 34, no. 4 (2010): 391–412.

53. L. P. Kyrgidou and M. Hughes, "Strategic Entrepreneurship: Origins, Core Elements and Research Directions," *European Business Review* 22, no. 1 (2010): 43–63.

Getting Personal *with* MORPHOLOGY

Founder:

KATE RYAN REILING

MBA, The Tuck School at Dartmouth College, 2009

Dialogue *with*
Kate Ryan Reiling

FIRST ENTREPRENEURIAL EXPERIENCE
Selling friendship bracelets when I was younger

BEST ADVICE I'VE RECEIVED
Believe in yourself (from my dad).

MY FAVORITE SMARTPHONE APP
Zillow

WHAT I DO WHEN I'M NOT WORKING
Go biking, cross country skiing or do something active

MY BIGGEST SURPRISE AS AN ENTREPRENEUR
How many decisions I have to make on a daily basis with little historical data to help guide me

BEST PART OF BEING A STUDENT
Time to think with friends

CHAPTER 3

Feasibility *Analysis*

OPENING PROFILE

MORPHOLOGY
The Value of Validating a Business Idea

Web: www.morphologygames.com
Twitter: morphologygames
Facebook: Morphology Games

It all started on a snowy Minnesota night in 2002. Kate Ryan Reiling was hanging out with friends and they decided to play a board game. They were bored with the board games they had to pick from, so they took wooden sticks from one game, glass beads from another, and took turns picking words from the dictionary, and the person who picked the word would try to depict the word with the sticks and beads to see if the others could guess the word. Reiling thought it was a really neat idea and asked the group if she could run with it and investigate it further. They said absolutely.

To flesh out the idea, Reiling started accumulating small objects for the game, such as shapes, strings, rocks, and anything that could be used to help depict a word. Luckily, there was a thrift shop near where she lived, where she could sift through these types of items and find what she needed. She also started learning about the board game industry. She went to Toys "R" Us, for example, to peruse the board game aisle, to see how different games were set up and packaged. She put together an early version of her game, which she named Fluster, so she could ask friends to play it and get their reaction. (The name of the game was later changed to Morphology because Fluster was already trademarked.) Morphology is played in teams. The basic idea is that each team has a person who chooses a word and attempts to build the word in such a way that his or her teammates can guess what it is. As a team guesses correctly, they move across the board and the first to the finish line wins. Reiling knew Morphology was engaging when she'd have friends over to play and the next day one of them would say something like, "I was thinking about the word *butterfly* and I wish I had used this piece . . ." or she'd be at a cocktail party and someone would start playfully arranging their food in a manner that depicted a word, just like they did in the game. Morphology had a certain type of stickiness that Reiling interpreted as a very positive thing.

LEARNING OBJECTIVES

After studying this chapter you should be ready to:

1. Explain what a feasibility analysis is and why it's important.

2. Discuss the proper time to complete a feasibility analysis when developing an entrepreneurial venture.

3. Describe the purpose of a product/service feasibility analysis and the two primary issues that a proposed business should consider in this area.

4. Explain a concept statement and its contents.

5. Describe the purpose of a buying intentions survey and how it's administered.

6. Explain the importance of library, Internet, and gumshoe research.

7. Describe the purpose of industry/market feasibility analysis and the two primary issues to consider in this area.

8. Discuss the characteristics of an attractive industry.

9. Describe the purpose of organizational feasibility analysis and list the two primary issues to consider in this area.

10. Explain the importance of financial feasibility analysis and list the most critical issues to consider in this area.

From 2002 until 2007, Reiling was employed full-time but continued to ask people to play Morphology so she could watch them play and collect feedback. After people played the game, she would ask them to fill out a short questionnaire about their experience. During this period, she observed the game being played many times, switching out game pieces when she observed that one piece worked better than another. She also carefully observed how adding a particular piece or subtracting a particular piece changed the pace and enjoyment level of the game. She eventually created 15 sample games that she put together in her basement. She went beyond family and friends and sent copies of the game to people she didn't know to get their feedback. The response was excellent. She continued working on Morphology. On one occasion she asked people running a local coffee shop, which had lots of board games available for its patrons to play, to schedule a time when customers could pilot test her game. Reiling remembers that on the day the pilot test was taking place, a man stuck his head in the door of the shop and asked what everyone was doing that was so fun. He was invited in to play and when he left, handed Reiling one of his business cards and asked to be contacted when the game was available for purchase. This type of experience was very motivating for Reiling. Reiling also wasn't bashful about asking people who were in a position to give her good quality feedback for advice. For example, when she was working on Morphology's packaging design, she called several stores that carried board games asking for general information on the board game industry and packaging. She incorporated the feedback she received into the final packaging design for the game.

To bolster her business knowledge, Reiling decided to pursue an MBA at the Tuck School at Dartmouth College. MBA students at Tuck complete a first-year project, in teams, and Reiling saw this as an opportunity to do additional work on Morphology. So she organized a team and convinced the members to focus on Morphology. The project resulted in a business plan and an investor presentation for Morphology. The team drilled deep in regard to the board game industry, an exercise that was particularly instructive to Reiling. Her group at Tuck also did a lot of play testing of the game.

After finishing her MBA in 2009, Reiling returned to Minnesota as the women's soccer coach at Macalester College in St. Paul. In 2010, Reiling took Morphology to the New York Toy Fair, which is the largest trade show in the United States for toys and games. It was well received, and was one of the top picks of the fair according to *TD Monthly*. It was also nominated as one of the best party games according to *Games*. Prior to previewing Morphology at the New York Toy Fair, Reiling figures she watched over 400 people play Morphology and collected 124 user surveys. Dozens of iterations in Morphology's game pieces, rules, style of play, and so forth took place as a result of this testing. Buoyed by Morphology's positive feedback, in mid-2010 Reiling was able to raise $150,000 to create 5,000 copies of Morphology for her initial inventory. Morphology is now being sold in more than 40 stores across the United States, with some distribution in Canada. Reiling hopes to have Morphology in additional stores soon.[1]

In this chapter, we'll discuss the importance of feasibility analysis. Failure to conduct a feasibility analysis can result in disappointing outcomes, as illustrated in this chapter's "What Went Wrong?" feature which deals with the failure of Visa Cash Cards in Hong Kong.

FEASIBILITY ANALYSIS

Feasibility analysis is the process of determining if a business idea is viable. As shown in Figure 3.1, the most effective businesses emerge from a process that includes (1) recognizing a business idea, (2) testing the feasibility of the idea, (3) writing a business plan, and (4) launching the business. If a business idea falls short on one or more of the four components of feasibility analysis, it should be dropped or rethought, as shown in the figure. Many entrepreneurs make the mistake of identifying a business idea and then jumping directly to writing a business plan to describe and gain support for the idea. This sequence often omits or provides little time for the important step of testing the feasibility of a business idea before the business plan is written.

A mental transition must be made when completing a feasibility analysis from thinking of a business idea as just an idea to thinking of it as a business. A feasibility analysis is an assessment of a potential business rather than strictly a product or service idea. The sequential nature of the steps shown in Figure 3.1 cleanly separates the investigative portion of thinking through the merits of a business idea from the planning and selling portion of the process. Feasibility analysis is investigative in nature and is designed to critique the merits of a proposed business. A business plan is more focused on planning and selling. The reason it's important to complete the entire process, according to John W. Mullins, the author of the highly regarded book *The New Business Road Test*, is to avoid falling into the "everything about my opportunity is wonder" mode. In Mullins's view, failure to properly investigate the merits of a business idea before the business plan is written runs the risk of blinding an entrepreneur to inherent risks associated with the potential business and results in too positive of a plan.[2] This scenario may explain the failure of the Visa Cash Card in Hong Kong as described in the "What Went Wrong?" feature.

This chapter provides a methodology for conducting a feasibility analysis by describing its four key areas: product/service feasibility, industry/market feasibility, organizational feasibility, and financial feasibility. We introduce supplemental material in two appendixes to the chapter. Appendix 3.1 contains a tool called First Screen, which is a template for completing a feasibility analysis. Appendix 3.2 contains an Internet Resource Table that provides information on Internet resources that are helpful in completing First Screen.

An outline for the approach to feasibility analysis depicted in this chapter is provided in Table 3.1. Completing a feasibility analysis requires both primary and secondary research. **Primary research** is research that is collected by the

LEARNING OBJECTIVE
1. Explain what a feasibility analysis is and why it's important.

LEARNING OBJECTIVE
2. Discuss the proper time to complete a feasibility analysis when developing an entrepreneurial venture.

FIGURE 3.1
Role of Feasibility Analysis in Developing Successful Business Ideas

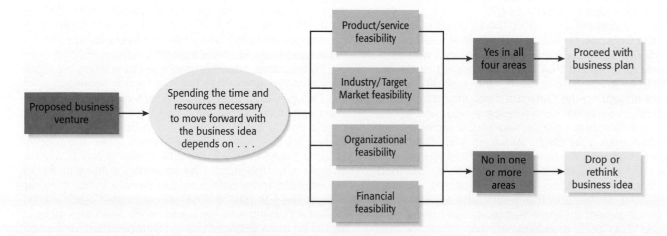

TABLE 3.1 FEASIBILITY ANALYSIS

Part 1: Product/Service Feasibility

    A. Product/service desirability

    B. Product/service demand

Part 2: Industry/Target Market Feasibility

    A. Industry attractiveness

    B. Target market attractiveness

Part 3: Organizational Feasibility

    A. Management prowess

    B. Resource sufficiency

Part 4: Financial Feasibility

    A. Total start-up cash needed

    B. Financial performance of similar businesses

    C. Overall financial attractiveness of the proposed venture

Overall Assessment

WHAT WENT WRONG?

Visa Cash in Hong Kong: How Feasible Was It?

Launched in 1996 in Hong Kong, Prime Visa Cash was a revolutionary e-money card released by a cooperation between Bank of China, Standard Chartered Bank, and Visa International. This e-money card is different from the Octopus card that has gained popularity throughout Hong Kong today. In August 1996, the Visa Cash card was introduced as a disposable card that could store up to HK$200 (US$26). In April 1997, it transformed into a reloadable card that could store up to HK$3000 (US$385). Cards can be reloaded at hundreds of designated ATMs. In 2001, about 4,500 retail merchants honored the cards. Unfortunately, in 2001, the Visa Cash service in Hong Kong was discontinued. In theory, Visa Cash sounded like a good idea, so what went wrong?

In 1997, a prepaid card called the Octopus was introduced. The Octopus, honored by *The Independent* as one of the "50 Great Ideas for the 21st Century," gained in popularity to the point that today 95 percent of people aged 16 to 65 in Hong Kong use it. With over 383 service providers accepting the Octopus card, including public transportation services, convenience stores, and phone booths, the Octopus card gained much wider market penetration than Visa Cash. Although Visa Cash was accepted in approximately 4,500 merchant terminals in various retail outlets, including supermarkets, fast-food chains, convenience stores, department stores, gasoline stations, book stores, and hair salons, the exclusive use of the Octopus card for mass transportation transactions weakened Visa Cash's market penetration.

In addition to the vendors accepting the cards, the design of both cards affected their usage rate. The Octopus card adopts RFID technology, while Visa Cash does not, forcing users to insert the card in reading machines for processing. Since the Octopus card can be used in many contactless ways, people do not need to take out their cards from their bags, allowing users to place their bags above the card reader. This design saves time and simplifies life for millions of public transportation passengers.

Since car ownership is low due to a lack of land supply and parking space in Hong Kong, people prefer to take mass transportation rather than drive their own cars. Therefore, the Octopus card's position as the sole e-money card used for transportation successfully captured a vast number of customers. The Octopus card succeeded in Hong Kong but not overseas due to its huge usage rate for mass transportation.

Furthermore, spending habits in Hong Kong are more conservative, which has led to a higher acceptance of the Octopus card than the Visa Cash card. The Octopus card opposed the buy-now-pay-later principle of most credit cards, including Visa Cash, and works on the instantaneous debit principle, which takes the money directly from the user's account, allowing practically no overdraft on the card. The spending culture in Asian countries is more cautious, and people in Hong Kong are not used to paying small amounts with credit cards, preferring paying with coins and notes. Therefore, people would be more willing to use the Octopus card for a small amount rather than a large amount since the money comes directly from their accounts rather than as a loan they would have to pay later.

Furthermore, the ramifications of losing an Octopus card are arguably much less than those of losing a Visa Cash card. An Octopus cardholder will only lose a maximum of HK$1,000 (approximately US$130) if the card is lost or stolen. If the Octopus cardholder reports the loss quickly, Octopus Cards Limited can lock the card to prevent its misuse, and will refund to the customer any value remaining on the lost card six hours after the loss has been reported. This provides a better guarantee than Visa Cash.

The approach to reloading the cards has also affected their use in Hong Kong. Visa Cash owners are only able to reload their cards at designated ATMs, which is not attractive for the Hong Kong public as saving time is their first priority. Owners of the Octopus card can reload their cards automatically.

The Octopus card has become the most widely used form of e-money in Hong Kong due to its exclusive use for public transportation transactions and its ability to be a faster and more convenient substitute for cash in retail payments.

Questions for Critical Thinking

1. Describe the difference between Visa Cash and Octopus cards.
2. What can a start-up learn from the experience of Visa Cash about the importance of a feasibility analysis?
3. Can Visa Cash significantly modify its business idea to attract more customers?
4. Would Visa Cash be more popular where you live? Carry out a comprehensive feasibility analysis to help you decide.

person or persons completing the analysis. It normally includes talking to industry experts, obtaining feedback from prospective customers, conducting focus groups, and administering surveys. **Secondary research** probes data that is already collected. The data generally includes industry studies, Census Bureau data, analyst forecasts, and other pertinent information gleaned through library and Internet research. The Internet Resource Table in Appendix 3.2 is useful for conducting secondary research.

It should be emphasized that while a feasibility analysis tests the merits of a specific idea, it allows ample opportunity for the idea to be revised, altered, and changed as a result of the feedback that is obtained and the analysis that is conducted. The key objective behind feasibility analysis is to put an idea to the test—by talking to industry experts, surveying prospective customers, studying industry trends, thinking through the financials, and scrutinizing it in other ways. These types of activities not only help determine whether an idea is feasible but also help shape and mold the idea.

Now let's turn our attention to the four areas of feasibility analysis. The first area we'll discuss is product/service feasibility.

Product/Service Feasibility Analysis

Product/service feasibility analysis is an assessment of the overall appeal of the product or service being proposed. Although there are many important things to consider when launching a new venture, nothing else matters if the product or service itself doesn't sell. There are two components to product/service feasibility analysis: product/service desirability and product/service demand.

> **LEARNING OBJECTIVE**
>
> 3. Describe the purpose of a product/service feasibility analysis and the two primary issues that a proposed business should consider in this area.

One of the best things prospective entrepreneurs can do, throughout the feasibility analysis process, is get out and talk to prospective customers about their product ideas. Surveys, designed properly, can be an effective way of gathering information.

©Sue Harper/Dreamstime.com

Product/Service Desirability   The first component of product/service feasibility is to affirm that the proposed product or service is desirable and serves a need in the marketplace. You should ask the following questions to determine the basic appeal of the product or service:

■ Does it make sense? Is it reasonable? Is it something consumers will get excited about?

■ Does it take advantage of an environmental trend, solve a problem, or fill a gap in the marketplace?

■ Is this a good time to introduce the product or service to the market?

■ Are there any fatal flaws in the product or service's basic design or concept?

The proper mind-set at the feasibility analysis stage is to get a general sense of the answers to these and similar questions, rather than to try to reach final conclusions. One way to achieve this objective is to administer a concept test.

Concept Test   A **concept test** involves showing a preliminary description of a product or service idea, called a **concept statement**, to industry experts and prospective customers to solicit their feedback. It is a one-page document that normally includes the following:

■ A description of the product or service. This section details the features of the product or service; many include a sketch of it as well.

■ The intended target market. This section lists the consumers or businesses who are expected to buy the product or service.

■ The benefits of the product or service. This section describes the benefits of the product or service and includes an account of how the product or service adds value and/or solves a problem.

■ A description of how the product or service will be positioned relative to competitors. A company's position describes how its product or service is situated relative to its rivals.

■ A brief description of the company's management team.

TABLE 3.2 SHORT SURVEY TO ATTACH TO THE CONCEPT STATEMENT

1. List three things you like about the product or service idea described in this statement.
2. Provide three suggestions for making the idea better.
3. Do you think the idea is feasible (i.e., is a realistic or viable business idea)?
4. Provide any additional comments or suggestions you think might be helpful (including red flags).

After the concept statement is developed, it should be shown to at least 10 people who are familiar with the industry that the firm plans to enter and who can provide informed feedback. The temptation to show it to family members and friends should be avoided because these people are predisposed to give positive feedback. Instead, it should be distributed to people who will provide candid and informed feedback and advice. A short survey should be attached to the statement. The items that should be placed in the survey are shown in Table 3.2. The information gleaned from the survey should be tabulated and carefully read. If time permits, the statement can be used in an iterative manner to strengthen the product or service idea. For example, you might show the statement to a group of prospective customers, receive their feedback, tweak the idea, show it to a second group of prospective customers, tweak the idea some more, and so on.

The concept statement for a fictitious company named New Venture Fitness Drinks is provided in Figure 3.2. New Venture Fitness Drinks sells a line of nutritious fitness drinks and targets sports enthusiasts. Its strategy is to place

FIGURE 3.2
New Venture Fitness Drinks' Concept Statement

New Business Concept
New Venture Fitness Drinks Inc.

Product

New Venture Fitness Drinks will sell delicious, nutrition-filled, all-natural fitness drinks to thirsty sports enthusiasts. The drinks will be sold through small storefronts (600 sq. ft.) that will be the same size as popular smoothie restaurants. The drinks were formulated by Dr. William Peters, a world-renowned nutritionist, and Dr. Michelle Smith, a sports medicine specialist, on behalf of New Venture Fitness Drinks and its customers.

Target Market

In the first three years of operation, New Venture Fitness Drinks plans to open three or four restaurants. They will all be located near large sports complexes that contain soccer fields and softball diamonds. The target market is sports enthusiasts.

Why New Venture Fitness Drinks?

The industry for sports drinks continues to grow. New Venture Fitness Drinks will introduce exciting new sports drinks that will be priced between $1.50 and $2.50 per 16-ounce serving. Energy bars and other over-the-counter sports snacks will also be sold. Each restaurant will contain comfortable tables and chairs (both inside and outside) where sports enthusiasts can congregate after a game. The atmosphere will be fun, cheerful, and uplifting.

Special Feature—No Other Restaurant Does This

As a special feature, New Venture Fitness Drinks will videotape select sporting events that take place in the sports complexes nearest its restaurants and will replay highlights of the games on video monitors in their restaurants. The "highlight" film will be a 30-minute film that will play continuously from the previous day's sporting events. This special feature will allow sports enthusiasts, from kids playing soccer to adults in softball leagues, to drop in and see themselves and their teammates on television.

Management Team

New Venture Fitness Drink is led by its cofounders, Jack Petty and Peggy Wills. Jack has 16 years of experience with a national restaurant chain, and Peggy is a certified public accountant with seven years of experience at a Big 4 accounting firm.

small restaurants, similar to smoothie restaurants, near large sports complexes. It is important to keep a concept statement relatively short (no more than one page) to increase the likelihood that it will be read.

Rather than developing a formal concept statement, some entrepreneurs conduct their initial product/service feasibility analysis by simply talking through their ideas with people or conducting focus groups to solicit feedback. While not a complete approach, there is merit to the give-and-take that entrepreneurs experience by talking with prospective customers rather than just handing them a concept statement and asking them to complete a questionnaire. The ideal combination is to do both—distribute a concept statement to 10 or more people who can provide informed feedback and engage in verbal give-and-take with as many industry experts and prospective customers as possible.

Product/Service Demand   The second component of product/service feasibility analysis is to determine if there is demand for the product or service. There are two techniques for making this determination: administering a buying intentions survey and conducting library, Internet, and gumshoe research.

Buying Intentions Survey   A **buying intentions survey** is an instrument that is used to gauge customer interest in a product or service. It consists of a concept statement or a similar description of a product or service with a short survey attached. The statement and survey should be distributed to 20 to 30 potential customers (people who completed the concept statement test should not be asked to complete this survey). Each participant should be asked to read the statement and complete the survey. The format for the survey is shown in Table 3.3.

To gauge customer interest, the number of people who indicate they definitely would buy is typically combined with the number of people who indicate they probably would buy. It's getting increasingly easy to administer buying intentions surveys. For example, Internet sites like SurveyMonkey and SurveyGizmo allow you to set up small-scale surveys for free or for a modest fee.[3]

One caveat is that people who say that they intend to purchase a product or service don't always follow through; as a result, the numbers resulting from this activity are almost always optimistic. The survey also doesn't normally tap a scientifically random sample. Still, the results give a potential entrepreneur a general sense of the degree of customer interest in the product or service idea.

> **LEARNING OBJECTIVE**
>
> **5.** Describe the purpose of a buying intentions survey and how it's administered.

TABLE 3.3   BUYING INTENTIONS SURVEY

Distributed to a different group of people than those who completed the initial concept statement test

How likely would you be to buy the product or service described above, if we make it?

____ Definitely would buy

____ Probably would buy

____ Might or might not buy

____ Probably would not buy

____ Definitely would not buy

Additional questions that are sometimes included in the survey:

How much would you be willing to pay for the product or service?

Where would you expect to find this product or service for sale?

If the optional questions shown in Table 3.3 are included in the survey, additional insights can be obtained regarding pricing and sales and distribution.

One approach to finding qualified people to talk to about a product or service idea or to react to a concept statement is to contact trade associations and/or attend industry trade shows. If your product idea is in the digital media space, for example, you may be able to call the Digital Media Association (which is a national trade association devoted primarily to the online audio and video industries) and get a list of members who live in your area. Attending trade shows in the industry you're interested in will place you in direct contact with numerous people who might be of assistance. A Web site that provides a directory of trade associations is included in the Internet Resource Table in Appendix 3.2.

Library, Internet, and Gumshoe Research The second way to assess demand for a product or service idea is by conducting library, Internet, and gumshoe research. While administrating a buying intentions survey is important, more data is needed. Think of yourself as a lawyer preparing to defend a client in court. You can't just tell the jury that you "think" your client is innocent or that 25 out of 30 people you surveyed think that acquitting him is a good idea. The jury will want more evidence. So you have to dig it up. In a feasibility analysis context, you have a similar task. Evidence that there will be healthy demand for your product or service must be accumulated. Three important ways to do this are via library, Internet, and gumshoe research.

As mentioned in Chapter 2, reference librarians can often point you toward resources to help investigate a business idea, such as industry-specific magazines, trade journals, and industry reports. For example, Sprig Toys makes super-safe, environmentally friendly, educational toys for children. Sounds like a good idea. But "sounds like a good idea" isn't enough—we need facts to discern whether there is a demand for products Sprig Toys plans to sell. What's the trajectory of the toy industry? What do industry experts say are the most important factors that parents consider when they buy their children toys? Has this idea been tried before? If so, what were the results? Is there an "educational toy" segment within the larger toy industry? If so, is this segment growing or shrinking? Is there a trade association for the makers of education toys that already has statistics about market demand for educational toys?

The overarching point is that for your particular product or service idea you need to accumulate evidence about likely demand. Your university or college library is a good place to start, and the Internet is a marvelous resource. By simply typing "market demand for education toys" into the Google search box, we quickly found two articles that bode well for Sprig Toys:

> Statistics show that the sales of toys and games have declined over the years. However, educational toys have been on the rise, as more parents opt to purchase products that would give them the most value for their money, as compared to, say, buying Bratz dolls and Hot Wheels.[4]

This article, which appeared in a computer and technology blog, is affirmed by an article that was found commenting on trends observed at the 2011 International Toy Fair in New York City. According to the article,

> After combing through 100,000+ products now on display at the Jacob K. Javits Convention Center in New York City, TIA's (Toy Industry Association) trend experts report that this year's top trends target every type of child—from those who like to learn through games and creative craft, to those who have a "need for speed" and enjoy active play—and they truly reflect the advancements being made across other industries, like technology and science. The top trends for 2011 also met the increasing demands of parents, the government and healthcare officials who are striving to amp up educational and active play to ensure a brighter, healthier future for today's kids.[5]

These two quotes tell us a lot about the likely demand for Sprig Toys' products, and it's just a start. It also gives us some important insights. Apparently parent groups, governmental officials, and health care officials are actively advocating educational toys. The second article also gives us the name of a trade association, the Toy Industry Association, which we can contact for more information.

Simple gumshoe research is also important for gaining a sense of the likely demand for a product or service idea. A gumshoe is a detective or an investigator that scrounges around for information or clues wherever they can be found. Don't be bashful. Ask people what they think about your product or service idea. If your idea is to sell educational toys, spend a week volunteering at a day care center and watch how children interact with toys. Take the owner of a toy store to lunch and discuss your ideas. Spend some time browsing through toy stores and observe the types of toys that get the most attention. If you actually launch a business, there is simply too much at stake to rely on gut instincts and cursory information to assure you that your product or service will sell. Collect as much information as you can within reasonable time constraints.

To supplement the techniques discussed previously, there is a growing number of tools that are available online for all facets of feasibility analysis, as shown in Table 3.4. These tools range from open-ended Q&A sites, like Quora, where an entrepreneur can pose questions pertaining to business ideas and get informed feedback, to sites that will conduct usability tests of Web sites and applications. These services are becoming increasingly affordable and should be utilized where appropriate.

The importance of library, Internet, and gumshoe research doesn't wane once a firm is launched. It's important to continually assess the strength of product or service ideas and learn from users. A colorful example of the value of ongoing gumshoe research is provided in the "Savvy Entrepreneurial Firm" feature. In this feature, a successful company made a 180-degree turn regarding how to position a particular product simply by watching how customers interacted with the product in retail stores.

TABLE 3.4   ONLINE TOOLS AVAILABLE FOR COMPLETING FEASIBILITY ANALYSIS

Tool	Source	Cost
A/B testing—meaning respondent is given two options (i.e., which logo is more appealing?)	Pick-fu (http://pickfu.com)	$5.00 for answers from 50 people.
Feedback on product ideas	Quirky (www.quirky.com)	Free.
Feedback on ideas or designs	Conceptshare (www.conceptshare.com)	Free 30-day trial; tiered pricing system based on level of feedback.
Q&A sites—open-ended questions	Quora (www.quora.com) LinkedIn Answers (www.linkedin.com/answers)	Free. Free.
Survey	SurveyMonkey (www.surveymonkey.com) SurveyGizmo (www.surveygizmo.com)	Free for basic survey; fee based for more extensive surveys. Tiered pricing based on nature of survey.
Web site usability tests	UserTesting (www.usertesting.com) Loop11 (www.loop11.com) OpenHallway (www.openhallway.com)	$39 for video of visitors speaking their thoughts as they use your Web site. Flat fee of $350 for user testing project. Tired pricing for usability studies of your Web site or application. Test can originate from social platforms like Facebook or Twitter.

SAVVY ENTREPRENEURIAL FIRM

How Learning from Customers Caused a Successful Firm to Make a 180-Degree Turn on the Positioning of a Product

Bill Gross is both a serial entrepreneur and the founder of Idealab, an incubator-type organization that has launched over 75 companies. He's also an Internet pioneer and the creator of the pay-per-click model of Internet advertising. In speaking to groups about entrepreneurship and in working with start-ups at Idealab, there is a story that Gross likes to tell about the importance of feasibility analysis and getting close to customers. It's an experience that has shaped his views about how important it is to learn from the potential users of your product.

In the early 1990s Gross started a software company named Knowledge Adventure. It started by making educational CD-ROM products for children, such as Space Adventure and Dinosaur Adventure. The firm also launched a line of products under the JumpStart brand. These products help kids with topics they encounter in school, such as math and science.

One Christmas, in the early 1990s, Gross really wanted his company to excel, so he decided to have employees spend weekends in places where Knowledge Adventure products were sold, to demo the products to parents and hopefully boost sales. So the company's 65 employees took turns traveling to electronics stores where they would set up booths at the end of aisles to demo their firm's products. Each Monday, following a weekend when employees were in stores, the employees met to talk about their experiences. One interesting theme emerged from these meetings. When looking at educational software products, parents were often confused about whether a particular product was age-appropriate for their child. They would often look at the back of the box (software was sold on CDs in boxes in those days), look at their child, look back at the box, and appear puzzled about whether the software was a good match for their child. Many companies, Knowledge Adventure included, would put wide age ranges on their products to broaden their appeal. Apparently, this practice inadvertently caused parents to wonder whether a product with a wide age range was really a good match for their particular child.

Thinking through what the employees had observed, Gross and his team came up with a novel idea. What if they produced educational software products that were targeted for a specific grade—like one for preschoolers, one for kindergarteners, one for first grade students, and so forth, to try to avoid confusion for parents. Gross remembers that there was a big fight in his company over this idea. The sales force said, "We can't convince stores to sell software for one age group. They'll never sell enough product." After listening to all the arguments, Gross concluded it was worth a try. So Knowledge Adventure created JumpStart Pre-School and JumpStart Kindergarten to test the concept. The result: The products sold 20 to 50 times the company's other products. Parents loved it—now they knew exactly what product was right for their child. There was even an aspirational quality to the products. Parents would see a product like JumpStart Kindergarten and buy it for their preschool child hoping to give them a head start in kindergarten. Knowledge Adventure has sold over 20 million copies of its grade-specific JumpStart products, and they are still for sale today.

What Gross likes to emphasize when telling this story is that he and his team would have never discovered the confusion that parents had in trying to determine if particular software products were age-appropriate for their children without directly observing them in stores. As a result of this experience, Gross is now a passionate advocate of start-ups directly interacting with potential users of their products.

Questions for Critical Thinking

1. In putting wide age ranges on their products (i.e., suitable for ages 4 through 7), do you think that software companies prior to the advent of JumpStart's grade-specific products ever thought that the wide age range caused parents angst in trying to determine if a particular product was suitable for their child? If your answer is "no," how could companies have missed such a fundamental factor? What is the broader implication of this lesson?

2. Could Gross and his team have gleaned the same type of insights they gained via directly observing parents shopping for educational software for their kids through surveys and focus groups? Explain your answer.

3. Design a program for InstyMeds, the subject of the "You Be the VC 3.1" feature, to directly observe its customers use its service. How should InstyMeds go about it? What type of insights might emerge from this initiative?

4. How can a start-up that hasn't already launched apply the lessons learned from Gross's experience with JumpStart and grade-specific software products?

Source: B. Gross, "A Devotion to New Ideas," Stanford Technology Ventures Entrepreneurial Thought Leaders Podcast (accessed March 11, 2011, originally posted on February 23, 2011).

Information pertaining to industry growth rates, trends, and future prospects is available via online databases like the one accessed here. IBISWorld and BizMiner are additional databases that provide particularly helpful industry information.

©MI12nan/ Dreamstime.com

Industry/Target Market Feasibility Analysis

LEARNING OBJECTIVE

7. Describe the purpose of industry/market feasibility analysis and the two primary issues to consider in this area.

Industry/target market feasibility is an assessment of the overall appeal of the industry and the target market for the product or service being proposed. There is a distinct difference between a firm's industry and its target market, which should be clearly understood. An **industry** is a group of firms producing a similar product or service, such as computers, children's toys, airplanes, or social networks. A firm's target market is the limited portion of the industry that it goes after or to which it wants to appeal. Most firms and certainly entrepreneurial start-ups typically do not try to service their entire industry. Instead, they select or carve out a specific target market and try to service that market very well. Sprig Toys is not trying to target the entire children's toy industry. Its target market is parents who are willing to pay a premium for super-safe, environmentally friendly, educational toys.

There are two components to industry/target market feasibility analysis: industry attractiveness and target market attractiveness.

LEARNING OBJECTIVE

8. Discuss the characteristics of an attractive industry.

Industry Attractiveness   Industries vary in terms of their overall attractiveness.[6] In general, the most attractive industries have the characteristics depicted in Table 3.5. The top three factors are particularly important. Industries that are young rather than old, are early rather than late in their life cycle, and are fragmented rather than concentrated are more receptive to new

TABLE 3.5   CHARACTERISTICS OF ATTRACTIVE INDUSTRIES

- ■ Are young rather than old
- ■ Are early rather than late in their life cycle
- ■ Are fragmented rather than concentrated
- ■ Are growing rather than shrinking
- ■ Are selling products or services that customers "must have" rather than "want to have"
- ■ Are not crowded
- ■ Have high rather than low operating margins
- ■ Are not highly dependent on the historically low price of a key raw material, like gasoline or flour, to remain profitable

entrants than industries with the opposite characteristics. You also want to pick an industry that is structurally attractive—meaning start-ups can enter the industry (in various target markets) and compete. Some industries are characterized by such high barriers to entry or the presence of one or two dominant players that potential new entrants are essentially shut out.

Other factors are also important. For example, the degree to which environmental and business trends are moving in favor rather than against the industry are important for the industry's long-term health and its capacity to spawn new target or niche markets. Are changing economic and societal trends helping or hurting industry incumbents? Are profit margins increasing or falling? Is innovation accelerating or waning? Are input costs going up or down? Are new markets for the industry's staple products opening up or are current markets being shut down by competing industries? You can't cover every facet of an industry; but you should gain a sense of whether the industry you're entering is a good one or a poor one for start-ups.

Information that addresses each of these issues is available via industry reports published by IBISWorld, Mintel, Standard & Poor's NetAdvantage, and similar fee-based databases that are typically free if assessed through a university or large public library's Web site. These resources are listed in the Internet Resource Table in Appendix 3.2. The First Screen, which is the feasibility analysis template included in Appendix 3.1, includes a section that draws attention to the most important issues to focus on regarding industry attractiveness during the feasibility analysis stage of investigating a business idea.

Target Market Attractiveness   As mentioned, a target market is a place within a larger market segment that represents a narrower group of customers with similar needs. Most start-ups simply don't have the resources needed to participate in a broad market, at least initially. Instead, by focusing on a smaller target market, a firm can usually avoid head-to-head competition with industry leaders and can focus on serving a specialized market very well. It's also not realistic, in most cases, for a start-up to introduce a completely original product idea into a completely new market. In most instances, it's just too expensive to be a pioneer in each area. Most successful start-ups either introduce a new product into an existing market (like Sprig Toys introducing new toys into the existing toy market) or introduce a new market to an existing product (like InstyMeds is introducing vending machine sales, which is a new market, to prescription medicines, which is an existing product).

The challenge in identifying an attractive target market is to find a market that's large enough for the proposed business but is yet small enough to avoid attracting larger competitors at least until the entrepreneurial venture can get off to a successful start. Tommy John, a maker of men's undershirts and the subject of Case 3.1, is an example of a company that has targeted a market that meets these criteria. Tommy John began in 2008 by making custom-fitted men's undershirts, and has recently expanded to men's briefs. The undershirts are sold under the brand name Second Skin, based on the idea that they fit so well they feel like a "second skin" when worn. Tommy John started by selling through a single retailer, and eventually persuaded Neiman Marcus to give its undershirts a try. Today, Tommy John undershirts are sold in Neiman Marcus stores nationwide, and are making their way into other retailers as well. Although Tommy John operates in the $30 billion worldwide market for men's undershirts, it has carved out a specialized target or niche market for itself and is gaining momentum. One key to its success is that it has remained laser-focused on a clearly defined target market. The number one question the company gets is when it will start producing women's undergarments. So far it's resisted, preferring to remain focused on its Second Skin line of men's undershirts.[7]

While it's generally easy to find good information to assess the attractiveness of an entire industry, discerning the attractiveness of a small target market within an industry is tougher, particularly if the start-up is pioneering the target market. Often, under these circumstances, information from more than one industry and/or market must be collected and synthesized to make an informed judgment. For example, H2OAudio, first introduced in Chapter 2, makes waterproof housings for the iPhone and the iPod. The waterproof housings permit iPhone and iPod users to listen to their devices while swimming, surfing, skiing, or engaging in any activity where the iPod might get wet. The question for a product like this is what market to assess? There are no SIC (Standard Industrial Classification) or NAICS (North American Industry Classification System) codes for the "waterproof iPhone and iPod housing" industry or market. Obviously, a combination of markets must be studied, including the iPhone and iPod markets, the iPhone and iPod accessories market, and the market for water and snow sports. It would be important to not only know how well iPhone and iPod accessories are selling but also what the current trends in water and snow sports are. If iPhone and iPod accessories are selling like hotcakes but water and snow sports are on a sharp decline, the target market that H2OAudio is pioneering would be much less attractive than if iPhone and iPods were selling well and interest in water sports and snow sports were rapidly increasing.

The sources of information to mine and tap are also not as transparent when investigating target market attractiveness opposed to industry attractiveness. Say you wanted to piggyback on H2OAudio's idea and create super-durable airtight housings (which are near indestructible and don't allow any dirt or dust in) for smartphones for people who participate in extreme sports (i.e., mountain biking, hang-gliding, skateboarding, motocross, etc.). How to best assess the attractiveness of this target market is not entirely clear. Table 3.6 includes a list of suggestions, which illustrates the type of creativity that's required to find information on a narrowly defined target market. Ultimately, it will require a synthesis of data and facts collected from various sources to get a sense of whether creating super-durable airtight housings for smartphones for extreme sports participants is an attractive target market. You'll need to construct a

---

TABLE 3.6   POTENTIAL SOURCES OF INFORMATION TO ASSESS TARGET MARKET ATTRACTIVENESS FOR SUPER-DURABLE AIRTIGHT SMARTPHONE HOUSINGS FOR EXTREME SPORTS PARTICIPANTS

■ Type "smartphone accessories industry" into the Google or Bing search bar to gain general information about the trajectory of smartphone accessory sales. You might also try "iPhone accessories," "Android Smartphone Accessories," and "BlackBerry Accessories."

■ Go to a site that reviews or sells smartphone accessories, such as CellPhoneShop.net, and see if a similar product is already for sales. If it is, go to the company's Web site to see what evidence it reports about market attractiveness. This company may have already done much of your work for you.

■ Try to determine if there is a trade association or an annual trade show for smartphone accessories manufacturers and the manufacturers of extreme sports clothing and gear. Contact the relevant organizations to ask if they have data that might be helpful.

■ Search for newspaper and magazine articles on smartphone accessories using public search engines such as Find Articles (http://findarticles.com) and MagPortal (www.magportal.com), and more powerful search engines such as ProQuest and LexisNexis Academic, which are usually available through a university or large public library Web site.

■ Search newspaper and magazine articles on extreme sports, looking specifically for how extreme sport enthusiasts protect the products they carry while participating in their sport. Search engines are also getting extremely smart. Try entering into Google or ProQuest "smartphone accessories + extreme sports" and see what happens.

■ Contact a company that focuses on extreme sports to ask for leads in finding industry-wide sales data and to ask if super-durable airtight housings for smartphones currently exist. If they don't, ask if it would carry the product if it were available (you might even get your first customer this way). Don't be shy. Adrenalina, which is a retail chain that specializes in extreme sports clothing and gear, lists the phone numbers and e-mail addresses of each of its retail stores and its corporate office right on its Web site.

similar list of potential sources of information to assess the attractiveness of the target market to which your product or service will attempt to appeal.

Organizational Feasibility Analysis

Organizational feasibility analysis is conducted to determine whether a proposed business has sufficient management expertise, organizational competence, and resources to successfully launch its business.[8] There are two primary issues to consider in this area: management prowess and resource sufficiency.

Management Prowess   A proposed business should evaluate the prowess, or ability, of its initial management team, whether it is a sole entrepreneur or a larger group.[9] This task requires the individuals starting the firm to be honest and candid in their self-assessments. Two of the most important factors in this area are the passion that the solo entrepreneur or the management team has for the business idea and the extent to which the management team or solo entrepreneur understands the markets in which the firm will participate.[10] There are no practical substitutes for strengths in these areas.[11]

A collection of additional factors help define management prowess. Managers with extensive professional and social networks have an advantage in that they are able to reach out to colleagues and friends to help them plug experience or knowledge gaps. In addition, a potential new venture should have an idea of the type of new-venture team that it can assemble. A **new-venture team** is the group of founders, key employees, and advisers that either manage or help manage a new business in its start-up years. If the founder or founders of a new venture have identified several individuals they believe will join the firm after it is launched and these individuals are highly capable, that knowledge lends credibility to the organizational feasibility of the potential venture. The same rationale applies for highly capable people a new venture believes would be willing to join its board of directors or board of advisers.

One thing that many potential business founders find while assessing management prowess is that they may benefit from finding one or more partners to help them launch their business. Tips for finding an appropriate business partner are provided in the "Partnering for Success" feature.

Resource Sufficiency   The second area of organizational feasibility analysis is to determine whether the proposed venture has or is capable of obtaining sufficient resources to move forward. The focus in organizational feasibility analysis is on nonfinancial resources. The objective is to identify the most important nonfinancial resources and assess their availability. An example is a start-up that will require employees with specialized skills. If a firm launches in a community that does not have a labor pool that includes people with the skill sets the firm needs, a serious resources sufficiency problem exists.

Another key resource sufficiency issue is the ability to obtain intellectual property protection on key aspects of the business. This issue doesn't apply to all start-ups but is critical to companies that have invented a new product or are introducing a new business process that adds value to the way a product is manufactured or a service is delivered. One quick test a start-up can administer is to see if a patent has already been filed for its product or business process idea. Google Patents (www.google.com/patents) is a user-friendly way to search for patents. This approach isn't a substitute for utilizing a patent attorney, but can give a start-up a quick assessment of whether someone has beaten them to the punch regarding a particular product or business process idea.

To test resource sufficiency, a firm should list the 6 to 12 most critical nonfinancial resources that it will need to move its business idea forward and determine if those resources are available. Table 3.7 provides a list of the types of nonfinancial resources that are critical to many start-ups' success.

PARTNERING FOR SUCCESS

Finding the Right Business Partner

One thing that becomes clear to many potential business founders, while conducting organizational feasibility analysis, is that they need one or more partners to help launch their business. You might be a Web developer who has a great idea for a Web 2.0 cooking site, for example, but have no experience in marketing or sales. In this instance, you may need to find a partner with marketing and sales experience to successfully launch and run the firm. There are five key criteria to look for in a business partner. You want to get this right because picking the wrong partner or partners can lead to a lot of heartaches and business challenges.

1. **Know the skills and experiences you need.**   Make an honest assessment of the skills and experience you bring to the business and the gaps that remain. Pick someone who fills the gaps. For example, if you're an experienced Web designer you probably don't want to partner with another experienced Web designer. Pick someone who brings other competencies that you need to the venture, like marketing or finance.
2. **Make sure your personalities and work habits are compatible.**   While you don't need someone who is just like yourself, you do need to be comfortable with the person you'll be in business with. For example, if you'd rather work 16 hours a day if that is what it takes to finish a project on time, and your partner would rather quit after 8 hours a day and try to renegotiate the due date for the project, that difference in work styles will invariably cause conflict. Similarly, if you like to wear a coat and tie when meeting with clients and your partner thinks wearing blue jeans is fine, obvious disagreements could arise.
3. **Make sure you and your partner have common goals and aspirations.**   Be sure that you and your partner are shooting for the same target. For example, if your goal is to build a billion-dollar company but your partner would be perfectly satisfied growing the company to $10 million in sales and then selling out, obvious problems could ensue.
4. **Look in the right places.**   If you don't have someone already in mind, it's important to know where to look for a potential partner. Generic networking events, like Chamber of Commerce mixers, are usually ineffective for finding a business partner. Instead, if you're looking for an engineer, contact engineering trade associations for leads or attend engineering trade fairs. Social networking sites for professionals, like LinkedIn, can be an effective way to make contacts. There are also Web sites like PartnerUp (http://partnerup.com), Founders Space (www.foundersspace.com), and foundrs.com (http://foundrs.com) that help people identify business partners.
5. **Hire a lawyer.**   When you have identified a potential partner and you're confident that the criteria shown previously have been satisfied, you should hire a lawyer to sit down with the two (or more) of you to help hammer out the details. You should decide what each partner will contribute to the business, how the equity in the business will be split, what form of business ownership to select, what each partner's role in the company will be, and so forth. It's important to hire someone who's not loyal to any specific partner (even if it's you). Hire someone who is impartial and everyone feels good about.

Questions for Critical Thinking

1. Think about your personality and work habits. What type of person (in terms of personality and work habits) do you think you'd work well with and what type of person do you think you'd be in constant conflict with?
2. Do you think it's a good idea or a bad idea to form a business partnership with a close friend? How could you go about discerning if a good friend would make for a good business partner?
3. Provide some suggestions, other than those mentioned in the feature, for places (online or offline) for finding a business partner.
4. Spend some time looking at LinkedIn. How could you use LinkedIn to help find a business partner?

TABLE 3.7   **TYPES OF NONFINANCIAL RESOURCES THAT ARE CRITICAL TO MANY START-UPS' SUCCESS**

- Affordable office space
- Lab space, manufacturing space, or space to launch a service business
- Contract manufacturers or service providers
- Key management employees (now and in the future)
- Key support personnel (now and in the future)
- Key equipment needed to operate the business (computers, machinery, delivery vehicles)
- Ability to obtain intellectual property protection on key aspects of the business
- Support of local governments and state government if applicable for business launch
- Ability to form favorable business partnerships

Financial Feasibility Analysis

Financial feasibility analysis is the final component of a comprehensive feasibility analysis. For feasibility analysis, a preliminary financial assessment is usually sufficient; indeed, additional rigor at this point is typically not required because the specifics of the business will inevitably evolve making it impractical to spend a lot of time early on preparing detailed financial forecasts.

The most important issues to consider at this stage are total start-up cash needed, financial performance of similar businesses, and the overall financial attractiveness of the proposed venture.

If a proposed new venture moves beyond the feasibility analysis stage, it will need to complete pro forma (or projected) financial statements that demonstrate the firm's financial viability for the first one to three years of its existence. In Chapter 8, we'll provide you with specific instructions for preparing these statements.

Total Start-Up Cash Needed   This first issue refers to the total cash needed to prepare the business to make its first sale. An actual budget should be prepared that lists all the anticipated capital purchases and operating expenses needed to get the business up and running. After determining a total figure, an explanation of where the money will come from should be provided. Avoid cursory explanations such as "I plan to bring investors on board" or "I'll borrow the money." Although you may ultimately involve investors or lenders in your business, a more thoughtful account is required of how you'll provide for your initial cash needs. We'll cover funding and financing in Chapter 10.

If the money will come from friends and family or is raised through other means, such as credit cards or a home equity line of credit, a reasonable plan should be stipulated to repay the money. Showing how a new venture's start-up costs will be covered and repaid is an important issue. Many new ventures look promising as ongoing concerns but have no way of raising the money to get started or are never able to recover from the initial costs involved. When projecting start-up expenses, it is better to overestimate rather than underestimate the costs involved. Murphy's Law is prevalent in the start-up world—things will go wrong. It is a rare start-up that doesn't experience some unexpected expenses during the start-up phase.

There are worksheets posted online that help entrepreneurs determine the start-up costs to launch their respective businesses. Start-up cost worksheets are available via SCORE (www.score.org) and the Small Business Administration (www.sba.gov).

Financial Performance of Similar Businesses   The second component of financial feasibility analysis is estimating a proposed start-up's potential financial performance by comparing it to similar, already established businesses.

LEARNING OBJECTIVE

10. Explain the importance of financial feasibility analysis and list the most critical issues to consider in this area.

Obviously, this effort will result in approximate rather than exact numbers. There are several ways of doing this, all of which involve a little gumshoe labor.

First, substantial archival data is available online, which offers detailed financial reports on thousands of individual firms. The easiest data to obtain is on publicly traded firms through Hoovers or a similar source. These firms are typically too large, however, for meaningful comparisons to proposed new ventures. The challenge is to find the financial performance of small, more comparable firms. Samples of Web sites that are helpful in this regard are provided in the Internet Resource table in Appendix 3.2. IBISWorld, BizMiner, and Mintel provide data on the average sales and profitability for the firms in the industries they track. Reference USA provides revenue estimates for many private firms, but fewer libraries subscribe to its service. (This resource is more commonly available at large city libraries.) On the expense side, a very useful Web site is BizStats.com, where an entrepreneur can type in the projected revenue of his or her firm, by industry classification (not all industries are covered), and receive a mock income statement in return that shows the average profitability and expense percentages of U.S. businesses in the same category. IBISWorld also normally provides a chart of the average expenses (as a percentage of sales) for major items like wages, rent, office and administrative expenses, and utilities for firms in the industries they follow. Another source to help estimate a firm's sales and net profit is BizMiner (www.bizminer.com). BizMiner provides a printout of the average sales and profitability for firms in the industries they follow and provides more detail than similar reports. BizMiner is a fee-based site, and the reports cost between $69 and $99.[12]

There are additional ways to obtain financial data on smaller firms. If a start-up entrepreneur identifies a business that is similar to the one he or she wants to start, and the business isn't likely to be a direct competitor, it's not inappropriate to ask the owner or manager of the business to share sales and income data. Even if the owner or manager is only willing to talk in general terms (i.e., our annual sales are in the $3 million range, and we're netting around 9 percent of sales), that information is certainly better than nothing. Simply Internet, ProQuest, and LexisNexis Academic searches are also helpful. If you're interested in the sports apparel industry, simply typing "sports apparel industry sales" and "sports apparel industry profitability" will invariably result in links to stories about sports apparel companies that will mention their sales and profitability.

Simple observation and legwork is a final way to obtain sales data for similar businesses. This approach is suitable in some cases and in others it isn't. For example, if you were proposing to open a new smoothie shop, you could gauge the type of sales to expect by estimating the number of people, along with the average purchase per visit, who patronize similar smoothie shops in your area. A very basic way to do this is to frequent these stores and count the number of customers who come in and out of the stores during various times of the day.

Overall Financial Attractiveness of the Proposed Venture A number of other factors are associated with evaluating the financial attractiveness of a proposed venture. These evaluations are based primarily on a new venture's projected sales and rate of return (or profitability), as just discussed. At the feasibility analysis stage, the projected return is a judgment call. A more precise estimation can be computed by preparing pro forma (or projected) financial statements, including one- to three-year pro forma statements of cash flow, income statements, and balance sheets (along with accompanying financial ratios). This work can be done if time and circumstances allow, but is typically done at the business plan stage rather than the feasibility analysis stage of a new venture's development.

To gain perspective, a start-up's projected rate of return should be weighed against the following factors to assess whether the venture is financially feasible.

- The amount of capital invested
- The risks assumed in launching the business
- The existing alternatives for the money being invested
- The existing alternatives for the entrepreneur's time and efforts

As promising as they seem on the surface, some opportunities simply may not be worth it financially. For example, it makes no economic sense for a group of entrepreneurs to invest $10 million in a capital-intense risky start-up that offers a 5 percent rate of return. Five percent interest can be earned through a money market fund with essentially no risk. The adequacy of returns also depends on the alternatives the individuals involved have. For example, an individual who is thinking about leaving a $150,000-per-year job to start a new firm requires a higher rate of return than the person thinking about leaving a $50,000-per-year job.[13]

Other factors used to weigh the overall financial attractiveness of a new business are listed in Table 3.8.

First Screen

First Screen, shown in Appendix 3.1, is a template for completing a feasibility analysis. It is called First Screen because a feasibility analysis is an entrepreneur's (or a group of entrepreneurs') initial pass at determining the feasibility of a business idea. If a business idea cuts muster at this stage, the next step is to complete a business plan.

The mechanics for filling out the First Screen worksheet are straightforward. It maps the four areas of feasibility analysis described in the chapter, accentuating the most important points in each area. The final section of the worksheet, "Overall Potential," includes a section that allows for suggested revisions to a business idea to improve its potential or feasibility. For example, a business might start out planning to manufacture its own product, but through the process of completing First Screen, learn that the capital needed to set up a manufacturing facility is prohibitive in terms of both the money that would need to be raised and the extended time to break even for the business. As a result, two of five items in Part 5, "Initial Capital Investment" and "Time to Break Even," might be rated "low potential." This doesn't need to be the end of the story, however. In the column labeled "Suggestions for Improving the Potential," the founders of the business might write, "Consider contract manufacturing or outsourcing as an alternative to manufacturing the product ourselves." The value of the First Screen worksheet is that it draws attention to issues like this one and forces the founders to think about alternatives. If this particular suggestion is realistic and is determined to be a better way to proceed, a revised version of First Screen might rate the two factors referred to previously, "Initial Capital Requirements" and "Time to Break Even," as "high potential" rather than "low potential" because of the change in the business concept

TABLE 3.8 FINANCIAL FEASIBILITY

- Steady and rapid growth in sales during the first five to seven years in a clearly defined market niche
- High percentage of recurring revenue—meaning that once a firm wins a client, the client will provide recurring sources of revenue
- Ability to forecast income and expenses with a reasonable degree of certainty
- Internally generated funds to finance and sustain growth
- Availability of an exit opportunity (such as an acquisition or an initial public offering) for investors to convert equity into cash

that was made. Business ideas, at the feasibility analysis stage, should always be seen as fluid and subject to change. Little is lost if several versions of First Screen are completed for the same business idea; however, there is much more to be lost if a start-up gets half way through writing a business plan and concludes that the business isn't feasible, or actually launches a business without having all the kinks worked out.

Although completing First Screen does take some research and analysis, it is not meant to be a lengthy process. It is also not meant to be a shot in the dark. The best ideas are ones that emerge from analysis that is based on facts and good information, rather than speculation and guesses, as emphasized throughout the chapter. Appendix 3.2 contains the Internet Resource Table that may be particularly helpful in completing a First Screen analysis. It is well worth your time to learn how to use these resources—they are rich in terms of their content and analysis.

It's important to be completely candid when completing First Screen for your business idea. No business scores "high potential" on every item. There is also no definitive way of discerning, after the worksheet is completed, if an idea is feasible. First Screen, like the feasibility analysis itself, is meant to convey an overall impression or sense of the feasibility of a business idea.*

CHAPTER SUMMARY

1. Feasibility analysis is the process of determining whether a business idea is viable. It is a preliminary evaluation of a business idea, conducted for the purpose of determining whether the idea is worth pursuing.

2. The proper time to conduct a feasibility analysis is early in thinking through the prospects for a new business idea. It follows opportunity recognition but comes before the development of a business plan.

3. Product/service feasibility analysis is an assessment of the overall appeal of the product or service being proposed. The two components of product/service feasibility analysis are product desirability and product demand.

4. A concept statement is a preliminary description of a product idea.

5. Two techniques for determining the likely demand for a product or service are administering a buying intentions survey and conducting library, Internet, and gumshoe research.

6. Industry/market feasibility analysis is an assessment of the overall appeal of the market for the product or service being proposed. For feasibility analysis, there are two primary issues that a business should consider in this area: industry attractiveness and target market attractiveness.

7. A target market is a place within a larger market segment that represents a narrower group of customers with similar needs. Most start-ups simply don't have the resources needed to participate in a broad market, at least initially. Instead, by focusing on a smaller target market a firm can usually avoid head-to-head competition with industry leaders and can focus on serving a specialized market very well.

8. Organizational feasibility analysis is conducted to determine whether a proposed business has sufficient management expertise, organizational competence, and resources to successfully launch its business. There are two primary issues to consider in this area: management prowess and resource sufficiency.

9. Financial feasibility analysis is a preliminary financial analysis of whether a business idea is worth pursuing. The most important areas to consider are the total start-up cash needed, financial performance of similar businesses, and the overall financial attractiveness of the proposed business.

10. First Screen is a template for completing a feasibility analysis. It is called First Screen because a feasibility analysis is an entrepreneur's (or group of entrepreneurs') initial pass at determining the feasibility of a business idea.

*Copies of the First Screen worksheet, in both MS Word and PDF format, are available at www.pearsonglobaleditions.com/barringer.

KEY TERMS

buying intentions survey, **110**
concept statement, **108**
concept test, **108**
feasibility analysis, **105**
financial feasibility analysis, **119**

industry, **114**
new-venture team, **117**
organizational feasibility
    analysis, **117**
primary research, **105**

product/service feasibility
    analysis, **107**
secondary research, **107**

REVIEW QUESTIONS

1. What is a feasibility analysis? What is it designed to accomplish?
2. Briefly describe each of the four areas that a properly executed feasibility analysis explores.
3. What is a product/service feasibility analysis?
4. Describe the difference between primary research and secondary research.
5. What is a concept statement?
6. What is a buying intentions survey, and what does it accomplish?
7. What are the two ways that entrepreneurs assess the likely product demand for the proposed product or service they are analyzing?
8. What is gumshoe research in the context of product/service feasibility analysis?
9. What is industry/target market feasibility analysis?
10. Describe the attributes of an attractive industry for a new venture.
11. What is a target market? Why do most start-ups focus on relatively small target markets to begin with rather than larger markets with more substantial demand?
12. What are some of the ways to determine the attractiveness of a small target market within a larger industry?
13. What is organizational feasibility analysis?
14. Briefly describe each of the two primary issues to consider when conducting an organizational feasibility analysis.
15. What is a new-venture team?
16. What is financial feasibility analysis?
17. Identify and briefly describe the three separate components of financial feasibility analysis.
18. What are some of the techniques a start-up can use to estimate its potential financial performance by comparing it to similar, already established businesses?
19. What are some factors that make a potential start-up attractive from an overall financial perspective?
20. What is the purpose of a First Screen analysis?

APPLICATION QUESTIONS

1. Kelly Myers, a friend of yours, just told you an interesting story. She was at her parents' house over the weekend and her father saw this book lying next to her backpack. He pickup it up and read Chapter 3. He told Kelly, "When you were growing up, I started and sold three successful businesses and never completed a feasibility analysis once. I wonder what the authors of your entrepreneurship book would say about that." If you could advise Kelly about how to respond to her father, what would you tell her to say?
2. Jason Willis just applied for a bank loan to finance a smoothie restaurant that he plans to open. The banker asked Jason if he conducted any primary research to assess the feasibility of the restaurant, and Jason replied that he spent countless evenings and weekends in the library and on the Internet collecting data on the feasibility of smoothie restaurants, and he is confident that his restaurant will be successful. He said that he even did careful research to make sure that smoothie restaurants do well in demographic areas that are similar to the area where he plans to open his restaurant. If you were the banker, how would you react to Jason's statements?

3. Assume that you were one of the recipients of New Venture Fitness Drink's concept statement. What type of feedback would you have given the company about the viability of its product idea?

4. Shelly Mills, who has considerable experience in the home security industry, is planning to launch a firm that will sell a new line of home security alarms that she believes will be superior to anything currently on the market. Shelly knows how to develop a concept statement and administer a buying intentions survey but is less clear about the type of library and Internet research that might be helpful in assessing the likely demand for her product. If Shelly turned to you for help, what would you tell her?

5. Assess the industry attractiveness for the industry that Songkick, the subject of the "You Be the VC 1.2" feature, will be participating in.

6. Skip ahead to Chapter 4 and look at the "You Be the VC 4.1" feature, which focuses on Secret Recipe. How would you assess the likely demand for Secret Recipe's service?

7. Suppose you're interested in opening a musical instruments store near the college or university you attend, to sell guitars, drums, and other types of musical instruments. What online resources would you draw on to conduct secondary research regarding the industry/target market feasibility of your business idea? How would you use the resources?

8. Suppose you were hired by the founders of ecoATM, the subject of the "You Be the VC 2.2" feature, to conduct a survey of potential users prior to the launch of the company. The purpose of the survey is to assess the product/service desirability and the product/service demand of ecoATM's service. The survey has 10 questions. What 10 questions would you ask?

9. Keith Ambrose, who is a physical therapist, is thinking about starting a firm to provide in-home therapy services for people who are suffering from sports-related injuries. Keith lives in Columbus, Ohio, and doesn't know whether his trade area is large enough to support such a service, or whether people would pay a premium for "in-home" therapy services for sports injuries. Provide Keith suggestions for conducting primary and secondary research to answer his questions.

10. Susan Campbell is thinking about launching a Web site to sell sports apparel for petite women. She's designed a Web site but isn't sure if it's user-friendly enough to launch. Provide Susan some concrete suggestions for how she can receive feedback on the usability of her site.

11. What do you think were the 8 to 10 most important nonfinancial resources that the founders of InstyMeds, the subject of the "You Be the VC 3.1" feature, needed to have in place before they launched their new venture?

12. Some neighbors of yours are hoping to open a Thai restaurant near a local community college. They have a limited budget so it is very important to them to have as good of an idea as possible of what their total start-up costs will be and what their first year's sales will be. How would you recommend that they estimate the total start-up costs of opening the restaurant and their first-year sales?

13. Look at the Web site of Rufus Shirts (www.rufusshirts.com), a company that was launched by first-time entrepreneur April Singer and makes high-end shirts for men and dresses for women. During the financial feasibility analysis stage of the process of investigating the merits of her new venture, how could Singer have gone about estimating the financial performance of Rufus Shirts by comparing it to similar, existing businesses?

14. What are some of the red flags that would suggest that the overall financial attractiveness of a proposed new venture is poor? Which of the red flags you identified would suggest that a proposed venture isn't realistically feasible?

15. A friend of yours just completed a First Screen analysis for an e-commerce site that she hoped to launch to sell horse riding supplies, including saddles, tack, lead ropes, and feed buckets. She's disappointed because she rated 10 of the 25 items on First Screen as either low or moderate potential. She says to you, "Well that's that. Good thing I completed a feasibility analysis. I sure don't want to start that business." Is your friend right? How would you advise her to interpret the results of her First Screen analysis?

YOU BE THE VC 3.1

Company: InstyMeds

Web: www.instymeds.com
Twitter: InstyMeds
Facebook: InstyMeds

Business Idea: Provide patients access to prescription medications instantly after they're prescribed by a doctor in a hospital emergency room or at an urgent care center. The prescriptions are dispensed via a vending machine that's present in the facility.

Pitch: There are many rural areas without 24-hour pharmacies. This make it difficult for people who visit an emergency room or an urgent care center late at night or on a weekend to quickly fill their prescriptions. Typically of course, we want to have immediate access to medications that a doctor has told us will make us feel better! In some cases, doctors will give patients a starter quantity of a medication, if they know the patient will not be able to get to a pharmacy soon. But there are two problems with this solution. First, it's costly for the doctors and hospitals. Second, a likely scenario is that the patient will take the starter medications, start feeling better, and never have the prescription filled. This leaves patients who started out with bronchitis, for example, susceptible to pneumonia if they don't take their full regiment of medication and their condition takes a turn for the worse.

InstyMeds provides a solution to these problems. The company has developed a vending machine for prescription drugs, to be located in hospitals and urgent care centers. Here's how it works. If you've just received a prescription from a doctor at an emergency room or an urgent care center that has an InstyMeds machine, your prescription will be accompanied by an InstyMeds private code. You approach the InstyMeds machine (which resembles an ATM) and enter the code. The online prompts then lead you through the process. If you have insurance, InstyMeds will ask for your insurance information and will determine the co-pay for your prescription. If you do not have insurance, InstyMeds' machine allows you to pay with cash or credit card. Following payment, your prescription will then be dispensed. InstyMeds doesn't work for all prescriptions, like those that need to be refrigerated, but does include the 100 or so most common medications prescribed by emergency room and urgent care physicians. If the patient has questions, each InstyMeds machine has a phone that directly connects the patient to InstyMeds' call center where licensed pharmacists are on duty.

The advantages of InstyMeds' operations create a "win-win" situation for both patients and hospitals and urgent care facilities. The facilities where the machines are present share in the income they produce. Hospitals and urgent care centers have also found that patients who are seen in the middle of the day, with a pharmacy nearby, still use the InstyMeds machine to avoid the wait time one normally experiences at a pharmacy. The InstyMeds machines are supported by a full support system. Each machine is connected to the Internet, which alerts InstyMeds' headquarters if certain medications need to be replenished or if there are any medications present that need to be replaced due to nearing expiration dates.

Q&A: Based on the material covered in this chapter, what questions would you ask the firm's founders before making your funding decision? What answers would satisfy you?

Decision: If you had to make your decision on just the information provided in the pitch and on the company's Web site, would you fund this company? Why or why not?

YOU BE THE VC 3.2

Company: CADI Scientific—SmartSense

Web: www.cadi.com.sg
Facebook: CADI Scientific

Business Idea: Produce and sell the first wireless patient monitoring system, enhancing patient care by continuously measuring vital medical data and transmitting the information to health practitioners.

Pitch: Monitoring a sick patient can be a delicate balancing act. Although they need uninterrupted sleep to aid their recovery, medical staff must also regularly check vital signs such as temperature and blood pressure. The two needs are not always fine bedfellows.

Four entrepreneurial scientists have come up with a solution: a wireless gadget called SmartSense, which is now being used in hospitals in Singapore, Bangkok, Taipei, and the Middle East. The 1.2-inch wide SmartSense is taped to a patient's body to continuously measure vital signs. Radio frequency technology then transfers the data wirelessly via ceiling-mounted transmitters, to computers in the nurses' station.

The inspiration for the idea came out of a coffee break conversation between CADI Scientific founder Zenton Goh and a colleague. The colleague had a sick child and said he and his wife were waking the infant every two hours through the night to take her temperature. Goh thought of the idea of an automated wireless sensing system to monitor a baby's body temperature, so that both parents and children could enjoy uninterrupted sleep. The idea evolved into SmartSense.

Nurses can now dispense with the task of manually checking temperatures and blood pressure every few hours, and patients get uninterrupted rest. SmartSense also cuts down on any possibility of human error in the checks and reduces nurses' workload. Doctors can

check on the data on-the-go too via WiFi-enabled digital assistants, or on PCs anywhere in the hospital.

Another bonus to introducing this system into crowded wards is it is now very easy to quickly spot clusters of patients developing a fever at the same time. At a time of growing incidences of hospital-acquired infections, this is an important early warning signal. Plans are also underway to introduce a consumer version of SmartSense, which can monitor temperature and blood pressure at home.

Q&A: Based on the material covered in this chapter, what questions would you ask the firm's founders before making your funding decision? What answers would satisfy you?

Decision: If you had to make your decision on just the information provided in the pitch and on the company's Web site, would you fund this firm? Why or why not?

CASE 3.1

Tommy John: The Role of Product and Industry Feasibility Analysis in Launching a Consumer Products Company

Web: www.tommyjohnwear.com
Twitter: TommyJohn
Facebook: Tommy John

Bruce R. Barringer, *Oklahoma State University*

R. Duane Ireland, *Texas A&M University*

Introduction

Just a few years ago, Tom Patterson was working as a medical device salesman. Today, his company, Tommy John, brings in about $2 million in revenue and makes the top selling men's undershirts at Neiman Marcus and Nordstrom. How does that happen? Patterson had no prior experience in the men's clothing industry—just a problem to solve and a lifetime desire to be an entrepreneur. It's an interesting story, and a good reminder of how important feasibility analysis is.

Tom Patterson and His Frustration with Undershirts

Tom Patterson grew up in South Dakota. He started wearing undershirts when he was 8. Like many boys and men, wearing an undershirt became part of his everyday life. But for Patterson, this was frustrating in that he

found himself constantly tucking his undershirt into his pants. Over time, he became increasingly aggravated with the way undershirts were made. To Patterson, men's undershirts were too baggy, too boxy, and they just weren't made to fit well. Patterson remembers when his frustration reached a boiling point. One day when he was working in medical sales, he had a presentation at a hospital. He remembers driving to the hospital and getting out of his car, and his undershirt had bunched up and was half way up his chest.

That day, following the presentation, Patterson went to several department stores and asked sales clerks if they carried men's undershirts that would solve his problem. None of them did. One clerk even told Patterson that if he found a solution to let him know—he'd like to buy the undershirts too. Patterson followed up by sketching the type of undershirt that he wanted—long and tailored—and took it to a dry cleaner that he was familiar with that employed a tailor. He showed the drawing to the tailor, who was unenthused about the idea but agreed to make him a prototype. He got the prototype and loved it. It solved the frustrations that he'd been having with undershirts since he was a boy. By this point, Patterson wondered if he had stumbled on a business idea.

Product and Industry Feasibility Analysis

Patterson went back to the tailor and asked for 15 more shirts. He sent them out to family and friends, asking that they give him feedback but keep his product idea to themselves. The most common response he got was, "Tom this is incredible, can I order five or six more?" He had no idea what to do next. He decided to keep his medical device sales job until he found out whether his undershirt idea really had legs. He then drove to the garment district in Los Angeles, not knowing a soul. He started asking around about who could make him some men's undershirts, and the 12th person he talked to called a friend and made an introduction. The garment maker he met that day became his first producer, and made about 200 more undershirts for Patterson.

After Patterson paid for the 200 undershirts, he contacted a patent attorney, based on a friend's advice. Through a friend of a friend he found a patent attorney who specialized in apparel products. He paid $300 for a preliminary patent search, and found that there was no comparable product. He filed a provisional patent and decided to keep his medical sales job and to spend the next year continuing to assess the potential for his product. After that, he'd decide whether to spend the money to file for a regular utility patent.

During the next several months, Patterson, buoyed by growing evidence that he had a unique idea, did a lot of online research about undershirts and the men's undershirt industry. He found that men's undergarments are a $30 billion industry worldwide. He also found that although the industry is dominated by major brands, such as Hanes and Fruit of the Loom, a number of small businesses had found success in the undergarments market as well, by identifying and filling niches the major brands ignored. He would go to stores and literally spend hours watching people buy men's undershirts. There were two things he found out by watching people buy undershirts. First, people either bought quickly or seemed a little confused when they looked at the alternatives. When he stopped people who bought quickly and politely asked about how they picked their brand, they would normally say that it's the brand of undershirt they've been buying for years. The second thing he found out was that men only buy undershirts for about 17 years of their life. From age zero to 17 their mothers buy their undershirts, and from age 34 (or whenever they get married) on their wives buy it. So the majority of the people who buy men's undershirts are women.

Tommy John Undershirts

During this period—early 2008—Patterson continued to work on prototypes for his undershirt, and decided on the name Tommy John. He studied all the major brands,

turning dozens of shirts inside out, measuring proportions, and testing fabric blends to develop the perfect combination of fit, function, comfort, breathability, and style. The design he settled on is made of a soft yet durable fabric named micro modal (it's derived from beech trees). It's cut to be form fitting without feeling snug and promises "not to ride up, bunch up, or come unbuckled." The shirts are machine wash and tumble dry.

Along with the shirt itself, Patterson felt that the package design was critical to the firm's success. All the packages for men's undershirts looked pretty much the same—they had the company's logo and a good looking guy on the front. Patterson designed a box with very feminine colors, chocolate brown and Tiffany blue, specifically to catch the eye of women, the primary purchasers of men's undershirts. The box clearly explained the problem the undershirt solved, and invited the shopper to feel the product for themselves. The box was designed to slide open easily, so a shopper could touch the undershirt. A survey confirmed Patterson's intuition about the colors for the box. Women had high positives for both chocolate and Tiffany jewelry, so the almost dessert-like color for the box turned out to be a big plus.

In late 2008, Patterson was laid off from his medical sales job. He knew he had a product that filled a need. The question was whether he could get distribution of his product. He decided to commit to Tommy John full-time and work toward landing the types of retail partners he'd need to make Tommy John a full-time effort.

Neiman Marcus

To get retail distribution, he first tried men's specialty stores. He called his undershirts *The Second Skin Collection*, based on the idea that they fit so well they felt like a "second skin." The first nine stores said no, but the 10th displayed interest and he had his first retailer. The question was whether he could land a department store as a customer. Through industry research, Patterson knew that the majority of men's undershirts were sold through department stores, so he'd need to land a department store to get significant sales. So with $800 left in his checking account, he got through to the Neiman Marcus buyer in Dallas and pitched Tommy John undershirts over the phone. Patterson had read that Neiman Marcus was known for giving new apparel companies a try. The buyer, who was a female, agreed to a meeting the following week. Before he hung up the phone, Patterson asked the buyer if she'd mind if he send samples of his undershirt to her husband and several men in her office to try before the meeting. The buyer agreed and the appointment was set.

When Patterson met the buyer the next week, she immediately said that she'd been getting rave feedback on his undershirts, and that she wanted to test them in 15 Neiman Marcus stores. She also said she never knew the struggles that men had with traditional undershirts. Within the first month, Patterson's undershirts achieved a 60 percent sell-through rate, nearly double the national rate for a successful clothing brand. By the third month,

(continued)

Neiman Marcus had expanded its test to 42 stores, and today Tommy John undershirts are in Neiman Marcus stores nationwide.

Neiman Marcus was the "crack in the door" (Patterson's words) that he needed. Three months later, Nordstrom signed on, and the Tommy John brand has now expanded to department stores and men's specialty stores across the United States.

Looking Forward

Looking forward, Patterson plans to continue to expand market penetration for Tommy John. One of the most frequent questions he gets is when Tommy John will expand into women's undergarments. So far, Patterson has resisted expanding into women's clothes. He feels the women's undergarment market is well served by existing companies, and wants to focus on his Second Skin line of men's undershirts for the foreseeable future.

Discussion Questions

1. Write a concept statement for Tommy John. If Tommy John was still in the start-up stage and Tom Patterson asked you to whom he should distribute the concept statement, what would you have told him?
2. What type of gumshoe research did Tom Patterson benefit from when he was developing Tommy John, and what additional gumshoe research could he have conducted while he was investigating the feasibility of his business?
3. Make a list of the people whom Tom Patterson talked to about his product during the design phase. What insight(s) does this list provide you about the nature of the feasibility analysis process? Were there any tactics that Tom Patterson used to get feedback about his product that you think were particularly clever?
4. Complete a First Screen analysis for Tommy John. What did you learn from the analysis?

Application Questions

1. What types of insights did Tom Patterson pick up by spending hours in stores watching people buy men's undershirts? What role did these insights play in the final design of the product? In what ways do you think Tommy John products might be different today if Tom Patterson hadn't spent the time watching people buy men's undershirts that he did?
2. Read the "You Be the VC 3.2" feature in this chapter. If you had started SmartSense, how would you have set up its product/service feasibility analysis?

Sources: Brian Freed and Tom Patterson, "Tom Patterson, Inventory & Founder of Tommy John Show," *Got Invention Radio Podcast,* www.gotinvention.com/listenshow.php?id=51 (accessed March 20, 2011, originally posted on July 15, 2010); Tommy John Web site, www.tommyjohnwear.com (accessed March 20, 2011).

CASE 3.2

What Segway Learned About the Value of Feasibility Analysis the Hard Way

Web: www.segway.com
Twitter: Segwayinc
Facebook: Segway

Bruce R. Barringer, *Oklahoma State University*

R. Duane Ireland, *Texas A&M University*

Introduction

The Segway PT is a two-wheeled, self-balancing transportation device that consists primarily of a set of tall handlebars on top of two disc-like wheels. There are no chains or visible mechanical workings. Riders lean forward to move forward and back to move backward. Turning is done mechanically via hand controls. The device is driven by a quiet, nonpolluting electric motor and can travel up to 10 miles per hour. The name "Segway PT" stands for "Segway Personal Transporter."

The Segway was built in secrecy and was unveiled on December 3, 2001, on the ABC program *Good Morning America*. The Segway PT was known as *Ginger* and *IT* before it was unveiled. The invention, development, and financing of the Segway were the subject of a book, *Code Name Ginger*, which was slated to be published after the Segway was introduced. The leak of information from the book led to rampant speculation about what the Segway was. Some people speculated it was an antigravity machine while others thought it might be a helicopter backpack. The initial reaction to the Segway PT was enthusiastic. Venture capitalist John Doerr predicted that it would be as important as the Internet. Apple's Steve Jobs predicted that cities would be built around it. To cope with the expected demand for the product, Segway's factory in Bedford, New Hampshire, was designed to build up to 40,000 units per month. Initial sales were targeted at between 10,000 and 50,000 units during the first 12 months. But, after 21 months, only 6,000 units had sold. What went wrong?

Feasibility Analysis

While the Segway was a technological marvel, in retrospect there were fundamental flaws in both its product/service feasibility analysis and its market/industry feasibility analysis. These issues are discussed next. When reviewing Segway's prelaunch and postlaunch behavior, one has to wonder how so many critical issues seemingly weren't analyzed or were missed. It provides lessons for future entrepreneurs to be more rigorous in their thinking regarding the feasibility of a new product or service, regardless of how much of a technological marvel it is.

Product/Service Feasibility

The Segway itself was extensively tested and it performed well both prelaunch and postlaunch. It was tested and retested during development, and was subjected to all the conditions it might experience in the field: extreme heat, extreme cold, rain, snow, high humidity, salt, dust, and so forth. It came through with flying colors. Its durability was also rigorously tested. In fact, when it was introduced, the company said that tens of thousands of hours had been dedicated to riding the Segway to see how it stood up under repeated use.

The testing was apparently successful. Despite all the knocks the Segway has taken over the years, there have been few reports of mechanical problems.

Yet, curiously, although the company put substantial effort into the Segway itself, people immediately questioned its price and how it could be used. First, it was priced at $4,950, which put it out of reach for many consumers. Second, while there were a few Segway dealers initially, there weren't many so it was unclear to people that if they bought a Segway, where they'd get it serviced. Finally, while most people admired what the Segway could do, they just couldn't see it fitting into their environments and lives. Imagine you owned a Segway. Try to answer the following questions:

- How do you take it with you in your car?
- How do you park it?
- How and where can you ride it? Sidewalks or roads?
- How do you get it up or down stairs?
- Can you take it on a bus or train?
- What kind of insurance do you need?
- Where and how do you charge it?
- If you park it outside a building, how do you keep it safe? Is it something you park like a motorcycle or a car, or do you chain it to a bike rack, as if it were a bike?
- Is it safe to drive on the street if it can only go 10 mph?
- Can you let your friends drive it, or does it take some getting used to for the driver to be safe?
- What if the battery runs out before you get it home?

There are even more penetrating questions. The Segway is best suited for densely populated areas where people could ride their Segway to work. But how would that work in a place like Manhattan, in New York City, where both the sidewalks and the streets are packed? It takes both hands to operate a Segway safely. So, how would

Segway PT

© Markhunt/ Dreamstime.com

(continued)

a businessperson carry a briefcase or a student carry books? The U.S. Postal Service, a large potential market for Segway, tested the device for use by mail carriers, who still deliver mail by foot. The postal service abandoned the idea after mail carriers complained that they couldn't sort mail or hold an umbrella while operating a Segway.

Segway's failure to address its potential users' questions in these areas provides an important reminder. When conducting product/service analysis, it's important to evaluate how the product or service will fit into the existing way that its potential customers live and behave. A company may have a product that on a stand-alone basis is fantastic. But people don't use products or services in isolation. They must fit into the existing framework of their environments and lives to be beneficial.

Segway scrambled to try to fix some of the usability issues, with mixed success. For example, the company hired lobbyists to try to persuade large city governments to make using the Segway on public sidewalks legal. Ironically, San Francisco, usually thought of as a progressive city, passed an ordinance specifically making the Segway illegal on its sidewalks as a result of safety concerns. The San Francisco Board of Supervisors was convinced that the Segway posed a risk to pedestrians.

Market/Industry Feasibility Analysis

In regard to markets, from the outset Segway positioned itself for a large rollout. It assumed success. A large amount of its capital, for instance, was dedicated toward production capacity and regulatory issues, rather than proving its concept. In most cases a more measured approach is pursued. A company rolls out incrementally and invests capital in production capacity once it validates that there is a market for its product.

Segway also went national from day one. Rather than identifying niche markets to penetrate and build from, the company saw its product as a solution in all markets. Many observers who have commented on Segway's missteps have singled out this issue, and feel that Segway should have gained traction in one market or a small number of markets before expanding. For example, what if Segway would have picked one city—say Boston—where in the downtown area a large number of people live near their jobs. They could have given Segways to 1,000 people to use for three months, free of charge, based on the condition that they use their Segways to travel back and forth to work each day. Had that test gone well, it would have generated tremendous positive publicity, and provided an example for people in other urban areas that the Segway could be used effectively. A similar approach would have been to ask a cross-section of bicycle clubs, for example, across the country to start using Segways when they weren't biking. If the test went

well, Segway could have started using bike shops to sell and service Segways. It could have then developed a more powerful version of the Segway PT and added motorcycle shops. This is how a company integrates itself into existing distribution channels rather than trying to create a new channel just for itself, which is costly and difficult.

Instead of pursuing these types of approaches, Segway went for the home run and never found a large market. As the company has downsized its expectations, it has had some success in niche markets. These include police departments, military bases, warehouses, corporate campuses, industrial sites, and theme parks. The Segway still, however, suffers from a usability stigma. At Walt Disney World in Orlando, Florida, for example, the Segway can be rented at the Disney Boardwalk and driven in specified areas, but can't be used in other parts of Disney World. It's more of a theme park attraction than a practical device.

Segway's decision to go for broad markets may also have been an artifact of its funding. It reportedly raised $80 million prior to launch. Its investors were most likely attracted by the "big opportunity" that it envisioned, and may not have settled for a slow-build approach.

Segway Pivots with No Significant Changes in Its Long-Term Prospects

Reeling from criticism and poor sales, in March 2003, Segway started a dealership expansion program. In October 2003, it launched the Segway HT p-series model, which was lighter and more portable than the original model, and was priced at $3,995. Around the same time, it dropped the price of the original Segway HT from $4,950 to $4,495. In March 2005, Segway introduced its 2005 product line-up, which featured three new models: the Segway HT i180 with enhanced range; the Segway XT, a cross terrain transporter; and the Segway GT, a golf transporter. It also launched an improved line of batteries.

While Segway experienced moderate success with each of its new offerings, none of them materially changed the long-range outlook for the company. Perceptions of the company also remain generally unchanged. For example, in 2008 Professor Karl Ulrich used the Segway in his undergraduate product-design class at the Wharton School of Business to demonstrate that creativity alone doesn't insure market acceptance, much less profits. He pointed out that although the Segway is potentially handy for a host of users, ranging from security guards to golfers, it's not ideal for any of them. It's not much faster than walking. And if you're going farther than a mile, a bike works much better. Plus, compare the cost of a Segway to a bike. Which value proposition do you find more attractive?

Segway Today

Segway was sold in early 2010 to a group led by British millionaire Jimi Heselden, chairman of Hesco Bastion. Sadly, he died in an accident involving a Segway on September 27, 2010. Segway continues to operate and serve several niche markets. According to the company's Web site, over 1,000 police and security agencies are using Segway PTs in their patrolling operations.

Discussion Questions

1. Why do you think Dean Kamen and his team didn't do a better job of anticipating the problems that beset the Segway?
2. Describe what you believe would have been an appropriate product/service feasibility analysis and an appropriate market/industry feasibility analysis for Segway during its development stage?
3. It what ways did Segway fail to build an ecosystem around its product? What could Segway have done, if anything, to ensure that its product would do a better job of fitting into its users' environments and lives?
4. What niche market or markets do you think Segway should have targeted initially and been successful in?

Application Questions

1. Describe a scenario in which Segway could have launched successfully, built its business, and be a large and thriving business today.
2. Think of a product you use that fits ideally into your day-to-day life. What makes the product so special? What design elements do you see in the product that makes it fit so nicely into your life. Spend a few minutes either looking at or thinking about the product. What can you learn from the product you're thinking about that could potentially make you a better entrepreneur?

Sources: Segway Web site, www.segway.com (accessed April 18, 2011); Wharton School: University of Pennsylvania, Entrepreneurial Programs, "Segway's Dilemma," http://wep.wharton.upenn.edu/gis/article.aspx?gisID=64 (accessed April 18, 2011, originally posted April 2008); Wikipedia, "Segway, Inc.," http://en.wikipedia.org/wiki/Segway_Inc. (accessed April 18, 2011).

ENDNOTES

1. Personal Conversation with Kate Ryan Reiling, March 15, 2011.
2. J. Mullins, *The New Business Road Test* (London: Prentice Hall, 2003).
3. SurveyMonkey homepage, www.surveymonkey.com (accessed May 21, 2011); SurveyGizmo homepage, www.surveygizmo.com (accessed May 21, 2011).
4. Computer and Technology Update Blog, www.humahost.com/educational-toys/the-rise-of-childrens-educational-games-and-toys.html (accessed May 21, 2011, originally posted on April 2, 2011).
5. "2011 Toy Trends Reflect 21st Century Values and Desires," Toy Industry Association, www.toyasso-ciation.org/AM/Template.cfm?Section=toy_Fair&CONTENTID=14846&SECTION=Toys&TEMPLATE=/CM/ContentDisplay.cfm (accessed May 21, 2011, originally posted on February 14, 2011).
6. R. D. Ireland, R. E. Hoskisson, and M. A. Hitt, *Understanding Business Strategy*, 3rd ed. (Cincinnati: SouthWestern Cengage Learning, 2012); P. Avida and I. Vertinsky, "Firm Exits as a Determinant of New Entry: Is There Evidence of Local Creative Destruction?" *Journal of Business Venturing* 23, no. 3 (2008): 257–79.
7. Brian Freed and Tom Patterson, "Tom Patterson, Inventory & Founder of Tommy John Show," Got Invention Radio Podcast, www.gotinvention.com/listenshow.php?id=51 (accessed March 20, 2011, originally posted on July 15, 2010).
8. D. A. Shepherd and H. Patzelt, "The New Field of Sustainable Entrepreneurship: Studying Entrepreneurial Action Linking 'What Is to Be Sustained' with "What Is to Be Developed,'" *Entrepreneurship Theory and Practice* 35, no. 1 (2011): 137–63; C. G. Brush, T. S. Manolova, and L. F. Edelman, "Properties of Emerging Organizations: An Empirical Test," *Journal of Business Venturing*, 23 no. 5 (2008): 547–66.
9. C.-J. Wang and L.-Y. Wu, "Team Member Commitments and Start-Up Competitiveness," *Journal of Business Research* (2011): in press.
10. G. T. Lumpkin, "From Legitimacy to Impact: Moving the Field Forward by Asking How Entrepreneurship Informs Life," *Strategic Entrepreneurship Journal* 5, no. 1 (2011): 3–9.
11. M. A. Hitt, R. D. Ireland, D. G. Sirmon, and C. A. Trahms, "Strategic Entrepreneurship: Creating Value for Individuals, Organizations, and Society," *Academy of Management Perspectives* 25, no. 2 (2011): 57–75.
12. BizMiner homepage, www.bizminer.com (accessed May 21, 2011).
13. T. Astebro and P. Thompson, "Entrepreneurs, Jacks of All Trades or Hobos?" *Research Policy* 40, no. 5 (2011): 637–49; H. A. Ndofor and R. L. Priem, "Immigrant Entrepreneurs, the Ethnic Enclave Strategy and Venture Performance," *Journal of Management* 37, no. 3 (2011): 790–818.

APPENDIX 3.1   FIRST SCREEN

Part 1: Strength of Business Idea

For each item, circle the most appropriate answer and make note of the (−1), (0), or (+1) score.

	Low Potential (−1)	Moderate Potential (0)	High Potential (+1)
1. Extent to which the idea: • Takes advantage of an environmental trend • Solves a problem • Addresses an unfilled gap in the marketplace	Weak	Moderate	Strong
2. Timeliness of entry to market	Not timely	Moderately timely	Very timely
3. Extent to which the idea "adds value" for its buyer or end user	Low	Medium	High
4. Extent to which the customer is satisfied by competing products that are already available	Very satisfied	Moderately satisfied	Not very satisfied or ambivalent
5. Degree to which the idea requires customers to change their basic practices or behaviors	Substantial changes required	Moderate changes required	Small to no changes required

Part 2: Industry-Related Issues

	Low Potential (−1)	Moderate Potential (0)	High Potential (+1)
1. Number of competitors	Many	Few	None
2. Stage of industry life cycle	Maturity phase or decline phase	Growth phase	Emergence phase
3. Growth rate of industry	Little or no growth	Moderate growth	Strong growth
4. Importance of industry's products and/or services to customers	"Ambivalent"	"Would like to have"	"Must have"
5. Industry operating margins	Low	Moderate	High

Part 3: Target Market and Customer-Related Issues

	Low Potential (−1)	Moderate Potential (0)	High Potential (+1)
1. Identification of target market for the proposed new venture	Difficult to identify	May be able to identify	Identified
2. Ability to create "barriers to entry" for potential competitors	Unable to create	May or may not be able to create	Can create
3. Purchasing power of customers	Low	Moderate	High
4. Ease of making customers aware of the new product or service	Low	Moderate	High
5. Growth potential of target market	Low	Moderate	High

Part 4: Founder- (or Founders-) Related Issues

	Low Potential (−1)	Moderate Potential (0)	High Potential (+1)
1. Founder's or founders' experience in the industry	No experience	Moderate experience	Experienced
2. Founder's or founders' skills as they relate to the proposed new venture's product or service	No skills	Moderate skills	Skilled
3. Extent of the founder's or founders' professional and social networks in the relevant industry	None	Moderate	Extensive
4. Extent to which the proposed new venture meets the founder's or founders' personal goals and aspirations	Weak	Moderate	Strong
5. Likelihood that a team can be put together to launch and grow the new venture	Unlikely	Moderately likely	Very likely

Part 5: Financial Issues

	Low Potential (−1)	Moderate Potential (0)	High Potential (+1)
1. Initial capital investment	High	Moderate	Low
2. Number of revenue drivers (ways in which the company makes money)	One	Two to three	More than three
3. Time to break even	More than two years	One to two years	Less than one year
4. Financial performance of similar businesses	Weak	Modest	Strong
5. Ability to fund initial product (or service) development and/or initial start-up expenses from personal funds or via bootstrapping	Low	Moderate	High

Overall Potential

Each part has five items. Scores will range from −5 to +5 for each part. The score is a guide—there is no established rule of thumb for the numerical score that equates to high potential, moderate potential, or low potential for each part. The ranking is a judgment call.

Score (−5 to +1)	Overall Potential of the Business Idea Based on Each Part	Suggestions for Improving the Potential
Part 1: Strength of Business Idea	High potential Moderate potential Low potential	
Part 2: Industry-Related Issues	High potential Moderate potential Low potential	
Part 3: Target Market and Customer-Related Issues	High potential Moderate potential Low potential	

Score (−5 to +1)	Overall Potential of the Business Idea Based on Each Part	Suggestions for Improving the Potential
Part 4: Founder- (or Founders-) Related Issues	High potential Moderate potential Low potential	
Part 5: Financial Issues	High potential Moderate potential Low potential	
Overall Assessment	High potential Moderate potential Low potential	

Summary
Briefly summarize your justification for your overall assessment:

APPENDIX 3.2 INTERNET RESOURCE TABLE

Resources to Help Complete the First Screen Worksheet in Appendix 3.1

Source	Description	Applicable Parts of First Screen	Cost/Availability
American Factfinder (www.factfinder.census.gov)	An easy-to-use portal for obtaining census data. One quick way to retrieve data is to get a "Fact Sheet" on a geographic area (by city, county, or zip code), which provides population, median household income, demographic breakdown (age, gender, race), and other information.	Part 3	Free
BizMiner (www.bizminer.com)	Industry statistics, sample pro forma financial statements by industry (and size of business), business start activity and failure rates by industry, and similar information. Provides data on small private firms.	Parts 2, 3, and 5	Fee based (more affordable than most); typically free if accessed through a university library
BizStats (www.bizstats.com)	Has a variety of detailed financial data on various retail categories. On the site, a user can type in the projected income of a firm, by industry, and receive a mock income statement in return.	Parts 2 and 5	Free
Business & Company Resource Center (www.gale.com/BusinessRC)	Access to information on the organization and structure of industries, current industry trends, and other information.	Parts 1 and 2	Free; premium version typically free if accessed through a university library
City-Data.com (www.city-data.com)	Contains detailed information on cities, including median resident age, median household income, ethnic mix of residents, and aerial photos.	Part 3	Free
County Business Patterns (www.census.gov/econ/chp/index.html)	Good resources for looking at business activity, including the number of competitors, at a city, county, or state level. For example, you can find the number of dry cleaners (or any other business) in a specific zip code or city.	Parts 2 and 3	Free
Hoovers Online (www.hoovers.com)	Brief histories and financial information on companies, industries, people, and products. Premium service provides access to detailed financial information and 10-K reports for publicly traded firms.	Parts 2, 3, and 5	Free; premium version available on a fee basis or typically for free if accessed through a university library

Source	Description	Applicable Parts of First Screen	Cost/Availability
IBISWorld (www.ibisworld.com)	Detailed reports available on hundreds of industries, including industry statistics, trends, buyer behavior, and expected returns.	Parts 1, 2, 3, and 5	Fee based; typically free if accessed through a university library
LexisNexis Academic (www.lexisnexis.com)	Provides access to sales data for public and private firms, which can be searched in a number of useful ways. Helps start-ups estimate the financial performance of similar businesses. Go to "Business" and then "Company Financial."	Part 5	Fee-based; typically free if accessed through a university library
MagPortal.com (www.magportal.com)	Search engine and directory for finding online magazine articles. Helps start-ups by providing access to magazine articles about their product/service and industry of interest. This information may be helpful in all areas of feasibility analysis.	Parts 1, 2, 3, 4, and 5	Free
Mergent Online (www.mergentonline.com)	Provides near instant access to financial data, including income statements, balance sheets, and cash flows, on more than 10,000 U.S. public corporations.	Parts 2 and 5	Fee based; typically free if accessed through a university library
Mintel (www.mintel.com)	Detailed reports available on hundreds of industries, including industry statistics, trends, buyer behavior, and expected returns.	Parts 1, 2, 3, and 5	Fee based; typically free if accessed through a university library
ProQuest (http://proquest.com)	Very robust search engine for searching publications such as the *Wall Street Journal* and the *New York Times*. Useful for all areas of feasibility analysis.	Parts 1, 2, 3, 4, and 5	Fee based; typically free if accessed through a university library
Quickfacts (http://quickfacts.census.gov)	A very quick way to access census bureau data, including population, median household income, census breakdowns by age and other demographic characteristics, and so on.	Parts 2 and 3	Free
ReferenceUSA (www.referenceusa.com)	Provides contact information, estimated annual sales, credit rating score, year established, news, and other information on both public and private companies. Contains more information on private firms than many similar sites. Helps start-ups estimate the financial performance of similar businesses.	Part 5	Fee based; typically free if accessed through a university library
Standard & Poor's NetAdvantage (www.netadvantage.standardpoor.com)	Detailed reports available on hundreds of industries, including industry statistics, trends, buyer behavior, and expected returns.	Parts 1, 2, 3, and 5	Free; premium version available on a fee basis or typically free if accessed through a university library
Trade (and Professional) Association Directories (http://idii.com/resource/associations.htm) (www.weddles.com/associations/index.cfm)	Directories provide access to the Web site addresses of trade associations in all fields. The trade associations can be contacted to obtain information on all areas of feasibility.	Parts 1, 2, 3, 4, and 5	Free
Valuation Resources (www.valuationresources.com)	Resources for information on over 400 industries. Each industry page lists resources and data available from trade associations, publication, and research firms, which addresses industry-related subjects such as industry overview, trends, financial rations, and valuation resources.	Parts 2, 3, and 5	Free
Yahoo! Industry Center (http://biz.yahoo.com/ic)	Provides a directory of industries, along with a list of the companies in each industry, the latest industry-related news, and performance data on the top companies in an industry.	Parts 2, 3, and 5	Free

Founder:

RANA EL CHEMAITELLY

Dialogue *with*
Rana El Chemaitelly

MY FAVORITE
SMARTPHONE APP
The tasks reminder

MY BIGGEST WORRY
AS AN ENTREPRENEUR
To be driven blindly to a more
challenging world

MY ADVICE FOR NEW
ENTREPRENEURS
Keep on dreaming, and never
fear failure

MY BIGGEST SURPRISE
AS AN ENTREPRENEUR
The ability and the perseverance
to convert an idea or a dream
into reality

WHAT I DO WHEN I'M NOT
WORKING
I spend quality time with my
three kids who miss their mom
when she's working

©Nathalie Moukadem

CHAPTER 4

Writing a *Business* Plan

OPENING PROFILE

THE LITTLE ENGINEER
Expanding on the Strength of a Winning Business Plan

Web: www.thelittleengineer.com
Twitter: TheLittleEngineer
Facebook: TheLittleEngineer

As a mother of three children, Rana El Chemaitelly was only too aware of how younger generations seemed hopelessly tied to electronic gizmos. Even her youngest, a 7-year-old boy, was addicted to games. Worse still, the more time he spent on them, the more unsociable he was when the time came to turn them off and interact with his family. El Chemaitelly decided that young people were in dire need of a place where they could learn and engage in more practical and sociable activities.

Being a mechanical engineer and a university instructor at the American University of Beirut meant El Chemaitelly had plenty of experience in practical, hands-on, activities to inspire and involve students. Her business idea was to set up an after-school activity center where young people from the ages of 4 to 16 could learn about science, technology, engineering, and mathematics. The key to its success would be to encourage critical thinking and yet still be fun. And so, The Little Engineer was born.

One of the first challenges in setting up the business was to find people to teach the classes and inspire the youngsters. El Chemaitelly turned to what she knew best and recruited a number of university graduates. This worked on a variety of levels. Many graduates were struggling to bridge the gap between school, university, and the professional world and were becoming increasingly demoralized about the prospects of finding a job. This venture gave them a chance to get away from the theory and into the real world. It also gave them valuable experience to put on their CVs too. Plus, as relative youngsters themselves, they were perfectly suited to relate to the children they were working with.

El Chemaitelly also had to design a range of courses to inspire the demanding audience. She found the most popular idea was one where children built and operated a robot using kits from major manufacturers, which could be anything from a car to a conveyor belt. Other courses were based on renewable energy, physics, electricity, manufacturing, and 3-D graphic design.

LEARNING OBJECTIVES

After studying this chapter you should be ready to:

1. Explain the purpose of a business plan.
2. Describe the two primary reasons for writing a business plan.
3. Describe who reads a business plan and what they're looking for.
4. Explain the difference between a summary business plan, a full business plan, and an operational business plan.
5. Explain why the executive summary may be the most important section of a business plan.
6. Describe a milestone and how milestones are used in business plans.
7. Explain why it's important to include separate sections on a firm's industry and its target market in a business plan.
8. Explain why the "Management Team and Company Structure" section of a business plan is particularly important.
9. Describe the purposes of a "sources and uses of funds" statement and an "assumptions sheet."
10. Detail the parts of an oral presentation of a business plan.

Children on the courses are encouraged to work in teams, which is something El Chemaitelly wanted to emphasize as a foil to the increasingly individualistic pressures of a virtual society. Key skills learned on the courses are time management, collaboration, and teamwork. The courses also cater to children from lower-income families, as well as those with learning difficulties or physical disabilities.

The first Little Engineer course opened in July 2009 with a six-week set of programs to test the market, and it quickly proved to be a hit. Both parents and children were immediately responsive to the idea of combining the how and wow of science, technology, and engineering. Within a year, El Chemaitelly had a total of four centers in Lebanon. Her thoughts then turned to how she would expand both in the Lebanese market and take the concept abroad. She had already received interest from Bahrain, Qatar, Cairo, Yemen, and Jordan.

In April 2010, with expansion in mind, El Chemaitelly decided to enter the MIT Arab Business Plan Competition, which offered the winner a cash prize of $50,000. The only challenge was she had to beat 1,850 applicants to win.

In her detailed plan, El Chemaitelly did her homework. Through her research, she found the children's education industry is estimated to be worth $60 billion worldwide in annual revenue and the edutainment industry, which The Little Engineer had so successfully broken into, was a relatively new but growing segment of this market. It is clear that parents are on the lookout for new intellectual activities, and schools are equally eager to incorporate more hands-on learning into the curriculum.

El Chemaitelly's plan was to grow her business by spreading out over the Lebanon and Arab region, then into Europe, through a combination of local centers and franchising. A key driver would be to open clubs attached to schools, particularly private schools, and also to target large shopping malls. She also argued that there was a market for The Little Engineer branded toys, as the brand grew in popularity.

The Little Engineer customers pay up to $250 each for around 16 learning hours at either after-school sessions or summer camps. El Chemaitelly's average cost per course, including expenses, is $60.

El Chemaitelly successfully argued that, as a first mover in the market, with the know how, know why, know what, and know where, the potential for The Little Engineer was huge. She planned to use the $50,000 for fast expansion and already had 18 trained educators lined up to grow the franchise incrementally in the region and then abroad. After a grueling three rounds, which included submitting a business plan and an oral presentation of the plan to three jurors, El Chemaitelly and The Little Engineer were one of nine finalists in a tough field from 13 Arab countries. El Chemaitelly won the competition and secured the cash prize while being recognized as one of the Middle East's and North Africa's most promising entrepreneurs.[1]

This chapter discusses the importance of writing a business plan. Although some new ventures simply "wing it" and start doing business without the benefit of formal planning, it is hard to find an expert who doesn't recommend preparing a business plan. A **business plan** is a written narrative, typically 25 to 35 pages long, that describes what a new business intends to accomplish and how it intends to accomplish it. For most new ventures, the business plan is a dual-purpose document used both inside and outside the firm. Inside the firm, the plan helps the company develop a "road map" to follow to execute its strategies and plans. Outside the firm, it introduces potential investors and other stakeholders to the business opportunity the firm is pursuing and how it plans to pursue it.[2]

To begin this chapter, we discuss issues with which entrepreneurs often grapple when facing the challenge of writing a business plan. Topics included in the first section of the chapter are reasons for writing a business plan, a description of who reads the business plan and what they're looking for, and guidelines to follow when preparing a written business plan. In the chapter's second section, we present an outline of a business plan with a description of the material in each section of the plan. The third section of the chapter deals with strategies for how to present the business plan to potential investors and others.

THE BUSINESS PLAN

LEARNING OBJECTIVE
1. Explain the purpose of a business plan.

As illustrated in the basic model of the entrepreneurial process shown in Chapter 1, the time to write a business plan is midway through the step of the entrepreneurial process titled "Developing Successful Business Ideas." It is a mistake to write a business plan too early. The business plan must be substantive enough and have sufficient details about the merits of the new venture to convince the reader that the new business is exciting and should receive support. Much of this detail is accumulated in the feasibility analysis stage of investigating the merits of a potential new venture.

A large percentage of entrepreneurs do not write business plans for their new ventures. In fact, only 31 percent of the 600 entrepreneurs who participated in a Wells Fargo/Gallup Small Business Study indicated that they had started their venture with a business plan.[3] This statistic should not deter an entrepreneur from writing a business plan, however. Consider that we do not know how many of the entrepreneurs participating in the Wells Fargo/Gallup Small Business study who did not write a business plan wish they had done so. We're also not sure how many aspiring entrepreneurs never got their businesses off the ground because they didn't have a business plan. One academic study found that potential entrepreneurs who completed a business plan were six times more likely to start a business than individuals who did not complete a business plan.[4]

Reasons for Writing a Business Plan

LEARNING OBJECTIVE
2. Discuss the two primary reasons for writing a business plan.

We show the two primary reasons to write a business plan in Figure 4.1. First, writing a business plan forces a firm's founders to systematically think through each aspect of their new venture.[5] This is not a trivial effort—it usually takes several days or weeks to complete a well-developed business plan—and the founders will usually meet regularly to work on the plan during this period. An example of how much work is sometimes involved, and how a well-planned new business unfolds, is provided by Gwen Whiting and Lindsey Wieber, the cofounders of The Laundress, a company that sells specially formulated laundry detergents and other fabric care products. Whiting and Wieber met at Cornell University while studying fabrics, and after graduating the pair decided to start

Internal Reason	External Reason
Forces the founding team to systematically think through every aspect of their new venture	Communicates the merits of a new venture to outsiders, such as investors and bankers

FIGURE 4.1
Two Primary Reasons for Writing a Business Plan

a business together. The following vignette comes from an interview they gave to Ladies Who Launch, a Web site that highlights the accomplishments of female entrepreneurs:

> *Gwen*: Lindsey and I went to college and studied textiles at Cornell together and always wanted to be in business together. We knew it was going to happen. We always talked about ideas. We were talking about this concept, and it was the right time for us. The first thing we did was the business plan and then a cash flow analysis. We wanted to do as much research as possible before developing the products.

> *Lindsey*: We spent Memorial Day weekend (2003) doing our business plan. We spent the Fourth of July weekend doing our cash flow. After we had our ideas on paper, we went back to Cornell, met with a professor there, and had a crash course in chemistry. She worked with us on the formulation of the products.

> *Gwen*: I found a manufacturer on Columbus Day. Every piece of free time we had, we dedicated to the business. We weren't at the beach with our friends anymore.[6]

The payoff for this level of dedication and hard work, which involved the preparation of a formal business plan, is that Whiting and Wieber now have a successful business. Their products are sold through their Web site and in many stores.

Consistent with Whiting and Wieber's experience, writing a business plan forces a firm's founders to intently study every aspect of their business, a process that's hard to replicate in any other way. Imagine the following. Two friends are thinking about opening a seafood restaurant. They spend the next two months meeting four nights a week to hash out every detail of the business. They study the restaurant industry, identify their target market, develop a marketing plan, settle on a hiring schedule, identify the type of people they want to employ, plan their facility, determine what their startup expenses will be, and put together five years of pro forma (projected) financial statements. After 32 meetings and several drafts, they produce a 30-page business plan that explains every aspect of their business. Regardless of how conscientious the founders of a business are, it's difficult to discipline oneself to cover this level of detail absent writing a business plan. As stated earlier, writing a business plan forces a business's founders to systematically think through every aspect of their business and develop a concrete blueprint to follow.

The second reason to write a business plan is to create a selling document for a company. It provides a mechanism for a young company to present itself to potential investors, suppliers, business partners, key job candidates, and others.[7] Imagine that you have enough money to invest in one new business. You chat informally with several entrepreneurs at a conference for start-ups and decide that there are two new ventures that you would like to know more about. You contact the first entrepreneur and ask for a copy of his business plan. The entrepreneur hesitates a bit and says that he hasn't prepared a formal business plan but would love to get together with you to discuss his ideas. You contact the second entrepreneur and make the same request. This time, the entrepreneur says that she would be glad to forward you a copy of a 30-page business plan, along with a 10-slide PowerPoint presentation that provides an overview of the plan. An hour or two later, the PowerPoint presentation is in your e-mail in-box with a note that the business plan will arrive the next morning. You look through the slides, which are crisp and to the point and do an excellent job of outlining the strengths of the business opportunity. The next day, the business plan arrives just as promised and is equally impressive.

Which entrepreneur has convinced you to invest in his or her business? All other things being equal, the answer is obvious—the second entrepreneur. The fact that the second entrepreneur has a business plan not only provides

This diverse group of entrepreneurs plans to launch a fashion-oriented Web site. Here, they are discussing how to integrate the results of their feasibility analysis into their business plan. A business plan is much more compelling if it contains primary research conducted by the entrepreneurs launching the business.

you with detailed information about the venture but also suggests that the entrepreneur has thought through each element of the business and is committed enough to the new venture to invest the time and energy necessary to prepare the plan. Having a business plan also gives an investor something to react to. Very few, if any, investors will free up time to "listen" to your idea for a new business, at least initially. Investors prefer to vet or evaluate business ideas by looking through business plans (or the executive summaries of business plans) initially before they are willing to invest more of their time and effort.[8]

Who Reads the Business Plan—And What Are They Looking For?

There are two primary audiences for a firm's business plan. Let's look at each of them.

A Firm's Employees   A clearly written business plan, which articulates the vision and future plans of a firm, is important for both the management team and the rank-and-file employees. Some experts argue that it's a waste of time to write a business plan because the marketplace changes so rapidly that any plan will become quickly outdated. Although it's true that marketplaces can and often do change rapidly, the process of writing the plan may be as valuable as the plan itself.

A clearly written business plan also helps a firm's rank-and-file employees operate in sync and move forward in a consistent and purposeful manner. The existence of a business plan is particularly useful for the functional department heads of a young firm. For example, imagine that you are the newly hired vice president for management information systems for a rapidly growing start-up. The availability of a formal business plan that talks about all aspects of the business and the business's future strategies and goals can help you make sure that what you're doing is consistent with the overall plans and direction of the firm.

Investors and Other External Stakeholders   External stakeholders who are being recruited to join a firm such as investors, potential business partners, and key employees are the second audience for a business plan.

To appeal to this group, the business plan must be realistic and not reflective of overconfidence on the firm's part. Overly optimistic statements or projections undermine a business plan's credibility, so it is foolish to include them. At the same time, the plan must clearly demonstrate that the business idea is viable and offers potential investors financial returns greater than lower-risk investment alternatives. The same is true for potential business partners, customers, and key recruits. Unless the new business can show that it has impressive potential, investors have little reason to become involved with it.

A firm must validate the feasibility of its business idea and have a good understanding of its competitive environment prior to presenting its business plan to others. Sophisticated investors, potential business partners, and key recruits will base their assessment of the future prospects of a business on facts, not guesswork or platitudes, as emphasized in Chapter 3. The most compelling facts a company can provide in its business plan are the results of its own feasibility analysis and the articulation of a distinctive and competitive business model. A business plan rings hollow if it is based strictly on an entrepreneur's predictions of a business's future prospects. Morphology, the board game company started by Dartmouth student Kate Ryan Reiling, is an example of a business that laid a firm foundation for its business plan via the feasibility analysis that it conducted very early on. Morphology is profiled in the opening feature for Chapter 3.

In addition to the previously mentioned attributes, a business plan should disclose all resource limitations that the business must meet before it is ready to start earning revenues. For example, a firm may need to hire service people before it can honor the warranties for the products it sells. It is foolhardy for a new venture to try to downplay or hide its resource needs. One of the main reasons new ventures seek out investors is to obtain the capital needed to hire key personnel, further develop their products or services, lease office space, or fill some other gap in their operations. Investors understand this, and experienced investors are typically willing to help the firms they fund plug resource or competency gaps.

Guidelines for Writing a Business Plan

There are several important guidelines that should influence the writing of a business plan. It is important to remember that a firm's business plan is typically the first aspect of a proposed venture that an investor will see. If the plan is incomplete or looks sloppy, it is easy for an investor to infer that the venture itself is incomplete and sloppy.[9] It is important to be sensitive to the structure, content, and style of a business plan before sending it to an investor or anyone else who may be involved with the new firm. Table 4.1 lists some of the "red flags" that are raised when certain aspects of a business plan are insufficient or miss the mark.

Structure of the Business Plan   To make the best impression, a business plan should follow a conventional structure, such as the outline shown in the next section. Although some entrepreneurs want to demonstrate creativity in everything they do, departing from the basic structure of the conventional business plan format is usually a mistake. Typically, investors are very busy people and want a plan where they can easily find critical information. If an investor has to hunt for something because it is in an unusual place or just isn't there, he or she might simply give up and move on to the next plan.[10]

Many software packages are available that employ an interactive, menu-driven approach to assist in the writing of a business plan. Some of these programs are very helpful.[11] However, entrepreneurs should avoid a boilerplate

TABLE 4.1 RED FLAGS IN BUSINESS PLANS

Red Flag	Explanation
Founders with none of their own money at risk	If the founders aren't willing to put their own money at risk, why should anyone else?
A poorly cited plan	A plan should be built on hard evidence and sound research, not guesswork or what an entrepreneur "thinks" will happen. The sources for all primary and secondary research should be cited.
Defining the market size too broadly	Defining the market for a new venture too broadly shows that the true target market is not well defined. For example, saying that a new venture will target the $550-billion-per-year pharmaceutical industry isn't helpful. The market opportunity needs to be better defined. Obviously, the new venture will target a segment or a specific market within the industry.
Overly aggressive financials	Many investors skip directly to this portion of the plan. Projections that are poorly reasoned or unrealistically optimistic lose credibility. In contrast, sober, well-reasoned statements backed by sound research and judgment gain credibility quickly.
Sloppiness in any area	It is never a good idea to make a reader wade through typos, balance sheets that don't balance, or sloppiness in any area. These types of mistakes are seen as inattention to detail, and hurt the credibility of the entrepreneur.

plan that looks as though it came from a "canned" source. The software package may be helpful in providing structure and saving time, but the information in the plan should still be tailored to the individual business. Some businesses hire consultants or outside advisers to write their business plans. Although there is nothing wrong with getting advice or making sure that a plan looks as professional as possible, a consultant or outside adviser shouldn't be the primary author of the plan. Along with facts and figures, a business plan needs to project a sense of anticipation and excitement about the possibilities that surround a new venture—a task best accomplished by the creators of the business themselves.[12]

Content of the Business Plan The business plan should give clear and concise information on all the important aspects of the proposed new venture. It must be long enough to provide sufficient information, yet short enough to maintain reader interest. For most plans, 25 to 35 pages (and typically closer to 25 than 35 pages) are sufficient. Supporting information, such as the résumés of the founding entrepreneurs, can appear in an appendix.

After a business plan is completed, it should be reviewed for spelling, grammar, and to make sure that no critical information has been omitted. There are numerous stories about business plans sent to investors that left out important information, such as significant industry trends, how much money the company needed, or what the money was going to be used for. One investor even told the authors of this book that he once received a business plan that didn't include any contact information for the entrepreneur. Apparently, the entrepreneur was so focused on the content of the plan that he or she simply forgot to provide contact information on the business plan itself. This was a shame, because the investor was interested in learning more about the business idea.[13]

Style or Format of the Business Plan The plan's appearance must be carefully thought out. It should look sharp but not give the impression that a lot of money was spent to produce it. Those who read business plans know that entrepreneurs have limited resources and expect them to act accordingly. A plastic spiral binder including a transparent cover sheet and a back sheet to support the plan is a good choice. When writing the plan, avoid getting carried

FIGURE 4.2
Types of Business
Plans

Summary Business Plan	Full Business Plan	Operational Business Plan
10–15 pages	25–35 pages	40–100 pages
Works best for new ventures in the early stages of development that want to "test the waters" to see if investors are interested in their idea	Works best for new ventures that are at the point where they need funding or financing; serves as a "blueprint" for the company's operations	Is meant primarily for an internal audience; works best as a tool for creating a blueprint for a new venture's operations and providing guidance to operational managers

away with the design elements included in word-processing programs, such as boldfaced type, italics, different font sizes and colors, clip art, and so forth. Overuse of these tools makes a business plan look amateurish rather than professional.[14]

One of the most common questions that the writers of business plans ask is, "How long and detailed should it be?" The answer to this question depends on the type of business plan that is being written. There are three types of business plans, each of which has a different rule of thumb regarding length and level of detail. Presented in Figure 4.2, the three types of business plans are as follows:

LEARNING OBJECTIVE

4. Explain the difference between a summary business plan, a full business plan, and an operational business plan.

■ **Summary plan:** A **summary business plan** is 10 to 15 pages and works best for companies that are very early in their development and are not prepared to write a full plan. The authors may be asking for funding to conduct the analysis needed to write a full plan. Ironically, summary business plans are also used by very experienced entrepreneurs who may be thinking about a new venture but don't want to take the time to write a full business plan. For example, if someone such as Mark Pincus, the founder and CEO of Zynga, was thinking about starting a new business, he might write a summary business plan and send it out to selected investors to get feedback on his idea. Most investors know about Pincus's success with Zynga and don't need detailed information. Zynga is the maker of FarmVille, the popular social networking game.

■ **Full business plan:** A **full business plan** is typically 25 to 35 pages long. This type of plan spells out a company's operations and plans in much more detail than a summary business plan, and it is the format that is usually used to prepare a business plan for an investor.

■ **Operational business plan:** Some established businesses will write an **operational business plan**, which is intended primarily for an internal audience. An operational business plan is a blueprint for a company's operations. Commonly running between 40 and 100 pages in length, these plans can obviously feature a great amount of detail that provide guidance to operational managers.

It's not uncommon for an investor to initially ask for a copy of the executive summary or a set of PowerPoint slides featuring an overview of the proposed business rather than a full business plan. This is normal so don't be alarmed if it happens to you. If the investor's interest is peaked, he or she will ask for more information. Don't misinterpret the signals that investors are sending by not asking for a full business plan. It's still important to write one. This sentiment is affirmed by Brad Feld, a venture capitalist based in Boulder, Colorado, who wrote:

Writing a good business plan is hard. At one point it was an entry point for discussion with most funding sources (angels and VCs). Today, while a formal business plan is less critical to get in the door, the exercise of writing a business plan is incredibly useful. As an entrepreneur, I was involved in writing numerous business plans. It's almost always tedious, time consuming, and difficult but resulted in me having a much better understanding of the business I was trying to create.[15]

A cover letter should accompany a business plan sent to an investor or other stakeholders through the mail. The cover letter should briefly introduce the entrepreneur and clearly state why the business plan is being sent to the individual receiving it. As discussed in Chapter 10, if a new venture is looking for funding, a poor strategy is to obtain a list of investors and blindly send the plan to everyone on the list. Instead, each person who receives a copy of the plan should be carefully selected on the basis of being a viable investor candidate.

Recognizing the Elements of the Plan May Change A final guideline for writing a business plan is to recognize that the plan will usually change as it is being written and as the business evolves, as illustrated in Case 6.1 on Airbnb. New insights invariably emerge when an entrepreneur or a team of entrepreneurs immerse themselves in writing the plan and start getting feedback from others. This process continues throughout the life of a company, and it behooves entrepreneurs to remain alert and open to new insights and ideas. As a result of this phenomenon, entrepreneurs who have written business plans and have launched successful businesses stress that a business plan is a living, breathing document, rather than something that is set in stone. This sentiment is affirmed by Calvin Tang, the founder of Newsvine, an online social news platform that was recently acquired by MSNBC. In regard to business plans being living, breathing documents, Tang said:

My advice to other entrepreneurs would be to stay true to your business plan and your vision. But at the same time, be nimble enough to be able to read the environment and weigh options against each other and try to make the best decision.[16]

The spirit of Tang's comment is reflected in the "Savvy Entrepreneurial Firm" feature. The feature focuses on the challenge of determining how closely to stick to your business plan once your business is launched.

OUTLINE OF THE BUSINESS PLAN

A suggested outline of the full business plan appears in Table 4.2. Specific plans may vary, depending on the nature of the business and the personalities of the founding entrepreneurs. Most business plans do not include all the elements introduced in Table 4.2; we include them here for the purpose of completeness.

Exploring Each Section of the Plan

Cover Page and Table of Contents The cover page should include the company's name, address, phone number, the date, the contact information for the lead entrepreneur, and the company's Web site address if it has one. The company's Facebook page and Twitter name can also be included. The contact information should include a land-based phone number, an e-mail address, and a cell phone number. This information should be centered at the top of the page. Because the cover letter and the business plan could get separated, it is wise to include contact information in both places. The bottom of the cover page should include information alerting the reader to the confidential nature of the plan. If the company already has a distinctive trademark, it should be

SAVVY ENTREPRENEURIAL FIRM

Know When to Hold Them, Know When to Fold Them

Exorogame. Web: www.exorogame.com, Facebook: Exorogame

mydestination.com. Web: www.mydestination.com, Twitter: MyDestination, Facebook: My Destination

Catcha Media. Web: www.catcha.com, Twitter: CatchaMedia, Facebook: Catcha Media

One of the challenges that business owners have is determining how closely to stick to their business plan once the business is launched and they start getting consumer feedback. In almost all cases, some changes will need to be made. But the degree to which business plans pan out as their founders' envisioned varies. In some cases, a business plan is spot-on and the worst thing a founder can do is vary from the plan. In other cases, a plan needs to be significantly tweaked, or even thrown out of the window completely, and the business needs to start over. The following are brief descriptions of businesses that have experienced these various outcomes.

No Changes Needed

ExoroGame is the brainchild of five undergraduates from the National University of Singapore (NUS) who wanted to spark students' interest in running a business. Their aim was to create a social enterprise to promote youth entrepreneurship more widely, rather than a commercial venture for pure profit.

In 2005, the team launched ExoroGame (*exoro* is Latin for "success through persuasion"), an interactive business simulation game dubbed "Entrepreneurship for Dummies." Players increase "their" company's valuation through strategic decisions on buying goods, marketing, sales development, and logistics management.

Students were initially reluctant to take up the challenge, but several months of further trials and enhancements saw the game's popularity soar among undergraduates. ExoroGame has gained a following in educational establishments across Singapore and China. Take-up has been enhanced by a series of ExoroGame Youth Challenge competitions. Although ExoroGame has an appeal among consumers as the "new board game in town," the team has stuck to its original plan to promote youth entrepreneurs. Online portals for universities and schools and even a computer game version are being developed.

Minor Changes Needed

Like so many students, U.K.-based business administration student Neil Waller could not help but get distracted by the thought of a beach holiday getaway, and the Spanish resort of Marbella particularly caught his eye. Unfortunately, when he turned to the Internet for information on hotels, restaurants, and local events, Waller was disappointed at what he found.

Waller was inspired to set up a Web site to help tourists, and Marbellainfo.com was born. While he quickly generated sponsorship from dozens of local companies that were understandably keen to get involved, when Waller studied the traffic on the rapidly growing site, he got a surprise. As well as attracting a strong tourist following, Marbellainfo.com had rapidly evolved into a community site used by local residents to find local services, exchange information, and even get real estate prices. So, his business plan shifted. Recognizing that there was an opportunity for combined tourist and community sites, he has rolled out the business as a worldwide franchise operation. The franchise, now named mydestination.com, has coverage from Cape Town to Sydney. It is run by local operators who have access to vital information about their destinations and who are well placed to understand and respond to the community around them.

Major Changes Needed

Catcha.com was the local icon in Malaysia in the 1990s dot-com craze, with its business formed out of the merger and rebranding of three local Web sites: Searchsingapore.com, Malaysiasearch.com, and Searchindonesia.com. The original strategy from the four entrepreneurs who began Catcha.com in 1999 was to rapidly build up a network of regional Web portals that included local content, community news, and listings, all supported by aggressive marketing of the Catcha.com brand.

Expansion was rapid into 2000, with sites for the Philippines, Thailand, and Australia added in as many months, but costs were high too. At the same time, U.S. search directories such as Yahoo! Inc. and Microsoft Corp's MSN all began to target the Asian market and were complementing their local sites with global Internet content. Lycos Inc. teamed up with Singapore Telecommunications in a US$50 million venture to set up sites in 10 Asian markets.

The writing was on the wall for Catcha.com. Portals and search engines make money from advertising and e-commerce, and they need as much traffic as possible. Only a handful of search engines can succeed in each market. By late 2000, Catcha.com did not have enough funds to maintain the business thanks to a combination of overexpansion, competition from established and well-financed companies, and the bursting of the dot-com bubble that spooked the markets and shelved Catcha.com's planned stock market flotation.

Catcha.com's founders were forced to completely rethink their business model, and using their local knowledge switched to media, publishing, and event management. Catcha Media Group has gone on to become one of the largest English-language publishing groups in Southeast Asia. It has also ventured back into the Internet arena with iProperty.com, which is now listed on the Australian Securities Exchange (ASX).

Questions for Critical Thinking

1. Does ExoroGame's evaluation of its current status and its decision to stick with its business plan make sense? Why or why not?
2. What do you think would have happened to Marbellainfo.com if it hadn't changed its business plan? What do you think would have happened to Catcha.com?
3. Why do you think some start-ups find it difficult to change their business plan, even when presented with evidence that their current business plan isn't working?
4. Look at the "You Be the VC" features at the end of Chapter 3, which focus on InstyMeds and SmartSense, and the "You Be the VC" features at the end of this chapter, which focus on Secret Recipe and PharmaJet. From the information in the features and on each of the company's Web sites, which company do you think will have the easiest time sticking to its original business plan? Which company do you think will have the hardest time? Explain your selections.

Sources: "Exoro-lating–The New Board Game in Town," *The Sun U!* April 15, 2008; "Interview with the Exoro Team," *SG Entrepreneurs*, October 11, 2006; "Catcha.com to Focus on Technology for Its Content Distribution," *ZDNet Asia*, May 15, 2000; "Once Bitten," *The Business Times*, February 19, 2009.

TABLE 4.2   BUSINESS PLAN OUTLINE

Cover Page
Table of Contents

I. Executive Summary
II. Industry Analysis
 Industry Size, Growth Rate, and Sales Projections
 Industry Structure
 Nature of Participants
 Key Success Factors
 Industry Trends
 Long-Term Prospects
III. Company Description
 Company History
 Mission Statement
 Products and Services
 Current Status
 Legal Status and Ownership
 Key Partnerships (if any)
IV. Market Analysis
 Market Segmentation and Target Market Selection
 Buyer Behavior
 Competitor Analysis
 Estimates of Annual Sales and Market Share
V. The Economics of the Business
 Revenue Drivers and Profit Margins
 Fixed and Variable Costs
 Operating Leverage, and Its Implications
 Start-up Costs
 Break-Even Chart and Calculation
VI. Marketing Plan
 Overall Marketing Strategy
 Product, Price, Promotions, and Distribution
 Sales Process (or Cycle)
 Sales Tactics
VII. Design and Development Plan
 Development Status and Tasks
 Challenges and Risks
 Projected Development Costs
 Proprietary Issues (Patents, Trademarks, Copyrights, Licenses, Brand Names)
VIII. Operations Plan
 General Approach to Operations
 Business Location
 Facilities and Equipment
IX. Management Team and Company Structure
 Management Team (Including a Skills Profile)
 Board of Directors
 Board of Advisers
 Company Structure
X. Overall Schedule
XI. Financial Projections
 Sources and Uses of Funds Statement
 Assumptions Sheet
 Pro Forma Income Statements
 Pro Forma Balance Sheets
 Pro Forma Cash Flows
 Ratio Analysis
Appendices

placed somewhere near the center of the page. A table of contents should follow the cover letter. It should list the sections and page numbers of the business plan and the appendices.

Executive Summary   The **executive summary** is a short overview of the entire business plan; it provides a busy reader with everything she needs to know about the new venture's distinctive nature.[17] As mentioned earlier, in many instances an investor will first ask for a copy of a firm's executive summary and will request a copy of the full business plan only if the executive summary is sufficiently convincing. The executive summary, then, is arguably the most important section of the business plan.[18] The most important point to remember when writing an executive summary is that it is not an introduction or preface to the business plan. Instead, it is meant to be a summary of the plan itself.[19]

An executive summary shouldn't exceed two single-spaced pages. The cleanest format for an executive summary is to provide an overview of the business plan on a section-by-section basis. The topics should be presented in the same order as they are presented in the business plan. Two identical versions of the executive summary should be prepared—one that's part of the business plan and one that's a stand-alone document. The stand-alone document should be used to accommodate people who ask to see the executive summary before they decide whether they want to see the full plan.

Even though the executive summary appears at the beginning of the business plan, it should be written last. The plan itself will evolve as it's written, so not everything is known at the outset. In addition, if you write the executive summary first, you run the risk of trying to write a plan that fits the executive summary rather than thinking through each piece of the plan independently.[20]

Industry Analysis   The main body of the business plan begins by describing the industry the business will enter in terms of its size, growth rate, and sales projections. It is important to focus strictly on the business's industry and not its industry and target market simultaneously. Before a business selects a target market, it should have a good grasp of its industry—including where its industry's promising areas are and where its points of vulnerability are located.

Industry structure refers to how concentrated or fragmented an industry is. Fragmented industries are more receptive to new entrants than industries that are dominated by a handful of large firms. You should also provide your reader a feel for the nature of the participants in your industry. Issues such as whether the major participants in the industry are innovative or conservative and are quick or slow to react to environment change are the types of characteristics to convey. You want your reader to visualize how your firm will fit in or see the gap that your firm will fill. The key success factors in an industry are also important to know and convey. Most industries have 6 to 10 key factors that all participants must be competent in to compete. Most participants try to then differentiate themselves by excelling in two or three areas.

Industry trends should be discussed, which include both environmental and business trends. The most important environmental trends are economic trends, social trends, technological advances, and political and regulatory changes. Business trends include issues such as whether profit margins in the industry are increasing or falling and whether input costs are going up or down. The industry analysis should conclude with a brief statement of your beliefs regarding the long-term prospects for the industry.

Company Description   This section begins with a general description of the company. Although at first glance this section may seem less critical than

If you plan to start a company in the fitness industry, it's important to document the health and future growth potential of the industry. A careful analysis of a firm's industry lays out what is realistically possible and what isn't realistically possible for a startup to achieve.

others, it is extremely important in that it demonstrates to your reader that you know how to translate an idea into a business.

The company history section should be brief, but should explain where the idea for the company came from and the driving force behind its inception. If the story of where the idea for the company came from is heartfelt, tell it. For example, in Case 2.1, we introduced you to Shane Taylor, the individual whose father is fighting both heart disease and cancer. You'll recall that Taylor's dad takes 26 different medications to fight his illnesses, and a concern that Taylor had was the possibility of a mistake being made in the types or dosages of prescription medications that his father takes. This concern motivated Taylor to start ScriptPad, a software platform that transforms an Apple iPhone or iPad into a digital prescription pad, which lessens the possibility of a prescription mistake from happening. Taylor's story is one that anyone can relate to. It might even cause a person reading ScriptPad's business plan to pause and think, "Someday I might be in the position of helping my mom or dad or another loved one deal with multiple prescriptions, and I'd like to see the prescription writing process become as safe as possible too."

A **mission statement** defines why a company exists and what it aspires to become. We further define a mission statement in Chapter 6. If carefully written and used properly, a mission statement can define the path a company takes and act as its financial and moral compass. Some businesses also include a tagline in their business plan. A **tagline** is a phrase that a business plans to use to reinforce its position in the marketplace. For example, Kazoo Toy's tagline is "Toys that play with imagination." Kazoo Toys is the subject of Case 4.1.

The products and services section should include an explanation of your product or service. Include a description of how your product or service is unique and how you plan to position it in the marketplace. A product or service's **position** is how it is situated relative to its rivals. If you plan to open a new type of smoothie shop, for example, you should explain how your smoothie shop differs from others and how it will be positioned in the market in terms of the products it offers and the clientele it attracts. This section is the ideal place for you to start reporting the results of your feasibility analysis. If the concept test, buying intentions survey, and library, Internet, and gumshoe research produced meaningful results, they should be reported here.

The current status section should reveal how far along your company is in its development. A good way to frame this discussion is to think in terms of milestones. A **milestone** is a noteworthy or significant event. If you have selected and registered your company's name, completed a feasibility analysis, written a business plan, and established a legal entity, you have already cleared several important milestones. The legal status and ownership section should indicate who owns the business and how the ownership is split up. You should also indicate what your current form of business ownership is (i.e., LLC, Subchapter S Corp., etc.) if that issue has been decided. We provide a full discussion of the different forms of business ownership in Chapter 7.

A final item a business should cover in this opening section is whether it has any key partnerships that are integral to the business. Many business plans rely on the establishment of partnerships to make them work. Examples of the types of partnerships that are common in business plans are shown in the "Partnering for Success" feature.

Market Analysis   The market analysis is distinctly different than the industry analysis. Whereas the industry analysis focuses on the industry that a firm will participate in (i.e., toy industry, software industry, men's clothing industry), the **market analysis** breaks the industry into segments and zeroes in on the specific segment (or target market) to which the firm will try to appeal. As mentioned in Chapter 3, most start-ups focus on servicing a specific target market within an industry.

The first task that's generally tackled in a market analysis is to segment the industry the business will be entering and then identify the specific target market on which it will focus. This is done through **market segmentation**, which is the process of dividing the market into distinct segments. Markets can be segmented in many ways, such as by geography (city, state, country), demographic variables (age, gender, income), psychographic variables (personality, lifestyle, values), and so forth. Sometimes a firm segments its market on more than one dimension to drill down to a specific segment that the firm thinks it is uniquely capable of serving. For example, in its market analysis, GreatCall, the cell phone service provided for older people, probably segmented the cell phone market by age and by benefits sought. Some start-ups create value by finding a new way to segment an industry. For example, before Tish Ciravolo started Daisy Rock Guitar, a company that makes guitars just for women, the guitar industry had not been segmented by gender. Daisy Rock Guitar's competitive advantage is that it makes guitars that accommodate a woman's smaller hands and build.

It's important to include a section in the market analysis that deals directly with the behavior of the consumers in a firm's target market. The more a start-up knows about the consumers in its target market, the more it can gear products or services to accommodate their needs. Many start-ups find it hard to sell products to public schools, for example, because purchase decisions are often made by committees (which draws out the decision-making process), and the funding often has to go through several levels of administrators to get approved. A **competitor analysis**, which is a detailed analysis of a firm's competitors,

PARTNERING FOR SUCCESS

Types of Partnerships That Are Common in Business Plans

Because new businesses are resource constrained, they often make partnering an essential part of their business plans. As illustrated throughout this book, effective partnering can help a start-up in many ways. The following are examples of the types of partnering scenarios that are common in business plans.

Smaller Companies Partnering with Larger Companies to Bring Their Products to Market

Because the cost of bringing a new drug to market is so high, biotech companies normally partner with large pharmaceutical companies to bring their products to market. Biotech companies specialize in discovering and developing new drugs—it's what they're good at. In most cases, however, they have neither the money nor the experience to bring the products to market. In contrast, the large drug companies, like Merck and Pfizer, specialize in marketing and selling drugs and in providing information to doctors about them. It's what they're good at. As a result, most biotech firms' business plans plainly state that their mission is to discover, develop, and patent new drugs and that they'll partner with larger pharmaceutical companies to bring the products to market.

Smaller Companies Partnering with Larger Companies to Produce, Fulfill, and/or Ship Their Products

Many new firms, from the get-go, structure their business plans on the notion that partners will produce, fulfill, and ship their products. As a result, a start-up that develops a new type of board game may have the game made by a contract manufacturer in China, have it shipped from China to a warehouse and fulfillment company in the United States, and when an order is placed (by a retailer like Barnes & Noble or Target) the warehouse and fulfillment company ships the product to the buyer. While there are costs involved at every step in the process, this arrangement frees the board game company to focus on designing and marketing products and reduces its initial capital requirements. A variation of this approach, for catalog and Web-based companies that sell other manufacturers' products, is a method called drop shipping. Drop shippers like eBags, which is an online retailer that sells luggage, backpacks, and similar items, doesn't warehouse anything it sells. Instead, when it receives an order it passes the order onto the original manufacturer (or distributor), which fulfills the order often in an eBags box with an eBags invoice so it looks like it came directly from eBags. This arrangement costs eBags money, but it is integral to eBags' business plan of offering a wide selection of products to customers at affordable prices and not getting caught with outdated merchandise.

Smaller Companies Outsourcing Human Resources Management Tasks

An increasingly common feature in business plans is outsourcing human resource management tasks that are labor intensive and take specialized expertise. Some start-ups outsource only administrative tasks, such as payroll processing and benefits administration. These firms partner with payroll accounting firms such as Paychex or Ceridian. Other start-ups outsource a broader range of their human resource management functions and partner with a company such as ADP or Administaff. These companies are called professional employer organizations (PEOs) and act like an off-site human resource department for a start-up or other firm. Along with doing everything that Paychex and Ceridian does, PEOs can help a start-up with hiring, firing, training, regulatory compliance, and other more in-depth human resource–related issues. Outsourcing these tasks can minimize a firm's investment in human resources management personnel and support (such as software products) and frees a company to focus on other core activities.

Questions for Critical Thinking

1. What factors in the business environment encourage firms to partner to compete?
2. What risks do small firms face when partnering with large, successful companies? What risks do large companies take when they partner with small start-ups?
3. What are three ways (that are not illustrated in the feature) that small firms can partner with larger firms to lessen their capital requirements?
4. The "You Be the VC 4.2" feature focuses on PharmaJet, a company that is producing a needle-free syringe and injection system. What types of partnerships could PharmaJet form to lower its capital requirements and allow its top management team to focus on its distinctive competencies?

should be included. A complete explanation of how to complete a competitor analysis is provided in Chapter 5.

The final section of the market analysis estimates a firm's annual sales and market share. There are four basic ways for a new firm to estimate its initial sales. If possible, more than one method should be used to complete this task. The most important outcome is to develop an estimate that is based on sound assumptions and seems both realistic and attainable. We show the four methods entrepreneurs can use to estimate sales in Table 4.3.

The Economics of the Business This section begins the financial analysis of a business, which is further fleshed out in the financial projections. It addresses the basic logic of how profits are earned in the business and how many units of a business's product or service must be sold for the business to "break even" and then start earning a profit.

The major revenue drivers, which are the ways a business earns money, should be identified. If a business sells a single product and nothing else, it has one revenue driver. If it sells a product plus a service guarantee, it has two revenue drivers, and so on. The size of the overall gross margin for each revenue driver should be determined. The gross margin for a revenue driver is the selling price minus the cost of goods sold or variable costs. The **costs of goods sold** are the materials and direct labor needed to produce the revenue driver. So, if a product sells for $100 and the cost of goods sold is $40 (labor and materials), the gross margin is $60 or 60 percent. The $60 is also called the **contribution margin**. This is the amount per unit of sale that's left over and is available to "contribute" to covering the business's fixed costs and producing a profit. If your business has more than one revenue driver, you

TABLE 4.3 THE FOUR METHODS FOR ESTIMATING A NEW FIRM'S INITIAL SALES

Method	Explanation
Utilize the Multiplication Method	There are two approaches that fit this category. Start-ups that plan to sell a product on a national basis normally use a top-down approach. This involves trying to estimate the total number of users of the product, estimate the average price customers pay, and estimate what percentage of the market your business will garner. Start-ups that plan to sell locally normally use a more bottom-up approach. This approach involves trying to determine how many customers to expect and the average amount each customer will spend.
Find a Comparable Firm	Find a comparable firm, and ask for an estimate of annual sales. For example, if you are planning to open a woman's clothing boutique, try to find a boutique that is similar to yours (and is not in your trade area) and simply call the owner and ask for a chance to talk to him or her about the business. Once a relationship has been established, you can ask for an estimate of the business's annual sales.
Contact Industry Trade Associations	Contact the premier trade associations in your industry and ask if they track the sales numbers for businesses that are similar to your business. If the trade association doesn't track actual sales numbers for comparable businesses, ask if there are other rules of thumb or metrics that help new companies estimate sales. For example, many industries collect statistics such as "average sales per square foot" or "average sales per employee" for firms in their industry.
Conduct Internet Searches	Internet searches will often reveal magazines and newspaper articles that focus on firms in your industry. On occasion, the articles will talk about the sales experiences of a similar early stage firm. If you know of a firm that is comparable to your firm, target the firm first in your search. You may get lucky, and find an article that says, "XYZ firm earned gross revenues of $250,000 per year its first three years." If the article is credible and XYZ firm is comparable to your firm, you've just found useful information.

should figure the contribution margin for each. If you have multiple products in a given revenue driver category, you can calculate the contribution margin for each product and take an average. (For example, if you're opening an office supply store, you may have several different computer printers under the revenue driver "printers.") You can then calculate the weighted average contribution margin for each of the company's revenue drivers by weighing the individual contribution margin of each revenue driver based on the percentage of sales expected to come from that revenue driver.

The next section should provide an analysis of the business's fixed and variable costs. The variable costs (or costs of goods sold) for each revenue driver was figured previously. Add a projection of the business's fixed costs. A firm's **variable costs** vary by sales, while its **fixed costs** are costs a company incurs whether it sells something or not. The company's operating leverage should be discussed next. A firm's **operating leverage** is an analysis of its fixed versus variable costs. Operating leverage is highest in companies that have a high proportion of fixed costs relative to their variable costs. In contrast, operating leverage is lowest in companies that have a low proportion of fixed costs relative to variable costs. The implications of the firm's projected operating leverage should be discussed. For example, a firm with a high operating leverage takes longer to reach breakeven, but once breakeven is reached more of its revenues fall to the bottom line.

The business's one-time start-up costs should be estimated and put in a table. These costs include legal expenses, fees for business licenses and permits, Web site design, business logo design, and similar one-time expenses. Normal operating expenses should not be included.

This section should conclude with a break-even analysis, which is an analysis of how many units of its product a business must sell before it breaks even and starts earning a profit. An explanation of how to compute a break-even analysis is included in Chapter 8.

Marketing Plan The marketing plan focuses on how the business will market and sell its product or service. It deals with the nuts and bolts of marketing in terms of price, promotion, distribution, and sales. For example, GreatCall, the firm that makes cell phones for older users, may have a great product, a well-defined target market, and a good understanding of its customers and competitors, but it still has to find customers and persuade them to buy its product.

The best way to describe a company's marketing plan is to start by articulating its marketing strategy, positioning, and points of differentiation, and then talk about how these overall aspects of the plan will be supported by price, promotional mix and sales process, and distribution strategy. Obviously, it's not possible to include a full-blown marketing plan in the four to five pages permitted in a business plan for the marketing section, but you should hit the high points as best as possible.

A firm's **marketing strategy** refers to its overall approach for marketing its products and services. A firm's overall approach typically boils down to how it positions itself in its market and how it differentiates itself from its competitors. Sprig Toys, the educational toy company introduced in Chapter 3, is positioning itself as a toy company selling premium products to parents with the ability to pay and differentiates itself through the educational and developmental value of its toys and their environmentally friendly and safe properties. This overall strategy sets the tone and provides guidance for how the company should reach its target market via its product, pricing, promotional, and distribution tactics. For example, it will invariably promote and advertise its products in places that people in its target market are most likely to see. Similarly, it will most likely sell its products through specialty toy stores (like Kazoo &

Company, the subject of Case 4.1) and its own Web site rather than through mass merchandisers like Walmart and Costco.

The next section should deal with your company's approach to product, price, promotion, and distribution. If your product has been adequately explained already, you can move directly to price. Price, promotion, and distribution should all be in sync with your positioning and points of differentiation, as described previously. Price is a particularly important issue because it determines how much money a company can make. It also sends an important message to your target market. If Sprig Toys advertised its toys as high-quality toys that are both educationally sound and environmentally friendly but also charged a low price, people in its target market would be confused. They would think, "This doesn't make sense. Are Sprig Toys high quality or aren't they?" In addition, the lower price wouldn't generate the profits that Sprig Toys needs to further develop its toys. You should also briefly discuss your plans regarding promotions and distribution.

The final section should describe the company's sales process or cycle and specific sales tactics it will employ. It's surprising how many business plans describe a business's overall marketing strategies, but never comment on how a product or service will actually be sold.

Product (or Service) Design and Development Plan If you're developing a completely new product or service, you need to include a section in your business plan that focuses on the status of your development efforts. Many seemingly promising start-ups never get off the ground because their product development efforts stall or the actual development of the product or service turns out to be more difficult than expected.

The first issue to address is to describe the present stage of the development of your product or service. Most products follow a logical path of development that includes product conception, prototyping, initial production, and full production. You should describe specifically the point that your product or service is at and provide a timeline that describes the remaining steps. If you are in the very early stages of your business and only have an idea, you should carefully explain how a prototype, which is the first physical depiction of a new product or service, will be produced. A **product prototype** is the first physical manifestation of a new product, often in a crude or preliminary form. The idea is to solicit feedback and then iterate. A **service prototype** is a representation of what the service will be like and how it will be experienced by the customer. For example, a service prototype for a Web-based company might consist of a preliminary or beta version of the site, with sufficient functionality built into the site for users to test it and then report their experiences. In some instances a virtual prototype is sufficient. A **virtual prototype** is a computer-generated 3-D image of a product or service idea. It displays the idea as a 3-D model that can be viewed from all sides and rotated 360 degrees.

A section labeled "Challenges and Risks" should be included and disclose any major anticipated design and development challenges and risks that will be involved in bringing the product or service to market. While you want to remain upbeat, the last thing you want to do is paint an overly rosy picture of how quickly and effortlessly your design and development process will unfold. Experienced readers know that product and service development is an inherently bumpy and challenging process and will want insights into the challenges and risks you anticipate with your particular offering.

A final section should describe any patents, trademarks, copyrights, or trade secrets that you have secured or plan to secure relative to the products or services you are developing. If your start-up is still in the early stages and you have not taken action on intellectual property issues yet, you should get legal advice so you can, at a minimum, discuss your plans in these areas. Intellectual property is discussed in Chapter 12.

Operations Plan   The operations plan section of the business plan outlines how your business will be run and how your product or service will be produced. You have to strike a careful balance between adequately describing this topic and providing too much detail. Your readers will want an overall sense of how the business will be run, but they generally will not be looking for detailed explanations. As a result, it is best to keep this section short and crisp.

A useful way to illustrate how your business will be run is to first articulate your general approach to operations in terms of what's most important and what the make-or-break issues are. You can then frame the discussion in terms of "back stage," or behind the scenes activities, and "front stage," or what the customer sees and experiences. For example, if you're opening a new fitness center, the back stage and the front stage issues might be broken down as follows:

Back Stage (Behind the Scenes Activities)	Front Stage (What the Members See)
• Staff selection	• Member tours
• Operations manual	• Operating hours
• Relationships with suppliers	• Staff assistance
• Relationships with city government	• Fitness classes and programs
• Development of marketing materials	• Fitness machines
• Employee orientation and training	• Workshops
• Emergency plans	• Monthly newsletter

Obviously you can't comment on each issue in the three to four pages you have for your operations plan, but you can lay out the key back stage and front stage activities and address the most critical ones.

The next section of the operations plan should describe the geographic location of your business. In some instances, location is an extremely important issue and in other instances it isn't. For example, one of the reasons why Jeff Bezos located Amazon.com in Seattle is that Seattle is a major distribution hub for several large book publishers. By locating near these distribution facilities, Amazon.com has enjoyed a cost advantage that it wouldn't have had otherwise. On a more fine-grained level, for restaurants and retail businesses, the specific location within a mall or shopping center, or a certain side of a busy street, may make a dramatic difference.

This section should also describe a firm's facilities and equipment. You should list your most important facilities and equipment and briefly describe how they will be (or have been) acquired, in terms of whether they will be purchased, leased, or acquired through some other means. If you will be producing a product and will contract or outsource your production, you should comment on how that will be accomplished. If your facilities are nondescript, such as a generic workspace for computer programmers, a lot of explanation is not needed.

Management Team and Company Structure   Many investors and others who read business plans look first at the executive summary and then go directly to the management team section to assess the strength of the people starting the firm. Investors read more business plans with interesting ideas and exciting markets than they are able to finance. As a result, it's often not the idea or market that wins funding among competing plans, but the perception that one management team is better prepared to execute their idea than the others.

LEARNING OBJECTIVE

8. Explain why the "Management Team and Company Structure" section of a business plan is particularly important.

The management team of a new firm typically consists of the founder or founders and a handful of key management personnel. A brief profile of each member of the management team should be provided, starting with the founder or founders of the firm. Each profile should include the following information:

■ Title of the position
■ Duties and responsibilities of the position
■ Previous industry and related experience
■ Previous successes
■ Educational background

Although they should be kept brief, the profiles should illustrate why each individual is qualified and will uniquely contribute to the success of the firm. Certain attributes of a management team should be highlighted if they apply in your case. For example, investors and others tend to prefer team members who've worked together before. The thinking here is that if people have worked together before and have decided to partner to start a new firm, it usually means that they get along personally and trust one another.[21] You should also identify the gaps that exist in the management team and your plans and timetable for filling them. The complete résumés of key management team personnel can be placed in an appendix to the business plan.

If a start-up has a board of directors and/or a board of advisers, their qualifications and the roles they play should be explained and they should be included as part of your management team. A **board of directors** is a panel of individuals elected by a corporation's shareholders to oversee the management of the firm, as explained in more detail in Chapter 9. A **board of advisers** is a panel of experts asked by a firm's management to provide counsel and advice on an ongoing basis. Unlike a board of directors, a board of advisers possess no legal responsibility for the firm and gives nonbinding advice.[22] Many start-ups ask people who have specific skills or expertise to serve on their board of advisers to help plug competency gaps until the firm can afford to hire additional personnel. For example, if a firm is started by two Web designers and doesn't have anyone on staff with marketing expertise, the firm might place one or two people on its board of advisers with marketing expertise to provide guidance and advice.

The final portion of this section of your business plan focuses on how your company will be structured. Even if you are a start-up, you should outline how the company is currently structured and how it will be structured as it grows. It's important that the internal structure of a company makes sense and that the lines of communication and accountability are clear. Including a description of your company's structure also reassures the people who read the plan that you know how to translate your business idea into a functioning firm.

The most effective way to illustrate how a company will be structured and the lines of authority and accountability that will be in place is to include an organizational chart in the plan. An **organizational chart** is a graphic representation of how authority and responsibility are distributed within the company. The organizational chart should be presented in graphical format if possible.

Overall Schedule A schedule should be prepared that shows the major events required to launch the business. The schedule should be in the format of milestones critical to the business's success, such as incorporating the venture, completion of prototypes, rental of facilities, obtaining critical financing, starting the production of operations, obtaining the first sale, and so forth. An effectively prepared and presented schedule can be extremely valuable in convincing potential investors that the management team is aware of what needs to take place to launch the venture and has a plan in place to get there.

Financial Projections   The final section of a business plan presents a firm's pro forma (or projected) financial projections. Having completed the previous sections of the plan, it's easy to see why the financial projections come last. They take the plans you've developed and express them in financial terms.

The first thing to include is a **sources and uses of funds statement**, which is a document that lays out specifically how much money a firm needs (if the intention of the business plan is to raise money), where the money will come from, and what the money will be used for. The next item to include is an **assumptions sheet**, which is an explanation of the most critical assumptions that your financial statements are based on. Some assumptions will be based on general information, and no specific sources will be cited to substantiate the assumption. For example, if you believe that the U.S. economy will gain strength over the next three to five years, and that's an underlying assumption driving your sales projections, then you should state that assumption. In this instance, you wouldn't cite a specific source—you're reflecting a consensus view. (It's then up to your reader to agree or disagree.) Other assumptions will be based on very specific information, and you should cite the source for your assumptions. For example, if Sprig Toys has credible data that shows the educational segment of the children's toy industry is expected to grow at a rate of 10 to 12 percent per year for the foreseeable future, and this figure plays a large role in its belief that it can increase its sales every year, then it should cite the sources of its information.

The importance of identifying the most critical assumptions that a business is based on and thoroughly vetting the assumptions is illustrated in the "What Went Wrong" feature. StyleHop, the company that is the focus of the feature, failed largely because it neglected to plan and at least one of the key assumptions that business was based upon turned out to be incorrect.

The **pro forma (or projected) financial statements** are the heart of the financial section of a business plan. Although at first glance preparing financial statements appears to be a tedious exercise, it's a fairly straightforward process if the preceding sections of your plan are thorough. The financial statements also represent the finale of the entire plan. As a result, it's interesting to see how they turn out.

A firm's pro forma financial statements are similar to the historical statements an established firm prepares, except they look forward rather than track the past. Pro forma financial statements include the pro forma income statement, the pro forma balance sheet, and the pro forma cash flow statement. The are usually prepared in this order because information flows logically from one to the next. Most experts recommend three to five years of pro forma statements. If the company you're writing your plan for already exists, you should also include three years of historical financial statements. Most business plan writers interpret or make sense of a firm's historical or pro forma financial statements through **ratio analysis**. Ratios, such as return on assets and return on sales, are computed by taking numbers out of financial statements and forming ratios with them. Each ratio has a particular meaning in regard to the potential of the business.

We present a complete explanation of how to complete pro forma financial statements and ratio analysis in Chapter 8.

LEARNING OBJECTIVE

9. Describe the purpose of a "sources and uses of funds" statement and an "assumptions sheet."

WHAT WENT WRONG?

What StyleHop Learned About the Value of Planning the Hard Way

It was a cool B2B business idea. While working at Liz Claiborne, David Reinke had the idea to use crowd-sourcing to help retailers select the women's clothing they would feature in their stores. Crowdsourcing is the act of outsourcing a task, traditionally performed by a company's employees, to a larger group of people or community (a crowd) through an open call. The essence of Reinke's idea was that a large group of women, drawing upon their collective intuitions and a sense of what they liked and what the women they knew liked, could do a better job of picking clothing for a retailer than a retailer's own buyers.

To execute the idea, Reinke skipped the business plan and jumped right in. He hired a chief technology officer to build a fashion-oriented social network for women with a back end that would be relevant to the B2B market. The social network allowed participants to create user profiles, upload favorites, and view affiliate feeds so they could rank new fashions and put them into wish lists. StyleHop signed up two big-box retailers as pilot customers, who used the service to select what women's fashion items to feature in their stores the following season. It worked. Reinke says that StyleHop panelist's predictions were seven time more accurate than the predictions of in-house buyers when comparing how each item sold versus how much inventory had been ordered.

Regrettably, despite these encouraging results, StyleHop failed in late 2009. Reinke, in a candid interview with Howard Greenstein of *Inc.* magazine, outlined three reasons that contributed to StyleHop's demise. First, rather than validating the crowdsourcing idea with retailers first, Reinke put a lot of effort into building the social networking site. In retrospect, he feels it would have been better to have validated the crowdsourcing idea with retailers first. As it turned out, buyers weren't ready to change the way they had always done their buying. This shot down a key assumption that Reinke had made—that buyers would opt for a new method of buying if proven to be more effective. Second, if the retail side had been validated first, Reinke feels he could have used Facebook, Twitter, and Google to assemble online focus groups, to make fashion-related predictions, rather

than via StyleHop's stand-alone social network, which was expensive to build and maintain. This approach would have resulted in higher operating margins, giving StyleHop more time to prove its concept. Finally, StyleHop got a little unlucky. The person they were working with at the larger of their two pilot firms switched roles in the company, putting StyleHop back to square one in terms of trying to show its value. This scenario illustrates the disadvantage of working with a single or small number of pilot firms.

Reinke is back in a traditional job but is still a believer in StyleHop's vision and approach. In the *Inc.* magazine article referred to previously Reinke remarked, "StyleHop was knowledge and methodology, not technology. Maybe we'll get a chance to try it again in some form."

Questions for Critical Thinking

1. In what ways do you think StyleHop suffered by not having a business plan?
2. What assumptions, other than those mentioned in the feature, do you think were integral to StyleHop's business? In what ways could StyleHop have addressed these assumptions? In what ways, if any, do you believe StyleHop's business would have evolved differently if StyleHop had seriously addressed these assumptions?
3. Do you think StyleHop conducted a feasibility analysis, prior to hiring a chief technology officer and starting to build the business? In what ways do you think a feasibility analysis could have helped StyleHop better anticipate the problems that eventually led to the firm's failure?
4. The "You Be the VC 4.1" feature focuses on Secret Recipe, a popular cafe chain that offers a range of unique cakes, pastries, designer ice creams, and beverages. What are some of the main assumptions that Secret Recipe's business plan is based on?

Source: H. Greenstein, "Start 2011 by Learning from Failure," *Inc.*, www.inc.com/howard-greenstein/start-2011-by-learning-from-failure.html (accessed February 15, 2011).

Appendix Any material that does not easily fit into the body of a business plan should appear in an appendix—résumés of the top management team, photos or diagrams of product or product prototypes, certain financial data, and market research projections. The appendix should not be bulky and add significant length to the business plan. It should include only the additional information vital to the plan but not appropriate for the body of the plan itself.

TABLE 4.4   THE 10 MOST IMPORTANT QUESTIONS A BUSINESS PLAN SHOULD ANSWER

1. Is the business just an idea, or is it an opportunity with real potential?

2. Is the product or service viable? Does it add significant value to the customer? Has a feasibility analysis been completed? If so, what are the results?

3. Is the business entering an exciting, growing industry, and has the firm identified an attractive position within the industry?

4. Does the business have a well-defined target market?

5. Does the business have points of differentiation that truly separate itself from its competitors? Are these points of differentiation sustainable?

6. Does the business have a sound marketing plan?

7. Is the management team experienced, skilled, and up to the task of launching the new firm?

8. Is the business's operations plan appropriate and sound?

9. Are the assumptions that the firm is basing its financial projections on realistic?

10. Are the financial projections completed correctly, and do they project a bright future for the firm?

Putting It All Together   In evaluating and reviewing the completed business plan, the writers should put themselves in the reader's shoes to determine if the most important questions about the viability of their business venture have been answered. Table 4.4 lists the 10 most important questions a business plan should answer. It's a good checklist for any business plan writer.

PRESENTING THE BUSINESS PLAN TO INVESTORS

If the business plan successfully elicits the interest of a potential investor, the next step is to meet with the investor and present the plan in person. The investor will typically want to meet with the firm's founders. Because investors ultimately fund only a few ventures, the founders of a new firm should make as positive an impression on the investor as possible.

The first meeting with an investor is generally very short, about one hour.[23] The investor will typically ask the firm to make a 15- to 20-minute presentation using PowerPoint slides and use the rest of the time to ask questions. If the investor is impressed and wants to learn more about the venture, the presenters will be asked back for a second meeting to meet with the investor and his or her partners. This meeting will typically last longer and will require a more thorough presentation.

The Oral Presentation of a Business Plan

When asked to meet with an investor, the founders of a new venture should prepare a set of PowerPoint slides that will fill the time slot allowed for the presentation portion of the meeting. The same format applies to most business plan competitions. The first rule in making an oral presentation is to follow instructions. If an investor tells an entrepreneur that he or she has one hour and that the hour will consist of a 20-minute presentation and a 40-minute

LEARNING OBJECTIVE
10. Detail the parts of an oral presentation of a business plan.

question-and-answer period, the presentation shouldn't last more than 20 minutes. The presentation should be smooth and well-rehearsed. The slides should be sharp and not cluttered with material.

The entrepreneur should arrive at the appointment on time and be well prepared. If any audiovisual equipment is needed, the entrepreneur should be prepared to supply the equipment if the investor doesn't have it. These arrangements should be made before the meeting. The presentation should consist of plain talk and should avoid technical jargon. Start-up entrepreneurs may mistakenly spend too much time talking about the technology that will go into a new product or service and not enough time talking about the business itself. The most important issues to cover in the presentation and how to present them are shown in Table 4.5. This presentation format

TABLE 4.5   TWELVE POWERPOINT SLIDES TO INCLUDE IN AN INVESTOR PRESENTATION

Topic	Explanation
1. Title slide	Introduce the presentation with your company's name, the names of the founders, and the company logo if available.
2. Problem	Briefly state the problem to be solved or the need to be filled.
3. Solution	Explain how your firm will solve the problem or how it will satisfy the need to be filled.
4. Opportunity and target market	Articulate your specific target market. Talk about business and environmental trends that are providing your target market momentum.
5. Technology	This slide is optional but is normally included. Talk about your technology or any unusual aspects of your product or service. Don't talk in an overly technical manner. Make your descriptions easy to understand.
6. Competition	Explain specifically the firm's competitive advantage in the marketplace and how it will compete against more established competitors.
7. Marketing and sales	Describe your overall marketing strategy. Talk about your sales process. If you've administered a buying intentions survey or conducted other primary research regarding how people feel about your product, report the results here.
8. Management team	Describe your existing management team. Explain how the team came together and how their backgrounds and expertise are keys to the success of your firm. If you have a board of advisers or board of directors, briefly mention the key individuals involved. If you have gaps in your team, explain how and when they will be filled.
9. Financial projections	Briefly discuss the financials. Stress when the firm will achieve profitability, how much capital it will take to get there, and when its cash flow will break even. Use additional slides if needed to properly display your information, but don't go overboard.
10. Current status	Describe the current status of your firm in the context of the milestones you've achieved to date. Don't diminish the value of your accomplishments.
11. Financing sought	Lay out specifically how much financing you're seeking and how you'll use the money.
12. Summary	Bring the presentation to a close. Summarize the strongest points of your venture and your team. Solicit feedback from your audience.

Source: B. Barringer, *Preparing Effective Business Plans: An Entrepreneurial Approach,* 1st Edition, © 2009, pp. 242–253. Adapted by permission of Pearson Education, Inc. Upper Saddle River, NJ.

calls for the use of 12 slides. A common mistake entrepreneurs make is to prepare too many slides and then try to rush through them during a 20-minute presentation.

Questions and Feedback to Expect from Investors

Whether in the initial meeting or on subsequent occasions, an entrepreneur will be asked a host of questions by potential investors. The smart entrepreneur has a good idea of what to expect and is prepared for these queries. Because investors often come across as being very critical,[24] it is easy for an entrepreneur to get discouraged, particularly if the investor seems to be poking holes in every aspect of the business plan. The same dynamic typifies the question-and-answer sessions that follow presentations in business plan competitions. In fact, an investor who is able to identify weaknesses in a business plan or presentation does a favor for the entrepreneur. This is because the entrepreneur can take the investor's feedback to heart and use it to improve the business plan and/or the presentation.

In the first meeting, investors typically focus on whether a real opportunity exists and whether the management team has the experience and skills to pull off the venture. The investor will also try to sense whether the managers are highly confident in their own venture. The question-and-answer period is extremely important. Here investors are typically looking for how well entrepreneurs think on their feet and how knowledgeable they are about the business venture. Michael Rovner, a partner of Rob Adam's at AV Labs, put it this way: "We ask a lot of peripheral questions. We might not want answers—we just want to evaluate the entrepreneur's thought process."[25]

CHAPTER SUMMARY

1. A business plan is a written narrative that describes what a new business intends to accomplish and how it plans to achieve its goals.

2. For most ventures, the business plan is a dual-purpose document used both inside and outside the firm. Inside the firm, it helps the company develop a road map to follow in executing its strategies. Outside the firm, it acquaints potential investors and other stakeholders with the business opportunity the firm is pursuing and describes how the business will pursue that opportunity.

3. There are two primary audiences for a firm's business plan: a firm's employees and investors and other external stakeholders.

4. A summary business plan is 10 to 15 pages and works best for companies in the early stages of development. These companies don't have the information needed for a full business plan but may put together a summary business plan to see if potential investors are interested in their idea. A full business plan, typically 25 to 35 pages, spells out a company's

operations and plans in much more detail than a summary business plan and is the usual format for a business plan prepared for an investor. An operational business plan is usually prepared for an internal audience. It is 40 to 100 pages long and provides a blueprint for a company's operations.

5. The executive summary is a quick overview of the entire business plan and provides busy readers with everything they need to know about the distinctive nature of the new venture. In many instances, an investor will ask for a copy of a firm's executive summary and will request a copy of the full business plan only when the executive summary is sufficiently convincing.

6. A milestone is a significant or noteworthy event in the life of a business. Milestones are used to track progress (i.e., milestones completed) and to identify the most important steps remaining to be completed.

7. An industry analysis describes the industry a business will enter. The market analysis,

which is a separate section, breaks the industry analysis into segments and zeroes in on the specific segments (or target markets) to which the firm will seek to appeal.

8. The management team and company structure section of a business plan is critical. Many investors and others who read business plans look first at the executive summary and then go directly to the management team section to assess the strength of the people starting the firm.

9. The sources and uses of funds statement is a document that lays out specifically how much money a firm needs (if it is raising money), where the money will come from, and what it will be used for. An assumptions sheet is an explanation of the most critical assumptions that a business's financial analysis is based on.

10. The oral presentation of a business plan typically consists of 15 to 20 minutes of formal remarks, accompanied by approximately 12 PowerPoint slides, and 30 minutes of questions and answers. The presentation should be smooth and well-rehearsed. The slides should be sharp and not cluttered with material.

KEY TERMS

assumptions sheet, **157**	market segmentation, **150**	ratio analysis, **157**
board of advisers, **156**	marketing strategy, **153**	service prototype, **154**
board of directors, **156**	milestone, **150**	sources and uses of funds
business plan, **138**	mission statement, **149**	statement, **157**
competitor analysis, **150**	operating leverage, **153**	summary business
contribution margin, **152**	operational business plan, **144**	plan, **144**
costs of goods sold, **152**	organizational chart, **156**	tagline, **149**
executive summary, **148**	position, **150**	variable costs, **153**
fixed costs, **153**	pro forma (or projected)	virtual prototype, **154**
full business plan, **144**	financial statements, **157**	
market analysis, **150**	product prototype, **154**	

REVIEW QUESTIONS

1. What is a business plan? What are the advantages of preparing a business plan for a new venture? Explain your answer.

2. When is the appropriate time to write a business plan?

3. What are the two primary reasons for writing a business plan?

4. A business plan is often called a selling document for a new company. In what ways does a business plan provide a mechanism for a young company to present itself to potential investors, suppliers, business partners, and key job candidates?

5. It is often argued that the process of writing a business plan is as important as the plan itself, particularly for the top management team of a young firm. How is this so?

6. Who reads the business plan and what are they looking for?

7. Why is it necessary for a business plan to be realistic? How will investors typically react if they think a business plan is based on estimates and predictions rather than on careful thinking and facts? Where can entrepreneurs obtain facts to substantiate their business plans?

8. Why is it important for a business plan to follow a conventional structure rather than be highly innovative and creative?

9. What are the differences among a summary business plan, a full business plan, and an operational business plan?

10. Why should the executive summary, which is one of the first things that appears in a business plan, be written last?

11. What is the difference between the industry analysis and the market analysis sections of a business plan?

12. What is the difference between a concentrated and a fragmented industry? What type of industry is usually more open to new firms?

13. What is the purpose of "The Economics of the Business" section of a business plan?

14. If you're developing a completely new product or service, what type of information should

you include in your business plan regarding the status of the development efforts?

15. What is the purpose of the "Operations Plan" section of a business plan?

16. Why is the "Management Team and Company Structure" section of a business plan often touted as one of the most important sections?

17. What is the purpose of a sources and uses of funds statement?

18. What is the purpose of an assumptions sheet? Why is it important to include an assumptions sheet in a business plan's financial section?

19. What are the differences between historical financial statements and pro forma financial statements?

20. What is the number one rule in making an investor presentation?

APPLICATION QUESTIONS

1. Shelly Jacobs is a high school math teacher, who has created an iPhone app centered on engaging games that require high school students to use math to master the games. The idea is that the games are both appealing and will help students improve their math skills. Shelly has set aside the next two weekends to write a business plan. Do you think she's proceeding in the right manner?

2. Michael and Jill Simpson just left their jobs with Microsoft to start a business that will sell a new type of fax machine. They wrote a full business plan that they've asked you to review. When reading the plan, you noticed that several key sections start with the phrase "We believe . . . " Is any knowledgeable person who reads this plan going to know what "We believe . . . " really means? What's the problem with the statement "We believe . . . " in a business plan?

3. A good friend or yours, Kelly Ford, has decided to leave his corporate job to launch a private Web marketing firm. He is putting together his business plan and asks you, "I've read several books and articles about how to write a business plan, and there is one point I'm still confused about. Is a business plan written more for learning and discovering, or is it written more for pitching and selling?" What would you tell Kelly?

4. Spend some time looking at SmartSense, the focus of the "You Be the VC 3.2" feature. Name five things that SmartSense could have done in its feasibility analysis that would have been particularly helpful in supporting its business plan.

5. Suppose you have been asked by your local chamber of commerce to teach a two-hour workshop on how to write an effective business plan. The workshop will be attended by people who are thinking about starting their own business but don't currently have a business plan. Write a one-page outline detailing what you'd cover in the two-hour session.

6. John Brunner is a biochemist at a major university. He is thinking about starting a business to commercialize some animal vaccines on which he has been working. John just registered for a biotech investment conference in Boston. A number of venture capitalists are on the program, and John hopes to talk to them about his ideas. John hasn't written a business plan and doesn't see the need to write one. When asked about this issue, he told a colleague, "I can sell my ideas without the hassle of writing a business plan. Besides, I'll have plenty of time to talk to investors at the conference. If they need additional information, I can always write something up when I get home." Explain to John why his approach to the development of a business plan is unwise.

7. Imagine you just received an e-mail message from a friend. The message reads, "Just wanted to tell you that I just finished writing my business plan. I'm very proud of it. It's very comprehensive and is just over 100 pages. The executive summary alone is 9 pages. I plan to start sending it out to potential investors next week. Do you have any words of advice for me before I start sending it out? Be honest—I really want to get funding." How would you respond to your friend's request for feedback?

8. d.light, the subject of Case 4.2, is a for-profit social enterprise. What, if any, special factors should be kept in mind when writing a business plan for a for-profit social enterprise?

9. Write a mission statement and a tagline for Secret Recipe, the subject of the "You Be the VC 4.1" feature. What is the rationale for the mission statement and the tagline you wrote?

10. Segment the wind-generated power industry in a way that shows where Windspire Energy, the subject of the "You Be the VC 1.1" feature, is located in the industry. How does Windspire's awareness of the segment it is in help it develop its marketing strategy?

11. Heather Smith and Katie Jones are launching a personal finance software company. They conducted a thorough feasibility analysis, and are now working on their business plan. Heather just sent you an e-mail message. The subject line of the message read, "Are we jumping the gun?" In the message Heather tells you that the plan is going well, but she and Katie have had to rewrite certain sections of the plan several times because they keep coming across new information that impacts the way they'd like to structure their business. Heather wants to know if this is normal, or if they should have had a more definite picture of what their business would look like before they started writing the plan. What would you tell Heather?.

12. Bill Sharp, a friend of yours, has an idea for a new type of kitchen utensil, which will make it easier for busy people to scramble eggs in the morning. He showed his business plan to a local SCORE counselor who told Bill that the business plan was strong, but he needed to produce an actual prototype of his product before anyone would take his idea seriously. Bill can't understand why he needs to produce a prototype—it's easy to see on paper what the device will look like and how it will work. What would you tell Bill?

13. Laura Carroll is thinking about opening a high-end fashion boutique in an affluent suburb of Miami, Florida. She contacts an angel investor who she knows has invested in fashion boutiques before, and asked if he would read her business plan. She receives the following reply from the angel investor: "I'd be glad to read your plan, but you should know that when I examine business plans for fashion boutiques, the section that I focus on the most is 'The Economics of the Business.'" Why do you think the angel investor focuses intently on "The Economics of the Business" section when evaluating fashion boutiques? What, specifically, do you think he'll be looking for in Laura's plan?

14. Spend some time searching the Internet for sample business plans. What site, or sites, do you think provide access to the best sample plans? In what ways do sample business plans serve a useful purpose?

15. Suppose you are asked to serve as a judge for a local business plan competition. In preparing for the competition, the organizer has asked you to write a very brief article titled "What the Judges of Business Plan Competitions Look For" that she plans to pass along to the entrepreneurs who enter the competition. Write a 500- to 600-word article to accommodate this request.

YOU BE THE VC 4.1

Company: Secret Recipe Cakes and Café

Web: www.secretrecipe.com.my

Facebook: Secret Recipe Malaysia

Business Idea: A café chain that integrates both local and international flavors for food enthusiasts all over the world.

Pitch: Secret Recipe Cakes and Café is no stranger to food enthusiasts, particularly in Malaysia. It has become a household name since its first establishment in 1997. With quality cakes, fusion food, and distinctive service as its core strategy, Secret Recipe has already developed a winning recipe for success. It is one of the leading and largest café chains in the country with more than 160 outlets in Malaysia serving a variety of dishes and desserts that appeal to a wide range of customers. Serving more than 20 types of fusion food, 40 different types of cake creations, and an assortment of pastries, designer ice creams, and beverages,

Secret Recipe has won the hearts of many Malaysians and has successfully established its brand name in the region.

The Secret Recipe business formula has also been successfully replicated internationally with more outlets located in Thailand, Singapore, Indonesia, the Philippines, China, Pakistan, and Brunei. In 14 years, Secret Recipe has expanded to a network of more than 250 cafés. In 2010 it began to expand into Australia and there are plans to open another 50 outlets in the country within the next five years.

Building a sustainable business with a strong brand was not an easy task for Secret Recipe. To be different, it had to identify features of its brand that could extend beyond one store or one country. Differentiation, innovation, adaptability, research and development, consistency, identity, and brand promise were the key ingredients that have allowed Secret Recipe to enjoy worldwide success. Secret Recipe is one of the most successful home-grown café chains in the country, having won several awards including the Homegrown Franchise of the Year, International Franchisor of the Year, Franchise of the Year Best Sales Growth Award, and Best Brand Food & Beverage Café Award. Moreover, Secret Recipe has also grabbed several international awards such as the International Franchisor of the Year Award 2007 in Singapore, Indonesia's Best Restaurant Award 2006, Best Casual Dining Restaurant of the Year 2007/2008 in the Philippines, and Philippine Tatler's Best Restaurant 2008.

Secret Recipe is not only a café that offers a wide variety of cakes but it also offers a flexible menu with different items available in different countries. However, to identify itself as a truly Malaysian brand, a customer will be able to find Malaysian all-time favorites like nasi lemak (rice with spicy gravy) and mee goreng (fried noodles) in some of the overseas outlets as well. Secret Recipe will continue striving to surpass its own accomplishments and aims to be recognized as a leader in the industry both locally and globally.

Q&A: Based on the material covered in this chapter, what questions would you ask the firm's founders before making your funding decision? What answers would satisfy you?

Decision: If you had to make your decision on just the information provided in the pitch and on the company's Web site, would you fund this company? Why or why not?

YOU BE THE VC 4.2

Company: PharmaJet

Web: www.pharmajet.com

Business Idea: Administer injections using a needle-free injection system.

Pitch: Administering injections is an integral part of both preventative health care and the treatment of sickness and disease. Traditional injections use a needle to penetrate the patient's skin and insert the vaccine or medicine. While this has been a staple practice in medicine for decades, it has drawbacks. Patients of all ages have a fear of needles, and for some the fear is so acute they avoid necessary injections. Needles are problematic for health care workers. Their sharp points require special containers to dispose of safely, and all health care workers worry about receiving an inadvertent needle "stick," which may contaminate them with someone else's blood and as a result, potentially someone else's disease.

In one fell swoop, PharmaJet addresses these problems with the development of a simple, safe needle-free injection system that's cleared for sale in the United States. Instead of using a needle, it delivers intramuscular or subcutaneous injections through a high velocity fluid jet that penetrates the skin in one-third of a second. The device is spring powered, so there are no gas canisters to dispose of. Many of the earlier iterations of needleless syringes used bottled gas to power the syringe, which was costly and cumbersome. The PharmaJet system is environmentally friendly in that two of its four parts are consumable and the other two are reused. The consumable components consist of the needle-free syringe and a filling adaptor. The reusable components consist of the injector and a reset station. The only component that

comes in contact with the patient's skin is the needle-free syringe, which is disposed of and replaced after each use. While a PharmaJet injection isn't painless, it's gentler than a needle stick for most patients. For most patients, the pain is analogous to being snapped by a small rubber band.

An ancillary benefit of the PharmaJet system is that there are an estimated 16 billion needle injections given each year in developing countries. In many instances, needles are reused. Because of this practice, the World Health Organization estimates that 50 percent of needle-syringe injections are unsafe, and that 21 million people contract hepatitis, HIV, and other diseases each year from previously used needles. Once used, the PharmaJet syringe auto-disables and cannot be reused. This feature may make it particularly attractive to nongovernmental organizations (NGOs) and other organizations that provide health care assistance in developing countries. The PharmaJet system may also be attractive in select niche markets. For example, detention facilities and prisons struggle with the use of needle syringes because needles are contraband in a detention setting.

Q&A: Based on the material covered in this chapter, what questions would you ask the firm's founders before making your funding decision? What answers would satisfy you?

Decision: If you had to make your decision on just the information provided in the pitch and on the company's Web site, would you fund this company? Why or why not?

CASE 4.1

Kazoo Toys: You Can Compete Against the Big Guys— If You Have the Right Plan

Web: www.kazootoys.com
Facebook: KazooToys.com

Bruce R. Barringer, *Oklahoma State University*
R. Duane Ireland, *Texas A&M University*

Introduction

There is no denying it. It's tough for an independent toy store to compete against Walmart, Target, Toys "R" Us, and other large retailers (including online giant retailer Amazon.com) selling products that entertain children and adults alike. So how is it that Kazoo Toys, an independent toy store in Denver, Colorado, is thriving? It's thriving because of two things—the firm has a doggedly determined entrepreneur at the helm and it has a good business plan. After you read about Kazoo Toys, you'll nod your head and think to yourself, yup—that's a good plan!

Diana Nelson

In the early 1990s, Diana Nelson left the corporate world with the intention of spending more time with her two young sons. In 1998, she decided to reenter the workforce, but this time as an entrepreneur. Rather than starting a company from scratch, she set out looking for a business to buy. After ruling out fast food and flower shops, she came across a toy store named Kazoo & Company. She saw untapped potential in the store and decided to buy it. It wasn't easy to get the money together to close the deal. To finance the purchase, she cashed out her retirement accounts, put $25,000 on credit cards, borrowed money from her father, and set up a $500,000 SBA-guaranteed bank loan. "I gambled everything to buy a toy store," she says. The actions Nelson took to finance her venture demonstrate the courage that characterizes virtually all entrepreneurs.

From the outset, Nelson had no illusions that owning a toy store would be easy. When she bought Kazoo, independent toy stores were being tattered to pieces by Walmart, Toys "R" Us, and other large retailers. So, she knew that the only way to beat them was to outthink them. In this regard, Nelson saw her challenge as that of designing and then implementing a business plan that would make a small toy store competitive. Here's how she did it.

Kazoo's Business Plan

The essence of Kazoo's business plan was to not try to be like Walmart or Toys "R" Us. Instead, Nelson set out to build a business that would offer unique products and services to its clientele. The mistake that many small businesses make, in Nelson's thinking, is that they set themselves up to compete against the chains (e.g., Toys "R" Us) or a big-box stores (Walmart) by trying to duplicate what they do. In these instances, the best an entrepreneurial venture can expect to do is to come close to being as effective at what the "big boys" are skilled at doing. Instead of falling into that trap, Nelson took Kazoo in a different direction. "We changed our whole merchandise mix to not carry the same product (as the nationwide chains did)," she recalls, "so price competition isn't an issue." As a result of this strategy, Kazoo doesn't carry Mattel, Crayola, or Fisher-Price. Instead, the store sells unique items like Gotz Dolls from Germany and a wide range of educational toys. The key to making this strategy work, Nelson found, is to build strong relationships with vendors. To help do this, Nelson invites many of Kazoo's vendors to demo and test new products in her store. Doing this gives Kazoo first crack at many of the new products that its vendors make. While they are in her store, the vendors also tip their hand from time to time regarding what the big retailers are buying. This gives Nelson and Kazoo a heads-up about what not to buy.

In 1999, Nelson opened a Yahoo! store online. The site sold the same type of toys being sold in the store. Over time, Nelson increased her Internet prowess and now her Kazoo Toys Web site sells many of the same products that are sold in the store, along with additional products that are drop shipped by vendors. At one point in the early 2000s, Nelson considered franchising Kazoo but decided to pass on the idea. Instead, she felt it was better to preserve Kazoo's "destination" image and build the e-commerce site. Now, with nearly 15 years of experience as Kazoo's owner under her belt, Nelson has decided to pursue franchising, and Kazoo & Company will begin franchising at some point in the near future.

Points of Differentiation

Through all of this, Kazoo has established strong points of differentiation between itself and its much larger competitors, which has been the heart of Kazoo's business plan from the beginning. Along with carrying different products than its competitors, Kazoo is different from Walmart, Toys "R" Us, and other large toy retailers in the following ways.

1. The company welcomes professionals, like speech therapists, to bring their patients into the store, to play with them and identify specific toys that might help them progress in their treatments. Observing professionals work with their patients (i.e., young children that have some type of disability) also helps Kazoo's staff know what to recommend when a parent comes in looking for a similar solution.
2. Kazoo's store design is unique. While the store itself is still fairly small, it is further broken down into smaller, more intimate departments. "When a particular consumer goes into a Toys "R" Us it has departments, but it's like a big warehouse," Nelson explains. "Here, it's very small. It's intimate, but it's also departmentalized, so you actually have a Playmobil department, and you have a Thomas the Tank Engine department."
3. The company focuses intently on customer service, from free gift wrapping to free parking. So whether it's a baby crying or a customer who can't find an item in the store, the company works hard to accommodate its customers in every way possible.
4. The company's specialty is selling educational, nonviolent toys, for birth to 12-year-old children. In fact, Kazoo's focus on selling toys that meet this criterion has won it a loyal clientele.
5. The inventory in the store is freshened up frequently, so regular customers see different toys each time they come into the store. "If you think about your regular customer, they don't want to see the same stuff on the shelf all the time, so we're always changing our inventory and our mix of what we do," Nelson said.

Kazoo's business plan and its sharp execution have paid off. Business is growing, and the company was named the number one toy store in Denver by Denver's *5280* magazine for 2002, 2003, 2004, 2005, 2006, 2007, 2008, and 2009. In 2010, Kazoo Toys made the *Inc.* 500 list of one of the 500 fastest-growing private companies in America.

Challenges Ahead

In spite of how well Kazoo & Company has done, the firm faces multiple challenges. For one, many of the manufacturers of specialty toys, which have been Kazoo's bread-and-butter since Nelson bought the firm in 1998, are now selling into broader channels. Thus, the toys that at one time only Kazoo and other specialty toy stores could get their hands on will be popping up in other types of stores. Economic pressures also tend to hit specialty retailers particularly hard. Tough economic times drive more people to Walmart and Target as opposed to specialty stores.

As far as Diana Nelson is concerned, she is very content with her decision to become an entrepreneur and the lifestyle that accompanies that decision as the owner of Kazoo & Company. Commenting on how her young sons fared over the years with her decision to buy a toy store, she said, "Their friends think—how cool are they that their mom has a toy store and a toy business." How cool indeed!

Discussion Questions

1. To what extent do you sense that Diana Nelson got up to speed quickly on the dynamics of the toy industry when she took over Kazoo & Company in 1998? What impact would it have had on the ultimate success of Kazoo if Nelson had spent more time initially focused on the specifics of her business (i.e., store layout, hiring personnel, placing ads in local newspapers, writing press releases, setting up the accounting system, and so on) rather than gaining a complete understanding of the toy industry as part of her work to carefully develop a business plan?
2. When she first bought the store, do you think that Nelson could have convinced an investor that Kazoo & Company could successfully compete against the likes of giants such as Walmart, Target, Toys "R" Us, and Amazon.com? If not, who needed to believe that the business plan would work? How does an entrepreneur's level of belief in his or her own business plan affect how successful the business is, particularly in the early years?
3. Based on the information contained in the case, write the one-page executive summary of Kazoo's original business plan.
4. What is drop shipping? What are the advantages and the risks for a company like Kazoo & Company to engage in drop-shipping arrangements with its vendors?

Application Questions

1. If you had taken over Kazoo & Company in 1998 instead of Diana Nelson, would you have thought of all the things that Nelson did? Would you have been able to write Kazoo's original business plan? If your answer is *no* to these questions, what steps can you take now to better prepare yourself for the day that you might become an entrepreneur? Make your answer as specific as possible.
2. If you decided to buy a specialty store that competes against Walmart, Target, or another big-box retailer, what type of store would you like to own? How would you differentiate your store from your larger competitors?

Sources: Kazoo & Company homepage, www.kazootoys.com (accessed February 15, 2011); B. Ruggiero, "Kazoo & Company Reaches Top 5…Again," *TD Monthly*, June 2005; J. M. Webb, "When the Tools of the Trade Are Toys," *TD Monthly*, March 2006.

CASE 4.2

d.light: How Bringing Its Business Plan to Life Helped a Social Enterprise Get Off to a Strong Start

Web: dlightdesign.com
Twitter: delight_design
Facebook: d.light design

Bruce R. Barringer, *Oklahoma State University*

R. Duane Ireland, *Texas A&M University*

Introduction

Imagine the following. You're in the audience of a business plan competition. The next team up to present is d.light, a for-profit social enterprise that plans to bring light to people without access to reliable electricity. Two young men introduce themselves as the founders of d.light, and say they're going to start their presentation with a demonstration. The lights go out. In a few seconds, you see a dim light at the front of the room, and smell smoke and burning kerosene. After about 30 seconds, your eyes start to water and it becomes slightly uncomfortable to breathe. The lights switch back on and the smoke clears. The young men apologize for the lack of light and smoke, but say the demonstration was staged to illustrate a point. Around 1.5 billion people, or more than one fifth of the world's population, have no access to electricity, and about a billion more have an unreliable or intermittent supply. A large share of these people use kerosene to light their homes at night. Kerosene fumes are extremely unhealthy, even fatal. In fact, the United Nations estimates that kerosene fumes kill 1.5 million people per year, and cause countless health complications for others.

Sam Goldman and the Origins of d.light

The scene described here actually took place—several times. It's the way Sam Goldman and Ned Tozen, the cofounders of d.light, introduced the company at business plan competitions and when they pitched investors. d.light is an international consumer products company serving "base of the pyramid" consumers who don't have access to reliable electricity. Although d.light technically started in a class at Stanford University, its beginning can be traced to Sam Goldman's youth and early adulthood. Growing up, Goldman's parents worked for the United States Agency for International Development (USAID), a government agency that provides economic and humanitarian assistance in countries across the globe. Goldman lived in Pakistan, Peru, India, Canada, and several other countries. As a young adult, while working for the Peace Corps, he lived for four years in a West African village that had no electricity. A neighbor boy was badly burned in a kerosene fire, an event that deeply impacted Goldman. At one point during his time in the village, Goldman was given a battery-powered LED headlamp, and was struck by the dramatic difference that simply having light at night can make in a person's life. He could now cook, read, and do things at night that were unimaginable without the benefits reliable lighting provides.

Impacted by this experience, Goldman sought out a graduate program that would provide him the opportunity to start thinking about creating a business to take light to people without access to reliable electricity. He landed at Stanford, which was starting a program in social enterprise. A pivotal class was Jim Patelli's 2006–2007 Entrepreneurial Design course. The class was divided into teams, and each team was challenged to address a significant issue in the developing world. Goldman was teamed up with Ned Tozen, a business classmate, and two engineering students, Erica Estrade and Xian Wu. The team tackled the problem of light for people without access to reliable electricity, and developed a rough prototype of a portable LED light that could be recharged via solar power. That spring, the team traveled to Burma for the purpose of going into villages that didn't have access to electricity to introduce their device. Villagers told them they spent up to 40 percent of their income on kerosene. When shown how their crude prototype could provide light at night and be recharged during the day simply by deploying small solar panels on their homes, the villagers were so taken that one women actually wept. According to one account of the team's trip, in one village the local police confiscated the prototypes. They, too, needed light at night.

Design and Distribution

After completing the Entrepreneurial Design course, the teammates headed their separate directions for the summer. In the fall, they reunited, and determined to continue to work on their business concept. The concept of using solar power to recharge portable lights in poor rural areas wasn't new. In fact, it had been tried many times. The problem, in Goldman and his team's estimation, was a combination of design and distribution. Previous models relied either on NGOs and governments "giving" fairly expensive lights to people without access to electricity, which they couldn't afford to replace when used up or if broken, or commercial enterprises buying extremely inexpensive lights in China and exporting them to Africa and elsewhere, where they performed poorly. It was clear to Goldman that neither of these models was sustainable.

So Goldman and his team, driven by the possibility of changing literally millions of people's lives throughout the world, recruited talented engineers and distribution experts, who worked on a near pro bono basis, to help with the project. The goal was to produce a solar-powered portable LED light that was exactly what rural villagers needed—nothing more and nothing less. It also had to be cheap enough that villagers could afford it yet produce sufficient margins for d.light to be profitable. The decision was made early on that d.light would be a for-profit company. The company's goal was not to impact 100,000 people or a million people but to impact hundreds of millions of people. Goldman and his team knew that their lofty ambitions would take cash and additional R&D efforts, which would require private-sector investment capital.

During this period, which covered the summer of 2007 until early 2008, Goldman and his cofounders continued traveling to remote areas for the purpose of obtaining feedback about their prototype. During Christmas break, instead of traveling home to see his family, Goldman was in the middle of Miyamairi doing research. The team thinned some in early 2008, with Goldman, Tozan, and Wu continuing. d.light was now up-and-running and opened its first international offices in India, Shenzhen, China, and Tanzania.

Business Plan Competitions and Investor Presentations

One thing Goldman stresses during talks about d.light is the instrumental role that the company's business plan played in helping the company take shape and in raising investment capital. Early on, d.light entered several business plan competitions. It the spring of 2007, it took second place in the University of California, Berkley's Social Venture Competition and won first prize at Stanford's Social E-Challenge. A big breakthrough happened in May 2007 when the team claimed the $250,000 first prize in the prestigious Draper Fisher Jurvetson Venture Challenge competition. This money provided seed funding for much of the work that was completed during the summer and fall of 2007.

What's particularly interesting is Goldman's reflections on why his company was so successful in business plan competitions and eventually investor presentations—reflections that are instructive for all young businesses. There are six reasons, shown in the table that follows.

Collectively, these attributes presented d.light as an organization with a compelling idea, a strong team, large markets, a product focus and a coherent, resolute, and extremely admirable vision for the future.

d.light Today

Today, d.light is fully up-and-running. In 2008, the company reached about 100,000 people in eight countries. Its numbers now exceed one million units sold in 37 countries, and d.light projects strong growth for the

Six Key Reasons d.light Was Successful in Business Plan Competitions

Told Stories and Showed Pictures	While many teams enter business plan competitions with impressive PowerPoint slides and bullet points, d.light focused on telling stories and showing pictures. They showed photographs of rural villagers using their device, and shared their testimonials. In one interview, Goldman remarked that he was confident that no matter how many plans or pitches a group of judges or investors heard during a day, he was confident they remembered d.light's presentation.
All In	The founders were fully committed to d.light. They passed on corporate jobs and focused on d.light full time. Along with talking the talk, they also walked the walk. Instead of saying that they planned to travel to remote villages to test their device, they just went out and did it. Some of the trips came before the business plan presentations.
Right Team	d.light put together a strong team, with a balance of business and engineering expertise. The team was well-suited for launching a global initiative. Goldman had lived overseas the majority of his life, in places like India and Pakistan. Other team members had demonstrated that they had no inhibitions about traveling to remote villages to talk about their device.
Big Market	d.light was tackling a large market, which investors like. To make their financials work, the team would have to scale the business and sell millions of units. While the challenge was great, so was the potential payoff.
Product Focus	The company iterated its device multiple times before settling on its first solar-powered portable LED light, called the Nova. The Nova sold for a U.S. equivalent of around $25. Early feedback indicated that the price was still too high, so more iterations took place.
Strong Vision	Although d.light was a social enterprise, it unashamedly presented itself as a for-profit venture. The team was resolute that getting to scale could only be accomplished via private sector capital. d.light also measured its success by the number of families it positively impacted. This sense of purpose and vision permeated the organization.

(continued)

Archivo Particular GDA Photo Service/Newscom

Indian mother of three
with her d.light Kiran
solar-powered lamp.

future. Its first product was the Nova, which was a solar-powered portable LED light that sold for a U.S. equivalent of about $25. It's most popular device is now the Kiran, which at U.S. equivalent $10 has been touted as the world's most affordable portable solar light. It has a life of 50,000 hours, and if used to replace kerosene, can pay for itself in just four months. In one study in rural India, having a Kiran LED light in the home increased the study time for school-aged children two to three hours per day. d.light continues to strength its distribution strategy. One strategy that has worked well is to employ "rural entrepreneurs" to sell the product. d.light likes to employ indigenous personnel, who know the local customs, people, and language, to sell its product on a commission basis. In India, d.light has established partnerships with NGOs and microfinance organizations. It has also scored $6 million in investment capital from U.S. and Indian investors.

Challenges Ahead

As it continues to grow, d.light faces a host of challenges. The primary challenge, as it continues to enter new areas, is to convince hesitant customers with little extra income to invest in unfamiliar technology. Although kerosene has many harmful side effects, it is an integral part of many villagers' lives. Another challenge is managing the tension between growth and profitability. d.light can actually accelerate profitability by slowing growth. Yet slowing growth is counter to its overall mission of reaching as many people as possible. Finally, while d.light's most basic lantern costs $10, the price will have to fall below $5 to make it universally affordable, according to a study by the International Finance Corporation, an arm of the World Bank. d.light has not yet reached this milestone.

Discussion Questions

1. Of the six reasons listed in the case that d.light was successful in business plan competitions, which reason do you find the most compelling? Explain your answer.
2. If you were the founders of d.light, what would your marketing strategy be? How would you educate people in remote areas about the existence of your device and the benefits of purchasing it?
3. Why do you think the problem of bringing light to people who don't have access to reliable electricity isn't being tackled in a meaningful way by a large lighting company, like General Electric? What qualities do Sam Goldman and his team have that will help them solve the problem of providing light to the 2.5 billion people in the world who don't have access to electricity or only have access to intermittent electricity, which General Electric or a similar large company is unlikely to muster?
4. Why do you think Sam Goldman goes out of his way to talk about the importance of d.light's business plan? In what ways do you think having a meticulously crafted business plan helped d.light?

Application Questions

1. Make a list of the ways in which Sam Goldman's passions and life experiences made him the ideal founder for d.light. Then, make a list of your most distinct passions and life experiences. Study the list. Is there a potential venture for which you might be the most ideal founder?
2. Find an example of an entrepreneurial company that is addressing a significant issue in the developing world (excluding companies featured in the "You Be the VC" features in this book). Briefly relate that company's story. What similarities, if any, do you see between the company you're reporting on and d.light?

Sources: d.light homepage, www.dlightdesign.com (accessed February 15, 2011); J. Wiener, "d.light's Lofty Goals Meet Practical Challenges in India," *Stanford Business Magazine*, May 24, 2010; Sheela Sethuraman and Sam Goldman, "Lighting the Way to Economic Development," *Social Innovation Conversations Podcast*, *http://sic.conversationsnetwork.org/shows/detail4238.html*, September 8, 2009.

ENDNOTES

1. MIT Enterprise Forum Arab Business Competition homepage, www.mitarabcompetition.com; Ebenezer, "Rana El Chemaitelly Itani Had the Will and Initiative and Then Won US $50,000 from MIT," *WowElle*, http://wowelle.com/2010/11/09/rana-shmaitelly-itani-had-the-will-and-the-initiative-and-then-won-us-50000-from-mit-to-engineer-her-little-dream/ (accessed September 5, 2011, originally posted November 9, 2010); R. El Chemaitelly, "The Little Engineer," www.medventures.biz/upload/LIB-LITTLE.pdf (accessed September 5, 2011, originally posted 2010).

2. S. Mariotti and C. Glackin, *Entrepreneurship: Starting and Operating a Small Business* (Upper Saddle River, NJ; Prentice Hall, 2010).

3. Wells Fargo, "How Much Money Does It Take to Start a Small Business?" Wells Fargo/Gallup Small Business Index, August 15, 2006.

4. J. Liao and W. Gartner, "The Influence of Pre-Venture Planning on New Venture Creation," *Journal of Small Business Strategy* 18, no. 2 (Fall/Winter 2008): 21–30.

5. J. Brinckmann, D. Grichnik, and D. Kapsa, "Should Entrepreneurs Plan or Just Storm the Castle? A Meta-analysis on Contextual Factors Impacting the Business Planning-Performance Relationship in Small Firms," *Entrepreneurship Theory and Practice* 25, no. 1 (January 2010): 24–40; K. Shah, "SMEs Need to Beef Up Business Plans, Warns Lotus," *Financial Advisor*, FT Business, October 2, 2008.

6. "Meet Lindsey Wieber and Gwen Whiting," Ladies Who Launch, www.ladieswholaunch.com (accessed July 20, 2007, originally posted January 16, 2007).

7. A. Burke, S. Fraser, and F. J. Greene, "The Multiple Effects of Business Planning on New Venture Performance," *Journal of Management Studies* 47, no. 3 (May 2010): 391–415; P. Kennedy, "20 Reasons Why You Need a Business Plan," growthink, www.growthink.com, April 9, 2008 (accessed December 1, 2008).

8. J. Mullins and R. Komisar, "Measuring Up: Dashboarding for Innovators," *Business Strategy Review* 22, no. 1 (2011): 7–16; D. Kennedy and M. Hughes, *Smart Business, Stupid Business* (Garden City, NY: Morgan Jones Publishers, 2010).

9. P. Mack-Turner, *What You Should Know before Starting a Business* (Bloomington, IN: AuthorHouse, 2010); Deloitte & Touche, *Writing an Effective Business Plan*, 4th ed., 2003.

10. P. Nadeau, "Venture Capital Investment Selection: Do Patents Attract Investors?" *Strategic Change* 19, no. 7/8 (2010): 325–42; G. Kawasaki, *The Art of the Start* (New York: Portfolio, 2004).

11. T. Needleman, "Business Plan Software Remains an Important App," *Accounting Today* 21, no. 3 (2007): 16.

12. "How to Present Your Business Plan," *Inc.*, www.inc.com, March 5, 2010; J. L. Nesheim, *The Power of Unfair Advantage* (New York: Free Press, 2005).

13. Personal conversation with Michael Heller, January 20, 2002.

14. G. Cassar, "Are Individuals Entering Self-Employment Overly Optimistic? An Empirical Test of Plans and Projections on Nascent Entrepreneur Expectations," *Strategic Management Journal* 31, no. 8 (August 2010): 822–40; *Entrepreneur's Toolkit* (Boston: Harvard Business School Publishing, 2005).

15. B. Feld, "Should You Hire Someone to Write Your Business Plan?" *Ask the VC*, www.askthevc.com/blog/archives/2007/02/should-you-hire.php (accessed November 12, 2008).

16. C. Tang, Interview with Calvin Tang, nPost homepage, www.npost.com (accessed November 15, 2008).

17. J. W. Mullins, "Voices: What to Do before You Write a Business Plan," *Business Strategy Review* 21, no. 4 (2010): 92–93.

18. U.S. Small Business Administration, "Business Plan Executive Summary," www.sba.gov. (accessed March 3, 2010); S. Rogers, *The Entrepreneur's Guide to Finance and Business* (New York: McGraw-Hill, 2003).

19. *Entrepreneur's Toolkit* (Boston: Harvard Business School Publishing, 2005).

20. B. Ford and J. Pruitt, *The Ernst & Young Business Plan Guide* (New York: Ernst & Young: 2007).

21. R. Rico, M. Sanchez-Manzanares, F. Gil, and C. Gibson, "Team Implicit Coordination Processes: A Team Knowledge-Based Approach," *Academy of Management Review* 33, no. 1 (2008): 163–84; K. Eisenhardt and C. Shoonhoven, "Organizational Growth: Linking Founding Team Strategy, Environment, and Growth Among U.S. Semiconductor Ventures, 1978–1988," *Administrative Science Quarterly* 35 (1990): 504–29.

22. B. Thomsen, *90 Days to Success as a Small Business Owner* (Cincinnati: Cengage Learning, 2012).

23. W. M. Pride, R. J. Hughes, and J. R. Kapoor, *Business*, 11th ed. (Cincinnati: Cengage Learning, 2012).

24. D. Cumming, D. Schmidt, and U. Waiz, "Legality and Venture Capital Governance around the World," *Jour-nal of Business Venturing* 25, no. 1 (2010): 54–72.

25. R. Adams, *A Good Hard Kick in the Ass* (New York: Crown Books, 2002), 150.

Getting Personal *with* ELEMENT BARS

Founder:

JONATHAN MILLER
MBA, Northwestern University, 2008

Dialogue *with*
Jonathan Miller

WHAT I DO WHEN I'M NOT WORKING
Woodworking, golf, flying

CURRENTLY IN MY SMARTPHONE
The Rolling Stones, Howlin' Wolf, Phish

MY ADVICE FOR NEW ENTREPRENEURS
You're never the number one with an idea—and that's OK. Check out the competition, buy their product, and figure out how you can do it better.

FIRST ENTREPRENEURIAL EXPERIENCE
Back in middle school, I wrote and sold games for my TI programmable calculator. We called the company Mildewsoft.

BEST ADVICE I'VE RECEIVED
Ready. Fire. Aim. You often have to take action in entrepreneurship before you have all of the facts. The trick is to be able to correct along the way.

MY FAVORITE SMARTPHONE APP
Chase app—I can direct deposit checks right from the phone.

CHAPTER 5

Industry and Competitor *Analysis*

OPENING PROFILE

ELEMENT BARS
Occupying a Unique Position in a Difficult Industry—and Thriving

Web: www.elementbars.com
Twitter: elementbars
Facebook: Element Bars

It was one of those lucky coincidences that sometimes happen to people. Jonathan Miller started tinkering with making energy bars in his kitchen. At the same time, his wife, Jennifer, was working with Maria Sutanto who was doing the same thing. Jennifer put Jonathan and Maria together, and they swapped stories about how to make energy bars at home. Both were energy bar eaters, but were dissatisfied with the surprisingly unhealthy ingredients contained in many of the energy bars on the market. Eventually one thing led to another and Jonathan and Maria cofounded Element Bars, a new energy bar company.

That's the short version of the story. But as is almost always the case, a great deal of thought was put into the type of company Element Bars would become and how it would position itself in the energy bar industry—before the company was launched.

Miller and Sutanto met in December 2007. At that time, Miller was an MBA student at Northwestern University's Kellogg School of Management, while Sutanto was a PhD candidate in molecular nutrition at the University of Chicago. That combination of expertise, marketing for Miller (his area of specialty within the MBA), and nutrition for Sutanto, led to Element Bars' basic value proposition. The company would offer fresh nutritious energy bars that could be "customized" by its customers. Sales would be made online and through special arrangements with businesses like spas and fitness centers that wanted to brand their own specialty energy bars.

Here's how the company was set up. Customers log onto Element Bars' Web site, and in five steps can "build" their own energy bar. They are first asked to pick a base texture, with options such as Chewy, Crispy, and Datey. They then add their choice of fruits, nuts, sweets, and boosts (such as whey protein, Omega-3, or fiber) to create their customized bar. A nutrition label on the right portion of the screen changes as ingredients are added, so the creator can see how different ingredients affect the calories or the grams of saturated fat in the bar. After the bar is built, the final step is for the customer to name the bar

LEARNING OBJECTIVES

After studying this chapter you should be ready to:

1. Explain the purpose of an industry analysis.

2. Identify the five competitive forces that determine industry profitability.

3. Explain the role of "barriers to entry" in creating disincentives for firms to enter an industry.

4. Identify the nontraditional barriers to entry that are especially associated with entrepreneurial firms.

5. List the four industry-related questions to ask before pursuing the idea for a firm.

6. Identify the five primary industry types and the opportunities they offer.

7. Explain the purpose of a competitor analysis.

8. Identify the three groups of competitors a new firm will face.

9. Describe ways a firm can ethically obtain information about its competitors.

10. Describe the reasons for completing a competitive analysis grid.

whatever he or she wants. Once the order is placed, the bar is made and is shipped in just a few days. Bars run $36 for a pack of 12, though shoppers can get a $6 discount if they purchase bars that are listed under the popular section of the site. A helpful twist—while users are free to create any customized energy bar that appeals to them, the site will warn them if one of their choices will result in a poor outcome in terms of taste or texture.

Shortly after Element Bars launched, Sutanto decided to focus on her academic career and Jonathan Kelley, a third cofounder, was added to the Element Bars team. The novel way the bars are made and sold, combined with the "freshness" factor of shipping the bars just a few days after they're made, describes Element Bars' position in the $3 billion per year energy bar industry. For discerning customers, this position is unique. Many of the best-known energy bars are made in large lots and pass through multiple hands before they're placed on store shelves. As a result, these bars are typically several months old before consumed, and taste suffers. Miller and his team believe that Element Bars' approach produces not only a more nutritious energy bar but a better tasting bar, product characteristics for which consumers are willing to pay.

Along with selling customizable energy bars via the Internet, Element Bars sells direct to specialty retailers who want to create their own branded energy bars. The problem that fitness centers, for example, have selling well-known energy bars, like Clif Bars, is that if they charge a premium price their members will quickly figure out that they can get the same energy bar at a local grocery store for less. Element Bars has an advantage in that it can customize an energy bar for a fitness center that the center can brand as its own, and sell at a premium price. The fact that the members can't get the same energy bar anywhere else reduces their sensitivity to a higher price.

Element Bars envisions a bright future, for two reasons. First, while its Web site is easy to navigate and the five-step process of building your own energy bar looks simple, the technology behind the Web site wasn't simple to create. There are trade secrets embedded in the functionality of the site, along with how the bars are baked and shipped in such an expedient manner. The company believes sufficient barriers to entry are in place so that it has a shot at becoming the premier provider of fresh, customizable energy bars in the United States. Second, the energy bar market has tremendous upside potential. While nearly 100 percent of Americans are familiar with what energy bars are, only about 15 percent of the population regularly buys them. As a result, to gain sales, Element Bars doesn't necessarily have to take sales from larger competitors. It can appeal to the growing population of health-conscious consumers to bring new customers into the energy bar industry.

Element Bars is a success in part because of Jonathan Miller's ability to analyze the energy bar industry and precisely position Element Bars within it. In this chapter, we'll look at industry analysis and competitor analysis. The first section of the chapter considers **industry analysis**, which is business research that focuses on the potential of an industry. An **industry** is a group of firms producing a similar product or service, such as music, fitness drinks, or electronic games. Once it is determined that a new venture is feasible in regard to the industry and the target market in which it will compete, a more in-depth analysis is needed to learn the ins and outs of the industry the firm plans to enter. This analysis helps a firm determine if the niche or target markets it identified during its feasibility analysis are accessible and which ones represent the best point of entry for the new firm.

We focus on competitor analysis in the second section of the chapter. A **competitor analysis** is a detailed evaluation of a firm's competitors. Once a firm decides to enter an industry and chooses a market in which to compete, it must gain an understanding of its competitive environment. We'll look at how a firm identifies its competition and the importance of completing a competitive analysis grid.

INDUSTRY ANALYSIS

When studying an industry, an entrepreneur must answer three questions before pursuing the idea of starting a firm. First, is the industry accessible—in other words, is it a realistic place for a new venture to enter? Second, does the industry contain markets that are ripe for innovation or are underserved? Third, are there positions in the industry that will avoid some of the negative attributes of the industry as a whole? It is useful for a new venture to think about its **position** at both the company level and the product or service level. At the company level, a firm's position determines how the company is situated relative to its competitors, as discussed in Chapter 4. For example Windspire Energy, the subject of the "You Be the VC 1.1" feature, has positioned itself as a maker of wind power turbines that home owners and businesses can buy to produce electricity. Individual units are priced at $9,000 to $12,000 fully installed, and each unit has a fairly modest physical footprint. This is a much different position than GE Wind Energy, which manufactures and sells the tall wind turbines that you see in some parts of the United States. GE Wind Energy units are up to 350 feet tall, have a fairly large physical footprint, and are sold primarily to utility companies.

LEARNING OBJECTIVE
1. Explain the purpose of an industry analysis.

The importance of knowing the competitive landscape, which is what an industry is, may have been first recognized in the fourth century B.C. by Sun-tzu, a Chinese philosopher. Reputedly he wrote *The Art of War* to help generals prepare for battle. However, the ideas in the book are still used today to help managers prepare their firms for the competitive wars of the marketplace. The following quote from Sun-tzu's work points out the importance of industry analysis:

> We are not fit to lead an army on the march unless we are familiar with the face of the country—its pitfalls and precipices, its marshes and swamps.[1]

These words serve as a reminder to entrepreneurs that regardless of how eager they are to start their businesses, they are not adequately prepared until they are "familiar with the face of the country"—that is, until they understand the industry or industries they plan to enter and in which they intend to compete.

It's also important to know that some industries are simply tougher than others in terms of survival rates and profit potential. For example, the four-year survival rate in the information sector is only 38 percent, while it is 55 percent in education and health care. What this means is that the average start-up in education and health care is roughly 50 percent more likely than the average start-up in the information sector to survive four years, which is a big difference.[2] These types of differences exist for comparisons across other types of industries. The differences can be mitigated some by firm-level factors, including a company's products, culture, reputation, and other resources.[3] Still, in various studies researchers have found that from 8 to 30 percent of the variation in firm profitability is directly attributable to the industry in which a firm competes.[4] As a result, the overall attractiveness of an industry should be part of the equation when an entrepreneur decides whether to pursue a particular opportunity. Studying industry trends and using the five forces model are two techniques entrepreneurs have available for assessing industry attractiveness.

Studying Industry Trends

The first technique that an entrepreneur has available to discern the attractiveness of an industry is to study industry trends. Environmental and business trends are the two most important trends for entrepreneurs to evaluate.

Environmental Trends As discussed in Chapter 2, environmental trends are very important. The strength of an industry often surges or wanes not so much because of the management skills of those leading firms in a particular industry, but because environmental trends shift in favor or against the products or services sold by firms in the industry.

Economic trends, social trends, technological advances, and political and regulatory changes are the most important environmental trends for entrepreneurs to study. For example, companies in industries selling products to seniors such as the eyeglasses industry and the hearing aid industry benefit from the social trend of the aging of the population. In contrast, industries selling food products that are high in sugar, such as the candy industry and the sugared soft-drink industry, are suffering as the result of a renewed emphasis on health and fitness. Sometimes there are multiple environmental changes at work that set the stage for an industry's future. This point is illustrated in the following statement from IBISWorld's assessment of the future of the motorcycle dealership and repair industry:

> Demand for motorcycle dealers is expected to speed up over the next five years. Industry revenue is anticipated to increase 2.5% to $24.2 billion in the five years to 2016. Disposable income is poised to increase over the next five years while the U.S. economy gains steam. With more money in their pockets, consumers will hit motorcycle lots again. Furthermore, the tight lending standards of the past are projected to dissipate, and more financing will be available for consumers to use when purchasing a motorcycle. High fuel prices will also feed into industry demand as some consumers switch from cars to motorcycles.[5]

This short assessment about sales in the motorcycle industry illustrates the degree to which environmental trends affect the prospects of an industry. Note that nothing is said about improvements in the management of motorcycle dealerships or enhancements in motorcycle product quality. The somewhat positive assessment of the future of the motorcycle industry is tied to an improved U.S. economy, a lessening of tight credit standards, and high fuel prices. High fuel prices work to the advantage of the motorcycle industry because motorcycles use less fuel than cars. Similar forces are at work in all industries.

Business Trends Other trends impact industries that aren't environmental trends per se but are important to mention. For example, the firms in some industries benefit from an increasing ability to outsource manufacturing or service functions to lower-cost foreign labor markets, while firms in other industries don't share this advantage. In a similar fashion, the firms in some industries are able to move customer procurement and service functions online, at considerable cost savings, while the firms in other industries aren't able to capture this advantage. Trends like these favor some industries over others.

It's important that start-ups stay on top of both environmental and business trends in their industries. One way to do this is via participation in industry trade associations, trade shows, and trade journals, as illustrated in the "Partnering for Success" feature.

PARTNERING FOR SUCCESS

Three Ts That Are Important for Becoming Active in an Industry: Trade Associations, Trade Shows, and Trade Journals

One thing that's important for a start-up is to become active in the industry it's entering. Activity leads to learning the ins and outs of an industry, finding business partners, and becoming recognized as an industry leader. Three important Ts that lead to industry activity are trade associations, trade shows, and trade journals. Start-ups should consider utilizing these Ts as a part of their early and ongoing activities.

Trade Associations

A trade association (or trade group) is an organization that's formed by firms in the same industry to collect and disseminate trade information, offer legal and technical advice, furnish industry-related training, and provide a platform for collective lobbying. In addition to promoting industry-related issues, trade associations typically provide their members a variety of other services. For example, the American Watchmakers-Clockmakers Institute, which is a trade association of watchmakers and clockmakers, provides its members training, a database of hard-to-find parts, technical support for watch and clock repair, bulletins with up-to-date product information, and an extensive library of industry-specific educational material.

Trade associations are typically governed by a paid staff and a volunteer board. Busy CEOs and entrepreneurs are motivated to serve on trade association boards, not only to influence the direction of the associations but because their service provides them visibility and a platform to network closely with other members of the association. These types of interactions can lead to businesses forming partnerships and working together in other ways.

There are 7,600 national trade associations in the United States. The vast majority have Web sites that list their activities and their members.

Trade Shows

A trade show (or a trade fair) is an exhibition organized so that companies in an industry can showcase and demonstrate their latest products and services. Some trade shows are open to the public while others can only be attended by company representatives and members of the press. In the Unites States, over 2,500 trade shows are held every year. There are several online directories, such as the Trade Show News Network (www.tsnn.com), that help organizers, attendees, and marketers identify the most appropriate trade shows to attend. The largest trade show in the United States is the International Consumer Electronics Trade Show, which is held every January in Las Vegas. In 2011, it included more than 2,700 exhibitors and over 140,000 attendees.

Along with displaying their latest products and services, businesses attend trade shows to study the activities of rivals, meet members of the press, and network with industry participants. Companies must rent exhibit space at trade shows. Some of the better shows, which usually last just under a week, cost upward of $20,000 to attend. Small companies are often able to share exhibit space and split the cost. Trade shows offer prime opportunities for networking to generate business, establish new relationships, and nurture existing ones. In fact, there are many articles and "how to" guides published in periodicals and posted on Web sites that teach businesses how to maximize their time at trade shows and establish business relationships.

Trade Journals

Trade journals, or magazines, are usually published by trade associations, and contain articles and advertising focused on a specific industry. Very little general-audience advertising appears in trade journals. They may also include industry-specific job notices and classified advertising.

Some trade journals are available to the general public, and others are very specifically controlled—meaning that you must participate in the industry to receive the journal. This practice ensures advertisers that their ads will be viewed by people in their target audience. Many of the articles in trade journals are written about companies in the industry. It enhances the stature and visibility of a company to have a favorable article written about it in a premier industry trade journal.

Along with trade journals, some industries have peer-reviewed journals that contain both technical articles and heavy advertising content. The articles are often coauthored by people who work for vendors who advertise in the journal. *BioTechniques* is an example of an industry-specific peer-reviewed journal that follows this format. These journals blur the distinction somewhat between trade journals and peer-reviewed journals.

Although trade journals do not provide the direct networking opportunities that trade associations and trade shows do, the visibility a company can obtain by being featured in an article or by running ads can result in multiple positive outcomes.

(continued)

The Five Forces Model

LEARNING OBJECTIVE

2. Identify the five competitive forces that determine industry profitability.

The five forces model is a framework for understanding the structure of an industry and was developed by Harvard professor Michael Porter. Shown in Figure 5.1, the framework is comprised of the forces that determine industry profitability.[6] These forces—the threat of substitutes, the entry of new competitors, rivalry among existing firms, the bargaining power of suppliers, and the bargaining power of buyers—determine the average rate of return for the firms competing in a particular industry (e.g., the insurance industry) or a particular segment of an industry (e.g., health insurance only).

Each of Porter's five forces impacts the average rate of return for the firms in an industry by applying pressure on industry profitability. Well-managed companies try to position their firms in a way that avoids or diminishes these forces—in an attempt to beat the average rate of return for the industry. For example, the rivalry among existing firms in the energy bar industry is high. Element Bars has diminished the impact of this threat to its profitability by selling customized energy bars online and through special arrangements with businesses like spas and fitness centers that want to brand their own specialty energy bars.

In his book *Competitive Advantage*, Porter points out that industry profitability is not a function of *only* a product's features. Although the book was published in 1980 and the dynamics of the industries mentioned have changed, Porter's essential point still offers important insights for entrepreneurs such as the insight suggested by the following quote:

> Industry profitability is not a function of what the product looks like or whether it embodies high or low technology but of industry structure. Some very mundane industries such as postage meters and grain trading are extremely profitable, while some more glamorous, high-technology industries such as personal computers and cable television are not profitable for many participants.[7]

The five competitive forces that determine industry profitability are described next. As mentioned in previous chapters, industry reports, produced by companies like Mintel, IBISWorld, and Standard & Poor's NetAdvantage, provide substantive information for analyzing the impact of the five forces on specific industries. All three of these resources are available free through many university library Web sites and are highlighted in the Internet Resources Table in Appendix 3.2.

Threat of Substitutes   In general, industries are more attractive when the threat of substitutes is low. This means that products or services from

FIGURE 5.1
Forces That Determine
Industry Profitability

other industries can't easily serve as substitutes for the products or services being made and sold in the focal firm's industry. For example, there are few if any substitutes for prescription medicines, which is one of the reasons the pharmaceutical industry is so profitable. When people are sick, they typically don't quibble with the pharmacist about the price of a medicine. In contrast, when close substitutes for a product do exist, industry profitability is suppressed because consumers will opt not to buy when the price is too high. Consider the price of airplane tickets. If the price gets too high, businesspeople will increasingly utilize videoconferencing as a substitute for travel. This problem is particularly acute if the substitutes are free or nearly free. For example, if the price of express mail gets too high, people will increasingly attach documents to e-mail messages rather than sending them via UPS or FedEx.

The extent to which substitutes suppress the profitability of an industry depends on the propensity for buyers to substitute alternatives. This is why the firms in an industry often offer their customers amenities to reduce the likelihood of their switching to a substitute product, even in light of a price increase. Let's look at the coffee restaurant industry as an example of this. The coffee sold at Starbucks is relatively expensive. A consumer could easily find a less expensive cup of coffee at a convenience store or brew coffee at home rather than pay more at Starbucks. To decrease the likelihood that customers will choose either of these alternatives, Starbucks offers high-quality fresh coffee, a pleasant atmosphere (often thought of as part of the "Starbucks experience"), and good service. Starbucks doesn't do this just so its customers don't go to a different coffee restaurant. It offers the service so its customers won't switch to substitute products as well. Although this strategy is still working for Starbucks, it isn't as effective as it once was, given Starbucks's recent slowdown in its growth rate. Because of this slowdown, Starbucks has been experimenting with offering less expensive coffees while maintaining its commitment to quality and providing customers with what the firm believes is the unique Starbucks experience.

Threat of New Entrants   In general, industries are more attractive when the threat of entry is low. This means that competitors cannot easily enter the industry to copy what the industry incumbents are doing. There are a number of ways that firms in an industry can keep the number of new entrants low. These techniques are referred to as barriers to entry. A **barrier to entry** is a condition that creates a disincentive way for a new firm to enter an industry.[8] Let's look at the six major sources of barriers to entry:

> LEARNING OBJECTIVE
> 3. Explain the role of "barriers to entry" in creating disincentives for firms to enter an industry.

■ **Economies of scale:** Industries that are characterized by large economies of scale are difficult for new firms to enter, unless they are willing to accept a cost disadvantage. **Economies of scale** occur when mass-producing a product results in lower average costs. For example, Intel has huge microchip factories that produce vast quantities of chips, thereby reducing the average cost of a chip. It would be difficult for a new entrant to match

This independently owned coffee shop doesn't just sell coffee. It also offers its patrons a convenient and pleasant place to meet, socialize, and study. The shop offers these amenities in part to decrease the likelihood that its customers will "substitute" coffee at this shop for a less expensive alternative.

© Scott Griessel/Dreamstime.com

Intel's advantage in this area. There are instances in which the competitive advantage generated by economics of scale can be overcome. For example, many microbreweries have successfully entered the beer industry by brewing their beer locally and relying on a local niche market clientele. By offering locally brewed, high-quality products, successful microbreweries counter the enormous economies of scale (and the lower price to consumers they permit) of national brewers such as Anheuser-Busch and MillerCoors.

■ **Product differentiation:** Industries such as the soft-drink industry that are characterized by firms with strong brands are difficult to break into without spending heavily on advertising. For example, imagine how costly it would be to compete head-to-head against Pepsi or Coca-Cola. Another way of achieving differentiation is through product innovation. Apple is an example of a company that has differentiated itself in laptop computers by regularly improving the features on its line of MacBooks. It does this to not only keep existing customers and win new ones, but to deter competitors from making a big push to try to win market share from Apple in the laptop computer industry.

■ **Capital requirements:** The need to invest large amounts of money to gain entrance to an industry is another barrier to entry. The automobile industry is characterized by large capital requirements, although Tesla, which launched in 2003, was able to overcome this barrier and raise substantial funds by winning the confidence of investors through its expertise and innovations in electric car technology.

■ **Cost advantages independent of size:** Entrenched competitors may have cost advantages not related to size that are not available to new entrants. Commonly, these advantages are grounded in the firm's history. For example, the existing competitors in an industry may have purchased land and equipment in the past when the cost was far less than new entrants would have to pay for the same assets at the time of their entry.

■ **Access to distribution channels:** Distribution channels are often hard to crack. This is particularly true in crowded markets, such as the convenience store market. For a new sports drink to be placed on a convenience store shelf, it typically has to displace a product that is already there. Similarly, Element Bars would find it difficult to gain sufficient shelf space in grocery stores where a large number of offerings from major producers are already available to consumers.

■ **Government and legal barriers:** In knowledge-intensive industries, such as biotechnology and software, patents, trademarks, and copyrights form major barriers to entry. Other industries, such as banking and broadcasting, require the granting of a license by a public authority.

When a new firm tries to enter an industry with powerful barriers to entry, it must have a plan to overcome those barriers. Scott McNealy, the cofounder of Sun Microsystems, says that Sun was able to overcome the barriers to entry in many of its industries primarily by partnering with other firms, largely in the form of strategic alliances that helped Sun overcome entry barriers to attractive markets.[9]

When start-ups create their own industries or create new niche markets within existing industries, they must create barriers to entry of their own to reduce the threat of new entrants. It is difficult for start-ups to create barriers to entry that are expensive, such as economies of scale, because money is usually tight. The biggest threat to a new firm's viability, particularly if it is creating a new market, is that larger, better-funded firms will step in and copy what it is doing. The ideal barrier to entry is a patent, trademark, or copyright, which prevents another firm from duplicating what the start-up is doing. Element Bars' trade secret associated with the functionality of its Web site is a barrier to entry in the niche-oriented customizable energy bar industry. Apart from these options, however, start-ups have to rely on nontraditional barriers to entry to discourage new entrants, such as assembling a world-class management team that would be difficult for another company to replicate. A list of nontraditional barriers to entry, which are particularly suited to start-up firms, is provided in Table 5.1.

Rivalry Among Existing Firms   In most industries, the major determinant of industry profitability is the level of competition among the firms already competing in the industry. Some industries are fiercely competitive to the point where prices are pushed below the level of costs. When this happens, industry-wide losses occur. In other industries, competition is much less intense and price competition is subdued. For example, the personal computer industry is so competitive that profit margins are extremely thin. ASUSTeK Computer, for example, was selling its Eee PC laptop for $350 in 2011. In contrast, the market for specialized medical equipment is less competitive, and profit margins are higher.

There are four primary factors that determine the nature and intensity of the rivalry among existing firms in an industry:

■ **Number and balance of competitors:** The more competitors there are, the more likely it is that one or more will try to gain customers by cutting prices. Price-cutting causes problems throughout the industry and occurs more often when all the competitors in an industry are about the same size and when there is no clear market leader.

■ **Degree of difference between products:** The degree to which products differ from one producer to another affects industry rivalry. For example, commodity industries such as paper products producers tend to compete on price because there is no meaningful difference between one manufacturer's products and another's.

TABLE 5.1   NONTRADITIONAL BARRIERS TO ENTRY

Barrier to Entry	Explanation	Example
Strength of management team	If a start-up puts together a world-class management team, it may give potential rivals pause in taking on the start-up in its chosen industry.	Zynga
First-mover advantage	If a start-up pioneers an industry or a new concept within an existing industry, the name recognition the start-up establishes may create a formidable barrier to entry.	Facebook
Passion of management team and employees	If the key employees of a start-up are highly motivated by its unique culture, are willing to work long hours because of their belief in what they are doing, and anticipate large financial gains through stock options, this is a combination that cannot be replicated by a larger firm. Think of the employees of a biotech firm trying to find a cure for a disease.	Amgen
Unique business model	If a start-up is able to construct a unique business model and establish a network of relationships that make the business model work, this set of advantages creates a barrier to entry.	Netflix
Internet domain name	Some Internet domain names are so "spot-on" in regard to a specific product or service that they give a start-up a meaningful leg up in terms of e-commerce opportunities. Think of www.1800flowers.com, www.1800gotjunk.com, and www.bodybuilding.com.	www.1800contacts. com
Inventing a new approach to an industry and executing the idea in an exemplary fashion	If a start-up invents a new approach to an industry and executes it in an exemplary fashion, these factors create a barrier to entry for potential imitators.	Cirque du Soleil

LEARNING OBJECTIVE

4. Identify the nontraditional barriers to entry that are especially associated with entrepreneurial firms.

■ **Growth rate of an industry:** The competition among firms in a slow-growth industry is stronger than among those in fast-growth industries. Slow-growth industry firms, such as insurance, must fight for market share, which may tempt them to lower prices or increase quality to get customers. In fast-growth industries, such as pharmaceutical products, there are enough customers to satisfy most firms' production capacity, making price-cutting less likely.

■ **Level of fixed costs:** Firms that have high fixed costs must sell a higher volume of their product to reach the break-even point than firms with low fixed costs. Once the break-even point is met, each additional unit sold contributes directly to a firm's bottom line. Firms with high fixed costs are anxious to fill their capacity, and this anxiety may lead to price-cutting.

Bargaining Power of Suppliers   In general, industries are more attractive when the bargaining power of suppliers is low. In some cases, suppliers can suppress the profitability of the industries to which they sell by raising prices or reducing the quality of the components they provide. If a supplier reduces the quality of the components it supplies, the quality of the finished product will suffer, and the manufacturer will eventually have to lower its price. If the suppliers are powerful relative to the firms in the industry to which they sell, industry profitability can suffer.[10] For example, Intel, with its Pentium chip, is a powerful supplier to the PC industry. Because most PCs feature Pentium chips, Intel can command a premium price from the PC manufacturers, thus directly affecting the overall profitability of the PC industry. Several factors have an impact on the ability of suppliers to exert pressure on buyers and suppress the profitability of the industries they serve. These include the following:

- **Supplier concentration:** When there are only a few suppliers to provide a critical product to a large number of buyers, the supplier has an advantage. This is the case in the pharmaceutical industry, where relatively few drug manufacturers are selling to thousands of doctors and their patients.

- **Switching costs:** Switching costs are the fixed costs that buyers encounter when switching or changing from one supplier to another. If switching costs are high, a buyer will be less likely to switch suppliers. For example, suppliers often provide their largest buyers with specialized software that makes it easy to buy their products. After the buyer spends time and effort learning the supplier's ordering and inventory management systems, it will be less likely to want to spend time and effort learning another supplier's system.

- **Attractiveness of substitutes:** Supplier power is enhanced if there are no attractive substitutes for the products or services the supplier offers. For example, there is little the computer industry can do when Microsoft and Intel raise their prices, as there are relatively few if any practical substitutes for these firms' products.

- **Threat of forward integration:** The power of a supplier is enhanced if there is a credible possibility that the supplier might enter the buyer's industry. For example, Microsoft's power as a supplier of computer operating systems is enhanced by the threat that it might enter the PC industry if PC makers balk too much at the cost of its software or threaten to use an operating system from a different software provider.

Bargaining Power of Buyers In general, industries are more attractive when the bargaining power of buyers (a start-up's customers) is low. Buyers can suppress the profitability of the industries from which they purchase by demanding price concessions or increases in quality. For example, even in light of the problems it has encountered over the past several years, the automobile industry remains dominated by a handful of large automakers that buy products from thousands of suppliers in different industries. This enables the automakers to suppress the profitability of the industries from which they buy by demanding price reductions. Similarly, if the automakers insisted that their suppliers provide better-quality parts for the same price, the profitability of the suppliers would suffer. Several factors affect buyers' ability to exert pressure on suppliers and suppress the profitability of the industries from which they buy. These include the following:

- **Buyer group concentration:** If the buyers are concentrated, meaning that there are only a few large buyers, and they buy from a large number of suppliers, they can pressure the suppliers to lower costs and thus affect the profitability of the industries from which they buy.

- **Buyer's costs:** The greater the importance of an item is to a buyer, the more sensitive the buyer will be to the price it pays. For example, if the component sold by the supplier represents 50 percent of the cost of the buyer's product, the buyer will bargain hard to get the best price for that component.

- **Degree of standardization of supplier's products:** The degree to which a supplier's product differs from its competitors' affects the buyer's bargaining power. For example, a buyer who is purchasing a standard or undifferentiated product from a supplier, such as the corn syrup that goes into a soft drink, can play one supplier against another until it gets the best combination of features such as price and service.

■ **Threat of backward integration:** The power of a buyer is enhanced if there is a credible threat that the buyer might enter the supplier's industry. For example, the PC industry can keep the price of computer monitors down by threatening to make its own monitors if the price gets too high.

The Value of the Five Forces Model

Along with helping a firm understand the dynamics of the industry it plans to enter, the five forces model can be used in two ways: (1) to help a firm determine whether it should enter a particular industry and (2) whether it can carve out an attractive position in that industry. Let's examine these two positive outcomes.

First, the five forces model can be used to assess the attractiveness of an industry or a specific position within an industry by determining the level of threat to industry profitability for each of the forces, as shown in Table 5.2. This analysis of industry attractiveness should be more in-depth than the less rigorous analysis conducted during feasibility analysis. For example, if a firm filled out the form shown in Table 5.2 and several of the threats to industry profitability were high, the firm may want to reconsider entering the industry or think carefully about the position it will occupy in the industry. In the restaurant industry, for example, the threat of substitute products, the threat of new entrants, and the rivalry among existing firms are high. For certain restaurants, such as fresh-seafood restaurants, the bargaining power of suppliers may also be high (the number of seafood suppliers is relatively small compared to the number of beef and chicken suppliers). Thus, a firm that enters the restaurant industry has several forces working against it simply because of the nature of the industry. To help sidestep or diminish these threats, it must establish a favorable position. One firm that has accomplished

TABLE 5.2   DETERMINING THE ATTRACTIVENESS OF AN INDUSTRY USING THE FIVE FORCES MODEL

Competitive Force	Threat to Industry Profitability		
	Low	Medium	High
Threat of substitutes			
Threat of new entrants			
Rivalry among existing firms			
Bargaining power of suppliers			
Bargaining power of buyers			

Instructions:

Step 1 Select an industry.
Step 2 Determine the level of threat to industry profitability for each of the forces (low, medium, or high).
Step 3 Use the table to get an overall feel for the attractiveness of the industry.
Step 4 Use the table to identify the threats that are most often relevant to industry profitability.

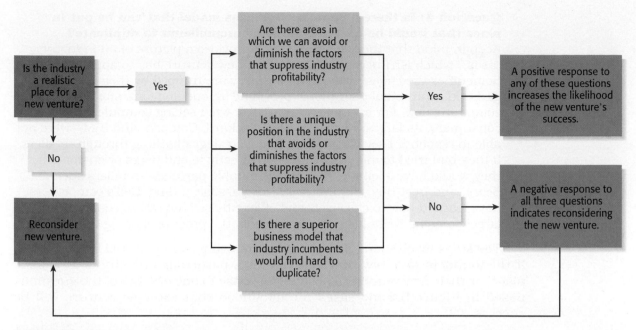

FIGURE 5.2
Using the Five Forces Model to Pose Questions to Determine the Potential Success of a New Venture

this is Panera Bread, as discussed in Case 5.1 in this chapter. By studying the restaurant industry, Panera found that some consumers have tired of fast food but don't always have the time to patronize a sit-down restaurant. To fill the gap, Panera helped to pioneer a new category called "fast casual," which combines relatively fast service with high-quality food. Panera has been very successful in occupying this unique position in the restaurant industry. You'll learn more about Panera Bread's success while reading Case 5.1.

The second way a new firm can apply the five forces model to help determine whether it should enter an industry is by using the model pictured in Figure 5.2 to answer several key questions. By doing so, a new venture can assess the thresholds it may have to meet to be successful in a particular industry:

Question 1: Is the industry a realistic place for our new venture to enter?   This question can be answered by looking at the overall attractiveness of an industry, as depicted in Table 5.2, and by assessing whether the window of opportunity is open. It's up to the entrepreneur to determine if the window of opportunity for the industry is open or closed.

Question 2: If we do enter the industry, can our firm do a better job than the industry as a whole in avoiding or diminishing the impact of the forces that suppress industry profitability?   A new venture can enter an industry with a fresh brand, innovative ideas, and a world-class management team and perform better than the industry incumbents. This was the case when Google entered the Internet search engine industry and displaced Yahoo! as the market leader. Outperforming industry incumbents can also be achieved if a new venture brings an attractive new product to market that is patented, preventing others from duplicating it for a period of time.

Question 3: Is there a unique position in the industry that avoids or diminishes the forces that suppress industry profitability?   As we've described, this is the advantage that both Element Bars and Panera Bread have captured.

LEARNING OBJECTIVE

5. List the four industry-related questions to ask before pursuing the idea for a firm.

Question 4: Is there a superior business model that can be put in place that would be hard for industry incumbents to duplicate?

Keep in mind that the five forces model provides a picture of an industry "as is," which isn't necessarily the way a new venture has to approach it. Sometimes the largest firms in an industry are trapped by their own strategies and contractual obligations, providing an opening for a start-up to try something new. For example, when Dell started selling computers directly to consumers, its largest rivals—Hewlett-Packard, Compaq, and IBM—were not able to respond. They were locked into a strategy of selling through retailers. If they had tried to mimic Dell and sell directly to end users or customers, they would have alienated their most valuable partners—retailers such as Sears, and Best Buy. However, with the passage of time, Dell's competitors have learned how to effectively and efficiently sell directly to consumers, largely erasing Dell's historic advantage in the process of doing so.

The steps involved in answering these questions are pictured in Figure 5.2. If the founders of a new firm believe that a particular industry is a realistic place for their new venture, a positive response to one or more of the questions posed in Figure 5.2 increases the likelihood that the new venture will be successful.

Industry Types and the Opportunities They Offer

LEARNING OBJECTIVE
6. Identify the five primary industry types and the opportunities they offer.

Along with studying the factors discussed previously, it is helpful for a new venture to study industry types to determine the opportunities they offer.[11] The five most prevalent industry types, depicted in Table 5.3, are emerging industries, fragmented industries, mature industries, declining industries, and global industries.[12] There are unique opportunities offered by each type of industry.

TABLE 5.3 INDUSTRY STRUCTURE AND OPPORTUNITIES

Industry Type	Industry Characteristics	Opportunities	Examples of Entrepreneurial Firms Exploiting These Opportunities
Emerging industries	Recent changes in demand or technology; new industry standard operating procedures have yet to be developed	First-mover advantage	■ Apple with its iTunes Music Store ■ Windspire in small-scale wind-generated power ■ Freedirectoryenquiries as an alternative to the fee-paying 118 companies
Fragmented industries	Large number of firms of approximately equal size	Consolidation	■ Starbucks in coffee restaurants ■ 1-800-GOT-JUNK? in junk removal ■ Geeks on Call in home computer repairs
Mature industries	Slow increases in demand, numerous repeat customers, and limited product innovation	Process and after-sale service innovation	■ InstyMeds in prescription drug sales ■ Fresh Health Vending in food vending ■ Daisy Rock Guitars in guitars
Declining industries	Consistent reduction in industry demand	Leaders, niche, harvest, and divest	■ Nucor in steel ■ JetBlue in airlines ■ Cirque du Soleil in circuses
Global industries	Significant international sales	Multinational and global	■ PharmaJet in needless injection systems ■ d.light in solar powered lanterns

Emerging Industries   An **emerging industry** is a new industry in which standard operating procedures have yet to be developed. The firm that pioneers or takes the leadership of an emerging industry often captures a first-mover advantage. A **first-mover advantage** is a sometimes insurmountable advantage gained by the first company to establish a significant position in a new market.

Because a high level of uncertainty characterizes emerging industries, any opportunity that is captured may be short-lived. Still, many new ventures enter emerging industries because barriers to entry are usually low and there is no established pattern of rivalry.

Fragmented Industries   A **fragmented industry** is one that is characterized by a large number of firms of approximately equal size. The primary opportunity for start-ups in fragmented industries is to consolidate the industry and establish industry leadership as a result of doing so. The most common way to do this is through a **geographic roll-up strategy**, in which one firm starts acquiring similar firms that are located in different geographic areas.[13] Zipcar, the car sharing company profiled in Case 6.2, is currently engaged in a geographic roll-up strategy to consolidate the car sharing industry and position itself as the industry leader. In 2007, it merged with Flexcar, its primary domestic competitor. It 2009, it acquired a minority interest in Avancar, the largest car sharing company in Spain. In April 2010, it acquired Streetcar, a London-based car sharing club.[14]

Mature Industries   A **mature industry** is an industry that is experiencing slow or no increase in demand, has numerous repeat (rather than new) customers, and has limited product innovation. Occasionally, entrepreneurs introduce new product innovations to mature industries, surprising incumbents who thought nothing new was possible in their industries. An example is Steve Demos, the founder of White Wave, a company that makes vegetarian food products. White Wave introduced a new product—Silk Soymilk—into a mature industry—consumer milk. Silk Soymilk became the best-selling soymilk in the country. Soymilk isn't really milk at all—it's a soybean-based beverage that looks like milk and has a similar texture. Still, it has made its way into the dairy section of most supermarkets in the United States and has positioned itself as a healthy substitute for milk. Who would have thought that a major innovation was possible in the milk industry?

The lure of mature industries, for start-ups, is that they're often large industries with seemingly vast potential if product and/or process innovations can be effectively introduced and the industry can be revitalized. In the case of White Wave it worked. Regrettably, it didn't work for Eclipse Aviation, a 1998 start-up that attempted to revitalize the private jet industry. Eclipse Aviation had a vision that literally thousands of people including investors, pilots, aviation experts, local government officials (where Eclipse facilities were located), and others desperately wanted to come true. It ultimately didn't come true as profiled in this chapter's "What Went Wrong?" feature. Eclipse Aviation's story is a reminder that some industries are nearly impossible to revitalize, despite a massive effort on the part of the people involved.

Declining Industries   A **declining industry** is an industry that is experiencing a reduction in demand, such as the retail photo finishing industry. Typically, entrepreneurs shy away from declining industries because the firms in the industry do not meet the tests of an attractive opportunity, described in Chapter 2. There are occasions, however, when a start-up will do just the opposite of what conventional wisdom would suggest and, by doing so, stakes out a position in a declining industry that isn't being hotly contested. That is what Cirque du Soleil did in the circus industry.

WHAT WENT WRONG?

Eclipse Aviation: Sometimes an Industry Can't Be Revitalized

Former Microsoft employee Vern Reborn founded Eclipse Aviation in 1998. The idea was to solve a problem in the aviation industry: although private jet service is safe and convenient, it is also very expensive. To remedy this problem, Eclipse, headquartered in Albuquerque, New Mexico, set out to design and build a six-passenger jet that could be produced in high volume and at a substantially lower price than existing private jets. In fact, Eclipse's goal was to create a new segment in the private jet industry called *very light jets*. The pitch Eclipse made to investors is that its jet would be so small and inexpensive to build and operate, that not only would private individuals buy it, but a new class of air taxi service would emerge to make private jet travel more accessible to middle-class individuals and smaller companies.

Eclipse set out to accomplish its ambitious goals by revolutionizing how airplanes are made. The conventional way of making airplanes does not deliver substantial economies of scale. Planes built by Boeing, Airbus, Cessna, and similar companies are largely hand-built, meaning that increasing the number of units produced only slightly decreases the cost per unit. Eclipse endeavored to change the way airplanes are built by introducing ultra-efficient manufacturing techniques that reduce costs and allow for high-volume manufacturing. The result, Eclipse promised, is that it would be able to sell a jet for around $1 million, which was roughly one-fourth the cost of the least expensive corporate jet on the market.

Eclipse worked toward its ambitious goal for almost 10 years. The firm designed and produced 260 copies of its Eclipse 500 very light twin-engine jet, and developed and sold a handful of copies of its Eclipse 400 single engine jet. Its vision of helping create an air-taxi industry came to fruition, at least for a short period of time. Dayjet, an air taxi service, was founded in 2002 largely on the premise of utilizing *very light jets* to ferry passengers to and from midsized cities. Dayjet was Eclipse's biggest customer, and had purchased 28 Eclipse 500 jets with plans to purchase 1,400 more when it went out of business in late 2008. Investors, suppliers, and state governments (through tax subsidies) invested over $1 billion in Eclipse. In the end, it wasn't enough. In November 2008, Eclipse filed for bankruptcy. What went wrong?

There are lots of things that went wrong with Eclipse. However, two factors are paramount among these and represent the essence of why Eclipse failed.

First, a number of people including investors, pilots, local governments (where Eclipse facilities were located), aviation experts, and others desperately wanted Eclipse's story and vision to be true. The idea of producing airplanes in high numbers, rather than essentially one-by-one, is one that had it came true would have revolutionized the industry. Ultimately Eclipse, like other aviation industry failures before it, couldn't make it work. According to aviation writer J. Mac McClellan, it cost Eclipse twice as much to build an Eclipse 500 aircraft than the company was selling it for. Particularly striking is how many people and companies bought into Eclipse's vision, even though it may have been unrealistic from the start. For example, there were over 5,000 creditors in the Eclipse bankruptcy filing alone. The fact that Eclipse was a start-up may have added to its allure. It wasn't trapped by the conventional thinking that characterized executives at established manufacturers such as Embracer, Cessna, and Boeing. But in the end, it turned out that the conventional thinking was true—at least for the time Eclipse Aviation was in business. As J. Mac McClellan has noted, building airplanes is like building houses. Whether a contractor builds one house or an entire sub-division, the houses still have to go up one at a time and each board has to be nailed separately. Similarly, airplanes are built one at a time and their parts are riveted or glued together piece by piece.

The second thing that sunk Eclipse, which is related to the first, is that its ambitions, which were integral to its business plan, were spectacular. Its plan called for deliveries of one thousand very light jets per year. To put that number in perspective, in 2007 about 4,000 corporate jets were built in the entire world. So Eclipse, which was a start-up with no production experience, set out to implement a plan that would increase the worldwide production of small jets by 25 percent. Eclipse's path to success then became predicated on price and not only production savvy but production breakthroughs. The only way to sell 1,000 jets per year was to dramatically lower the product's price. The only way to dramatically lower the price was to dramatically lower production costs. When that didn't happen, the company had no path forward.

Ultimately, Eclipse's investors, customers, suppliers, and state governments that supported it lost over $1 billion—the largest financial failure in the history of general aviation.

Questions for Critical Thinking

1. What lessons does Eclipse's failure have for entrepreneurs who are studying the industry or industries they are about to enter?
2. Why do you think more people, including Eclipse employees, suppliers, and customers, weren't more skeptical of Eclipse's ability to implement its ambitious plans? Do you think Eclipse's failure will slow down or accelerate new innovation in the airplane industry?

3. Interestingly, no current manufacturer of corporate jets is using the term *very light jets*. Embraer calls its Phenom 100 an "entry-level jet" and Stratos describes its jet as a "very light personal jet." Do you think these companies are deliberately avoiding the term *very light jet* to avoid conjuring up memories of Eclipse? If so, can you think of another term or name that been tainted by the failure of the firm that first started using it?

4. Eclipse Aviation has been revitalized as Eclipse Aerospace by new owners and a new management team. Spend some time studying Eclipse Aerospace. How is Eclipse Aerospace positioning itself in the airplane industry differently than Eclipse Aviation did?

Sources: Wikipedia, "History of Eclipse Aviation," http://en.wikipedia.org/wiki/Eclipse_Aviation (accessed March 3, 2011); J. Mac McClellan, "What Went Wrong with Eclipse?" *Flying*, March 9, 2009, www.flyingmag.com/what-went-wrong-eclipse (accessed March 1, 2011).

Entrepreneurial firms employ three different strategies in declining industries. The first is to adopt a **leadership strategy**, in which the firm tries to become the dominant player in the industry. This is a rare strategy for a start-up in a declining industry. The second is to pursue a **niche strategy**, which focuses on a narrow segment of the industry that might be encouraged to grow through product or process innovation. The third is a **cost reduction strategy**, which is accomplished through achieving lower costs than industry incumbents through process improvements. Achieving lower costs allows a firm to sell its product or service at a lower price, creating value for consumers in the process of doing so. Initially a small firm but now quite large as a result of its success, Nucor Steel revolutionized the steel industry through the introduction of the "minimill" concept, and is an example of an entrepreneurially minded firm that pursued this strategy. Most steel mills in the United States use large blast furnaces that produce a wide line of products and require enormous throughput in order to be profitable. Nucor's minimills are smaller and produce a narrower range of products. They are, however, energy efficient and make high-quality steel.[15]

Nucor proved its concept and quickly found growth markets within the largely declining U.S. steel industry.

Global Industries A **global industry** is an industry that is experiencing significant international sales. Many start-ups enter global industries and from day one try to appeal to international rather than just domestic markets. The two most common strategies pursued by firms in global industries are the multidomestic strategy and the global strategy. Firms that pursue a **multidomestic strategy** compete for market share on a country-by-country basis and vary their product or service offerings to meet the demands of the local market. In contrast, firms pursuing a **global strategy** use the same basic approach in all foreign markets. The choice between these two strategies depends on how similar consumers' tastes are from market to market. For example, food companies typically are limited to a multidomestic strategy because food preferences vary significantly from country to country. Firms that sell more universal products, such as athletic shoes, have been successful with global strategies. A global strategy is preferred because it is more economical to sell the same product in multiple markets.[16]

COMPETITOR ANALYSIS

After a firm has gained an understanding of the industry and the target market in which it plans to compete, the next step is to complete a competitor analysis. A competitor analysis is a detailed analysis of a firm's competition. It helps a firm understand the positions of its major competitors and the opportunities that are available to obtain a competitive advantage in one or more areas.

> **LEARNING OBJECTIVE**
> **7.** Explain the purpose of a competitor analysis.

These are important issues, particularly for new ventures.[17] In the words of Sun-tzu, quoted earlier in this chapter, "Time spent in reconnaissance is seldom wasted."

First we'll discuss how a firm identifies its major competitors, and then we'll look at the process of completing a competitive analysis grid, which is a tool for organizing the information a firm collects about its primary competitors.

Identifying Competitors

The first step in a competitive analysis is to determine who the competition is. This is more difficult than one might think. For example, take a company such as 1-800-FLOWERS. Primarily, the company sells flowers. But 1-800-FLOWERS is not only in the flower business; in fact because flowers are often given for gifts, the company is also in the gift business. If the company sees itself in the gift business rather than just the flower business, it has a broader set of competitors and opportunities to consider. In addition, some firms sell products or services that straddle more than one industry. For example, a company that makes computer software for dentists' offices operates in both the computer software industry and the health care industry. Again, a company like this has more potential competitors but also more opportunities to consider.

The different types of competitors a business will face are shown in Figure 5.3. The challenges associated with each of these groups of competitors are described here:

■ **Direct competitors:** These are businesses that offer products identical or similar to those of the firm completing the analysis. These competitors are the most important because they are going after the same customers as the new firm. A new firm faces winning over the loyal followers of its major competitors, which is difficult to do, even when the new firm has a better product.

■ **Indirect competitors:** These competitors offer close substitutes to the product the firm completing the analysis sells. These firms' products are also important in that they target the same basic need that is being met by the new firm's product. For example, when people told Roberto Goizueta, the late CEO of Coca-Cola, that Coke's market share was at a maximum, he countered by saying that Coke accounted for less than 2 percent of the 64 ounces of fluid that the average person drinks each day. "The enemy is coffee, milk, tea [and] water," he once said.[18]

■ **Future competitors:** These are companies that are not yet direct or indirect competitors but could move into one of these roles at any time. Firms are always concerned about strong competitors moving into their markets. For example, think of how the world has changed for Barnes & Noble, Borders and other brick-and-mortar bookstores since Amazon.com was founded. And, think of how smartphone technology continues changing the nature of competition for a variety of firms including those selling entertainment services, telephone services, and the like.

FIGURE 5.3
Types of Competitors
New Ventures Face

Direct Competitors	Indirect Competitors	Future Competitors
Businesses offering identical or similar products	Businesses offering close substitute products	Businesses that are not yet direct or indirect competitors but could be at any time

It is impossible for a firm to identify all its direct and indirect competitors, let alone its future competitors. However, identifying its top 5 to 10 direct competitors and its top 5 to 10 indirect and future competitors makes it easier for the firm to complete its competitive analysis grid.

If a firm does not have a direct competitor, it shouldn't forget that the status quo can be the toughest competitor of all. In general, people are resistant to change and can always keep their money rather than spend it.[19] A product or service's utility must rise above its cost, not only in monetary terms but also in terms of the hassles associated with switching or learning something new, to motivate someone to buy a new product or service.[20]

Creating meaningful value and sharp differentiation from competitors are actions small firms in crowded industries can take to remain competitive and gain market share. Three firms that have successful accomplished this are profiled in the "Savvy Entrepreneurial Firm" feature.

SAVVY ENTREPRENEURIAL FIRM

Thriving in a Crowded Industry by Creating Meaningful Value and Differentiation from Competitors

HomeMade Pizza Company: Web: www.homemadepizza.com; Twitter: HomeMadePizzaCo
Hot Mama: Web: www.shopmama.com; Twitter: Hot Mama; Facebook: Hot Mama
J. Hilburn: Web: www.jhilburn.com; Twitter: Hil_Davis; Facebook: JHilburn

Firms do well in a crowded industry when two conditions exist: (1) they create meaningful value for customers at a fair price and (2) they effectively differentiate themselves from competitors. In fact, diminishing the impact of three of Porter's five forces rests largely on these factors. A firm is able to withstand rivalry among existing firms and is able to deter substitutes and new entrants by creating value for its customers and offering something that people can't get anywhere else.

The following are examples of three businesses that are creating unique value in their industries and have differentiated themselves from their competitors. Each industry is very competitive, yet these companies are growing and thriving.

HomeMade Pizza Company

In 1997, when Eric Fosse told his family and friends that he was leaving his job to open a pizza business in Chicago, they probably thought he was crazy. Seriously, how many pizza delivery services do you think already existed in Chicago? Yet Fosse had a new idea. His pizzas would be made to order and delivered, just like the others, but rather than delivering the pizzas hot and ready-to-eat, his pizzas would be delivered uncooked and unboxed. Customers would slide the pizza, which came on heatable parchment paper, into

their ovens at 425 degrees and in 10 to 15 minutes have a fresh pizza. The advantage: the pizza would be filled with fresh ingredients and would be piping hot from the oven.

Sound simple? It wasn't. Fosse's distinctive advantage, other than delivering pizzas in a new way, is fresh ingredients and a dough recipe that was rolled out after months of taste testing. To get the freshest ingredients possible, the company works with local farmers to acquire produce. Along with pizza, HomeMade Pizza Company also makes and delivers signature salads and desserts. Its products are premium-priced. A large veggie pizza with mushrooms, crisp red onions, and a twist of poblano pepper and fresh-cut oregano cost upward of $18.00.

HomeMade Pizza has company-owned stores and franchise locations in four locations: Illinois, Minnesota, D.C./Virginia, and New York/New Jersey. It's reported to be profitable and growing.

Hot Mama

Who could think of a tougher and more competitive industry than women's and children's clothing? And retail to boot. The competitiveness of the industry didn't deter Hot Mama founder/CEO Megan Temte. In November 2004, Temte and her husband Mike opened the first Hot Mama clothing boutique in Edina, Minnesota, a suburb of Minneapolis. Since then, the company has expanded. Hot Mama opened six new stores in 2010, bringing the

(continued)

total to 17 locations in seven states. The company planned to establish at least 14 additional stores in 2011 and 2012.

What's different about Hot Mama is the layout of the store and the product selection. It's a store that's designed specifically for mothers to shop with small children in tow. Each location entertains kids with movies, toys, video games, and coloring books, all centrally located so mothers can keep an eye on their kids. Every aisle is wide enough to accommodate a two-seat stroller, and the floors are made so strollers don't get stuck. Sales employees double as babysitters, and often hold infants as their mothers try on clothes. The goal is to give moms a small amount of "shopping peace" in the midst of a hectic day. Most shoppers stay in the store more than an hour. Sales employees are specially trained to help mothers find clothes that fit, whether they are pregnant, have just had a baby, or have older children. In regard to selection, the stores feature products from more than 200 brands.

Hot Mama's revenue is expected to top $20 million in 2011, and the company plans to have 50 locations by 2014.

J. Hilburn

Another tough industry is men's shirts. Founded in 2007, J. Hilburn reportedly sold 60,000 shirts in 2010 through a very unique approach. It sends salespeople to customers' homes and offices to take measurements and suggest fabrics and styles.

J. Hilburn was started by Veeral Rathod and Hill Davis, two men who saw shopping as a chore. The company employs a direct sales model, similar to Avon or Pampered Chef. The company has 650 part-time "style advisers" who earn commissions of up to 25 percent on the clothing they sell. Most style advisers are women of school-aged

children looking for extra income. Once a shirt is ordered, it's sent to a factory near Macau, China, where it's made from Italian fabric and is ready in two to three weeks. Shirts cost between $79 and $149. While that may sound like a lot, it's less than half the price of comparable shirts in high-end stores.

According to J. Hilburn, some 30,000 people have bought clothing or accessories from the company, and 93 percent of its customers reorder. Since the company was founded, its sales have tripled each year and topped $9 million in 2010.

Questions for Critical Thinking

1. What are the common attributes across the three companies in this feature? How do these attributes help the companies thrive in otherwise competitive industries?
2. In what ways are each company's features redefining the customer experience in their industries?
3. Of the three companies featured, which one do you think has the most potential to remain competitive? Which company do you think is the most vulnerable to increased competition from competitors? Explain your answers.
4. Find an example of another company that is thriving in a highly competitive industry. Analyze the company and discern what sets it apart from its competitors.

Sources: Stephanie Schomer, HomeMade Pizza Company homepage, www.homemadepizza (accessed March 31, 2011); Stephanie Schomer, "How Retailer Hot Mama Is Rethinking Shopping for Moms." *FastCompany.com*, www.fastcompany.com/magazine/152/mums-the-word.html (accessed March 31, 2011, posted on February 1, 2011); "Borrowing from Avon and Dell to Sell Shirts," *Bloomberg Businessweek*, December 13–December 19, 2010.

Sources of Competitive Intelligence

LEARNING OBJECTIVE

9. Describe ways a firm can ethically obtain information about its competitors.

To complete a meaningful competitive analysis grid, a firm must first understand the strategies and behaviors of its competitors. The information that is gathered by a firm to learn about its competitors is referred to as **competitive intelligence**. Obtaining sound competitive intelligence is not always a simple task. If a competitor is a publicly traded firm, a description of the firm's business and its financial information is available through annual reports filed with the Securities and Exchange Commission (SEC). These reports are public records and are available at the SEC's Web site (www.sec.gov). If one or more of the competitors is a private company, the task is more difficult given that private companies are not required to divulge information to the public. There are a number of ways that a firm can ethically obtain information about its competitors. A sample of the most common techniques is shown in Table 5.4.

TABLE 5.4 SOURCES OF COMPETITIVE INTELLIGENCE

Source	Description/Benefit
Attend conferences and trade shows	Participants talk about the latest trends in the industry and display their most current products.
Purchase competitors' products	Purchasing and using a competitor's products can provide insight into their benefits and shortcomings. The purchase process itself can provide data about how a competitor treats its customers.
Study competitors' Web sites	Many companies put a lot of information on their Web sites, including product information and the latest news about the company.
Set up Google and Yahoo! e-mail alerts	E-mail alerts are updates of the latest Google or Yahoo! results, including press releases, news articles, and blog posts, on any keywords of interest. You can set up e-mail alerts using your company's name or the name of a competitor.
Read industry-related books, magazines, and eb sites	Many of these sources contain articles or features that contain information about competitors.
Talk to customers about what motivated them to buy your product as opposed to your competitor's product	Customers can provide a wealth of information about the advantages and disadvantages of competing products.

Many companies attend trade shows to display their products and see what their competitors are up to. This is a photo of the 2011 Consumer Electronics Trade Show, held in Las Vegas, which is America's largest annual tradeshow of any kind.

© Davewebbphoto/Dreamstime.com

Completing a Competitive Analysis Grid

As we mentioned previously, a **competitive analysis grid** is a tool for organizing the information a firm collects about its competitors. It can help a firm see how it stacks up against its competitors, provide ideas for markets to pursue, and, perhaps most importantly, identify its primary sources of competitive advantage. To be a viable company, a new venture must have at least one clear competitive advantage over its major competitors.

LEARNING OBJECTIVE
10. Describe the reasons for completing a competitive analysis grid.

TABLE 5.5   COMPETITIVE ANALYSIS GRID FOR ELEMENT BARS

Name	Element Bars	Power Bar	Clif Bar	Balance Bar	Larabar
Nutritional value	Advantage	Even	Even	Even	Even
Taste	Even	Disadvantage	Even	Even	Disadvantage
Freshness	Advantage	Disadvantage	Disadvantage	Disadvantage	Disadvantage
Price	Disadvantage	Advantage	Advantage	Advantage	Advantage
Packaging	Advantage	Even	Even	Even	Even
Branding	Disadvantage	Advantage	Advantage	Even	Even
Customizable	Advantage	Disadvantage	Disadvantage	Disadvantage	Disadvantage
Social consciousness/ philanthropy	Disadvantage	Disadvantage	Advantage	Disadvantage	Even

An example of a competitive analysis grid is provided in Table 5.5. This grid is for Element Bars, the energy bar start-up featured at the beginning of the chapter. The main competitive factors in the industry are nutritional value, taste, freshness, price, and packaging. Some industry participants, such as Clif Bar, also engage in philanthropy (Clif Bar gives away 1 percent of its revenue to community causes). These factors are placed on the vertical axis of Element Bars' competitive analysis grid. The horizontal axis contains Element Bars and its five main competitors. In each box, Element Bars rates itself against its main competitors. The purpose of this exercise is for a company to see how it stacks up against its competitors and to illustrate the areas in which it has an advantage (and has a disadvantage). For example, Element Bars rates itself as superior to its competitors in terms of nutritional value and freshness. It will likely use this information in its advertising and promotions. An additional benefit of completing a competitive analysis grid is that it helps a company fine-tune its offering. For example, Element Bars rates itself at a disadvantage to its competitors on price. Its bars are roughly two and a half times the cost of a Clif Bar or a Balance Bar. It may want to confront this issue head-on in its advertising and promotions, by acknowledging that it's not the cheapest bar but has the most nutritional value, is the freshest, and is the only bar that's customizable. It can back up its freshness claim by explaining that all Element Bars are "made to order," and are shipped just several days after they come out of the oven.

CHAPTER SUMMARY

1. Industry analysis is business research that focuses on an industry's potential. The knowledge gleaned from this analysis helps a firm decide whether to enter an industry and if it can carve out a position in that industry that will provide it a competitive advantage. Environ-mental trends and business trends are the two main components of "industry trends" that firms should study. Environmental trends include economic trends, social trends, technological advances, and political and regulatory changes. Business trends include other business-related trends that aren't environmental trends but are important to recognize.

2. Porter's five forces model includes threat of substitutes, threat of new entrants, rivalry among existing firms, bargaining power of suppliers, and bargaining power of buyers.

3. The threat of new entrants is one of the five forces that determine industry profitability.

Firms try to keep other firms from entering their industries by erecting barriers to entry. A barrier to entry is a condition that creates a disincentive for a new firm to enter an industry. Economies of scale, product differentiation, capital requirements, cost advantages independent of size, access to distribution channels, and government and legal barriers are examples of barriers to entry.

4. The nontraditional barriers to entry that are particularly well suited to entrepreneurial firms include strength of the management team, first-mover advantage, passion of the management team and employees, a unique business model, special Internet domain name, and inventing a new approach to an industry and executing the approach in an exemplary manner.

5. The four industry-related questions that a firm should ask before entering an industry are the following: Is the industry a realistic place for a new venture? If we do enter the industry, can our firm do a better job than the industry as a whole in avoiding or diminishing the threats that suppress industry profitability? Is there a unique position in the industry that avoids or diminishes the forces that suppress industry profitability? Is there a superior business model that can be put in place that would be hard for industry incumbents to duplicate?

6. The five primary industry types and the opportunities they offer are as follows: emerging industry/first-mover advantage; fragmented industry/consolidation; mature industry/emphasis on service and process innovation; declining industry/leadership, niche, harvest, and divest; and global industry/multidomestic strategy or global strategy.

7. A competitor analysis is a detailed analysis of a firm's competition. It helps a firm understand the positions of its major competitors and the opportunities that are available to obtain a competitive advantage in one or more areas.

8. Direct competitors, indirect competitors, and future competitors are the three groups of competitors a new firm faces.

9. There are a number of ways a firm can ethically obtain information about its competitors, including attending conferences and trade shows; purchasing competitors' products; studying competitors' Web sites; setting up Google and Yahoo! e-mail alerts; reading industry-related books, magazines, and Web sites; and talking to customers about what motivated them to buy your product as opposed to your competitor's product.

10. A competitive analysis grid is a tool for organizing the information a firm collects about its competitors. This grid can help a firm see how it stacks up against its competitors, provide ideas for markets to pursue, and, perhaps most importantly, identify its primary sources of competitive advantage.

KEY TERMS

barrier to entry, **179**
competitive analysis grid, **193**
competitive intelligence, **192**
competitor analysis, **175**
cost reduction strategy, **189**
declining industry, **187**
economies of scale, **179**

emerging industry, **187**
first-mover advantage, **187**
fragmented industry, **187**
geographic roll-up strategy, **187**
global industry, **189**
global strategy, **189**
industry, **174**

industry analysis, **174**
leadership strategy, **189**
mature industry, **187**
multidomestic strategy, **189**
niche strategy, **189**
position, **175**

REVIEW QUESTIONS

1. What is an industry? Provide an example of an industry and several firms in it.
2. What is the purpose of industry analysis?

3. What are the four primary categories of environmental trends? Provide an example of how a trend in each category could affect the toy industry.

4. Identify the five forces that determine industry profitability.

5. Describe how the threat of substitute products has the potential to suppress an industry's profitability.

6. How does the threat of new entrants have the potential to suppress an industry's profitability?

7. What is meant by the term *barrier to entry*? Describe the six major sources of barriers to entry that can restrict a firm's entry into a market.

8. How does rivalry among existing firms have the potential to suppress an industry's profitability?

9. Describe the four primary factors that play a role in determining the nature and intensity of the bargaining power of suppliers. How does the bargaining power of suppliers have the potential to suppress an industry's profitability?

10. Describe the four primary factors that play a role in determining the nature and intensity of the bargaining power of buyers. How does the bargaining power of buyers have the potential to suppress an industry's profitability?

11. Identify the nontraditional barriers to entry that are particularly suitable for entrepreneurial firms.

12. How can a start-up avoid or sidestep the pressure applied by one of the five forces on industry profitability by establishing a unique "position" in an industry?

13. Describe the characteristics of a fragmented industry. What is the primary opportunity for new firms in fragmented industries?

14. Describe the characteristics of a mature industry. What is the primary opportunity for new firms in a mature industry?

15. What is a global industry? Describe the two most common strategies pursued by firms in global industries.

16. What is the purpose of a competitor analysis? Make your answer as complete as possible.

17. Describe the differences between direct competitors, indirect competitors, and future competitors.

18. What is meant by the term *competitive intelligence*? Why is it important for firms to collect intelligence about their competitors?

19. Identify three sources of competitive intelligence.

20. What is the purpose of completing a competitive analysis grid?

APPLICATION QUESTIONS

1. Jason Murphy is thinking about starting a firm in the fitness drinks industry. When asked by a potential investor if he had studied the industry, Jason replied, "The fitness drink industry is so full of potential, it doesn't need formal analysis." Will Jason's answer satisfy the investor? In what ways will Jason limit his potential if his current attitude about the importance of industry analysis doesn't change?

2. The "You Be the VC 5.1" feature focuses on Xeros, the maker of a virtually waterless laundry machine. Spend some time studying Xeros's Web site (www.xerosltd.com) as well as additional information you can find about the company. How would you describe Xeros's positioning strategy? How will the strategy help Xeros avoid any downward pressure on the laundry machine manufacturing business that might be imposed by Porter's five forces?

3. Karen Sharp lives in a town of approximately 10,000 in Western Kentucky. There isn't a furniture store in the town and Karen is thinking about starting one. She has good business and marketing skills and is confident she can run the store, but she's not sure whether the furniture store industry is a good industry to enter. Karen's turned to you for help. What would you tell her?

4. The "You Be the VC 5.2" feature focuses on SRS Aviation, a company in the South African airline industry. Spend some time studying the airline industry and Sibongile

Sambo's unique approach to the industry. Which environmental and business trends favor SRS Aviation's offering, and which environmental and business trends are likely to work against it?

5. Jackson Sprout, a long-time friend of yours, is disenchanted with what he perceives to be a lack of quality in the local restaurants serving Italian-based foods. In talking to you about this, Jackson says, "My grandparents are Italian. Over the years, I have learned a great deal about cooking great Italian dishes just by watching them in the kitchen. There is no doubt in my mind that I could easily open a restaurant and be quite successful." How would you respond to Jackson's comments? Relying on the insights associated with Porter's five forces model, what areas of competition would you recommend he consider before trying to open an Italian restaurant?

6. Your friend Lisa Ryan is opening a smoothie shop that will sell a variety of smoothie drinks in the $4 to $5 price range. When you ask her if she is worried that the steep price of smoothies might prompt potential customers to buy a soda or a sports drink instead of a smoothie, Lisa answers, "You're right. Someone could substitute a soda or a sports drink for a smoothie and save a lot of money. Is there anything I can do to discourage that?" What do you tell her?

7. Starbucks has been very successfully selling high-priced coffee despite the fact that consumers could easily substitute Starbucks coffee for less expensive coffee or substitute its coffee for less expensive drinks like soda, bottled water, or fitness drinks. Why do you think Starbucks has historically been so successful avoiding substitutes? Do you think its advantage is eroding in this area? If so why? If its advantage is eroding, what could the firm do to change this situation?

8. Kendall Jones is in the process of opening a new pet store. The store will sell pet food, pet supplies, and a select variety of pets (excluding dogs and cats). It will also offer grooming services and dog obedience classes. In a recent *Fortune* magazine article, Kendall read that in industries where the bargaining power of suppliers is high, industry profitability suffers. Help Kendall determine if the bargaining power of suppliers is high in the pet store industry.

9. Read Case 5.1, which focuses on Panera Bread. What are some of the entry barriers a firm would have to deal with and try to overcome if it tried to compete against Panera Bread in the casual dining segment of the restaurant industry?

10. Think of at least three entrepreneurial firms, not listed in Table 5.1, that benefit greatly from their Internet domain names. In each case, to what extent do you think the strength of their Internet domain names is instrumental to their ability to limit the number of new entrants in their industries?

11. As mentioned in this chapter, White Wave Inc. produces Silk Soymilk, a product that has done surprisingly well in the mature milk industry. Based on the material we've covered so far, why do you think Silk Soymilk has been so successful?

12. Look again at Case 5.1 dealing with Panera Bread. Using the Internet to search for information, make a list of this firm's direct competitors, indirect competitors, and future competitors. On a scale of 1 to 5 (5 is high), how concerned should Panera Bread be about each category of competitors?

13. The founders and initial management team at Xeros want to do as good a job as possible collecting competitive intelligence in an ethical manner to determine if large-scale manufacturers of washing machines (e.g., Whirlpool, GE, and LG Electronics) are trying to copy its innovative washing machine. Suggest some specific trade shows, industry-related magazines and periodicals, and Web sites the company should pay attention to as part of its competitive intelligence efforts.

14. Dana Smith will soon be opening a fitness club in Tucson, Arizona. Having identified his competitors, he wants to display the information he has collected in a way that will help him determine how he'll stack up against his competitors and pinpoint his sources of competitive advantage. Describe to Dana a technique that he could use to help achieve his objectives.

15. Complete a competitive analysis grid for Panera Bread.

YOU BE THE VC 5.1

Company: Xeros

Web: www.xerosltd.com

Facebook: Xeros Ltd

Business Idea: Create a "virtually waterless" laundry machine that washes clothes and is quicker, uses less detergent, uses less water, and produces a smaller carbon footprint than conventional washing machines.

Pitch: Remember when you were a kid and you sat in front of a washing machine and watched the soaked clothes tumble through the suds? Although enjoyable for many, that experience may be a thing of the past. Researchers at Leeds University (located in the United Kingdom), which is home to one of the world's most advanced textile institutes, have created a washing machine that uses 90 percent less water than traditional machines. Xeros, the company that will bring the technology to market, is a spin-out of the university. Here's how it works. The patented technology cleans clothes using reusable nylon polymer beads. The beads have an inherent polarity that attracts stains, and are designed to gently but fully penetrate into a large load of laundry. Only a small amount of water is needed to dampen the garments, loosen stains, and create the water vapor that activates the cleaning properties of the beads. The beads are then tumbled with the clothes, allowing the polarizing properties of polymer to attract and absorb dirt. After a wash cycle is complete, the beads are automatically removed by the washing machine. The beads last for about 100 loads (six months for the average family) before they need to be replaced. The system is virtually waterless, uses 30 percent less energy (the tumble dry cycle is eliminated), and uses considerably less detergent. Clothes emerge from the system just as clean as if they were washed in a conventional manner. As an added benefit, the energy savings and reduction of waste water dramatically reduces the carbon footprint of the device, compared to traditional washing machines. In fact, based on independent assessments, if the Xeros system replaced all washing machines in the United Kingdom, the environmental impact would be equivalent to taking two million cars off the road.

The Xeros system is undergoing advanced prototyping to prepare for commercial launch. The company's initial target market will be the commercial washing market, including hotels, nursing homes, and Laundromats. Downstream, the company plans to license its technology to mainstream washing machine companies to penetrate the consumer market. To reach its initial target markets, Xeros is partnering with Kansas City–based GreenEarth Cleaning, which has been a pioneer in the development of low-environmental impact dry cleaning solutions. The global market for laundry products is around $50 billion per year. This market's size is a strong indicator of Xeros's commercial potential.

Q&A: Based on the material covered in this chapter, what questions would you ask the firm's founders before making your funding decision? What answers would satisfy you?

Decision: If you had to make your decision on just the information provided in the pitch and on the company's Web site, would you fund this company? Why or why not?

YOU BE THE VC 5.2

Company: SRS Aviation

Web: www.srsaviation.co.za

Twitter: srsaviation

Facebook: SRS-Aviation

Business Idea: Build a network of professional private jet services across Africa that will offer personalized flight options to destinations around the world.

Pitch: Sibongile Sambo was meant to fly. The South African entrepreneur grew up close to an Air Force base and always had a love of planes. After a successful seven-year career in human resources, Sambo seized the opportunity presented by South Africa's Black Economic Empowerment Act of 2003 to realize her lifelong dream of setting up her own aviation company. The Act promotes affirmative action for previously disadvantaged groups, although Sambo conceded that her main obstacle to setting up and running an airline was being "young and female" in the male-dominated aviation industry.

In 2004, Sambo founded SRS Aviation, the first black female–owned aviation company in South Africa. From her previous work at diamond giant De Beers, Sambo could see that there was a significant demand for high-quality private jets in the increasingly prosperous business community. Although initially access to funding was difficult, the Black Economic Empowerment Act made all the difference in convincing the government to award Sambo her first contract; after all, the legislation was designed to promote economic transformation by enabling "meaningful participation of black people in the economy." The contract encouraged many companies who had previously refused support and partnership to open their doors to SRS Aviation. The government also provided business training and a consultant to help her with her business plan.

In 2005, SRS Aviation's first full year of trading, the firm generated revenues of $5 million, with three-quarters of the business coming from the government. With growing competition, the company keeps overhead low by employing a skeleton staff of nine employees, yet it is still committed to empowering socially disadvantaged groups, such as South African women, by training them to become pilots, cabin crew, technicians, and engineers. SRS also keeps costs down by only commissioning planes immediately before the flight, once the revenue has been received.

From its early beginnings as simply a broker of flights, the company now holds government licenses in helicopter operations and air transport for large and small aircraft. It undertakes VIP, cargo, and tourist charters, as well as emergency work such as medical evacuations and firefighting with the mission to offer flexibility, security, and "unparalleled service." Sambo won the international Black Woman in Business Award in 2007 and was selected for the prestigious Fortune mentoring program for women in the United States.

With South Africa as the transport hub for many goods coming into Africa, or being exported to Asia or the United States, Sambo now has plans to expand the business throughout the continent. SRS Aviation is also targeting international contracts for supplying food and other products to emergency areas across southern Africa.

Q&A: Based on the material covered in this chapter, what questions would you ask the firm's founders before making your funding decision? What answers would satisfy you?

Decision: If you had to make your decision on just the information provided in the pitch and on the company's Web site, would you fund this firm? Why or why not?

CASE 5.1

Panera Bread: Occupying a Favorable Position in a Highly Competitive Industry

Web: www.panerabread.com
Twitter: Panera Bread
Facebook: Panera Bread

Bruce R. Barringer, *Oklahoma State University*
R. Duane Ireland, *Texas A&M University*

Introduction

If you analyzed the restaurant industry using Porter's five forces model, you wouldn't be favorably impressed. Three of the threats to profitability—the threat of substitutes, the threat of new entrants, and rivalry among existing firms—are high. Despite these threats to industry profitability, one restaurant chain is moving forward in a very positive direction. St. Louis–based Panera Bread, a chain of specialty bakery-cafés, has grown from 602 company-owned and franchised units in 2003 to 1,450 today. In 2010, sales increased by 7.9 percent. In 2010 and 2009, combined sales jumped 10.1 percent. These numbers reflect a strong performance for a restaurant chain, particularly during a difficult economic period. So what's Panera's secret? How is it that this company flourishes

while its industry as a whole is experiencing difficulty? As we'll see, Panera Bread's success can be explained in two words: positioning and execution.

Changing Consumer Tastes

Panera's roots go back to 1981, when it was founded under the name of Au Bon Pain Co. and consisted of three Au Bon Pain bakery-cafés and one cookie store. The company grew slowly until the mid-1990s, when it acquired Saint Louis Bread Company, a chain of 20 bakery-cafés located in the St. Louis area. About that time, the owners of the newly combined companies observed that people were increasingly looking for products that were "special"—that were a departure from run-of-the-mill restaurant food. Second, they noted that although consumers were tiring

(continued)

of standard fast-food fare, they didn't want to give up the convenience of quick service. This trend led the company to conclude that consumers wanted the convenience of fast food combined with a higher-quality experience. In slightly different words, they wanted good food served quickly in an enjoyable environment.

The Emergence of Fast Casual

As the result of these changing consumer tastes, a new category in the restaurant industry, called "fast casual," emerged. This category provided consumers the alternative they wanted by capturing the advantage of both the fast-food category (speed) and the casual dining category (good food), with no significant disadvantages. The owners of Au Bon Pain and Saint Louis Bread Company felt that they could help pioneer this new category, so they repositioned their restaurants and named them Panera Bread. The position that Panera moved into is depicted in the graphic titled "Positioning Strategy of Various Restaurant Chains." A market positioning grid provides a visual representation of the positions of various companies in an industry. About Panera's category, industry expert T. J. Callahan said, "I don't think fast casual is a fad; I think it's a structural change starting to happen in the restaurant industry."

Panera's Version of Fast Casual

To establish itself as the leader in the fast-casual category and to distinguish itself from its rivals, Panera (which is Latin for "time for bread") added a bonus to the mix— specialty food. The company has become known as the nation's bread expert and offers a variety of artisan and other specialty breads, along with bagels, pastries, and baked goods. Panera Bread's restaurants are open for breakfast, lunch, and dinner and also offer hand-tossed salads, signature sandwiches, and hearty soups served in edible sourdough bread bowls, along with hot and cold coffee drinks and other beverages. The company also provides catering services through its Via Panera catering business. Its restaurants provide an inviting neighborly atmosphere, adding to their appeal. Panera even

suggests a new time of day to eat specialty foods, calling the time between lunch and dinner "chill-out" time.

With high hopes for future expansion, Panera Bread is now the acknowledged leader in the fast-casual category. Systemwide sales were $1.5 billion in 2010. Its unique blend of fast-casual service and specialty foods also continues to gain momentum. This sentiment is captured in the following quote from Mark von Waaden, an investor and restaurateur who signed an agreement to open 20 Panera Bread restaurants in the Houston, Texas, area early in the company's recent growth spurt. Commenting on why he was attracted to Panera Bread as opposed to other restaurant chains, von Waaden said,

> My wife, Monica, and I fell in love with the fresh-baked breads and the beautiful bakery-cafés. We think the Panera Bread concept of outstanding bread coupled with a warm, inviting environment is a natural fit with the sophistication that the Houston market represents.

The spirit of von Waaden's statement captures the essence of Panera's advantage. It isn't just another restaurant. By observing trends and listening to customers, its leaders helped the firm carve out a unique and favorable position in a difficult industry.

Present Status and Goal for the Future

Panera's leadership in the fast-casual category and its financial performance has drawn considerable attention to the company. The company serves nearly six million customers a week systemwide, and is currently one of the largest restaurant chains in the United States. The company is counting on its unique positioning strategy, its signature foods, and savvy execution to continue its positive momentum.

Discussion Questions

1. How has Panera Bread established a unique position in the restaurant industry? How has this unique position

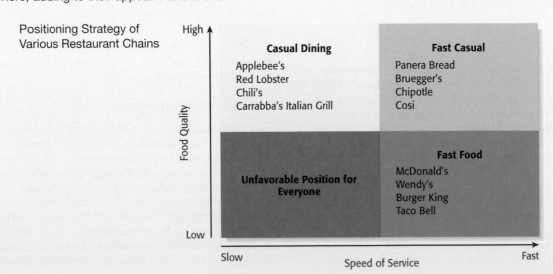

Positioning Strategy of Various Restaurant Chains

Casual Dining
Applebee's
Red Lobster
Chili's
Carrabba's Italian Grill

Fast Casual
Panera Bread
Bruegger's
Chipotle
Cosi

Unfavorable Position for Everyone

Fast Food
McDonald's
Wendy's
Burger King
Taco Bell

Food Quality — High / Low
Speed of Service — Slow / Fast

contributed to the firm's success? Do you think Panera Bread will reach its goal of becoming a leading national brand in the restaurant industry? Why or why not?

2. Analyze the restaurant industry using Porter's five forces model. In what ways has Panera Bread successfully positioned itself against the forces that are suppressing the profitability of the restaurant industry as a whole?

3. What barriers to entry has Panera Bread created for potential competitors? How significant are these barriers?

4. What are Panera Bread's primary sources of competitive advantage? In your judgment, are these sources of advantage sustainable? Why or why not?

Application Questions

1. What are the ways that Panera Bread can conduct ethical and proper forms of competitive analysis to learn about potential competitors entering the fast-casual category?

2. Think of at least two other businesses that have established unique positions in their industries. How have their unique positions contributed to their success?

Sources: Panera Bread homepage, www.panerabread.com, (accessed May 10, 2011); Panera Bread Annual Report 2010; "Industry by Industry: A Look at the Start, Their Stocks—and Their Latest Picks, *Wall Street Journal*, May 12, 2003, R8.

CASE 5.2

Plumgarths

Web: www.plumgarths.co.uk

For consumers in the United Kingdom, when it comes to their weekly grocery shopping, buying local is important. Research released by Mintel in April 2011 showed that 76 percent of UK consumers strongly agree or agree that buying local or regional food supports jobs and gives the economy a boost, especially at a time when the economy is weak. The findings led one industry commentator to compare the popularity of local to the previous boom in organic foods.

The UK supermarket giants are never ones to miss a growing trend for long, but for them, this "buy local" initiative is a challenge. Even selling relatively small amounts of local food presents enormous logistical problems. In the past, supermarkets' entire regional distribution policy has centered on large volumes to make a profit. Now, they are being faced with a whole new business model.

Imagine the following scenario. The produce buyer at Tesco in a city in the south west of the country wants to buy sweet corn from local producers. She's familiar with half a dozen local farms that grow sweet corn and could call each one asking them to e-mail, fax, or drop their price list by the store. The day to choose the supplier and place the order will arrive. The produce buyer will lay the price sheets out on her desk and pick out the name of the two or three farmers from whom she wants to buy food products. She will then start trying to get in touch with all those farmers. When she finally gets to speak to them in person, she has to ask whether they still have the product, if it is still the same price, and how soon they can deliver it to the store. She also has to talk through the complex ordering process and standard requirements such as plastic crates to a pre-agreed size for delivery. She genuinely wants to buy local and it is the policy of the supermarket giant, but what a hassle! If she

gets distracted or busy, she has a quick and easy alternative. She can go online and get anything she wants from Tesco's regional distribution center.

This is what happens in the highly fragmented food industry. There are potentially dozens of small sweet corn producers within driving distance of each individual Tesco store across the United Kingdom, all looking for buyers. Plus, Tesco is not the only store in the area looking for sweet corn. Other industry leaders such as Asda, Sainsburys, and Waitrose have all indicated they want to sell more local produce.

You'd think that buyers and sellers would connect easily, but often they don't. It's not the price, the quality of the product, or the fact that it is grown locally that's the problem. The reason local buyers and sellers have difficulty connecting is because it is difficult and a time-consuming hassle for everyone involved.

John Geldard

John Geldard and his wife Rachel had some understanding of the problem thanks to their long-term experience as farmers. John had grown up on his family farm in Kendal, Cumbria, and continued the family trade after getting married. In 1989, he bought a large livestock farm next to the Kent Estuary at the southern tip of the county.

When John acquired the farm, it was not an easy time for farming. The pound's value had skyrocketed, livestock prices had plummeted, and John's budgets were exceeded. He had overstretched himself financially and had to generate some cash flow. He immediately put 500 free-range chickens in a hut and he and his wife began selling eggs door-to-door.

The enterprising egg operation coincided with the opening of an Asda supermarket in Kendal. Rachel Geldard wasted no time in contacting the manager, asking

(continued)

if the store would like to sell their locally laid eggs. She persuaded Asda to take their eggs into stores in Lancaster, Barrow, and Kendal on a 12-week trial. In that time, egg sales in those Asda stores soared 30 percent.

Plumgarths

While the egg business continued to grow steadily, John Geldard was busily looking at other ways to make money. Following the death of his parents, John, together with other members of his family. had inherited Plumgarths, the farm where he'd been raised. By this time, thanks to various changes through the years, the farm had several buildings but not much land.

What should he do? Take the easy option, sell it and go on a world cruise? Or, take on another mortgage and buy out the other family members with an interest in Plumgarths?

In weighing his decision, John thought carefully about the food market. It seemed to him that consumers were becoming increasingly interested in where their food came from, particularly after various food crises, such as BSE (bovine spongiform encephalopathy, also known as mad cow disease). He correctly predicted a surge in interest in locally sourced food.

John decided to take the second option and invest in six food manufacturing units and a farm shop. He redeveloped the Plumgarths site at a cost of $815,000. Half the money was raised by re-mortgaging the property, with the rest as a grant from the government's Department for Environment, Food and Rural Affairs.

Although it had taken almost two and a half years to get planning permission to develop the units, almost the moment they opened, Asda got in touch wanting to do business. Following the success of the egg trial, Asda wanted to collaborate with John on establishing and delivering a wider local sourcing initiative. The supermarket suggested setting up a trial in the Kendal store.

In 2002, Plumgarths became the hub for 18 local food producers, who together introduced 80 new products onto the shelves of Kendal Asda.

Local Hub Business Model

Plumgarths has become what is known as a "local hub" where producers pitch their products to Plumgarths, and if a product is accepted, Plumgarths buys the product directly from the producer. The producer then supplies the required amount to Plumgarths and it supplies the product to Asda.

Since the trial, the service has been extended to 18 stores, with plans for more. Asda sends Plumgarths orders electronically for all the 18 stores. Plumgarths then invoices Asda for those products and delivers them to the various stores in its van. When Asda pays Plumgarths, it pays the other producers.

The system works perfectly for all parties. Asda, like all supermarkets, specifies a number of strict criteria for distribution of the products it buys, such as barcoding, which is an ability many small suppliers do not have. Plumgarths is able to provide this service to the suppliers, so that they can provide products to Asda. By working

with the local hub, producers are able to get their products on supermarket shelves without having to negotiate complete order systems and distribution networks, and without having to make multiple deliveries. The local suppliers are also exposed to a far wider customer base, without the need to fulfill the sometimes onerous requirements of being a "listed supplier."

Likewise, the supermarkets get the benefits of a great range of local produce with a simple, one-stop, ordering system from one supplier. By dealing with Plumgarths, rather than multiple small companies, the supermarket doesn't have to put up with their delivery bays being congested with dozens of suppliers dropping off their goods. Frequent deliveries from Plumgarths keep stock levels in stores to a minimum, which ensures the freshness of the products.

Plumgarths also benefits as the successful enterprise at the center of the local hub and is able to spread the costs of dealing with Asda to sell its own goods, through the margin taken on the other products. By dealing with a wider range of suppliers, the venture has been able to invest in better transport of the goods, because it is being used across all the suppliers. Plus, any over-orders from suppliers are sold through Plumgarths' farm shop. Shoppers too are the winners as they are now afforded the option of buying local products in a major supermarket.

Benefits

Selling local helps supermarkets foster closer relationships with its customers, which is particularly important at a time when many large store groups have been accused of pushing out local retailers. It is a visible sign of investment in the community.

Asda estimates that around 42 percent of its customers buy local goods at least once a week and two-thirds do so because they see it as a way of helping the local economy and supporting their neighbors. Following the successful pilot with Plumgarths, Asda has spun off the local hub concept to 14 regions across the United Kingdom.

Discussion Questions

1. Make a list of the environmental trends and the business trends that are working both for and against Plumgarths and its business proposition.
2. To what degree has Plumgarths established a new approach to interface with businesses in the agricultural and food sales industries? How well do you think Plumgarths is executing its approach? What do you think of Plumgarths' business model? What are the pluses and minuses of its approach?
3. What barriers to entry is Plumgarths erecting to prevent competitors from moving into its space? Do you believe first-mover advantage Plumgarths is creating will prevent competitors from entering the firm's industry?
4. Are you surprised that Plumgarths received funding from the Department for Environment, Food and Rural Affairs? What do you think the government saw in the company that prompted it to make the investment?

Application Questions

1. Address the most significant challenges that Plumgarths has in growing and reaching its full potential. Briefly describe how you'd address each of the challenges.
2. Think of a fragmented industry, other than agriculture, in which a local hub connecting buyers and sellers might work. Name the industry and describe the type of local hub that you'd build to connect buyers and sellers in the industry.

Sources: V. Matthews, "Local Is the New Organic," *The Grocer*, www.thegrocer.co.uk/Articles.aspx?page=articles&ID=216485 (accessed September 4, 2011, originally posted on March 5, 2011); "Triumph of a Local Hero," *The Northern Farmer,* www.northernfarmer.co.uk/diversification/8745728.print/ (accessed September 4, 2011, originally posted on December 17, 2010); "Local Sourcing: Distribution Advice for Regional Food and Drink Producers," *IGD.com*, www.igd.com/index.asp?id=1&fid=1&sid=3&tid=53&folid=0&cid=553 (accessed September 4, 2011); "Supporting Local Food and Drink: An Introduction to the English Food and Drink Alliance," regionalandlocalfood.co.uk/?EFADAbrochure.pdf (accessed September 4, 2011, originally posted September 2010).

ENDNOTES

1. Sun-tzu, *The Art of War* (Mineola, NY: Dover Publications, 2002), chap. 7.
2. A. Knaup, "Survival and Longevity in Business Employment Dynamics Data," *Monthly Labor Review* (May 2005): 50–56.
3. D. R. King and R. J. Slotegraaf, "Industry Implications of Value Creation and Appropriation Investment," *Decision Sciences* 42, no. 2 (2011): 511–29; P. J. Derfus, P. G. Maggitti, C. M. Grimm, and K. G. Smith, "The Red Queen Effect: Competitive Actions and Firm Performance," *Academy of Management Journal* 51, no. 1 (2008): 61–80; R. P. Rumelt, "How Much Does Industry Matter?" *Strategic Management Journal* 12, no. 3 (1991): 167–85.
4. Y. E. Spanos, G. Zaralis, and S. Lioukas, "Strategy and Industry Effects on Profitability: Evidence from Greece," *Strategic Management Journal* 25 (2004): 139–65.
5. J. Molavi, "Motorcycle Dealership and Repair in the US," *IBISWorld Industry Report 44122a*, February 2011.
6. M. Porter, *Competitive Strategy: Techniques for Analyzing Industries and Competitors* (New York: Free Press, 1980).
7. Porter, *Competitive Strategy*.
8. J. Levie and E. Autio, "Regulatory Burden Rule of Law, and Entry of Strategic Entrepreneurs: An International Panel Study," *Journal of Management Studies* 48, (2011): 1392–1419.
9. S. McNealy, "A Winning Business Model," in *The Book of Entrepreneurs' Wisdom*, ed. Peter Krass (New York: John Wiley & Sons, 1999), 171–89.
10. T. Jambulingam, R. Kathuria, and J. R. Nevin, "Fairness-Trust-Loyalty Relationship Under Varying Conditions of Supplier-Buyer Interdependence," *Journal of Marketing Theory and Practice* 19, no.1 (2011): 39–56.
11. J. Hayton, G. N. Chandler, and D. R. DeTienne, "Entrepreneurial Opportunity Identification and New Firm Development Processes: A Comparison of Family and Non-family Ventures," *International Journal of Entrepreneurship and Innovation Management* 13, no. 1 (2011): 12–31; R. E. Hosskison, J. Covin, H. W. Volberda, and R. A. Johnson, "Revitalizing Entrepreneurship: The Search for New Research Opportunities," *Journal of Management Studies* 48 (2011): 1141–1168.
12. J. F. Porac, H. Thomas, and C. Baden-Fuller, "Competitive Groups as Cognitive Communities: The Case of Scottish Knitwear Manufacturers Revisited," *Journal of Management Studies* 48, no. 3 (2011): 646–64; A. Potter and H. D. Watts, "Evolutionary Agglomeration Theory: Increasing Returns, Diminishing Returns, and the Industry Life Cycle," *Journal of Economic Geography* 11, no. 3 (2010): 417–55.
13. D. A. Aaker, *Brand Relevance: Making Competitors Irrelevant* (Hoboken, NJ: Jossey-Bass Publishers, 2011).
14. Zipcar homepage, www.zipcar.com (accessed May 6, 2011).
15. W. A. Cohen, "Absolute Integrity is the Basis of Heroic Leadership," *Executive Forum* 50 (2011): 46–51; J. Rodengen, *The Legend of Nucor Corporation* (Ft. Lauderdale, FL: Write Stuff Enterprises, 1997).
16. S. H. Appelbaum, M. Roy, and T. Gilliland, "Globalization of Performance Appraisals: Theory and Application," *Management Decision* 49, no. 4 (2011): 570–85; K. E. Meyer, R. Mudambi, and R. Narula, "Multinational Enterprises and Local Contexts: The Opportunities and Challenges of Multiple Embeddedness," *Journal of Management Studies* 48, no. 2 (2011): 235–52.
17. H. A. Ndofor, D. G. Sirmon, and X. He, "Firm Resources, Competitive Actions and Performance: Investigating a Mediated Model with Evidence from the In-Vitro Diagnostics Industry," *Strategic Management Journal* 32, no. 6 (2011): 640–57; M-J. Chen, K-H. Su, and W. Tsai, "Competitive Tension: The Awareness-Motivation-Capability Perspective," *Academy of Management Journal* 50, no. 1 (2007): 101–18; M-J. Chen, "Competitor Analysis and Inter-Firm Rivalry: Toward a Theoretical Integration," *Academy of Management Review* 21, no. 1 (1996): 100–34.
18. P. Kotler, *Marketing Insights from A to Z* (Hoboken, NJ: Wiley, 2003), 23.
19. C. Baumann, G. Elliott, and H. Hamin, "Modelling Customer Loyalty in Financial Services: A Hybrid of Formative and Reflective Constructs," *International Journal of Bank Marketing* 29, no. 3 (2011): 247–67.
20. L. Grzybowski and P. Pereira, "Subscription Choices and Switching Costs in Mobile Telephony," *Review of Industrial Organization* 38, no. 1 (2011): 23–42.

Getting Personal *with* STROOME

Cofounders:

NONNY DE LA PEÑA
Master's in Communications,
University of Southern California, 2009

TOM GRASTY
Master's in Communications,
University of Southern California, 2009

Dialogue *with*
Nonny de la Peña

BEST ADVICE I'VE RECEIVED
Solve a problem

**MY ADVICE FOR NEW
ENTREPRENEURS**
"No" often means "not now"

**FIRST ENTREPRENEURIAL
EXPERIENCE**
Selling my Wacky-Packy card
collection to my brother

**MY FAVORITE SMARTPHONE
APP**
Newsy

**MY BIGGEST WORRY
AS AN ENTREPRENEUR**
Timing

**MY BIGGEST SURPRISE
AS AN ENTREPRENEUR**
People want you to succeed

CHAPTER 6

Developing an *Effective* Business Model

OPENING PROFILE

STROOME

Working to Find a Viable Business Model for an Exciting New Web-Based Service for Editing and Remixing Video

Web: www.stroome.com
Twitter: Stroome
Facebook: Stroome

If you took an evening class at University of Southern California (USC) in spring 2010, you may have noticed two students who frequently stood by one of their cars after class heatedly discussing a classroom topic. If you did, it's likely you noticed Tom Grasty and Nonny de la Peña, two masters of communications students. The two were enrolled in the program that instead of a thesis, required students to create an online community as their final project. Grasty and de la Peña were working on a Web-based application that anyone could use to post, cooperatively edit, share, and remix video. The application went beyond YouTube, where people simply upload videos. Instead, Grasty and de la Peña's service allowed people to upload video, and then edit and remix it, collaborating with either a closed group of collaborators or an open community to do so. Grasty and de la Peña's conversations weren't focused on how to get the project done on time or what grade they thought they'd get. Rather, the two were beginning to realize that they may be onto something that might translate into a business after they graduated.

The origin of Grasty and de la Peña's Web-based collaborative video editing and remixing idea is an interesting story. de la Peña was a documentarian and produced stories and reports for *The New York Times*, *Time*, and *Newsweek*. She was given a story to write for *The New York Times* about the sounds that fish make to communicate. The story ran in 2008, and gained lots of traction. As a result, *The New York Times* asked her to produce a video component for the story. de la Peña reached out to several people to provide snippets of video illustrating how fish communicate by sound, planning to splice the different video segments together to produce the final segment. She found the process to be cumbersome. People would use FedEx to send video to her, but only just in time to meet her deadline; as a result, she had to scramble to include them. Others would send video in a format she couldn't easily convert. Toward the end of the project de la Peña thought,

LEARNING OBJECTIVES

After studying this chapter you should be ready to:

1. Describe a business model.
2. Explain business model innovation.
3. Discuss the importance of having a clearly articulated business model.
4. Discuss the concept of the value chain.
5. Identify a business model's two potential fatal flaws.
6. Identify a business model's four major components.
7. Explain the meaning of the term *business concept blind spot*.
8. Define *core competency* and describe its importance.
9. Explain the concept of supply chain management.
10. Explain the concept of fulfillment and support.

"This isn't working." What she needed was a Web-based platform where people could upload video and where tools were available to help them edit and remix the video in a collaborative manner.

Grasty and de la Peña ran with this idea, and obtained further validation that they were onto something while the project was unfolding. They put a crude version of it up on the Web, so they could work on it together, and got a call from the New School in New York, asking if they could use it. Somehow they had stumbled on the project and asked permission to use it for their students' final project in a class called Mashup Culture. A few months later, Grasty and de la Peña entered the idea in the 2009 USC New Venture Competition and took first place.

Grasty graduated in spring 2009 and de la Peña graduated the following summer. The two decided to continue working on the project, now called Stroome. USC became Stroome's first customer, licensing the beta version of the site that had been created for the course project. Stroome received two additional boosts in 2010. It won the Audience Award from the Online News Association and was one of 12 projects to win the *Knights News* Challenge, which includes a $200,000 grant. The *Knights News* Challenge is an award for initiatives likely to "impact the future of news."

Stroome has now settled in and Grasty and de la Peña are fashioning it into a for-profit business. While journalists are Stroome's initial target market, the vision is to allow any person or groups of people to upload video to the firm's Web site, and then share, edit, and mix the video in a collaboration setting. The site also has a social component. As video is shared, either in a closed group or to the entire Stroome community, users can exchange comments, build communities, and find new collaborators. An example of how Stroome could be used is a group of friends attending the same sporting event. They could all shoot video of the event upload their individual videos to Stroome's Web site, and then work together to create a highlight video of the event. The same approach could be used to create documentaries or to chronicle breaking news events.

Stroome is gaining traction in terms of traffic to its Web site and industry visibility. Given this positive momentum, a key challenge the firm now faces is to develop a viable business model that includes specific and detailed actions it can take to earn money from the services it offers. In this regard, Stroome is thinking there are two ways the firm can make money. The first is via a freemium model on its Web site. Freemium is a business model that works by offering a basic product or service free of charge while charging a premium for advanced features. Grasty and de la Peña are carefully tracking which features Stroome's users find most useful, so they can properly structure their freemium strategy. The second way the company plans to make money is via white labeling its site—Stroome, for a fee, will allow other companies to use its video editing platform and rebrand it as their own. These companies could then make the service available to their customers.

This chapter introduces the business model and explains why it's important for a new venture to develop a business model early in its life. In everyday language, a model is a plan that's used to make or describe something. More formally, a **business model** is a firm's plan or diagram for how it competes, uses its resources, structures its relationships, interfaces with customers, and creates value to sustain itself on the basis of the profits it earns.[1] As you'll see later in this chapter, a successful business model has four components.

It's important to understand that a firm's business model takes it beyond its own boundaries. Almost all firms partner with others to make their business models work. Stroome's business model is based on the idea that users will voluntarily upload video and then work together to edit and mix the video in a collaborative manner. In addition, Stroome plans to partner with companies and organizations that use its technology to create their own collaborative video editing platforms. In both instances, Stroome is relying on outsiders to help its business model coalesce and add value.

It's important to note that a company's business model involves its network of partners along with its products. It encompasses the capabilities of multiple individuals and entities, all of which must be willing and motivated to play along. An example is Apple and in particular the Apple App Store. As of May 2011, more than 350,000 apps were available through the Apple App Store, created by over 30,000 developers. It's a win-win situation for both Apple and the developers. The developers get access to a platform to sell their apps, and Apple shares in the revenue that's generated. Positive scenarios like this often allow businesses to not only strengthen but to expand their business models. As a result of its collaboration with app developers, Apple launched iAds, the platform that allows app companies to sell advertising on the apps they make available via the Apple App Store. Apple shares in the revenue generated by the advertising.

When partners abandon a company the opposite can happen to its business model and future prospects. For example, the newspaper industry is suffering from the shift in readership from print to online, which has caused a number of the industry's advertisers and partners to shift their advertising dollars to digital news providers and aggregators. In 2009, newspapers took in $27.5 billion in advertising revenue, compared to $48.7 billion in 2000. That's a massive decline. Some newspapers, like Denver's *Rocky Mountain News*, haven't survived. Others are adjusting. For example, in March 2009, the *Seattle Post-Intelligencer* dropped its print edition, after 146 years in business, and moved strictly online. This shift brought with it an entirely different business model. The company is now an online community platform, which provides value to Seattle area residents via breaking news, columns from prominent Seattle residents, community databases, photo galleries, citizen bloggers, and links to other journalistic outlets.[2]

In this chapter, we'll first discuss business models and their importance. Then we'll look at how business models emerge and examine some of their potential "fatal flaws." Finally, we'll examine the components of effective business models.

BUSINESS MODELS

There is no standard business model, no hard-and-fast rules that dictate how a firm in a particular industry should compete. In fact, it's dangerous for the entrepreneur launching a new venture to assume that the venture can be successful by simply copying the business model of another firm—even if that other firm is the industry leader. This is true for two reasons. First, it is difficult to precisely understand all of the components of another firm's business model. Second, a firm's business model is inherently dependent on the collection of resources it controls and the capabilities it possesses. For example, if UPS employs the best group of supply chain managers in the country and has established long-term trusting relationships with key suppliers, it may be the only company in the world that can effectively implement its business model. No other firm would have this unique set of capabilities, at least initially.

To achieve long-term success though, all business models need to be modified across time. The reason for this is that competitors can eventually learn how to duplicate the benefits a particular firm is able to create through its business model. In the late 2000s, for example, financial returns suggested that competitors such as Hewlett-Packard had learned how to successfully duplicate the benefits of Dell Inc.'s "build-to-order" (BTO) business model. When Dell's BTO business model was first introduced, it was a **business model innovation**, which refers to a business model that revolutionizes how a product is produced, sold, or supported after the sale.[3] Figure 6.1 depicts Dell's initial approach to

LEARNING OBJECTIVE
1. Describe a business model.

LEARNING OBJECTIVE
2. Explain business model innovation.

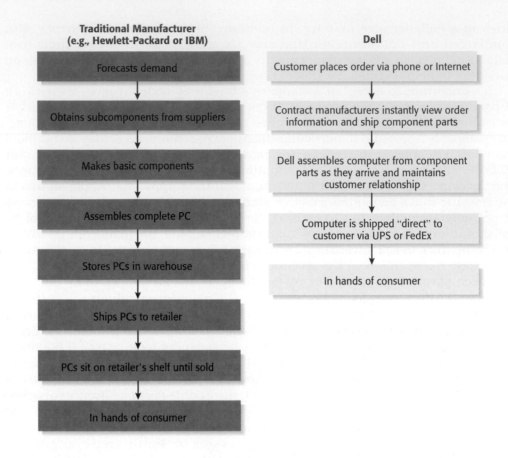

selling computers versus traditional manufacturers. As we've noted, Dell's competitors (e.g., Hewlett-Packard, Lenovo, Sony, Toshiba, and others) have been able to duplicate the benefits of Dell's business model. Nonetheless, at the time of its introduction, Dell's business model was very innovative.

Firms are continually introducing business model innovations to find ways to add value in unique ways and revolutionize how products and services are sold in their industries. The "Savvy Entrepreneurial Firm" feature for this chapter provides examples of business model innovations in eyewear, retail shopping, and solar power.

A firm's business model is developed after the feasibility analysis stage of launching a new venture. If a firm has conducted a successful feasibility analysis and knows that it has a product or service with potential, the business model stage addresses how to surround it with a core strategy, a partnership model, a customer interface, distinctive resources, and an approach to creating value that represents a viable business.

The Importance and Diversity of Business Models

Having a well-thought-out business model is important for several reasons. Although some models are better than others, it is dangerous to link the performance of a firm solely to the configuration of its business model. In most cases, performance is a function of both the *choice* of a business model and how effectively it's implemented. For example, eBay's business model is straightforward. In exchange for providing a virtual meeting place for people to buy and sell things, it earns a fee. It isn't a complicated model. The challenge is executing the model in a way that satisfies customers and makes a profit for eBay. If the customers aren't satisfied, the business model fails. If eBay can't make a profit, the business model fails.

SAVVY ENTREPRENEURIAL FIRM

Three Industries, Three Business Model Innovators

Warby Parker: Web: www.warbyparker.com; Twitter: warbyparker; Facebook: Warby Parker Eyewear
Shopkick: Web: www.shopkick.com; Twitter: Shopkick; Facebook: Shopkick
SunRun: Web: www.sunrunhome.com; Twitter: SunRun; Facebook: SunRun

Business model innovation is an important part of the entrepreneurial process. Not only do entrepreneurs bring new products and services to market, but new business models often revolutionize how products and services are sold and have the potential to bring considerable value to businesses and consumers. The following are examples of business model innovations in three industries.

Warby Parker

Warby Parker is pitching itself as an alternative to what it calls the overpriced and bland eyewear available today. By circumventing traditional channels, such as selling through optometrist offices and eyeglass stores, like Pearle Vision, and selling only online, Warby Parker is able to provide high-quality, fashionable glasses for $95.

How can this firm sell glasses at such a low price? The secret is not doing it the traditional way. Most branded eyewear is designed and manufactured by contract manufacturers, who resell their products to optometrist offices, eyewear shops, and other places where glasses are sold. The contract manufacturer must not only pay for the manufacturing costs of the glasses, but must also pay the brand, like Dior or Gucci, for using their name and logo. Then, the optometrist office or retail shop marks up the glasses an additional two to three times, which results in $300 to $500 glasses.

Warby Parker's business model is different in two ways. First, it creates its own designs, which eliminates fees to brands like Dior or Gucci, and second, it sells directly to the consumer, eliminating the two- to three-time markup at the retail level. The result: $95 prescription glasses that are equal in vision correction, quality, and durability to the $300 to $500 branded eyewear.

Warby Parker also has a social component to its business model. For every pair of glasses it sells for $95, it donates a pair of glasses to a charity that distributes glasses to people in need.

Shopkick

There are many businesses that help Internet retailers drive traffic to their Web sites. Examples include Google (click ads), Tribal Fusion (banner ads), and Commission Junction (affiliate programs). But what about fresh ideas for driving foot traffic to brick and mortar stores?

Enter Shopkick. Shopkick gives its users rewards for simply walking into its partners' retail stores. Shopkick launched in August 2010 and quickly signed up Best Buy, Sports Authority, American Eagle, and Macy's. To accomplish this, Shopkick has created an iPhone app that automatically recognizes when a user enters a partner's retail store. After the user enters the store, several things happen. First, the user is given a certain quantity of a virtual currency called "kickbucks," which can be redeemed for Facebook credits, iTunes gift cards, DVDs, or immediate cash-back awards at the partner's store, simply for walking in. A certain number of accumulated kickbucks are required for specific rewards. Alternatively, users can donate their kickbucks to charity. Second, a store discount will appear, such as 10 percent off any one item in the store. Often, additional offers will be made, such as 15 percent off certain big screen TVs or 20 percent off DVDs. Sometimes the offer will be a teaser. For example, it might say, "There is an offer waiting for you in the home theater department, but you must go to the department to receive the offer." You can also earn additional kickbucks for performing certain activities within stores. At some clothing stores, for example, you receive additional kickbucks for stepping into dressing rooms.

This Shopkick process, of course, encourages people to spend time in its partners' retail stores, and hopefully make spontaneous purchases. While Shopkick's business model is still evolving, it likely receives a small commission for items that are bought via Shopkick offers and promotional campaigns.

SunRun

Solar energy seems like an ideal alternative to fossil fuels. However, the reality is that purchasing and installing a solar energy system is simply too expensive given the potential cost savings in most instances. Installing a solar energy system also requires a consumer or business to make a substantial capital outlay for future cost savings. Although there are obvious environmental benefits to consider, how would you like to pay your next five years of electric bills in advance? There's also the issue of maintenance. Once you buy a solar energy system you own it and are responsible for upkeep and repairs.

So how can solar energy be an affordable alternative energy source? One innovative business model, pioneered

(continued)

by SunRun, is to provide solar power to consumers via a power purchase agreement. Under the agreement, SunRun purchases, installs, and maintains solar panels on its customers' homes in exchange for a long-term commitment by the consumer to buy the power generated from the solar panels from SunRun and to pay a set rate for the electricity. This approach reduces the initial capital outlay required by the home owner. Along with a solar power purchase agreement, SunRun also offers a solar lease program where SunRun is responsible for installation, maintenance, monitoring, and repairs. With the lease, which is available in states and cities that do not accommodate power purchase agreements, customers pay a low monthly fee to lease the firm's system and use the solar electricity for their homes.

Questions for Critical Thinking

1. Which of the business models described here strikes you as the most innovative and even revolutionary? Which business model do you think will have the largest long-term impact on its industry? Why?

2. Select one of the three businesses in the feature, and conduct online research to better familiarize yourself with the business and its business model. Evaluate the four separate components (core strategy, strategic resources, partnership network, and customer interface) of its business model, and how the separate components reinforce one another. On a scale of 1 to 10 (10 is high), how strong of a business model does the company have? Explain your answer.

3. Do you think Warby Parker stands to capture a first-mover advantage in the discount eyewear industry if its business model catches on? If so, how important of an advantage do you think this will be for Warby Parker?

4. Name two additional business model innovations not mentioned in the chapter. How is each business model innovation "adding value" in its industry?

Sources: Warby Parker Web site, www.warbyparker.com (accessed March 20, 2011); Shopkick Web site, www.shopkick.com (accessed March 20, 2011); SunRun Web site, www.sunrunhome.com (access March 20, 2011).

The challenge for all firms is to *create* or *develop* a sensible business model and then effectively *implement* it.[4]

LEARNING OBJECTIVE

3. Discuss the importance of having a clearly articulated business model.

Importance of Business Models   Having a clearly articulated business model is important because it does the following:

■ Serves as an ongoing extension of feasibility analysis (a business model continually asks the question, Does the business make sense?)

■ Focuses attention on how all the elements of a business fit together and how they constitute a working whole

■ Describes why the network of participants needed to make a business idea viable is willing to work together

■ Articulates a company's core logic to all stakeholders, including the firm's employees

A good way to illustrate the importance of these points is to describe a business model that *didn't* work. WebHouse Club was launched by Priceline.com founder Jay Walker in fall 1999 and failed just a year later after eating up nearly $350 million of its investors' money. Priceline.com allowed customers to "bid" for airline tickets, hotel rooms, and home mortgages. WebHouse was set up to mimic Priceline.com's business model and extend it to grocery store items. WebHouse worked like this: A shopper obtained a plastic card with a unique number and a magnetic strip from a local grocery store or a newspaper insert. The card was used to activate an account on the WebHouse Internet site. Once an account was established, the shopper could then make a bid for a supermarket item, say $3.75 for a box of toasted corn flakes cereal. The shopper could specify the price but not the brand. In seconds, the shopper would learn whether a maker of toasted corn flakes cereal was willing to accept the price. If so, the shopper would pay WebHouse for the cereal with a credit card and would then pick up the cereal at a participating store using the WebHouse card. The cereal could be Kellogg's, General Mills, or any other brand.

Behind the scenes, WebHouse followed the same formula that Priceline.com had invented to sell airline tickets and hotel rooms. By aggregating shopper demand for products such as cereal, tuna, or diapers, WebHouse could go to producers such as Kellogg's and General Mills and negotiate discounts. The company could then pass along the discounts to consumers and take a small fee for bringing buyers and sellers together.[5]

Why didn't the WebHouse business model work? Actually, several reasons describe the business model's failure in grocery stores. First, it assumed that companies such as Kellogg's would be willing to participate—not a wise assumption when you consider that Kellogg's has spent millions of dollars over many years for the purpose of convincing consumers that Kellogg's Corn Flakes is better than competing brands. The WebHouse model teaches consumers to select products strictly on the basis of price rather than brand identity. So why would Kellogg's or any other producer want to help WebHouse do that? Second, the WebHouse model assumed that millions of shoppers would take the time to sit down at their computers and bid on grocery store items. It's easy to see why a consumer might take the time to get a better deal on an airline ticket or a stay in a four-star hotel room. But how many people have the time to sit down, log on to their computer, and interact with a Web site to save 50 cents on a box of cereal without even being able to choose the brand? As it turned out, not many people were willing to do so.

Ultimately, WebHouse failed because its business model was flawed. The company just couldn't motivate its suppliers or customers to participate at a sufficient scale to support the overhead of the business. WebHouse was asking suppliers to act against their self-interest and was asking shoppers to take too much time to save too little money. As busy as people are today, shoppers want to make the very best use of their limited time, meaning that they'll likely reject a time-consuming process that doesn't create obvious value for them.

Diversity of Business Models   As mentioned, there is no standard business model that guarantees success when used in a particular industry or a specific segment of an industry. Firms approach their markets in different ways and devise different ways to make money. For example, there are six distinct ways that online companies make money. These approaches, shown in Table 6.1, are the core piece of their respective company's business models. The table illustrates one of the beauties of the Internet—you don't have to have a product or service to sell to make money online. If you know a great deal about a particular topic, such as cooking or home repair, you can launch a Web site; populate it with articles, tips, and other useful information; and make money online by essentially selling access to the people you attract to your Web site. This is possible by becoming an affiliate of another company, allowing pay-per-click ads to be placed on your Web site, or by selling direct ads that are placed on your Web site, as described in Table 6.1. All of these approaches were developed and pioneered by business model innovators. The result is that the Internet is essentially an ecosystem of varying business models that allow both online and offline companies to make money. A Web site that promotes BMX biking, for example, makes money by selling ads to companies that make BMX bikes and related equipment. The advertisers, in turn, make money when people respond to the ads and buy their products. The search engines, like Google and Bing, make money by bringing Web sites and advertisers together.

Over time, the most successful business model (or models) in an industry predominate and the weaker models fall by the wayside. There are always opportunities for business model innovation, as illustrated in the "Savvy Entrepreneurial Firm" feature. Netflix in movie rentals, Amazon.com's Kindle in digital books, Cirque du Soleil in live entertainment, and Apple's iTunes in the way music is purchased are familiar examples of successful business model innovations.

TABLE 6.1 SIX DISTINCT WAYS OF MAKING MONEY ONLINE (THE WAY AN ONLINE COMPANY MAKES MONEY LARGELY DEFINES ITS BUSINESS MODEL)

Method for Making Money	Description
Affiliate programs	An affiliate program is a way for online merchants, like 1-800-FLOWERS, to get more exposure by offering a commission to Web sites and blogs that are willing to feature ads for its products or services. The merchant *pays* the affiliate a small commission every time someone clicks on the ads and buys one of its products.
Pay-per-click programs	A Web site or blog allows an advertiser's link to be placed on its site and gets *paid* a small commission every time someone clicks the ad. Examples include Google AdSense and Yahoo! Search Marketing. You've seen many Google AdSense ads. They are easy to spot because they have an emblem underneath that says "Ads by Google."
Direct ads	These are banner ads, skyscraper ads (all ads that run along the side of a Web page), or ads with pictures embedded in the content of a Web site. Web sites, blogs, and other online companies get *paid* for allowing these ads to be placed on their Web sites.
E-commerce	Direct sale of products online (i.e., Amazon.com, Dell.com). Online companies get *paid* directly by the individuals and businesses that buy their products.
Subscription services	These online companies provide services that have sufficient value that people in their niche market are willing to *pay* for on a yearly on monthly basis. For example, eHarmony charges an annual fee for access to its matchmaking service.
Freemium models	These Web sites offer a basic service for free and offer premium services on tiered pricing plans. An example is SurveyMonkey, a service that allows users to create their own online surveys. The basic service (10 questions, 100 respondents) is free, the Select service is $17.00 per month (unlimited questions, unlimited respondents), and the Gold ($25.00 per month) and Platinum ($65.00 per month) plans offer additional features.

Sources: SurveyMonkey Web site, www.surveymonkey.com (accessed May 3, 2011); Bruce R. Barringer and R. Duane Ireland, *What's Stopping You?: Shatter the 9 Most Common Myths Keeping You from Starting Your Own Business,* 1st Edition, © 2008, pp.162–170. Adapted by permission of Pearson Education, Inc., Upper Saddle River, NJ.

How Business Models Emerge

LEARNING OBJECTIVE

4. Discuss the concept of the value chain.

The value chain is a model developed by an academic researcher[6] that many businesspeople as well as entrepreneurs use to identify opportunities to enhance their competitive strategies. The value chain also explains how business models emerge and develop. The **value chain** is the string of activities that moves a product from the raw material stage, through manufacturing and distribution, and ultimately to the end user. Shown in Figure 6.2, the value chain consists of primary activities and support activities. The primary activities have to do with the physical creation, sale, and service of a product or a service, while the support activities provide reinforcement for the primary activities. Individual parts of the chain either add or do not add value as a product moves through the different stages of the value chain. The final product or service is an aggregate of the individual contributions of value made at the different stages of the chain.

Entrepreneurs look at the value chain of a product or a service to pinpoint where the value chain can be made more effective or to spot where additional "value" can be added in some meaningful way. This type of analysis may focus on (1) a single primary activity of the value chain (such as marketing and sales), (2) the interface between one stage of the value chain and another (such as the interface between marketing and sales and service), or (3) one of

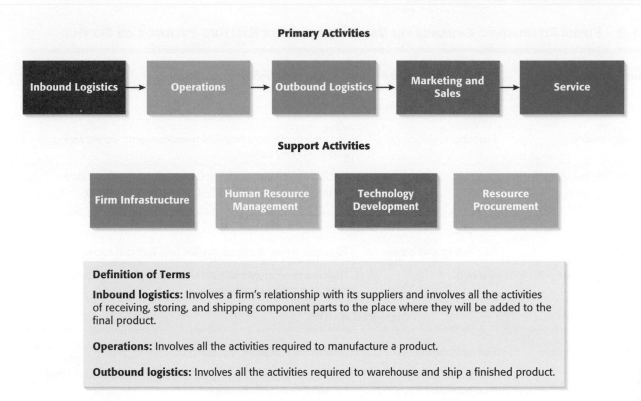

Primary Activities

Inbound Logistics → Operations → Outbound Logistics → Marketing and Sales → Service

Support Activities

Firm Infrastructure | Human Resource Management | Technology Development | Resource Procurement

Definition of Terms

Inbound logistics: Involves a firm's relationship with its suppliers and involves all the activities of receiving, storing, and shipping component parts to the place where they will be added to the final product.

Operations: Involves all the activities required to manufacture a product.

Outbound logistics: Involves all the activities required to warehouse and ship a finished product.

FIGURE 6.2
The Value Chain

the support activities (such as human resource management). If a product's value chain can be strengthened in any one of these areas, it may represent an opportunity for the formation of a new firm to perform that activity. For example InstyMeds, the focus of the "You Be the VC 3.1 feature, recognized a limitation in the marketing and sales component of the value chain for prescription medicine in rural areas. There are many rural areas without 24-hour pharmacies. This makes it difficult for people who visit an emergency room or an urgent care center late at night to quickly fill their prescriptions. To address the problem, InstyMeds has developed a vending machine for prescription drugs to be located in hospitals and urgent care centers in rural areas. This gives people access to the most commonly prescribed medications, like antibiotics, instantly rather than having to wait until the next morning. InstyMeds' solution improves the value chain for prescription medications.

Table 6.2 provides examples of entrepreneurial firms that have enhanced the value chain of existing products or services by focusing on one of the three previously mentioned areas. Some of the firms shown in Table 6.2 are older now, but had entrepreneurial beginnings and were launched to address a flaw or a limitation in the value chain of the respective industry in which each firm now competes.

Potential Fatal Flaws of Business Models

Two fatal flaws can render a business model untenable from the beginning: a complete misread of the customer and utterly unsound economics. Business models that fall victim to one of these two flaws have lost the race before leaving the starting gate.

LEARNING OBJECTIVE

5. Identify a business model's two potential fatal flaws.

TABLE 6.2   FIRMS FOUNDED TO ENHANCE THE VALUE CHAIN OF AN EXISTING PRODUCT OR SERVICE

New Venture's Current Name	Value Chain Activity	Reason New Venture Was Started
Primary Activities		
Con-way, MercuryGate	Inbound logistics	To provide efficient material management, warehousing, and inventory control
Celestica, Pier Components	Operations	To provide efficient contract manufacturing services for companies such as IBM, Microsoft, and Ericsson
FedEx, UPS	Outbound logistics	To provide new ways to warehouse and move goods effectively to the end user
Costco, Overstock.com	Marketing and sales	To provide new ways to market and sell products
Contact America, iQor	Service	To provide efficient call center, e-mail, and Web-based customer contact services
Support Activities		
Accenture, Booz & Company	Firm infrastructure	To provide management support
Administaff, Paychex	Human resource management	To provide payroll, tax, benefits administration, and other human resource services
Booz Allen, Rural Sourcing	Technology development	To help firms integrate emerging technologies into existing business systems
BASF, Grainger	Resource procurement	To help firms procure the raw materials and supplies needed for their production processes
The Interface Between One Stage of the Value Chain and Another		
Ariba, JDA Software	Inbound logistics/ operations	To help firms with the interface between inbound logistics and operations
ASW Global, UPS	Operations/outbound logistics	To help firms with the interface between operations and outbound logistics
Interstate Cold Storage	Outbound logistics/ marketing and sales	To help firms with the interface between outbound logistics and marketing and sales
InsightsNow, ClickSpeed	Marketing and sales/service	To help firms with the interface between marketing and sales/service

In plain terms, a product must have customers to be successful. In the previously mentioned WebHouse example, the savings that were possible by bidding on grocery store items just weren't large enough to make it worthwhile for a sufficient number of paying customers to participate. A similar misread of the customer sank Pets.com, a high-profile e-commerce flameout. Although it was convenient for consumers to have pet food and supplies delivered directly to their homes, the orders took several days to arrive—too long for customers who have access to the same products at the grocery store and at pet superstores such as PetSmart. Pets.com didn't realize that fast delivery was essential to its customers.

The second fatal flaw is pursuing unsound economics, as shown by the failure of many e-Bay drop-off stores. The idea behind eBay drop-off stores (like iSoldit and QuickDrop) was that nearly everyone has something they'd like to sell on eBay, but many people don't want the hassles associated with setting up an eBay account, listing an item, following the auction, shipping the item to the buyer, and so forth.[7] While there are still some eBay drop-off stores still open and presumably making money, most store owners couldn't make the business model work. Their profit margins were just too small to justify their time and investment.[8]

COMPONENTS OF AN EFFECTIVE BUSINESS MODEL

Although not everyone agrees precisely about the components of a business model, many agree that a successful business model has a common set of attributes. For example, one team of academics thinks of a business model as a coordinated plan to design strategy along three vectors: customer interaction, asset configuration, and knowledge leverage.[9] Similarly, a noted business professor and writer, Gary Hamel, believes that a business model consists of four components: core strategy, strategic resources, customer interface, and value network.[10] We adopt a similar view here and talk about a business model consisting of the following components:

> **LEARNING OBJECTIVE**
>
> **6.** Identify a business model's four major components.

■ Core strategy (how a firm competes)

■ Strategic resources (how a firm acquires and uses its resources)

■ Partnership network (how a firm structures and nurtures its partnerships)

■ Customer interface (how a firm interfaces with its customers)

Each of these components has several subcomponents; we provide a summary of each component and its respective subcomponents in Figure 6.3.

Core Strategy

The first component of a business model is the **core strategy**, which describes how a firm competes relative to its competitors.[11] The primary elements of a core strategy are the firm's mission statement, the product/market scope, and the basis for differentiation.

Experience suggests that things can go wrong quickly for a company that doesn't have a focused core strategy. This is what happened to Joost, the subject of this chapter's "What Went Wrong?" feature. As illustrated in the feature, an unfocused core strategy and miscues in other areas related to use of its business model contributed to Joost's failure.

Core Strategy	Strategic Resources	Partnership Network	Customer Interface
• Business mission • Product/market scope • Basis for differentiation	• Core competencies • Strategic assets	• Suppliers • Partners • Other key relationships	• Target customer • Fulfillment and support • Pricing structure

FIGURE 6.3

Components of a Business Model

WHAT WENT WRONG?

Joost: Why Its Important to Be Sensitive to *All* Aspects of Your Business Model

Joost was a hot start-up when it launched. If you're familiar with Hulu, Joost was Hulu before Hulu existed. Joost launched in 2006 as a premier online video service that aggregated and streamed premium video online. It quickly struck partnership agreements with media companies including CBS and Viacom. It raised $45 million in funding from top-tier venture capital firms such as Sequoia Capital and Index Ventures. It also generated incredible buzz. It was what everyone was waiting for—a service that allowed people to watch high-quality content online rather than on a television set. It also had successful celebrity founders, Niklas Zennström and Janus Friis, who started Skype and just a year earlier sold it to eBay for $2.6 billion.

Incredibly, just three years after Joost launched, in mid-2009, it failed. It remained in business by licensing its technology to cable, satellite, and other Web sites, but laid off the majority of its employees and set its original vision aside. What went wrong for this firm after what appeared to be such a successful and promising beginning?

Several things went wrong with Joost. The most obvious problems are that the firm grew too big too fast, and never behaved like a start-up. From day one, according to technology blogger Om Malik, it felt more like a large company than a small company, with all the bureaucratic trappings that large companies have. It was also based in multiple geographic locations—New York, London, and the Netherlands. Maintaining a good communication flow across multiple locations is difficult for all firms—particularly new ones. Joost also may have suffered from too much hype too soon. Start-ups rarely launch perfect products or services; they often have to adjust based on customer feedback. Joost had many people eagerly awaiting its release—250,000 people signed up for the beta version of the site alone. However, lots of people quickly became upset with some early technical hiccups. Buzz can quickly turn into buzz kill when a hyped-up company fails to deliver on its promises.

But Joost's most critical mistakes dealt with subtle aspects of its business model. Its core strategy wasn't focused. Instead of building an online service that streamed sporting events, for example, it built an online service to stream any content—from sporting events to television shows to full-length movies. In terms of customer interface, rather than being a browser-based service, like YouTube was at the time, it asked its customers to download a clunky piece of software. It was also slow to fix technical problems, an error that frustrated its users. Joost's biggest problems, however, resulted in the way it configured its partnership network. First, in a rush to sign up partners, some observers feel that Joost signed unfavorable deals giving it little ad inventory to sell to generate revenue. The weakness of these agreements may have done Joost in when Hulu came along.

Joost was blindsided by Hulu, which was backed by NBC, Universal, News Corp, and Disney. Hulu was better than Joost on almost all metrics. It was browser-based rather than requiring a download, had more premium content than Joost did, and because of the richness of its premium content, could sell more ads and pass along more revenue to its content providers. When Joost's partners compared what they could get from Joost versus Hulu, many abandoned Joost for Hulu.

Questions for Critical Thinking

1. In regard to putting together an effective business model, what are the lessons you can learn from Joost's failure?
2. What do you think was Joost's single biggest mistake?
3. Spend some time looking at Hulu. Describe the four components (core strategy, strategic resources, partnership network, and customer interface) of Hulu's business model. Evaluate Hulu's model. To what degree is Hulu vulnerable to being blindsided by a start-up in its space, similar to how Joost was blindsided by Hulu?
4. One point made in the feature is that Joost grew too big too fast, and never acted like a start-up. In what ways can growing too big too fast and not acting like a start-up hinder a start-up firm?

Sources: Michael Learmouth, "Web TV Pioneer Joost Gives Up Dream, Restructures," *Advertising Age*, http://adage.com/digital/article?article_id=13767, June 30, 2009 (accessed February 28, 2011); Om Malik, "What Went Wrong with Joost?" *Gigoma.com* blog, http://gigaom.com/2009/06/30/what-went-wrong-with-joost, June 20, 2009 (accessed February 28, 2011).

Mission Statement   A firm's mission, or **mission statement**, describes why it exists and what its business model is supposed to accomplish.[12] Table 6.3 provides examples of the mission statements of five firms from very different industries. To varying degrees, the statements articulate the overarching priorities of the firms and set criteria to measure performance.

TABLE 6.3 EXAMPLES OF MISSION STATEMENTS

Google

Organize the world's information and make it universally accessible and useful.

Facebook

Give people the power to share and make the world more open and connected.

d.light

Enable households without reliable electricity to attain the same quality of life as those with electricity. We will begin by replacing every kerosene lantern with clean, safe and bright light.

Southwest Airlines

The mission of Southwest Airlines is dedication to the highest quality of customer service delivered with a sense of warmth, friendliness, individual pride, and company spirit.

Zynga

To connect people through games.

It is important that a firm's mission not be defined too narrowly. If it is, the business model that evolves may become too singularly focused and resistant to change. Take Xerox, for example—a firm that styled itself as "The Document Company" with an implicit mission that focused on copiers and copying. This mission created what some call a **business concept blind spot**, which prevents a firm from seeing an opportunity that might fit its business model. Xerox viewed itself as a company that *reproduced* documents that already existed, causing the firm to be a late entrant into the market for computer printers, which print original documents stored electronically. This narrow focus allowed Hewlett-Packard to gain control of the printer market.[13]

LEARNING OBJECTIVE
7. Explain the meaning of the term *business concept blind spot*.

Product/Market Scope A company's **product/market scope** defines the products and markets on which it will concentrate. The choice of product has an important impact on a firm's business model. For example, Amazon.com started out as an online bookseller but has evolved to sell a host of diverse products including CDs, DVDs, shoes, apparel, furniture, and even groceries and gourmet food. Similarly, Yahoo! started as a company offering free Internet search services in an attempt to generate enough traffic to sell advertising space on its Web site. This business model worked until the e-commerce bubble burst in early 2000 and advertising revenues declined. Yahoo! is continually revising its business model to include additional subscription services to generate a more consistent income stream.[14]

The markets on which a company focuses are also an important element of its core strategy. For example, Dell Inc. targets business customers and government agencies, while Hewlett-Packard targets individuals, small businesses, and first-time computer buyers. For both firms, their choices have had a significant impact on the shaping of their business models.

New ventures should be particularly careful not to expand their product/market offerings beyond their capabilities. Even Dell had to resist this temptation, during its early rapid growth stage, as illustrated by Michael Dell in his book *Direct from Dell*:

Growing a company much faster than the industry is growing is great, but when your company grows by as much as 127 percent in one year, you can quickly outstrip your ability to manage it effectively. Our problem was not that Dell was in serious decline or that our customers didn't want to buy our products. Quite the opposite, we learned that it was possible to grow too quickly. The problem was that we had been over enthusiastically pursuing every opportunity that presented itself. We needed to learn that not only did we not have to jump at each and every one, as we once did—but that we couldn't or shouldn't, for our overall well-being.[15]

Basis for Differentiation   A new venture should differentiate itself from its competitors in some way that is important to its customers and is not easy to copy.[16] If a new firm's products or services aren't different from those of its competitors, why should anyone try them?[17]

From a broad perspective, firms typically choose one of two generic strategies (cost leadership and differentiation) to establish a defensible position in the marketplace. Firms that have a **cost leadership strategy** strive to have the lowest costs in the industry, relative to competitors' costs, and typically attract customers by offering them a low, if not the lowest, price for the products they sell. Warby Parker, the company that sells $95 prescription glasses, clearly uses a cost-leadership strategy as do some large firms such as Walmart and Dollar General. In contrast, firms using a **differentiation strategy** compete on the basis of providing unique or different products, typically on the basis of quality, service, timeliness, or some other dimension that is important to customers.[18] Historically, it has been difficult for a new venture to use a cost leadership strategy because effective use of this strategy demands that a firm develop economies of scale as a path to continuously reducing its costs. The issue is that time and experience are required for a firm to develop economies of scale.

Firms within the same industry often use different generic strategies. In the retail clothing industry, for example, Ross follows a cost leadership strategy by offering slightly out-of-date merchandise at a deep discount. In contrast, Abercrombie & Fitch uses a differentiation strategy. It rarely cuts prices and instead competes on the basis that its products are different and stylish enough that they should command a premium price.

The strategy a firm chooses greatly affects its business model.[19] A cost leadership strategy requires a business model that is focused on efficiency, cost minimization, and large volume. As a result, a cost leader's facilities typically aren't fancy, as the emphasis is on keeping costs low rather than on creating products that differ substantially from competitors' products in terms of features. Conversely, a differentiation strategy requires a business model focused on developing products and services that are unique in ways that are important to targeted customers and that command a premium price.

Strategic Resources

A firm is not able to implement a strategy without adequate resources. This reality means that a firm's resources substantially affect how its business model is used. For a new venture, its strategic resources may initially be limited to the competencies of its founders, the opportunity they have identified, and the unique way they plan to service their market. Core competencies and strategic assets are a firm's most important resources.

LEARNING OBJECTIVE

8. Define *core competency* and describe its importance.

Core Competencies   A **core competency** is a resource or capability that serves as a source of a firm's competitive advantage over its rivals. It is a unique skill or capability that transcends products or markets, makes a significant contribution to the customer's perceived benefit, and is difficult to imitate.[20] Examples of core competencies include Apple's competence in designing consumer products, Zappos's competence in customer service, and Netflix's competence in supply chain management. A firm's core competencies determine where a firm is able to create the most value. In distinguishing its core competencies, a firm should identify the skills it has that are

Pizza Fusion, whose motto is "Saving the Earth One Pizza at a Time," differentiates itself by selling organic pizzas that are delivered in hybrid cars and placed in boxes that are made of material that will decompose within 50 days. The company's core competencies focus on its understanding of organic and specialty foods. Its current menu is more than 75% organic, and it offers selections for vegans and products that are gluten free.

p77/Zuma Press/Newscom

(1) unique, (2) valuable to customers, (3) difficult to imitate, and (4) transferable to new opportunities.[21]

A firm's core competencies are important in both the short and the long term. In the short term, it is a company's core competencies that allow it to differentiate itself from its competitors and create unique value. For example, Dell's core competencies historically have included supply chain management, efficient assembly, and serving corporate customers, so its business model of providing corporate customers computers that are price competitive, are technologically up-to-date, and have access to after-sale support makes sense. If Dell suddenly started assembling and selling musical instruments, analysts would be skeptical of the new strategy and justifiably ask, "Why is Dell pursuing a strategy that is outside its core competency?"

In the long term, it is important to have core competencies to grow and establish strong positions in complementary markets. For example, Dell has taken its core competencies in the assembly and sale of PCs and has moved them into the market for computer servers and other electronic devices. This process of adapting a company's core competencies to exploit new opportunities is referred to as **resource leverage**.

Strategic Assets **Strategic assets** are anything rare and valuable that a firm owns. They include plant and equipment, location, brands, patents, customer data, a highly qualified staff, and distinctive partnerships. A particularly valuable strategic asset is a company's brand, which is discussed in detail in Chapter 11. Starbucks, for example, has worked hard to build the image of its brand, and it would take an enormous effort for another coffee retailer to achieve this same level of brand recognition. Companies ultimately try to combine their core competencies and strategic assets to create a **sustainable competitive advantage**. This factor is one to which investors pay close attention when evaluating a business.[22] A sustainable competitive advantage is achieved by implementing a value-creating strategy that is unique and not easy to imitate.[23] This type of advantage is achievable when a firm has strategic resources and the ability to use them in unique ways that create value for a group of targeted customers.[24]

Partnership Network

A firm's network of partnerships is the third component of a business model. New ventures, in particular, typically do not have the resources to perform all the tasks required to make their businesses work, so they rely on partners to perform key roles.[25] In most cases, a business does not want to do everything itself because the majority of tasks needed to build a product or deliver a service are not core to a company's competitive advantage.[26] For example, Dell historically sought to differentiate itself from competitors through its expertise in assembling computers but buys chips from others, primarily Intel. Dell could manufacture its own chips, but it didn't have a core competency in this area. Similarly, Dell relies on UPS and FedEx to deliver its products because it would be silly for Dell to build a nationwide system to deliver its computers. Firms also rely on partners to supply intellectual capital needed to produce complex products and services, as illustrated in the following observation from two authorities on business partnerships:

> Neither Boeing nor Airbus has one-tenth of the intellectual capital or coordination capacity to cost-effectively mine metals, create alloys, make fasteners, cast and machine parts, design avionics, produce control systems, make engines, and so on. The complex systems we call airplanes come together through the voluntary agreements and collaborations of thousands of companies operating in the global marketplace.[27]

One thing that firms must often work hard at, particularly when they are in their start-up stage, is convincing other firms to partner with them. Partnering with a start-up is risky, particularly if its business model is new and untested in the marketplace. A firm's partnership network includes suppliers and other partners. Let's look at each of them.

Suppliers   A **supplier** (or vendor) is a company that provides parts or services to another company. A **supply chain** is the network of all the companies that participate in the production of a product, from the acquisition of raw materials to the final sale. Almost all firms have suppliers who play vital roles in the functioning of their business models.

Traditionally, firms maintained an arm's-length relationship with their suppliers and viewed them almost as adversaries. Producers needing a component part would negotiate with several suppliers to find the best price. Today, however, firms want to move away from contentious relationships with their suppliers and seek to partner with them to achieve mutually beneficial goals.[28] This shift resulted from competitive pressures that motivated managers to look up and down their value chains to find opportunities for cost savings, quality improvement, and improved speed to market. More and more, managers are focusing on **supply chain management**, which is the coordination of the flow of all information, money, and material that moves through a product's supply chain. The more efficiently an organization can manage its supply chain, the more effectively its entire business model will perform.[29]

When collaborating with suppliers, firms seek to find ways to motivate them to perform at a higher level. Many firms are reducing the number of their suppliers and working more closely with a smaller group. Procter & Gamble (P&G), for example, maintains close relationships with its suppliers and uses sophisticated systems to enhance the performance of its supply chain. P&G has accomplished a level of rigor in its supply chain that supports its core strategy of offering technologically up-to-date computers at affordable prices. Additionally, P&G continues working with its suppliers for the purpose of developing "environmentally sustainable supply chain practices."[30]

TABLE 6.4   **THE MOST COMMON TYPES OF BUSINESS PARTNERSHIPS**

Partnership Form	Description
Joint venture	An entity created by two or more firms pooling a portion of their resources to create a separate, jointly owned organization
Network	A hub-and-wheel configuration with a local firm at the hub organizing the interdependencies of a complex array of firms
Consortia	A group of organizations with similar needs that band together to create a new entity to address those needs
Strategic alliance	An arrangement between two or more firms that establishes an exchange relationship but has no joint ownership involved
Trade associations	Organizations (typically nonprofit) that are formed by firms in the same industry to collect and disseminate trade information, offer legal and technical advice, furnish industry-related training, and provide a platform for collective lobbying

Source: B. Barringer and J. Harrison, "Walking a Tightrope: Creating Value Through Interorganizational Relationships," *Journal of Management* 26, no. 3 (2000): 367–403. Reprinted by permission of Sage Publications.

Other Key Relationships   Along with its suppliers, firms partner with other companies to make their business models work. As described in Table 6.4, strategic alliances, joint ventures, networks, consortia, and trade associations are common forms of these partnerships. A survey by PricewaterhouseCoopers found that more than half of America's fastest-growing companies have formed multiple partnerships to support their business models. According to the research, these partnerships have "resulted in more innovative products, more profit opportunities, and significantly high growth rates" for the firms involved.[31]

There are also hybrid forms of business partnerships that allow companies to maximize their efficiencies. One relatively new approach, referred to as **insourcing**, takes place when a service provider comes inside a partner's facilities and helps the partner both design and manage its supply chain. An example is a unique partnership between Papa John's and UPS. Since 1996, UPS has managed, routed, and scheduled the delivery of tomatoes, pizza sauce, cheese, and other ingredients from Papa John's food service centers across the United States to its more than 3,500 pizza delivery stores twice a week. The ingredients are delivered in UPS trailers marked with Papa John's insignias.[32]

Partnerships do carry risks, particularly if a single partnership is a key component of a firm's business model. For a number of reasons, many partnerships fall short of meeting participants' expectations. When this happens, partnerships are thought to have *failed*. Many of the failures result from poor planning or the difficulties involved with meshing the cultures of two or more organizations to achieve a common goal. There are also potential disadvantages to participating in alliances, including loss of proprietary information, management complexities, financial and organizational risks, risk of becoming dependent on a partner, and partial loss of decision autonomy.[33] The percentage of alliances that fail remains an unresolved issue with some suggesting that the failure rate is around 50 percent[34] while others suggest that the failure rate is as high as 70 percent.[35]

Still, for the majority of start-ups, the ability to establish and effectively manage partnerships is a major component of their business models' success. Two start-ups that have been able to form successful partnerships for this reason are Getwine and WaveSecure, as illustrated in the "Partnering for Success" feature.

PARTNERING FOR SUCCESS

Getwine, South Africa, and WaveSecure, Singapore: Forging Valuable Relationships by Elevating the Performance of Their Partners

Getwine: Web: www.getwine.co.za, Twitter: getwine, Facebook: GETWINE

WaveSecure: Web: www.wavesecure.com, Twitter: wavesecure, Facebook: McAfee WaveSecure

All firms must partner with others to make their business models work. A challenge that new firms have is forging partnerships and obtaining the cooperation they need to move forward. It's easy for new firms to face resistance, particularly if it looks like their business models will only benefit themselves. A better approach is to build a business model that not only works for yourself but elevates your partners. Firms that meet this criterion find it easier to establish partnerships and build an upbeat, can-do culture.

Getwine

Getwine is a wine company based in Cape Town, South Africa. It doesn't own a single vineyard or processing facility, but buys unlabelled surplus wines from vineyards and distributors and sells them online to consumers at very affordable prices. While Getwine competes with other wines that are available to consumers, it actually helps the industry by buying its excess wine.

Although South African wines are competing well on the world stage, the strengthening of the rand has considerably pushed up the cost of a bottle abroad. The practice of selling unlabelled wines, or clearskins as they are also known, works well in periods of currency imbalance. Many top estates are unable to export all of their annual wine harvests and are keen to shift surplus stock while avoiding the negative consequences of heavily discounting their brands. Getwine sources the unlabelled excess wines and sells them at cut prices across South Africa via an efficient e-commerce operation. The business model is a win-win proposition for everyone involved, and the country's wine experts have feted the Getwine selection.

WaveSecure

Mobile phones today host a whole suite of functions, such as a phone book, a camera, calendar, and e-mail; and users are becoming increasingly dependent on them. Losing one is not just frustrating, it can make life very difficult indeed. Like so many good entrepreneurial ideas, the origin for WaveSecure was a simple problem. One of the cofounders kept losing his mobile phone, and the team of graduates from the National University of Singapore put their heads together to find a solution.

WaveSecure phone security software allows users to lock their phones remotely, track its usage, back up personal contacts through the Internet, and even remotely wipe private data off the phone once it is lost. The phone can even be programmed to emit a piercing scream when stolen, even if in silent mode, in a bid to embarrass the finder of the device.

The idea was an immediate hit with the authorities, gaining high-profile clients such as the Singapore Police and the Defense Ministry. The consumer version, which was launched in December 2007, saw 60,000 users sign up to the $2-a-month service within three months. Large phone corporations were a little reluctant to partner with the unknown start-up at first, but once they saw the response from consumers, they became convinced that WaveSecure is a product that mobile phone users needed.

WaveSecure has now been adopted by most of the major phone companies including Nokia, O2, Sony Ericsson, and Motorola, with some offering it as a bundle with the phone contract and others including it as a value-added service charge on subscribers' bills.

Questions for Critical Thinking

1. Describe a firm, other than Getwine or WaveSecure, that has created a win-win business model for itself and its partners.
2. One a scale of 1 to 5 (5 is high), how do you rate the strength of both Getwine's and WaveSecure's business models? Explain your ratings.
3. Describe Getwine's core strategy and its customer interface. Do the same for WaveSecure's.
4. Look at the "You Be the VC 6.2" feature, which focuses on Minted, a company that utilizes an innovative business model to produce stationery and invitations. In what ways, if any, does Minted's business model elevate the performance of its partners?

Sources: "GetWine!" *The Times*, May 15, 2008; "New Code to Track Your Lost Mobile," *Economic Times*, October 25, 2008; "*Asia* WaveSecure Software to Go Commercial Soon," *CNET*, October 6, 2008.

Customer Interface

Customer interface—how a firm interacts with its customers—is the fourth component of a business model. The type of customer interaction depends on how a firm chooses to compete. For example, Amazon.com sells books solely over the Internet, while Barnes & Noble sells through both its traditional bookstores and online. Sometimes a company's customer interface will change as conditions change. For example, until 2001, Apple sold its products through retailers like Sears and CompUSA (CompUSA is now a part of a larger firm called TigerDirect.com). Apple experienced sales declines in the late 1990s, and in 2001 made the strategic decision to take control of retail sales of its products, in part to "own" the customer retail experience. The first two Apple stores opened in 2001 in McLean, Virginia, and Glendale, California. The Apple stores have been a hit, and are partly responsible for Apple's surge in popularity. In 2002, Apple enhanced its stores by adding the Genius Bar, which is a place where customers can receive technical advice or set up service and repairs for their Apple products. This added dimension of Apple's customer interface has provided the company a forum to physically interact with people who have questions about Apple's products or need help with a repair.[36]

For a new venture, the customer interface that it chooses is central to how it plans to compete and where it is located in the value chain of the products and services it provides.[37] The three elements of a company's customer interface are target market, fulfillment and support, and pricing structure. Let's look at each of these elements closely.

Target Market   A firm's **target market** is the limited group of individuals or businesses that it goes after or tries to appeal to, as discussed earlier in this book. The target market a firm selects affects everything it does, from the strategic resources it acquires to the partnerships it forges to its promotional campaigns. For example, the clothing retailer Abercrombie & Fitch

Apple interfaces directly with its customers in its Apple stores. Here, an Apple customer tries out an Apple iPad 2 for the first time. Apple has over 300 stores, including this store in Eaton Center in Toronto, Canada. Merchandise is displayed in "solution zones" for hands-on experimentation.

Zou Zheng Xinhua News Agency/Newscom

targets 18- to 22-year-old men and women who are willing to pay full price for trendy apparel. So the decisions it makes about strategic resources, partnerships, and advertising will be much different from the decisions made by Chico's, a clothing store that targets 30- to 60-year-old women.

Typically, a firm greatly benefits from having a clearly defined target market. Because of the specificity of its targeted customer, Abercrombie & Fitch can keep abreast of the clothing trends for its market, it can focus its marketing and promotional campaigns, and it can develop deep core competencies pertaining to its specific marketplace. A company such as Gap Inc. has a larger challenge because its stores appeal to a broader range of clientele. In fact, when a retailer such as Gap starts offering too many products, it typically begins breaking itself down into more narrowly focused markets so that it can regain the advantages that are enjoyed by a singularly focused retailer such as Abercrombie & Fitch. Gap has done this successfully and now has a diversified collection with five brands Gap, Old Navy, Banana Republic, Piperlime, and Athleta.

LEARNING OBJECTIVE

10. Explain the concept of fulfillment and support.

Fulfillment and Support   **Fulfillment and support** describes the way a firm's product or service "goes to market," or how it reaches its customers. It also refers to the channels a company uses and what level of customer support it provides.[38] All these issues impact the shape and nature of a company's business model.

Firms differ considerably along these dimensions. Suppose that a new venture developed and patented an exciting new smartphone technology. In forming its business plan, the firm might have several options regarding how to take its technology to market. It could (1) license the technology to existing smartphone companies such as Nokia and Samsung, (2) manufacture the smartphone itself and establish its own sales channels, or (3) partner with a smartphone company such as Samsung and sell the phone through partnerships with the smartphone service providers such as AT&T and Verizon. The choice a firm makes about fulfillment and service has a dramatic impact on the type of company that evolves and the business model that develops. For example, if the company licenses its technology, it would probably build a business model that emphasized research and development to continue to have cutting-edge technologies to license to the cell phone manufacturers. In contrast, if it decides to manufacture its own cell phones, it needs to establish core competencies in the areas of manufacturing and design and needs to form partnerships with cell phone retailers such as AT&T, Sprint, and Verizon.

The level of customer support a firm is willing to offer also affects its business model. Some firms differentiate their products or services and provide extra value to their customers through high levels of service and support. Customer service can include delivery and installation, financing arrangements, customer training, warranties and guarantees, repairs, layaway plans, convenient hours of operation, convenient parking, and information through toll-free numbers and Web sites.[39] Dell Inc. for example has a broad menu of tiered services available to provide its corporate clients the exact level of support they need and for which they are willing to pay. Making this choice of services available is a key component of Dell's business model.

Pricing Structure   A third element of a company's customer interface is its pricing structure, a topic that we discuss in more detail in Chapter 11. Pricing structures vary, depending on a firm's target market and its pricing philosophy. For example, some consultants charge a flat fee for performing a service (e.g., helping an entrepreneurial venture write a business plan), while others charge an hourly rate. In some instances, a company must also choose whether to charge its customers directly or indirectly through a service provider. A popular way to sell a service on the Internet is via the freemium pricing structure, as described in Table 6.1. The word *freemium* is a blend of the words *free* and *premium.* Businesses that utilize a freemium pricing model give away a basic product or service for free, and offer premium services on a tiered pricing plan.

Firms differentiate themselves on the basis of their pricing structure in both common and unusual ways. In general, it is difficult for new ventures to differentiate themselves on price, which is a common strategy for larger firms with more substantial economies of scale, as discussed earlier in the chapter. There are exceptions such as Warby Parker in eyewear and in graphic design—firms that have been price leaders since their inception. Similarly, there are several examples of firms that have started primarily on the basis of featuring innovative pricing models. The most noteworthy is Priceline.com, which pioneered the practice of letting customers explicitly set prices they are willing to pay for products and services. CarMax, which features a "no-haggle" pricing policy and sells new and used cars through its showrooms and Web site, is another example. The company's slogan is "The Way Car Buying Should Be." CarMax offers its customers a low-stress environment by presenting them with what it believes to be a fair price, with no negotiations.

In summary, it is very useful for a new venture to look at itself in a holistic manner and understand that it must construct an effective "business model" to be successful. Everyone that does business with a new firm, from its customers to its partners, does so on a voluntary basis. As a result, a firm must motivate its customers and partners to play along. The primary elements of a firm's business model are its core strategy, strategic resources, partnership network, and customer interface. Close attention to each of these elements is essential for a new venture's success.

CHAPTER SUMMARY

1. A firm's business model is its plan or diagram for how it intends to compete, use its resources, structure relationships, interface with customers, and create value to sustain itself on the basis of the profits it generates.

2. Business model innovation refers to initiatives such as those undertaken by Michael Dell when he established the firm now known as Dell Inc. that revolutionized how products are sold in an industry.

3. The main reasons that having a clearly articulated business model is important are as follows: It serves as an ongoing extension of feasibility analysis, it focuses attention on how all the elements of a business fit together, it describes why the network of participants who are needed to make a business idea viable would be willing to work together, and it articulates the core logic of a firm to all its stakeholders.

4. The value chain shows how a product moves from the raw-material stage to the final consumer. The value chain helps a firm identify opportunities to enhance its competitive strategies and to recognize new business opportunities.

5. A complete misread of the customer and utterly unsound economics are the two fatal flaws that can make a business model a failure from the outset.

6. Core strategy, strategic resources, partnership networks, and customer interface are the four major components of a firm's business model.

7. A business concept blind spot prevents a firm from seeing an opportunity that might fit its business model.

8. A core competency is something that a firm does particularly well. It is a resource or capability that serves as a source of a firm's competitive advantage over its rivals.

9. Supply chain management refers to the flow of all information, money, and material that moves through a product's supply chain. The more efficiently an organization can manage its supply chain, the more effectively its entire business model will perform.

10. A firm's target market is the limited group of individuals or business that it goes after or tries to appeal to at a point in time.

KEY TERMS

business concept blind spot, **217**

business model, **206**

business model innovation, **207**

core competency, **218**

core strategy, **215**

cost leadership strategy, **218**

customer interface, **223**

differentiation strategy, **218**

fulfillment and support, **224**

insourcing, **221**

mission statement, **216**

product/market scope, **217**

resource leverage, **219**

strategic assets, **219**

supplier, **220**

supply chain, **220**

supply chain management, **220**

sustainable competitive advantage, **219**

target market, **223**

value chain, **212**

REVIEW QUESTIONS

1. Define the term *business model*. How can entrepreneurial firms benefit by developing and using a business model? What are the downsides for entrepreneurial ventures when an effective business model isn't put in place?

2. Explain what business model innovation means. Provide an example of business model innovation other than the examples included in the chapter.

3. List at least three reasons that demonstrate why having a business model is important.

4. Why did WebHouse's business model fail?

5. How does an understanding of the value chain help explain how business models emerge?

6. What are the two fatal flaws that can render a business model untenable?

7. What are the four primary components of a firm's business model? Briefly describe the importance of each component.

8. Describe what is meant by the term *core strategy* and why it is important.

9. Describe the purpose of a mission statement.

10. What is meant by the term *business model blind spot*? Provide an original example of a firm that suffered as the result of having a business model blind spot.

11. What is a firm's product/market scope? Why is the concept of product/market

scope important in regard to crafting a successful business model?

12. Why is it important for firms to differentiate themselves from competitors?

13. In what ways does a focus on a cost leadership strategy lead to a very different business model than a focus on a differentiation strategy?

14. Define the term *core competency* and describe why it's important for a firm to have one or more core competencies. How do a company's core competencies help shape its business model?

15. What is meant by the term *resource leverage*? How does an understanding of this term help a firm exploit new product or service opportunities?

16. What is meant by the term *strategic asset*? Provide examples of the strategic assets of three well-known firms.

17. Why do firms typically need partners to make their business models work?

18. What is meant by the term *supply chain management*?

19. What is meant by the term *customer interface*? Explain how Dell and Hewlett-Packard differ from each other on this core dimension.

20. Describe the impact of a firm's pricing structure on its business model.

APPLICATION QUESTIONS

1. Write a brief critique of Stroome's business model. What do you think are the strengths and weaknesses of the model? Do you think that Stroome has a sustainable competitive advantage? Why or why not?

2. Write a brief description of Apple Inc.'s business model.

3. Spend some time thinking about Warby Parker, the eyewear company (highlighted in the "Savvy Entrepreneurial Firm" feature) that is pioneering a new business model. Which of the four components of a business model does Warby Parker's business model emphasize? To what extent does the success or failure of Warby Parker's business model rest on how much value its patients see in this portion of its model?

4. Carol Schmidt plans to open a company that will make accessories for smartphones. She has read that having a clearly articulated business model will help "all the elements of her business fit together." Carol isn't quite sure what that statement means. If Carol asked you to explain it to her, what would you say?

5. Do you consider the founders of Zipcar to be business model innovators? If so, why do you think a traditional car rental company, like Hertz or Avis, didn't bring car sharing, as an alternative to car ownership or car rentals, to America rather than Zipcar?

6. Jane Rowan is an experienced business consultant. Through working with clients, she has noticed that many companies have "business concept blind spots." How can having a business concept blind spot affect the strength of a firm's business model?

7. Write a mission statement for WaveSecure, one of the companies highlighted in the "Partnering for Success" feature. How can this statement help clarify and direct the core strategy component of WaveSecure's business model?

8. Select one of the following companies: Facebook, Foursquare, or Zynga. For the company you selected, identify its core competency and explain how its core competency strengthens its business model and how it contributes to the firm's competitive advantage.

9. Using the same firm you selected for question 8, make a list of the firm's strategic assets. How does each of its strategic assets strengthen its business model?

10. Twitter (http://twitter.com) is a free networking and micro-blogging service that allows its users to send and read other users' updates (otherwise known as "tweets"). Although Twitter has millions of users and is growing rapidly, it has been criticized for not having a viable long-term business model. Spend some time researching Twitter. How does the company make money? Does it have a viable long-term business model? If so, describe it.

11. What are some examples of instances in which location is an important part of a firm's business model?

12. Shannon Jones just received an e-mail message from an angel investor who has agreed to listen to her pitch her business idea. The investor said, "Your timing is good—I just happen to be sitting on $500,000 that I'm anxious to invest. One thing I'll warn you about ahead of time, however, is that you must show me that your business has the potential to achieve a sustainable competitive advantage. If you can't show me that, I won't invest." Shannon has read about sustainable competitive advantage but is still a little hazy about the concept. Explain the concept to Shannon.

13. Spend some time studying SunRun, the solar power company highlighted in the "Savvy Entrepreneurial Firm" feature. What is found in the "strategic resources" component of SunRun's business model? How do this firm's strategic resources strengthen its business model and contribute to its success?

14. Do you think that the business models of daily newspapers are viable in the long run? If you were the owner of a daily newspaper in a major American city, would you try to maintain the print edition of your paper, evolve to strictly an online presence, or do something else?

YOU BE THE VC 6.1

Company: Home Plus

Web: www.homeplus.co.kr

Business Idea: Create a virtual supermarket targeting busy customers in Korea. The "shop" is in the form of a screen door that has been covered with images of real-life store shelves stacked with goods, each carrying a small bar code. Target customers, who are too busy to go to the supermarket to shop, will be able to make purchases by taking photos of the bar codes. The goods will be sent to the customers' houses in the evening if buyers make purchases in the morning.

Pitch: Home Plus, a subsidiary of the British giant Tesco, has opened a virtual store in a busy Seoul subway station. It is a virtual supermarket that offers more than 500 items than regular Tesco stores, including food, electronics, office supplies, and toiletries. Customers can download a related app on their smartphones and make purchases by taking photos of an item's bar code.

This is a new store that integrates current online and offline shopping space, and has great potential. The virtual shop is located on the wall of the busy subway station. Customers can browse images of products and order them using applications on their mobile phones while they are waiting for trains. One of the reasons that Home Plus has chosen this market to target is that Koreans are very hard-working people who often do not have the time to shop frequently. With this innovative "store," customers can simply make purchases on the way to work and will have their shopping delivered by the time they get home. Another reason is that the smartphone market in Korea is well-developed. Most people in Korea have at least one smartphone that they carry with them at all times and therefore, the market for the Home Plus app is very large. This platform decreases the distance between customers and the shop and allows the shop to come to the customers.

Home Plus is now the third largest supermarket in Korea. Its online store for smartphone users achieves sales of 30 million won a week, but it hopes it can get a big boost from some of the 200,000 people who pass through the station daily. Online sales of all types last year were worth 160 billion won, and Home Plus's total revenue was 11 trillion won. From a state telecommunication official estimation, smartphone use will surge from 30 percent of the population to 80 percent within three to four years. That means the virtual market's sales will keep growing.

Q&A: Based on the material covered in this chapter, what questions would you ask the firm's founders before making your funding decision? What answers would satisfy you?

Decision: If you had to make your decision on just the information provided in the pitch and on the company's Web site, would you fund this company? Why or why not?

YOU BE THE VC 6.2

Company: FastPencil

Web: www.fastpencil.com
Twitter: fastpencil
Facebook: FastPencil

Business Idea: Provide a user-friendly, affordable, and effective platform for authors to self-publish books, and obtain real-time feedback on the books they're working on.

Pitch: Not long ago, the only way to publish a book was to pitch the book or a proposal for a book to a book agent or publisher, and hope that the book would be one of the few they'd accept. That's no longer the case. FastPencil is a leader among companies helping writers self-publish books.

Here's how it works. Once registered on FastPencil's Web site, an author can use the company's Web-based software to write a book. Once completed, easy-to-use tools are available for the purpose of customizing the book and prepare it for printing. A single copy of a 200-page 6-by 3-inch paperback book can be obtained for as little as $9.30. A single copy of a 300-page hardback book in a 7-by 10-inch format can be obtained for $18.00. Premium services such as professional design, editing, proofing, and expert advice are also available. The services, which are sold in "publishing packages," range from $999 for the bronze service to $1,999 for the gold service. The gold service, for example, includes online coaching, manuscript setup, editorial review, formatting review, distribution of the finished book to FastPencil's Web site, Amazon.com, BarnesAndNoble.com, and other book stores, and related services. A differentiating feature of FastPencil's approach, whether an author wants to create the book essentially for free or whether the author avails himself or herself of one of the premium services, is the support that's provided. Authors can obtain real-time feedback for free by allowing friends and colleagues to access their book while it's being written on FastPencil's

Web site. Another option is to solicit feedback from a like-minded author through FastPencil's online forum. For those paying for one of the premium services, more advanced forms of advice are available.

FastPencil's service is timely in that sales of digital books have taken off, and companies like Apple and Amazon.com have created marketplaces for self-published authors. FastPencil helps the majority of its authors convert their books into a digital format. Generally, authors of self-published digital books obtain a 70 percent royalty on net sales compared to authors of hardback, paperback, and digital books sold through traditional publishers, which receive a royalty in the 10 percent to 18 percent range. The number of digital books being sold in the United States is impressive, a number attributed to the popularity of digital

book readers like the Amazon Kindle and the Apple iPad. According to the Association of American Publishers, U.S. book sales fell 1.8 percent last year to $23.9 billion, but digital book sales tripled to $313 million. In late 2010, Amazon.com announced that it was now selling more digital books than paperback and hardback books through its Web site.

Q&A: Based on the material covered in this chapter, what questions would you ask the firm's founders before making your funding decision? What answers would satisfy you?

Decision: If you had to make your decision on just the information provided in the pitch and on the company's Web site, would you fund this company? Why or why not?

CASE **6.1**

Airbnb: How Listening to Customers and Iterating the Business Model Helped Shape and Mold a Successful Start-up

Web: www.airbnb.com
Twitter: airbnb
Facebook: Airbnb

Bruce R. Barringer, *Oklahoma State University*
R. Duane Ireland, *Texas A&M University*

Introduction

It all started because two aspiring designers needed money to pay their rent. It was October 2007, and Brian Chesky and Joe Gebbia were sharing an apartment in San Francisco. There was an international design conference coming to town. The two noticed that on the conference's Web site, all the hotels that were listed were sold out. The thought occurred to them that they could make extra money by renting out space in their apartment to people attending the conference.

They proceeded to pull out a couple of air beds they had in a closet and said to each other, "This is it. We're going to be the air bed and breakfast—at least for the weekend." They quickly designed a Web site, put it up, and filled the three spots they had available in their apartment. They figured they'd get a couple of guys in their twenties who decided to attend the conference at the last minute. They ended up with three people who broke all their assumptions—about the business, the market, everything. The first person was a guy from India, who just couldn't believe they put up a Web site offering space in their apartment. The second was a 35-year-old woman from Boston. And the third person was a 45-year-old father of five from Utah.

This experience got Chesky and Gebbia thinking there might be a bigger opportunity here. They made good money, about $1,000, renting their space for the conference. They also got to meet three amazing designers in the exact same field they aspired to enter. They also started thinking about the feedback their guests had provided regarding staying in their apartment. They had liked the social element of the experience. Instead of being in a sterile hotel, they got to stay with other designers who knew San Francisco and were eager to show them around. And they saved a little money to boot.

Initial Business Model

Chesky and Gebbia started talking to friends and family about their idea. They knew if they wanted to formulate a business they'd need programming help, so they approached a good friend and expert programmer, Nate Blecharczyk, who agreed to sign on. The next big conference was South by Southwest in Austin, Texas, in February 2008. South by Southwest is an annual film, music, and emerging technologies conference. Chesky and Gebbia wanted a more robust site than the quick site they put up for the design conference in San

(continued)

Francisco. So they worked night and day to build the site and get it up. The business model at this point was simple. Air Bed & Breakfast, as it was now called, was a way to help people find housing, at a private residence rather than a hotel, when attending a conference. Air Bed & Breakfast didn't accept money. Similar to Craigslist, people would simply exchange money when they met each other during the stay. Their own revenue model wasn't worked out in that they weren't quite sure at this point how to charge for the service.

There was one interesting twist to their Web site at this point that differentiated themselves from two sites, Couch Surfing and Craigslist, which were providing a similar service. On Couch Surfing you saw a photo of the person you'd be staying with. On Craigslist you saw a photo of the place. On Air Bed & Breakfast you saw the person, the place, and it focused strictly on conferences and events. So the social element was stronger. At least you'd be staying with someone who was attending the same conference or event you were attending.

Iteration 1—Motivated by Using Their Own Service

Encouraged by their reception at South by Southwest (they hooked up 30 to 40 people), Chesky and Gebbia tried a third conference, in April 2008, and this time decided to use their own service. They picked a place to stay, and their host offered to pick them up at the airport because his girlfriend was making them a Vietnamese dinner. Things were going great until the host turned to them and said something like, "OK, where is my money?" The mood changed and Chesky and Gebbia realized that exchanging cash in person is awkward. It felt a little shady and they realized that they couldn't have people all over the world exchanging money in this manner. Air Bed & Breakfast had to handle the money. This was also the revenue model they were looking for. They would take a transaction fee for facilitating payment through the site. Handling the money this way would also improve the user experience.

They realized something else during the April 2008 event. People started saying things like they'd love to use the site next month when they're in London, but they weren't attending a conference or event. So they started thinking, "Maybe this is bigger than conferences." At that point, there was no way to list a room for rent other than for a conference or event. The site was set up for conferences and events and once the conference was over, the opportunity to list in the location of the conference was taken down.

These two insights—Air Bed & Breakfast should handle the money and the site is bigger than conferences—transformed the company. The business model quickly iterated to Air Bed & Breakfast handling the payments and broadening beyond conferences and events.

Iteration 2—Motivated by Joining Y Combinator and Interacting with Users

In early 2009, things were going well but not great for Air Bed & Breakfast. The team, consisting of Chesky,

Gebbia, and Blecharczyk, the programmer who became part of the team just before South by Southwest, joined Y Combinator. Y Combinator is a start-up incubator, located in Silicon Valley, which in exchange for about 6 percent equity in a start-up provides a small amount of seed-stage funding and three months of intense mentorship. It's run by Paul Graham, a very experienced investor and entrepreneur.

At that time, the majority of business Air Bed & Breakfast was getting was from New York City. Graham told the Air Bed & Breakfast team to go to New York City, rather than sit in California, and get to know their customers. So they started shuffling back and forth from California, to attend Y Combinator events, to New York City, to meet their customers. They set out to meet every single one of their users in New York City. They took pictures of their customers' places. They hosted parties for their customers to talk about the service. Two things started to happen. First, booking in New York started to go up. Apparently, their customers appreciated being asked for their feedback and started talking up the service. Second, every time they went to New York they used their own service. They started realizing that many things they thought about their service were not as good as they thought they were. They'd try to book a room on their Web site and think, "This is annoying." They also realized that the pictures of the rooms for rent needed to be bigger. They'd look at the small picture of an apartment listed on their site and then actually go to the place and think "Wow, this place is beautiful—I would have never known from the small photos." As a result of their experiences as customers of their own business, they put a lot of effort into redesigning the site.

Spending time with their users caused the Air Bed & Breakfast team to think about a piece of advice that's often given to start-up entrepreneurs. Often, entrepreneurs who are trying to build a big business are told to not try to visit or speak to users one-on-one because it "doesn't scale." The thinking is that if you want a million users, you can't get out and talk to everyone, so it's best to develop systems to interface with customers. Paul Graham, their Y Combinator mentor, told them to talk to users anyway. He said that while they were still small was the opportune time to meet users and learn from them. Looking back, the Air Bed & Breakfast team now thinks that meeting users in New York City in the spring of 2009 was the fundamental thing that changed their company for the better. Not only did they talk to their users, they booked rooms with them, slept in their homes, hung out with them, and picked their brains for hours on end for advice. It shaped their business, shaped the design of their Web site, and shaped the policies of their company. It goes back to a basic Paul Graham quote, "Make something people want."

Iteration 3—Meeting Barry Manilow's Drummer

At this point, the summer of 2009, the business model was set, or so the Air Bed & Breakfast team thought. The site was redesigned, the revenue model was in place, and the firm's business model had established a clear niche— namely, Air Bed & Breakfast helped people find spaces in people's homes while on a trip, and helped people who had rooms or other spaces to rent find travelers to rent to. Then, while on a trip to New York City, the Air Bed & Breakfast team met a guy who had a beautiful apartment across the street from Carnegie Hall in New York City. It turns out he was Barry Manilow's drummer, an individual who was traveling with Barry Manilow several months a year while Manilow was on tour. He loved Air Bed & Breakfast's service but didn't want to rent out a room or two occasionally; he wanted to rent his whole apartment for several months a year. That was an idea, and an entire market, the team had never considered. So they redesigned their site again to add the ability to rent an entire house or apartment, on a weekly or monthly basis. This type of rental arrangement is now a large part of Air Bed & Breakfast's business.

Current Status

The Air Bed & Breakfast team recently changed the firm's name to Airbnb. In July 2010, to get to know his users even better, Chesky moved out of the three-bedroom apartment where the company started, and announced he'd be "living on Airbnb" until the end of the year. He used his own site to book rooms in the San Francisco area for two to three nights a piece, and moved from place to place for the rest of 2010. In November 2010, the company raised $7.2 million in Series A venture capital funding to fund global expansion, hire staff, translate their service into multiple languages, and offer additional payment options.

On February 24, 2011, Airbnb announced a milestone: Since its launch, one million nights had been booked through its service. It now has bookings available in 170 countries. Here is a set of fun stats related to this business (as of February 2011): Longest single reservation: 200 nights; Most expensive listing: $10,000 per night; Most reservations by a single guest: 28; Number of marriage proposals between guest and host: 1.

Epilogue

In hindsight, each of the iterations of Airbnb's business model seems obvious. How could the founders not know that facilitating payment was an obvious revenue model or that some people would be interested in renting their apartments or homes for weeks or months rather than just days at a time? But in fairness Airbnb's entire business, in hindsight, is obvious. Why didn't someone start it before Chesky, Gebbia, and Blecharczyk did? This is the magic of entrepreneurship. With hindsight, eBay, Facebook, and even Walmart, use obvious business models to serve customers in ways that create value for them. While it's easy to look backward, it's more difficult to look forward.

Not all business models follow Airbnb's path—some coalesce more quickly, others take longer, still others never come together at all. It's a judgment call on the part of a firm's founders. In Airbnb's case, it's fortunate that the founders didn't stop and say, "We're done," after iteration 1, iteration 2, and probably iteration 3. Instead, they kept engaging, watching, listening, and

Progression of Airbnb's Business Model

Initial Business Model
- Help people find housing when traveling to conferences or events.
- No revenue model in place

After Iteration #1
- Broaden beyond conferences and events and help people find housing while traveling for any purpose.
- Charge a transaction fee for handling payments.

After Iteration #2
- Broaden beyond conferences and events and help people find housing while traveling for any purpose.
- Charge a transaction fee for handling payments.
- Add bigger pictures, more detailed explanations, and more functionality to Web site.

After Iteration #3
- Broaden beyond conferences and events and help people find housing while traveling for any purpose.
- Charge a transaction fee for handling payments.
- Add bigger pictures, more detailed explanations, and more functionality to Web site.
- Open to weekly and monthly rentals.

(continued)

remaining open to change—actions that are typically required for a business model to be successfully developed.

Discussion Questions

1. Comment on the propensity of Airbnb's founders to solicit customer feedback. Based on the information in the case, do you think they did it too often, not often enough, or just right? Is there anything in their approach to obtaining feedback that you think you'll emulate if you start a business?
2. Comment on each of the four elements of Airbnb's business model. Spend some time looking at Airbnb's Web site and do some outside reading on the company if every element of its business model is not apparent from the case.
3. There's an old saying that "all of us are smarter than any of us." In what ways does this saying remind you of Airbnb's approach to its business?
4. Is there anything in Airbnb's approach to business that you're uncomfortable with? For example, if you took a

trip to London, would you feel comfortable booking a room at an individual's private residence? How does Airbnb help assure people who may have concerns in this area?

Application Questions

1. Spend some time looking at Airbnb's Web site and do some outside reading about the company. If you could give the founders of Airbnb one piece of advice, what would it be?
2. Identify Airbnb's major competitors. Place the competitors' business models side by side with Airbnb's business model. Comment on the strengths and weaknesses of Airbnb's business model compared to those of its major competitors.

Sources: Andrew Warner, Brian Chesky, and Joe Gebbia (Airbnb), *Mixergy,* www.mixergy.com (accessed March 28, 2011, originally posted on January 28, 2010); Airbnb Web site, www.airbnb.com (accessed March 28, 2011); R. Wauters, "Airbnb Hits 1 Million Nights Booked as European Clone Emerges," *TechCrunch,* www.techcrunch.com (accessed March 25, 2011, originally posted on February 24, 2011).

CASE 6.2

Zipcar: A Business Model Innovator That's Changing the Way People Think About Cars

Web: www.zipcar.com
Twitter: Zipcar
Facebook: Zipcar

Bruce R. Barringer, *Oklahoma State University*
R. Duane Ireland, *Texas A&M University*

Introduction

Zipcar is a car sharing service that Cambridge, Massachusetts, residents Robin Chase and Antje Danielson launched in 2000. Scott Griffith, a former Boeing engineer, now leads the firm. Although Zipcar didn't pioneer the idea of car sharing—it first emerged in Europe—it is the largest car sharing company, and is changing the way people think about car ownership in urban areas. From its start in 2000, the company now has over 500,000 members. A total of 40 percent of its

members say they've either sold a car or have decided to not purchase a car because of their Zipcar membership.

Business Model

Zipcar is a membership-based system. It charges a one-time application fee of $25 and an annual membership fee of $50. Zipcar cars have permanent parking spots in convenient locations in urban areas. Each member is given a membership card (called the Zipcard) that gets them into the cars. Reservations can be made from

1. Join **2. Reserve** **3. Unlock** **4. Drive**

How It Works: Four Simple Steps to Zipcar Freedom

minutes before a car is needed up to a year in advance. Once a reservation is made, the member simply approaches the car, opens it with the Zipcard, and drives it away. It costs about $9 an hour or $65 per day to rent a car. The cost includes the car, gas, and insurance. The car must be returned to its original parking space. The member simply leaves the keys in the car, locks it with the Zipcard, and walks away.

Zipcar is an entirely self-service business. As much as it loves it members, it tries to talk to them as infrequently as possible. None of its locations are manned. Cars are available 24 hours a day, seven days a week. As of December 2010, Zipcar offered a fleet of over 8,000 vehicles in urban areas throughout 28 North American states and Canadian providences, as well as London. Zipcar's goal is to take the concept of car ownership and turn it into a service. As a result, it doesn't see its competition as car rental companies, like Avis or Hertz; rather, it sees its major competition as car owners.

Piggybacking on Environmental Trends

Zipcar envisions itself as ideally positioned to take advantage of environmental trends. Currently, about 50 percent of the world's population lives in urban areas, a number that's steadily on the increase. According to surveys conducted by Zipcar, the two biggest complaints that people who live in urban areas have are (1) the high cost of living and (2) traffic and congestion. Zipcar sees itself as at least a partial solution for both problems. In regard to the high cost of living, Zipcar has found that only about 10 percent to 15 percent of the people who live in urban areas and own cars need them on a daily basis. It costs anywhere from $6,000 to $10,000 a year to own a car in an urban area, considering the cost of the car, insurance, maintenance, gas, and parking. In some areas of New York City, for example, it cost upward of $500 per month just to park a car. According to independent research firm Frost and Sullivan, Zipcar (along with other car sharing programs) can save urban residents 70 percent of their total transit costs, because they only pay for the hours they use the vehicle, with no responsibility for gas, insurance, maintenance, or parking. In regard to congestion, Zipcar has documented what it calls its "1 to 15 phenomenon." For every parking place that a city designates for a Zipcar, about 15 cars are taken off the road. This number results from the 40 percent of Zipcar members who say they either sell their car or decide not to purchase one as a result of their Zipcar membership. This statistic hasn't gone unnoticed by city governments, which are trying to develop comprehensive strategies to address traffic congestion. London, for example, has literally removed traffic meters in some locations and has given the parking spots to Zipcar and other car sharing services because they help relieve congestion.

Zipcar also contributes to environmental sustainability, although that's not the point that the company emphasizes in its advertising and promotions. Its cars are energy efficient. Studies have shown that when people rely on a car sharing service rather than owning a car, they drive about 50 percent fewer miles per year. Based on 500,000 members, Zipcar members reduce CO_2 emissions by more than 500,000 tons a year as a result of fewer miles driven.

Another trend favoring Zipcar is that an increasing number of young professionals are either moving to or staying in urban areas. There are upscale neighborhoods opening in the inner-city in places like Miami, St. Louis, and Atlanta, where young professionals are deciding to locate and start families rather than moving to the suburbs. This demographic is an ideal target market for Zipcar.

How Zipcar's Business Model Changes Its Members' Behaviors

A particularly interesting aspect of Zipcar's business model is how it changes its members' behaviors. The reason people drive less when they use a car sharing service rather than owning a car is that when they pay for a car an hour at a time, they tend to group their trips more efficiently to save money. In addition, they tend to think of alternatives to driving that they might not have thought of otherwise. Through surveys, Zipcar has found that its members not only drive less but use public transportation more often and walk and bike more as a result of their Zipcar memberships. When people own cars, they tend to want to use them to get the full value from the car. When people rent cars by the hour, they tend to not want to use them to save the hourly rental charge. Zipcar is fine with this. It believes by saving individual members money, they will spread the word about Zipcar's service which will lead to more members.

University, Organization, and Business Partnerships

Zipcar has several programs aimed specifically at universities and businesses. In 2004, it launched a program called Zipcar for Business, to allow businesses to use the firm's service in the same way individuals do. Since 2004, it's signed up 10,000 small, medium, and large companies. The program works nicely for both Zipcar and the businesses. Rates are cut for Monday to Friday driving, when businesses use vehicles the most, which helps businesses control/reduce their costs. Zipcar can then rent the same cars to individuals on the weekends, when individuals tend to use cars the most. Zipcar is also active on many university and college campuses. More than 225 universities and colleges are now partnering with Zipcar and providing parking spaces on their campuses.

In 2009, Zipcar launched a service called FastFleet, to help cities use the cars they own more efficiently. Rather than having different departments maintain their own car pools, cities can now maintain a single fleet of vehicles, strategically located throughout the city, and have city employees reserve them and use them in the same manner that Zipcar members reserve and use cars. Zipcar provides the back-end functionality for the system. Washington DC, which was the first city to use the system, reportedly saved more than $1 million in the first 12 months.

(continued)

Continual Expansion of the Business and Business Model

Zipcar is still growing rapidly relying on organic growth as well as mergers and acquisitions to do so. In 2007, it merged with Flexcar, its primary domestic competitor. In 2009, it acquired a minority interest in Avancar, the largest car sharing company in Spain. In April 2010, it acquired Streetcar, a London-based car sharing club.

Zipcar pegs the worldwide market for car sharing at about 8 million users. It's currently at 500,000. While it sees continual growth in North America and Europe, it sees its biggest potential market in Asia, an area where it currently doesn't have operations. It's not clear how Zipcar will penetrate Asian markets.

Zipcar feels that it has just scratched the surface of its markets and the possibilities its business model presents.

Discussion Questions

1. How does Zipcar's business model motivate its customers and its partners (such as the cities, businesses, and universities it partners with) to participate with its business? On a scale of 1 to 5 (5 is high), how motivated do you think each group is to do business with Zipcar and help it succeed?
2. At the beginning of this chapter, the statement is made that "at its simplest level, a business model is a story of how a company operates." Do you think Zipcar has a good story to tell? When it goes to a city, a business, or a university to pitch its idea, do you think it's easy or hard for Zipcar's employees to clearly explain what it does and what the benefits of its service are?
3. Look at Figure 6.3 in the chapter. Explain Zipcar's business model in each of the four areas. Is there anything in Zipcar's business model that makes what it is doing hard to replicate? Explain your answer to this final question.
4. Do you think Zipcar is growing too rapidly? In what ways can rapid growth jeopardize the strengths of Zipcar's business model?

Application Questions

1. What are the main challenges that you feel Zipcar will face in both the immediate and the long-term future?
2. In San Francisco, Zipcar competes with City Car Share, another car sharing service. Compare City Car Share and Zipcar's business models. Use information you find about each firm to determine the ways these companies are similar and the ways in which they are different. Are there any areas in which you feel City Car Share's business model is superior to Zipcar's?

Sources: Zipcar Web site, www.zipcar.com (accessed April 17, 2011); Wikipedia, "Zipcar," www.wikipedia.org (accessed April 17, 2011); Scott Griffin, "IdeaCity 2007," Available via YouTube, www.youtube.com/watch?v=7uPA0C8r7oE&playnext=1&list=PLBD CA72F19ADF9CB4 (accessed April 17, 2011).

ENDNOTES

1. G. George and A. J. Bock, "The Business Model in Practice and Its Implications for Entrepreneurship Research," *Entrepreneurship Theory and Practice* 35, no. 1 (2011): 83–111; H. Chesbrough and R. S. Rosenbloom, "The Role of the Business Model in Capturing Value from Innovation: Evidence from Xerox Corporation's Technology Spin-off Companies," *Industrial and Corporate Change* 11, no. 3 (2002): 529–55.
2. D. Richman and A. James, "Seattle P-I to Publish Last Edition Tuesday," *seattlepi*, www.seattlepi.com/default/article/Seattle-P-I-to-publish-last-edition-Tuesday-1302597.php (accessed May 2, 2011, originally posted on March 16, 2011).
3. R. A. Baron and J. Tang, "The Role of Entrepreneurs in Firm-Level Innovation: Joint Effects of Positive Affect, Creativity, and Environmental Dynamism," *Journal of Business Venturing* 26 no. 1 (2011): 49–60; G. Hamel, *Leading the Revolution* (New York: Plume, 2002).
4. M. S. Cardon, C. E. Stevens, and D. R. Potter, "Misfortunes or Mistakes? Cultural Sensemaking of Entrepreneurial Failure," *Journal of Business Venturing* 26, no. 1 (2011): 79–92; C. Jordan, "Are Hidden Flaws in Your Business Preventing Your Success?" e-Firm Consultants, www.event-vibe thevibe.com/Hidden_Flaws.asp (accessed November 16, 2008).
5. N. Wingfield, "New Battlefield for Priceline Is Diapers, Tuna," *Wall Street Journal*, September 20, 1999, B1.
6. M. Porter, *Competitive Advantage: Creating and Sustaining Superior Performance* (New York: Free Press, 1985).
7. H. Chu and S. Liao, "Defining and Categorizing Consumer Resale Behavior in Consumer-to-Consumer (C@C) E-Commerce," *International Journal of Business and Information* 2, no. 2 (2007): 159–84.
8. S. Pooler, "If You Own a QuickDrop eBay Drop Store Franchise What Will You Do Now?" http://ezinearticles.com/?If-You-Own-A-Quickdrop-Ebay-Drop-Store-Franchise-What-Will-You-Do-Now?&id=930650 (accessed September 27, 2008, posted January 15, 2008); F. Fortunato, "The State of eBay Drop-Off Stores," www.ecommerce-guide.com/news/news/article.pha/3631266 (accessed September 27, 2008, posted September 11, 2006).

9. N. Venkataraman and J. C. Henderson, "Real Strategies for Virtual Organizations," *Sloan Management Review* 40, no. 1 (1998): 33–48.

10. Hamel, *Leading the Revolution*.

11. R. D. Ireland, R. E. Hoskisson, and M. A. Hitt, *Understanding Business Strategy*, 3rd ed. (Mason, OH: South-Western Cengage Learning, 2012); M. E. Porter, *On Competition* (Boston: Harvard Business School Press, 1996).

12. S. Desmidt, A. Prinzie, and A. Decramer, "Looking for the Value of Mission Statements: A Meta-Analysis of 20 Years of Research," *Management Decision* 49, no. 3 (2011): 468–83.

13. Hamel, *Leading the Revolution*.

14. Yahoo! Inc., *Standard and Poor's Stock Report*, www.standardandpoors.com, May 3, 2011.

15. M. Dell, *Direct from Dell* (New York: HarperBusiness, 1999), 57.

16. H. Gebauer, A. Gustafsson, and L. Wite, II, "Competitive Advantage through Service Differentiation by Manufacturing Companies," *Journal of Business Research* (2011): in press.

17. Hamel, *Leading the Revolution*.

18. Porter, *Competitive Advantage*.

19. R. Casadesus-Masanell and J. E. Ricart, "From Strategy to Business Models and onto Tactics," *Long Range Planning* 43, no. 2/3 (2010): 195–215; C. Zott and R. Amit, "Business Model Design: An Activity System Perspective," *Long Range Planning* 43, no. 2/3 (2010): 216–26.

20. E. Rasmussen, S. Mosey, and M. Wright, "The Evolution of Entrepreneurial Competencies: A Longitudinal Study of University Spin-Off Venture Emergence," *Journal of Management Studies* (2011): in press.

21. J. S. Harrison, D. A. Bosse, and R. A. Phillips, "Managing for Stakeholders, Stakeholder Utility Functions, and Competitive Advantage," *Strategic Management Journal* 31, no. 1 (2010): 58–74.

22. D. J. Teece, "Business Models, Business Strategy and Innovation," *Long Range Planning* 43, no. 2/3 (2010): 172–94.

23. L.-Y. Wu, "Applicability of the Resource-Based and Dynamic-Capability Views Under Environmental Volatility," *Journal of Business Research* 63, no. 1 (2010): 27–31. S. L. Newbert, "Value, Rareness, Competitive Advantage, and Performance: A Conceptual-Level Empirical Investigation of the Resource-Based View of the Firm," *Strategic Management Journal* 29, no 7, 2008: 745–68.

24. R. F. Lusch, S. L. Vargo, and M. Tanniru, "Service, Value Networks and Learning," *Journal of the Academy of Marketing Science* 38, no. 1 (2010): 19–31; I. C. MacMillan and L. Selden, "The Incumbent's Advantage," *Harvard Business Review* 86, no. 10 (2008).

25. R. L. Sorenson, C. A. Folker, and K. H. Brigham, "The Collaborative Network Orientation: Achieving Business Success Through Collaborative Relationships," *Entrepreneurship Theory and Practice* 32, no. 4 (2008): 615–34; F. T. Rothaermel and D. L. Deeds, "Alliance Type, Alliance Experience and Alliance Management Capability in High-Technology Ventures," *Journal of Business Venturing* 21 (2006): 429–60.

26. M. N. Young, D. Ahlstrom, and G. D. Bruton, "What Do Firms from Transition Economies Want from Their Strategic Alliance Partners?" *Business Horizons* 54, no. 2 (2011): 163–74; G. P. Pisano and R. Verganti, "Which Kind of Collaboration Is Right for You?" *Harvard Business Review* 86, no. 12 (2008).

27. E. Pinchot and G. Pinchot, "Leading Organizations into Partnerships," in *Partnering*, eds. L. Segil, M. Goldsmith, and J. Belasco (New York: AMACOM Books, 2002), 41–55.

28. H. Lockett, M. Johnson, S. Evans, and M. Basti, "Product Service Systems and Supply Network Relationships: An Exploratory Case Study," *Journal of Manufacturing Technology Management* 22, no. 3 (2011): 293–313.

29. D. J. Ketchen, Jr., and G. T. M. Hult, "Building Theory about Supply Chain Management: Some Tools from the Organizational Sciences," *Journal of Supply Chain Management*, vol. 47, no. 2, (2011): 12–18.

30. Procter & Gamble moves forward with sustainable supply chain scorecard, Sustainable Business.Com, www.sustainablebusiness.com (accessed April 8, 2011).

31. PricewaterhouseCoopers, "Partnerships Have Big Payoffs for Fast-Growth Companies," *Trendsetter Barometer*, August 26, 2002.

32. Business First, "UPS Logistics Provides Variety of Services at Local Center," April 19, 2002; Y.-C. Chao, "Decision-Making Biases in the Alliance Life Cycle: Implications for Alliance Failure," *Management Decision* 49, no. 3 (2011): 350–64.

33. B. Barringer and J. Harrison, "Walking a Tightrope: Creating Value Through Interorganizational Relationships," *Journal of Management* 26, no. 3 (2000): 367–403.

34. T. K. Das, "Regulatory Focus and Opportunism in the Alliance Development Process," *Journal of Management* 37, no. 3 (2011): 682–708.

35. Chao, "Decision-Making Biases in the Alliance Life Cycle: Implications for Alliance Failure."

36. ifoAppleStore.com, www.ifoapplestore.com/the_stores.html (accessed May 5, 2011).

37. M. Sambasivan, L. Siew-Phaik, Z. A. Mohamed, and Y. C. Leong, "Impact of Interdependence Between Supply Chain Partners on Strategic Alliance Outcomes: Role of Relational Capital as a Mediating Construct," *Management Decision* 49, no. 4 (2011): 548–69.

38. Y. Amer, L. Luong, M. A. Ashraf, and S.-H. Lee, "A Systems Approach to Order Fulfillment," *International Journal of Operational Research* 9, no. 4 (2010): 443–65.

39. L. Ryals, "Customer Assets and Customer Equity: Management and Measurement Issues," *Marketing Theory* 10, no. 4 (2010): 417–36.

PART 3

Moving from an Idea to an Entrepreneurial Firm

CHAPTER 7
Preparing the Proper *Ethical and Legal* Foundation

CHAPTER 8
Assessing a New Venture's *Financial Strength* and Viability

CHAPTER 9
Building a *New-Venture* Team

CHAPTER 10
Getting *Financing* or Funding

Getting Personal *with* XPLOSAFE

Founder:

SHOAIB SHAIKH

MBA, Spears School of Business, Oklahoma State University, 2009

Dialogue *with* Shoaib Shaikh

FAVORITE PERSON I FOLLOW ON TWITTER
Guy Kawasaki

WHAT I DO WHEN I'M NOT WORKING
Hang out with friends, meet new people, put in a decent workout

MY BIGGEST WORRY AS AN ENTREPRENEUR
Complacency is not an entrepreneur's virtue. It is highly recommended to acknowledge and celebrate every milestone or setback but one must pay special attention to not dwell in past successes or failures.

MY FAVORITE SMARTPHONE APP
Pandora

MY ADVICE FOR NEW ENTREPRENEURS
Entrepreneurship is all about working as much as you can towards the goals you establish for the venture. It is not about working 8 hours a day for 5 days a week, it is about operating to meet the goals irrespective of the days or the schedule.

CURRENTLY IN MY SMARTPHONE
The Black Keys, The Rolling Stones, Beatles, Led Zeppelin, The Who, Pink Floyd, Jimi Hendrix, Warren Zevon, Jay-Z, Eminem, Lil Wayne

CHAPTER 7

Preparing the Proper *Ethical and Legal* Foundation

OPENING PROFILE

XPLOSAFE
Proceeding on a Firm Legal Foundation

Web: www.xplosafe.com
Twitter: XploSafe
Facebook: XploSafe, LLC

Imagine the following scenario. You're next in line to walk through the metal detector at airport security. Shortly after you walk through, you observe an interesting scene at the security line next to you. A backpack that passed through the scanning device for carry-on luggage has raised concern. A TSA agent identifies the owner of the backpack and pulls the owner along with the backpack aside. The backpack is searched and a bottle of water is revealed. Instead of asking the backpack's owner to throw the bottle of water away, the TSA agent removes a small bottle from his shirt pocket, opens the bottle, and places two drops of an ink-like substance in the water. The ink is initially dark blue and starts to change to pale yellow. The TSA agent immediately alerts a uniformed police officer who is nearby. The police officer asks the owner of the bag to "step aside" and they start moving away. Within seconds, you see several other TSA agents and another uniformed police officer gather around the owner of the backpack.

This scenario may someday happen as a result of work being done by XploSafe, an explosives detection start-up. The ink-like substance in the product described previously, called XploSens KT, contains metal-oxide particles. When the particles come in contact with peroxide-based explosives, which are a favorite of terrorists, they change color alerting authorities to the presence of an explosive. XploSafe now sells a full line of explosive-detection devices, including a spray version of the product described previously, which can be sprayed on suspicious packages or objects to detect explosives.

The manner in which XploSafe was started, and the work that was done to place it on a firm legal foundation, is an interesting story. XploSafe was started by Shoaib Shaikh, Jessie Loeffler, and Liviu Pavel, three MBA students at Oklahoma State University.

LEARNING OBJECTIVES

After studying this chapter you should be ready to:

1. Describe how to create a strong ethical culture in an entrepreneurial venture.

2. Explain the importance of "leading by example" in terms of establishing a strong ethical culture in a firm.

3. Explain the importance of having a code of conduct and an ethics training program.

4. Explain the criteria important to selecting an attorney for a new firm.

5. Discuss the importance of a founders' agreement.

6. Provide several suggestions for how entrepreneurial firms can avoid litigation.

7. Discuss the importance of nondisclosure and noncompete agreements.

8. Provide an overview of the business licenses and business permits that a start-up must obtain before it starts conducting business.

9. Discuss the differences among sole proprietorships, partnerships, corporations, and limited liability companies.

10. Explain why most fast-growth entrepreneurial ventures organize as corporations or limited liability companies rather than sole proprietorships or partnerships.

The three were part of an honors class and were matched with two scientists who were working on explosive-detection technologies. The students' task was to write a business plan to commercialize the technology. The three completed the plan in the fall of 2008, which they found fascinating, and in early 2009 entered it into *Venture Challenge*, a business plan competition hosted by San Diego State University. While they didn't advance to the finals, they received positive feedback and encouragement from the judges. Shortly after returning from San Diego, the three met with Dr. Michael Morris, the head of the School of Entrepreneurship at Oklahoma State. Dr. Morris encouraged the team and pledged the school's support, and the three decided to commit to XploSafe and make it a reality.

The two scientists behind the explosive detection technologies are Dr. Allen Apblett and Dr. Nick Materer, both chemistry professors and active researchers at Oklahoma State. At this point, the XploSafe team consisted of the three students, Shaikh, Loeffler, and Pavel, and the two scientists. All three students graduated in spring 2009. Although the team was eager to move forward with developing products, one thing they realized is that XploSafe needed to be on a firm legal foundation. Here are the steps they took, led by Shaikh, who was emerging as the leader of the group, to establish a firm legal foundation:

■ Obtained a Federal Tax ID Number.
■ Registered XploSafe as a Limited Liability Company.
■ Obtained a business license.
■ Obtained an exclusive option to license the technologies underlying XploSafe's potential products from Oklahoma State University.
■ Drafted and executed an operating agreement, between the five cofounders, that laid out how XploSafe would be structured, how it would operate, the equity split between the cofounders, and similar details.
■ Obtained the appropriate Internet domain name(s).
■ Established a pattern for the type of distribution agreements that would be executed with distributors of XploSafe's products.
■ Drafted prospective nondisclosure agreements.
■ Opened a bank account.

Shaikh did not take on these tasks on his own. Part of the process involved finding an attorney who was a good fit for the firm and could help with the items identified previously. XploSafe was based in Stillwater, Oklahoma, the home of Oklahoma State University. Shaikh and his team interviewed four attorneys, one in Stillwater, one in Tulsa, and two in Oklahoma City. They picked the attorney in Tulsa for two reasons. First, he had the most experience working with start-ups. Second, he agreed to alter his fee structure to charge less at the beginning and more as XploSafe grew and became profitable.

With these legal steps completed, XploSafe moved forward. It wasn't long before the operating agreement, in particular, was needed. One of the co-founders, Jessie Loeffler, decided to pursue a full-time job and left XploSafe before the operating agreement was signed. The second student cofounder, Liviu Pavel, left shortly after the agreement was signed. His departure was handled consistent with the operating agreement, which he had signed. Fortunately, the operating agreement had clauses in it that addressed how a cofounder's "exit" would be handled in regard to equity distribution and other issues. Pavel's exit from XploSafe was handled smoothly and wasn't a distraction.

XploSafe is now moving forward on sound legal footing. It routinely utilizes legal documents in everyday business dealings including nondisclosure agreements, mutual confidentiality agreements, and formal agreements with distributors. When needed, the documents are run by an attorney for approval or advice. It's also progressing as a business. It's generating sales, has been awarded a Small Business Innovation Research grant, and has secured sales from customers across the world including NASA, the Department of Energy, and multiple pharmaceutical companies. It is also hoping to play an ever expanding role in the fight against harmful explosives.[1]

This chapter begins by discussing the most important initial ethical and legal issues facing a new firm, including establishing a strong ethical organizational culture, choosing a lawyer, drafting a founders' agreement, and avoiding litigation. Next, we discuss the different forms of business organization, including sole proprietorships, partnerships, corporations, and limited liability companies.

Chapter 12 discusses the protection of intellectual property through patents, trademarks, copyrights, and trade secrets. This topic, which is also a legal issue, is becoming increasingly important as entrepreneurs rely more on intellectual property rather than physical property as a source of a competitive advantage. Chapter 15 discusses legal issues pertaining to franchising. The chapter next discusses the licenses and permits that may be needed to launch a business, along with the different forms of business organization, including sole proprietorships, partnerships, corporations, and limited liability companies.

INITIAL ETHICAL AND LEGAL ISSUES FACING A NEW FIRM

As the opening case about XploSafe suggests, new ventures must deal with important ethical and legal issues at the time of their launching. Ethical and legal errors made early on can be extremely costly for a new venture down the road. And there is a tendency for entrepreneurs to overestimate their knowledge of the law. In fact, in one study 254 small retailers and service company owners were asked to judge the legality of several business practices.[2] A sample of the practices included in the survey is shown next. Which practices do you think are legal and which ones do you think aren't legal?

- Avoiding Social Security payments for independent contractors
- Hiring only experienced help
- Preempting potential competition with prices below costs
- Agreeing to divide a market with rivals

The first two practices are legal, while the second two are illegal. How did you do? For comparison purposes, you might want to know that the participants in the survey were wrong 35 percent of the time about these four practices. The study doesn't imply that entrepreneurs break the law intentionally or that they do not have ethical intentions. What the study does suggest is that entrepreneurs tend to overestimate their knowledge of the legal complexities involved with launching and running a business.

As a company grows, the legal environment becomes even more complex. A reevaluation of a company's ownership structure usually takes place when investors become involved. In addition, companies that go public are required to comply with a host of Securities and Exchange Commission (SEC) regulations, including regulations spawned by the Sarbanes-Oxley Act of 2002. We provide more information about the Sarbanes-Oxley Act in Chapter 10.

Against this backdrop, the following sections discuss several of the most important ethical and legal issues facing the founders of new firms.

Establishing a Strong Ethical Culture for a Firm

LEARNING OBJECTIVE

1. Describe how to create a strong ethical culture in an entrepreneurial venture.

One of the most important things the founders of an entrepreneurial venture can do is establish a strong ethical culture for their firms. The data regarding business ethics are both encouraging and discouraging. The most recent version of the National Business Ethics Survey was published in 2009. This survey is the only longitudinal study that tracks the experiences of employees within organizations regarding business ethics. According to the survey, 49 percent of the 2,852 employees surveyed reported that they had observed misconduct or unethical behavior in the past year.

Of the employees who observed misconduct, 63 percent reported their observation to a supervisor or another authority in their firm.[3] The 10 most common types of misconduct or unethical behavior observed by the employees surveyed are shown in Table 7.1.

While the percentage of employees who have observed misconduct or unethical behavior (49 percent) is discouraging, it's encouraging that 63 percent of employees reported the behavior. According to the survey, the majority of employees also have a positive view of their leaders' transparency and accountability. A total of 80 percent said they were satisfied with the information they were getting from top management about "what's going on in my company." Seventy-four percent said they trusted that top management would keep their promises and commitment. A full 89 percent said top management talks about the importance of workplace ethics and "doing the right thing." And when asked if they believe top managers would be held accountable if caught violating the organization's ethical standards, 82 percent said yes.[4] Overall, these numbers are heartening.

TABLE 7.1 PERCENTAGE OF U.S. WORKFORCE OBSERVING SPECIFIC FORMS OF MISCONDUCT OR UNETHICAL BEHAVIOR (BASED ON 2009 NATIONAL BUSINESS ETHICS SURVEY)

Form of Misconduct or Unethical Behavior	Percentage of U.S. Workforce Observing Behavior
Company resource abuse	23%
Abusive behavior	22%
Lying to employees	19%
E-mail or Internet abuse	18%
Conflicts of interest	16%
Discrimination	15%
Lying to outside stakeholders	12%
Employee benefits violations	11%
Health or safety violations	11%
Employee privacy breach	10%

Source: 2009 National Business Ethics Survey Ethics in the Recession (Washington, DC: Ethics Resource Center, 2009).

In analyzing the results of its survey, the Ethics Resource Center concluded that the most important thing an organization can do to combat the figures its study revealed is to establish a strong ethical culture.[5] But strong ethical cultures don't emerge by themselves. It takes entrepreneurs who make ethics a priority and organizational policies and procedures that encourage ethical behavior (and punish unethical behavior) to make it happen. The following are specific steps that an entrepreneurial organization can take to build a strong ethical culture.

Lead by Example   Leading by example is the most important thing that any entrepreneur, or team of entrepreneurs, can do to build a strong ethical culture in their organization. This is being done in many organizations, as indicated by the transparency and accountability figures shown previously. Three things are particularly important in building a strong ethical culture in a firm:

LEARNING OBJECTIVE

2. Explain the importance of "leading by example" in terms of establishing a strong ethical culture in a firm.

- Leaders who intentionally make ethics a part of their daily conversations and decision making
- Supervisors who emphasize integrity when working with their direct reports
- Peers who encourage each other to act ethically

In companies where these attributes are present, a stronger ethical culture exists. This reality demonstrates the important role that everyone involved with a start-up plays in developing a strong ethical culture for their firm.

Establish a Code of Conduct   A **code of conduct** (or code of ethics) is a formal statement of an organization's values on certain ethical and social issues.[6] The advantage of having a code of conduct is that it provides specific guidance to managers and employees regarding expectations of them in terms of ethical behavior. Consider what Google has done in this area. The company's informal corporate motto is "Don't be evil," but it also has a formal code of conduct, which explicitly states what is and isn't permissible in the organization. The table of contents for Google's code of conduct is shown in Table 7.2. It illustrates the ethical issues that Google thinks can be bolstered and better explained to employees via a written document to which they are required to adhere. A copy of Google's full code of conduct is available at http://investor.google.com/conduct.html.

LEARNING OBJECTIVE

3. Explain the importance of having a code of conduct and an ethics training program.

TABLE 7.2   TABLE OF CONTENTS OF GOOGLE'S CODE OF CONDUCT

1. Serve Our Users
1. Integrity
2. Usefulness
3. Privacy and Freedom of Expression
4. Responsiveness
5. Take Action

2. Respect Each Other
1. Equal Opportunity Employment
2. Positive Environment
3. Drugs and Alcohol
4. Safe Workplace
5. Dog Policy

(Continued)

TABLE 7.2 CONTINUED

3. Avoid Conflicts of Interest

1. Personal Investments
2. Outside Employment and Inventions
3. Outside Board Membership
4. Business Opportunities
5. Friends and Relatives; Co-Worker Relationships
6. Gifts, Entertainment, and Payments
7. Reporting

4. Preserve Confidentiality

1. Confidential Information
2. Google Partners
3. Competitors; Former Employees
4. Outside Communications and Research

5. Protect Google's Assets

1. Intellectual Property
2. Company Equipment
3. The Network
4. Physical Security
5. Use of Google's Equipment and Facilities
6. Employee Data

6. Ensure Financial Integrity and Responsibility

1. Spending Google's Money
2. Signing a Contract
3. Recording Transactions
4. Reporting Financial or Accounting Irregularities
5. Hiring Suppliers
6. Retaining Records

7. Obey the Law

1. Trade Controls
2. Competition Laws
3. Insider Trading Laws
4. Anti-Bribery Laws

8. Conclusion

Source: Google Web site, http://investor.google.com/corporate/code-of-conduct.html (accessed May 13, 2011). Google Code of Conduct © Google Inc. and is used with permission.

In practice, some codes of conduct are very specific, like Google's. Other codes of conduct set out more general principles about an organization's beliefs on issues such as product quality, respect for customers and employees, and social responsibility. The 2009 National Business Ethics Survey, mentioned previously, found that employees are much more likely to report ethical misconduct in their firms when specific compliance mechanisms like codes of conduct are in place.

Implement an Ethics Training Program   Firms also use ethics training programs to promote ethical behavior. **Ethics training programs** teach business ethics to help employees deal with ethical dilemmas and improve their overall ethical conduct. An **ethical dilemma** is a situation that involves doing something that is beneficial to oneself or the organization, but may be unethical. Most employees confront ethical dilemmas at some point during their careers.

Ethics training programs can be provided by outside vendors or can be developed in-house. For example, one organization, Character Training International (CTI), provides ethics training programs for both large organizations and smaller entrepreneurial firms. The company offers a variety of ethics-related training services, including on-site workshops, speeches, a train-the-trainer curriculum, videos, and consulting services. A distinctive attribute of CTI is its focus on the moral and ethical roots of workplace behavior. In workshops, participants talk about the reasons behind ethical dilemmas and are provided practical, helpful information about how to prevent problems and how to deal appropriately with the ethical problems and temptations that do arise. The hope is that this training will significantly cut down on employee misconduct and fraud and will increase morale.[7]

In summary, ethical cultures are built through both strong ethical leadership and administrative tools that reinforce and govern ethical behavior in organizations. Building an ethical culture motivates employees to behave ethically and responsibly from the inside out, rather than relying strictly on laws that motivate behavior from the outside in.[8] There are many potential payoffs to organizations that act and behave in an ethical manner. A sample of the potential payoffs appears in Figure 7.1.

The strength of a firm's ethical culture and fortitude is put to the test when it faces a crisis or makes a mistake and has to determine how to respond. Amazon.com provides an example of this. In April 2011, Amazon.com's Web hosting service experienced a massive glitch, which led to a shutdown of its servers for several days. The shutdown caused many of its customers' Web sites, including popular sites like Foursquare, HootStuite, Reddit, and Quora, to go down and in some cases lose data. In addition to its e-commerce site, Amazon.com provides Web services for businesses. Amazon.com publicly apologized for the glitch and took full responsibility. It also offered a credit to those affected. At the end of a lengthy explanation of what led to the failure, Amazon.com said "Last, but certainly not least, we want to apologize. We know how critical our services to our customers' businesses are, and we will do everything we can to learn from this event and use it to drive improvement across our services."[9] In addition to making technical changes, Amazon.com said it also would improve the way it communicates with customers. Some users were frustrated during the outage that they weren't getting timely information from Amazon.com about when the outage would be fixed.

FIGURE 7.1
Potential Payoffs for Establishing a Strong Ethical Culture

By showing contrition, a concern for its customers, and a commitment to do better next time, Amazon hopefully not only repaired its reputation with its users but showed the true nature of its corporate character.

Choosing an Attorney for a Firm

It is important for an entrepreneur to select an attorney as early as possible when developing a business venture. Selecting an attorney was instrumental in helping XploSafe, the company profiled in the opening feature, establish a firm legal foundation. Table 7.3 provides guidelines to consider when selecting an attorney. It is critically important that the attorney be familiar with start-up issues and that he or she has successfully shepherded entrepreneurs through the start-up process before. It is not wise to select an attorney just because she is a friend or because you were pleased with the way he prepared your will. For issues dealing with intellectual property protection, it is essential to use an attorney who specializes in this field, such as a patent attorney, when filing a patent application.[10]

Entrepreneurs often object to the expense of hiring an attorney when there are many books, Web sites, and other resources that can help them address legal issues on their own. However, these alternatives should be chosen with extreme caution. Many attorneys recognize that start-ups are short on cash and will work out an installment plan or other payment arrangement to get the firm the legal help it needs without starving it of cash, as was the case with XploSafe. This is particularly true if the attorney senses that the new venture has strong commercial potential and may develop into a steady client in the future. There are also ways for entrepreneurs to save on legal fees and to increase the value of their relationship with their attorney. Here are several ways for entrepreneurs to achieve these dual objectives:

- **Group together legal matters:** It is typically cheaper to consult with an attorney on several matters at one time rather than schedule several separate meetings. For example, in one conference, a team of start-up entrepreneurs and their attorney could draft a founders' agreement, decide on a form of business organization, and discuss how to best draft nondisclosure and noncompete agreements for new employees. (We discuss these issues later in the chapter.)

- **Offer to assist the attorney:** There are excellent resources available to help entrepreneurs acquaint themselves with legal matters. An entrepreneur could help the attorney save time by writing the first few drafts of a founders' agreement or a contract or by helping gather the documents needed to deal with a legal issue.

- **Ask your attorney to join your advisory board:** Many start-ups form advisory boards (discussed in Chapter 9). Advisory board members typically serve as volunteers to help young firms get off to a good start. An attorney serving on an advisory board becomes a coach and a confidant as well as a paid service provider. However, entrepreneurs must be careful not to give the impression that the attorney was asked to serve on the advisory board as a way of getting free legal advice.

- **Use nonlawyer professionals:** Nonlawyer professionals can perform some tasks at a much lower fee than a lawyer would charge. Examples include management consultants for business planning, tax preparation services for tax work, and insurance agents for advice on insurance planning.

One thing entrepreneurs should guard themselves against is ceding too much control to an attorney. While an attorney should be sought out and relied

TABLE 7.3 How to Select an Attorney

1. Contact the local bar association and ask for a list of attorneys who specialize in business start-ups in your area.

2. Interview several attorneys. Check references. Ask your prospective attorney whom he or she has guided through the start-up process before and talk to the attorney's clients. If an attorney is reluctant to give you the names of past or present clients, select another attorney.

3. Select an attorney who is familiar with the start-up process. Make sure that the attorney is more than just a legal technician. Most entrepreneurs need an attorney who is patient and is willing to guide them through the start-up process.

4. Select an attorney who can assist you in raising money for your venture. This is a challenging issue for most entrepreneurs, and help in this area can be invaluable.

5. Make sure your attorney has a track record of completing his or her work on time. It can be very frustrating to be prepared to move forward with a business venture, only to be stymied by delays on the part of an attorney.

6. Talk about fees. If your attorney won't give you a good idea of what the start-up process will cost, keep looking.

7. Trust your intuition. Select an attorney who you think understands your business and with whom you will be comfortable spending time and having open discussions about the dreams you have for your entrepreneurial venture.

8. Learn as much about the process of starting a business yourself as possible. It will help you identify any problems that may exist or any aspect that may have been overlooked. Remember, it's your business start-up, not your attorney's. Stay in control.

upon for legal advice, the major decisions pertaining to the firm should be made by the entrepreneurs. Entrepreneurs should also develop a good working knowledge of business law. This notion is affirmed by Constance E. Bagley, a professor at Yale University, who wrote, "Just as a lawyer needs a sufficient understanding of how business operates and the strategies for success to be an effective partner (in an attorney–client relationship with an entrepreneur), the manager and entrepreneur need to have some knowledge of legal nomenclature and the legal principles most relevant to their business."[11]

Drafting a Founders' Agreement

It is important to ensure that founders are in agreement regarding their interests in the venture and their commitment to its future. It is easy for a team of entrepreneurs to get caught up in the excitement of launching a venture and fail to put in writing their initial agreements regarding the ownership of the firm. A **founders' agreement** (or shareholders' agreement) is a written document that deals with issues such as the relative split of the equity among the founders of the firm, how individual founders will be compensated for the cash or the "sweat equity" they put into the firm, and how long the founders will have to remain with the firm for their shares to fully vest.[12] Having a founders' agreement served the initial founders of XploSafe well when shortly after the agreement was signed one of the founders left the firm. The exit of the departing founder went smoothly and didn't result in any hard feelings because the exit was handled in accordance with the written agreement.

The items typically included in a founders' agreement are shown in Table 7.4.

An important issue addressed by most founders' agreements is what happens to the equity of a founder if the founder dies or decides to leave the firm. Most founders' agreements include a **buyback clause**, which legally obligates departing founders to sell to the remaining founders their interest in the firm if the remaining founders are interested.[13] In most cases, the agreement also specifies the formula for computing the dollar value to be paid. The presence of a buyback clause is important for at least two reasons. First, if a founder leaves the firm, the remaining founders may need the

> LEARNING OBJECTIVE
> 5. Discuss the importance of a founders' agreement.

TABLE 7.4   ITEMS INCLUDED IN A FOUNDERS' (OR SHAREHOLDERS') AGREEMENT

- Nature of the prospective business
- Identity and proposed titles of the founders
- Legal form of business ownership
- Apportionment of stock (or division of ownership)
- Consideration paid for stock or ownership share of each of the founders (may be cash or "sweat equity")
- Identification of any intellectual property signed over to the business by any of the founders
- Description of the initial operating capital
- Buyback clause, which explains how a founder's shares will be disposed of if she or he dies, wants to sell, or is forced to sell by court order

SAVVY ENTREPRENEURIAL FIRM

Vesting Ownership in Company Stock: A Sound Strategy for Start-Ups

If you're not familiar with vesting, the idea is that when a firm is launched, instead of issuing stock outright to the founders, the stock is distributed over a period of time, typically three to four years, as the founder or founders "earn" the stock. The same goes for employees who join the firm later and receive company stock. Instead of giving someone stock all at once, the stock is distributed over a period of time.

The reason vesting is a smart move is that although everyone is normally healthy and on the same page when launching an entrepreneurial venture, you never know what might happen. You want everyone involved with the firm to stay engaged. You also want a way of determining the price of a departing employees' stock, if the firm has a "buy-back" clause in its corporate bylaws and wants to repurchase a departing employee's shares. Vesting provides a mechanism for accomplishing both of these objectives. A typical start-up's vesting schedule lasts 36 to 48 months and includes a 12-month cliff. The cliff represents the period of time that the person must work for the company in order to leave with any ownership interest. Thus, if a company has a 48-month vesting schedule and offers 1,000 shares of stock to an employee, if the employee leaves after 10 months, the employee keeps no equity. If the employee leaves after 28 months, the employee gets to keep 28/48 of the equity promised, or 583 of the 1,000 shares. The shares will be issued at a specific price. If an employee leaves and the company is entitled to buy back the employee's shares, normally the buy-back clause will stipulate that the shares can be repurchased at the price at which they were issued.

Vesting avoids three problems. First, it helps keep employees motivated and engaged. If the employee in the example mentioned in the previous paragraph received his or her entire allotment of 1,000 shares on day one, the employee could walk away from the firm at any point and keep all the shares. Second, if an employee's departure is acrimonious, there isn't any squabbling about how many shares the employee gets to leave with—the answer to this question is spelled out in the vesting schedule. In addition, if a buy-back clause is in place and it stipulates the formula for determining the value of the departing employee's stock, the company can repurchase the shares without an argument. It's never a good thing to have a former employee, particularly one that left under less than ideal conditions, remain a partial owner of the firm. Finally, investors are generally reluctant to invest in a firm if a block of stock is owned by a former employee. It just spells trouble, which investors are eager to avoid.

Questions for Critical Thinking

1. Investors are often criticized for insisting that a vesting schedule be put in place for stock that's issued to employees. After reading this feature, do you think this criticism is justified? If a company anticipated that it will never take money from an investor, is it still a good idea to establish a vesting schedule? Explain your answer.

2. Why do you think start-ups launch and distribute stock to founders and others members of their new-venture team without vesting schedules?

3. Is it typically necessary to hire an attorney to set up a vesting schedule for a firm, or can the firm do it on its own?

4. If a company started with a single founder and no employees, is it necessary to set up a vesting schedule for the founder?

shares to offer to a replacement person. Second, if founders leave because they are disgruntled, the buyback clause provides the remaining founders a mechanism to keep the shares of the firm in the hands of people who are fully committed to a positive future for the venture.

Vesting ownership in company stock is another topic most founders' agreements address. The idea behind vesting is that when a firm is launched, instead of issuing stock outright to the founder or founders, it is distributed over a period of time, typically three to four years, as the founder or founders "earn" the stock. Not only does vesting keep employees motivated and engaged, but it also solves a host of potential problems that can result if employees are given their stock all at once. More on the concept of vesting ownership in company stock is provided in the "Savvy Entrepreneurial Firm" feature.

Avoiding Legal Disputes

Most legal disputes are the result of misunderstandings, sloppiness, or a simple lack of knowledge of the law. Getting bogged down in legal disputes is something that an entrepreneur should work hard to avoid. It is important early in the life of a new business to establish practices and procedures to help avoid legal disputes. Legal snafus, particularly if they are coupled with ethical mistakes can be extremely damaging to a new firm, as illustrated in this chapter's "What Went Wrong?" feature.

There are several steps entrepreneurs can take to avoid legal disputes and complications, as discussed next.

Meet All Contractual Obligations It is important to meet all contractual obligations on time. This includes paying vendors, contractors, and employees as agreed and delivering goods or services as promised. If an obligation cannot be met on time, the problem should be communicated to the affected parties as soon as possible. It is irritating for vendors for example, when they are not paid on time, largely because of the other problems the lack of prompt payments create. The following comments dealing with construction

One of the simplest ways to avoid misunderstandings and ultimately legal disputes is to get everything in writing.

© Graham Stewart/Dreamstime.com

WHAT WENT WRONG?

How Legal Snafus Can Stop a Business in Its Tracks

Building a coffee chain in China, a country famous for its taste in tea, might seem a challenge for some companies, but not for global coffee giant Starbucks. However, when the Seattle-based chain decided to target the Chinese market in the late 1990s, the choice of beverage of potential customers was not the biggest problem. The challenge to its international expansion plans came from copycat chain Shanghai Xingbake and the resultant legal row over copyright infringement embroiled the two companies in a lengthy and complex legal battle.

The row centred on the name *Xingbake*. In Chinese, *xing* means "star" and *bake* sounds very much like *bucks*. Although the American coffee company registered the name Starbucks and trademark pictures associated with it in China in 1996, it did not register the Xing Bake trademark until December 28, 1999.

While Starbucks' application for the trademark "Xing Bake" was pending, local company Shanghai Xingbake preregistered the corporate name Xing Bake and gained approval. Shanghai Xingbake's principle business was the sale of hot drinks and Western-style meals in a chain of restaurants in Shanghai, which appeared to emulate Starbucks' style of upholstered chairs and roomy seating.

To compound the potential confusion, Shanghai Xingbake printed "Starbuck Coffee" on its price list, which was hard to distinguish from the American company's trademark *Starbucks*. Shanghai Xingbake's logo, which was featured on menus, café windows, receipts, and business cards, also appeared to be copying Starbuck's distinctive logo using one small circle inside a larger one, with white characters on a green background and two stars embedded in the circles' overlapped area. The only difference was the Chinese company used a coffee cup in the circle instead of Starbucks' ubiquitous mermaid. Finally, Shanghai Xingbake used the slogan "Xing Bake Coffee" prominently on its storefront and price lists.

Although Starbucks immediately launched a legal action, Shanghai Xingbake appeared to have a strong case because it had succeeded in registering its Chinese name first. Under Chinese law, trademark rights are normally bestowed on the company that first files for a trademark. The case eventually went to court and, breaking with tradition, the Shanghai court ruled that, as a direct Chinese translation of "Starbucks," Xingbake infringed on the American coffee maker's trademark, even though the Chinese company was first to register its name. The court ruled that Shanghai Xingbake intentionally used Xingbake in its name to mislead the public, violating trademark law and basic commercial ethics of equality, honesty, and good faith. Starbucks won the exceptional ruling on the strength that it is one of the world's best-known brands and is well recognized in China too.

Shanghai Xingbake was fined 500,000 yuan (US$64,000) for infringing Starbucks' trademark and ordered to change its name and apologize publicly through a local newspaper. Despite losing subsequent appeals, Shanghai Xingbake hesitated to change its name for some time. Eventually, after the courts ordered a freezing of the defendant's assets and garnishment of its bank accounts, Shanghai Xingbake changed its name to Fangyun Coffee and agreed to pay the compensation by installments. Trademark lawsuits can be both lengthy and prohibitively expensive, and Fangyun has never fully recovered from the experience.

Questions for Critical Thinking

1. To what extent do you believe establishing a strong ethical culture could have helped Shanghai Xingbake avoid its difficulties?
2. Imagine you were given the job of writing a code of conduct for Shanghai Xingbake when the company was founded. Using the table of contents of Google's code of conduct as a guide (Table 7.1), construct a table of contents for Shanghai Xingbake's code of conduct. Make Shanghai Xingbake's code of conduct fit its industry and individual circumstances.
3. If you had been one of the entrepreneurs founding Shanghai Xingbake, what would you have done differently compared to the actions described in this feature?

companies demonstrate this situation: "Not getting paid on time can be devastating to construction companies that have costs to (their) vendors and employees that sometimes require payment weekly. Cash flow problems can send a company into a hole from which they will often not recover."[14] Being forthright with vendors or creditors if an obligation cannot be met and providing the affected party or parties a realistic plan for repaying the money is an appropriate path to take and tends to maintain productive relationships between suppliers and vendors.

Avoid Undercapitalization   If a new business is starved for money, it is much more likely to experience financial problems that will lead to litigation.[15] A new business should raise the money it needs to effectively conduct business or should stem its growth to conserve cash. Many entrepreneurs face a dilemma regarding this issue. Most entrepreneurs have a goal of retaining as much of the equity in their firms as possible, but equity must often be shared with investors to obtain sufficient investment capital to support the firm's growth. This issue is discussed in more detail in Chapter 10.

Get Everything in Writing   Many business disputes arise because of the lack of a written agreement or because poorly prepared written agreements do not anticipate potential areas of dispute.[16] Although it is tempting to try to show business partners or employees that they are "trusted" by downplaying the need for a written agreement, this approach is usually a mistake. Disputes are much easier to resolve if the rights and obligations of the parties involved are in writing. For example, what if a new business agreed to pay a Web design firm $7,500 to design its Web site? The new business should know what it's getting for its money, and the Web design firm should know when the project is due and when it will receive payment for its services. In this case, a dispute could easily arise if the parties simply shook hands on the deal and the Web design firm promised to have a "good-looking Web site" done "as soon as possible." The two parties could easily later disagree over the quality and functionality of the finished Web site and the project's completion date.

The experiences and perspectives of Maxine Clark, the founder of Build-A-Bear Workshop, provide a solid illustration of the practical benefits of putting things in writing, even when dealing with a trusted partner:

> While I prefer only the necessary contracts (and certainly as few pages as possible), once you find a good partner you can trust, written up-front agreements are often a clean way to be sure all discussed terms are acceptable to all parties. It's also a good idea after a meeting to be sure someone records the facts and agree-to points, and distribute them to all participants in writing. E-mail is a good method for doing this. Steps like this will make your life easier. After all, the bigger a business gets, the harder it is to remember all details about every vendor, contract, and meeting. Written records give you good notes for doing follow-up, too.[17]

There are also two important written agreements that the majority of firms ask their employees to sign. A **nondisclosure agreement** binds an employee or another party (such as a supplier) to not disclose a company's trade secrets. A **noncompete agreement** prevents an individual from competing against a former employer for a specific period of time. A sample nondisclosure and noncompete agreement is shown in Figure 7.2.

LEARNING OBJECTIVE
7. Discuss the importance of nondisclosure and noncompete agreements.

Set Standards   Organizations should also set standards that govern employees' behavior beyond what can be expressed via a code of conduct. For example, four of the most common ethical problem areas that occur in an organization are human resource ethical problems, conflicts of interest, customer confidence, and inappropriate use of corporate resources. Policies

FIGURE 7.2
Sample Nondisclosure
and Noncompete
Agreement

Nondisclosure and Noncompetition. (a) At all times while this agreement is in force and after its expiration or termination, [employee name] agrees to refrain from disclosing [company name]'s customer lists, trade secrets, or other confidential material. [Employee name] agrees to take reasonable security measures to prevent accidental disclosure and industrial espionage.

(b) While this agreement is in force, the employee agrees to use [his/her] best efforts to [describe job] and to abide by the nondisclosure and noncompetition terms of this agreement; the employer agrees to compensate the employee as follows: [describe compensation]. After expiration or termination of this agreement, [employee name] agrees not to compete with [company name] for a period of [number] years within a [number] mile radius of [company name and location]. This prohibition will not apply if this agreement is terminated because [company] violated the terms of this agreement.

Competition means owning or working for a business of the following type: [specify type of business employee may not engage in].

(c) [Employee name] agrees to pay liquidated damages in the amount of $[dollar amount] for any violation of the covenant not to compete contained in subparagraph (b) of this paragraph.

IN WITNESS WHEREOF, [company name] and [employee name] have signed this agreement.

_____
[company name]

_____
[employee's name]

Date: _____

and procedures should be established to deal with these issues. In addition, as reflected in the "Partnering for Success" boxed features throughout this book, firms are increasingly partnering with others to achieve their objectives. Because of this, entrepreneurial ventures should be vigilant when selecting their alliance partners. A firm falls short in terms of establishing high ethical standards if it is willing to partner with firms that behave in a contrary manner. This chapter's "Partnering for Success" feature illustrates how two firms, Patagonia and Build-A-Bear Workshop, deal with this issue.

When legal disputes do occur, they can often be settled through negotiation or mediation, rather than more expensive and potentially damaging litigation. **Mediation** is a process in which an impartial third party (usually a professional mediator) helps those involved in a dispute reach an agreement. At times, legal disputes can also be avoided by a simple apology and a sincere pledge on the part of the offending party to make amends. Yale Professor Constance E. Bagley illustrates this point.[18] Specifically, in regard to the role a simple apology plays in resolving legal disputes, Professor Bagley refers to a *Wall Street Journal* article in which the writer commented about a jury awarding $2.7 million to a woman who spilled scalding hot McDonald's coffee on her lap. The *Wall Street Journal* writer noted that "A jury awarded $2.7 million to a woman who spilled scalding hot McDonald's coffee on her lap. Although this case is often cited as an example of a tort (legal) system run amok, the *Wall Street Journal* faulted McDonald's for not only failing to respond to prior scalding incidents but also for mishandling the injured woman's complaints by not apologizing."[19]

A final issue important in promoting business ethics involves the manner in which entrepreneurs and managers demonstrate accountability to their investors and shareholders. This issue, which we discuss in greater detail in Chapter 10, is particularly important in light of the corporate scandals observed during the early 2000s as well as scandals that may surface in future years.

PARTNERING FOR SUCCESS

Patagonia and Build-A-Bear Workshop: Picking Trustworthy Partners

Patagonia: Web: www.patagonia.com; Twitter: Patagonia; Facebook: Patagonia

Build-A-Bear Workshop: Web: www.buildabear.com; Twitter: buildabear; Facebook: Build a Bear

Patagonia

Patagonia sells rugged clothing and gear to mountain climbers, skiers, and other extreme-sport enthusiasts. The company is also well known for its environmental stands and its commitment to product quality. Patagonia has never owned a fabric mill or a sewing shop. Instead, to make a ski jacket, for example, it buys fabric from a mill, zippers and facings from other manufacturers, and then hires a sewing shop to complete the garment. To meet its own environmental standards and ensure product quality, it works closely with each partner to make sure the jacket meets its rigid standards.

As a result of these standards, Patagonia does as much business as it can with as few partners as possible and chooses its relationships carefully. The first thing the company looks for in a partner is the quality of its work. It doesn't look for the lowest-cost provider, who might sew one day for a warehouse store such as Costco and try to sew the next day for Patagonia. Contractors that sew on the lowest-cost basis, the company reasons, wouldn't hire sewing operators of the skill required or welcome Patagonia's oversight of its working conditions and environmental standards. What Patagonia looks for, more than anything, is a good fit between itself and the companies it partners with. It sees its partners as an extension of its own business, and wants partners that convey Patagonia's own sense of product quality, business ethics, and environmental and social concern.

Once a relationship is established, Patagonia doesn't leave adherence to its principles to chance. Its production department monitors its partners on a consistent basis. The objective is for both sides to prosper and win. In fact, in describing the company's relationship with its partners, Patagonia founder Yvon Chouinard says, "We become like friends, family—mutually selfish business partners; what's good for them is good for us."

Build-A-Bear Workshop

A similar set of beliefs and actions describe Build-A-Bear Workshop. Build-A-Bear lets its customers, who are usually children, design and build their own stuffed animals, in a sort of Santa's workshop setting. Like Patagonia, Build-A-Bear is a very socially conscious organization, and looks for partners that reflect its values. Affirming this point, Maxine Clark, the company's founder, said, "The most successful corporate partnerships are forged between like-minded companies with similar cultures that have come together for a common goal, where both sides benefit from the relationship."

Also similar to Patagonia, Build-A-Bear thinks of its partners as good friends. Reflecting on her experiences in this area, Clark said, "I tend to think of partners as good business friends—companies and people who would do everything they could to help us succeed and for whom I would do the same." In a book she wrote about founding and building Build-A-Bear into a successful company, Clark attributes having good partners to careful selection. She also likens business partnership to a marriage, which has many benefits but also takes hard work: "Good business partnerships are like successful marriages. To work, they require compatibility, trust and cooperation. Both parties need to be invested in one another's well-being and strive for a common goal."

Both Patagonia and Build-A-Bear make extensive use of partnerships and are leaders in their respective industries.

Questions for Critical Thinking

1. To what extent do you believe that Patagonia and Build-A-Bear Workshop's ethical cultures drive their views on partnering?
2. Assume you were assigned the task of writing a code of conduct for Patagonia. Write the portion of the code of conduct that deals with business partnership relationships.
3. List the similarities that you see between the partnership philosophies of Patagonia and Build-A-Bear Workshop.
4. Spend some time studying Patagonia by looking at the company's Web site, its Facebook account, and via other Internet searches. Describe Patagonia's general approach to business ethics, social responsibility, and environmental concerns. What, if anything, can start-ups learn from Patagonia's philosophies and its experiences?

Sources: M. Clark, *The Bear Necessities of Business* (New York: Wiley, 2006); Y. Chouinard, *Let My People Go Surfing* (New York: The Penguin Press, 2005).

OBTAINING BUSINESS LICENSES AND PERMITS

Before a business is launched, a number of licenses and permits are typically needed. What is actually needed varies by city, county, and state, as well as by type of business, so it's important for the entrepreneur to study local regulations carefully. Some licenses are difficult to get—such as liquor licenses. For example, in some states, the only way to get a liquor license is to buy a preexisting license. This stipulation often results in a bidding war when a business is willing to give up its liquor license, which increases the price.

Business Licenses

In most communities, a business needs a license to operate. A **business license** can be obtained at the city clerk's office in the community where the business will be located. If the business will be run out of the founder's home, a separate home occupation business license is often required. When a business license is applied for, the city planning and zoning departments usually check to make sure the business's address is zoned for the type of business that is being planned. If a business will be located outside a city or town's jurisdiction, the county courthouse will issue the business license.

If a business is a sole proprietorship, it can usually stop here, as far as obtaining a business license goes. If a business has employees, or is a corporation, limited liability company, or limited partnership, it will usually need a state business license in addition to its local one. Individual states may have additional provisions with which you might need to comply. If you're starting a retail business or a service business, you'll need to obtain a sales tax license, which enables you to collect taxes on the state's behalf. Special licenses are needed to sell liquor, lottery tickets, gasoline, or firearms. People in certain professions, such as barbers, chiropractors, nurses, and real estate agents, must normally pass a state examination and maintain a professional license to conduct business. Certain businesses also require special state licenses. Examples of these types of businesses include child care, health care facilities, hotels, and restaurants. It's important to check to see which licenses your business needs.

A narrow group of businesses are required to have a federal business license, including investment advising, drug manufacturing, firms preparing meat products, broadcasting, interstate trucking, and businesses that manufacture tobacco, alcohol, or firearms, or sell firearms. These licenses are obtained through the Federal Trade Commission.

Nearly all businesses are required to obtain a federal **employer identification number (EIN)**, also known as a tax identification number, which is used in filing various business tax returns. The only exception is sole proprietors who do not have employees. In this instance the sole proprietor uses his or her social security number as the tax identification number. A tax identification number can be obtained from the Internal Revenue Service by calling 800-829-4933.

Business Permits

Along with obtaining the appropriate licenses, some businesses may need to obtain one or more permits. The need to obtain a permit or permits depends on the nature and location of the business. For example, if you plan to sell food, either as a restaurateur or as a wholesaler to other retail businesses, you'll need a city or county health permit. If your business will be open to the public or will use flammable material, you may need a fire department permit. Some communities require businesses to obtain a permit to put up a sign. If you're occupying a building, there may also be building code requirements that need to be complied with.

All businesses that plan to use a fictitious name, which is any name other than the business owner's name, need a **fictitious business name permit** (also called a *dba* or *doing business as*). If a business is a sole proprietorship, the permit can be obtained at the city or county level. The way this works is that if your name is Justin Ryan and you apply for a business license, your business will be registered as Justin Ryan. If you want to use another name, like *Snake River Computer Consulting*, then you'll need a fictitious name permit. You'll typically need a fictitious name permit to obtain a checking account in your business's name. It's also important to have a fictitious name permit if you execute any contracts, sign any agreements, or pay bills or accept payments under your business's name. Selecting a name for a business and obtaining a fictitious business name permit if needed is an important task, not only to comply with the law but because a business's name is a critical part of its branding strategy.[20] It's also one of the first things that people associate with a business. Appendix 7.1 contains a set of guidelines and suggestions for picking a business's name. As illustrated in the appendix, it is important that a business choose a name that facilitates rather than hinders how it wants to differentiate itself in the marketplace.

Several resources are available to assist business founders in identifying the proper licenses and permits to apply for. The SBA maintains a Web site, at www.sba.gov/content/search-business-licenses-and-permits, that features links, which provide information on how to obtain a business license in each state or zip code. Many city governments also publish documents or maintain online resources that provide guidance for doing business in their city. Good places to look for these publications or resources are the city government's Web site, the city library's Web site, or the Web site for the local Chamber of Commerce. For example, the Dallas Public Library maintains an excellent online resource titled "Starting a Small Business in Dallas." The site is available at www.dallaslibrary2.org/government/smallbiz.php.

Choosing a Form of Business Organization

When a business is launched, a form of legal entity must be chosen. Sole proprietorship, partnerships, corporations, and limited liability companies are the most common legal entities from which entrepreneurs make a choice. Choosing a legal entity is not a one-time event. As a business grows and matures, it is necessary to periodically review whether the current form of business organization remains appropriate. In most cases, a firm's form of business entity can be changed without triggering adverse tax implications.

There is no single form of business organization that works best in all situations. It's up to the owners of a firm and their attorney to select the legal entity that best meets their needs. The decision typically hinges on several factors, which are shown in Figure 7.3. It is important to be careful in selecting

> LEARNING OBJECTIVE
> 9. Discuss the differences among sole proprietorships, partnerships, corporations, and limited liability companies.

FIGURE 7.3
Factors Critical in Selecting a Form of Business Organization

| The Cost of Setting Up and Maintaining the Legal Form | The Extent to Which Personal Assets Can Be Shielded from the Liabilities of the Business | Tax Considerations | The Number and Types of Investors Involved |

a legal entity for a new firm because each form of business organization involves trade-offs among these factors and because an entrepreneur wants to be sure to achieve the founders' specific objectives.

This section describes the four forms of business organization and discusses the advantages and disadvantages of each. A comparison of the four legal entities, based on the factors that are typically the most important in making a selection, is provided in Table 7.5.

Sole Proprietorship

The simplest form of business entity is the sole proprietorship. A **sole proprietorship** is a form of business organization involving one person, and the person and the business are essentially the same. Sole proprietorships are the most prevalent form of business organization. The two most important advantages of a sole proprietorship are that the owner maintains complete control over the business and that business losses can be deducted against the owner's personal tax return.[21]

Setting up a sole proprietorship is cheap and relatively easy compared to the other forms of business ownership. The only legal requirement, in most states, is to obtain the appropriate license and permits to do business as described in the previous section of the chapter.

If the business will be operated under a trade name (e.g., West Coast Graphic Design) instead of the name of the owner (e.g., Samantha Ryan), the owner will have to file an assumed or fictitious name certificate with the appropriate local government agency, as mentioned earlier in the chapter. This step is required to ensure that there is only one business in an area using the same name and provides a public record of the owner's name and contact information.

A sole proprietorship is not a separate legal entity. For tax purposes, the profit or loss of the business flows through to the owner's personal tax return document and the business ends at the owner's death or loss of interest in the business. The sole proprietor is responsible for all the liabilities of the business, and this is a significant drawback. If a sole proprietor's business is sued, the owner could theoretically lose all the business's assets along with personal assets. The liquidity of an owner's investment in a sole proprietorship is typically low. **Liquidity** is the ability to sell a business or other asset quickly at a price that is close to its market value.[22] It is usually difficult for a sole proprietorship to raise investment capital because the ownership of the business cannot be shared. Unlimited liability and difficulty raising investment capital are the primary reasons entrepreneurs typically form corporations or limited liability companies as opposed to sole proprietorships. Most sole proprietorships are salary-substitute or lifestyle firms (as described in Chapter 1) and are typically a poor choice for an aggressive entrepreneurial firm.

To summarize, the primary advantages and disadvantages of a sole proprietorship are as follows:

Advantages of a Sole Proprietorship

- Creating one is easy and inexpensive.
- The owner maintains complete control of the business and retains all the profits.
- Business losses can be deducted against the sole proprietor's other sources of income.
- It is not subject to double taxation (explained later).
- The business is easy to dissolve.

TABLE 7.5 COMPARISON OF FORMS OF BUSINESS OWNERSHIP

Factor	Proprietorship	Partnership		Corporation		Limited Liability Company
	Sole Proprietorship	General	Limited	C Corporation	S Corporation	
Number of owners allowed	1	Unlimited number of general partners allowed	Unlimited number of general and limited partners allowed	Unlimited	Up to 100	Unlimited number of "members" allowed
Cost of setting up and maintaining	Low	Moderate	Moderate	High	High	High
Personal liability of owners	Unlimited	Unlimited for all partners	Unlimited for general partners; limited partners only to extent of investment	Limited to amount of investment	Limited to amount of investment	Limited to amount of investment
Continuity of business	Ends at death of owner	Death or withdrawal of one partner unless otherwise specified	Death or withdrawal of general partner	Perpetual	Perpetual	Typically limited to a fixed amount of time
Taxation	Not a taxable entity; sole proprietor pays all taxes	Not a taxable entity; each partner pays taxes on his or her share of income and can deduct losses against other sources of income	Not a taxable entity; each partner pays taxes on his or her share of income and can deduct losses against other sources of income	Separate taxable entity	No tax at entity level; income/loss is passed through to the shareholders	No tax at entity level if properly structured; income/loss is passed through to the members
Management control	Sole proprietor is in full control	All partners share control equally, unless otherwise specified	Only general partners have control	Board of directors elected by the shareholders	Board of directors elected by the shareholders	Members share control or appoint manager
Method of raising capital	Must be raised by sole proprietor	Must be raised by general partners	Sale of limited partnerships, depending on terms of operating agreement	Sell shares of stock to the public	Sell shares of stock to the public	It's possible to sell interests, depending on the terms of the operating agreement
Liquidity of investment	Low	Low	Low	High, if publicly traded	Low	Low
Subject to double taxation	No	No	No	Yes	No	No

Disadvantages of a Sole Proprietorship

■ Liability on the owner's part is unlimited.

■ The business relies on the skills and abilities of a single owner to be successful. Of course, the owner can hire employees who have additional skills and abilities.

■ Raising capital can be difficult.

■ The business ends at the owner's death or loss of interest in the business.

■ The liquidity of the owner's investment is low.

Partnerships

If two or more people start a business, they must organize as a partnership, corporation, or limited liability company. Partnerships are organized as either general or limited partnerships.

General Partnerships   A **general partnership** is a form of business organization where two or more people pool their skills, abilities, and resources to run a business. The primary advantage of a general partnership over a sole proprietorship is that the business isn't dependent on a single person for its survival and success. In fact, in most cases, the partners have equal say in how the business is run. Most partnerships have a partnership agreement, which is a legal document that is similar to a founders' agreement. A **partnership agreement** details the responsibilities and the ownership shares of the partners involved with an organization. The business created by a partnership ends at the death or withdrawal of a partner, unless otherwise stated in the partnership agreement. General partnerships are typically found in service industries. In many states, a general partnership must file a certificate of partnership or similar document as evidence of its existence. Similar to a sole proprietorship, the profit or loss of a general partnership flows through to the partner's personal tax returns. If a business has four general partners and they all have equal ownership in the business, then one-fourth of the profits or losses would flow through to each partner's individual tax return.[23] The partnership files an informational tax return only.

The primary disadvantage of a general partnership is that the individual partners are liable for all the partnership's debts and obligations. If one partner is negligent while conducting business on behalf of the partnership, all the partners may be liable for damages. Although the non-negligent partners may later try to recover their losses from the negligent one, the joint liability of all partners to the injured party remains. It is typically easier for a general partnership to raise money than a sole proprietorship simply because more than one person is willing to assume liability for a loan. One way a general partnership can raise investment capital is by adding more partners. Investors are typically reluctant to sign on as general partners, however, because of the unlimited liability that follows each one.

In summary, the primary advantages and disadvantages of a general partnership are as follows:

Advantages of a General Partnership

■ Creating one is relatively easy and inexpensive compared to a corporation or limited liability company.

■ The skills and abilities of more than one individual are available to the firm.

■ Having more than one owner may make it easier to raise funds.

■ Business losses can be deducted against the partners' other sources of income.

■ It is not subject to double taxation (explained later).

Disadvantages of a General Partnership

■ Liability on the part of each general partner is unlimited.

■ The business relies on the skills and abilities of a fixed number of partners. Of course, similar to a sole proprietorship, the partners can hire employees who have additional skills and abilities.

■ Raising capital can be difficult.

■ Because decision making among the partners is shared, disagreements can occur.

■ The business ends at the death or withdrawal of one partner unless otherwise stated in the partnership agreement.

■ The liquidity of each partner's investment is low.

Limited Partnerships A **limited partnership** is a modified form of a general partnership. The major difference between the two is that a limited partnership includes two classes of owners: general partners and limited partners. There are no limits on the number of general or limited partners permitted in a limited partnership. Similar to a general partnership, the general partners are liable for the debts and obligations of the partnership, but the limited partners are liable only up to the amount of their investment. The limited partners may not exercise any significant control over the organization without jeopardizing their limited liability status.[24] Similar to general partnerships, most limited partnerships have partnership agreements. A **limited partnership agreement** sets forth the rights and duties of the general and limited partners, along with the details of how the partnership will be managed and eventually dissolved.

A limited partnership is usually formed to raise money or to spread out the risk of a venture without forming a corporation. Limited partnerships are common in real estate development, oil and gas exploration, and motion picture ventures.[25]

Corporations

A **corporation** is a separate legal entity organized under the authority of a state. Corporations are organized as either C corporations or subchapter S corporations. The following description pertains to C corporations, which are what most people think of when they hear the word *corporation*. Subchapter S corporations are explained later.

C Corporations A **C corporation** is a separate legal entity that, in the eyes of the law, is separate from its owners. In most cases, the corporation shields its owners, who are called **shareholders**, from personal liability for the debts and obligations of the corporation. A corporation is governed by a board of directors, which is elected by the shareholders (more about this in Chapter 9). In most instances, the board hires officers to oversee the day-to-day management of the organization. It is usually easier for a corporation to raise investment capital than a sole proprietorship or a partnership because the shareholders are not liable beyond their investment in the firm. It is also easier to allocate partial ownership interests in a corporation through the distribution of stock. Most C corporations have two classes of stock: common and preferred. **Preferred stock**

> **LEARNING OBJECTIVE**
> **10.** Explain why most fast-growth entrepreneurial ventures organize as corporations or limited liability companies rather than sole proprietorships or partnerships.

is typically issued to conservative investors who have preferential rights over common stockholders in regard to dividends and to the assets of the corporation in the event of liquidation. **Common stock** is issued more broadly than preferred stock. The common stockholders have voting rights and elect the board of directors of the firm. The common stockholders are typically the last to get paid in the event of the liquidation of the corporation, that is, after the creditors and the preferred stockholders.[26]

Establishing a corporation is more complicated than a sole proprietorship or a partnership. A corporation is formed by filing **articles of incorporation** with the secretary of state's office in the state of incorporation. The articles of incorporation typically include the corporation's name, purpose, authorized number of stock shares, classes of stock, and other conditions of operation.[27] In most states, corporations must file papers annually, and state agencies impose annual fees. It is important that a corporation's owners fully comply with these regulations. If the owners of a corporation don't file their annual paperwork, neglect to pay their annual fees, or commit fraud, a court could ignore the fact that a corporation has been established and the owners could be held personally liable for actions of the corporation. This chain of effects is referred to as "**piercing the corporate veil**."[28]

A corporation is taxed as a separate legal entity. In fact, the "C" in the title "C corporation" comes from the fact that regular corporations are taxed under subchapter C of the Internal Revenue Code. A disadvantage of corporations is that they are subject to **double taxation**, which means that a corporation is taxed on its net income and, when the same income is distributed to shareholders in the form of dividends, is taxed again on shareholders' personal income tax returns. This complication is one of the reasons that entrepreneurial firms often retain their earnings rather than paying dividends to their shareholders. The firm can use the earnings to fuel future growth and at the same time avoid double taxation. The hope is that the shareholders will ultimately be rewarded by an appreciation in the value of the company's stock.

The ease of transferring stock is another advantage of corporations. It is often difficult for a sole proprietor to sell a business and even more awkward for a partner to sell a partial interest in a general partnership. If a corporation is listed on a major stock exchange, such as the New York Stock Exchange or the NASDAQ, an owner can sell shares at almost a moment's notice. This advantage of incorporating, however, does not extend to corporations that are not listed on a major stock exchange. There are approximately 2,800 companies listed on the New York Stock and 2,850 the NASDAQ. These firms are **public corporations**. The stockholders of these 5,650 companies enjoy a **liquid market** for their stock, meaning that the stock can be bought and sold fairly easily through an organized marketplace. It is much more difficult to sell stock in closely held or private corporations. In a **closely held corporation**, the voting stock is held by a small number of individuals and is very thinly or infrequently traded.[29] A **private corporation** is one in which all the shares are held by a few shareholders, such as management or family members, and are not publicly traded.[30] The vast majority of the corporations in the United States are private corporations. The stock in both closely held and private corporations is fairly **illiquid**, meaning that it typically isn't easy to find a buyer for the stock.

A final advantage of organizing as a C corporation is the ability to share stock with employees as part of an employee incentive plan. Because it's easy to distribute stock in small amounts, many corporations, both public and private, distribute stock as part of their employee bonus or profit-sharing plans. Such incentive plans are intended to help firms attract, motivate, and retain high-quality employees.[31] **Stock options** are a special form of incentive compensation. These plans provide employees the option or right to buy a certain number of shares of their company's stock at a stated price over a certain period of time. The most compelling advantage of stock options is the potential rewards to participants when (and if) the stock price increases.[32] Many employees receive stock options at the time they are hired and then periodically receive additional options. As employees accumulate stock options, the link between their potential reward and their company's stock price becomes increasingly clear. This link provides a powerful inducement for employees to exert extra effort on behalf of their firm in hopes of positively affecting the stock price.[33]

To summarize, the advantages and disadvantages of a C corporation are as follows:

Advantages of a C Corporation

- Owners are liable only for the debts and obligations of the corporation up to the amount of their investment.
- The mechanics of raising capital is easier.
- No restrictions exist on the number of shareholders, which differs from subchapter S corporations.
- Stock is liquid if traded on a major stock exchange.
- The ability to share stock with employees through stock option or other incentive plans can be a powerful form of employee motivation.

Disadvantages of a C Corporation

- Setting up and maintaining one is more difficult than for a sole proprietorship or a partnership.
- Business losses cannot be deducted against the shareholders' other sources of income.
- Income is subject to double taxation, meaning that it is taxed at the corporate and the shareholder levels.
- Small shareholders typically have little voice in the management of the firm.

Subchapter S Corporation A **subchapter S corporation** combines the advantages of a partnership and a C corporation. It is similar to a partnership in that the profits and losses of the business are not subject to double taxation. The subchapter S corporation does not pay taxes; instead, the profits or losses of the business are passed through to the individual tax returns of the owners. The S corporation must file an information tax return. An S corporation is similar to a C corporation in that the owners are not subject to personal liability for the behavior of the business. An additional advantage of the subchapter S corporation pertains to self-employment tax. By electing the subchapter S corporate status, only the earnings actually paid out as salary are subject to payroll taxes. The ordinary income that is disbursed by the business to the shareholders is not subject to payroll taxes or self-employment tax.

Because of these advantages, many entrepreneurial firms start as subchapter S corporations. There are strict standards that a business must meet to qualify for status as a subchapter S corporation:

- The business cannot be a subsidiary of another corporation.
- The shareholders must be U.S. citizens. Partnerships and C corporations may not own shares in a subchapter S corporation. Certain types of trusts and estates are eligible to own shares in a subchapter S corporation.
- It can have only one class of stock issued and outstanding (either preferred stock or common stock).

■ It can have no more than 100 members. Husbands and wives count as one member, even if they own separate shares of stock. In some instances, family members count as one member.

■ All shareholders must agree to have the corporation formed as a subchapter S corporation.

The primary disadvantages of a subchapter S corporation are restrictions in qualifying, expenses involved with setting up and maintaining the subchapter S status, and the fact that a subchapter S corporation is limited to 100 shareholders.[34] If a subchapter S corporation wants to include more than 100 shareholders, it must convert to a C corporation or a limited liability company.

Limited Liability Company

The **limited liability company (LLC)** is a form of business organization that is rapidly gaining popularity in the United States. The concept originated in Germany and was first introduced in the United States in the state of Wyoming in 1978. Along with the subchapter S corporation, it is a popular choice for start-up firms. As with partnerships and corporations, the profits of an LLC flow through to the tax returns of the owners and are not subject to double taxation. The main advantage of the LLC is that all partners enjoy limited liability. This differs from regular and limited partnerships, where at least one partner is liable for the debts of the partnership. The LLC combines the limited liability advantage of the corporation with the tax advantages of the partnership.[35]

Some of the terminology used for an LLC differs from the other forms of business ownership. For example, the shareholders of an LLC are called "members," and instead of owning stock, the members have "interests." The LLC is more flexible than a subchapter S corporation in terms of number of owners and tax-related issues. An LLC must be a private business—it cannot be publicly traded. If at some point the members want to take the business public and be listed on one of the major stock exchanges, it must be converted to a C corporation.

The owners of an S corporation are required to file an informational tax return, even though the profits or losses are "passed through" to the owners and are assessed on their individual tax returns. These provisions allow S corporations to avoid double taxation on the corporate income.

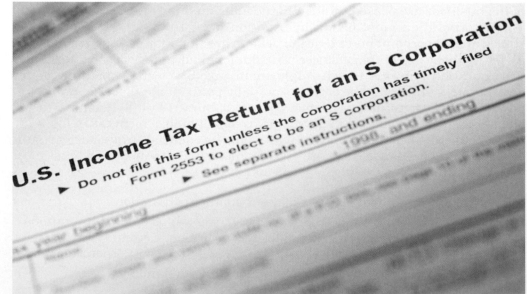

FogStock LLC/Newscom

The LLC is rather complex to set up and maintain, and in some states the rules governing the LLC vary. Members may elect to manage the LLC themselves or may designate one or more managers (who may or may not be members) to run the business on a day-to-day basis. The profits and losses of the business may be allocated to the members anyway they choose. For example, if two people owned an LLC, they could split the yearly profits 50–50, 75–25, 90–10, or any other way they choose.[36]

In summary, the advantages and disadvantages of an LLC are as follows:

Advantages of a Limited Liability Company

■ Members are liable for the debts and obligations of the business only up to the amount of their investment.

■ The number of shareholders is unlimited.

■ An LLC can elect to be taxed as a sole proprietor, partnership, S corporation, or corporation, providing much flexibility.

■ Because profits are taxed only at the shareholder level, there is no double taxation.

Disadvantages of a Limited Liability Company

■ Setting up and maintaining one is more difficult and expensive.

■ Tax accounting can be complicated.

■ Some of the regulations governing LLCs vary by state.

■ Because LLCs are a relatively new type of business entity, there is not as much legal precedent available for owners to anticipate how legal disputes might affect their businesses.

CHAPTER SUMMARY

1. Establishing a strong ethical culture in their firms is the single most important thing the founders of an entrepreneurial venture can do. Three important ways to do this are (1) lead by example, (2) establish a code of conduct, and (3) implement an ethics training program.

2. In the context of "leading by example," three keys to building a strong ethical culture in a firm are (1) having leaders who intentionally make ethics a part of their daily conversations and decision making, (2) supervisors who emphasize integrity when working with their direct reports, and (3) peers who encourage each other to act ethically.

3. A code of ethics and ethics training program are two techniques entrepreneurs use to promote high standards of business ethics in their firms. A code of conduct describes the general value system, moral principles, and

specific ethical rules that govern a firm. An ethics training program provides employees with instructions for how to deal with ethical dilemmas when they occur.

4. The criteria important for selecting an attorney for a new firm are shown in Table 7.3. Critical issues include selecting an attorney familiar with the start-up process, selecting an attorney who can assist you in raising money, and making certain that the attorney has a track record of completing work on time.

5. It is important to ensure that a venture's founders agree on their relative interests in the venture and their commitment to its future. A founders' (or shareholders') agreement is a written document dealing with issues such as the split of equity between or among the founders of the firm, how individual founders will be compensated for the cash

or the "sweat equity" they put into the firm, and how long the founders will have to stay with the firm for their shares to fully vest.

6. Suggestions for how new firms can avoid litigation include meeting all contractual obligations, avoiding undercapitalization, getting everything in writing, and promoting business ethics in the firm.

7. A nondisclosure agreement is a promise made by an employee or another party (such as a supplier) not to disclose a company's trade secrets. A noncompete agreement prevents an individual from competing against a former employer for a specific period of time.

8. Before a business is launched, a number of licenses and permits are typically needed. They vary by city, county, and state, as well as by type of business, so it's important to study local regulations carefully. In most

communities, a business needs a license to operate. Along with obtaining the appropriate licenses, some businesses may need to obtain one or more permits.

9. The major differences among sole proprietorships, partnerships, corporations, and limited liability companies are shown in Table 7.5. These forms of business organization differ in terms of the number of owners allowed, cost of setting up and maintaining, personal liability of owners, continuity of the business, methods of taxation, degree of management control, ease of raising capital, and ease of liquidating investments.

10. Fast-growth firms tend to organize as corporations or limited liability companies for two main reasons: to shield the owners from personal liability for the behavior of the firm and to make it easier to raise capital.

KEY TERMS

articles of incorporation, **260**
business license, **254**
buyback clause, **247**
C corporation, **259**
closely held corporation, **260**
code of conduct, **243**
common stock, **260**
corporation, **259**
double taxation, **260**
employer identification number (EIN), **254**
ethical dilemma, **245**
ethics training programs, **244**

fictitious business name permit, **255**
founders' agreement, **247**
general partnership, **258**
illiquid, **260**
limited liability company (LLC), **262**
limited partnership, **259**
limited partnership agreement, **259**
liquid market, **260**
liquidity, **256**
mediation, **252**

noncompete agreement,**251**
nondisclosure agreement, **251**
partnership agreement, **258**
piercing the corporate veil, **260**
preferred stock, **259**
private corporation, **260**
public corporations, **260**
shareholders, **259**
sole proprietorship, **256**
stock options, **260**
subchapter S corporation, **261**

REVIEW QUESTIONS

1. When should your friend, who is considering launching a consulting firm to provide financial services to small businesses, think about the ethical climate she wants to establish in her venture?

2. In general, do entrepreneurs tend to overestimate or underestimate their knowledge of the laws that pertain to starting a new firm? What does the answer to this question suggest that entrepreneurs do before they start a firm?

3. Why is it important for an entrepreneur to build a strong ethical culture for his or her firm? What are some of the

specific steps that can be taken in an entrepreneurial venture for the purpose of building a strong ethical culture?

4. Describe what is meant by the terms *code of conduct* and *ethics training programs*. What is their purpose?

5. What are some of the more important criteria to consider when selecting an attorney for a new firm?

6. Describe what a founders' agreement is and why it's important for a team of entrepreneurs to have one in place when launching a venture.

7. Describe the purpose of a nondisclosure agreement and the purpose of a noncompete agreement.

8. Describe several ways entrepreneurial ventures can avoid legal disputes.

9. Explain what mediation is and how mediation is used to resolve disputes.

10. At what point, during the process of starting a firm, does a business need to focus on the business licenses and permits that it needs? Are business licenses and permits the same in all cities and states or do they vary?

11. Why is it important for a firm's founders to think carefully about the name they pick for their company?

12. The following statement appears in this chapter: "Choosing a legal entity (for an entrepreneurial venture) is not a one-time event." Why isn't choosing a legal entity a one-time event? What might trigger a firm's decision to change how it is legally organized?

13. What are the advantages and disadvantages of organizing a new firm as a sole proprietorship? Is a sole proprietorship an appropriate form of ownership for an aggressive entrepreneurial firm? Why or why not?

14. Describe the differences between a general partnership and a limited partnership. Is a general partnership an appropriate form of ownership for two people pooling their resources to start a high-growth entrepreneurial firm?

15. What are the major advantages and disadvantages of a C corporation? How is a C corporation subject to double taxation?

16. What is the difference between preferred stock and common stock? Who gets paid first in the event of liquidation—the preferred stockholders or the common stockholders?

17. What is meant by the term *piercing the corporate veil*? What are the implications for the owners of a corporation if the corporate veil is pierced?

18. What are the differences between a public corporation, a closely held corporation, and a private corporation? Which type of corporation enjoys the highest level of liquidity for its stock?

19. What are stock options? Why would a corporation offer stock options to its employees?

20. What are the advantages and disadvantages of a limited liability company? Is a limited liability company an appropriate form of ownership for an aggressive entrepreneurial firm?

APPLICATION QUESTIONS

1. Assume that Shoaib Shaikh, the founder of XploSafe (the company focused on at the beginning of the chapter), has asked you to help him write a code of conduct for his firm. Given your understanding of XploSafe's business model and its priorities, put together a table of contents for XploSafe's code of conduct.

2. Under what circumstances should ethical considerations be part of a company's business plan? Should a company periodically measure its ethical performance? If so, what are the best ways for a company to measure its ethical performance?

3. Suppose you have been asked by your school newspaper to write a short article about business ethics and entrepreneurship. The editor of the paper has asked you to write a 300-word piece. She's asked that you start the article with the words "An ethical entrepreneurial firm is one that . . ." Complete the article.

4. The "You Be the VC 7.1" feature focuses on Velib, a company that is encouraging people to give up their cars in favour of pedal power with an easy-to-use, self-service, bike-for-hire system. Spend some time studying Velib. Other than the ethical and legal issues that confront all firms, what special issues do you think Velib should be particularly attentive to?

5. Tom Andersen owns an electronics firm in Wichita. He has told you that he has been suffering some cash flow problems, but has avoided having to borrow money by letting some of his bills run late and by cutting corners on meeting some of his contractual obligations. When you raised your eyebrows as he told you this, he said,

"Don't worry; I'm really not nervous about it. I have some big orders coming in, and am confident I can catch up on my bills and renegotiate my contracts then." Do you think Tom has a sound strategy? What could he be doing differently? What are the downsides to what Tom is currently doing?

6. Nancy Wills is purchasing a business named Niagara Laser Optics near Buffalo, New York. The business has had several brushes with the law during the past several years, dealing with claims of false advertising and wrongful termination of employees. As a result, Nancy is very concerned about the ethical culture of the firm. What specific techniques could Nancy use to increase the emphasis placed on business ethics when she takes control of the firm?

7. Assume you are opening a restaurant near the college or university you attend and have decided to name it *Campus Burger, Wraps, Fries, and Shakes.* Based on the location of the college or university, identify the specific business licenses and permits you would need to open your business.

8. A classmate of yours is starting a company that is designed to help high school athletes maximize their chances of obtaining a college scholarship. The company will help athletes put together highlight films of their high school accomplishments, write letters of introduction to college coaches, and manage the process of prospecting and communicating with college coaches and administrators. Based on the material in Appendix 7.1, suggest three potential names for the business. Settle on an Internet domain name for each suggestion (the domain name must be available). Explain how the name will help the company communicate its purpose and build its brand.

9. Of the "You Be the VC" features included in Chapters 1 through 7 of this book, which do you think has the best name for its business, and which do you think has the worst name? Explain your selections and the criteria you used to make your determinations.

10. Reacquaint yourself with ScriptPad, the subject of Case 2.1. Imagine that ScriptPad's founders are writing an operating manual that describes the administrative processes they'll use in running their business. They'd like to include in the manual a description of when it's appropriate to ask for nondisclosure and noncompete agreements to be signed, and have asked you for your advice. Please write this portion of ScriptPad's operating manual for them.

11. Kimberly Smith, a friend of yours, is a freelance journalist. She writes articles on business topics and sells them to business periodicals, newspapers, and online sites. Kimberley just read an article about the advantages of organizing as a subchapter S corporation or an LLC but doesn't know if the article applies to her. She's currently organized as a sole proprietorship, and doesn't know if it's appropriate or advisable for a freelance journalist to set up a subchapter S corporation or an LLC. Kimberly has turned to you for advice. What would you tell her?

12. Brian just formed a C corporation. The shareholders of the corporation will be Brian and his wife Carrie and his father Bob, who put $35,000 of cash into the business. Brian explained to his wife and dad that he organized the business as a C corporation because of the ease of transfer of ownership of the stock. He said that if any of the three of them wanted his or her money out of the corporation, that person could simply find a buyer for the stock, just like the shareholders of Google and other large public corporations do, and transfer the ownership. Does Brian have realistic expectations regarding the ease of getting out of his investment if he wants to? Why or why not? What would be a better choice for form of business ownership for Brian?

13. You have been approached by a close family friend who is putting together a limited liability company to purchase a condominium complex near Cocoa Beach in Florida. He is asking you along with a number of family members and friends to each invest $10,000 in his company. The condominium complex is for sale for $5 million. Your friend hopes to convince

50 people to invest $10,000 apiece, which will raise $500,000, and borrow the remaining $4.5 million to close the deal. You told your friend, "I don't mind investing the $10,000, but I'm really nervous about being on the hook for a $4.5 million loan if the deal goes bad. Your friend insists that all you will have at risk is your $10,000 and you won't be liable for anything else, no matter what happens. Is your friend right or wrong? Explain your answer.

14. Determine specifically what the requirements are for starting a limited liability company in your state. Indicate what forms need to be filed, where they can be obtained, how the filing process works, and what fees are involved.

15. Laura just took a job with Cisco Systems in San Jose, California. One of the things that attracted her to Cisco was the stock option plan that Cisco offers its employees. Explain what is meant by a stock option plan and why a company such as Cisco Systems would offer stock options to its employees.

YOU BE THE VC 7.1

Company: Velib

Web: www.velib.paris.fr
Twitter: Velib Paris
Facebook: Vélib'

Business Idea: Reduce traffic congestion, air pollution, and wear and tear on the nation's highways by introducing an easy-to-use, self-service, bike-for-hire system.

Pitch: Traffic congestion is stressful; it causes air pollution and costs millions in tax revenue to keep roads in good repair. Now one company is encouraging people to give up their cars in favor of pedal power. Velib, located in Paris, France, is pioneering the concept of a public bicycle rental program.

On July 15, 2007, 10,000 bicycles were introduced to the city, along with 750 automated rental stations, which hold 15 bicycles each. Customers pay a deposit of $200 for an unlimited number of rentals and are then given a charge card, which also detaches the bikes from the cycle racks. The first half an hour is free and thereafter it costs as little as $1.30 an hour, and there is unlimited access for 24 hours a day. The bike does not need to be returned to the same pick-up point. Customers can pick up one of the distinctive gray bicycles from a rack near the Eiffel Tower, cycle to the Pantheon, and leave it at the nearest Velib stand there. Twenty trucks are used each night to redistribute the machines to high-demand stations.

Theft is kept to a minimum by the heavy design of the bikes. The parking facilities are also secure, and the credit card deposit system deters users from "forgetting" to return the bikes, because fines can be collected directly from the card. The service is primarily aimed at people who are making short journeys, and there are currently more than 190,000 people signed up for the service, with 94 percent saying they are very satisfied with the service. Each bicycle is used on average 30 times a day, and the average trip time is just 18 minutes. Visitors to the city can take out short-term subscriptions by simply using their credit cards directly at the cycle rack terminals.

The service is financed by family-controlled advertising company JCDecaux that provides the bikes in return for an exclusive contract to sell outdoor advertising in prime locations around Paris. JCDecaux paid start-up costs of around $115 million and is signed up to operate and repair the bikes for 10 years.

Since the launch, the number of bicycles available for hire has doubled to 20,000, and the number of rental stations has increased to 1,450. City officials say traffic has been reduced by 5 percent in the French capital.

Q&A: Based on the material covered in this chapter, what questions would you ask the firm's founders before making your funding decision? What answers would satisfy you?

Decision: If you had to make your decision on just the information provided in the pitch and on the company's Web site, would you fund this firm? Why, or why not?

YOU BE THE VC 7.2

Company: Prefense

Web: www.prefense.com
Twitter: Prefense
Facebook: Prefense Hand Sanitizer

Business Idea: Develop a hand sanitizer that a person applies once a day and which retains its potency for 24 hours.

Pitch: Everyday people are exposed to germs and diseases that are invisible to the naked eye. Ideally, to combat this danger, people should wash their hands several times a day, or at the minimum use a hand sanitizer like Purell. The problem is that washing is a chore, and a hand sanitizer isn't always available. An everyday activity as ordinary as greeting someone with a handshake and then later placing your hand near your mouth can expose you to harmful germs. Even if you do wash or use an ordinary sanitizer, the benefits quickly dissipate. In fact, alcohol-based hand sanitizers, which are the most common kind, have been the subject of scrutiny because they have a short duration, they need to be constantly reapplied, and they have the potential to leave skin dry and are a safety concern for children.

Finally, there is a hand sanitizer that does a better job. Prefense proactively and persistently offers protection from bacteria and fungi such as staph, strep, E.coli, H1N1 (swine flu), and many more for up to 24 hours and 10 hand washings without reapplication. What sets Prefense apart is a completely safe patented silica compound that attaches to the outside of the washer's hands, forming microscopic needle-shaped structures that kill germs by rupturing their cells when they come into contact with skin. Other sanitizers kill germs by basically dehydrating them and shrinking the germ cells. Prefense is also so eco-friendly that you can drink it without experiencing any harmful effects, making it safe for all ages.

Prefense, which has gotten off to a strong start, is available at Whole Foods and REI stores across the country. The company is hoping to expand to mainstream retailers. Prefense is currently seeking FDA approval, which will allow it to sell into regulated industries and medical markets. The company's founders believe that Prefense's core technology can be applied to additional personal care products for the purpose of improving their safety.

Q&A: Based on the material covered in this chapter, what questions would you ask the firm's founders before making your funding decision? What answers would satisfy you?

Decision: If you had to make your decision on just the information provided in the pitch and on the company's Web site, would you fund this company? Why or why not?

CASE 7.1

Preparing a Proper Legal Foundation: A Start-Up Fable

Bruce R. Barringer, *Oklahoma State University*

R. Duane Ireland, *Texas A&M University*

Introduction

Jack Peterson and Sarah Jones are planning to start a business. Their plan is to locate and operate 10 kiosks in malls and other high-traffic areas to sell accessories for Apple iPhones, iPads, and iPods. To complement their accessory sales, the two have created a series of short videos that help users learn how to make better use of their iPhones, iPads, and iPods. The videos will be available on Jack and Sarah's Web site for a one-time fee of $10.99 or on an app they are developing for a $10.99 one-time download fee. Both the Web site and the mobile app will include promotions to buy additional iPhone, iPad, and iPod accessories via Jack and Sarah's kiosks or by mail.

iUser Accessories is the tentative name for the business. Jack and Sarah like to use the word *tentative* because they aren't completely sold on the name. The Internet domain name, www.iuseraccessories.com, was available, so they registered it on GoDaddy.com. Part of their start-up funding will be used to hire a trademark attorney to do a formal trademark search before they use the name or do any advertising.

Jack and Sarah met in an introduction to entrepreneurship course at their local university. They hit it off while working on the initial business plan for iUser Accessories, which they completed as an assignment for the class. Their senior year, they refined the plan by working on it during a business planning class. They took first place in a university-wide business plan competition just before graduation. The win netted them $10,000 in cash and $10,000 in "in-kind" services for the business. Their plan was to use the money to establish a relationship with an accountant affiliated with the university.

Feasibility Analysis and Business Plan

As part of their business plan, Jack and Sarah completed a product feasibility analysis for iUser Accessories. They first developed a concept statement and distributed it to a total of 16 people, including professors, electronic store owners, iPhone, iPad and iPod users, and the parents of young iPhone, iPad and iPod users. The responses were both positive and instructive. The idea to distribute videos dealing with how to better use your iPhone, iPad, and iPod via streaming video over the Internet or via the mobile app came directly from one of the concept-statement participants. Jack and Sarah's original idea was to distribute this material in a more conventional manner. The person who came up with the idea wrote on the bottom of the concept statement, "Not only will this approach save you money (by not having to distribute actual videos) but it will drive traffic to your Web site and your app and provide you with additional e-commerce opportunities."

Following the concept statement, Jack and Sarah surveyed 410 people in their target market, which is 15- to 35-year-olds. They did this by approaching people wherever they could and politely asking them to complete the survey. They persuaded one of their marketing professors to help them with the survey's design, to make sure it generalized to a larger population. They learned that 58 percent of the people in their target market own an iPod or iPhone or plan to get one soon. The survey also listed a total of 36 iPhone, iPad and iPod accessories, which are available through vendors that Jack and Sarah have access to. The results affirmed Jack and Sarah's notion that the vast majority of people in their target market don't realize the number of iPhone, iPad and iPod accessories that exist, let alone know where to get them. They also were pleased with the high degree of interest expressed by the survey participants in learning more about many of the accessories.

Start-Up Capital

As part of their business plan, Jack and Sarah completed one- and three-year pro forma financial statements, which demonstrate the potential viability of their business. They have commitments for $66,000 of funding from friends and family. According to their projections, they should be cash-flow positive within four months and will not need any additional infusions of cash, unless they expand the business beyond the scope of their original business plan. The projections include salaries of $32,000 per year for both Jack and Sarah, who will both work more than 40 hours a week manning the kiosks and running the business.

Jack and Sarah are fortunate in that they are able to each contribute $3,000 to the business personally and were able to gain commitments of $30,000 each from their respective groups of friends and family. A year or so ago they participated in a class offered by their local Small Business Development Center (SBDC) about how to start a business and remembered an attorney saying that's it all right to talk to people about funding prior to talking to an attorney but don't actually accept any money until you have your legal ducks in order. As a result, other than their own money, Jack and Sarah didn't actually have the $66,000 yet. They can accumulate it within 30 days once they are confident that the business is a go.

Preparing for the Meeting with the Attorney

Jack and Sarah plan to launch their business on September 15, just two months prior to the start of the busy Christmas season. They spent some time asking around the business school and the technology incubator attached to their university to identify the name of a good small-business attorney. They identified an attorney and made the appointment. The appointment was scheduled for 2:15 P.M. on July 16 at the attorney's office.

Another take-away that Jack and Sarah gleaned from the SBDC class was to plan carefully the time you spend with an attorney, to make best use of your time and minimize expenses. As a result, prior to the meeting, Jack and Sarah planned to spend several evenings at a local Borders bookstore, looking at books that deal with forms of business ownership and other legal issues and making a concise list of issues to discuss with the attorney. They had also gone over this material in preparing their business plan. In the meeting with the attorney, they want to be as well informed as possible and actually lead the discussion and make recommendations. Sarah's dad is a real estate agent and had dealt with many attorneys during his career. One thing he told her, in helping her prepare for this meeting, is that attorneys are helpful and necessary but shouldn't make your decisions for you. Sarah shared this insight with Jack, and they were both determined to follow that advice in their upcoming meeting.

Jack and Sarah's Recommendations

To put their list on paper and get started, Jack created the document at the top of the next column.

Jack and Sarah spent the next several evenings completing this list and talking about their business. When they made the call to set up the meeting with the attorney, the attorney told them that she wasn't an intellectual property lawyer, and if it looked like the business was a go after their meeting, she could arrange for them to talk to one of her partners who specialized in patent and trademark law. As a result, Jack and Sarah knew that this meeting would focus more on forms of business ownership and general legal issues, and they would address their intellectual property questions at another meeting.

(continued)

Jack Peterson and Sarah Jones

Founders, iUser Accessories

List of Legal Issues to Discuss with Attorney

Issue	Jack and Sarah's Recommendation

The Day Arrives

The day for the meeting arrived, and Jack and Sarah met at the attorney's office at 2:15 P.M. They had e-mailed the attorney their list of issues along with their recommendations a week prior to the meeting. The attorney greeted them with a firm handshake and opened a file labeled "iUser Accessories, Jack Peterson and Sarah Jones." Seeing their names like that, on an attorney's file, made it seem like their company was already real. The attorney looked at both of them and placed a copy of the list they had e-mailed in front of her. The list already had a number of handwritten notes on it. The attorney smiled and said to Jack and Sarah, "Let's get started."

Discussion Questions

1. Complete Jack and Sarah's list for them, including the issues you think they will place on the list along with their recommendations. Which of the issues do you think will stimulate the most discussion with the attorney, and which issues do you think will stimulate the least?
2. Make a list of the things you think Jack and Sarah did right in preparing for their meeting with the attorney.
3. Comment on the product feasibility analysis that Jack and Sarah completed. Do you think the way Jack and Sarah approached this task was appropriate and sufficient?
4. What advantages do Jack and Sarah have starting iUser Accessories together, rather than one of them starting it as a sole entrepreneur? What challenges do you think Jack and Sarah will have keeping their partnership together?

Application Questions

1. Suggest an alternative to iUser Accessories for the name of Jack and Sarah's firm. Check to see if the ".com" version of the Internet domain name is available. If it isn't, select another name and continue selecting names until you can match a name with an available domain name.
2. Do you think it is too early for Jack and Sarah to start laying an ethical foundation for their firm? What steps can they take now to lay a solid ethical foundation for their firm?

CASE 7.2

Smarty Pants and DonorsChoose: How For-Profit and Nonprofit Start-Ups Build Credibility and Trust

SmartyPants Web: www.wearesmartypants.com
Twitter: SmartyPantsKids
Facebook: SmartyPants Vitamins
DonorsChoose Web: www.donorschoose.org
Twitter: DonorsChoose
Facebook: DonorsChoose.org

Bruce R. Barringer, *Oklahoma State University*
R. Duane Ireland, *Texas A&M University*

Introduction

Credibility is a vital part of any start-up's persona. Whether a prospective customer in a for-profit context, or a prospective donor in a nonprofit context, it's important that the company or organization presents itself in a manner that builds credibility and trust during first encounters. Both consumers and donors have multiple options for allocating their money. As a result, it's essential that a start-up make a favorable first impression and give its patrons reasons to trust it.

How Companies and Organizations Build Credibility and Trust

There are several ways companies and organizations can build credibility and trust. We present eight techniques that are essential in nearly all cases in the following list.

The following are examples of how two organizations—one for-profit and one nonprofit—are building credibility and trust via these techniques.

SmartyPants

Launched in 2010, SmartyPants sells children's vitamins via the Internet. While there are many companies that sell children's vitamins, SmartyPants is unique in that it's the only company solely dedicated to children's vitamins. It's also an advocate for "brain health." The scientific link between healthy brains, healthy bodies, cognitive development, and emotional well-being is well-documented. All children benefit from appropriate daily supplements of three micronutrients that support brain health—Omega 3, DHA, and Vitamin D. Until now, these micronutrients could be bought separately, but were not available in a single tablet. SmartyPants Gummy Multi-Vitamins include each of these micronutrients, plus 11 others.

That's the product. Here's how SmartyPants is building credibility and trust via the eight techniques described previously.

1. It has a professional logo design, beautiful Web site, and corporate e-mail address.
2. It's attracted considerable press. Its founders have been interviewed on MSNBC. It's been featured by Daily Candy, ModernMom, ecomom, ecofabulous, and in various other media outlets.
3. It's pediatrician approved. According to Dr. Robert Kramer, chairman of the Department of Pediatrics (retired) Baylor University Medical Center,

Techniques for Engendering Credibility, Legitimacy, and Trust

Technique	Explanation
1. Have an attractive logo, corporate e-mail address, and professional looking Web site.	Prospective customers and donors have a mental image of what *real* companies and organizations looks like. If your logo, Web site, or e-mail address look amateurish or suspect, the game is up. Always have a corporate .com or .org e-mail address. A Gmail or Yahoo! e-mail address makes a company or organization look amateurish.
2. Receive media coverage.	Display prominently on your Web site the media coverage you've received. If you're new, start by asking bloggers in your industry to cover you. Media coverage is a tacit sign of legitimacy and support.
3. Obtain expert testimonials.	Get expert testimonials and feature them on your Web site and in your literature. An expert doesn't have to be someone who is famous. If you're selling surgery-related software, ask a surgeon to test it and comment. If you're starting a nonprofit to provide a place for at-risk kids to hang out after school, ask the local police chief or a school principal to comment on your service.
4. Obtain customer testimonials.	Ask customers, donors, or recipients of the good or service you provide to test that good or service and then to comment about their experiences. Include their pictures if possible. Positive quotes from real people are often the most persuasive.
5. Give people a reason to care.	Make sure to convey your start-up's relevance, but don't use buzz words like you're "revolutionary," or "are the industry's best." These terms are too slick. Instead, be genuine. Explain in everyday language why your customers or donors should care.
6. Tell your story.	Why do you care? There is nothing that builds credibility and trust faster than a founder telling the sincere story of why he or she is launching a company or starting a nonprofit. Include your picture and put a real e-mail address next to it.
7. Have a presence on Twitter, Facebook, or both.	Like it or not, people will look for you on Twitter and Facebook. If you're not there, it's a red flag. Establish a presence on one or both sites and provide frequent updates.
8. Tell people how you'll use and/or protect their money.	If you're a for-profit business, offer a money-back guarantee. If you're a nonprofit, explain in specific terms how your donor's money will be spent.

(continued)

"SmartyPants helps parents ensure their children are getting all the nutrients they need."

4. Prime real estate on its Web site is devoted to "What Parents Are Saying about SmartyPants Multi-Vitamins." Pictures of parents and kids are included. Samantha S. from New York, New York, for example, says "My girl is a very picky eater and I love that she loves SmartyPants."

5. The company prominently displays material about the connection between brain health and mental, physical, and emotional well-being. Vitamins are part of the route to achieving brain health.

6. An "Our Story" tab is included on the toolbar at the top of SmartyPants's Web site. It was started by parents and entrepreneurs who have the same dreams and aspirations that all parents have for their children.

7. The company is active on both Twitter and Facebook. As of April 2011, it had 2,274 Twitter followers and 10,826 Facebook friends.

8. The firm provides a 100 percent money-back guarantee. In addition, it's partnered with Vitamin Angels, a nonprofit organization, which distributes micronutrients, especially Vitamin A, to infants and children in developing nations. Every time someone buys a SmartyPants bottle of vitamins, the company makes a one-to-one nutrient grant through Vitamin Angels. It says it cares about kids. This proves it.

SmartyPants prominently features this information on its Web site. It's tastefully done, provides useful information, conveys the company's values, and provides multiple opportunities (i.e., newsletter, blog, Twitter, Facebook) for prospective customers to get to know the company before trying it out. While these techniques serve multiple purposes, they're essential in helping SmartyPants build credibility and trust with its target market.

DonorsChoose

DonorsChoose is a nonprofit organization that provides a way for people to donate directly to specific projects at public schools. Charles Best, a middle school science teacher at a public school in the Bronx, launched this firm in 2000. Since then, it's grown to serve public schools across the United States.

DonorsChoose collects proposals from teachers and posts them on its Web site. A typical project is a request that was posted in March 2011 by a teacher at Christine O'Donovan Middle Academy in Los Angeles—a public school. The teacher requested $549.48 for two high-quality exercise mats to help students learn basic exercises. The rationale is that physically active children are more likely to thrive academically and socially. A 17 percent overhead to cover DonorsChoose's costs, which donors can opt out of, was added bringing the request to $646.45. As of the date this case was written, 16 people had donated a total of $553.45 with only $93.05 to go. If the project is funded, DonorsChoose will buy the mats and deliver them to the teacher. A fax or e-mail message will then be sent to the school principal indicating that the gift had been made. In addition, if any teachers in the same school have raised money through DonorsChoose, those teachers will be notified of the gift. DonorsChoose never sends cash to a teacher to buy the items included in the request. It makes the purchases and delivers the items.

What happens next is heartwarming and special. Anyone who donates $1 or more receives a written thank-you note from the teacher. Donors who contribute $100 more to a project, or complete the funding for a project, receive a "thank-you package" from all the students that are affected, along with photographs of the projects and a letter from the teacher. DonorsChoose is funded by the administrative overhead it collects from donors and through private funding sources. The photo shows a second grade class at Hancock Elementary School in San Diego, California. The students are sitting on a new carpet they received from DonorsChoose.

That's what DonorsChoose is about. Like any charity, it relies on the trust and support of its donors. Here's how DonorsChoose covers the eight techniques shown previously for building credibility and support.

1. It has a professional logo design, beautiful Web site, and .org e-mail address.

2. Despite having been active for more than 10 years, the company still draws attention to the press it's received. It's been featured by *The Wall Street Journal*, NPR, CNN, *Time*, *USA Today*, *The Oprah Winfrey Show,* and others.

3. DonorsChoose has been endorsed by two organizations that rate nonprofits: BBB Accredited Charity and Charity Navigator. It consistently meets the BBB Wise Giving Alliance's standards for charity accountability, and has received a four-star rating (the highest possible) from Charity Navigator, America's premier independent charity evaluator.

4. DonorsChoose prominently displays donor feedback in real time on its Web site. You can log onto the Web site and depending on the time of day see feedback as current as within 10 minutes of the time it was written.

5. The entire premise of the company provides people a reason to care. Multiple pictures of children and the projects that are being funded are posted on its Web site.

6. The "About Us" tab provides extensive information about why the organization was started and who's behind it.

7. DonorsChoose is active on both Twitter and Facebook. As of April 2011, it had 35,096 Twitter followers and 81,080 Facebook friends.

8. DonorsChoose prominently displays the impact it makes. In the final week of March 2011, which was a typical week, it collected money from 31,615 donors, 1,525 projects were completed, and 90,577 students were affected. Its financial records are audited by a public accounting firm, and its records are available to the public upon request.

Discussion Questions

1. On a scale of 1 to 10 (10 is high), rate both SmartyPants and DonorsChoose in their efforts to build credibility and trust. Highlight one thing that particularly impresses you about both organizations.

2. Is it appropriate for a company to comment on its ethical standards on its Web site or in its marketing literature? If so, how should a firm or organization approach this task?

3. How can building credibility and trust help a firm or organization avoid legal disputes?

4. What are things that start-ups, whether they are for-profit or nonprofit, do that have the opposite effect of the techniques described in this feature: they engender a lack of credibility and mistrust?

Application Questions

1. What techniques can a firm or organization use to build credibility and trust that aren't mentioned in this feature? Provide examples of firms that are using the techniques that you suggest.

2. The "You Be the VC 7.2" feature focuses on Prefense, a company that's making a hand sanitizer that a person has to apply only once a day. Spend some time studying the company. Based on the information you find, comment on the job that Prefense is doing to build credibility and trust with its target market.

Sources: SmartyPants Web site, www.wearesmartypants.com (accessed April 4, 2011); DonorsChoose Web site, www.donorchoose.org (accessed April 4, 2011).

ENDNOTES

1. Personal Conversation with Shoaib Shaikh, May 10, 2011.

2. R. T. Peterson, "Small Retailers and Service Company Accuracy in Evaluating the Legality of Specified Practices,"*Journal of Small Business Management* 39, no. 4 (2001): 312–19.

3. 2009 *National Business Ethics Survey,Ethics in the Recession* (Washington, DC: Ethics Resource Center, 2009).

4. *National Business Ethics Survey,* 2009.

5. *National Business Ethics Survey,* 2009.

6. A. E. Singer, "Organizing Ethics and Entrepreneurship," *Human Systems Management* 29, no. 2 (2010): 69–78.

7. Character Training International homepage, www.character-ethics.org (accessed May 13, 2011).

8. A. Fayolle, O. Basso, and V. Bouchard, "Three Levels of Culture and Firms' Entrepreneurial Orientation: A Research Agenda," *Entrepreneurship & Regional Development: An International Journal* 22, nos. 7 and 8 (2010): 707–30; T. Friedman, *Hot, Flat, and Crowded* (New York: Farrar, Straus and Giroux, 2008).

9. N. Oliverez-Giles, "Amazon Apologizes for Server Outage, Offers Credit," *Mercury News*, www.mercurynews.com/business/ci_17957957?source=rss&nclick_check=1 (accessed May 13, 2011, originally posted on April 29, 2011).

10. A. Fernandez-Ribens, "International Patent Strategies of Small and Large Firms: An Empirical Study of Nanotechnology," *Review of Policy Research* 27, no. 4 (2010): 457–73.

11. C. E. Bagley, *Legal Aspects of Entrepreneurship: A Conceptual Framework* (Cambridge, MA: Harvard Business School Publishing, 2002).

12. E. Gimmon and J. Levie, "Founder's Human Capital, External Investment and the Survival of New High-Technology Ventures," *Research Policy* 39, no. 9 (2010): 1214–26.

13. T. M. Marcum and E. S. Blair, "Entrepreneurial Decisions and Legal Issues in Early Venture Stages: Advice That Shouldn't Be Ignored," *Business Horizons* 54, no. 2 (2011): 143–52.

14. J. Poole, "What to Do If You're Not Getting Paid," *Constructionimics*, www.constructionmics.com, July 5, 2010.

15. Y. Sheffi, "What Does Not Kill Me, Makes Me Stronger," *Journal of Supply Chain Management* 46, no. 1 (2010): 8; C. Sutton, "Cash Is King, Hard Lessons Some Small-Business Owners and Managers Forgot!" www.smallbusinessanswers.com (accessed July 28, 2008) .

16. C. Frank, "Get Everything in Writing," The Kauffman Foundation, www.entrepreneurship.org/Resources/Detail/Default.aspx?id=11328 (accessed December 12, 2008, originally posted on July 1, 2000).

17. M. Clark, *The Bear Necessities of Business* (New York: Wiley, 2006), 112.

18. C. E. Bagley, *Legal Aspects of Entrepreneurship: A Conceptual Framework* (Cambridge, MA: Harvard Business School Publishing, 2002), 17.

19. A. Gerlin, "A Matter of Degree: How a Jury Decided That a Coffee Spill Is Worth $2.7 Million,"*Wall Street Journal*, September 1, 1994.

20. Marcum and Blair, "Entrepreneurial Decisions and Legal Issues in Early Venture Stages."

21. K. G. Stewart and L. Zheng, "Treating Cross-Dependence in Event Studies: The Canadian Income Trust Leak," *Applied Financial Economics* 21, no. 6 (2011): 369–77; H. R. Cheeseman, *The Legal Environment of Business and Online Commerce,* 6th ed. (Upper Saddle River, NJ: Pearson Education, 2009).

22. J. C. Leach and R. W. Mellcher, *Entrepreneurial Finance*, 4th ed. (Cincinnati: Cengage Learning, 2012).

23. R. L. Miller and G. A. Jentz, *Business Law Today*, 9th ed. (Cincinnati: Cengage Learning, 2012).

24. J. E. Adamson and A. Morrison, *Law for Business and Personal Use*, 19th ed. (Cincinnati: Cengage Learning, 2012).

25. D. J. McKenzie, R. M. Betts, and C. A. Jensen, *Essentials of Real Estate Economics* (Cincinnati: Cengage Learning, 2011).

26. C. S. Warren, J. M. Reeve, and J. Duchac, *Accounting*, 24th ed. (Cincinnati: Cengage Learning, 2012).

27. J. Dammann and M. Schundein, "The Incorporation Choices of Privately Held Corporations," *Journal of Law, Economics and Organization* 27, no. 1 (2011): 79–112.

28. F. B. Cross and R. L. Miller, *The Legal Environment of Business*, 8th ed. (Cincinnati: Cengage Learning, 2012).

29. Investorwords.com homepage, www.investorwords.com (accessed May 15, 2011).

30. Investorwords.com homepage, www.investorwords.com (accessed May 15, 2011).

31. Y. Ertimur, F. Ferri, and V. Muslu, "Shareholder Activism and CEO Pay," *Review of Financial Studies* 24, no. 2 (2010): 535–92.

32. M. Abudy and S. Benniga, "Taxation and the Value of Employee Stock Options," *International Journal of Managerial Finance* 7, no. 1 (2011): 9–37; E. J. McElvaney, "The Benefits of Promoting Employee Ownership Incentives to Improve Employee Satisfaction, Company Productivity and Profitability," *International Review of Business Research Papers* 7, no. 1 (2011): 201–10.

33. A. Pendleton and A. Robinson, "Employee Share Ownership, Involvement, and Productivity: An Interaction-Based Approach," *Industrial & Labor Relations Review* 46, no. 1 (2010): 3–29.

34. C. H. Green, *The SBA Loan Book* 3rd ed. (Avon, MA: Adams Business, 2011).

35. J. M. Malcomson, "Do Managers with Limited Liability Take More Risky Decisions? An Information Acquisition Model," *Journal of Economics & Management Strategy* 20, no. 1 (2011): 83–120.

36. L. Gray, "The Three Forms of Governance: A New Approach to Family Wealth Transfer and Asset Protection, Part III," *Journal of Wealth Management* 14, no. 1 (2011): 41–54.

APPENDIX 7.1   WHAT'S IN A BUSINESS NAME?: A LOT OF TROUBLE IF YOU AREN'T CAREFUL

Introduction

While at first glance naming a business may seem like a minor issue, it is an extremely important one. A company's name is one of the first things people associate with a business, and it is a word or phrase that will be said thousands or hundreds of thousands of times during the life of a firm. A company's name is also the most critical aspect of its branding strategy. A company brand is the unique set of attributes that allow consumers to separate it from its competitors. As a result, it is important that a business choose its name carefully so that it will facilitate rather than hinder how the business wants to differentiate itself in the marketplace.

If an entrepreneur isn't careful, the process of naming a business can also result in a peck of trouble. There are a number of legal issues involved in naming a business, which should be taken seriously. If a business selects a name and later finds out that it's already been legally taken, the business may have to (1) amend its articles of incorporation, (2) change its Internet domain name, (3) obtain new listings in telephone and other directories, (4) purchase new stationery and business cards, (5) redo signage and advertising, and (6) incur the expense and potential embarrassment of introducing a new name to its customers. These are complications that no entrepreneur wants to endure. The following case describes the strategies for naming a business along with the legal issues involved.

Strategies for Naming a Business

The primary consideration in naming a company is that the name should complement the type of business the company plans to be. It is helpful to divide companies into four categories to discuss this issue.

Consumer-Driven Companies

If a company plans to focus on a particular type of customer, its name should reflect the attributes of its clientele. For example, a high-end clothing store that specializes in small sizes for women is called La Petite Femme. The name was chosen to appeal specifically to its target market or clientele.

Product- or Service-Driven Companies

If a company plans to focus on a particular product or service, its name should reflect the advantages that its product or service brings to the marketplace. Examples include Jiffy Print, ServiceMaster, and 1-800-FLOWERS. These names were chosen to reflect the distinctive attributes of the product or service the company offers, regardless of the clientele.

Industry-Driven Companies

If a company plans to focus on a broad range of products or services in a particular industry, its name should reflect the category it is participating in. Examples include General Motors, Bed Bath & Beyond, and Home Depot. These companies have names that are intentionally broad and are not limiting in regard to target market or product selection.

Personality- or Image-Driven Companies

Some companies are founded by individuals who put such an indelible stamp on the company that it may be smart to name the company after the founder. Examples include Liz Claiborne, Walt Disney, Charles Schwab, and Magic Johnson Enterprises. These companies have names that benefit from a positive association with a popular or distinctive founder. Of course, this strategy can backfire if the founder falls out of favor in the public's eye.

While names come to some business owners easily, for others it's a painstaking process. It was a painstaking process for JetBlue, as described in the book *Blue Streak*, which is a chronology of the early years of JetBlue. According to Barbara Peterson, the book's author, David Neeleman, the founder of JetBlue, and his initial management team agonized over what to name the company and considered literally hundreds of names before settling on JetBlue. JetBlue was launched in 1999. Neeleman felt that a strong brand would surmount the handicap of being a new airline and believed that the company's name was the key to building its brand. A list of some of the alternative names that Neeleman and his management team seriously considered for JetBlue is shown at the top of the next page. Today, it's hard to think of JetBlue as anything other than JetBlue, which illustrates the power of branding.

**Names That Were Seriously
Considered for JetBlue**

Air Hop	Egg
Scout Air	It
Competition	Blue
Home	Fair Air
Air Taxi	Scout
Avenues	Hi! Way
Civilization Airways	True Blue

Legal Issues Involved in Naming a Business

The general rule for business names is that they must be unique. In other words, in most instances, there may not be more than one business per name per state. In addition, a business may not have a name that is confusingly similar to another business. This regulation prevents a software company from naming itself Macrosoft, for example, which Microsoft would undoubtedly claim is confusingly similar to its name.

To determine if a name is available in a particular state, the entrepreneur must usually contact the secretary of state's office to see if a particular name is available. The inquiry can typically be accomplished over the phone or by mail. If the name is available, the next step is to reserve it in the manner recommended by the secretary of state's office. Many attorneys and incorporation services include this step in the fee-based services they offer to entrepreneurs and their ventures.

Once a name that is available has been chosen, it should be trademarked. The process for obtaining a trademark is straightforward and relatively inexpensive, given the protection it provides. A full explanation of how to obtain a trademark is provided in Chapter 12 of this book.

The entire process of naming a business is often very frustrating for entrepreneurs, because it is becoming increasingly difficult to find a name that isn't already taken. For example, if an entrepreneur was planning to open a new quick-printing service, almost every possible permutation of the word *printing* with words like *quick*, *swift*, *fast*, *rapid*, *speedy*, *jiffy*, *express*, *instant*, and so forth are taken. In addition, sometimes names that work in one culture don't work in another, which is something that should be taken into consideration. The classic example of this is the Chevy NOVA. After much advertising and fanfare, the car received a very cool reception in Mexico. It turned out that the phrase *no va* in Spanish means "Doesn't Go." Not surprisingly, the NOVA didn't sell well in Mexico.

As a result of these complications, and for other reasons, entrepreneurs use a variety of other strategies when naming their business. Some names are simply made up, because the firm wants a name that is catchy or distinctive, or because it needs to make up a name to get an Internet domain name that isn't already taken (more about this later). Examples of names that were made up include Exxon, Verizon, eBay, Google, and Xerox. Some of these names are made up with the help of marketing research firms that use sophisticated methodologies such as an evaluation of the "linguistic properties" (will a consumer read the name properly?), the "phonetic transparency" (is it spelled as it sounds?), and the "multilingual functionality" (is it as intelligible in Japanese as in English?) of a particular name. All of these issues are potentially important. Several years ago Anderson Consulting changed its name to Accenture. The pronunciation of "Accenture" isn't obvious, which has been a problem for the firm ever since.

Internet Domain Names

A final complicating factor in selecting a name for a company is registering an Internet domain name. A domain name is a company's Internet address (e.g., www.facebook.com). Most companies want their domain name to be the same as their company's name. It is easy to register a domain name through an online registration service such as GoDaddy.com (www.godaddy.com). The standard fee for registering and maintaining a domain name is about $10 per year.

Because no two domain names can be exactly the same, frustrations often arise when a company tries to register its domain name and the name is already taken. There are two reasons that a name may already be taken. First, a company may find that another company with the same name has already registered it. For example, if an entrepreneur started a company called Delta Semiconductor, it would find that the domain name www.delta.com is already taken by Delta Airlines. This scenario plays itself out every day and represents a challenge for new firms that have chosen fairly ordinary names. The firm can either select another domain name (such as www.deltasemiconductor.com) or try to acquire the name from its present owner. However, it is unlikely that Delta Airlines would give up www.delta.com for any price. The second reason that a domain name may already be taken is that it might be in the hands of someone who has registered the name with the intention of using it at a later date or of someone who simply collects domain names in hopes that someone will want to buy the name at a higher price.

Still, a little imagination goes a long way in selecting a company name and an Internet domain name. For example, we (your book's authors) made up the name iUser Accessories for the business described in Case 7.1. The Internet domain name www.iuseraccessories.com was available, which we registered on GoDaddy.com for $10 per year. What might we do with this Internet domain name? We aren't certain. But, another party deciding to launch an entrepreneurial venture with this name will discover that the hoped-for name is already registered.

Getting Personal *with* KLYMIT

Founder:

NATE ALDER
Brigham Young University, anticipated at some point in the future

Dialogue *with*
Nate Alder

**MY FAVORITE
SMARTPHONE APP**
E-mail, GPS navigator, Expensify

BEST ADVICE I'VE RECEIVED
Get the right people on the bus, the wrong people off, then figure out where to take the bus. You can never be successful without the right team.

**MY BIGGEST WORRY
AS AN ENTREPRENEUR**
Being able to manage rapid growth

**MY BIGGEST SURPRISE
AS AN ENTREPRENEUR**
How long it can take and how much money it can cost to start a business

**FIRST ENTREPRENEURIAL
EXPERIENCE**
Mowing lawns, babysitting, swim lessons

**BEST PART OF BEING
A STUDENT**
You have a lot of great resources and mentors at your disposal for free.

CHAPTER 8

Assessing a New Venture's *Financial Strength* and Viability

OPENING PROFILE

KLYMIT
The Critical Importance of Cash Flow

Web: www.klymit.com
Twitter: klymit
Facebook: Klymit

In summer 2006, Nate Alder was scuba diving off the east coast of Brazil. Alder learned that divers using dry suits in Arctic conditions used noble gases to insulate their wet suits when they were in cold water. Back home in Utah, Alder was a snowboard instructor and knew all about being cold. He wondered why noble gases couldn't be used in ski jackets to keep skiers and snowboarders warm.

The idea stuck with Alder, and when he returned home he enlisted the help of business student Nick Sorensen and engineering PhD candidate Brady Woolford to see if noble gases could be used to warm jackets. The basic idea was to create a jacket with a series of connected, airtight chambers. A small cartridge, filled with pressurized argon gas, would be stored in a pocket, and would have a small dial on it. When the dial was turned to the right, gas would flow into the chambers and the skier would get warmer. Turn the dial to the left and gas would escape and the skier would cool down. The secret to how the system works is grounded in the properties of argon gas. The benefits of using argon gas to warm a jacket instead of bulky fabrics is that the gas creates a thinner, lighter, and more comfortable jacket.

Alder and his team entered a number of business plan competitions in spring 2007 through spring 2008. Incredibly, the team placed first or second in 11 business plan or innovation competitions, winning more than $200,000 in prize money and services. Klymit formally launched in 2007, intending to license its technology to major outdoor apparel companies. It spent the next year building prototypes of the jacket, aided by $220,000 in funds from an angel investor. In late 2008 and early 2009, Alder and his team started approaching large apparel companies hoping to ink licensing deals. This is when they hit their first snag. While large apparel companies routinely license new innovations from technology provider companies such as 3M, DuPont, Gore-Tex, etc., they had never seen anything like Klymit's product before and weren't

LEARNING OBJECTIVES

After studying this chapter you should be ready to:

1. Explain the two functions of the financial management of a firm.
2. Identify the four main financial objectives of entrepreneurial ventures.
3. Explain the difference between historical and pro forma financial statements.
4. Explain the purpose of an income statement.
5. Explain the purpose of a balance sheet.
6. Explain the purpose of a statement of cash flows.
7. Discuss how financial ratios are used to analyze and interpret a firm's financial statements.
8. Discuss the role of forecasts in projecting a firm's future income and expenses.
9. Explain what a completely new firm bases its forecasts on.
10. Explain what is meant by the term *percent-of-sales method*.

equipped to manufacture it. In addition, the timing was bad. Early 2009 was the depth of the recent economic downturn. Large apparel companies were in no mood to license designs from other companies, regardless of how promising they seemed. If Klymit wanted to bring its novel gas-insulated ski jacket to market, it would have to do it itself.

The Klymit team decided to move forward, focusing intently on three topics: jacket production, raising capital, and careful financial management. Klymit had about six months of cash available. If it couldn't raise additional capital in that time, it would have to close up shop. Alder and his team also knew they had to make every penny count to be able to build the product and gain traction in the marketplace to incent investors to come on board.

The basic design of the first product, named the Klymit Kinetic Vest featuring the NobleTek insulation, was set. The challenge was to get it manufactured and into retail outlets with the cash the company had on hand. To produce the vest, they located manufacturers in Asia—but there was a catch. The catch was that for a small company, like Klymit, offshore manufacturers want 30 to 50 percent of the cost up front, with the remainder assured by a letter of credit from a bank. Klymit was able to swing this for the first shipment of its NobleTek vests. Through trade shows and the publicity Klymit had generated, it was able to secure retailers for its initial batches of product. Once in stores, the vests started to sell and gain traction. Armed with evidence that it could build a product that would sell, from September to November 2009, Alder and his team landed $2 million in venture capital and angel funding. It was a turning point for Klymit. Without the additional investment, Klymit wouldn't have had the cash to go on.

Klymit used the $2 million to hire a VP of sales and to build inventory. It also started building prototypes of a second product, an inflatable sleeping pad, called the Klymit Inertia X-Frame. Packed up, the sleeping pad is about the size of a 12 ounce can of Coke, making it easy for a hiker to carry. It inflates by mouth with air or with argon gas, the same gas used in the NobleTec vest. The Inertia X-Frame was ready to go in August 2010, and was introduced at trade shows, with rave reviews. The product is now selling in a number of retail outlets in over 25 countries around the world, with some major camping and sporting goods chains about ready to sign on as Inertia X-Frame retailers. Its basic NobleTec jacket has also evolved. It now has several versions of what it calls its Kinetic jackets/shells and its Kinetic vests.

Klymit is now at a point where its earnings are funding its operations, although additional capital may be needed. Cash flow challenges persist. While it's gained the trust of its Asian manufacturers, they still want 30 to 50 percent of the cost up front and the remainder upon shipment. Retailers typically pay Klymit 30 days after they receive product. This means there's a considerable gap between paying the manufacturer of the product and getting paid by the retailers who sell the product. Ironically, the more successful a product-based firm is, the more capital it needs to pay up front for inventory and the more strain is placed on its cash flow.

In terms of overall financial management, Alder is comfortable with where Klymit is today. Many lessons have been learned, however, about the importance of cash flow and the need for sharp financial management for a growing company.

In this chapter, we'll look at how new ventures manage their finances and assess their financial strength and viability. For the purposes of completeness, we'll look at how both existing firms and entrepreneurial ventures accomplish these tasks. First, we'll consider general financial management and discuss the financial objectives of a firm and the steps involved in the financial management process. **Financial management** deals with two activities: raising money and managing a company's finances in a way that achieves the highest rate of return.[1] We cover the process of raising money in Chapter 10. This chapter focuses on how a company manages its finances in an effort to increase its financial strength and earn the highest rate of return. Next, we'll examine how existing firms track their financial progress through preparing, analyzing, and maintaining past financial statements. Finally, we'll discuss how both existing firms and start-up ventures forecast future income and expenses and how the forecasts are used to prepare pro forma (i.e., projected) financial statements. Pro forma financial statements, which include the pro forma income statement, the pro forma balance sheet, and the pro forma statement of cash flows, are extremely helpful to firms in financial planning.

INTRODUCTION TO FINANCIAL MANAGEMENT

An entrepreneur's ability to pursue an opportunity and turn the opportunity into a viable entrepreneurial firm hinges largely on the availability of money. Regardless of the quality of a product or service, a company can't be viable in the long run unless it is successful financially. Money either comes from external sources (such as investors or lenders) or is internally generated through earnings. It is important for a firm to have a solid grasp of how it is doing financially. One of the most common mistakes young entrepreneurial firms make is not placing an emphasis on financial management and putting in place appropriate forms of financial controls.[2]

LEARNING OBJECTIVE

1. Explain the two functions of the financial management of a firm.

Entrepreneurs and those managing established companies must be aware of how much money they have in the bank and if that amount is sufficient to satisfy their firm's financial obligations. Just because a firm is successful doesn't mean that it doesn't face financial challenges.[3] For example, many of the small firms that sell their products to larger companies such as IBM, General Electric (GE), and The Home Depot aren't paid for 30 to 60 days from the time they make a sale. Think about the difficulty this scenario creates. The small firm must buy parts, pay its employees, pay its routine bills, ship its products, and then wait for one to two months for payment. Unless a firm manages its money carefully, it is easy to run out of cash, even if its products or services are selling like hotcakes.[4] Similarly, as a company grows, its cash demands often increase to service a growing clientele. It is important for a firm to accurately anticipate whether it will be able to fund its growth through earnings or if it will need to look for investment capital or borrowing to raise needed cash.

The financial management of a firm deals with questions such as the following on an ongoing basis:

■ How are we doing? Are we making or losing money?
■ How much cash do we have on hand?
■ Do we have enough cash to meet our short-term obligations?
■ How efficiently are we utilizing our assets?
■ How do our growth and net profits compare to those of our industry peers?
■ Where will the funds we need for capital improvements come from?
■ Are there ways we can partner with other firms to share risk and reduce the amount of cash we need?
■ Overall, are we in good shape financially?

A properly managed firm stays on top of the issues suggested by these questions through the tools and techniques that we'll discuss in this chapter.

Financial Objectives of a Firm

Most entrepreneurial firms—whether they have been in business for several years or they are start-ups—have four main financial objectives: profitability, liquidity, efficiency, and stability. Understanding these objectives sets a firm on the right financial course and helps it track the answers to the previously posed questions. Figure 8.1 describes each of these objectives.

Profitability is the ability to earn a profit. Many start-ups are not profitable during their first one to three years while they are training employees and building their brands, but a firm must become profitable to remain viable and provide a return to its owners.

Liquidity is a company's ability to meet its short-term financial obligations. Even if a firm is profitable, it is often a challenge to keep enough money in the bank to meet its routine obligations in a timely manner. To do so, a firm must keep a close watch on accounts receivable and inventories. A company's **accounts receivable** is money owed to it by its customers. Its **inventory** is its merchandise, raw materials, and products waiting to be sold. If a firm allows the levels of either of these assets to get too high, it may not be able to keep sufficient cash on hand to meet its short-term obligations.[5]

Efficiency is how productively a firm utilizes its assets relative to its revenue and its profits. Southwest Airlines, for example, uses its assets very productively. Its turnaround time, or the time that its airplanes sit on the ground while they are being unloaded and reloaded, is the lowest in the airline industry. As Southwest officials are quick to point out, "Our planes don't make any money sitting on the ground—we have to get them back into the air."[6]

Stability is the strength and vigor of the firm's overall financial posture. For a firm to be stable, it must not only earn a profit and remain liquid but also keep its debt in check. If a firm continues to borrow from its lenders and its **debt-to-equity ratio**, which is calculated by dividing its long-term debt by its shareholders' equity, gets too high, it may have trouble meeting its obligations and securing the level of financing needed to fuel its growth.

An increasingly common way that small companies improve their prospects across several of these areas is to join buying groups or co-ops, where businesses band together to attain volume discounts on products and services. Gaining access to products and services this way facilitates smaller firms' efforts to compete on more of a "level playing field" with larger, more established companies. The way buying groups work, and how they're able to help businesses cut costs without adversely affecting their competitiveness, is described in this chapter's "Partnering for Success" feature.

FIGURE 8.1
Primary Financial Objectives of Entrepreneurial Firms

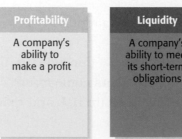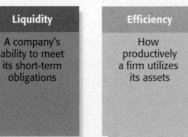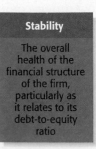

Profitability	Liquidity	Efficiency	Stability
A company's ability to make a profit	A company's ability to meet its short-term obligations	How productively a firm utilizes its assets	The overall health of the financial structure of the firm, particularly as it relates to its debt-to-equity ratio

The Process of Financial Management

To assess whether its financial objectives are being met, firms rely heavily on analyses of financial statements, forecasts, and budgets. A **financial statement** is a written report that quantitatively describes a firm's financial health. The income statement, the balance sheet, and the statement of cash flows are the financial statements entrepreneurs use most commonly. **Forecasts** are an estimate of a firm's future income and expenses, based on its past performance, its current circumstances, and its future plans.[7] New ventures typically base their forecasts on an estimate of sales and then on industry averages or the experiences of similar start-ups regarding the cost of goods sold (based on a percentage of sales) and on other expenses. **Budgets** are itemized forecasts of a company's income, expenses, and capital needs and are also an important tool for financial planning and control.[8]

The process of a firm's financial management is shown in Figure 8.2. It begins by tracking the company's past financial performance through the preparation and analysis of financial statements. These statements organize and report the firm's financial transactions. They tell a firm how much money it is making or losing (income statement), the structure of its assets and liabilities (balance sheet), and where its cash is coming from and going (statement of cash flows). The statements also help a firm discern how it stacks up against its competitors and industry norms. Most firms look at two to three years of past financial statements when preparing forecasts.

The next step is to prepare forecasts for two to three years in the future. Then forecasts are used to prepare a firm's pro forma financial statements, which, along with its more fine-tuned budgets, constitute its financial plan.

The final step in the process is the ongoing analysis of a firm's financial results. **Financial ratios**, which depict relationships between items on a firm's financial statements, are used to discern whether a firm is meeting its financial

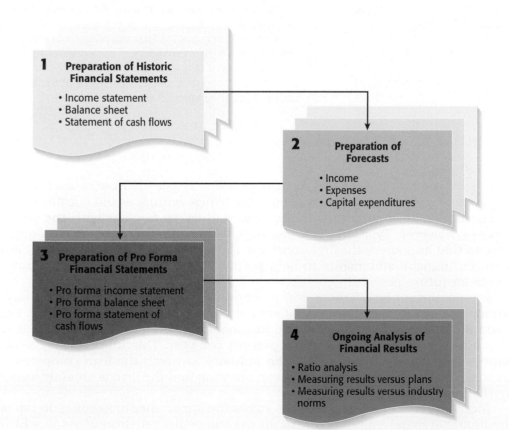

FIGURE 8.2
The Process of Financial Management

1 Preparation of Historic Financial Statements
- Income statement
- Balance sheet
- Statement of cash flows

2 Preparation of Forecasts
- Income
- Expenses
- Capital expenditures

3 Preparation of Pro Forma Financial Statements
- Pro forma income statement
- Pro forma balance sheet
- Pro forma statement of cash flows

4 Ongoing Analysis of Financial Results
- Ratio analysis
- Measuring results versus plans
- Measuring results versus industry norms

PARTNERING FOR SUCCESS

Organizing Buying Groups to Cuts Costs and Maintain Competitiveness

One challenge that businesses confront is cutting costs in ways that don't erode their ability to remain competitive. Many cost-cutting techniques, such as scaling back on hiring, lowering marketing expenses, or reducing inventory, may save money but may also decrease a business' chances to remain competitive. One technique that can help to conserve a product-based business' financial assets without adverse side effects is to join or organize a buying group.

A buying group, or buying co-op, is a partnership that bands small businesses and start-up firms together to attain volume discounts on products and services. An example is the independent supermarket consortium Coopernic, a not-for-profit European grocery buying group that combines the buying power of retailers in Belgium, France, Switzerland, Germany, and Italy. The cost of running the organization is split among the members, as is the savings made on grocery products. A similar buying group is the U.K.-based United Aftermarket Network, which supplies its members in the vehicle trade with parts from leading motor manufacturers that have been bought at a group discount.

In Thailand, Stockbuz is another successful example of a group-buying operation, which has solved a problem for both yarn producers and manufacturers of apparel. The clothes makers forecast demand based on sales data, seasonality, and retailer feedback and buy fabrics in bulk from the yarn producers. This, in turn, helps reduce market uncertainty for the fabric producers and ensures orders are honored. There are similar buying co-ops in other industries.

The beauty of buying groups is that they generally allow businesses to obtain the exact same product for a lower price, with no undesirable impact (other than the membership fee) on the other parts of their operations. The money that's freed up can go directly to a business' bottom line or be used to invest in customer service or other methods to increase competitiveness. There is no national directory of industry buying groups. The best way to find out whether there are buying groups servicing an industry is to conduct Internet research and ask among industry participants.

Questions for Critical Thinking

1. Which of the four financial objectives of a firm—profitability, liquidity, efficiency, or stability—does participating in a buying cooperative contribute to the most?
2. Do some Internet and/or library research to discern whether there is a small business buying group or groups that New Venture Fitness Drinks, the fictitious company introduced in Chapter 3 and used as an example throughout this chapter, could benefit from. New Venture Fitness Drinks' products contain all the ingredients used to make smoothies and similar fitness drinks and shakes.
3. Identify three ways, other than buying cooperatives, that small businesses partner with other small businesses to cut costs without sacrificing their competitiveness?
4. In an effort to improve the financial position of their firms, do you think the majority of entrepreneurs spend an equal amount of time focusing on (1) cost cutting and (2) increasing revenues? If not, which of the two do you think they spend more time on and why?

objectives and how it stacks up against its industry peers. These ratios are also used to assess trends. Obviously, a completely new venture would start at step 2 in Figure 8.2. It is important that a new venture be familiar with the entire process, however. Typically, new ventures prepare financial statements quarterly so that as soon as the first quarter is completed, the new venture will have historic financial statements to help prepare forecasts and pro forma statements for future periods.

It is important for a firm to evaluate how it is faring relative to its industry. Sometimes raw financial ratios that are not viewed in context are deceiving. For example, a firm's past three years' income statements may show that it is increasing its sales at a rate of 15 percent per year. This number may seem impressive—until one learns that the industry in which the firm competes is growing at a rate of 30 percent per year, showing that the firm is steadily losing market share.

Many experienced entrepreneurs stress the importance of keeping on top of the financial management of a firm. In the competitive environments in which most firms exist, it's simply not good enough to shoot from the hip when making financial decisions. Reinforcing this point, Bill Gates, the founder of Microsoft, said,

> The business side of any company starts and ends with hard-core analysis of its numbers. Whatever else you do, if you don't understand what's happening in your business factually and you're making business decisions based on anecdotal data or gut instinct, you'll eventually pay a big price.[9]

FINANCIAL STATEMENTS AND FORECASTS

Historical financial statements reflect past performance and are usually prepared on a quarterly and annual basis. Publicly traded firms are required by the Securities and Exchange Commission (SEC) to prepare financial statements and make them available to the public. The statements are submitted to the SEC through a number of required filings. The most comprehensive filing is the **10-K**, which is a report similar to the annual report except that it contains more detailed information about the company's business.[10] The 10-K for any publicly traded firm is available through the SEC's Web site (www.sec.gov/index.htm).

LEARNING OBJECTIVE

3. Explain the difference between historical and pro forma financial statements.

Pro forma financial statements are projections for future periods based on forecasts and are typically completed for two to three years in the future. Pro forma financial statements are strictly planning tools and are not required by the SEC. In fact, most companies consider their pro forma statements to be confidential and reveal them to outsiders, such as lenders and investors, only on a "need-to-know" basis.

To illustrate how these financial instruments are prepared, let's look at New Venture Fitness Drinks, the fictitious sports drink company to which you were introduced in Chapter 3. New Venture Fitness Drinks has been in business for five years. Targeting sports enthusiasts, the company sells a line of nutritional fitness drinks. It opened a single location in 2009, added a second location in 2011, and plans to add a third in 2012. The company's strategy is

Keeping good records is the first step toward prudent financial management. This entrepreneur, who is the owner of a fast casual restaurant, takes a minute during a hectic day to update his financial records. Good record keeping is essential for tax reporting and generating accurate financial statements.

to place small restaurants, similar to smoothie restaurants, near large outdoor sports complexes. The company is profitable and is growing at a rate of 25 percent per year.

Historical Financial Statements

Historical financial statements include the income statement, the balance sheet, and the statement of cash flows. The statements are usually prepared in this order because information flows logically from one to the next. In start-ups, financial statements are typically scrutinized closely to monitor the financial progress of the firm. On the rare occasion when a company has not used financial statements in planning, it should prepare and maintain them anyway. If a firm goes to a banker or investor to raise funds, the banker or investor will invariably ask for copies of past financial statements to analyze the firm's financial history. If a firm does not have these statements, it may be precluded from serious consideration for an investment or a loan. Let's look at each of these statements.

LEARNING OBJECTIVE

4. Explain the purpose of an income statement.

Income Statement   The **income statement** reflects the results of the operations of a firm over a specified period of time.[11] It records all the revenues and expenses for the given period and shows whether the firm is making a profit or is experiencing a loss (which is why the income statement if often referred to as the "profit-and-loss statement"). Income statements are typically prepared on a monthly, quarterly, and annual basis. Most income statements are prepared in a multiyear format, making it easy to spot trends.

The consolidated income statement for the past three years for New Venture Fitness Drinks is shown in Table 8.1. The value of the multiperiod

TABLE 8.1   CONSOLIDATED INCOME STATEMENTS FOR NEW VENTURE FITNESS DRINKS, INC.

	December 31, 2011	December 31, 2010	December 31, 2009
Net sales	$586,600	$463,100	$368,900
Cost of sales	268,900	225,500	201,500
Gross profit	317,700	237,600	167,400
Operating expenses			
Selling, general, and administrative expenses	117,800	104,700	90,200
Depreciation	13,500	5,900	5,100
Operating income	186,400	127,000	72,100
Other income			
Interest income	1,900	800	1,100
Interest expense	(15,000)	(6,900)	(6,400)
Other income (expense), net	10,900	(1,300)	1,200
Income before income taxes	184,200	119,600	68,000
Income tax expense	53,200	36,600	18,000
Net income	131,000	83,000	50,000
Earnings per share	1.31	0.83	0.50

format is clear. It's easy to see that the company's sales are increasing at the rate of about 25 percent per year, it is profitable, and its net income is increasing. The numbers are used to evaluate the effect of past strategies and to help project future sales and earnings.

The three numbers that receive the most attention when evaluating an income statement are the following:

- **Net sales: Net sales** consist of total sales minus allowances for returned goods and discounts.

- **Cost of sales (or cost of goods sold): Cost of sales** includes all the direct costs associated with producing or delivering a product or service, including the material costs and direct labor. In the case of New Venture Fitness Drinks, this would include the ingredients that go into the fitness drinks and the labor needed to produce them.

- **Operating expenses: Operating expenses** include marketing, administrative costs, and other expenses not directly related to producing a product or service.

One of the most valuable things that entrepreneurs and managers do with income statements is to compare the ratios of cost of sales and operating expenses to net sales for different periods. For example, the cost of sales for New Venture Fitness Drinks, which includes the ingredients for its fitness drinks and the labor needed to make them, has been 55, 49, and 46 percent of sales for 2009, 2010, and 2011, respectively. This is a healthy trend. It shows that the company is steadily decreasing its material and labor costs per dollar of sales. This is the type of trend that can be noticed fairly easily by looking at a firm's multiyear income statements.

Profit margin is a ratio that is of particular importance when evaluating a firm's income statements. A firm's **profit margin**, or return on sales, is computed by dividing net income by net sales. For the years 2009, 2010, and 2011, the profit margin for New Venture Fitness Drinks has been 13.6, 17.9, and 22.3 percent, respectively. This is also a healthy trend. A firm's profit margin tells it what percentage of every dollar in sales contributes to the bottom line. An increasing profit margin means that a firm is either boosting its sales without increasing its expenses or that it is doing a better job of controlling its costs. In contrast, a declining profit margin means that a firm is losing control of its costs or that it is slashing prices to maintain or increase sales.

One ratio that will not be computed for New Venture Fitness Drinks is **price-to-earnings ratio, or P/E ratio**. New Venture Fitness Drinks is incorporated, so it has stock, but its stock is not traded on a public exchange such as the NASDAQ or the New York Stock Exchange. P/E is a simple ratio that measures the price of a company's stock against its earnings.[12] Generally, the higher a company's price-to-earnings ratio goes, the greater the market thinks it will grow. In 2008, New Venture Fitness Drinks earned $1.31 per share. If it was listed on the NASDAQ and its stock was trading at $20 per share, its P/E would be 15.3. This is what is meant when you hear that a company is selling for "15 times earnings."

The importance of looking at several years of income statements rather than just one is illustrated in this chapter's "Savvy Entrepreneurial Firm" feature.

Balance Sheet   Unlike the income statement, which covers a specified *period* of time, a **balance sheet** is a snapshot of a company's assets, liabilities, and owners' equity at a specific *point* in time.[13] The left-hand side of a balance sheet (or the top, depending on how it is displayed) shows a firm's assets, while the right-hand side (or bottom) shows its liabilities and owners' equity. The assets are listed in order of their "liquidity," or the length of time it takes to

LEARNING OBJECTIVE

5. Explain the purpose of a balance sheet.

SAVVY ENTREPRENEURIAL FIRM

Know the Facts Behind the Numbers

Let's say that New Venture Fitness Drinks was interested in hiring a new chief executive officer (CEO) and was interviewing the CEOs of three small restaurant chains. To get a sense of how savvy each candidate was at managing a firm's finances, the board of directors of New Venture Fitness Drinks asked each person to submit the 2011 income statement for his or her current firm. An analysis of an abbreviated version of each firm's income statement is shown here.

	Candidate 1: CEO of New Venture Soup and Salad	Candidate 2: CEO of New Venture Beef	Candidate 3: CEO of New Venture Sea Food
Net sales	$326,400	$281,200	$486,700
Cost of sales	150,500	143,900	174,700
Gross profit	175,900	137,300	312,000
All expenses, including taxes and depreciation	114,200	112,400	150,000
Net income	61,700	24,900	162,000

By glancing at these statements, it would appear that the shrewdest financial manager of the three is the CEO of New Venture Sea Food. The company's net income is more than double that of the other two firms. In addition, New Venture Sea Food's cost of sales was 35.9 percent of net sales in 2011, compared to 46.1 percent for New Venture Soup and Salad and 51 percent for New Venture Beef. Similarly, New Venture Sea Food's expenses were 30.9 percent of sales, compared to 35.0 percent for New Venture Soup and Salad and 40 percent for New Venture Beef.

Fortunately, one of the board members of New Venture Fitness Drinks asked a series of questions during the personal interviews of the candidates and uncovered some revealing information. As it turns out, New Venture Sea Food was in the hottest segment of the restaurant industry in 2011. Seafood restaurants of comparable size produced about 1.5 times as much net income as New Venture Sea Food did. So if candidate 3 had done his job properly, his company's net income should have been in the neighborhood of $240,000 instead of $162,000. New Venture Soup and Salad was in a slow-growth area and at midyear feared that it might not meet its financial targets. So the CEO pulled several of his best people off projects and reassigned them to marketing to develop new menu items. In other words, the company borrowed from its future to make its numbers work today.

As for New Venture Beef, the CEO found herself in a market that was losing appeal. Several reports that gained national publicity were published early in the year warning consumers of the risks of eating red meat. To compensate, the CEO quickly implemented a productivity improvement program and partnered with a local beef promotion board to counter the bad press with more objective research results about beef's nutritional value. The company also participated in several volunteer efforts in its local community to raise the visibility of its restaurants in a positive manner. If the CEO of New Venture Beef hadn't moved quickly to take these actions, its 2011 performance would have been much worse.

Ultimately, New Venture Fitness Drinks decided that candidate 2, the CEO of New Venture Beef, was the best candidate for its job. This example illustrates the need to look at multiple years of an income statement rather than a single year to fairly assess how well a firm is performing financially. It also illustrates the need to look beyond the numbers and understand the circumstances that surround a firm's financial results.

Questions for Critical Thinking

1. Show the income statements for the three candidates to two or three friends who are majoring in business. Ask them to select the best CEO from among these three people on the basis of these income statements. In addition, ask your friends to explain their choices to you. Did your friends choose the same candidate? If not, what do you think caused the differences in their choices?

2. Based on material presented in this chapter, earlier chapters in this book, and your general business knowledge, where would you go to find information about the growth of the different segments of the restaurant industry? Where would you go to find information about the profitability of the restaurant industry in general?

3. What would have been the appropriate financial information to request from the three candidates for the job?

4. What are the three most important insights you gained from studying this feature? Which of these insights surprised you, and why?

convert them to cash. The liabilities are listed in the order in which they must be paid. A balance sheet must always "balance," meaning that a firm's assets must always equal its liabilities plus owners' equity.[14]

The major categories of assets listed on a balance sheet are the following:

■ **Current assets: Current assets** include cash plus items that are readily convertible to cash, such as accounts receivable, marketable securities, and inventories.

■ **Fixed assets: Fixed assets** are assets used over a longer time frame, such as real estate, buildings, equipment, and furniture.

■ **Other assets: Other assets** are miscellaneous assets, including accumulated goodwill.

The major categories of liabilities listed on a balance sheet are the following:

■ **Current liabilities: Current liabilities** include obligations that are payable within a year, including accounts payable, accrued expenses, and the current portion of long-term debt.

■ **Long-term liabilities: Long-term liabilities** include notes or loans that are repayable beyond one year, including liabilities associated with purchasing real estate, buildings, and equipment.

■ **Owners' equity: Owners' equity** is the equity invested in the business by its owners plus the accumulated earnings retained by the business after paying dividends.

Balance sheets are somewhat deceiving. First, a company's assets are recorded at cost rather than fair market value. A firm may have invested $500,000 in real estate several years ago that is worth $1 million today, but the value that is reflected on the firm's current balance sheet is the $500,000 purchase price rather than the $1 million fair market value. Second, intellectual property, such as patents, trademarks, and copyrights, receive value on the balance sheet in some cases and in some cases they don't, depending on the circumstances involved. In many cases, a firm's intellectual property will receive no value on its balance sheet even though it may be very valuable from a practical standpoint.[15] Third, intangible assets, such as the amount of training a firm has provided to its employees and the value of its brand, are not recognized on its balance sheet. Finally, the goodwill that a firm has accumulated is not reported on its balance sheet, although this may be the firm's single most valuable asset.

The consolidated balance sheet for New Venture Fitness Drinks is shown in Table 8.2. Again, multiple years are shown so that trends can be easily spotted. When evaluating a balance sheet, the two primary questions are whether a firm has sufficient short-term assets to cover its short-term debts and whether it is financially sound overall. There are two calculations that provide the answer to the first question. In 2011, the **working capital** of New Venture Fitness Drinks, defined as its current assets minus its current liabilities, was $82,500. This number represents the amount of liquid assets the firm has available. Its **current ratio**, which equals the firm's current assets divided by its current liabilities, provides another picture of the relationship between its current assets and current liabilities and can tell us more about the firm's ability to pay its short-term debts.

New Venture Fitness Drink's current ratio is 3.06, meaning that it has $3.06 in current assets for every $1.00 in current liabilities. This is a healthy number and provides confidence that the company will be able to meet its current liabilities. The company's trend in this area is also positive. For the years 2009, 2010, and 2011, its current ratio has been 2.35, 2.26, and 3.06, respectively.

TABLE 8.2   CONSOLIDATED BALANCE SHEETS FOR NEW VENTURE FITNESS DRINKS, INC.

Assets	December 31, 2011	December 31, 2010	December 31, 2009
Current assets			
Cash and cash equivalents	$63,800	$54,600	$56,500
Accounts receivable, less allowance for doubtful accounts	39,600	48,900	50,200
Inventories	19,200	20,400	21,400
Total current assets	122,600	123,900	128,100
Property, plant, and equipment			
Land	260,000	160,000	160,000
Buildings and equipment	412,000	261,500	149,000
Total property, plant, and equipment	672,000	421,500	309,000
Less: accumulated depreciation	65,000	51,500	45,600
Net property, plant, and equipment	607,000	370,000	263,400
Total assets	729,600	493,900	391,500
Liabilities and shareholders' equity **Current liabilities**			
Accounts payable	30,200	46,900	50,400
Accrued expenses	9,900	8,000	4,100
Total current liabilities	40,100	54,900	54,500
Long-term liabilities			
Long-term debt	249,500	130,000	111,000
Long-term liabilities	249,500	130,000	111,000
Total liabilities	289,600	184,900	165,500
Shareholders' equity			
Common stock (100,000 shares)	10,000	10,000	10,000
Retained earnings	430,000	299,000	216,000
Total shareholders' equity	440,000	309,000	226,000
Total liabilities and shareholders' equity	729,600	493,900	391,500

Computing a company's overall debt ratio will give us the answer to the second question, as it is a means of assessing a firm's overall financial soundness. A company's debt ratio is computed by dividing its total debt by its total assets. The present debt ratio for New Venture Fitness Drinks is 39.7 percent, meaning that 39.7 percent of its total assets are financed by debt and the remaining 60.3 percent by owners' equity. This is a healthy number for a young firm. The trend for New Venture Fitness Drinks in this area is also encouraging. For the years 2009, 2010, and 2011, its debt ratio has been 42.3, 37.4, and 39.7 percent, respectively. These figures indicate that, over time, the company is relying less on debt to finance its operations. In general, less debt creates more freedom for the entrepreneurial firm in terms of taking different actions.

The numbers across all the firm's financial statements are consistent with one another. Note that the $131,000 net income reported by New Venture

Fitness Drinks on its 2011 income statement shows up as the difference between its 2011 and 2010 retained earnings on its 2011 balance sheet. This number would have been different if New Venture Fitness Drinks had paid dividends to its stockholders, but it paid no dividends in 2011. The company retained all of its $131,000 in earnings.

Statement of Cash Flows   The **statement of cash flows** summarizes the changes in a firm's cash position for a specified period of time and details why the change occurred. The statement of cash flows is similar to a month-end bank statement. It reveals how much cash is on hand at the end of the month as well as how the cash was acquired and spent during the month.

The statement of cash flows is divided into three separate activities: operating activities, investing activities, and financing activities. These activities, which are explained in the following list, are the activities from which a firm obtains and uses cash:

> **LEARNING OBJECTIVE**
> **6.** Explain the purpose of a statement of cash flows.

- **Operating activities: Operating activities** include net income (or loss), depreciation, and changes in current assets and current liabilities other than cash and short-term debt. A firm's net income, taken from its income statement, is the first line on the corresponding period's cash flow statement.
- **Investing activities: Investing activities** include the purchase, sale, or investment in fixed assets, such as real estate, equipment, and buildings.
- **Financing activities: Financing activities** include cash raised during the period by borrowing money or selling stock and/or cash used during the period by paying dividends, buying back outstanding stock, or buying back outstanding bonds.

Interpreting and analyzing cash flow statements takes practice. On the statement, the *uses* of cash are recorded as negative figures (which are shown by placing them in parentheses) and the *sources* of cash are recorded as positive figures. An item such as depreciation is shown as a positive figure on the statement of cash flows because it was deducted from net income on the income statement but was not a cash expenditure. Similarly, a decrease in accounts payable shows up as a negative figure on the cash flow statement because the firm used part of its cash to reduce its accounts payable balance from one period to the next.

The statement of cash flows for New Venture Fitness Drinks is shown in Table 8.3. As a management tool, it is intended to provide perspective on the following questions: Is the firm generating excess cash that could be used to pay down debt or returned to stockholders in the form of dividends? Is the firm generating enough cash to fund its investment activities from earnings, or is it relying on lenders or investors? Is the firm generating sufficient cash to pay down its short-term liabilities, or are its short-term liabilities increasing as the result of an insufficient amount of cash?

Again, a multiperiod statement is created so that trends can easily be spotted. A large increase in a firm's cash balance is not necessarily a good sign. It could mean that the firm is borrowing heavily, is not paying down its short-term liabilities, or is accumulating cash that could be put to work for a more productive purpose. On the other hand, it is almost always prudent for a young firm to have a healthy cash balance.

Table 8.3 shows the consolidated statement of cash flows for New Venture Fitness Drinks for two years instead of three because it takes three years of balance sheets to produce two years of cash flow statements. The statements show that New Venture Fitness Drinks is funding its investment activities from a combination of debt and earnings while at the same time it is slowly decreasing its

TABLE 8.3   CONSOLIDATED STATEMENT OF CASH FLOWS FOR NEW VENTURE FITNESS DRINKS, INC.

	December 31, 2011	December 31, 2010
Cash flows from operating activities		
Net income	$131,000	$83,000
Additions (sources of cash)		
Depreciation	13,500	5,900
Decreases in accounts receivable	9,300	1,300
Increase in accrued expenses	1,900	3,900
Decrease in inventory	1,200	1,000
Subtractions (uses of cash)		
Decrease in accounts payable	(16,700)	(3,500)
Total adjustments	9,200	8,600
Net cash provided by operating activities	140,200	91,600
Cash flows from investing activities		
Purchase of building and equipment	(250,500)	(112,500)
Net cash flows provided by investing activities	(250,500)	(112,500)
Cash flows from financing activities		
Proceeds from increase in long-term debt	119,500	19,000
Net cash flows provided by financing activities		19,000
Increase in cash	9,200	(1,900)
Cash and cash equivalents at the beginning of year	54,600	56,500
Cash and cash equivalents at the end of each year	63,800	54,600

accounts receivable and inventory levels (which is good—these items are major drains on a company's cash flow). It is also steadily increasing its cash on hand. These are encouraging signs for a new venture.

LEARNING OBJECTIVE

7. Discuss how financial ratios are used to analyze and interpret a firm's financial statements.

Ratio Analysis   The most practical way to interpret or make sense of a firm's historical financial statements is through ratio analysis. Table 8.4 is a summary of the ratios used to evaluate New Venture Fitness Drinks during the time period covered by the previously provided financial statements. The ratios are divided into profitability ratios, liquidity ratios, and overall financial stability ratios. These ratios provide a means of interpreting the historical financial statements for New Venture Fitness Drinks and provide a starting point for forecasting the firm's financial performance and capabilities for the future.

Comparing a Firm's Financial Results to Industry Norms
Comparing its financial results to industry norms helps a firm determine how it stacks up against its competitors and if there are any financial "red flags" requiring attention. This type of comparison works best for firms that are of similar size, so the results should be interpreted with caution by new firms. Many sources provide industry-related information. For example, both Hoover's premium service and BizMiner provide industry norms to which a

TABLE 8.4   RATIO ANALYSIS FOR NEW VENTURE FITNESS DRINKS, INC.

Ratio	Formula	2011	2010	2009
Profitability ratios: associate the amount of income earned with the resources used to generate it				
Return on assets	ROA = net income/average total assets[a]	21.4%	18.7%	14.7%
Return on equity	ROE = net income/average shareholders' equity[b]	35.0%	31.0%	24.9%
Profit margin	Profit margin = net income/net sales	22.3%	17.9%	13.6%
Liquidity ratios: measure the extent to which a company can quickly liquidate assets to cover short-term liabilities				
Current	Current assets/current liabilities	3.06	2.26	2.35
Quick	Quick assets/current liabilities	2.58	1.89	1.96
Overall financial stability ratio: measures the overall financial stability of a firm				
Debt	Total debt/total assets	39.7%	37.4%	42.3%
Debt to equity	Total liabilities/owners' equity	65.8%	59.8%	73.2%

[a] Average total assets = beginning total assets + ending total assets ÷ 2.
[b] Average shareholders' equity = beginning shareholders' equity + ending shareholders' equity ÷ 2.

new firm can compare itself and are typically free of charge if accessed via a university library. BizMiner (www.bizminer.com) is particularly good for providing comparison data for private firms. Several suggestions for obtaining comparison data for private firms are provided in Chapter 3.

Forecasts

As depicted in Figure 8.2, the analysis of a firm's historical financial statement is followed by the preparation of forecasts. **Forecasts** are predictions of a firm's future sales, expenses, income, and capital expenditures. A firm's forecasts provide the basis for its pro forma financial statements. A well-developed set of pro forma financial statements helps a firm create accurate budgets, build financial plans, and manage its finances in a proactive rather than a reactive manner.

As mentioned earlier, completely new firms typically base their forecasts on a good-faith estimate of sales and on industry averages (based on a percentage of sales) or the experiences of similar start-ups for cost of goods sold and other expenses. As a result, a completely new firm's forecast should be preceded in its business plan by an explanation of the sources of the numbers for the forecast and the assumptions used to generate them. This explanation is called an **assumptions sheet**, as mentioned in Chapter 4. Investors typically study assumptions sheets like hawks to make sure the numbers contained in the forecasts and the resulting financial projections are realistic. For example, the assumptions sheet for a new venture may say that its forecasts are based on selling 500 units of its new product the first year, 1,000 units the second year, and 1,500 units the third year and that its cost of goods sold will remain stable (meaning that it will stay fixed at a certain percentage of net sales) over the three-year period. It's up to the reader of the plan to determine if these numbers are realistic.[16] If the reader feels they are not, then the credibility of the entire plan is called into question.

LEARNING OBJECTIVE
8. Discuss the role of forecasts in projecting a firm's future income and expenses.

LEARNING OBJECTIVE
9. Explain what a completely new firm bases its forecasts on.

Sales Forecast   A **sales forecast** is a projection of a firm's sales for a specified period (such as a year), though most firms forecast their sales for two to five years into the future.[17] It is the first forecast developed and is the basis for most of the other forecasts.[18] A sales forecast for an existing firm is based on (1) its record of past sales, (2) its current production capacity and product demand, and (3) any factor or factors that will affect its future production capacity and product demand. To demonstrate how a sales forecast works, Figure 8.3 is a graph of the past sales and the forecasted future sales for New Venture Fitness Drinks. The company's sales increased at a rate of about 26 percent per year from 2009 to 2011 as the company became established and more people became aware of its brand. In forecasting its sales for 2012 and 2013, the company took into consideration the following factors:

■ The fitness craze in America continues to gain momentum and should continue to attract new people to try its fitness drinks.

■ The interest in intramural sports, especially soccer, baseball, and softball, should continue to provide a high level of traffic for its restaurants, which are located near large intramural sports complexes.

■ The company expanded from a single location in 2008 to two locations in 2011 (the second restaurant was added in November 2011), and this should increase its capacity to serve fitness drinks by approximately 50 percent. The second restaurant is smaller than the first and is located in an area where the company is not as well known. The company will be actively promoting the new restaurant but knows it will take time to win market share.

■ The general economy in the city where the company is located is flat—it is neither growing nor shrinking. However, layoffs are rumored for a larger employer near the location of the new restaurant.

The combination of these factors results in a forecast of a 40 percent increase in sales from 2011 to 2012 and a 25 percent increase in sales from 2012 to 2013. It is extremely important for a company such as New Venture Drinks to forecast future sales as accurately as possible. If it overestimates the demand for its products, it might get stuck with excess inventory and spend too much on overhead. If it underestimates the demand for its product, it might have to turn away business, and some of its potential customers might get into the habit of buying other firms' fitness drinks.

Note that sophisticated tools are available to help firms project their future sales. One approach is to use **regression analysis**, which is a statistical

FIGURE 8.3
Historical and
Forecasted Annual
Sales for New Venture
Fitness Drinks

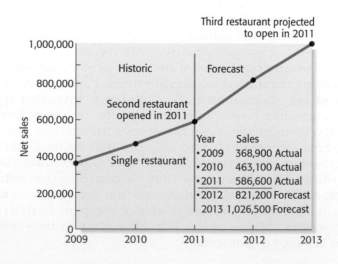

technique used to find relationships between variables for the purpose of predicting future values.[19] For example, if New Venture Fitness Drinks felt that its future sales were a function of its advertising expenditures, the number of people who participate in intramural sports at the sports complexes near its restaurants, and the price of its drinks, it could predict future sales using regression analysis as long as it had historical data for each of these variables. If the company used simpler logic and felt that its future sales would increase a certain percentage over its current sales, regression analysis could be used to generate a more precise estimate of future sales than was predicted from the information contained in Figure 8.3. For a new firm that has limited years of "annual data," monthly data could be used to project sales.

Forecast of Costs of Sales and Other Items   After completing its sales forecast, a firm must forecast its cost of sales (or cost of goods sold) and the other items on its income statement. The most common way to do this is to use the **percent-of-sales method**, which is a method for expressing each expense item as a percentage of sales.[20] For example, in the case of New Venture Fitness Drinks, its cost of sales has averaged 47.5 percent over the past two years. In 2011, its sales were $586,600 and its cost of sales was $268,900. The company's sales are forecast to be $821,200 in 2012. Therefore, based on the percent-of-sales method, its cost of sales in 2012 will be $390,000, or 47.5 percent of projected sales. The same procedure could be used to forecast the cost of each expense item on the company's income statement.

LEARNING OBJECTIVE

10. Explain what is meant by the term *percent-of-sales method.*

Once a firm completes its forecast using the percent-of-sales method, it usually goes through its income statement on an item-by-item basis to see if there are opportunities to make more precise forecasts. For example, a firm can closely estimate its depreciation expenses, so it wouldn't be appropriate to use the percent-of-sales method to make a forecast for this item. In addition, some expense items are not tied to sales. For those items, the firm makes reasonable estimates.

Obviously, a firm must apply common sense in using the percent-of-sales method. If a company is implementing cost-cutting measures, for example, it might be able to justify projecting a smaller percentage increase in expenses as opposed to sales. Similarly, if a firm hires an upper-level manager, such as a chief financial officer, toward the end of the year and plans to pay the person $100,000 the next year, that $100,000 may not have an immediate impact on sales. In this case, the firm's forecast for administrative expenses may have to be adjusted upward beyond what the percent-of-sales method would suggest.

If a firm determines that it can use the percent-of-sales method and it follows the procedure described previously, then the net result is that each expense item on its income statement (with the exception of those items that may be individually forecast, such as depreciation) will grow at the same rate as sales. This approach is called the **constant ratio method of forecasting**. This approach will be used in preparing the pro forma financial statements for New Venture Fitness Drinks in the next section.

A summary of the forecasts used to prepare the pro forma financial statements for New Venture Fitness Drinks is provided in Table 8.5.

In addition to computing sales forecasts, when a company like New Venture Fitness Drinks considers opening a new restaurant or producing a new product, it often calculates a break-even analysis to determine if the proposed initiative is feasible. The **break-even point** for a new restaurant or product is the point where total revenue received equals total costs associated with the output of the restaurant or the sale of the product.[21] In the case of opening a new restaurant, New Venture Fitness Drinks could use break-even analysis as one way of determining whether the proposed initiative is feasible. The formula for break-even analysis is as follows: Total fixed costs/(price – average variable costs). In most instances, average variable cost is the same number as average

**TABLE 8.5   FORECASTS USED TO PREPARE PRO FORMA FINANCIAL STATEMENTS FOR NEW VENTURE
FITNESS DRINKS, INC.**

Pro Forma Income Statements

Net sales

Historic	Average sales increase of 25% per year
2012	Increase to 40% as the result of increased brand awareness and the opening of a second service location
2013	Increase 25% as the result of increased brand awareness (a third service location will be opened late in the year)

Cost of goods sold (COGS)

Historic	Average of 47.5% of sales the past two years
2012	47.5% of sales
2013	47.5% of sales

Selling, general, and administrative expenses

Historic	Average 22% of sales the past two years
2012	Increase to 25% of sales as the result of the opening of a second service location (the increase will not be any larger as the result of increased operating efficiencies)
2013	25% of sales

Interest expense

Historic	6% to 7% of long-term debt
2012	7% of long-term debt
2013	7% of long-term debt

Other income

Historic	Licensing income of $10,900 per year
2012	Licensing income will increase to $20,000 as the result of the renegotiation of the licensing contract
2013	Licensing income will be $20,000

Pro Forma Balance Sheets

Accounts receivable

Historic	Accounts receivable have trended down to 6.8% of sales in 2008 from 13.6% of sales in 2007
2012	7% of sales
2013	7% of sales

Inventories

Historic	Inventories have trended down to 3.3% of sales in 2008 from 4.4% of sales in 2007
2012	4% of sales (reflecting slight increase over 2003 as the result of the opening of a second service location)
2013	4% of sales

Land, buildings, and equipment

2012	$100,000 in equipment purchases and capital improvements made to existing buildings
2013	$275,000 in capital improvements, including a $100,000 real estate purchase and $175,000 in buildings and equipment

(Continued)

TABLE 8.5   CONTINUED

Accounts payable

Historic	Accounts payable have trended down to 5.1% of sales in 2008 from 13.6% of sales in 2007 because of the implementation of more effective collection methods (a slightly higher level of accounts payable will be projected for the future)
2012	7% of sales
2013	7% of sales

Long-term debt

2012	$75,000 reduction in long-term debt from earnings
2013	$150,000 will be borrowed to finance $275,000 to acquire land, equipment, and buildings (the balance of the acquisition costs will be funded from earnings)

cost of goods sold. As a result, if the total fixed cost associated with opening a new restaurant is $101,000 per year, the average price for a fitness drink is $2.75, and the variable cost (or cost of goods sold) for each drink is $1.10, then the break-even point for the new restaurant is as follows:

$$\$101,000 \text{ (total fixed costs)}/(\$2.75-\$1.10) \text{ or } \$1.65 = 61,212 \text{ units}$$

This number means that the new restaurant will have to sell 61,212 "units" or fitness drinks per year to "break even" at the current price of the drinks. That number breaks down to the sale of 170 fitness drinks per day, on average, based on a 360-day year. To determine whether opening the new restaurant is feasible, the managers of New Venture Fitness Drinks would compare this number against the historic sales figures for their other restaurants, making adjustments as appropriate (e.g., the new restaurant may have a better or worse location than the existing restaurants). If selling 170 fitness drinks per day seems unrealistic, then the managers of New Fitness Drinks might opt to not open the new restaurant, or find ways to lower fixed or variable costs or increase revenues. An obvious way to increase revenues is to raise the price of the fitness drinks, if that option is realistic given the competitive nature of the marketplace.

PRO FORMA FINANCIAL STATEMENTS

A firm's pro forma financial statements are similar to its historical financial statements except that they look forward rather than track the past. New ventures typically offer pro forma statements, but well-managed established firms also maintain these statements as part of their routine financial planning process and to help prepare budgets. The preparation of pro forma statements also helps firms rethink their strategies and make adjustments if necessary. For example, if the pro forma statements predict a downturn in profitability, a firm can make operational changes, such as increasing prices or decreasing expenses, to help prevent the decrease in profitability from actually happening.[22]

A firm's pro forma financial statements should not be prepared in isolation. Instead, they should be created in conjunction with the firm's overall planning activities. For example, it's often critical to have a good sense of how quickly a firm can raise money. Sometimes a firm has a good product or service, good demand, and knows how much capital it needs to maintain a sufficient cash flow, but can't raise the money in time. This is what happened to Wise Acre

Frozen Treats, as illustrated in the "What Went Wrong?" feature. The Wide Acre Frozen Treats case is a good example of how one aspect of financial management (i.e., raising money) can have a dramatic impact on another aspect of financial management (i.e., maintaining a sufficient cash flow).

The following sections explain the development of pro forma financial statements for New Venture Fitness Drinks.

WHAT WENT WRONG?

Be Careful What You Wish For: How Growing Too Quickly Overwhelmed One Company's Cash Flow

When Jim Picariello started Wise Acre Frozen Treats, no other company was making organic popsicles from unrefined sweeteners. Working out of a makeshift kitchen in 2006, Picariello developed his recipes using maple syrup and honey. He worked alone for a year and a half before hiring his first employee. About that time, his frozen popsicles really took off; by 2008, Wise Acre Frozen Treats had 15 employees, a 3,000-square-foot manufacturing facility, and was distributing its product to natural food stores and supermarkets across the East Coast. The company was awarded a contract to distribute to the West Coast. Then, abruptly, Wise Acre Frozen Treats failed. What went wrong?

Here's what happened. In its first year, Wise Acre Frozen Treats grew at a measured pace. It was filling orders for eight stores for a few hundred dollars each, nothing Picariello couldn't handle. Early in its second year, it won the "Most Innovative Product" award out of more than 2,000 products at a large food show called Expo East. That award increased Wise Acre Frozen Treats' profile, and it landed a contract with United National Foods, a huge national distributor, for freezer space in premier stores like Whole Foods and Wegmans. At that time, it seemed that things couldn't have worked out better.

Picariello knew he'd need to raise capital to cover the increased pace of activity. Operating expenses including labor, equipment, ingredients, packaging material, insurance, and design and marketing would all increase. Picariello obtained $300,000 from a local bank and $200,000 from an investment firm. But because Wise Acre Frozen Treats had so many orders to fill, it needed about $1 million to make things work. Picariello approached a local high net worth individual who agreed to invest $1 million, and assured Picariello that he could put together the money quickly. Based on that promise, Picariello placed orders for the additional material and equipment Wise Acre Frozen Treats needed.

The timing of the investor's promise couldn't have been worse. In short order, the economy tanked and the investor reneged on his promise. At that point, Picariello characterized his life as a mad dash between running the company and meeting with potential investors. In regard to potential investors, Wise Acre Frozen Treats found itself in somewhat of a no man's land. Although its future was bright, the entrepreneurial venture wasn't big enough yet for investors to take notice. As time went on, serious cash flow difficulties kicked in. According to a blog post that Picariello wrote about Wise Acre Frozen Treats' failure, the company was burning through about $30,000 a month at its peak but didn't have the capital to back it up.

In retrospect, many things lined up well for Wise Acre Frozen Treats. It had a product that sold well, it had national distribution, and it had a business plan that indicated that it would take about two years for the company to break even. Its fatal flaw was that it didn't raise the money it needed before it hit major milestones, like getting the big orders. It literally went from eight stores to dozens to hundreds in a matter of months. From a cash standpoint, the firm lacked what it needed to keep up with its growth.

Questions for Critical Thinking

1. What lessons can be learned from Jim Picariello's agreement with the high net worth individual, who agreed to invest $1 million in Wise Acre Frozen Treats and then reneged on the agreement when the economy turned sour?

2. Why is it that a company can grow too fast? If Wise Acre Frozen Treats significantly increased its sales, why wouldn't its increased income provide more than enough cash to even out its cash flow?

3. Besides cash flow difficulties, what other problems can a firm experience by growing too quickly?

4. If Jim Picariello starts another company, make a list of the things you think he'll do differently as a result of his Wise Acre Frozen Treats experience.

Sources: J. Picariello, "My Company Grew Too Fast—and Went Out of Business," BNET blog, www.bnet.com/blog/smb/my-company-grew-too-fast-and-went-out-of-business/1795 (accessed February 28, 2011); L. Petrecca, "Fast Growth Isn't Always Good: A Big Influx of Orders Can Be Overwhelming," *USA Today*, September 13, 2010, 1B.

Pro Forma Income Statement

Once a firm forecasts its future income and expenses, the creation of the **pro forma income statement** is merely a matter of plugging in the numbers. Table 8.6 shows the pro forma income statement for New Venture Fitness Drinks. Recall that net sales for New Venture Fitness Drinks are forecast to increase by 40 percent from 2011 to 2012 and by 25 percent from 2012 to 2013 and that its cost of sales has averaged 47.5 percent of net sales. In the pro forma income statement, the constant ratio method of forecasting is used to forecast the cost of sales and general and administrative expense, meaning that these items are projected to remain at the same percentage of sales in the future as they were in the past (which is the mathematical equivalent of saying that they will increase at the same rate of sales). Depreciation, other income, and several other items that are not directly tied to sales are figured separately—using reasonable estimates. The most dramatic change is "other income," which jumps significantly from 2011 to 2012. New Venture Fitness Drinks anticipates a significant increase in this category as the result of the renegotiation of a licensing agreement for one of its fitness drinks that is sold by another company.

Pro Forma Balance Sheet

The **pro forma balance sheet** provides a firm a sense of how its activities will affect its ability to meet its short-term liabilities and how its finances will evolve over time. It can also quickly show how much of a firm's money will be tied up in accounts receivable, inventory, and equipment. The pro forma balance sheet

TABLE 8.6   PRO FORMA INCOME STATEMENT FOR NEW VENTURE FITNESS DRINKS, INC.

	2011 Actual	2012 Projected	2013 Projected
Net sales	$586,600	$821,200	$1,026,500
Cost of sales	268,900	390,000	487,600
Gross profit	317,700	431,200	538,900
Operating expenses			
Selling, general, and administrative expenses	117,800	205,300	256,600
Depreciation	13,500	18,500	22,500
Operating income	186,400	207,400	259,800
Other income			
Interest income	1,900	2,000	2,000
Interest expense	(15,000)	(17,500)	(17,000)
Other income (expense), net	10,900	20,000	20,000
Income before income taxes	184,200	211,900	264,800
Income tax expense	53,200	63,600	79,400
Net income	131,000	148,300	185,400
Earnings per share	1.31	1.48	1.85

is also used to project the overall financial soundness of a company. For example, a firm may have a very aggressive set of pro forma income statements that project rapidly increasing growth and profitability. However, if this rapid growth and profitability push the firm's debt ratio to 75 percent (which is extremely high), investors may conclude that there is too much risk involved for the firm to be an attractive investment.

The pro forma balance sheet for New Venture Fitness Drinks is shown in Table 8.7. Note that the company's projected change in retained earnings each year is consistent with its projected net income for the same period on its pro forma income statements. The same approach was used to construct the pro forma balance sheets as the pro forma income statements. For each item listed under current assets and current liabilities, the item's historical

TABLE 8.7 PRO FORMA BALANCE SHEETS FOR NEW VENTURE FITNESS DRINKS, INC.

Assets	December 31, 2011	Projected 2012	Projected 2013
Current assets			
Cash and cash equivalents	$63,800	$53,400	$80,200
Accounts receivable, less allowance for doubtful accounts	39,600	57,500	71,900
Inventories	19,200	32,900	41,000
Total current assets	122,600	143,800	193,100
Property, plant, and equipment			
Land	260,000	260,000	360,000
Buildings and equipment	412,000	512,000	687,000
Total property, plant, and equipment	672,000	772,000	1,047,000
Less: accumulated depreciation	65,000	83,500	106,000
Net property, plant, and equipment	607,000	688,500	941,000
Total assets	729,600	832,300	1,134,100
Liabilities and shareholders' equity			
Current liabilities			
Accounts payable	30,200	57,500	71,900
Accrued expenses	9,900	12,000	14,000
Total current liabilities	40,100	69,500	85,900
Long-term liabilities			
Long-term debt	249,500	174,500	274,500
Total long-term liabilities	249,500	174,500	274,500
Total liabilities	289,600	244,000	360,400
Shareholders' equity			
Common stock (100,000 shares)	10,000	10,000	10,000
Retained earnings	430,000	578,300	763,700
Total shareholders' equity	440,000	588,300	773,700
Total liabilities and shareholders' equity	729,600	832,300	1,134,100

percentage of sales was used to project its future percentage of sales. Several of the numbers were adjusted slightly upward, such as inventory levels and accounts payable, to reflect the potential impact of the opening of the second restaurant.

In regard to property, plant, and equipment, New Venture Fitness Drinks plans to invest $100,000 in 2012 and $275,000 in 2013. The pro forma balance sheet shows a corresponding increase in valuation in this category for 2012 and 2013, respectively. The company's projected long-term debt for 2012 and 2013 reflects changes resulting from principal reductions from cash flow and increased borrowing to fund the property, plant, and equipment purchases just mentioned. These transactions are reflected in the pro forma statement of cash flows for New Venture Fitness Drinks.

Pro Forma Statement of Cash Flows

The **pro forma statement of cash flows** shows the projected flow of cash into and out of the company during a specified period. The most important function of the pro forma statement of cash flows is to project whether the firm will have sufficient cash to meet its needs. As with the historical statement of cash flows, the pro forma statement of cash flows is broken into three activities: operating activities, investing activities, and financing activities. Close attention is typically paid to the section on operating activities because it shows how changes in the company's accounts receivable, accounts payable, and inventory levels affect the cash that it has available for investing and finance activities. If any of these items increases at a rate that is faster than the company's annual increase in sales, it typically raises a red flag. For example, an increase in accounts receivable, which is money that is owed to a company by its customers, decreases the amount of cash that it has available for investment or finance activities. If accounts receivable gets out of hand, it may jeopardize a company's ability to fund its growth or service its debt.

The pro forma consolidated statement of cash flows for New Venture Fitness Drinks is shown in Table 8.8. The figures appearing on the statement come directly, or are calculated directly, from the pro forma income statement and the pro forma balance sheet. The one exception is that the last line of each

TABLE 8.8 PRO FORMA STATEMENT OF CASH FLOWS FOR NEW VENTURE FITNESS DRINKS, INC.

	December 31, 2011	Projected 2012	Projected 2013
Cash flows from operating activities			
Net income	$131,000	$148,300	$185,400
Changes in working capital			
Depreciation	13,500	18,500	22,500
Increase (decrease) in accounts receivable	9,300	(17,900)	(14,400)
Increase (decrease) in accrued expenses	1,900	2,100	2,000
Increase (decrease) in inventory	1,200	(13,700)	(8,100)
Increase (decrease) in accounts payable	(16,700)	27,300	14,400
Total adjustments	9,200	16,300	16,400
Net cash provided by operating activities	140,200	164,600	201,800

(Continued)

TABLE 8.8   CONTINUED

	December 31, 2011	Projected 2012	Projected 2013
Cash flows from investing activities			
Purchase of building and equipment	(250,500)	(100,000)	(275,000)
Net cash flows provided by investing activities	(250,500)	(100,000)	(275,000)
Cash flows from financing activities			
Proceeds from increase in long-term debt	119,500	—	100,000
Principle reduction in long-term debt		(75,000)	
Net cash flows provided by financing activities			
Increase in cash	9,200	(10,400)	26,800
Cash and cash equivalents at the beginning of the year	54,600	63,800	53,400
Cash and cash equivalents at the end of the year	63,800	53,400	80,200

statement of cash flows, which reflects the company's cash balance at the end of the period, becomes the first line of the company's balance sheet for the next period. The pro forma statement of cash flows for New Venture Fitness Drinks shows healthy cash balances at the end of each projected period and shows that investment activities are being funded more by earnings than by debt. This scenario reflects a company that is generating sufficient cash flow to fund the majority of its growth without overly relying on debt or investment capital.

In regard to dividends, the pro forma statement of cash flows shows that New Venture Fitness Drinks is not planning to pay a dividend to its stockholders in 2012 and 2013. Recall that New Venture Fitness Drinks is incorporated and has stockholders even though it is not traded on an organized exchange. If New Venture Fitness Drinks were planning to pay a dividend, the projected

These entrepreneurs own a greenhouse and nursery. They prepare pro forma statements of cash flow each quarter to assure that they'll have sufficient cash available to fund the inventory of product they need to maintain in their nursery.

dividend payments would show up under financing activities and would reduce the amount of cash available for investing and financing activities. It is common for a new firm to invest the majority of its cash in activities that fund its growth, such as property, plant, and equipment purchases, rather than pay dividends.

Ratio Analysis

The same financial ratios used to evaluate a firm's historical financial statements should be used to evaluate the pro forma financial statements. This work is completed so the firm can get a sense of how its projected financial performance compares to its past performance and how its projected activities will affect its cash position and its overall financial soundness.

The historical financial ratios and projected ratios for New Venture Fitness Drinks are shown in Table 8.9. The profitability ratios show a slight decline from the historical period to the projected. This indicates that the projected increase in assets and corresponding sales will not produce income quite as efficiently as has been the case historically. Still, the numbers are strong, and no dramatic changes are projected.

The liquidity ratios show a consistently healthy ratio of current assets to current liabilities, suggesting that the firm should be able to cover its short-term liabilities without difficulty. The overall financial stability ratios indicate promising trends. The debt ratio drops from an actual of 39.7 percent in 2011 to a projected 31.8 percent in 2013. The debt-to-equity ratio shows an even more dramatic drop, indicating that an increasing portion of the firm's assets is being funded by equity rather than debt.

In summary, it is extremely important for a firm to understand its financial position at all times and for new ventures to base their financial projections on solid numbers. As mentioned earlier, regardless of how successful a firm is in other areas, it must succeed financially to remain strong and viable.

TABLE 8.9 **RATIO ANALYSIS OF HISTORICAL AND PRO FORMA FINANCIAL STATEMENTS FOR NEW VENTURE FITNESS DRINKS, INC.**

	Historical			Projected	
Ratio	2009	2010	2011	2012	2013
Profitability ratios					
Return on assets	14.7%	18.7%	21.4%	19.0%	18.9%
Return on equity	24.9%	31.0%	35.0%	28.9%	27.2%
Profit margin	13.6%	17.9%	22.3%	18.1%	18.1%
Liquidity ratios					
Current	2.35	2.26	3.05	2.07	2.24
Quick	1.96	1.89	2.58	1.60	1.78
Overall financial stability ratios					
Debt	42.3%	37.4%	39.7%	29.3%	31.8%
Debt to equity	73.2%	59.8%	65.8%	41.5%	46.6%

CHAPTER SUMMARY

1. Financial management deals with two activities: raising money and managing a company's finances in a way that achieves the highest rate of return.

2. Profitability, liquidity, efficiency, and stability are the four main financial objectives of entrepreneurial firms.

3. Historical financial statements reflect past performance. Pro forma financial statements are projections for expected performance in future periods.

4. An income statement reflects the results of a firm's operations over a specified period of time. It records all the revenues and expenses for the given period and shows whether the firm is making a profit or is experiencing a loss.

5. A balance sheet is a snapshot of a company's assets, liabilities, and owners' equity.

6. A statement of cash flows summarizes the changes in a firm's cash position for a specified period of time.

7. Financial ratios depict relationships between items on a firm's financial statement and are used to discern if a firm is meeting its financial objectives and how it stacks up against its competitors.

8. Forecasts are predictions of a firm's future sales, expenses, income, and capital expenditures. A firm's forecasts provide the basis for its pro forma financial statements.

9. Completely new firms typically base their forecasts on a good-faith estimate of sales and on industry averages (based on a percentage of sales) or the experiences of similar start-ups for cost of goods sold and other expenses.

10. Once a firm has completed its sales forecast, it must forecast its costs of sales as well as the other items on its income statement. The most common way to do this is to use the percent-of-sales method, which is a method for expressing each expense item as a percentage of sales.

KEY TERMS

REVIEW QUESTIONS

1. What are the two primary functions of the financial management of a firm?
2. What are the four main financial objectives of a firm?
3. Why is it important for a company to focus on its liquidity? What special challenges do entrepreneurial firms have in regard to remaining liquid?
4. What is meant by the term *efficiency* as it relates to the financial management of a firm?
5. What is meant by the term *stability* as it relates to the financial management of a firm?
6. What is the purpose of a forecast? What factors does a firm use to create its forecasts of future income and expenses?
7. On what factors or conditions do completely new firms base their forecasts?
8. What is the purpose of an income statement? What are the three numbers that receive the most attention when evaluating an income statement? Why are these snumbers important?
9. How does a firm compute its profit margin? What is the significance of this ratio?
10. How does a firm compute its price-to-earnings ratio? Why does a high price-to-earnings ratio indicate that the stock market thinks the firm will grow?
11. What is the purpose of a balance sheet?
12. What are the major categories of assets and liabilities on a balance sheet? Briefly explain each category.
13. What is meant by the term *working capital*? Why is working capital an important consideration for entrepreneurial firms?
14. How does a firm compute its current ratio? Is this a relatively important or unimportant financial ratio? Explain your answer.
15. What is the purpose of a statement of cash flows?
16. What are the three separate categories of activities that are reflected on a firm's statement of cash flows? Briefly explain the importance of each activity.
17. What is the purpose of financial ratios? Why are financial ratios particularly useful in helping a firm interpret its financial statements?
18. What is the purpose of an assumptions sheet?
19. Describe why a firm's sales forecast is the basis for most of the other forecasts.
20. Explain what is meant by the percent-of-sales method as it relates to forecasts.

APPLICATION QUESTIONS

1. Refer to the opening feature, which focuses on Klymit, a company that makes ultra light and hyperefficient cold weather apparel and related products. Make a list of the things that you believe Nate Alder, the founder of Klymit, has done "right" in regard to the financial management of the company.
2. Kirsten, a friend of yours, plans to open a fashion boutique that will sell women's clothing and accessories. She told you that she leafed through several books on how to prepare forecasts and pro forma financial statements but that the books were geared toward existing firms that have several years of historical financial statements on which to base their projections. If Kirsten asked you your advice for how to prepare forecasts for a completely new women's fashion boutique, what would you tell her?
3. Suppose a friend of yours showed you the pro forma income statements for his start-up and exclaimed excitedly that during the first three years of operations his firm will make a net income of $150,000 per year, which is just the amount of money ($450,000) the firm will need to pay off a three-year loan. Explain to your friend why he might not actually have $450,000 in cash, even though his pro forma income statements say that he will earn that amount of money.
4. Kate Snow just retired from a career with Walmart, cashing out a sizable retirement fund at the time of doing so. To start a second career, she is looking at the possibility of buying three different businesses.

She has three years' historical financial statements for each business and has been pouring over the numbers. She was puzzled when she read the following statement in a book about small business financial management, "Be careful when looking at balance sheets to fully understand what you're looking at. In some respects balance sheets are very revealing, and in other respects they can be very deceiving." What do you think the author of the book meant by that statement?

5. The "You Be the VC 1.1" feature focuses on Windspire, a company that's making wind turbines to generate electricity that can be used by businesses and home owners. If the founder of Windspire asked you to help the company complete a break-even analysis for its business, how would you go about it?

6. Chipotle Mexican Grill is a publicly traded company. Calculate the firm's price-to-earnings ratio (P/E). What does Chipotle's P/E ratio tell you about investors' expectations regarding the company's growth? Analyze how Chipotle's financial ratios compare to restaurant industry norms.

7. Jarrett Baker is the founder of an enterprise software company located in Chevy Chase, Maryland. By looking at the income statements for Jarrett's business over the past three years, you see that its working capital has declined from $42,400 in 2009 to $17,900 in 2010 to $3,100 in 2011. If this trend continues, in what ways could it jeopardize the future of Jarrett's business?

8. Jorge Martinez is thinking about buying an existing printing business and has been carefully studying the records of the business to get a good handle on its historical financial performance. Jorge heard that you are taking a class in entrepreneurship and asks you, "What suggestions do you have for me to make the best use of this financial information (i.e., three years of audited income statements, balance sheets, and statements of cash flow)?" What suggestions would you give Jorge for making the maximum use of the financial statements?

9. Casey Cordell is the owner of a digital photography service in Madison, Wisconsin. The company has been profitable every year of its existence. Its debt ratio is currently 68 percent, its current ratio is 1.1, and its debt-to-equity ratio is 72.2 percent. Do these financial numbers cause any reason to be concerned? Why or why not?

10. Spend some time studying Nila, the subject of the "You Be the VC 8.1" feature. Given the nature of its business, what financial management issues should Nila be most attentive to and why?

11. Describe the items that receive the most scrutiny on the left side (or top) and the right side (or bottom) of a firm's balance sheet. In regard to each of these items, what are the most important factors that a new venture should focus on to maintain its overall financial health?

12. Suppose a colleague of yours is gearing up to write a business plan for a business she intends to start. She told you she plans to prepare the financial statements first to get that job out of the way before she tackles the rest of the plan. Explain to your colleague the flaw in her approach.

13. Refer to the "You Be the VC 5.1" feature, which focuses on Xeros, the company that produces a "virtually waterless" washing machine. If the founders of Xeros asked you what ratios they can use to discern whether they're maintaining sufficient short term assets to meet their short term obligations, what would you tell them?

14. Josh Lee has owned a fitness center for the past four years. He has historical financial statements but has never put together a set of pro forma financial statements. He just applied for a bank loan and has been told he needs a set of pro forma financial statements for the next two years. If Josh asked you to help him, how would you tell him to proceed?

15. Brenda Wilson owns a restaurant chain named Rhapsody Cuisine. She is planning to expand her chain from 9 restaurants to 15. Brenda is now working to put together a set of pro forma financial statements for an investor who expressed interest in her expansion project. Brenda used a combination of common sense and industry norms to project her future income and expenses. Shortly after she submitted the financial statements, she received them back with a handwritten note from the investor, who wrote, "I'm comfortable with your sales forecasts but think you would be on firmer ground if you used the percent-of-sales method to forecast expenses. Please redo the statements." If Brenda asked you what the investor was talking about, what would you tell her?

YOU BE THE VC 8.1

Company: Nila

Web: www.nila.tv
Twitter: nilaLED
Facebook: Nila

Business Idea: Produce durable and powerful LED lighting systems that significantly reduce electricity usage and reduce heat in digital video, live events, concerts, houses of worship, movie and television sets, and still photography.

Pitch: An LED (light-emitting diode) is a solid state semiconductor device that converts electricity into light. It consumes far less energy and has a substantially longer life span than traditional lighting. It's also more environmentally sound. Right now, 20 percent of the world's electricity is used for lighting. Experts estimate that number can be reduced to 4 percent with LED lighting.

Large lighting systems, like those used on movie sets, in concerts, and in other live events, are particularly problematic. Not only do they use a lot of electricity, but they're bright, hot, and difficult to move. Movie studios, in particular, suffer as a result of the heat generated from large banks of lights, not only via the electricity used by the lights but in air conditioning that is used to cool the studio. Nila has introduced a revolutionary new lighting system for the entertainment industry, based on LED technology that addresses these problems. While its lights vary in size, they all share the beneficial properties of LED lights: They're energy efficient, do not produce significant amounts of heat, and have the potential to be much "smarter" than traditional lights. LED lights, like those produced by Nila, have the potential to have intelligent functionality built into them, such as motion sensors, smoke detectors, dimming capabilities, and color adaptation.

Nila's modular JNH unit is particularly well-suited for studio and location work. The relatively small units are locked together in panels, and can deliver useful levels of light up to 100 feet without any noticeable heat. Since each unit draws 65 watts of power, locking 10 of these units together still only equals the amount of power a hair dryer might use. Each light can be controlled from another unit or through DMX control.

The worldwide market for lighting products tops $100 billion per year. As a first mover, Nila has the potential to dominate its industry as it provides efficient and effective LED lights to the entertainment industry.

Q&A: Based on the material covered in this chapter, what questions would you ask the firm's founders before making your funding decision? What answers would satisfy you?

Decision: If you had to make your decision on just the information provided in the pitch and on the company's Web site, would you fund this company? Why or why not?

YOU BE THE VC 8.2

Company: Cool Palms

Web: www.betterexerciseexperience.com
Twitter: bexrunner
Facebook: Bexrunner

Business Idea: Create a padded bracelet that slides into the palm of a runner's hand, and helps bring down the body's core temperature (the device must be frozen before use), which extends peak performance during exercise.

Pitch: Whether you're a professional athlete or an occasional walker, you've probably been disappointed from time to time because it was just too hot to exercise.

An alternative to prematurely giving up is the Cool Palms cooling device referred to as the BEX Runner. The BEX (which stands for Better Exercise Experience) Runner is a frozen gel pack that fits in a runner's or walker's palm. The hand is a natural radiator for the body, and cooling the palm can result in a cooler body core. When their body core is lowered, runners and walkers normally feel fewer effects from the heat. The theory is that by cooling the palm, the blood flowing through the palm and returning from the arteries to the veins is cooled as it returns to the body's core. Depending on how hot it is, the BEX Runner can stay cool for 30 minutes to a couple of hours. The device's relatively small size is its largest asset because other cooling devices on the market include vests that are filled with ice water and are much bulkier to handle and heavier to wear.

The BEX Runner device, which is pictured on the company's Web site, attaches to the user's palm with a Velcro strap. It's lightweight and will not contribute to strain during exercise. To prepare it for use, the product must be frozen for at least four hours. When worn, the strap should be adjusted so the BEX Runner device is in full contact with the palm. The device is hand washable and its durable construction makes it practical for multiple uses. Like any device that affects a person's physiology it should be scrutinized before use. For

example, it should not be used by people with diabetes, circulatory problems, or those sensitive to temperature extremes. Exercisers should also follow a normal routine of drinking water and warming up and cooling down prior to and following exercise, even if the BEX Runner device is used.

The BEX Runner is Cool Palms' initial product. In 2009, to obtain user feedback and gain visibility for its device, Cool Palms became a national sponsor for USA Fit marathon training programs.

Q&A: Based on the material covered in this chapter, what questions would you ask the firm's founders before making your funding decision? What answers would satisfy you?

Decision: If you had to make your decision on just the information provided in the pitch and on the company's Web site, would you fund this firm? Why or why not?

CASE 8.1

Heartache and Financial Failure: What Happens When Financial Challenges Become Overwhelming

Web: www.coldstonecreamery.com
Twitter: Cold Stone Creamery
Facebook: Cold Stone Creamery

Bruce R. Barringer, *Oklahoma State University*

R. Duane Ireland, *Texas A&M University*

Introduction

When a business struggles financially, not only is its budget stressed, but the people who own and operate the business are often stressed as well. That's why it's so important that a business practice prudent financial management. While most people launch a business to satisfy a consumer need, they also do it to improve their lives and to achieve financial security. The worst-case scenario is to work hard to launch a business and invest a lot of money only to have the business deteriorate your quality of life and leave you worse off financially than you were before.

Cold Stone Creamery

Susan and Donald Sutherland founded Cold Stone Creamery in 1988. The couple liked ice cream that was neither hard-packed nor soft-serve, and opened the first Cold Stone Creamery in Tempe, Arizona. The "Cold Stone" name comes from the frozen granite stone used

to mix "mix-ins" like candy, Oreo cookies, nuts, or other edibles into ice cream in Cold Stone stores. In 1995, Cold Stone opened its first franchise in Tucson, Arizona, and grew quickly through the late 1990s and early to mid-2000s. At its peak it had around 1,400 franchise stores in the United States and several foreign countries. The number of stores doubled from 2003 to 2005 alone.

In June 2008, a *Wall Street Journal* article, by Richard Gibson, examined the unusually high number of Cold Stone Creamery franchises that had closed or been put up for sale by their owners, many of whom had suffered severe financial losses and emotional distress. The article lays out both sides of the story—including the claims made by disgruntled Cold Stone franchisees and the company's counterclaims. While the article examines the financial plight of a number of Cold Stone franchisees, it makes a larger point. The Cold Stone Creamery story illustrates the financial and emotional hardships that beset business owners if their costs are too high relative to their revenues and/or they're trying to sell a premium-priced product in a tough economy. It also illustrates some of the most important financial issues that business founders should be mindful of when setting up a new business.

Since 2008, the situation regarding Cold Stone Creamery and its franchises remains largely unchanged. According to CNNMoney.com, the failure rate for Cold Stone Creamery franchises, based on SBA loan data from October 2000 through September 2009, was 31 percent, the second worst of the franchise organizations it follows. Commenting on the failure rate, CNNMoney.com said, "The product is sweet, but the financials can be bitter. In the last 10 years almost one in three SBA-backed (Cold Stone Creamery) franchisees defaulted on their loan." In December 2010, Cold Stone Creamery threatened a lawsuit against CNBC because in an upcoming documentary, entitled "Behind the Counter: The Untold Story of Franchising," CNBC planned to portray Cold Stone Creamery in a very unfavorable light. The program aired as scheduled, and it's unclear whether a lawsuit was actually filed.

Challenges Facing Cold Stone Creamery Franchisees

The following are the financial challenges confronting Cold Stone Creamery franchisees:

1. High prices in a tough economy. It's hard to sell enough $4.00 scoops of ice cream in a difficult economy to support the overhead of a business that has a high overhead. Many Cold Stone Creamery franchises are located in the food courts of enclosed malls or high-traffic strip malls. Rent alone can exceed $7,000 per month. When you add the franchisee fees and other expenses, it requires a franchisee to sell a lot of scoops of ice cream per day just to break even.
2. Saturated market. Cold Stone expanded rapidly and many franchisees complain that the stores are too close together. Its competitors also expanded in the 1990s and early to mid-2000s. Combine the growing number of ice cream shops with the increased availability of premium ice cream (like Häagen-Dazs and Ben & Jerry's) in grocery stores, and it makes for a crowded market. An example of the problems created by opening stores too close to one another and the response of franchisees is illustrated in an article published in the *Brown Daily Herald*, a newspaper servicing the Brown University community in Providence, Rhode Island. The October 2009 article reported on a Cold Stone Creamery franchise that was closing. The owners of the franchise, Kristina and Craig Gedutis, said sales were down 30 percent from 2008. Citing one reason for the failure of her franchise, Kristina Gedutis said that in February 2009, a joint Tim Hortons–Cold Stone location opened near their location, and she saw her sales drop. "I'm bitter

towards that," she told the newspaper. "It really wasn't fair."
3. Believing the hype. Many Cold Stone franchisees bought in when the buzz surrounding the company was the strongest. At one time Cold Stone was a hot franchise and was frequently talked up in the press. While it's exciting to hear about a successful business concept, it's important to maintain a healthy sense of skepticism, particularly for a business that relies on a healthy economy to generate significant sales.
4. Franchisor control. In regard to specific financial issues, Cold Stone Creamery franchisees have complained about the way they are required to operate their businesses. An example is a former Cold Stone franchisee, quoted in an article titled "Cold Stone, Delicious but Financially Questionable" posted on the Franchise Hound blog, who commented on his Cold Stone Creamery experience by saying, "I paid above market prices for ingredients from the company's distributor. I also paid too much for equipment. Cold Stone actually profits on both the ingredients and equipment, putting us, the franchisee, at a significant disadvantage."

The cumulative result of this and similar points is that many current and former Cold Stone franchisees say that it's extremely difficult to make money owning and operating a Cold Stone Creamery franchise. Some go so far as to say that the company's business model is "broken." Based on the data reported by *Entrepreneur*, the number of Cold Stone Creamery franchises in the United States continues to drop. The company had 1,163 domestic franchises in 2010, 1,221 in 2009, and 1,394 in 2008. That's a net decrease of 231 units in three years.

Emotional and Financial Toll

A Web search will produce many articles and blog posts from former Cold Stone Creamery franchisees who talk about both the financial toll and the emotional toll that losing their Cold Stone franchise has imposed on their lives. As of 2010, there were still more than 1,100 Cold Stone Creamery stores open in the United States, and the company continues to sell franchises. The company argues that the ultimate success of an individual store depends on how well it's operated.

Discussion Questions

1. If you were thinking about buying a franchise, like a Cold Stone Creamery store, what financial information would you look at and analyze before you completed the purchase? Be specific.
2. After reading the case, do you sympathize with the disgruntled Cold Stone franchisees, or do you believe the company's explanations?
3. Do you think that some businesses that have financial trouble might never have had a chance to begin

(continued)

with? If so, what can a business owner (including a franchisor of a Cold Store Creamery) do ahead of time to make sure the business is financially feasible? Use the concepts conveyed in this chapter and Chapter 3 to formulate your answer.

4. At some point in your career, could you see yourself buying a franchise? If so, what type of franchise do you think you'd enjoy owning?

Application Questions

1. What lessons, regardless of the type of business involved, can a prospective business owner learn by reading this case?
2. Do some Internet research to see what the status of Cold Stone Creamery and its franchisees are today.

Has the business environment for Cold Stone Creamery franchisees improved or are a number of them still going out of business? Make a list of the business and environmental factors working for and factors working against Cold Stone Creamery franchisees.

Sources: CNNMoney.com, "10 Most Popular Franchises," http://money.cnn.com/galleries/2010/smallbusiness/1004/gallery. Franchise_failure_rates/4.html (accessed June 3, 2011); "Cold Stone: Delicious but Financially Questionable," The Franchise Hound blog, http://thefranchisehound.com/2011/01/28/coldstone-delicious-but-financially-questionable (accessed June 3, 2011, originally posted on January 28, 2011); L. Fedor, "Like It, Love It—Can't Have It," www.browndailyherald.com/like-it-love-it-can-t-have-it-1.1940197 (accessed June 3, 2011, originally posted on October 6, 2009); R. Gibson, "The Inside Scoop," *Wall Street Journal*, June 12, 2008.

CASE 8.2

Dell Inc.: How Its Business Model Sweetens Its Financial Statements

Web: www.dell.com
Twitter: DELL
Facebook: dell

Bruce R. Barringer, *Oklahoma State University*

R. Duane Ireland, *Texas A&M University*

Introduction

There are many reasons that Dell Inc. has been successful over the years. Two of the most compelling reasons are its direct sales model and its ultra-efficient global supply chain. While a start-up can't quickly emulate what Dell has done, there are lessons to be learned from Dell's experiences that any start-up can benefit from. Historically at least, Dell's approach to business made it the preferred computer brand for many businesses and consumers. Additionally, the business approach has sweetened Dell's financial statements and its ability to make money.

Dell's Hybrid Sales Approach (Combining Direct Sales and Retail Sales)

Dell was founded in 1988 touting a direct sales model. Rather than selling through stores, like Sears and Circuit City, Dell sold direct, first over the phone and then via the Internet. Its business model not only allowed businesses and consumers to "customize" their computers, but had profound positive effects on Dell's

supply chain and financial activities. Other PC manufacturers had to forecast demand, build computers, ship them to retailers, hope they'd sell, and then wait 30 days or more for payment. Dell sidestepped all of this via its direct sales model. It received orders, built computers, and then shipped them to the buyers via UPS or FedEx. There was no "forecasting" of demand because demand was determined in real time, and Dell never got stuck with outdated computers because it maintained no inventory. Its customers also essentially financed its operations by paying in advance.

Dell maintained this business model from 1988 until 2007, when it shifted its sales strategy. Rather than selling exclusively direct, it decided to transition to a hybrid model, where it would continue to emphasize direct sales, but also sell a portion of its product line through retailers like Best Buy, Staples, and Walmart. The main reason for the change was that Dell was shifting its emphasis from targeting businesses to targeting businesses, consumers, and international markets. The thinking was that it needed to have its computers side-by-side with its competitors in consumer channels, if it hoped to become the preferred computer vendor for consumers along with businesses. It was also problematic to sell exclusively direct in some international markets.

Dell doesn't disclose the percentage of its sales that originate through its Web site or over the phone (its original direct sales model) versus the percentage of its sales that come through retail outlets. It's clear though that a significant portion of its sales now occur online and over the phone and an increasing percentage of its sales are generated through retail outlets.

Dell's Supply Chain and Manufacturing Strategy

Dell's hybrid sales model has a significant impact on its supply chain and manufacturing strategy. It can produce computers in a highly efficient manner, because it does not have to forecast demand and keep excess inventory on hand for a large percentage of its sales. In fact, when Dell receives an order, via the Internet or on the phone, its suppliers are alerted in real time, and periodically throughout the day deliver parts to Dell's assembly facilities where the computers are assembled, configured, and shipped. It also sources the world for the best combinations of quality and cost for parts, which results in a complex yet highly efficient supply chain. In fact, in his 2005 book *The World Is Flat,* Thomas Friedman asked Dell to retrace the supply chain for his laptop computer, to determine where it was made, how many suppliers were involved, and how it reached his front door. The total supply chain for Friedman's Dell Inspiron 600m notebook computer, including suppliers of suppliers, involved about 400 companies in North America, Europe, and primarily Asia. The computer was codesigned in Austin, Texas, in Taiwan by a team of Dell engineers, and by a team of Taiwanese notebook designers (a globally distributed team can work 24 hours a day). Its final assembly was in a Dell factory in Penang, Malaysia. It was flown from Penang, Malaysia, to Nashville, Tennessee, on a China Airlines 747, the only 747 that lands in Nashville, other than when Air Force One is in town. It was delivered to Friedman's home via UPS.

To further increase efficiencies and reduce the amount of capital it must maintain, Dell is currently transitioning from this model and is relying increasingly on contract manufacturers.

Financial Advantages of Dell's Hybrid Sales Approach and Its Supply Chain and Manufacturing Strategy

There are direct financial benefits to Dell's hybrid sales approach and its approach to supply chain management and manufacturing. One of the biggest advantages is its inventory turnover. Dell turns its inventory over 40.1 times a year, compared to 14.6 times a year for Hewlett-Packard and 11.8 times a year for the S&P 500 average. Inventory turnover is determined by the following formula: (the higher the number the better)

$$\text{Inventory Turnover} = \frac{\text{Cost of Goods Sold}}{\text{Average Inventories}}$$

A high inventory turnover means that a company is converting its inventory into cash quickly. Turning its inventory over quickly allows Dell to generate cash that's used to fund its growth, and to not get caught with out-of-date inventory. An often-told joke in the PC industry is that unsold inventory is like unsold vegetables—it spoils quickly. So maintaining a favorable inventory turnover ratio is critical.

Another ratio that's important is the asset turnover ratio. Asset turnover reflects the amount of sales generated for every dollar's worth of assets. It's calculated using the following formula: (the higher the number the better)

$$\text{Asset Turnover} = \frac{\text{Sales}}{\text{Assets}}$$

Dell's asset turnover ratio is 1.70 compared to 1.06 for Hewlett-Packard and 0.80 for the S&P 500 average. Asset turnover denotes the amount of sales generated for every dollar's worth of assets. It's a measure of efficiency in regard to a firm's ability to use its assets to generate sales.

Along with crunching numbers, savvy managers assess the impact of their financial strategies on their overall goals and levels of customer satisfaction. Ultimately, it doesn't matter that a company has attractive-looking financial statements if its customers are starting to go elsewhere. Dell's hybrid sales approach and its supply chain and manufacturing strategy shine in this area too. Because it turns its inventory over quickly, it offers its customers the latest technologies rather than saddling them with products that likely will soon be outdated. It can also pass along the advantages of falling component costs quicker than its competitors can.

The Downside of Pushing Cost Savings Too Far

Although the majority of the decisions that Dell has made have both sweetened its financial statements and pleased its customers, Dell is learning the hard way that cost savings can be pushed too far. In the early 1990s, partly in response to the challenges imposed by its rapid growth, Dell started outsourcing the majority of its call center activities to low-wage countries in Asia and Central America. This strategy led to a chorus of growing complaints about long wait times for customer service calls and poor postsales support. In response, Dell has spent over $100 million to revive its customer service, including an effort to increase the percentage of full-time Dell employees who man customer service support lines and reduce its use of part-time and contract workers. The jury is still out on whether Dell has done enough to stem the tide of customer dissatisfaction. Another downside is that Dell pushes its suppliers hard. While most suppliers respond positively, it's hard to

(continued)

gauge the long-term impact in supplier relations by assuming the role of "taskmaster," as Dell does, in its relationships with its suppliers.

It's also unclear how long Dell's hybrid sales approach will maintain an advantage. Although its inventory turnover number is still strong, it isn't as strong as it once was, when Dell sold primarily online and over the phone. In 2004, its inventory turnover was 107.1, in 2006 it was 88.8, and in 2008 it was 53.8. It's now 41.0 as reported previously. It's also unclear whether Dell will be able to maintain the same degree of quality control as it continues to rely on more contract manufacturers to fulfill its manufacturing activities.

Discussion Questions

1. Investigate the financial ratio of inventory turnover. Find current information about Dell (www.hoovers.com is a good starting place) and report whether its inventory turnover is still as impressive as the number mentioned in the case. How does Dell's current inventory turnover ratio compare to that of its direct competitors? Do the same for Dell's asset turnover ratio.

2. Locate Dell's most recent 10-K report and either locate or compute what you believe are the three most important financial ratios for Dell. Are the ratios impressive or do they provide you reason for concern?

3. If you were the CEO of HP, how would you respond to Dell's hybrid sales approach?

4. What lessons can a young entrepreneurial firm learn from Dell's experiences?

Application Questions

1. Find an example of a start-up that is emulating Dell in one or more ways as it pertains to the topics in this case. Provide a brief description of what the company is doing, and how what the company is doing resembles either Dell's hybrid sales approach or its approach to supply chain management and manufacturing.

2. Write a brief analysis of what you believe the future holds for Dell. Include in the analysis whether you think Dell will be able to maintain its edge in supply chain management and manufacturing excellence, or whether you think switching to a hybrid sales model will result in Dell starting to resemble other computer companies, rather than remaining unique.

Sources: B. Breen, "Living in Dell Time," *Fast Company*, December 19, 2007; Dell Inc. 10-K report submitted to the Securities and Exchange Commission, filed March 15, 2011; HP Investor Relations, http://h30261.www3.hp.com/phoenix.zhtml?c=71087&p=irol-fundratios (accessed June 3, 2011).

ENDNOTES

1. R. C. Moyer, J. R. McGuigan, R. P. Rao, and W. J. Kretlow, *Contemporary Financial Management*, 12th ed. (Cincinnati: SouthWestern Cengage Learning, 2012).

2. J. Brinckmann, S. Salomo, and H. G. Gemuenden, "Financial Management Competence of Founding Teams and Growth of New Technology-Based Firms," *Entrepreneurship Theory and Practice* 35, no. 2 (2011): 217–43.

3. C. Keen and H. Etemad, "The Impact of Entrepreneurial Capital and Rapidly Growing Firms: The Canadian Example," *International Journal of Entrepreneurship and Small Business* 12, no. 3 (2011): 273–89.

4. J. C. Leach and R. W. Melicher, *Entrepreneurial Finance*, 4th ed. (Cincinnati: SouthWestern Cengage Learning, 2012).

5. J. K. Smith, R. L. Smith, and R. T. Bliss, *Entrepreneurial Finance: Strategy, Evaluation & Deal Structure* (Palo Alto: Stanford University Press, 2011).

6. J. H. Gittell, *The Southwest Airlines Way* (New York: McGraw-Hill, 2003), 7.

7. A. S. Dunk, "Product Innovation Budgetary Control, and the Financial Performance of Firms," *British Accounting Review* 43, no. 2 (2011): 102–11.

8. K. G. Palepu and P. M. Healy, *Business Analysis and Valuation: Using Financial Statements*, 4th ed. (Mason, OH: Cengage South-Western, 2008).

9. B. Gates, *Business @ the Speed of Thought* (New York: Time Warner, 1999), 214.

10. SEC homepage, www.sec.gov (accessed June 5, 2011).

11. D. Kuratko and J. Hornsby, *New Venture Management* (Upper Saddle River, NJ: Prentice Hall, 2008).

12. J. Keefe, "Price-Earnings Ratios: Woulds, Coulds and Shoulds for 2011," *MoneyWatch*, www.moneywatch.bnet.com, January 16, 2011.

13. H. Van Auken and S. M. Carraher, "How Do Small Firms Use Financial Statements?" *Academy of Accounting and Financial Studies Proceedings* 16, no. 1 (2011): 35–42.

14. B. E. Needles and M. Powers, *Financial Accounting*, 11th ed. (Cincinnati: SouthWestern Cengage Learning, 2012).

15. E. Autio and Z. Acs, "Intellectual Property Protection and the Formation of Entrepreneurial

Growth," *Strategic Entrepreneurship Journal* 4, no. 3 (2010): 234–51.

16. G. Cassar, "Are Individuals Entering Self-Employment Overly Optimistic? An Empirical Text of Plans and Projections on Nascent Entrepreneur Expectations," *Strategic Management Journal* 31, no. 8 (2010): 822–40.

17. F. J. H. M. Verhees, M. T. G. Meulenberg, and J. M. E. Pennings, "Performance Expectations of Small Firms Considering Radical Product Innovation," *Journal of Business Research* 63, no. 7 (2010): 772–77.

18. M. Schindehutte, M. H. Morris, and L. F. Pitt, *Rethinking Marketing: The Entrepreneurial Imperative* (Upper Saddle River, NJ: Prentice Hall, 2009).

19. D. R. Anderson, D. J. Sweeney, and T. A. Williams, *Statistics for Business and Economics*, 11th ed. (Cincinnati: South-Western Cengage Learning, 2012).

20. E. F. Brigham and J. F. Houston, *Fundamentals of Financial Management, Concise Edition*, 7th ed. (Cincinnati: South-Western Cengage Learning 2012).

21. M. Knockaert, B. Clarysse, and A. Lockett, "Are Technology VC Investors a Distinct Species on the Investment Market?" *Venture Capital: An International Journal of Entrepreneurial Finance* 12, no. 4 (2010): 267–83.

22. J. M. Kaplan and A. Warren, *Patterns of Entrepreneurship Management*, 3rd ed. (New York: John Wiley & Sons, 2009).

Getting Personal *with* SCRIPPED

Cofounders:

SUNIL RAJARAMAN
MBA, UCLA, 2008

ZAK FREER
Peter Stark Producers Program, USC, 2002

RYAN BUCKLEY
Joint Program—MPP, JFK School of Public Policy, Harvard University 2009; MBA, Sloan School of Management, 2009

Dialogue *with* Sunil Rajaraman

MY BIGGEST SURPRISE AS AN ENTREPRENEUR
5% idea, 95% execution

BEST ADVICE I'VE RECEIVED
Listen first

MY FAVORITE SMARTPHONE APP
Instagram

MY BIGGEST WORRY AS AN ENTREPRENEUR
Not working hard enough

FAVORITE PERSON I FOLLOW ON TWITTER
@edward_burns

WHAT I DO WHEN I'M NOT WORKING
Play tennis

CHAPTER 9

Building a *New-Venture* Team

OPENING PROFILE

SCRIPPED
Hitting the Ground Running

Web: www.scripped.com
Twitter: scripped
Facebook: Scripped

Scripped.com offers Web-based screenwriting software on a freemium model. The basic service is free, and a premium version of the service costs $9.95 per month or $89.95 for a lifetime. The software is used by screenwriters who are writing scripts for short films, television shows, and Hollywood movies. Scripped.com's innovative text editor functions like a standard word processor but automatically formats and catalogs each screenplay element according to industry standards. Scripped.com also hosts contests where thousands of writers submit scripts, the best of which are passed along to Hollywood producers. Sound like an impressive company? It is—and it was started by three graduate school students.

The idea for Scripped.com emerged in 2006, when Sunil Rajaraman was about to start his MBA program at UCLA's Anderson School of Management. Rajaraman was concerned about his friend, Zak Freer. Freer, who had graduated from the Peter Stark Producing Program at the USC School of Cinema & Television in 2002, was an aspiring screenwriter, but couldn't get his work in front of Hollywood execs. He had even won a prestigious film festival award for a short film he directed. Rajaraman and Freer had kicked around the idea of starting a screenwriting magazine to help aspiring screenwriters build their careers, but the idea never took root. At the same time these discussions were taking place, another friend of Rajaraman, Ryan Buckley, was developing software that made it easier for writers to collaborate on projects. Buckley was in a joint program at MIT and Harvard's Kennedy School of Government in Boston. Rajaraman shared with Buckley his concern for Freer. Eventually, the three came together and started talking about the lack of good online screenplay text editing software for screenwriters. That awareness, along with their shared passion for film, prompted the three to start working on a screenwriting platform of their own, and Scripped.com was born. In the photo, the three are enjoying a lighthearted moment together. Zak Freer is on the left, Sunil Rajaraman is in the middle, and Ryan Buckley is on the right.

LEARNING OBJECTIVES

After studying this chapter you should be ready to:

1. Identify the primary elements of a new-venture team.

2. Explain the term *liability of newness*.

3. Discuss the difference between heterogeneous and homogeneous founding teams.

4. Identify the personal attributes that strengthen a founder's chances of successfully launching an entrepreneurial venture.

5. Describe how to construct a "skills profile" and explain how it helps a start-up identify gaps in its new-venture team.

6. Describe a board of directors and explain the difference between inside directors and outside directors.

7. Identify the two primary ways in which the nonemployee members of a start-up's new-venture team help the firm.

8. Describe the concept of signaling and explain its importance.

9. Discuss the purpose of forming an advisory board.

10. Explain why new ventures use consultants for help and advice.

Rajaraman and Buckley continued with their studies, and Scripped.com was officially incorporated in June 2007. The vision for the company from the beginning was to make screenwriting software accessible to writers at all levels and provide the tools that screenwriters need to bring their ideas from inception to completion. Scripped.com was also envisioned to be a marketplace for developing, buying, and selling screenplays. A producer provides specifications to Scripped users as to what type of script he or she is looking for. Scripped users submit screenplays to a contest, and the producer buys the rights to the winning contest screenplay. Scripped has worked with Spike TV and other media entities interested in buying scripts.

Scripped.com's first product was launched in January 2008. Each cofounder contributed $10,000, and they raised another $50,000 from friends and family. Scripped.com gained momentum through late 2008 into 2009, as both writers and producers became aware of the service, but needed money to grow. Rajaraman took a full-time job in late 2008, as a way of helping bootstrap the company, and the team tried to raise money in early 2009. They received an offer from an investor, with terms weighed heavily in the investor's favor. The three cofounders experienced some tense moments as they disagreed about how to respond to the offer. They eventually decided to pass and continued to bootstrap Scripped.com's operations and growth.

In early 2010, things improved for Scripped.com as the company raised $250,000 from two angel investors. It also merged with Zhura, a company featuring a similar screenwriting software platform. The merger didn't affect Scripped.com's management structure, and the three original cofounders remained at the helm. The merger did nearly double Scripped.com's user base, which at this point was 60,000 strong. Although Scripped.com's service is available to anyone, the core demographic is student writers and young writers who may not write the next *Citizen Kane*, but may write the next viral video hit. Scripped.com's founders feel that short video as a medium is about to take off, and that their service is uniquely capable of helping screenwriters in this area.

When asked how it's worked building a company with three cofounders, Rajaraman said that the three have agreed 95 percent of the time. He said that Scripped.com has been fortunate in that the cofounders have complementary skills. He also said that he's glad he started the company with friends because trust is such a critical issue in a start-up setting. Rajaraman is quick to point to Scripped.com's advisory board in playing a meaningful role in the company's success. The company has a 10- to 12-member formal advisory board and calls on a wider number of people from time to time for advice. Members of the advisory board include Break Media CEO Keith Richman, producer, director, and screenwriter Steven de Souza, and actor Edward Burns. Advisers are provided a small equity stake in Scripped.com in exchange for their participation.

Scripped.com has avoided building a large staff. Its formal employees consist of the three cofounders and an individual obtained in the Zhura merger. To fill programming and business development gaps, Scripped.com gets graphic help from freelancers in India and utilizes development resources in San Francisco. The company also continually solicits feedback from its users. In early 2010, Scripped.com moved from Los Angeles to San Francisco to become part of technology incubator i/o Ventures.[1]

We focus on how the founders of an entrepreneurial venture build a new-venture team as well as the importance of the team to the firm's overall success in this chapter.[2] A **new-venture team** is the group of founders, key employees, and advisers that move a new venture from an idea to a fully functioning firm. Usually, the team doesn't come together all at once.

Instead, it is built as the new firm can afford to hire additional personnel. The team also involves more than paid employees. Many firms have a board of directors, a board of advisers, and other professionals on whom they rely for direction and advice.

In this chapter's first section, we discuss the role of an entrepreneurial venture's founder or founders and emphasize the substantial effect that founders have on their firm's future. We then turn our attention to a discussion about how the founders build a new-venture team, including the recruitment and selection of key employees and the forming of a board of directors. The chapter's second section examines the important role of advisers and other professionals in shaping and rounding out a new-venture team.

As we note throughout this textbook, new ventures have a high propensity to fail. The high failure rate is due in part to what is known as the **liability of newness**, which refers to the fact that companies often falter because the people who start them aren't able to adjust quickly enough to their new roles and because the firm lacks a "track record" with outside buyers and suppliers.[3] Assembling a talented and experienced new-venture team is one path firms can take to overcome these limitations. Indeed, experienced management teams that get up to speed quickly are much less likely to make a novice's mistakes. In addition, firms able to persuade high-quality individuals to join them as directors or advisers quickly gain legitimacy with a variety of people, such as some of those working inside the venture as well as some outside the venture (e.g., suppliers, customers, and investors). In turn, legitimacy opens doors that otherwise would be closed.

Another way entrepreneurs overcome the liability of newness is by attending entrepreneurship-focused workshops, speaker series, boot camps, and similar events. These types of activities are often sponsored by local universities, small business development centers, and economic development commissions.

> **LEARNING OBJECTIVE**
> **2.** Explain the term *liability of newness*.

CREATING A NEW-VENTURE TEAM

Those who launch or found an entrepreneurial venture have an important role to play in shaping the firm's business concept. Stated even more directly, it is widely known that a well-conceived business plan cannot get off the ground unless a firm has the leaders and personnel to carry it out. As one expert put it, "People are the one factor in production . . . that animates all the others."[4] Often, several start-ups develop what is essentially the same idea at the same time. When this happens, the key to success is not the idea but rather the ability of the initial founder or founders to assemble a team that can execute the idea better than anyone else.

The way a founder builds a new-venture team sends an important signal to potential investors, partners, and employees. Some founders like the feeling of control and are reluctant to involve themselves with partners or hire managers who are more experienced than they are. In contrast, other founders are keenly aware of their own limitations and work hard to find the most experienced people to bring on board. Similarly, some new firms never form an advisory board, whereas others persuade the most important (and influential) people they can find to provide them with counsel and advice. In general, the way to impress potential investors, partners, and employees is to put together as strong a team as possible.[5] Investors and others know that experienced personnel and access to good-quality advice contributes greatly to a new venture's success.

The elements of a new-venture team are shown in Figure 9.1. It's important to carefully think through each element. Miscues regarding whether team

FIGURE 9.1
Elements of a
New-Venture Team

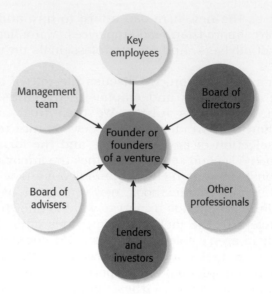

members are compatible, whether the team is properly balanced in terms of areas of expertise, and how the permanent members of the team will physically work together can be fatal, as illustrated in the "What Went Wrong?" feature. Conversely, careful attention in each of these areas can help a firm get off to a good start and provide it a leg up on competitors.

There is a common set of mistakes to avoid when putting together a new-venture team. These mistakes raise red flags when a potential investor, employee, or business partner evaluates a new venture. The most common mistakes are shown in Table 9.1.

Next, we look at each of the elements included in Figure 9.1. While reading these descriptions, remember that entrepreneurial ventures vary in how they use the elements.

The Founder or Founders

A founder's or founders' characteristics and their early decisions significantly affect the way an entrepreneurial venture is received and the manner in which the new-venture team takes shape. The size of the founding team and the qualities of the founder or founders are the two most important issues in this matter.

Size of the Founding Team   The first decision that most founders face is whether to start a firm on their own or whether to build an initial **founding team**. Studies show that more than one individual starts 50 to 70 percent of all new firms.[6] However, experts disagree about whether new ventures started by

**TABLE 9.1   COMMON MISTAKES MADE IN PUTTING TOGETHER
                      A NEW-VENTURE TEAM**

■ Placing unqualified friends or family members in management positions.
■ Assuming that previous success in other industries automatically translates to your industry.
■ Presenting a "one man team" philosophy—meaning that one person (or a small group of people) is wearing all hats with no plans to bolster the team.
■ Hiring top managers without sharing ownership in the firm.
■ Not disclosing or talking dismissively of management team skill or competency gaps.
■ Vague or unclear plans for filling the skill or competency gaps that clearly exist.

Devver: How Miscues in Regard to the Composition and Management of a New-Venture Team Can Kill a Start-up

Devver (pronounced like "developer," not "devious") launched in 2008 to help software developers use cloud-based services to "test" their code in a more expedient manner than current practices. The firm started by focusing on Ruby on Rails software applications. One of its flagship products, Caliper, provided quality metrics to Ruby on Rails developers for their Ruby on Rails code. By using Caliper, a Ruby on Rails developer could quickly discover problems like code duplication, complex code, and code "smells." In computer programming, a code smell is any symptom in the source code of a program that possibly indicates a deeper and potentially more serious problem.

Dan Mayer and Ben Brinckerhoff are Devver's cofounders. The two met in high school and started a Web business before their high school graduations. Both studied computer programming in college, Mayer at the University of Colorado and Brinckerhoff at Washington University in St. Louis. The two reunited in 2008 to launch Devver. They are graduates of TechStars, a Boulder, Colorado-based mentorship-driven seed stage investment fund. Devver operated from early 2008 until early 2010, when it went out of business. In announcing its plans to close, the company indicated that although it had worked hard to achieve its vision—to use the cloud to build tools that would change software developers' lives—it couldn't generate sufficient revenue to sustain and grow the company.

In a thoughtful blog post, Ben Brinckerhoff reflected on the reasons he feels resulted in Devver's failure. While the reasons were varied, the key reasons focused on the composition of the founding team, difficulties in communications, and product development.

In regard to the founding team, both Mayer and Brinckerhoff thought of themselves as geeks. Looking back, Brinckerhoff feels it would have been to their advantage to have had another cofounder who loved the business side of running a start-up. In reflecting on this observation, Mayer challenged the oft-repeated statement that "You can teach a hacker business, but you can't teach a businessman how to hack." This statement is sometimes used by technical founders to justify not needing a businessperson on the team. While Mayer acknowledges that it's possible to teach a hacker business, you can't force a hacker to get excited about it, or give it the proper amount of attention. According to Mayer, what hackers like to do is hack. So they measure progress in lines of code written or use a similar metric. It's equally important to have someone in a start-up measuring progress on business metrics—like number of

customers talked to or how well distribution channels are being developed. Not enough of that happened at Devver.

In regard to communication, Devver embraced working remotely. The company started in Boulder, where the two cofounders worked together. Devver's first key hire worked in Pennsylvania, and Mayer later moved to Washington, DC. The idea was that by embracing working remotely, Devver could hire the best talent available without requiring people to relocate to Colorado. In addition, they felt that by allowing team members to work remotely they would experience minimal distractions, which is important when it comes to effective code writing. Regrettably, achieving these objectives was more difficult than the founders anticipated. Communication was a challenge. It was also an administrative hassle. Mayer and Brinckerhoff found that it was a pain to manage payroll, benefits, and so forth in several states simultaneously. In addition, pair programming was difficult to do remotely—a challenge for which the Devver team never found a good solution.

Finally, Brinckerhoff believes Devver should have spent more time on customer development and finding a minimum viable product. A minimum viable product has just those features that allow a product to be deployed, and no more. It's typically deployed to early adopters for testing. The idea is to avoid building bells and whistles into products that customers don't need or want. Instead of doing this, Devver did minimal testing of its first product, the Ruby test accelerator, and then focused intently on building out the product without additional interaction with potential users. As a result, its Ruby test acceleration and additional products never really met market needs until Devver ran out of steam. In retrospect, Brinckerhoff believes Devver should have deployed individual products sooner, and solicited more customer feedback about pricing, market size, and technical challenges. Eventually, they learned that their market was too small and their price point needed to be too low to sustain the company.

Questions for Critical Thinking

1. In retrospect, Brinckerhoff believes that it would have been to Devver's advantage to have had a business-oriented cofounder as part of Devver's new-venture team. Do you think the reverse is true? If two businesspeople are set to launch a technology-oriented firm, do you think it's to their advantage to have a technology-oriented cofounder, or is it sufficient to hire technology-oriented personnel?

(continued)

2. Make a list of the pluses and minuses of adopting a philosophy of allowing workers to work remotely. Is this philosophy better for some types of start-ups than others? What is your opinion of this philosophy?
3. The "You Be the VC 9.1" feature focuses on YouTern, a Web-site that matches companies looking for interns with college students interested in internship opportunities. What do you think a minimal viable product would have looked like for YouTern? How could YouTern have used

the minimal viable product methodology to get user feedback about its site before committing substantial time and resources to building it out?
4. Do some Internet research to try to determine what Dan Mayer and Ben Brinckerhoff are doing today.

Source: Ben Brinckerhoff, "Lessons Learned." *Devver Blog*, http://devver.wordpress.com/2010/04/26/lessons-learned (accessed March 12, 2011, originally posted on April 26, 2010).

a team have an advantage over those started by a sole entrepreneur. Teams bring more talent, resources, ideas, and professional contacts to a new venture than does a sole entrepreneur.[7] In addition, the psychological support that cofounders of a business can offer one another can be an important element in a new venture's success.[8] Conversely, a lot can go wrong in a partnership—particularly one that's formed between people who don't know each other well. Team members can easily differ in terms of work habits, tolerances for risk, levels of passion for the business, ideas on how the business should be run, and similar key issues.[9] If a new-venture team isn't able to reach consensus on these issues, it may be handicapped from the outset.

When a new venture is started by a team, several issues affect the value of the team. First, teams that have worked together before, as opposed to teams that are working together for the first time, have an edge. If people have worked together before and have decided to partner to start a firm together, it usually means that they get along personally and trust one another.[10] They also tend to communicate with one another more effectively than people who are new to one another.[11] Second, if the members of the team are **heterogeneous**, meaning that they are diverse in terms of their abilities and experiences, rather than **homogeneous**, meaning that their areas of expertise are very similar to one another, they are likely to have different points of view about technology, hiring decisions, competitive tactics, and other important activities. Typically, these different points of view generate debate and constructive conflict among the founders, reducing the likelihood that decisions will be made in haste or without the airing of alternative points of view.[12] A founding team can be too big, causing communication problems and an increased potential for conflict. A founding team larger than four people is typically too large to be practical.[13]

There are three potential pitfalls associated with starting a firm as a team rather than as a sole entrepreneur. First, the team members may not get along. This is the reason investors favor teams consisting of people who have worked together before. It is simply more likely that people who have gotten along with one another in the past will continue to get along in the future. Second, if two or more people start a firm as "equals," conflicts can arise when the firm needs to establish a formal structure and designate one person as the chief executive officer (CEO). If the firm has investors, the investors will usually weigh in on who should be appointed CEO. In these instances, it is easy for the founder that wasn't chosen as the CEO to feel slighted. This problem is exacerbated if multiple founders are involved and they all stay with the firm. At some point, a hierarchy will have to be developed, and the founders will have to decide who reports to whom. Some of these problems can be avoided by developing a formal organizational chart from the beginning, which spells out the roles of each founder. Finally, as illustrated in the "What Went Wrong?" feature, if the founders of a firm have similar areas of expertise, it can be problematic. The founders of Devver were both technically oriented leaving the firm without a leader on the business side.

LEARNING OBJECTIVE
3. Discuss the difference between heterogeneous and homogeneous founding teams.

If a new venture is started by more than one person, it's important that the founders have a good rapport and complement one another rather than duplicate one another in terms of skills and backgrounds. Here, the founders of an educational software company have worked together before and are comfortable with each other's demeanors and work habits. The young woman on the left is a former teacher, the young woman in the middle is a software engineer, and the young man on the right has a business background.

Qualities of the Founders   The second major issue pertaining to the founders of a firm is the qualities they bring to the table. In the previous several chapters, we described the importance investors and others place on the strength of the firm's founders and initial management team. One reason the founders are so important is that in the early days of a firm, their knowledge, skills, and experiences are the most valuable resource the firm has. Because of this, new firms are judged largely on their "potential" rather than their current assets or current performance. In most cases, this results in people judging the future prospects of a firm by evaluating the strength of its founders and initial management team.

Several features are thought to be significant to a founder's success. The level of a founder's education is important because it's believed that entrepreneurial abilities such as search skills, foresight, creativity, and computer skills are enhanced through obtaining a college degree. Similarly, some observers think that higher education equips a founder with important business-related skills, such as math and communications. In addition, specific forms of education, such as engineering, computer science, management information systems, physics, and biochemistry, provide the recipients of this education an advantage if they start a firm that is related to their area of expertise.[14]

Prior entrepreneurial experience, relevant industry experience, and networking are other attributes that strengthen the chances of a founder's success. Indeed, the results of research studies somewhat consistently suggest that **prior entrepreneurial experience** is one of the most consistent predictors of future entrepreneurial performance.[15] Because launching a new venture is a complex task, entrepreneurs with prior start-up experience have a distinct advantage. The impact of **relevant industry experience** on an entrepreneur's ability to successfully launch and grow a firm has also been studied.[16] Entrepreneurs with experience in the same industry as their current venture will have a more mature network of industry contacts and will have a better understanding of the subtleties of their respective industries.[17] The importance of this factor is particularly evident for entrepreneurs who start firms in technical industries such as biotechnology. The demands of biotechnology are sufficiently intense that it would be virtually impossible for someone to start a biotech firm while at the

Zero Creatives Cultura/Newscom

LEARNING OBJECTIVE

4. Identify the personal attributes that strengthen a founder's chances of successfully launching an entrepreneurial venture.

same time learning biotechnology. The person must have an understanding of biotechnology prior to launching a firm through either relevant industry experience or an academic background. Some entrepreneurs, who come from a nonbusiness background, fear that a lack of business experience will be their Achilles' heel. There are several steps, techniques, or approaches to business that entrepreneurs can utilize to overcome a lack of business experience. These steps and approaches are highlighted in the "Savvy Entrepreneurial Firm" feature.

A particularly important attribute for founders or founding teams is the presence of a mature network of social and professional contacts.[18] Founders must often "work" their social and personal networks to raise money or gain access to critical resources on behalf of their firms.[19] **Networking** is building and maintaining relationships with people whose interests are similar or whose relationship could bring advantages to a firm. The way this might play out in practice is that a founder calls a business acquaintance or friend to ask for an introduction to a potential investor, business partner, or customer. For some founders, networking is easy and is an important part of their daily routine. For others, it is a learned skill.

Table 9.2 shows the preferred attributes of a firm's founder or founders. Start-ups that have founders or a team of founders with these attributes have the best chances of early success.

Recruiting and Selecting Key Employees

Once the decision to launch a new venture has been made, building a management team and hiring key employees begins. Start-ups vary in terms of how quickly they need to add personnel. In some instances, the founders work alone for a period of time while the business plan is being written and the venture begins taking shape. In other instances, employees are hired immediately.

One technique available to entrepreneurs to help prioritize their hiring needs is to maintain a skills profile. A **skills profile** is a chart that depicts the most important skills that are needed and where skills gaps exist. A skills profile for New Venture Fitness Drinks, the fictitious company introduced in

> **LEARNING OBJECTIVE**
> **5.** Describe how to construct a "skills profile" and explain how it helps a start-up identify gaps in its new-venture team.

TABLE 9.2 PREFERRED ATTRIBUTES OF THE FOUNDER OR FOUNDERS OF AN ENTREPRENEURIAL VENTURE

Attribute	Explanation
Firm started by a team	New ventures that are started by a team can provide greater resources, a broader diversity of viewpoints, and a broader array of other positive attributes than ventures started by individuals.
Higher education	Evidence suggests that important entrepreneurial skills are enhanced through higher education.
Prior entrepreneurial experience	Founders with prior entrepreneurial experience are familiar with the entrepreneurial process and are more likely to avoid costly mistakes than founders new to the rigors of the entrepreneurial process.
Relevant industry experience	Founders with experience in the same industry as their new venture will most likely have better-established professional networks and more applicable marketing and management expertise than founders without relevant industry experience.
Broad social and professional network	Founders with broad social and professional networks have potential access to additional know-how, capital, and customer referrals.

Overcoming a Lack of Business Experience

Many people who start businesses do not have prior business experience. This is especially true with the recent innovations in IT, where people have started businesses in areas that have never existed before. Some of these new business owners who lack business experience worry that people with experience in accounting, finance, and management will generally have an easier time starting a business than those who are tackling these challenges for the first time.

There are several methods and approaches to starting a business that people can take to compensate for their lack of business experience. However, first let's look at some of the characteristics a new business owner should have. A successful business owner should be:

1. Creative
2. Sure about the business
3. Realistic
4. Fast
5. Honest
6. Firm
7. Friendly
8. Careful
9. Sincere
10. Prepared to face failure

In Malaysia, there are several ways for a person to successfully launch a business even with a lack of prior experience.

Get Business Assistance and Advice

There are many places for business founders to get business assistance and advice. SME Corporation Malaysia (SME Corp. Malaysia), for example, is a government agency that provides management assistance and coaching to business owners. It is a central point of reference for information and advisory services for all small and medium enterprises (SMEs) in Malaysia. You will be able to find your local SME Corp. at www.smecorp.gov.my.

You may also find information from SME Toolkit Malaysia, which is a project by Dun & Bradstreet (D&B) Malaysia Sdn Bhd and the Small and Medium Enterprise (SME) Department of the World Bank Group. It is an organization that provides consulting services to small businesses. You can find your local SME Toolkit at www.malaysia.smetoolkit.org. There are also many other organizations that provide coaching, advice, and support to specific groups of business owners and tailor their offerings to fit the groups. An example is the National Association for Women Entrepreneurs of Malaysia (NAWEM), an organization that promotes, develops, and enhances the efforts and activities of women entrepreneurs. You may visit their Web site at www.nawem.org.my.

If you're looking for a support group in your area and can't find one, check the Meetup Web site. Meetup (www.meetup.com/cities/my) is an online platform that allows individuals to organize local groups via the Internet. Once a group is formed, its members "meet up" on a regular basis off-line. You may simply follow the directions on Meetup's home page to discover if there is a small business or entrepreneurship Meetup group in your area. The following is a sample of small business Meetup groups that have taken place in Malaysia:

■ Business networks
■ Social media training
■ Discussion and sharing on expanding your business across national borders

Participate in Online Forums and Q&A Sites

There are a growing number of online forums that provide support and advice to business owners. An example is the SMI SME Business Directory (www.smibusinessdirectory.com.my), which sponsors online forums that cover topics such as selecting a business, successful business planning, start-up funding, and financial management. The general tone of forums tends to be supportive and upbeat, which is exactly what business owners with limited experience need. There are also other growing numbers of Web sites for entrepreneurs that can be very helpful, especially to those who lack business experience.

Pick a Type of Business That Minimizes the Need for Prior Experience

There are also other alternatives for starting a business that minimize the need for prior experience. These alternatives allow people to pursue an opportunity in which fundamentals of the business have already been thought out. Franchising, for example, provides an individual the opportunity to own a business using a tested and refined business system. Other than that, a second alternative would be direct sales or multilevel marketing. These options require minimum experience and have been successful even for those who lack business experience.

Questions for Critical Thinking

1. Identify the sources of business assistance available in your area free of charge.
2. Identify three sources of business assistance or advice, particularly useful for someone who's starting a business without prior business experience, not mentioned in this feature.
3. How valuable do you believe that online forums, like the one mentioned previously, can be to someone who's trying to learn the "business" aspect of starting a business?
4. What other techniques, not mentioned previously, can people who don't have prior business experience utilize to compensate for their lack of experience?

FIGURE 9.2
Skills Profile for New
Venture Fitness Drinks

	Executive Leadership	Store Operations	Supply Chain Management	Marketing and Sales	HR/Recruiting	Accounting and Finance	Community Relations	Information Systems	Franchise Operations
Jack Petty	X								
Peggy Wells		X				X			
Jill Petersen				X					
Cameron Ivey			X						
Gap 1						O			
Gap 2								O	
Gap 3									O

X = position filled
O = position vacant

Chapter 3, is shown in Figure 9.2. Along with depicting where a firm's most important skills gaps exist, a skills profile should explain how current skills gaps are being dealt with. For example, two of New Venture Fitness Drink's skills gaps are being covered (on a short-term basis) by members of the board of advisers and the third skills gap does not need to be filled until the firm initiates a franchising program, which is still three to five years in the future.

Evidence suggests that finding good employees today is not an easy task. A 2011 survey conducted by the University of Maryland's School of Business and Network Solutions asked small business owners how well they competed with other companies for good employees, and only 46 percent said they were successful. Respondents said that recruiting workers who were comfortable in a small business setting is difficult.[20] Similarly, a 2008 survey asked the CEOs of 245 rapid-growth firms if finding qualified workers was a concern. A total of 40 percent of the CEOs, in the first quarter of 2008, reported that a lack of qualified workers is a potential barrier to growth for their firms over the next 12 months.[21]

Founders differ in their approach to the task of recruiting and selecting key employees. Some founders draw on their network of contacts to identify candidates for key positions. Others ask their existing employees for referrals. Safilo USA, a luxury eyewear company, pays its employees for referrals. An employee who refers someone who joins the company gets $500 after the new hire has been with Safilo for six months and another $500 after a year.[22] Across all types of firms, employee referral programs account for about 20 percent of all hiring.[23] Many companies use interns to help fill personnel needs. Other companies rely on job search Web sites like Monster.com or CareerBuilder.com.

An increasingly important approach for recruiting employees is via social media sites like LinkedIn, Twitter, and Facebook. The founder of a small firm can broadcast to his or her LinkedIn contacts or Facebook friends that s/he is interested in hiring qualified employees, without paying for a job posting. Similarly, some companies have Twitter accounts specifically for recruiting. ModCloth, the online retailer of vintage and vintage-inspired clothing for women, has a Twitter account named ModCloth Careers, which is specifically designed for people interested in pursuing a career with ModCloth. As of May 2011, it had over 1,100 followers. Table 9.3 provides additional information about how to use social media sites to recruit employees.

Many founders worry about hiring the wrong person for a key role. Because most new firms are strapped for cash, every team member must make a

TABLE 9.3   HOW TO USE SOCIAL MEDIA SITES TO RECRUIT EMPLOYEES

Social Media Site	Technique	Implementation
Facebook	Post job opening on your fan page.	Just like any other message, a company can post job openings on its fan page.
	Send out messages about job openings to fans of your company's fan page.	On Facebook, you can "send an update" to your fans via the "promote your page" function.
	Recruit new employees via current employees.	Ask your employees to send out job postings with links to your Facebook fan page or your recruiting Web site.
LinkedIn	Post a job listing.	Access the "jobs" link on LinkedIn's homepage. This is a paid service.
	Notify your contacts on LinkedIn that you are looking to hire, without paying for a job listing. Ask for a referral of a qualified candidate.	Simply send a message to your contacts via the "Share an update" function on LinkedIn.
	Search for candidates among LinkedIn members.	You can search for candidates via keywords. If you're looking for a CFO, simple type "CFO" in the search box and you can see profiles for CFOs who are LinkedIn members.
	Recruit new employees via current employees.	Ask your employees to notify their LinkedIn contacts that the company they work for is looking to hire, and include a link to your recruiting Web site.
Twitter	Post job listings on the company's Twitter account.	A company can post job listings on its general Twitter account just like it posts any other type of information.
	Create a separate Twitter account for job listings.	The account should include the words *jobs* or *careers*. Examples of Twitter accounts sent up for this purpose include Accenture_Jobs, JobsatIntel, and VerizonCareers.
	Ask your CEO to tweet.	Ask your CEO to create a Twitter account and post job listings along with other information. Some CEOs have incredible Twitter followings. Examples include Tony Hsieh, CEO of Zappos, 1.8 million followers; Eric Schmidt, chairman of Google, 297,000 followers; Richard Branson, CEO Virgin Group, 985,000 followers.

valuable contribution, so it's not good enough to hire someone who is well intended but who doesn't precisely fit the job. On some occasions, key hires work out perfectly and fill the exact roles that the founders of the firm need. For example, Dave Olsen was one of the first hires made by Starbucks founder Howard Schultz. At the time of his hiring, Olsen was the owner of a popular coffeehouse in the university district of Seattle, the city where Starbucks was launched. In his autobiography, Schultz recalls the following about the hiring of Olsen:

> On the day of our meeting, Dave and I sat on my office floor and I started spreading the plans and blueprints out and talking about my idea. Dave got it right away. He had spent ten years in an apron, behind a counter, serving espresso drinks. He had experienced firsthand the excitement people can develop about espresso, both in his café and in Italy. I didn't have to convince him that this idea had big potential. He just knew it in his bones. The synergy was too good to be true. My strength was looking outward: communicating the vision, inspiring investors, raising money, finding real estate, designing the stores, building the brand, and planning for the future. Dave understood the inner workings: the nuts and bolts of operating a retail café, hiring and training baristas (coffee brewers), ensuring the best quality coffee.[24]

Investors place high value on the attribute of flexibility, especially when founders are willing to assume the role that makes the most sense for them in their venture rather than insisting on being the CEO. This is a difficult task for some founders who become entrepreneurs to "be their own boss" or put their distinctive stamp on a firm. Founders who do remain flexible, however, often have an easier time obtaining financing or funding. The way many founders look at this issue is that it is better to be the vice president of a $100-million firm than the CEO of a $10-million firm.

The Roles of the Board of Directors

If a new venture organizes as a corporation, it is legally required to have a **board of directors**—a panel of individuals who are elected by a corporation's shareholders to oversee the management of the firm.[25] A board is typically made up of both inside and outside directors. An **inside director** is a person who is also an officer of the firm. An **outside director** is someone who is not employed by the firm. A board of directors has three formal responsibilities: (1) appoint the firm's officers (the key managers), (2) declare dividends, and (3) oversee the affairs of the corporation. In the wake of corporate scandals such as Enron, WorldCom, and others, there is a strong emphasis on the board's role in making sure the firm is operating ethically. One outcome of this movement is a trend toward putting more outsiders on boards of directors, because people who do not work for the firm are usually more willing to scrutinize the behavior of management than insiders who work for the company. Most boards meet formally three or four times a year. Large firms pay their directors for their service. New ventures are more likely to pay their directors in company stock, as in the case with Scripped, the start-up profiled at the beginning of the chapter, or ask them to serve without direct compensation—at least until the company is profitable. The boards for publicly traded companies are required by law to have audit and compensation committees. Many boards also have nominating committees to select stockholders to run for vacant board positions.

If handled properly, a company's board of directors can be an important part of the new-venture team. Providing expert guidance and legitimacy in the eyes of others (e.g., customers, investors, and even competitors) are two ways a board of directors can help a new firm get off to a good start and develop what, it is hoped, will become a sustainable competitive advantage.

Provide Guidance   Although a board of directors has formal governance responsibilities, its most useful role is to provide guidance and support to the firm's managers.[26] Many CEOs interact with their board members frequently and obtain important input. The key to making this happen is to pick board members with needed skills and useful experiences who are willing to give advice and ask insightful and probing questions. The extent to which an effective board can help shape a firm and provide it a competitive advantage in the marketplace is expressed by Ram Charan, an expert on the role of boards of directors in corporations:

> They (effective boards) listen, probe, debate, and become engaged in the company's most pressing issues. Directors share their expertise and wisdom as a matter of course. As they do, management and the board learn together, a collective wisdom emerges, and managerial judgment improves. The on-site coaching and consulting expand the mental capacity of the CEO and the top management team and give the company a competitive edge out there in the marketplace.[27]

Because managers rely on board members for counsel and advice, the search for outside directors should be purposeful, with the objective of filling gaps in the experience and background of the venture's executives and the other directors. For example, if two computer programmers started a software firm and neither one of them had any marketing experience, it would make sense to place a marketing executive on the board of directors. Indeed, a board of directors has the foundation to effectively serve its organization when its members represent many important organizational skills (e.g., manufacturing, human resource management, and financing) involved with running a company.

Lend Legitimacy   Providing legitimacy for the entrepreneurial venture is another important function of a board of directors. Well-known and respected board members bring instant credibility to the firm. For example, just imagine the positive buzz a firm could generate if it could say that Jack Dorsey of Twitter or Mark Pincus of Zynga had agreed to serve on its board of directors. This phenomenon is referred to as **signaling**. Without a credible signal, it is difficult for potential customers, investors, or employees to identify high-quality start-ups. Presumably, high-quality individuals would be reluctant to serve on the board of a low-quality firm because that would put their reputation at risk. So when a high-quality individual does agree to serve on a board of a firm, the individual is in essence "signaling" that the company has potential to be successful.[28]

Achieving legitimacy through high-quality board members can result in other positive outcomes. Investors like to see new-venture teams, including the board of directors that have people with enough clout to get their foot in the door with potential suppliers and customers. Board members are also often instrumental in helping young firms arrange financing or funding. As we will discuss in Chapter 10, it's almost impossible for an entrepreneurial venture's founders to get the attention of an investor without a personal introduction. One way firms deal with this challenge is by placing individuals on their boards that are acquainted with people in the investment community.

A list of the most desirable qualities in a board of directors and the most desirable qualities in individual board members is provided in Table 9.4.

LEARNING OBJECTIVE

7. Identify the two primary ways in which the nonemployee members of a start-up's new-venture team help the firm.

LEARNING OBJECTIVE

8. Describe the concept of signaling and explain its importance.

TABLE 9.4 ATTRIBUTES OF EFFECTIVE BOARDS OF DIRECTORS AND EFFECTIVE BOARD MEMBERS

Attributes of Effective Boards of Directors

- Strong communication with the CEO
- Customer-focused point of view
- Complementary mix of talents
- Decisiveness
- Mutual respect and regard for each other and the management team of the firm
- Ability and willingness to stand up to the CEO and top managers of the firm
- Strong ethics

Attributes of Strong Board Members

- Strong personal and professional networks
- Respected in their field
- Willingness to make personal introductions on behalf of the firm
- Strong interpersonal communication skills
- Pattern recognition skills
- Investment and/or operating experience
- Ability and willingness to mentor the CEO and the top managers of the firm

ROUNDING OUT THE TEAM: THE ROLE OF PROFESSIONAL ADVISERS

Along with the new-venture team members we've already identified, founders often rely on professionals with whom they interact for important counsel and advice. In many cases, these professionals become an important part of the new-venture team and fill what some entrepreneurs call "talent holes."

Next, we discuss the roles that boards of advisers, lenders, investors, and other professionals play in rounding out new-venture teams.

Board of Advisers

LEARNING OBJECTIVE
9. Discuss the purpose of forming an advisory board.

Some start-up firms are forming advisory boards to provide them direction and advice.[29] An **advisory board** is a panel of experts who are asked by a firm's managers to provide counsel and advice on an ongoing basis. Unlike a board of directors, an advisory board possesses no legal responsibility for the firm and gives nonbinding advice.[30] As a result, more people are willing to serve on a company's board of advisers than on its board of directors because it requires less time and no legal liability is involved. A board of advisers can be established for general purposes or can be set up to address a specific issue or need. For example, some start-ups set up customer advisory boards shortly after they are founded to help them fine-tune their initial offerings. Similar to a board of directors, the main purpose of a board of advisers is to provide guidance and lend legitimacy to a firm. Both of these attributes are seen in the advisory board set up by Sunil Rajaraman, the cofounder of Scripped, the company profiled at the beginning of the chapter. As noted previously, Scripped's advisory board includes Break Media CEO Keith Richman, producer, director and screenwriter Steven de Souza, and actor Edward Burns. These are individuals who can not only provide Scripped business and operations advice, but are people who command respect in Scripped's industry. An example of a firm that set up a customer advisory board for a different reason, to help develop its initial product, is highlighted in the "Partnering for Success" feature.

Most boards of advisers have between 5 and 15 members. Entrepreneurial firms typically pay the members of their board of advisers a small honorarium for their service either annually or on a per-meeting basis. Boards of advisers interact with each other and with a firm's managers in several ways. Some advisory boards meet three or four times a year at the company's headquarters or in another location. Other advisory boards meet in an online environment. In some cases, a firm's board of advisers will be scattered across the country, making it more cost-effective for a firm's managers to interact with the members of the board on the telephone or via e-mail rather than to bring them physically together. In these situations, board members don't interact with each other at all on a face-to-face basis, yet still provide high levels of counsel and advice.

The fact that a start-up has a board of directors does not preclude it from having one or more board of advisers. For example, Coolibar, a maker of sun protective clothing, has a board of directors and a medical advisory board. According to Coolibar, its medical advisory board "provides advice to the company regarding UV radiation, sunburn, and the science of detecting, preventing, and treating skin cancer and other UV-related medical disorders, such as lupus."[31] The board currently consists of seven medical doctors, all with impressive credentials. Similarly, Intouch Health, a medical robotics and instruments company, has a board of directors along with a Business & Strategy advisory board, an Applications & Clinical advisors board, and a Scientific & Technical advisory board. Intouch Health says that its "diversified Advisory Board draws on the talents of seasoned executives, clinical and scientific authorities, clinical and scientific authorities, and pioneers from a variety of technical areas. Their expertise encompasses international business management, robotics, telemedicine, and computer software, hardware and networking."[32]

There are several guidelines to organizing a board of advisers. First, a board of advisers should not be organized just so a company can boast of it. Advisers will become quickly disillusioned if they don't play a meaningful role in the firm's development and growth. Second, a firm should look for board members who are compatible and complement one another in terms of experience and expertise. Unless the board is being established for a specific purpose, a board that includes members with varying backgrounds is preferable to a board of people with similar backgrounds. Third, when inviting a person to serve on its board of advisers, a company should carefully spell out to the individual the rules in terms of access to confidential information.[33] Some firms ask the members of their advisory board to sign nondisclosure agreements, which are described in Chapter 7. Finally, firms should caution their advisers to disclose that they have a relationship with the venture before posting positive comments about it or its products on blogs or on social networking sites. A potential conflict of interest surfaces when a person says positive things about a company without disclosing an affiliation with the firm, particularly if there is a financial stake in the company.

Although having a board of advisers is widely recommended in start-up circles, most start-ups do not have one. As a result, one way a start-up can make itself stand out is to have one or more boards of advisers.

Lenders and Investors

As emphasized throughout this book, lenders and investors have a vested interest in the companies they finance, often causing these individuals to become very involved in helping the firms they fund. It is rare that a lender or investor will put money into a new venture and then simply step back and wait to see what happens. In fact, the institutional rules governing banks and investment firms typically require that they monitor new ventures fairly closely, at least during the initial years of a loan or an investment.[34]

PARTNERING FOR SUCCESS

Need Help with Product Development? Consider Establishing a Customer Advisory Board

Although most firms that have a customer advisory board set them up after their firm is started, primarily to assess customer satisfaction and brainstorm new product ideas, customer advisory boards can be useful before a firm has customers as well. An example of a firm that did this is iConclude, an IT solutions company that was recently acquired by Opsware (www.opsware.com). iConclude was founded to help other companies troubleshoot mission critical software and hardware problems, but when it came to producing an actual product, the company wasn't exactly sure what its product should look like. To make certain it didn't stumble and produce a product that wasn't what its clients needed, the company decided to form a customer advisory board to dig deep into its future customers' problems and discern the exact features its product should include. Reflecting on the nature of the customer advisory board that was set up, and what the effort accomplished, Sunny Gupta, iConclude's founder, recalls:

"We were very upfront with all of the companies we spoke with. We realized we needed real customer input in order for us to really get the right product into the market. That led us to form a customer advisory board of 7 to 8 of these (firms with large IT departments) companies mostly out of Seattle. They met with us every second week and really tried to hone down on exactly what their problems were and what would be the ideal solution from their perspective.

This got them on board much, much earlier with us which was pretty instrumental because we identified real requirements which enabled us to build the right product."

Ultimately, iConclude built a successful product and was acquired shortly after by a much larger firm.

Questions for Critical Thinking

1. Why do you think iConclude was able to persuade other companies to serve on its customer advisory board?
2. What insight or insights do you believe that iConclude gained by assembling a customer advisory board before rather than after its product was fully developed? What benefits, other than getting good quality advice, did iConclude glean from putting together a customer advisory board?
3. How do you think iConclude utilized its customer advisory board after its product was launched?
4. Look at YouTern (www.youtern.com), the focus of the "You Be the VC 9.1" feature. What type of advisory board or advisory boards would make the most sense for YouTern?

Source: nPost, "Sunny Gupta, CEO of iConclude," www.npost.com/?s=iConclude (accessed May 11, 2011, originally posted on April 4, 2006).

The amount of time and energy a lender or investor dedicates to a new firm depends on the amount of money involved and how much help the new firm needs. For example, a lender with a well-secured loan may spend very little time with a client, whereas a venture capitalist may spend an enormous amount of time helping a new venture refine its business model, recruit management personnel, and meet with current and prospective customers and suppliers. In fact, evidence suggests that an average venture capitalist is likely to visit each company in a portfolio multiple times a year.[35] This number denotes a high level of involvement and support.

As with the other nonemployee members of a firm's new-venture team, lenders and investors help new firms by providing guidance and lending legitimacy and assume the natural role of providing financial oversight.[36] In some instances, lenders and investors also work hard to help new firms fill out their management teams. Sometimes this issue is so important that a new venture will try to obtain investment capital not only to get access to money, but also to obtain help hiring key employees.

For example, during its beginning stages, eBay's partners, Pierre Omidyar and Jeff Skoll, decided to recruit a CEO. They wanted someone who was not only experienced, but who also had the types of credentials that are valued by

Wall Street investors. They soon discovered that every experienced manager they tried to recruit asked if they had venture capital backing—which at that time they did not. For a new firm trying to recruit a seasoned executive, venture capital backing is a sort of seal of legitimacy. To get this valuable seal, Omidyar and Skoll obtained funding from Benchmark Venture Capital, even though eBay didn't really need the money. Writer Randall Stross recalls this event as follows:

> eBay was an anomaly: a profitable company that was able to self-fund its growth and that turned to venture capital solely for contacts and counsel. No larger lesson can be drawn. When Benchmark wired the first millions to eBay's bank account, the figurative check was tossed into the vault—and there it would sit, unneeded and undisturbed.[37]

This strategy worked for eBay. Soon after affiliating with Benchmark, Bob Kagle, one of Benchmark's general partners, led eBay to Meg Whitman, an executive who had experience working for several top firms, including Procter & Gamble, Disney, and Hasbro. In March 2008, Whitman stepped down as eBay's president and CEO. However, Whitman continues serving as a member of the firm's board of directors.

Bankers also play a role in establishing the legitimacy of new ventures and their initial management teams. Research evidence rather consistently suggests that the presence of bank loans is a favorable signal to other capital providers.[38] Investors often take a seat on the boards of directors of the firms they fund to provide oversight and advice. For example, Fitbit, which makes a wireless-enabled wearable device that measures data such as the number of steps walked, quality of sleep, and other personal metrics, received $2 million in funding in October 2008. At the same time, Doug Levin, the company's angel investor, joined Fitbit's board of directors. It is less common for a banker to take a seat on the board of directors of an entrepreneurial venture, primarily because bankers provide operating capital rather than large amounts of investment capital to new firms.

There are additional ways that lenders and investors add value to a new firm beyond financing and funding. These roles are highlighted in Table 9.5.

TABLE 9.5 BEYOND FINANCING AND FUNDING: WAYS LENDERS AND INVESTORS ADD VALUE TO AN ENTREPRENEURIAL VENTURE

- Help identify and recruit key management personnel
- Provide insight into the industry and markets in which the venture intends to participate
- Help the venture fine-tune its business model
- Serve as a sounding board for new ideas
- Provide introductions to additional sources of capital
- Recruit customers
- Help to arrange business partnerships
- Serve on the venture's board of directors or board of advisers
- Provide a sense of calm in the midst of the emotional roller-coaster ride that many new-venture teams experience

Other Professionals

At times, other professionals assume important roles in a new venture's success. Attorneys, accountants, and business consultants are often good sources of counsel and advice. The role of lawyers in helping firms get off to a good start is discussed in Chapter 7, and the role of accountants is discussed in Chapter 8. So here, let's take a look at the role a consultant may play.

LEARNING OBJECTIVE

10. Explain why new ventures use consultants for help and advice.

Consultants   A **consultant** is an individual who gives professional or expert advice. New ventures vary in terms of how much they rely on business consultants for direction. In some ways, the role of the general business consultant has diminished in importance as businesses seek specialists to obtain advice on complex issues such as patents, tax planning, and security laws. In other ways, the role of general business consultant is as important as ever; it is the general business consultant who can conduct in-depth analyses on behalf of a firm, such as preparing a feasibility study or an industry analysis. Because of the time it would take, it would be inappropriate to ask a member of a board of directors or board of advisers to take on one of these tasks on behalf of a firm. These more time-intensive tasks must be performed by the firm itself or by a paid consultant.

Those leading an entrepreneurial venture often turn to consultants for help and advice because while large firms can afford to employ experts in many areas, new firms typically can't. If a new firm needs help in a specialized area, such as building a product prototype, it may need to hire an engineering consulting firm to do the work. Consultants' fees are typically negotiable. If a new venture has good potential and offers a consulting firm the possibility of repeat business, the firm will often be willing to reduce its fee or work out favorable payment arrangements.

Consultants fall into two categories: paid consultants and consultants who are made available for free or at a reduced rate through a nonprofit or government agency. The first category includes large international consulting firms, such as Bearing Point, Accenture, IBM Global Services, and Bain & Company. These firms provide a wide array of services but are beyond the reach of most start-ups because of budget limitations. But there are many smaller, localized firms. The best way to find them is to ask around for a referral.

Consultants are also available through nonprofit or government agencies. SCORE, for example, is a nonprofit organization that provides free consulting

There are many resources available to entrepreneurs for counsel and advice. Here, a couple is meeting with counselors who are helping them set up their accounting system. The couple is starting a medical products firm. The counselors are volunteers for a nonprofit organization that provides free counseling services to small business owners.

services to small businesses. SCORE currently has over 13,000 volunteers, 360 local chapters, and can provide assistance in over 500 areas. An increasing number of score volunteers, called mentors, assist clients via e-mail rather than face-to-face. Commonly, SCORE mentors are retired business owners who counsel in areas as diverse as cash flow management, operations, and sales.[39] The Small Business Administration, a government agency, provides a variety of consulting services to small businesses and entrepreneurs, primarily through its network of Small Business Development Centers (SBDC), which are spread throughout the United States. There is evidence that these centers are effective in providing advice and helping entrepreneurial ventures get off to a good start. For example, one study found that the rates of survival, growth, and innovation of SBDC-counseled firms are higher than the population of start-ups in general.[40]

In summary, putting together a new-venture team is one of the most critical activities that a founder or founders of a firm undertake. Many entrepreneurs suffer by not thinking broadly enough or carefully enough about this process. Ultimately, people must make any new venture work. New ventures benefit by surrounding themselves with high-quality employees and advisers to tackle the challenges involved with launching and growing an entrepreneurial firm.

CHAPTER SUMMARY

1. A new-venture team is the group of people who move a new venture from an idea to a fully functioning firm. Company founders, key employees, the board of directors, the board of advisers, lenders and investors, and other professionals are the primary elements of a new-venture team.

2. The liability of newness refers to the fact that entrepreneurial ventures often falter or even fail because the people who start them can't adjust quickly enough to their new roles and because the firm lacks a "track record" with customers and suppliers. These limitations can be overcome by assembling a talented and experienced new-venture team.

3. A heterogeneous founding team has members with diverse abilities and experiences. A homogeneous founding team has members who are very similar to one another.

4. The personal attributes that affect a founder's chances of launching a successful new firm include level of education, prior entrepreneurial experience, relevant industry experience, and the ability to network. Networking is building and maintaining relationships with people who are similar or whose friendship could bring advantages to the firm.

5. A skills profile is a chart that depicts the most importance skills that are needed in a new venture and where skills gaps exist.

6. Providing guidance and lending legitimacy are the two primary ways in which the non-employee members of a start-up's new-venture team help the firm.

7. A board of directors is a panel of individuals who is elected by a corporation's shareholders to oversee the management of the firm. It is typically made up of both inside and outside directors. An inside director is a person who is also an officer of the firm. An outside director is someone who is not employed by the firm.

8. When a high-quality individual agrees to serve on a company's board of directors, the individual is in essence expressing an opinion that the company has potential (why else would the individual agree to serve?). This phenomenon is referred to as signaling.

9. An advisory board is a panel of experts who are asked by a firm's management team to provide counsel and advice on an ongoing basis.

10. The primary reason that new ventures turn to consultants for help and advice is that while large firms can afford to employ experts in many areas, new firms typically can't. Consultants can be paid or can be part of a nonprofit or government agency and provide their services for free or for a reduced rate.

KEY TERMS

advisory board, **328**
board of directors, **326**
consultant, **332**
founding team, **318**
heterogeneous, **320**
homogeneous, **320**

inside director, **326**
liability of newness, **317**
networking, **322**
new-venture
   team, **316**
outside director, **326**

prior entrepreneurial
   experience, **321**
relevant industry experience,
   321
signaling, **327**
skills profile, **322**

REVIEW QUESTIONS

1. What is a new-venture team? Who are the primary participants in a start-up's new-venture team?
2. What is liability of newness? What can a new venture do to overcome the liability of newness?
3. Do new ventures started by a team have an advantage over new ventures started by a sole entrepreneur, or is the opposite the case?
4. Describe the difference between a heterogeneous and a homogeneous founding team.
5. Describe the two potential pitfalls of using a team to start a firm.
6. What are the personal attributes that affect a founder's chances of launching a successful new firm? In your judgment, which of these attributes are the most important? Why?
7. Explain why having relevant industry experience helps the founder of a firm.
8. Define *networking*. Why is it important for an entrepreneur to have a vibrant social and professional network?
9. What are the reasons for completing a skills profile for a new firm?
10. What is a board of directors? What is the difference between inside and outside directors?
11. Describe the three formal responsibilities of a board of directors.
12. Explain why recruiting a well-known and highly respected board of directors lends legitimacy to a firm.
13. Define *signaling* and explain its potential value for a new venture.
14. Discuss the purpose of forming an advisory board. If you were the founder of an entrepreneurial firm, would you set up an advisory board? Why or why not?
15. Describe the different ways advisory boards meet and conduct their business.
16. Describe several of the guidelines to setting up a board of advisers.
17. In what ways do lenders and investors lend legitimacy to a firm?
18. Explain why new ventures often turn to consultants for advice.
19. Describe the purpose of SCORE. What type of advice and counsel do SCORE volunteers provide?
20. As noted in the chapter, SBDCs (Small Business Development Centers) seem to contribute positively to the launch of an entrepreneurial venture. In your opinion, what accounts for this positive relationship? If you were launching an entrepreneurial venture today, would you seek the services of an SBDC? Why or why not?

APPLICATION QUESTIONS

1. Reread this chapter's opening case. What factors did Sunil Rajaraman have working in his favor, and what factors did he have working against him as the cofounder of Scripped?
2. Ann Perkins is a sales representative for The Pampered Chef, a direct sales organization that sells kitchen utensils and related products. Ann, who lives near Houston, is thinking about leaving The Pampered Chef to open a combination cookware store and cooking school near where she lives. Ann's background is in cooking and sales. She's thinking about taking on a partner. What qualities should she look for in a potential partner or "cofounder" for her new business? What type of board of advisors should she set up?
3. Neil Frasier, a friend of your family, is a very proficient accountant. He's 61 and has spent his entire career working at the Sears Holdings Corp. headquarters in Chicago. He just got a call from a high school buddy that still lives in the small town in Wisconsin that they both grew up in. Neil's buddy tells him

that the sole accountant in town is retiring and has his business for sale. Neil has always wanted to return to his home town. He thinks about it for a few minutes and then tells his buddy, "As much as I'd absolutely love to come back home, I don't have any business experience and I'm 61 years old. Those are two strikes against me—I'll have to pass on buying the business." Is Neil's thinking sound? What would tell Neil if he asked you for your advice?

4. According to the chapter, prior entrepreneurial experience, relevant industry experience, and networking are attributes that strengthen a person's chances of launching a successful venture. Think about the type of company that you might launch someday. Which of these attributes do you currently possess? What steps can you take now to build strengths in each of these areas?

5. Spend some time looking at the "Team" section of Songkick's Web site (under the "About Us" tab). Songkick is the subject of the "You Be the VC 1.2" feature. On a scale of 1 to 10 (10 is high), rate the team's ability to operate and grow Songkick. Justify your rating.

6. Select a company that has a Twitter account established specifically for the purpose of recruiting. Follow the site for a week or look at its archive of postings and read the tweets for the past week. Describe how the company uses the site for recruiting. Make an assessment regarding whether you believe the account will be effective for recruiting potential employees.

7. Amanda King has spent the past 15 years as a consultant for a national consulting company. She's worked with a range of organizations, from *Fortune* 500 companies to start-ups to nonprofits. Recently, she was approached by a start-up in the fashion industry that just received $1 million in angel funding. The founder of the firm was referred to Amanda by the angel investor, who knows Amada through a professional organization. Amanda is inclined to accept but has never worked with a single client in the fashion industry, so she really doesn't know what she can contribute. She's asked you for advice. What would you tell Amanda? In what ways, if any, can she contribute to the fashion company's success, even though she doesn't know much about the fashion industry?

8. Three days ago Peggy Armstrong sent a lengthy e-mail message to a long-time business acquaintance, asking the acquaintance if she'd consider cofounding a tutoring service with her. Peggy attached a first draft of her business plan. The acquaintance just replied to Peggy's message and said that she'd be interested under three conditions. After reading the conditions, Peggy thought to herself, "Boy did I make the right decision approaching her. These conditions are tough but smart." Speculate on what the conditions might have been.

9. Kim Simpson owns a successful fitness center in an affluent suburb of St. Louis. She just received funding and plans to open six new fitness centers in the St. Louis area over the next two years. She'll need to hire a general manager and staff for each center, and is concerned about making intelligent hiring decisions. Kim has turned to you for advice. Up to this point she has only operated the one center. Her questions to you are, "What recruiting techniques would you suggest I use? How do I make smart hiring decisions?" Craft answers for Kim's questions.

10. Sharon Burns, an attorney you know, was recently asked by a technology start-up to serve on its board of advisors. Sharon has a very busy practice. She's leaning toward turning down the offer, but has turned to you for advice. She says to you, "I'd like to help these guys, but confidentially I'm wondering what's in it for me?" What would you say to Sharon?

11. Early in the chapter, under the section titled "Creating a New Venture Team," a quote is provided that reads as follows: "People are the one factor in production . . . that animates all others." In the context of everything you know and have learned about entrepreneurship, what does this quote mean to you?

12. Cindy Coombs, a professional investor, was having lunch with a colleague recently and said, "Do you remember Peter Kennedy, the entrepreneur we met the other day, who created an iPhone app that helps busy families keep track of their activities? I checked up on him, and he has all the right personal attributes not only to be an app developer but to be a successful entrepreneur. He's thinking about creating some additional family-focused apps, and I'm inclined to invest." Cindy's dinner companion said, "Really, tell me about him." What do you think Cindy would say if she were describing a person who had all the right personal attributes to be a successful entrepreneur?

13. Jim Lane is an executive with General Electric. A former coworker of his recently started a company and raised $1 million from a well-known angel investor even though he didn't need the money to launch the business. Jim thinks his friend is foolish and can't think of one reason to take money from an investor if you don't need it. If you were talking to Jim, what would you tell him about this situation?

14. Charlie Berry, Shelly Jones, Nancy Harder, Keith Hawkins, Jennifer Atwood, and Cliff Barnes are all experienced software engineers. For some time, they've been talking about starting a company—the six of them—around a software solution in which all of them have an interest. Based on the material in the chapter, what challenges are these six individuals likely to encounter co-founding a firm?

15. What type of networking opportunities are available via your college or university, or entrepreneurial-minded organizations in the city or town that you live in, which could be helpful to you in your entrepreneurial career?

YOU BE THE VC 9.1

Company: YouTern

Web: www.youtern.com
Twitter: YouTern
Facebook: YouTern

Business Idea: Create an online community that links interns (primarily college students) with entrepreneurial start-ups and change-oriented nonprofit organizations.

Pitch: Internships can help students prepare for professional careers through mentorship and on-the-job training. In many cases, internships lead to permanent employment in that they give an employer a good look at an individual (in terms of skills and work ethic, for example) that they may want to hire upon graduation. Internship opportunities are becoming more coveted than ever. According to the National Association of Colleges and Employers (NACE), the number of college students seeking internships in their field of study has increased from 10 percent to 70 percent in recent years. The tight job market and the leg up that having one or more internships on a résumé can provide a job seeker are the primary reasons for the increased interest in internships.

Until now, there hasn't been a good way for entrepreneurial-minded college students to connect with start-ups that are interested in providing internship opportunities. YouTern was created to fill this need. The company allows students interested in internships with start-ups to create profiles, which describe their aspirations, degree/major, location, and hours of availability. Start-ups create similar profiles describing their business, location, the type of intern they're looking for, and hours available. YouTern's proprietary software looks for matches, and then introduces the matched parties. The ability to place students as interns in both for-profit and not-for-profit organizations increases the number of people YouTern has a chance to serve or help.

As part of its commitment to helping college students land good jobs, YouTern is very active in providing interviewing tips and general career guidance. The company channels most of its advice through social media, such as its Facebook page and via Twitter. In fact, as of February 2011, the company had posted 7,072 tweets on its Twitter account and had 1,850 followers. YouTern also maintains a blog titled *The Savvy Intern*. The blog is available at www.youtern.com/thesavvyintern.

YouTern launched in mid-2010 and focused initially on California and Illinois. Its initial plans were to be nationwide by mid-2011.

Q&A: Based on the material covered in this chapter, what questions would you ask the firm's founders before making your funding decision? What answers would satisfy you?

Decision: If you had to make your decision on just the information provided in the pitch and on the company's Web site, would you fund this company? Why or why not?

YOU BE THE VC 9.2

Company: Foodspotting

Web: www.foodspotting.com
Twitter: foodspotting
Facebook: Foodspotting

Business Idea: Create a Web site and a smartphone app that provides a visual guide to great food and where to find it. Instead of reviewing restaurants, users will share where to find their favorite dishes and see what dishes other people have liked at the restaurants they visit.

Pitch: Foodspotting began in 2009 when its cofounders realized that while there were many restaurant review Web sites and apps, there was no easy way to find or rate specific dishes. As a result, if a person craved grilled salmon there was no way to discover the restaurant in their area that customers concluded served the best grilled salmon. Similarly, if a person visited a particular restaurant, there was no way to know what dishes the restaurant served that were its patrons' favorites.

Foodspotting was founded to fill these gaps. Here's how it works. The site includes two groups of people: foodspotters and foodseekers. Foodspotters share where to find specific foods they like, such as grilled salmon or crab cakes, by taking photos of the dishes as they're delivered to their table and then uploading them to Foodspotting's Web site. The photos are tagged with the restaurant name, dish name, location, and more so others can find it. Foodspotters can also "nom" (or nominate) their favorite dishes to give them extra visibility and attention. In exchange for their efforts, foodspotters earn badges and virtual tips, and can also become a dish expert by spotting five or more foods of the same type. Foodseekers are the opposite and do one of two things. They either look up a restaurant to find what the best

dishes are (as reported by the foodspotters), or search for a specific dish they're craving, like barbecue ribs, to see where the best barbecue rib dishes are being served in their area. Once a dish is posted on Foodspotting's Web site, users vote on the dish. The dishes are listed, by geographic area, in an attractive scrolling interface.

Foodspotting's service is free and is available on its Web site and iPhone app. The format doesn't provide restaurant reviews—only reviews of dishes. Every review comes with a picture of the food being reviewed. To make finding great food easier, Foodspotting recommends that foodspotters should upload only pictures of food they like. It's more of a recommendation app than a review app. As of early 2011, Foodspotting reported that its iPhone app had been downloaded more than 600,000 times. Apps for Android and BlackBerry smartphones are expected to be released soon.

Foodspotting will make money in two ways with the first being through its collaborations with brands like the Travel Channel for the purpose of creating local food guides. The second way the firm intends to generate income is by partnering with local restaurants to alert nearby Foodspotters to specials and discounts.

Q&A: Based on the material covered in this chapter, what questions would you ask the firm's founders before making your funding decision? What answers would satisfy you?

Decision: If you had to make your decision on just the information provided in the pitch and on the company's Web site, would you fund this company? Why or why not?

CASE 9.1

DRY Soda: How One Company Put the Right People in Place both Prelaunch and Postlaunch

Web: www.DRYsoda.com
Twitter: DRYSODA
Facebook: DRY Soda Co.

Bruce R. Barringer, *Oklahoma State University*
R. Duane Ireland, *Texas A&M University*

Introduction

In 2005, Sharelle Klaus was lamenting the lack of beverage choices for women who like upscale dining but can't drink alcohol while they're pregnant. A mother of

four, she had experienced this frustration before. Klaus would frequently dine out with her husband and others, but felt left out when he and their dinner companions ordered wine to complement their meals. The restaurants

(continued)

had sodas, like Coke and Pepsi, available along with teas and mineral water. But the choices seemed like a poor substitute for wine and Klaus felt they often detracted rather than added to her dining experience.

Thinking about this problem caused Klaus to formulate a business idea. What if she were to create an elegant soda that was nonalcoholic and dry—meaning it wasn't sweet—that could be paired with fine food? That would give anyone who didn't drink alcohol a special beverage to drink with fine food. And what if it was a high-margin drink that came in different flavors with the flavors paired differently with different types of food? That would be good for the waitstaff and the restaurant. If someone ordered a Diet Coke or sweet tea, the waitstaff could suggest one of her drinks that would not only bring out the flavor in the food and make the guest feel more special, but make the waitstaff (via the size of their tip) and the restaurant more money.

This was the idea that became DRY Soda, a sophisticated nonalcoholic beverage company that launched in 2005. DRY Soda launched with four flavors—lavender, lemongrass, rhubarb, and kumquat—and has since expanded to seven flavors. The firm experienced fast growth from the start; and, its products are now available throughout the United States, Canada, Europe, and parts of the Middle East. Some high-end restaurants are so taken with the concept that they have eliminated nonalcoholic alternatives such as soda, tea, fruit drinks, and mineral water, and now offer DRY Soda as their exclusive alternative to alcoholic beverages. DRY Soda is also available in a growing number of high-end grocery stores.

Prelaunch Advisers

One aspect of DRY Soda's story that's particularly interesting is the way the company came together, from a new-venture team perspective. Sharelle Klaus was one of the least likely people to have started DRY Soda. Klaus launched an Internet company, named Planet Squid, shortly after the Internet came online. It was an early version of MySpace for 8- to 13-year-old children. The company failed during the dot-com implosion, losing its investor's money. She next became the president of the Forum for Women Entrepreneurs (FEW), an advocacy group for female business owners. It was an organization that she had relied on during her Planet Squid days. Following that job, Klaus became a consultant for a company that helped airports privatize. The privatization of airports never caught on, and Klaus was between jobs when the DRY Soda idea occurred to her.

Klaus had no beverage industry experience—just a passion for food and wine and a lifelong interest in entrepreneurship. She did, however, quickly reach out to people who did have beverage experience to test whether DRY Soda was a viable concept. Her husband worked for DaVinci Gourmet, a food company, and she tapped several of his colleagues for advice—from the VP of sales to the woman who was in charge of customer education to a food chemist. The food chemist was particularly instrumental in helping her understand the process of developing and testing a new

beverage product. He laid out the process and explained to Klaus that beverage products are tested a minimum of 1,000 times before they're perfected.

Following the food chemist's advice, Klaus bought the testing equipment she needed and started working on the DRY Soda concept in her kitchen. She was put in touch with a flavor company that provided flavors. She had everyone she knew test the four flavors that made it and some that didn't, and tweaked the successful flavors as she went. Once she was satisfied with her initial four flavors, she took them to six influential people in the food business and asked for feedback. She also had a well-known Seattle-area chef (Klaus lived in Seattle) visit her home and try the flavors. She contacted a bottle company that had just the right off-the-shelf bottle that could be used for her beverages.

Getting initial distribution was a major hurdle. Klaus approached two major beverage distributors, Columbia and Alaska, and they both told her to get traction and then come to see them again. A key advantage of working with large distributors is that they go beyond warehousing and delivering product and actually help win customers. The second tier of distributors Klaus went to only warehoused and delivered product, so she became the sales force. She went from restaurant to restaurant in the Seattle area and had good luck explaining her concept and getting orders. Positive reviews in local press sources accelerated orders and she started gaining traction. She went back to Alaska, one of the major distributors she had talked to earlier, and they took her on. With Alaska on board, DRY Soda started taking off. Klaus funded the initial inventory and operations of the company with an SBA loan.

Postlaunch Team

In 2006, once DRY Soda started gaining significant traction, Klaus raised $750,000 in investment capital to scale the company and hire a management team. She hired four key people: a marketing director with 12 years of food and beverage industry experience, a COO (chief operating officer) with 10 years of experience as a supply chain manager with HP and a stint at a beverage company as COO, a PR person with a public relations firm that was helping DRY Soda with its marketing, and a sales executive who had six years of feet-on-the-ground sales experience with a beverage company. The COO had also at one time been a partner at a venture capital firm. Interestingly, every member of the initial management team signed on without a steady paycheck. Instead, they all agreed to start their careers with DRY Soda by receiving an equity stake in the business.

Subsequent Additions to the New-Venture Team

DRY Soda is now approximately six years old. The company remains private and by all outward appearances appears to be growing in a healthy, organic manner. In May 2007, during a period of particularly rapid growth, DRY Soda appointed Dan Ginsberg, the former CEO of Red Bull, to its board of directors. At that time, the board consisted of the following members:

DRY Soda Board During a Period of Rapid Growth in 2007

Sharelle Klaus	Founder/CEO
Dan Ginsberg	Former CEO of Red Bull
Paul Shipman	Redhook Ale Brewery
Stan Baty	Corus Estates and Vineyards

In regard to its core management team, since its initial hires were put in place in 2006, the company has added a chief financial officer and a director of communications.

Future Growth

DRY Soda has remained true to its initial vision in that the firm is still a premium-priced sophisticated bottled beverage that's sold primarily in high-end restaurants. It's tinkered with its flavors some, and its seven flavors now include cucumber, vanilla bean, juniper berry, lavender, lemongrass, blood orange, and rhubarb. The only products it sells beyond its staple bottled drinks are pack and shipping boxes, T-shirts, beverage accessories, and gifts. It also has a company store in Seattle, where it has an upscale "tasting room" for its drinks, similar to a wine bar in a winery. The tasting room is staffed by hosts who can recommend what DRY flavors will pair best with your next evening of entertaining or local dining spots where you can find DRY Soda.

Discussion Questions

1. Sharelle Klaus created DRY Soda with no beverage industry experience. Make a list of the ways that she dealt with her lack of industry experience. On a scale of 1 to 10 (10 is highest), how successful do you think Klaus has been in overcoming her lack of industry experience?
2. Evaluate Klaus's initial management team. Why do you think she selected the people that she did? What are some common attributes the people she selected possess?
3. What do you think would have happened if Klaus had decided to "go it alone" and create DRY soda without reaching out to people with beverage industry experience? Do you think it would have hurt her more in the prelaunch phase of the business, the postlaunch phase of the business, or equally in both phases?
4. Why do you think Klaus added Dan Ginsberg, the former CEO of Red Bull, to her board of directors in 2007? In your judgment, was Ginsberg a good choice? Evaluate Klaus's 2007 board of directors. Do some Internet research on each member of the board, and speculate on why Klaus added each of them to her board.

Application Questions

1. If DRY Soda had put together a board of advisers when the company was founded, what type of people should it have asked to participate?
2. Look at the "You Be the VC" 9.2 feature. What type of new-venture team should Foodspotting assemble? Make up a simulated new-venture team for Foodspotting that would be capable of growing the company.

Sources: Greg Galant and Sharelle Klaus, "VV Show #35," *Venture Voice Podcast*, www.venturevoice.com/2006/06/vv_show_35_sharelle_klaus_of_d.html (accessed March 20, 2011, originally posted on June 14, 2006); Bloomberg Businessweek, "DRY Soda Co.," http://investing.businessweek.com/research/stocks/private/snapshot.asp?privcapId=39796169, March 28, 2011; DRY Soda Web site, www.DRYsoda.com (accessed march 28, 2011).

CASE 9.2

Zappos: Making Human Resources the Key to Customer Service

Web: Zappos
Twitter: zappos
Facebook: Zappos.com

Bruce R. Barringer, *Oklahoma State University*
R. Duane Ireland, *Texas A&M University*

Introduction

Zappos.com is an online shoe and apparel retailer that has built a strong brand and has shown impressive sales growth since its founding. It's based in Henderson, Nevada, just outside Las Vegas. The company had zero sales in 1990, $370 million in 2005, and over $1 billion in 2008. In 2009, Amazon.com acquired Zappos for $1.2 billion with the agreement that it could operate

(continued)

autonomously and maintain its unique culture. Zappos's formula for success is seemingly simple. It acquires customers through word-of-mouth and search engine marketing (SEM) and then wows them with customer service that keeps them coming back. The popular press often touts Zappos as the classic example of what can be accomplished through exemplary customer service.

But what's really behind Zappos's extraordinary success? Its prices are slightly on the high end. Its Web site isn't fancy. And it sells shoes and clothing for crying out loud! How does Zappos consistently deliver such a high level of customer service that people are willing to buy shoes, clothing, and a variety of other items to the tune of $1 billion plus per year? Read on.

Why Shoes?

Zappos was founded by Nick Swinmurn. Swinmurn had such a hard time finding shoes that he started an e-commerce company to help people just like himself. He was turned away by investors who thought it was crazy to think that people would buy shoes online. Seriously—who buys shoes without trying them on first? Swinmurn persevered, heartened by the fact that over $2 billion in shoes are sold via mail order catalogs every year—so people do buy shoes without trying them on. Selling shoes is also a fundamentally good business. You don't need to educate people about the product—people know shoes. The brands are strong, and the margins are good. The average order on Zappos.com is over $100, and the margin is 50 percent. That leaves a lot of room for profit. It's also possible to run an effective SEM campaign for shoes. Try this: Search Google for "Nike shoes," "New Balance shoes," and "soccer shoes," one by one. How many times do you see search engine ads for Zappos to the right of the results? Many, right?

Customer Service

According to reliable reports, customer service is what makes Zappos special. Call center employees don't use scripts and aren't pressed to keep calls short. The longest recorded call was over five hours. Shipping and returns are free. The warehouse is open 24/7 so customers can place an order as late as 11 P.M. and still receive quick delivery. Behind the scenes, most orders are upgraded to next-day delivery so customers are pleasantly surprised when their order arrives before expected. Normally, the early arrival is accompanied by an e-mail message from Zappos saying that the order was upgraded to next-day delivery because you are a "valued customer."

Zappos also has a very liberal return policy. It will take returns for up to 365 days no questions asked. When a customer is on the phone with a Zappos employee and is struggling with which pair of shoes to buy, the Zappos employees will suggest that the customer buy both pairs, and simply return the less desirable shoes. If Zappos's warehouse is out of a pair of shoes a customer wants, Zappos will e-mail the customer links to other Web sites where the shoes are for sale. Zappos also does little things to help its

customers out. For example, its toll-free phone number is listed at the top of every page on its Web site. Employees are given sufficient autonomy so they can do what they believe is "right" for the customer. For example, on one occasion a woman called Zappos to return a pair of boots for her husband because he died in a car accident. The next day she received a flower delivery, which the call center employee had billed to Zappos without checking with her supervisor.

What all this effort has gotten Zappos is a loyal customer base and word-of-mouth advertising. Approximately 75 percent of Zappos's orders come from existing customers.

Tony Hsieh

CEO Tony Hsieh is at the center of everything Zappos does. In his early 20s, Hsieh started a company called LinkExchange, which let small companies barter for banner ads. Hsieh insisted that every e-mail coming into the company was answered promptly and politely. In college, Hsieh made money by selling pizzas out of his Harvard dorm room. A classmate, Alfred Lin, bought whole pizzas from Hsieh and resold them piece by piece, making more money. Hsieh sold LinkExchange to Microsoft for $265 million in 1998 and he and Lin started an angel investment fund. Zappos's founder Nick Swinmurn pitched Hsieh and Lin, trying to raise money. Hsieh was so impressed with Zappos's market opportunity that he invested in the firm and briefly served as Zappos's co-CEO with Swinmurn. It wasn't long before Hsieh and Lin were running Zappos. Hsieh became Zappos's CEO and Lin became the CFO in the early 2000s.

Hsieh isn't the typical CEO, and his values, personality, and approach to doing business have clearly shaped Zappos's culture. Hsieh works in an open space amid a cluster of employee cubicles. He hosts employee parties and barbecues at his home, encourages employees to hang out after work, and spends his spare time studying the science of happiness. Zappos employees are encouraged to decorate their work spaces. Hsieh's desk features jungle vines and an inflatable monkey.

Human Resources

While exemplary customer service may be what keeps Zappos's customers coming back, the root of the company's competitive advantage is its human resource management policies. The company is fiercely protective of its culture, which has been crafted to facilitate its high level of customer service. It's 10 core values, which define its culture, brand, and business strategies, are shown next. Every new employee, regardless of their assignment, is required to undergo a four-week customer loyalty training course, which includes at least two weeks of talking on the phone with customers in the call center. Employees enjoy free lunches, no-charge vending machines, a company library, a nap room, and free health care (although employees do pay for their dependents).

Zappos's 10 Core Values

1. Deliver WOW Through Service
2. Embrace and Drive Change
3. Create Fun and a Little Weirdness
4. Be Adventurous, Creative, and Open-Minded
5. Pursue Growth and Learning
6. Build Open and Honest Relationships with Communication
7. Build a Positive Team and Family Spirit
8. Do More with Less
9. Be Passionate and Determined
10. Be Humble

That's not all. After training, each new hire is given what Zappos calls "the offer." The company says to each new hire, "If you quit today, we'll pay you for the amount of time you've worked, plus $2,000." Why would Zappos do this? The answer to this question is simply—because the firm wants employees to quit if they don't like the Zappos' culture. The $2,000 payoff is small potatoes, Hsieh and his top management team believe, opposed to having a half-hearted employee on the payroll. Over 97 percent of employees who complete training turn down the offer.

Social Media

Another distinctive aspect of Zappos is its extensive use of social media, which includes Twitter, Facebook, and YouTube. More than 450 Zappos employees have Twitter accounts, one of which is Hsieh who has over 1.8 million followers. The company encouragement of Twitter use coincides with core value 6: Build Open and Honest Relationships with Communication. Employees do not use Twitter to spam followers about Zappos's products. Instead, they provide updates about what they're doing and what it's like to work at Zappos. Hsieh himself is very authentic in his tweets. For example, on one occasion, before going onstage for a tech conference, Hsieh tweeted: "Spilled Coke on left leg of jeans, so poured some water on right leg so looks like denim fade." Hsieh also uses Twitter to solicit customer feedback. In his tweets, he frequently refers to something Zappos is doing and asks, "What do you think about this?" The replies he gets are from Zappos employees, customers, and others.

What Lies Ahead

Not much has changed at Zappos since it was bought by Amazon.com in late 2009. It's still quirky and is reportedly profitable and growing. It has added to its product line—along with shoes and clothing, it now sells bags, housewares, beauty products, eyewear, jewelry, and several other categories of products.

Two main challenges lie ahead for Zappos. First is competition in its primary categories—shoes and clothing. Zappos is a mainstream online retailer that carries shoes and clothing across the price gamut. Its women's heels, for example, range from $525 Robert Clergerie Chantos to $39.50 Soft Style Angel IIs. The challenge with this strategy is that Zappos is now being attacked by niche players at both ends of the price spectrum. In shoes, for example, it's being attacked from the top by high-end online retailers like Bluefly (www.bluefly.com), which have a larger selection of high-end shoes than Zappos does, and from the bottom by low-end online shoe retailers like Payless Shoes (www.payless.com), which sells shoes for as little as $9.99. A similar dynamic exists in online clothing. Zappos also has competition from mainline online shoe and clothing retailers that sell across the price spectrum like it does. Competitors include Endless.com, Shoebuy.com, and JCPenny.com.

The second challenge is whether Zappos will be able to maintain its unique culture. Often, the quirky nature of a start-up culture gives way to a more formal culture as a company grows and matures. So far, Zappos has successfully resisted this trajectory, even though the firm now generates over $1 billion annually in sales revenue. A wild card regarding Zappos's culture is whether Amazon.com, its owner, will honor its commitment to allow Zappos to operate autonomously. If at some point Amazon.com decided to fold Zappos into its existing management structure, Zappos's culture would clearly change.

Discussion Questions

1. What are some key points/traits that make Tony Hsieh and Zappos so successful?
2. How would you describe Zappos's approach to human resource management? Do you think Zappos's approach to human resource management is unique to Zappos, or do you think many of the policies Zappos has adopted could be used successfully in other firms?
3. To what extent do you believe the story that Zappos excels because of customer service and its customer service excels because of savvy human resource management? If you believe the story, what can other entrepreneurs learn from Zappos's experiences?
4. Reflect on the two primary challenges facing Zappos identified at the end of the case. How do you think Zappos should respond to these challenges? In your opinion, what is Zappos's third primary challenge?

Application Questions

1. What can start-ups learn about building a successful company culture by familiarizing themselves with Zappos and Zappos's story?
2. Spend several days following Tony Hsieh's Twitter account. Describe your reaction to what you read. Also, access Zappos's YouTube channel at www.youtube.com/zappos. What seems to be the purpose of this initiative? Watch several of the videos that Zappos has posted. What did you learn about Zappos by watching these videos?

Sources: Zappos homepage, www.zappos.com (accessed May 11, 2011); M. Chafkin, "The Zappos Way of Managing," www.inc.com/magazine/20090501/the-zappos-way-of-managing_pagen_4.html (accessed May 11, 2011, originally posted on May 1, 2009); T. Hsieh, *Delivering Happiness* (New York: Hachette Book Group, 2010).

ENDNOTES

1. Personal interview with Sunil Rajaraman, March 25, 2011.

2. R. Zarutskie, "The Role of Top Management Team Human Capital in Venture Capital Markets: Evidence from First-Time Funds," *Journal of Business Venturing* 25, no. 1 (2010): 155–72; D. A. Harper, "Towards a Theory of Entrepreneurial Teams," *Journal of Business Venturing* 23, no. 6 (2008): 613–26.

3. J. Wiklund, T. Baker, and D. Shepherd, "The Age-Effect of Financial Indicators as Buffers Against the Liability of Newness," *Journal of Business Venturing* 25, no. 4 (2010): 423–37; A. Stinchcombe, "Social Structure and Organization," in *Handbook of Organizations*, ed. James G. March (Chicago: Rand McNally, 1965), 142–93.

4. C. Read, J. Ross, J. Dunleavy, D. Schulman, and J. Bramante, *eCFO* (Chichester, UK: John Wiley & Sons, 2001), 117.

5. R. Zoli, A. Kuckertz, and T. Kautonen, "Human Resource Flexibility and Strong Ties in Entrepreneurial Teams," *Journal of Business Research* (2011): in press; P. G. Klein, "Opportunity Discovery, Entrepreneurial Action, and Economic Organization," *Strategic Entrepreneurship Journal* 2, no. 3 (2008): 175–90.

6. D. Miller, I. Le Breton-Miller, and R. H. Lester, "Family and Lone Founder Ownership and Strategic Behaviour: Social Context, Identity, and Institutional Logics," *Journal of Management Studies* 48, no. 1 (2011): 1–25; L. He, "Do Founders Matter? A Study of Executive Compensation, Governance Structure and Firm Performance," *Journal of Business Venturing* 23, no. 3 (2008): 257–79.

7. D. Iacobucci and P. Rosa, "The Growth of Business Groups by Habitual Entrepreneurs: The Role of Entrepreneurial Teams," *Entrepreneurship Theory and Practice* 34, no. 2 (2010): 351–77; C. E. Shalley and J. E. Perry-Smith, "The Emergence of Team Creative Cognition: The Role of Diverse Outside Ties, Sociocognitive Network Centrality, and Team Evolution," *Strategic Entrepreneurship Journal* 2, no. 1 (2008): 23–41; D. P. Forbes, P. S. Borchert, M. E. Zellmer-Bruhn, and H. J. Sapienza, "Entrepreneurial Team Formation: An Exploration of New Member Addition," *Entrepreneurship Theory and Practice* 30, no. 3 (2006): 225–48.

8. M. S. Wood and W. McKinley, "The Production of Entrepreneurial Opportunity: A Constructivist Perspective," *Strategic Entrepreneurship Journal* 4, no. 1 (2010): 66–84.

9. M. Suster, "The Co-Founder Mythology," Both Sides of the Table Blog, www.bothsidesofthetable.com/2011/05/09/the-co-founder-mythology (accessed May 10, 2011, originally posted on May 9, 2011).

10. M.-D. Foo, "Teams Developing Business Ideas: How Member Characteristics and Conflict Affect Member-Rated Team Effectiveness," *Small Business Economics* 36, no. 1 (2011): 33–46; K. Eisenhardt and C. Schoonhoven, "Organizational Growth: Linking Founding Team, Strategy, Environment, and Growth Among U.S. Semiconductor Ventures, 1978–1988," *Administrative Science Quarterly* 35 (1990): 504–29.

11. M.-D. Foo, "Member Experience, Use of External Assistance and Evaluation of Business Ideas," *Journal of Small Business Management* 48, no. 1 (2010): 32–43.

12. J. W. Webb, D. A. Ketchen, Jr., and R. D. Ireland, "Strategic Entrepreneurship Within Family-Controlled Firms: Opportunities and Challenges," *Journal of Family Business Strategy* 1, no. 2 (2010): 67–77.

13. B. Vissa, "A Matching Theory of Entrepreneurs' Tie Formation Intentions and Initiation of Economic Exchange," *Academy of Management Journal* 54, no. 1 (2011): 137–58.

14. S. Gedeon, "Trust, Ethics, Character and Competence in Angel Investing," *Entrepreneurial Practice Review* 1, no. 4 (2011): 12–26.

15. H. Hoang and J. Gimeno, "Becoming a Founder: How Founder Role Identity Affects Entrepreneurial Transitions and Persistence in Founding," *Journal of Business Venturing* 25, no. 1 (2010): 41–53; D. B. Audretsch, W. Bonte, and M. Keilbach, "Entrepreneurial Capital and Its Impact on Knowledge Diffusion and Economic Performance," *Journal of Business Venturing* 23, no. 6 (2008): 687–98.

16. D. Sardanna and D. Scott-Kemmis, "Who Learns What?—A Study of Entrepreneurs from Biotechnology New Ventures," *Journal of Small Business Management* 48, no. 3 (2010): 441–68.

17. J. Brinckmann and M. Hoegl, "Effects of Initial Teamwork Capability and Initial Relational Capability on the Development of New Technology-Based Firms," *Strategic Entrepreneurship Journal* 5, no. 1 (2011): 37–57; K. Foss and N. J. Foss, "Understanding Opportunity Discovery and Sustainable Advantage: The Role of Transaction Costs and Property Rights," *Strategic Entrepreneurship Journal* 2, no. 3 (2008): 191–207.

18. C.-M. Lau, "Team and Organizational Resources, Strategic Orientations, and Firm Performance in a Transitional Economy," *Journal of Business Research* (2011): in press; P. C. Patel and S. Terjesen "Complementary Effects of Network Range and Tie Strength in Enhancing Transnational Venture Performance," *Strategic Entrepreneurship Journal* 5, no. 1 (2011): 58–80; T. E. Stuart and O. Sorenson, "Strategic Networks and

Entrepreneurial Ventures," *Strategic Entrepreneurship Journal* 1, nos. 3 and 4 (2008): 211–27.

19. M. Hughes, R. E. Morgan, R. D. Ireland, and P. Hughes, "Network Behaviours, Social Capital, and Organisational Learning in High-Growth Entrepreneurial Firms," *International Journal of Entrepreneurship and Small Business* 12, no. 3 (2011): 257–72; C. Sousa, M. Fontes, and P. Videira, "The Role of Entrepreneurs' Social Networks in the Creation and Early Development of Biotechnology Companies," *International Journal of Entrepreneurship and Small Business* 12, no. 2 (2011): 227–44.

20. *Small Business Digest*, "Finding the Right Employees Vexes Small-Business Leaders," www.2sbdigest.com/small-business-hires (accessed May 11, 2011, originally posted on May 11, 2011).

21. Trendsetter Barometer Business Outlook 3Q 2008, www.barometersurveys.com/production/barsurv.nsf/Barometer_Trendsetter, Fall 2008 (accessed November 15, 2008).

22. M. Henricks, "A Look Ahead," *Entrepreneur*, January 2007, 70–76.

23. D. Medland, "Employee Referrals: 'Our Hiring Created a Monoculture.'" *FT.com*, www.ft.com/cms/s/0/cd1 E38126-2eb7-11e0-9877-00144feabdc0.html# axzz1M3Hv5ux3 (accessed May 11, 2011, originally posted on February 3, 2011).

24. H. Schultz, *Pour Your Heart into It* (New York: Hyperion, 1997), 82.

25. T. Dalziel, R. J Gentry, and M. Bowerman, "An Integrated Agency-Resource Dependence View of the Influence of Directors' Human and Relational Capital on Firms' R&D Spending," *Journal of Management Studies* (2011): in press; R. H. Lester, A. Hillman, A. Zardkoohi, and A. A. Cannella, Jr., "Former Government Officials as Outside Directors: The Role of Human and Social Capital," *Academy of Management Journal* 51, no. 5 (2008): 999–1013.

26. D. P. Boyd, "Lessons from Turnaround Leaders," *Strategy & Leadership* 39, no. 3 (2011): 36–43; A. J. Hillman, C. Shropshire, and A. A. Cannella, Jr., "Organizational Predictors of Women on Corporate Boards," *Academy of Management Journal* 50, no. 4 (2007): 941–952.

27. R. Charan, *Boards at Work* (San Francisco: Jossey-Bass Publishers, 1998), 3.

28. B. L. Connelly, S. T. Certo, R. D. Ireland, and C. R. Reutzel, "Signaling Theory: An Assessment and Review," *Journal of Management* (2011): in press.

29. T. Mazzaroi, S. Reboud, and T. Volery, "The Influence of Size, Age and Growth on Innovation Management in Small Firms," *International Journal of Technology Management* 52, nos. 1–2 (2010): 98–117; P. Devorak, "Board of Advisers Can Help Steer Small Firms to Right Track," *Wall Street Journal*, March 3, 2008, B4.

30. A. Sherman, *Fast-Track Business Growth* (Washington, DC: Kiplinger Books, 2001).

31. Coolibar homepage, www.coolibar.com (accessed May 11, 2011).

32. Intouch Technologies homepage, www.intouch health.com (accessed May 11, 2011).

33. M. R. Bowers and I. Alon, "An Exploratory Comparison of US and International Academically Based Entrepreneurship Centres," *International Journal of Business and Globalisation* 5, no. 2 (2010): 115–34.

34. F. Bertoni, A. Croce, and D. D'Adda, "Venture Capital Investments and Patenting Activity of Hihg-Tech Start-Ups: A Micro-Econometric Firm-Level Analysis," *Venture Capital: An International Journal of Entrepreneurial Finance* 12, no. 4 (2010): 307–26; D. Dimov and D. De Clercq, "Venture Capital Investment Strategy and Portfolio Failure Rate: A Longitudinal Study," *Entrepreneurship Theory and Practice* 30 (2006).

35. J. S. Petty and M. Gruber, "In Pursuit of the Real Deal: A Longitudinal Study of VC Decision Making," *Journal of Business Venturing* 26, no. 2 (2011): 172–88; Y. Li, "Duration Analysis of Venture Capital Staging: A Real Options Perspective," *Journal of Business Venturing* 23, no. 5 (2008): 497–512.

36. G. D. Bruton, I. Filatochev, S. Chahine, and M. Wright, "Governance, Ownership Structure, and Performance of IPO Firms: The Impact of Different Types of Private Equity Investors and Institutional Environments," *Strategic Management Journal* 31, no. 5 (2010): 491–509.

37. R. Stross, *eBoys* (New York: Crown Books, 2000), 29.

38. T. Feng and G. Wang, "How Private Enterprises Establish Organizational Legitimacy in China's Transitional Economy," *Journal of Management Development* 29, no. 4 (2010): 377–93; D. Cumming, "Adverse Selection and Capital Structure: Evidence from Venture Capital," *Entrepreneurship Theory and Practice* 30 (2006): 155–83.

39. SCORE homepage, www.score.org (accessed May 11, 2011).

40. J. J. Chrisman and W. E. McMullan, "A Preliminary Assessment of Outsider Assistance as a Knowledge Resource: The Longer-Term Impact of New Venture Counseling," *Entrepreneurship Theory and Practice* 24, no. 1 (2000): 37–53.

Getting Personal *with* INDINERO

Cofounders:

JESSICA MAH
Computer Science
University of California Berkeley, 2010

ANDY SU
Computer Science
University of California Berkeley, 2010

Dialogue *with*
Jessica Mah

CURRENTLY IN MY SMARTPHONE
Born This Way by Lady Gaga

MY BIGGEST WORRY AS AN ENTREPRENEUR
Making bad hiring decisions

FIRST ENTREPRENEURIAL EXPERIENCE
Selling drawings as a 1st grader

BEST ADVICE I'VE RECEIVED
Be skeptical about all the advice you receive, even from people who seem successful and experienced.

WHAT I DO WHEN I'M NOT WORKING
Reading and playing video games

FAVORITE PERSON I FOLLOW ON TWITTER
Tony Hsieh

CHAPTER 10

Getting *Financing* or Funding

OPENING PROFILE

INDINERO
Raising Money Carefully and Deliberately

Web: www.indinero.com
Twitter: inDinero
Facebook: inDinero.com

Jessica Mah and Andy Su like to describe inDinero as the fastest way for small businesses to manage their finances. A small business owner can go to inDinero's Web site, establish an account, and enter his or her financial information. Once the information is entered, inDinero will fetch the individual's financial information and organize it into different categories. The system then periodically updates its users' budgets and provides them with an easy to use financial dashboard.

Mah's personal experiences were the inspiration for inDinero. Although Mah was only 20 when inDinero launched, she had owned businesses before and had come up empty-handed when she looked for a way to manage her business's finances online. When Mah and Su started investigating the possibility of launching an online financial dashboard for small businesses, they became even more convinced that it was a good idea. Their research showed that about 80 percent of small business owners are sole proprietors; unfortunately, experience suggests that they generally don't do a good job tracking their finances. Although there are products like QuickBooks and FreshBooks available, Mah and Su found that these types of products are used by small business accountants and bookkeepers, but not so much by small businesspeople themselves.

The idea for inDinero originated in mid-2009 while Mah and Su were still in college. They knew from the beginning that their business idea would be capital intensive, because a service provider would need to be employed to download their users' financial information from banks, credit card companies, investment funds, and the like. Mint.com, a financial dashboard for personal finances, used a company named Yodlee, which is capable of performing these tasks. The problem with Yodlee is that it's expensive. Mah and Su didn't have a lot of money. Their burn rate was almost zero since they were still in college. But they needed enough to pay Yodlee for a year of service and get

LEARNING OBJECTIVES

After studying this chapter you should be ready to:

1. Explain why most entrepreneurial ventures need to raise money during their early life.

2. Identify the three sources of personal financing available to entrepreneurs.

3. Provide examples of how entrepreneurs bootstrap to raise money or cut costs.

4. Identify the three steps involved in properly preparing to raise debt or equity financing.

5. Discuss the difference between equity funding and debt financing.

6. Explain the role of an elevator speech in attracting financing for an entrepreneurial venture.

7. Describe the difference between a business angel and a venture capitalist.

8. Explain why an initial public offering (IPO) is an important milestone in an entrepreneurial venture.

9. Discuss the SBA Guaranteed Loan Program.

10. Explain the advantages of leasing for an entrepreneurial venture.

inDinero up and running. They started by trying to obtain angel funding; but, their efforts were unsuccessful. In 2009, they also applied to TechStars, which is a Boulder, Colorado-based seed stage fund/incubator. TechStars provides seed funding and a three-month mentorship program in exchange for a flat 6 percent equity stake in the companies it accepts. They didn't get accepted. Fortunately, Mah and Su became aware of a grant program offered by Lightspeed Venture Partners, a Silicon Valley venture capital fund. They won a grant for $35,000, which was enough to bring Yodlee on board and get inDinero off the ground.

Over the next few months, late 2009 into early 2010, Mah and Su put a beta version of inDinero up and tried to obtain angel funding to further develop the company. No takers. What kept them going was the fact that they had users who were satisfied with the service. In April 2010, they applied to Y Combinator, which, similar to TechStars, is an organization that provides seed stage funding, mentorship, and networking opportunities to its participants in two three-month sessions per year. Y Combinator, which is run by Paul Graham, a highly regarded investor, takes an average 6 percent equity in the firms that it accepts in exchange for about $17,000 in funding. While the $17,000 would be helpful, what Mah and Su were really looking for was the network of potential investors to which Y Combinator could expose them. They were accepted and went through the Y Combinator experience in mid-2010. Mah and Su were unusual Y Combinator participants in that they already had an up-and-running business and customers. The Y Combinator experience couldn't have worked out better. They were introduced to a number of potential angel investors, received one-on-one mentorship from Paul Graham and others, and enhanced their legitimacy as a result of their association with the Y Combinator brand.

Fresh from the Y Combinator experience, Mah and Su were able to raise approximately $1 million from a group of angel investors. They weren't exposed to all the investors via Y Combinator. Instead, once they engaged an investor, they would ask him or her for the names of other investors that might be interested. The $1 million didn't come all at once. One thing Mah and Su learned, through the process of engaging angel investors, is that raising money takes patience. Some investors are quick to commit while others want to spend time getting to know the entrepreneurs they invest in before making a decision.

inDinero is currently using its investors' money to bolster its staff and the robustness of its service. It reportedly has over 15,000 users and is building for the future.

In general, start-ups often have difficulty raising money because they are unknown and untested. Founders must frequently use their own money, try to secure grants, or go to friends and family for help. This effort is often a grueling endeavor. Many entrepreneurs hear "no" multiple times before they are able to obtain funding for their venture.

In this chapter, we focus on the process of getting financing or funding. We begin by discussing why firms raise capital. We follow this with a description of personal financing and the importance of personal funds, capital from friends and family, and bootstrapping in the early life of a firm. We then turn to the different forms of equity, debt, and creative financing available to entrepreneurial ventures. We also emphasize the importance of preparing to secure these types of financing.

THE IMPORTANCE OF GETTING FINANCING OR FUNDING

Few people deal with the process of raising investment capital until they need to raise capital for their own firm. As a result, many entrepreneurs go about the task of raising capital haphazardly because they lack experience in this area and because they don't know much about their choices.[1] This shortfall may cause a business owner to place too much reliance on some sources of capital and not enough on others.[2] Entrepreneurs need to have as full an understanding as possible of the alternatives that are available in regard to raising money. And raising money is a balancing act. Although a venture may need to raise money to survive, its founders usually don't want to deal with people who don't understand or care about their long-term goals.

The need to raise money surprises a number of entrepreneurs in that many of them launch their firms with the intention of funding all their needs internally. Commonly, though, entrepreneurs discover that operating without investment capital or borrowed money is more difficult than they anticipated. Because of this, it is important for entrepreneurs to understand the role of investment capital in the survival and subsequent success of a new firm.

Why Most New Ventures Need Funding

There are three reasons that most entrepreneurial ventures need to raise money during their early life: cash flow challenges, capital investments, and lengthy product development cycles. These reasons are laid out in Figure 10.1. Let's look at each reason so we can better understand their importance.

> **LEARNING OBJECTIVE**
> 1. Explain why most entrepreneurial ventures need to raise money during their early life.

Cash Flow Challenges   As a firm grows, it requires an increasing amount of cash to operate as the foundation for serving its customers. Often, equipment must be purchased and new employees hired and trained before the increased customer base generates additional income. The lag between spending to generate revenue and earning income from the firm's operations creates cash flow challenges, particularly for new, often small, ventures as well as for ventures that are growing rapidly.

If a firm operates in the red, its negative real-time cash flow, usually computed monthly, is called its burn rate. A company's **burn rate** is the rate at which it is spending its capital until it reaches profitability. Although a negative cash flow is sometimes justified early in a firm's life—to build plants and buy equipment, train employees, and establish its brand—it can cause severe complications. A firm usually fails if it burns through all its capital before it becomes profitable. This is why inadequate financial resources is a primary reason new firms fail.[3] A firm can simply run out of money even if it has good products and satisfied customers.

Cash Flow Challenges	Capital Investments	Lengthy Product Development Cycles
Inventory must be purchased, employees must be trained and paid, and advertising must be paid for before cash is generated from sales.	The cost of buying real estate, building facilities, and purchasing equipment typically exceeds a firm's ability to provide funds for these needs on its own.	Some products are under development for years before they generate earnings. The up-front costs often exceed a firm's ability to fund these activities on its own.

FIGURE 10.1
Three Reasons Start-Ups Need Funding

Being an entrepreneur in the biotech industry requires a lot of determination and drive. The path to getting a new drug approved takes approximately eight years. This "tortoise-like pace" of new product development normally takes a substantial up-front investment before a payoff is realized.

To prevent their firms from running out of money, most entrepreneurs need investment capital or a line of credit from a bank to cover cash flow shortfalls until their firms can begin making money. It is usually difficult for a new firm to get a line of credit from a bank (for reasons discussed later). Because of this, new ventures often look for investment capital, bootstrap their operations, or try to arrange some type of creative financing.

Capital Investments   Firms often need to raise money early on to fund capital investments. Although it may be possible for the venture's founders to fund its initial activities, it becomes increasingly difficult for them to do so when it comes to buying property, constructing buildings, purchasing equipment, or investing in other capital projects. Many entrepreneurial ventures are able to delay or avoid these types of expenditures by leasing space or co-opting the resources of alliance partners. However, at some point in its growth cycle, the firm's needs may become specialized enough that it makes sense to purchase capital assets rather than rent or lease them.

Lengthy Product Development Cycles   In some industries, firms need to raise money to pay the up-front costs of lengthy product development cycles. For example, it typically takes between one and a half and two years to develop an electronic game. In the biotech industry, the path to commercial licensing takes approximately eight years.[4] This tortoise-like pace of product development requires substantial up-front investment before the anticipated payoff is realized. While the biotech industry is an extreme example, lengthy product development cycles are the realities ventures face in many industries.

Sources of Personal Financing

2. Identify the three sources of personal financing available to entrepreneurs.

Typically, the seed money that gets a company off the ground comes from the founders' own pockets. There are three categories of sources of money in this area: personal funds, friends and family, and bootstrapping. These sources are depicted in Figure 10.2 and are explained next.

Personal Funds	Friends and Family	Bootstrapping
Involves both financial resources and sweat equity. Sweat equity represents the value of the time and effort that a founder puts into a firm.	Often comes in the form of loans or investments, but can also involve outright gifts, foregone or delayed compensation, or reduced or free rent.	Finding ways to avoid the need for external financing through creativity, ingenuity, thriftiness, cost-cutting, obtaining grants, or any other means.

FIGURE 10.2
Sources of Personal Financing

Personal Funds   The vast majority of founders contribute personal funds along with sweat equity to their ventures.[5] In fact, the results of a Kauffman Foundation survey of nearly 5,000 new business owners indicate that just 10 percent of those surveyed used external sources of funds their first year of operation.[6] The numbers change some but not as much as you might think as firms get older. Results from a number of studies that have examined firms that have been in business for just a few years up to a total of eight years show that close to 50 percent of the firms received no external funding—the money came strictly from the personal funds of the founders and the profits of the firms. **Sweat equity** represents the value of the time and effort that a founder puts into a new venture. Because many founders do not have a substantial amount of cash to put into their ventures, it is often the sweat equity that makes the most difference.

Friends and Family   Friends and family are the second source of funds for many new ventures. This type of contribution often comes in the form of loans or investments, but can also involve outright gifts, foregone or delayed compensation (if a friend or family member works for the new venture), or reduced or free rent. For example, Cisco Systems, the giant producer of Internet routers and switches, started in the house of one of its cofounder's parents.

There are three rules of thumb that entrepreneurs should follow when asking friends and family members for money. First, the request should be presented in a businesslike manner, just like one would deal with a banker or investor. The potential of the business along with the risks involved should be carefully and fully described. Second, if the help the entrepreneur receives is in the form of a loan, a promissory note should be prepared, with a repayment schedule, and the note should be signed by both parties. Stipulating the terms of the loan in writing reduces the potential of a misunderstanding and protects both the entrepreneur and the friend or family member providing the funding. Third, financial help should be requested only from those who are in a legitimate position to offer assistance. It's not a good idea to ask certain friends or family members, regardless of how much they may have expressed a willingness to help, for assistance if losing the money would cripple them financially. Entrepreneurs who are unable to repay a loan to a friend or family member risk not only damaging their business relationship with them, but their personal relationship as well.[7]

LendingKarma (www.lendingkarma.com) helps people involved with friends and family develop loan documents and then track the loans. Following a simple set of online commands, a user can select a loan amount, designate if he or she is the borrower or lender, and set various options such as interest rate, payment frequency, and length of loan. A promissory note, in PDF format, can then be created along with an amortization schedule. LendingKarma will track the loan repayment. E-mail reminders can even be sent to the borrower, reminding the borrower of the amount and due date of an upcoming payment. LendingKarma has three different levels to their loan documenting service,

TABLE 10.1   EXAMPLES OF BOOTSTRAPPING METHODS

- Buy used instead of new equipment
- Coordinate purchases with other businesses
- Lease equipment instead of buying
- Obtain payments in advance from customers
- Minimize personal expenses
- Avoid unnecessary expenses, such as lavish office space or furniture
- Buy items cheaply, but prudently, through discount outlets or online auctions such as eBay, rather than at full-price stores
- Share office space or employees with other businesses
- Hire interns

starting at $14.95 for the basics and working up to $59.95 for the premium service.[8] Accountants, attorneys, and bankers can also help people structure loan agreements.[9]

Bootstrapping   Bootstrapping is a third source of seed money for new ventures. **Bootstrapping** is finding ways to avoid the need for external financing or funding through creativity, ingenuity, thriftiness, cost-cutting, or any means necessary.[10] (The term comes from the adage "pull yourself up by your bootstraps.") It is the term attached to the general philosophy of minimizing start-up expenses by aggressively pursuing cost-cutting techniques and money-saving tactics. There are many well-known examples of entrepreneurs who bootstrapped to get their companies started. Legend has it that Steve Jobs and partner Steve Wozniak sold a Volkswagen van and a Hewlett-Packard programmable calculator to raise $1,350, which was the initial seed capital for Apple Computer.

There are many ways entrepreneurs bootstrap to raise money or cut costs. Some of the more common examples of bootstrapping are provided in Table 10.1. A simple example of bootstrapping is that fax machines are no longer an absolute necessity, in most cases. There are several Web-based services that allow anyone to fax a document for free, as long as they have a scanner and are able to scan the document into a word processing program. The document can then be sent to the recipient's fax machine and it will print out as a normal fax. Examples of companies that offer variations of this service are FaxZero, Got Free Fax, and MyFax. The overarching point is that a little ingenuity (learning how to fax for free) can save an entrepreneur the cost of purchasing a fax machine.

While bootstrapping and using personal funds are highly recommended actions in almost all start-up situations, there are subtle downsides. Cost-cutting and saving money are admirable practices, but pushing these practices too far can hold a business back from reaching its full potential. For example, renting space in a community incubator or building where other start-ups are located, rather than working from home, may be worth it if it provides entrepreneurs access to a network of people who can be relied on to provide social support and business advice.[11]

Preparing to Raise Debt or Equity Financing

Once a start-up's financial needs exceed what personal funds, friends and family, and bootstrapping can provide, debt and equity are the two most common sources of funds. The most important thing an entrepreneur must do at this point is determine precisely what the company needs and the most appropriate source to use to obtain those funds. A carefully planned approach to raising money increases a firm's chance of success and can save an entrepreneur considerable time.

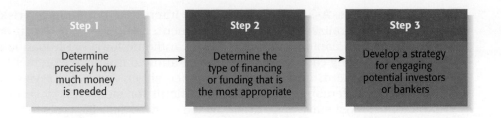

FIGURE 10.3
Preparation for Debt
or Equity Financing

The steps involved in properly preparing to raise debt or equity financing are shown in Figure 10.3 and are discussed next.

Step 1 **Determine precisely how much money the company needs** Constructing and analyzing documented cash flow statements and projections for needed capital expenditures are actions taken to complete this step. This information should already be in the business plan, as described in Chapter 4.

Knowing exactly how much money to ask for is important for at least two reasons. First, a company doesn't want to get caught short, yet it doesn't want to pay for capital it doesn't need. Second, entrepreneurs talking to a potential lender or investor make a poor impression when they appear uncertain about the amount of money required to support their venture.

Step 2 **Determine the most appropriate type of financing or funding** Equity and debt financing are the two most common alternatives for raising money. **Equity financing** (or funding) means exchanging partial ownership of a firm usually in the form of stock for funding in return. Angel investors, private placement, venture capital, and initial public offerings are the most common sources of equity funding (we discuss all these sources later in the chapter). Equity funding is not a loan—the money that is received is not paid back. Instead, equity investors become partial owners of the firm. Some equity investors invest "for the long haul" and are content to receive a return on their investment through dividend payments on their stock. More commonly, equity investors have a three- to five-year investment horizon and expect to get their money back, along with a substantial capital gain, through the sale of their stock. The stock is typically sold following a **liquidity event**, which is an occurrence that converts some or all of a company's stock into cash. The three most common liquidity events for a new venture are to go public, find a buyer, or merge with another company.

Because of the risks involved, equity investors are very demanding and fund only a small percentage of the business plans they consider.[12] An equity investor considers a firm that has a unique business opportunity, high growth potential, a clearly defined niche market, and proven management to be an ideal candidate. In contrast, businesses that don't fit these criteria have a hard time getting equity funding. Many entrepreneurs are not familiar with the standards that equity investors apply and get discouraged when they are repeatedly turned down by venture capitalists and angel investors. Often, the reason they don't qualify for venture capital or angel investment isn't because their business proposal is poor, but because they don't meet the exacting standards equity investors usually apply.[13]

Debt financing is getting a loan. The most common sources of debt financing are commercial banks and Small Business Administration (SBA) guaranteed loans. The types of bank loans and SBA guaranteed loans available to entrepreneurs are discussed later in this chapter. In general, banks lend money that must be repaid with interest. Banks

LEARNING OBJECTIVE
4. Identify the three steps involved in properly preparing to raise debt or equity financing.

LEARNING OBJECTIVE
5. Discuss the difference between equity funding and debt financing.

are not investors. As a result, bankers are interested in minimizing risk, properly collateralizing loans, and repayment, as opposed to return on investment and capital gains. The ideal candidate for a bank loan is a firm with a strong cash flow, low leverage, audited financial statements, good management, and a healthy balance sheet. A careful review of these criteria demonstrates why it's difficult for start-ups to receive bank loans. Most start-ups are simply too early in their life cycle to have the set of characteristics bankers want.

Table 10.2 provides an overview of three common profiles of new ventures and the type of financing or funding that is appropriate for each one. This table illustrates why most start-ups must rely on personal funds, friends and family, and bootstrapping at the outset and must wait until later to obtain equity or debt financing. Indeed, most new ventures do not have the characteristics required by bankers or investors until they have proven their product or service idea and have achieved a certain measure of success in the marketplace.

Step 3   **Developing a strategy for engaging potential investors or bankers**   There are three steps to developing a strategy for engaging potential investors or bankers. First, the lead entrepreneurs in a new venture should prepare an **elevator speech (or pitch)**—a brief, carefully constructed statement that outlines the merits of a business opportunity. Why is it called an elevator speech? If an entrepreneur stepped into an elevator on the 25th floor of a building and found that by a stroke of luck a potential investor was in the same elevator, the

TABLE 10.2   **MATCHING AN ENTREPRENEURIAL VENTURE'S CHARACTERISTICS WITH THE APPROPRIATE FORM OF FINANCING OR FUNDING**

Characteristics of the Venture	Appropriate Source of Financing or Funding
The business has high risk with an uncertain return:	Personal funds, friends, family, and other forms of bootstrapping
Weak cash flow	
High leverage	
Low-to-moderate growth	
Unproven management	
The business has low risk with a more predictable return:	Debt financing
Strong cash flow	
Low leverage	
Audited financials	
Good management	
Healthy balance sheet	
The business offers a high return:	
Unique business idea	Equity
High growth	
Niche market	
Proven management	

entrepreneur would have the time it takes to get from the 25th floor to the ground floor to try to get the investor interested in the business opportunity. Most elevator speeches are 45 seconds to 2 minutes long.[14]

There are many occasions when a carefully constructed elevator speech might come in handy. For example, many university-sponsored centers for entrepreneurship hold events that bring investors and entrepreneurs together. Often, these events include social hours and refreshment breaks designed specifically for the purpose of allowing entrepreneurs looking for funding to mingle with potential investors. An outline for a 60-second elevator speech is provided in Table 10.3.

The second step in developing a strategy for engaging potential investors or bankers is more deliberate and requires identifying and contacting the best prospects. First, the new venture should carefully assess the type of financing or funding it is likely to qualify for, as depicted in Table 10.2. Then, a list of potential bankers or investors should be compiled. If venture capital funding is felt to be appropriate, for example, a little legwork can go a long way in pinpointing likely investors. A new venture should identify the venture funds that are investing money in the industry in which it intends to compete and target those firms first. To do this, look to the venture capital firms' Web sites. These reveal the industries in which the firms have an interest. Sometimes, these sites also provide a list of the companies the firm has funded. For an example, access Sequoia Capital's Web site (www.sequoiacap.com), a well-known venture capital firm.

A cardinal rule for approaching a banker or an investor is to get a personal introduction. Bankers and investors receive many business plans, and most of them end up in what often becomes an unread stack of paper in a corner in their offices. To have your business plan noticed, find someone who knows the banker or the investor and ask for an introduction.

The third step in engaging potential investors or bankers is to be prepared to provide the investor or banker a completed business plan and make a presentation of the plan if requested. We looked at how to present a business plan in Chapter 4. The presentation should be as polished as possible and should demonstrate why the new venture represents an attractive endeavor for the lender or investor.

Because the process of raising money is complicated, it is important to obtain as much advice as possible for how to navigate the funding process. One source for obtaining seed funding and advice is to apply for admittance to a mentorship-driven seed stage fund/incubator. The two best known seed stage funds/incubators, which cater primarily to technology firms, are TechStars and Y Combinator. Both are described in this chapter's "Partnering for Success" feature.

TABLE 10.3   GUIDELINES FOR PREPARING AN ELEVATOR SPEECH

The elevator speech is a very brief description of your opportunity, product idea, qualifications, and market. Imagine that you step into an elevator in a tall building and a potential investor is already there; you have about 60 seconds to explain your business idea.

Step 1 Describe the opportunity or problem that needs to be solved	20 seconds
Step 2 Describe how your product or service meets the opportunity or solves the problem	20 seconds
Step 3 Describe your qualifications	10 seconds
Step 4 Describe your market	10 seconds
Total	60 seconds

TechStars and Y Combinator: A New Breed of Start-Up Incubators

TechStars: Web: www.techstars.org; Twitter: techstars; Facebook: TechStars
Y Combinator: Web: www.ycombinator.com; Twitter: ycombinator; Facebook: Y Combinator

There are two mentorship-driven seed stage funds/incubators that have been started in the past several years that have had considerable success: TechStars and Y Combinator. These are programs that must be applied for, and once accepted a start-up surrenders a small amount of equity for a similarly small amount of seed funding. The biggest advantage of getting into one of these programs is the mentorship opportunities the programs provide. In addition, being a TechStars or Y Combinator graduate is an increasingly valuable label for a technology start-up. Both TechStars and Y Combinator focus exclusively on technology firms.

TechStars

TechStars was started in Boulder, Colorado, in 2006, by David Cohen, Brad Feld, Jared Polis, and David Brown. It provides seed funding and three-month mentorship programs in exchange for a flat 6 percent stake in each company. The programs are run three times a year—spring, summer, and fall. TechStars has expanded beyond Boulder, and now runs its programs in New York City, Boston, and Seattle as well as in Boulder. The seed stage funding is up to $18,000. Start-ups get $6,000 per founder, up to three founders. TechStars also provides space for their start-ups to work from during the three-month experience.

The strength of TechStars, according to its founders, is the mentorship it provides. For the entrepreneurs it's an intense three-month immersion experience, in which each company is assigned four to six mentors who focus solely on that company. The program cumulates each session with an event in which the start-ups pitch their ideas to hundreds of investors. To date, over 70 percent of TechStars companies have either raised outside funding or become financially self-sustaining, which is an impressive success rate.

The TechStars program is designed to give start-ups a healthy start and improve their chances of success. David Cohen and Brad Feld, two of TechStars' founders, recently published a book titled *Do More Faster,* which describes the TechStars experience, and includes chapters written by TechStars' graduates and mentors.

Y Combinator

Y Combinator was started by in Boston, Massachusetts, in March 2005 by Paul Graham, Robert Morris, Trevor Blackwell, and Jessica Livingston. The firm has since been moved to the Silicon Valley. Similar to TechStars, it provides seed stage funding, mentorship, and networking opportunities to its participants in two three-month sessions per year. It takes an average of 6 percent equity in the firms that participate in exchange for about $17,000 in funding. Participants are asked to move to the San Francisco Bay area during their Y Combinator experience. Each cycle cumulates with Demo Day, in which the start-ups pitch their companies to a large audience of investors.

The Y Combinator experience is based largely around individual mentorship opportunities and weekly dinners, in which high-profile entrepreneurs are invited to speak to the group. Speakers speak strictly "off the record" and are encouraged to tell the inside story of how their companies overcame obstacles and became successful. Talks end with an intense Q&A period. Each dinner lasts several hours.

Individual mentorship opportunities happen during office hours the start-ups book online. Y Combinator maintains a staff that provides mentorship and advice, and utilizes select outside mentors. There is no limit to the amount of mentorship an individual start-up can obtain. About halfway through each cycle, Y Combinator holds an event called Angel Day, in which each start-up is paired with two angel investors. These angels meet regularly with the start-ups until Demo Day, when the program concludes. Earlier in the program, Y Combinator sponsors an event called Prototype Day. At Prototype Day, all the start-ups present to one another for the first time.

Clones

Several TechStars and Y Combinator clones have launched recently, and more are expected. An example is Imagine K12, an education-focused start-up accelerator that is modeled closely after Y Combinator. The first class was scheduled for the summer of 2011. K12 takes 6 percent equity in each of its participants in exchange for $15,000 to $20,000 in funding and participation in a mentorship program. Similarly, Rock Health is a new start-up accelerator in the health care industry. Its first class was also slated to start in the summer of 2011. It will grant each participant $20,000 in seed funding for an unspecified amount of equity.

Questions for Critical Thinking

1. If you were starting a technology company, do you think you'd benefit from participating in either

TechStars or Y Combinator? If so, what do you think the primary benefits would be?

2. Find an example of a start-up accelerator not mentioned in this feature. Describe the amount of equity the accelerator takes, how much seed funding is awarded, and in general how the program works.

3. If a business or entrepreneurship student has a technology-related business idea, what should the student do while in college to improve his or her chances of getting accepted by a program like TechStars or Y Combinator?

4. Why do you think being a TechStar or Y Combinator graduate is an increasingly valuable label for a technology start-up?

Sources: TechStars Web site, www.techstars.org (accessed April 5, 2011); Y Combinator Web site, www.ycombinator.com (accessed April 5, 2011); Michael Arrington, "Startup Veterans Launch Imagine K12, a 'Y Combinator for Education Startups,'" TechCrunch, http://techcrunch.com/2011/03/17/startup-veterans-launch-imagine-k12-a-y-combinator-for-education-startups (accessed April 2, 2011, originally posted on March 17, 2011); Rock Health Web site, http://rockhealth.com (accessed April 2, 2011).

SOURCES OF EQUITY FUNDING

The primary disadvantage of equity funding is that the firm's owners relinquish part of their ownership interest and may lose some control. The primary advantage is access to capital. In addition, because investors become partial owners of the firms in which they invest, they often try to help those firms by offering their expertise and assistance. Unlike a loan, the money received from an equity investor doesn't have to be paid back. The investor receives a return on the investment through dividend payments and by selling the stock.

The three most common forms of equity funding are described next.

Business Angels

Business angels are individuals who invest their personal capital directly in start-ups. The term *angel* was first used in conjunction with finance to describe wealthy New Yorkers who invested in Broadway plays. The prototypical business angel, who invests in entrepreneurial start-ups, is about 50 years old, has high income and wealth, is well educated, has succeeded as an entrepreneur, and invests in companies that are in the region where he or she lives.[15] These investors generally invest between $10,000 and $500,000 in a single company and are looking for companies that have the potential to grow 30 to 40 percent per year before they are acquired or go public.[16] Jeffrey Sohl, the director of the University of New Hampshire's Center for Venture Research, estimates that only 10 to 15 percent of private companies meet that criterion.[17] Many well-known firms have received their initial funding from one or more business angels. For example, Apple received its initial investment capital from Mike Markkula, who obtained his wealth as an executive with Intel. In 1977, Markkula invested $91,000 in Apple and personally guaranteed another $250,000 in credit lines. When Apple went public in 1980, his stock in the company was worth more than $150 million.[18] Similarly, in 1998, Google received its first investment from Sun Microsystems' cofounder Andy Bechtolsheim, who gave Larry Page and Sergey Brin (Google's cofounders) a check for $100,000 after they showed him an early version of Google's search engine.[19] Can you image what Bechtolsheim's investment was worth when Google went public in 2005?

The number of angel investors in the United States, which is estimated to be around 265,400, has increased dramatically over the past decade.[20]

LEARNING OBJECTIVE
7. Describe the difference between a business angel and a venture capitalist.

The rapid increase is due in part to the high returns that some angels report. In 2010, angels invested $20.1 billion in 61,900 small companies.[21] By comparison, during that same period, venture capital funds invested about $21.8 billion in 3,276 deals.[22] Health care services/medical devices and equipment accounted for the largest share of angel investment in 2010, with 30 percent of total investment, followed by software (16 percent), biotech (15 percent), industrial/energy (8 percent), retail (5 percent), and IT services (5 percent).[23] While most venture capitalists have a three- to five-year investment horizon, business angels are typically more patient, although at some point will look for an exit. In 2010, mergers and acquisitions represented 66 percent of angel exits, and bankruptcies accounted for 27 percent. About half of the angel exits were at a profit. Annual returns for angel exits (mergers and acquisitions and initial public offerings—IPOs) were between 24 and 36 percent, although the returns vary widely.

Business angels are valuable because of their willingness to make relatively small investments. This gives access to equity funding to a start-up that needs just $50,000 rather than the $1 million minimum investment that most venture capitalists require. Many angels are also motivated by more than financial returns; they enjoy the process of mentoring a new firm. Most angels remain fairly anonymous and are matched up with entrepreneurs through referrals. To find a business angel investor, an entrepreneur should discretely work a network of acquaintances to see if anyone can make an appropriate introduction. An advantage that college students have in regard to finding business angels is that many angels judge college- or university-sponsored business plan competitions. The number of organized groups of angels continues to grow. Typically, each group consists of 10 to 150 angel investors in a local area that meet regularly to listen to business plan presentations. While some groups focus on a specific industry, most are open to a variety of areas and select those markets with which some of their members have expertise. The Angel Capital Education Foundation provides a list of angel groups in the United States and Canada on its Web site (www.angelcapital-education.org). In many areas, local governments and nonprofit organizations are active in trying to bring entrepreneurs and angel investors together. According to the Center for Venture Research, approximately 18.4 percent of people who are provided the opportunity to pitch to business angels receive an investment.[24]

There are a growing number of organizations dedicated to helping entrepreneurs connect with business angels. Some are free to the entrepreneurs and others are not, as described in the "Savvy Entrepreneurial Firm" feature.

Venture Capital

Venture capital is money that is invested by venture capital firms in start-ups and small businesses with exceptional growth potential.[25] There are about 800 venture capital firms in the United States, which have approximately $179 billion under management.[26] In 2010, venture capital firms invested $21.8 billion in just over 3,276 deals.[27] The peak year for venture capital investing was 2000, when $98.6 billion was invested at the height of the e-commerce craze. A distinct difference between angel investors and venture capital firms is that angels tend to invest earlier in the life of a company, whereas venture capitalists come in later. The majority of venture capital money goes to follow-on funding for businesses originally funded by angel investors, government programs (which are discussed later in the chapter), or by some other means.

Venture capital firms are limited partnerships of money managers who raise money in "funds" to invest in start-ups and growing firms. The funds, or

Many business angels are "hands on" and like to involve themselves in the start-ups they invest in. Here, an angel investor is providing feedback to the cofounders of a Web-based company that he recently invested in.

© Kablonk/SuperStock

pools of money, are raised from high net worth individuals, pension plans, university endowments, foreign investors, and similar sources. The investors who invest in venture capital funds are called **limited partners**. The venture capitalists, who manage the fund, are called **general partners**. In 2009, the average fund size was $151 million.[28] The venture capitalists who manage the fund receive an annual management fee in addition to 20 to 25 percent of the profits earned by the fund. The percentage of the profits the venture capitalists get is called the **carry**. So if a venture capital firm raised a $100 million fund and the fund grew to $500 million, a 20 percent carry means that the firm would get, after repaying the original $100 million, 20 percent of the $400 million in profits, or $80 million. Some venture capital "funds" invest in specific areas. For example, Khosla Ventures invests strictly in clean tech and information technology companies.[29] Similarly, BEV Capital invests exclusively in consumer-oriented businesses, such as 1800diapers, Inc., and Cool Cuts 4 Kids.[30]

Because of the venture capital industry's lucrative nature and because in the past venture capitalists have funded high-profile successes such as Google, Cisco Systems, eBay, and Facebook, the industry receives a great deal of attention. But actually, venture capitalists fund very few entrepreneurial ventures in comparison to business angels and relative to the number of firms seeking funding. Remember, venture capitalists fund about 3,000 to 4,000 companies per year, compared to 61,900 funded by business angels. As mentioned earlier in this chapter, many entrepreneurs become discouraged when they are repeatedly rejected for venture capital funding, even though they may have an excellent business plan. Venture capitalists are looking for the "home run," a focus causing venture capitalists to reject the majority of the proposals they consider.

Venture capitalists know that they are making risky investments and that some of them will not be successful. In fact, most venture firms anticipate that about 20 percent or less of their investments will be home runs, 40 percent will

SAVVY ENTREPRENEURIAL FIRM

Open Angel Forum and AngelList: New Options for Getting in Front of Angel Investors

Open Angel Forum: Web: http://openangelforum.com; Twitter: openangelforum
AngelList: Web: http://angel.co; Twitter: angellist

There are three ways of getting in front of angel investors. First, contact the angel investor directly, either yourself or via a referral. Second, enroll in a "pay to pitch" forum such as DEMO (www.demo.com). And third, try out one of the new services that allow entrepreneurs to pitch angel investors for free. Of the three, the most controversial is the pay-to-pitch forums. There is no guarantee that paying a fee, which can run from several hundred dollars to $5,000 or more, will win a start-up an investor's support. In addition, outspoken critics of pay-to-pitch services argue that the services take advantage of entrepreneurs who are desperate to obtain investment capital but often have very little chance of doing so.

As a counter to pay-to-pitch services, several initiatives have launched that bring together entrepreneurs and angel investors at no cost to the entrepreneur. These services are open to anyone with promising business plans. One is Open Angel Forum, which holds free pitch events several times a year across the United States and will soon expand overseas. It is run by Jason Calacanis, the founder/CEO of Mahalo, and host of This Week in Startups, a popular start-up-focused podcast. Calacanis screens applicants, picks the most promising, and then allows them to pitch to a room of 20 to 30 angel investors. In Open Angel Forum's first event in February 2010, three of the six companies that pitched found new investors. The investors are also pre-screened. Each of the 20 to 30 angel investors who are included must have made at least three or four notable angel investments within the last year. Open Angel Forum is funded via sponsorships and by selling seats to service providers.

Another free service, AngelList, was started in 2010 by angels Naval Ravikant and Babak Nivi. Any start-up can post its business idea and funding request, and the managers of the site vet the start-ups and pick the most promising ones. The most promising ones are

placed on a "list" that's e-mailed each week to a group of 200 active angel investors. The start-ups that have the best shot at making the list typically have some traction (i.e., sales), have social proof (i.e., are able to cite two to three influential people who are on their board of advisers), and have a clear value proposition. A start-up can also be recommended by a current angel investor. It's not uncommon for a start-up to pitch an angel investor, for example, who doesn't invest, not because they don't believe in the start-up but because the timing isn't right or the start-up is in an industry the angel isn't investing in. AngelList provides an opportunity for the investor to help the start-up by recommending that it be placed on the list. The angel investor's name will appear as recommending the start-up to others.

Questions for Critical Thinking

1. At what point do you think a start-up should be before applying to Open Angel Forum or AngelList? Spend some time looking at the Web sites of both organizations before formulating your answer.
2. According to DEMO's Web site, it cost $18,500 to pitch at a DEMO event. Spend some time looking at DEMO's Web site. Do you think it's worth $18,500 to pitch at a DEMO event? To what degree do you agree with the critics who feel that pay-to-pitch events are inappropriate?
3. What do you believe are the keys, from the entrepreneur's point of view, to making it through the vetting process for both Open Angel Forum and AngelList, and having the opportunity to pitch to angel investors?
4. Why do you think angel investors participate in services like Open Angel Forum and AngelList?

Source: S. Austin, "Start-Ups Get Free Change to Pitch to Angel Investors," *Wall Street Journal*, June 17, 2010, B5.

return modest amounts of capital, and 40 percent will fail.[31] The home runs must be sensational to make up for the modest-return firms and the failures.

Still, for the firms that qualify, venture capital is a viable alternative to equity funding. An advantage to obtaining this funding is that venture capitalists are extremely well connected in the business world (by this we mean that they have a large number of useful contacts with customers, suppliers, government representatives, and so forth) and can offer a firm considerable assistance beyond funding. Firms that qualify typically obtain their money in stages that correspond to their own stage of development. Once a venture capitalist makes an investment in a firm, subsequent investments are made in **rounds** (or stages) and are referred to as **follow-on funding**. Table 10.4 shows the various stages in the venture capital process, from the seed stage to buyout financing.

An important part of obtaining venture capital funding is going through the **due diligence** process, which refers to the process of investigating the merits of a potential venture and verifying the key claims made in the business plan. Firms that prove to be suitable for venture capital funding should conduct their own due diligence of the venture capitalists with whom they are working to ensure that they are a good fit. An entrepreneur should ask the following questions and scrutinize the answers to them before accepting funding from a venture capital firm:

■ Do the venture capitalists have experience in our industry?

■ Do they take a highly active or passive management role?

■ Are the personalities on both sides of the table compatible?

■ Does the firm have deep enough pockets or sufficient contacts within the venture capital industry to provide follow-on rounds of financing?

■ Is the firm negotiating in good faith in regard to the percentage of our firm they want in exchange for their investment?

Along with traditional venture capital, there is also **corporate venture capital**. This type of capital is similar to traditional venture capital except that the money comes from corporations that invest in start-ups related to their areas of interest. In 2010, there were 469 corporate venture capital deals involving $1.89 billion.[32]

Just because a firm receives venture capital funding doesn't mean it's a sure success. In fact, venture-funded firms are under extreme pressure to perform to meet the expectations of their investors. A firm that received venture capital funding, Letsbuyit.com, and regrettably failed, is profiled in the "What Went Wrong?" feature.

TABLE 10.4   STAGES (OR ROUNDS) OF VENTURE CAPITAL FUNDING

Stage or Round	Purpose of the Funding
Seed funding	Investment made very early in a venture's life to fund the development of a prototype and feasibility analysis.
Start-up funding	Investment made to firms exhibiting few if any commercial sales but in which product development and market research are reasonably complete. Management is in place, and the firm has its business model. Funding is needed to start production.
First-stage funding	Funding that occurs when the firm has started commercial production and sales but requires financing to ramp up its production capacity.
Second-stage funding	Funding that occurs when a firm is successfully selling a product but needs to expand both its capacity and its markets.
Mezzanine financing	Investment made in a firm to provide for further expansion or to bridge its financing needs before launching an IPO or before a buyout.
Buyout funding	Funding provided to help one company acquire another.

WHAT WENT WRONG?

How One Start-up Caught the Attention of VCs, Raised Money, and Still Failed

In January 1999, a group of serial Swedish entrepreneurs, including John Palmer and Johan Stael von Holstein, launched a Pan European Internet company with a promise to reinvent the retail market.

On face value, their internet start-up, Letsbuyit.com, did appear to have a genuinely original business model. Members would request products or services on the site and the company would find a wholesaler and negotiate a bulk discount for them. Thus, for example, if 49 people signed up to buy a stainless steel cafetiere, the price would drop from $25 to only $10. If the company went on to find 99 buyers, the price dropped again to $9.

Letsbuyit was not likely to be overlooked by its potential customers either. The company spent $100 million on an ambitious worldwide advertising campaign—a figure which was in the same league as the amount being spent by Amazon.com and American Online at that time. Before long, global TV screens were invaded by commercials showing armies of cartoon ants extolling the virtues of Letsbuyit.

In the early months, this was all funded by investments from VCs after Letsbuyit completed an exhausting seven rounds of funding to raise more than $180 million. Early stage investors included the London-based Henderson Capital, Deutsche Bank, ProSieben, and the Netherlands-based Glide and NesBic. The cash was invested in the advertising, the sophisticated IT system that backed the group buying model, and in opening a succession of European offices.

This was, however, apparently not enough. In early 2000, Letsbuyit announced plans to raise up to $110 million in a flotation on Germany's Neuer Markt, valuing the company at several hundred million euros. By this time though, investors were beginning to get nervous.

Letsbuyit's timing could not have been worse. By the time it announced its floatation, technology shares were in steady decline. The much-expected bursting of the dot-com bubble had begun.

Yet, the problems did not just stem from the fact that dot-com stocks were beginning to lose their value in stock markets across the world. It seemed that investors were starting to question the Letsbuyit business model altogether and asked if it would ever realize the profits it would need to justify this sky-high valuation.

Their concerns were founded on many fronts. Investors wondered if Letsbuyit had simply stretched itself too thin for a start-up. From day one, the founders had been highly ambitious and were soon operating across 14 European countries, in 12 different languages. This translated into high marketing and infrastructure costs, and, it emerged, much of the network was failing to pull its weight. Letsbuyit was deriving a disproportionate amount of revenue from Germany and Austria.

Worse still were the miniscule margins that Letsbuyit were working with. Many of the much-vaunted discounts were actually pretty unimpressive compared to those available elsewhere, or simply unobtainable because of a lack of scale. After finding it hard to persuade enough people to sign up, Letsbuyit assigned most of the advantages of bulk buying to customers as an incentive. The firm's shareholders received virtually no advantages at all. Under the harsh spotlight of fund-raising, Letsbuyit's model was becoming highly questionable.

Then there were the rumors of bickering among the senior managers at Letsbuyit and among the heads of each of the 14 European centers, all who were keen to push their own agenda and make their voice heard.

What followed next was what can only be called a rollercoaster ride for Letsbuyit. The share listing was initially postponed, then when it did float in July 2000 it only managed to raise $60 million, which was well short of what it hoped for. It was also well short of the $180 million the firm needed in order to break even by the end of 2002.

By October 2000, Letsbuyit started to look for a strategic partner, but was unsuccessful. Four months later, the firm's management board resigned en masse. In December 2000, Letsbuyit sought the European equivalent of the U.S. Chapter 11 bankruptcy, with its shares trading at little more than 1 cent on the Neuer Markt.

Questions for Critical Thinking

1. Examine each of the four problems that Letsbuyit encountered. How could the company have avoided or navigated around each problem?
2. One of the problems that Letsbuyit encountered is that it went out to too many markets too quickly. How should a start-up find the sweet spot of launching to a broad enough market, but not overstretching itself?
3. Why do start-ups raise money in rounds? Knowing that the fund-raising process is very time consuming, wouldn't it be better to raise all the money at once?
4. In recent years, group buying Web sites have really taken off, with big names such as Groupon, Groupola, Crowdity, and Incahoot. If you were given the task of starting a group buying company to capture some of this energy, what type of company would you start?

Sources: "Letsbuyit.com—Another Internet Start Falls," *Economist*, www.eiu.com/index.asp?layout=ib3PrintArticle&article_id=1586041158& printer=printer&rf=0 (accessed September 5, 2001, originally posted January 8, 2001); "Letsbuyit.com Shares Suspended," BBC News, http://news.bbc.co.uk/2/hi/business/1092257.stm (accessed September 5, 2011, originally accessed December 29, 2000); D. Milmo, "Showdown Looms for Letsbuyit.com," *Guardian.co.uk*, www.guardian.co.uk/media/2001/jan/04/citynews.newmedia (accessed September 5, 2011, originally posted January 19, 2001); "Letsbuyit Foundered as Failure Fouled the Air," *The Times*, http:// business.timesonline.co.uk (accessed September 5, 2011, originally posted November 8, 2002).

Initial Public Offering

Another source of equity funding is to sell stock to the public by staging an **initial public offering (IPO)**. An IPO is the first sale of stock by a firm to the public. Any later public issuance of shares is referred to as a **secondary market offering**. When a company goes public, its stock is typically traded on one of the major stock exchanges. Most entrepreneurial firms that go public trade on the NASDAQ, which is weighted heavily toward technology, biotech, and small-company stocks.[33] An IPO is an important milestone for a firm.[34] Typically, a firm is not able to go public until it has demonstrated that it is viable and has a bright future.

Firms decide to go public for several reasons. First, it is a way to raise equity capital to fund current and future operations. Second, an IPO raises a firm's public profile, making it easier to attract high-quality customers, alliance partners, and employees. Third, an IPO is a liquidity event that provides a mechanism for the company's stockholders, including its investors, to cash out their investments. Finally, by going public, a firm creates another form of currency that can be used to grow the company. It is not uncommon for one firm to buy another company by paying for it with stock rather than with cash.[35] The stock comes from "authorized but not yet issued stock," which in essence means that the firm issues new shares of stock to make the purchase. Examples of well-known American firms that have gone public in recent years include Vitamin Shoppe, LinkedIn, Rosetta Stone, Rackspace, and Team Health.

Although there are many advantages to going public, it is a complicated and expensive process and subjects firms to substantial costs related to SEC reporting requirements. Many of the most costly requirements were initiated by the **Sarbanes-Oxley Act** of 2002. The Sarbanes-Oxley Act is a federal law that was passed in response to corporate accounting scandals involving prominent corporations, like Enron and WorldCom. This wide-ranging act established a number of new or enhanced reporting standards for public corporations.

The first step in initiating a public offering is for a firm to hire an investment bank. An **investment bank** is an institution that acts as an underwriter or agent for a firm issuing securities.[36] The investment bank acts as the firm's advocate and adviser and walks it through the process of going public. The most important issues the firm and its investment bank must agree on are the amount of capital needed by the firm, the type of stock to be issued, the price of the stock when it goes public (e.g., $20 per share), and the cost to the firm to issue the securities.

There are a number of hoops the investment bank must jump through to assure the Securities and Exchange Commission (SEC) that the offer is legitimate. During the time the SEC is investigating the potential offering, the investment bank issues a **preliminary prospectus** that describes the offering to the general public. The preliminary prospectus is also called the "red herring." After the SEC has approved the offering, the investment bank issues the **final prospectus**, which sets a date and issuing price for the offering.

In addition to getting the offering approved, the investment bank is responsible for drumming up support for the offering. As part of this process, the investment bank typically takes the top management team of the firm wanting to go public on a **road show**, which is a whirlwind tour that consists of meetings in key cities where the firm presents its business plan to groups of investors.[37] Until December 1, 2005, the presentations made during these road shows were seen only by the investors physically present in the various cities; an SEC regulation went into effect at that time requiring that road show presentations be taped and made available to the public. Road show presentations can be viewed online at www.retailroadshow.com. If enough interest in a potential public offering is created, the offering will take place on the date scheduled in the prospectus. If it isn't, the offering will be delayed or canceled.

An initial public offering is a big step for an entrepreneurial firm. LinkedIn staged its IPO on May 22, 2011. It opened the day at $45 a share and its shares skyrocketed 80 percent before the end of the first day of trading.

Stan Honda/AFP/Getty Images/Newscom

Timing and luck play a role in whether a public offering is successful. For example, a total of 332 IPOs raised about $50 billion in 1999, the height of the Internet bubble. When the bubble burst in early 2001, the IPO marketplace all but dried up, particularly for technology and telecom stocks. Since then, the market has recovered some, although it is still not robust, and most firms cannot count on an IPO to raise capital or as an exit strategy. There were 157 IPOs in 2010, 63 in 2009, and 32 in 2008. The vitality of the IPO market hinges largely on the state of the overall economy and the mood of the investing public, as evidenced by the sharp downturn in numbers in 2008, a bad year for the U.S. economy. Analysts project that the 2011 and the 2012 numbers of IPOs will exceed those recorded in 2010. However, even when facing a strong economy and a positive mood toward investing, an entrepreneurial venture should guard itself against becoming caught up in the euphoria and rushing its IPO.

A variation of the IPO is a **private placement**, which is the direct sale of an issue of securities to a large institutional investor. When a private placement is initiated, there is no public offering, and no prospectus is prepared.

SOURCES OF DEBT FINANCING

Debt financing involves getting a loan or selling corporate bonds. Because it is virtually impossible for a new venture to sell corporate bonds, we'll focus on obtaining loans.

There are two common types of loans. The first is a **single-purpose loan**, in which a specific amount of money is borrowed that must be repaid in a fixed amount of time with interest. The second is a **line of credit**, in which a borrowing "cap" is established and borrowers can use the credit at their discretion. Lines of credit require periodic interest payments.

There are two major advantages to obtaining a loan as opposed to equity funding. The first is that none of the ownership of the firm is surrendered—a major advantage for most entrepreneurs. The second is that interest payments on a loan are tax deductible in contrast to dividend payments made to investors, which aren't.

There are two major disadvantages of getting a loan. The first is that it must be repaid, which may be difficult in a start-up venture in which the entrepreneur is focused on getting the company off the ground. Cash is typically "tight" during a new venture's first few months and sometimes for a year or more. The second is that lenders often impose strict conditions on loans and insist on ample collateral to fully protect their investment. Even if a start-up is incorporated, a lender may require that an entrepreneur's personal assets be collateralized as a condition of the loan. In addition, a lender may place a stipulation on a loan, such that the borrower must "maintain a cash balance of $25,000 or more" in its checking account or the loan will become due and payable.

The three common sources or categories of debt financing available to entrepreneurs are described next.

Commercial Banks

Historically, commercial banks have not been viewed as practical sources of financing for start-up firms.[38] This sentiment is not a knock against banks; it is just that banks are risk averse, and financing start-ups is risky business. Instead of looking for businesses that are "home runs," which is what venture capitalists seek to do, banks look for customers who will reliably repay their loans. As shown in Table 10.2, banks are interested in firms that have a strong cash flow, low leverage, audited financials, good management, and a healthy balance sheet. Although many new ventures have good management, few have the other characteristics, at least initially. But banks are an important source of credit for small businesses later in their life cycles.

There are two reasons that banks have historically been reluctant to lend money to start-ups. First, as mentioned previously, banks are risk averse. In addition, banks frequently have internal controls and regulatory restrictions prohibiting them from making high-risk loans. So when an entrepreneur approaches a banker with a request for a $250,000 loan and the only collateral he or she has to offer is the recognition of a problem that needs to be solved, a plan to solve it, and perhaps some intellectual property, there is usually no practical way for the bank to help. Banks typically have standards that guide their lending, such as minimum debt-to-equity ratios that work against start-up entrepreneurs.

The second reason banks have historically been reluctant to lend money to start-ups is that lending to small firms is not as profitable as lending to large firms, which have historically been the staple clients of commercial banks. If an entrepreneur approaches a banker with a request for a $50,000 loan, it may simply not be worth the banker's time to complete the due diligence necessary to determine the entrepreneur's risk profile. Considerable time is required to digest a business plan and investigate the merits of a new firm. Research shows that a firm's size is an important factor in determining its access to debt capital.[39] The $50,000 loan may be seen as both high risk and marginally profitable (based on the amount of time it would take to do the due diligence involved), making it doubly uninviting for a commercial bank.[40]

Despite these historical precedents, some banks are starting to engage start-up entrepreneurs—although the jury is still out regarding how significant these lenders will become. When it comes to start-ups, some banks are rethinking their lending standards and are beginning to focus on cash flow and the strength of the management team rather than on collateral and the strength of the balance sheet. Entrepreneurs should follow developments in this area closely.

SBA Guaranteed Loans

LEARNING OBJECTIVE

9. Discuss the SBA
   Guaranteed Loan
   Program.

Approximately 50 percent of the 9,000 banks in the United States participate in the **SBA Guaranteed Loan Program**. The most notable SBA program available to small businesses is the **7(A) Loan Guaranty Program**. This program accounts for 90 percent of the SBA's loan activity. The program operates through private-sector lenders who provide loans that are guaranteed by the SBA. The loans are for small businesses that are unable to secure financing on reasonable terms through normal lending channels. The SBA does not currently have funding for direct loans, other than a program to fund direct loans for businesses in geographic areas that are hit by natural disasters.

Almost all small businesses are eligible to apply for an SBA guaranteed loan. The SBA can guarantee as much as 75 percent (debt to equity) on loans up to $5 million. For loans of $150,000 or under, the guaranteed amount is 85 percent. Guaranteed loan funds can be used for almost any legitimate business purpose. The maximum length of the loans are 10 years for working capital, 10 years for equipment (or useful life of equipment), and 25 years for real estate purchase. To obtain an SBA guaranteed loan, an application must meet the requirements of both the SBA and the lender.[41] Typically, individuals must pledge all of their assets to secure the loan.

Although SBA guaranteed loans are utilized more heavily by existing small businesses than start-ups, they should not be dismissed as a possible source of funding. Diane Nelson, the woman who built Kazoo & Company into a successful business and is the subject of Case 4.1, got her start through a $500,000 SBA guaranteed loan. There is a misconception that the SBA is a "lender of last resort" and only distressed businesses qualify for SBA Guaranteed loans. Just the opposite is true. Only viable businesses are eligible under the SBA 7(A) Guaranteed Loan Program.[42]

Other Sources of Debt Financing

There are a variety of other avenues business owners can pursue to borrow money or obtain cash. **Vendor credit** (also known as trade credit) is when a vendor extends credit to a business in order to allow the business to buy its products and/or services up front but defer payment until later. Vendor credit is quite heavily used, particularly during economic downturns when it's harder for businesses to obtain bank financing. According to a survey conducted by the National Small Business Association, between August 2008 and December 2009, the worst portion of the recent economic slowdown, between 22 and 29 percent of business owners utilized vendor credit.[43] Factoring is a hybrid method for obtaining cash. Not really debt financing per se, **factoring** is a financial transaction whereby a business sells its accounts receivable to a third party, called a factor, at a discount in exchange for cash.[44]

A fairly new channel for borrowing money is peer-to-peer networks like Prosper. **Peer-to-peer lending** is a financial transaction that occurs directly between individuals or "peers." Prosper, which is the best known peer-to-peer lending network, is a Web site where individuals can buy loans and request to borrow money. Prosper evaluates the credit risk of individuals requesting loans, and then lists the loans for others to consider taking on. For the matches that are made, Prosper manages the loan repayment. The loans are unsecured loans that are fully amortized over a period of one, three, or five years. Lending Club, another peer-to-peer lender, has a similar program. Another source is Kickstarter, as profiled in Case 10.1, and similar "crowdfunding" sites. **Crowdfunding** is the modern-day version of "passing the hat." Crowdfunding sites allow entrepreneurs to create a profile, list their fund-raising goals, and provide an explanation of how the funds will be used. Individuals can then pledge money, in exchange for some type of amenity, like being one of the first 100 people to try the company's product, instead of equity or a promissory note. The site typically takes a small percentage of the funds raised by the individual for its service. Kickstarter does not fund start-ups, per se. Instead, it funds "creative projects," but some start-ups fit that criterion. Similar crowdfunding sites include IndieGoGo and RocketHub.

There are also organizations that lend money to specific demographic groups. For example, Count Me In, founded in 1999, is an advocacy group for female business owners. The group provides loans of $500 to $10,000 to women starting or growing a business.[45] Make Mine a Million $ Business, which is aligned with Count Me In and American Express, lends up to $50,000 to female-owned start-ups that have been in business for at least two years and have $250,000 or more in annual revenue.

Some lenders specialize in microfinance, which are very small loans. For example, ACCION USA, with a mission of giving people the financial tools they need to work their way out of poverty, gives $500 credit-builder loans to people with no credit history. While $500 might not sound like much, it could be enough to open a home-based business.[46]

CREATIVE SOURCES OF FINANCING AND FUNDING

Because financing and funding are difficult to obtain, particularly for start-ups, entrepreneurs often use creative ways to obtain financial resources. Even for firms that have financing or funding available, it is prudent to search for sources of capital that are less expensive than traditional ones. The following sections discuss three of the more common creative sources of financing and funding for entrepreneurial firms.

Leasing

A **lease** is a written agreement in which the owner of a piece of property allows an individual or business to use the property for a specified period of time in exchange for payments. The major advantage of leasing is that it enables a company to acquire the use of assets with very little or no down payment. Leases for facilities and leases for equipment are the two most common types of leases that entrepreneurial ventures undertake.[47] For example, many new businesses lease computers from Dell Inc. or other PC manufacturers. The advantage for the new business is that it can gain access to the computers it needs with very little money invested up-front.

There are many different players in the leasing business. Some vendors, such as Dell, lease directly to businesses. As with banks, the vendors look for lease clients with good credit backgrounds and the ability to make the lease payments. There are also **venture-leasing firms** that act as brokers, bringing the parties involved in a lease together. These firms are acquainted with the producers of specialized equipment and match these producers with new ventures that are in need of the equipment. One of the responsibilities of these firms is conducting due diligence to make sure that the new ventures involved will be able to keep up with their lease payments.

Most leases involve a modest down payment and monthly payments during the duration of the lease. At the end of an equipment lease, the new venture typically has the option to stop using the equipment, purchase it at fair market value, or renew the lease. Lease deals that involve a substantial amount of

LEARNING OBJECTIVE
10. Explain the advantages of leasing for an entrepreneurial venture.

money should be negotiated and entered into with the same amount of scrutiny as when getting financing or funding. Leasing is almost always more expensive than paying cash for an item, so most entrepreneurs think of leasing as an alternative to equity or debt financing. Although the down payment is typically lower, the primary disadvantage is that at the end of the lease, the lessee doesn't own the property or equipment.[48] Of course, this may be an advantage if a company is leasing equipment, such as computers or copy machines, that can rather quickly become technologically obsolete.

SBIR and STTR Grant Programs

The Small Business Innovation Research (SBIR) and the Small Business Technology Transfer (STTR) programs are two important sources of early stage funding for technology firms. These programs provide cash grants to entrepreneurs who are working on projects in specific areas. The main difference between the SBIR and the STTR programs is that the STTR program requires the participation of researchers working at universities or other research institutions. For the purpose of the program, the term *small business* is defined as an American-owned for-profit business with fewer than 500 employees. The principle researcher must also be employed by the business.[49]

The **SBIR Program** is a competitive grant program that provides over $1 billion per year to small businesses for early stage and development projects. Each year, 11 federal departments and agencies are required by the SBIR to reserve a portion of their research and development funds for awards to small businesses. Table 10.5 shows the agencies that participate, along with the types of areas that are funded. Guidelines for how to apply for the grants are provided on each agency's Web site, along with a description of the types of projects the agencies are interested in supporting. The SBIR is a three-phase program, meaning that firms that qualify have the potential to receive more than one grant to fund a particular proposal. These three phases, along with the amount of funding available for each phase, are as follows:

- **Phase I** is a six-month feasibility study in which the business must demonstrate the technical feasibility of the proposed innovation. Funding available for Phase I research ranges from $75,000 to $100,000, depending on the agency involved.

- **Phase II** awards for up to $750,000 are granted for as long as two years to successful Phase I companies. The purpose of a Phase II grant is to develop and test a prototype of Phase I innovations. The funding that is available for Phase II research ranges from $300,000 to $750,000, depending on the agency involved. Some agencies have **fast-track programs** where applicants can simultaneously submit Phase I and Phase II applications.

- **Phase III** is the period during which Phase II innovations move from the research and development lab to the marketplace. No SBIR funds are involved. At this point, the business must find private funding or financing to commercialize the product or service. In some cases, such as with the Department of Defense, the government may be the primary customer for the product.

Historically, less than 15 percent of all Phase I proposals are funded, and about 30 percent of all Phase II proposals are funded. The payoff for successful proposals, however, is high. The money is essentially free. It is a grant, meaning that it doesn't have to be paid back and no equity in the firm is at stake. The recipient of the grant also retains the rights to the intellectual

TABLE 10.5 SMALL BUSINESS INNOVATION RESEARCH: THREE-PHASE PROGRAM

Phase	Purpose of Phase	Duration	Funding Available (Varies by Agency)
Phase I	To demonstrate the proposed innovation's technical feasibility.	Up to 6 months	Up to $100,000
Phase II	Available to successful Phase I companies. The purpose of a Phase II grant is to develop and test a prototype of the innovation validated in Phase I.*	Up to 2 years	Up to $750,000
Phase III	Period in which Phase II innovations move from the research and development lab to the marketplace.	Open	No SBIR funding available, however, federal agencies may award non-SBIR-funded follow-on grants or contracts for products or processes that meet the mission needs of those agencies, or for further R&D.

*Some agencies have a fast-track program where applicants can submit Phase I and Phase II applications simultaneously. Government agencies that participate in this program include the following: Department of Agriculture, Department of Commerce, Department of Defense, Department of Education, Department of Energy, Department of Health and Human Services, Department of Homeland Security, Department of Transportation, Environmental Protection Agency, NASA, National Institutes of Health, and National Science Foundation.

property developed while working with the support provided by the grant. The real payoff is in Phase III if the new venture can commercialize the research results.

The **STTR Program** is a variation of the SBIR for collaborative research projects that involve small businesses and research organizations, such as universities or federal laboratories. In 2010, over $100 million in grants were awarded through the program. More information about the SBIR and STTR programs can be obtained at www.sbir.gov.

Other Grant Programs

There are a limited number of other grant programs available to entrepreneurs. Obtaining a grant takes a little detective work. Granting agencies are, by nature, low-key, so they normally need to be sought out. A typical scenario of a small business that received a grant is provided by Rozalia Williams, the founder of Hidden Curriculum Education, a for-profit company that offers college life skills courses. To kick-start her business, Williams received a $72,500 grant from Miami-Dade Empowerment Trust, a granting agency in Dade County, Florida. The purpose of the Miami-Dade Empowerment Trust is to encourage the creation of businesses in disadvantaged neighborhoods of Dade County. The key to Williams's success, which is true in most grant-awarding situations, is that her business fit nicely with the mission of the granting organization, and she was willing to take her business into the areas the granting agency was committed to improving. After being awarded the grant and conducting her college prep courses in four Dade County neighborhoods over a three-year period, Williams received an additional $100,000 loan from the Miami-Dade Empowerment Trust to expand her business. There are also private foundations that grant money to both existing and start-up firms. These grants are usually tied to specific objectives or a specific project, such as research and development in a specific area.

The federal government has grant programs beyond the SBIR and STTR programs described previously. The full spectrum of grants available is listed at www.grants.gov. State and local governments, private foundations, and philanthropic organizations also post grant announcements on their Web sites.

Finding a grant that fits your business is the key. This is no small task. It is worth the effort, however, if you can obtain some or all of your start-up costs through a granting agency.

One thing to be careful of is grant-related scams. Business owners often receive unsolicited letters or e-mail messages from individuals or organizations that assure them that for a fee they can help the business gain access to hundreds of business-related grants. The reality is that there aren't hundreds of business-related grants that fit any one business. Most of these types of offers are a scam.

Strategic Partners

Strategic partners are another source of capital for new ventures.[50] Indeed, strategic partners often play a critical role in helping young firms fund their operations and round out their business models.

Biotechnology companies, for example, rely heavily on partners for financial support, as related in the "Partnering for Success" feature in Chapter 1. Biotech firms, which are typically fairly small, often partner with larger drug companies to conduct clinical trials and bring products to market. Most of these arrangements involve a licensing agreement. A typical agreement works like this: A biotech firm licenses a product that is under development to a pharmaceutical company in exchange for financial support during the development of the product and beyond. This type of arrangement gives the biotech firm money to operate while the drug is being developed. The downside to this approach is that the larger firm ultimately markets the drug and retains a large share of the income for itself. Sometimes strategic partnerships take on a different role in helping biotech firms take products to market and allow them to keep a larger share of the income than licensing arrangements permit.

Finally, many partnerships are formed to share the costs of product or service development, to gain access to a particular resource, or to facilitate speed to market.[51] In exchange for access to plant and equipment and established distribution channels, new ventures bring an entrepreneurial spirit and new ideas to these partnerships. These types of arrangements can help new ventures lessen the need for financing or funding.

CHAPTER SUMMARY

1. For three reasons—cash flow challenges, capital investment needs, and the reality of lengthy product development cycles—most new firms need to raise money at some point during the early part of their life.

2. Personal funds, friends and family, and bootstrapping are the three sources of personal financing available to entrepreneurs.

3. Entrepreneurs are often very creative in finding ways to bootstrap to raise money or cut costs. Examples of bootstrapping include minimizing personal expenses and putting all profits back into the business, establishing partnerships and sharing expenses with partners, and sharing office space and/or employees with other businesses.

4. The three steps involved in properly preparing to raise debt or equity financing are as follows: Determine precisely how much money is needed, determine the type of financing or funding that is most appropriate, and develop a strategy for engaging potential investors or bankers.

5. An elevator speech is a brief, carefully constructed statement outlining a business opportunity's merits.

6. Equity funding involves exchanging partial ownership in a firm, which is usually in the form of stock, for funding. Debt financing is getting a loan.

7. Business angels are individuals who invest their personal capital directly in start-up

ventures. These investors tend to be high net worth individuals who generally invest between $25,000 and $150,000 in a single company. Venture capital is money that is invested by venture capital firms in start-ups and small businesses with exceptional growth potential. Typically, venture capitalists invest at least $1 million in a single company.

8. An initial public offering (IPO) is an important milestone for a firm for four reasons: It is a way to raise equity capital, it raises a firm's public profile, it is a liquidity event, and it creates another form of currency (company stock) that can be used to grow the company.

9. The main SBA program available to small businesses is referred to as the 7(A) Loan Guaranty Program. This program operates through private-sector lenders providing loans that are guaranteed by the SBA. The loans are for small businesses that are unable to secure financing on reasonable terms through normal lending channels.

10. A lease is a written agreement in which the owner of a piece of property allows an individual or business to use the property for a specified period of time in exchange for payments. The major advantage of leasing is that it enables a company to acquire the use of assets with very little or no down payment.

KEY TERMS

REVIEW QUESTIONS

1. What are the three most common reasons most entrepreneurial ventures need to raise money in their early life?

2. What is meant by the term *burn rate*? What are the consequences of experiencing a negative burn rate for a relatively long period of time?

3. What is meant by the term *sweat equity*?

4. To what extent do entrepreneurs rely on their personal funds and funds from friends and families to finance their ventures? What are the three rules of thumb that a business owner should follow when asking friends and family members for start-up funds?

5. What is bootstrapping? Provide several examples of how entrepreneurs bootstrap to raise money or cut costs. In your judgment, how important is the art of bootstrapping for an entrepreneurial venture?

6. Describe the three steps involved in properly preparing to raise debt or equity financing.

7. Briefly describe the difference between equity funding and debt financing.

8. Describe the most common sources of equity funding.

9. Describe the most common sources of debt financing.

10. What is the purpose of an elevator speech? Why is preparing an elevator speech one of the first things an entrepreneur should do in the process of raising money?

11. Why is it so important to get a personal introduction before approaching a potential investor or banker?

12. Describe the three steps required to effectively engage potential investors or bankers.

13. Identify the three most common forms of equity funding.

14. Describe the nature of business angel funding. What types of people typically become business angels, and what is the unique role that business angels play in

the process of funding entrepreneurial firms?

15. Describe what is meant by the term *venture capital*. Where do venture capital firms get their money? What types of firms do venture capitalists commonly want to fund? Why?

16. Describe the purpose of an initial public offering (IPO). Why is an initial public offering considered to be an important milestone for an entrepreneurial firm?

17. What is the purpose of the investment bank in the initial public offering process?

18. In general, why are commercial banks reluctant to loan money to start-ups?

19. Briefly describe the SBA's 7(A) Loan Guaranty Program. Do most start-up firms qualify for an SBA guaranteed loan? Why or why not?

20. What is a Small Business Innovation Research (SBIR) grant? Why would a firm want to apply for such a grant if it so qualified?

APPLICATION QUESTIONS

1. Write a 60-second elevator speech for Joby Energy, which is the "You Be the VC 10.1" feature in this chapter.

2. Samantha Smith, a friend of yours, was recently telling you about a company that her father is starting in the solar power industry. Samantha's father is using a technology he developed, which has received favorable write-ups in several technical publications, and has been approached by two angel investors eager to invest. He's also been offered a spot in a prestigious technology incubator, where he can maintain an office and a lab to work on his project. Samantha says that her dad has turned away the potential investors and is opting to work out of a shop on some property he owns, rather than move into the incubator. He'll be able to fund the company from personal savings, at least for the first two years. Do you think Samantha's dad is making good decisions? What are the pluses and minuses of the decisions he's making?

3. Jim Carter, a classmate of yours, is preparing to launch an e-commerce company to sell home repair guidebooks, tools, how-to videos, and related material for home repair and remodeling projects. He just told you that he talked to his paternal grandmother over the weekend, and she has agreed to lend him $25,000 to launch the firm. When you asked Jim what arrangements he has made with his grandmother to formalize the loan, he looked puzzled and said, "She plans to send me a check in a week or so—she just needs to get the money out of her savings account." Jim seemed concerned by the worried look on your face and said, "Tell me what you're thinking. I really want to do the right thing here." What would you say to Jim?

4. Kathy Baker is in the midst of starting a computer hardware firm and thinks she has identified a real problem that her company will be able to solve. She needs investment capital, but doesn't know much about the process and doesn't know where to begin. She's turned to you for advice. Write Kathy a 250- to 300-word e-mail message introducing her to the process of raising investment capital.

5. One criticism of the venture capital industry is that the majority of the money is invested in a small number of geographic areas in the United States. In fact, historically, over 50 percent of venture capital investments have been made in just two states. Do some research on the venture capital industry, and determine which two states are the perennial leaders for venture capital funding. How much of a disadvantage do you believe that entrepreneurs who live in states like North Dakota and Wyoming have just because of their distance from the majority of venture capital firms?

6. Study the two "You Be the VC" features at the end of Chapter 9 and the two "You Be the VC" features at the end of this chapter. In your judgment, which of the four firms is the better candidate for venture capital funding? Which is the poorest candidate? Justify your answers.

7. A handful of business schools are experimenting with giving their students the opportunity to run venture capital funds with real money. Identify one or more of these business schools, and describe the nature of its student-run venture capital fund. Would you enjoy participating in running a student-run venture capital fund? What do you think you'd learn from the experience?

8. Identify a company that recently graduated from TechStars and a company that recently graduated from Y Combinator. Briefly describe the companies, and provide an

update on how they're doing. Identify whether either or both of the companies have received outside funding.

9. According to information in the chapter, the three areas that receive the most funding from business angels are health care services/ medical devices and equipment, software, and biotech. Why do you think business angels are attracted to start-ups in these areas? Why wouldn't someone starting a new soup and salad restaurant, for example, be equally interesting to business angels?

10. The "You be the VC 6.2" feature focuses on FastPencil, a company that provides a user-friendly, affordable, and effective platform for authors to self-publish books, and obtain real-time feedback on the books they're working on. Consider each of the 4Ps and comment on the most important issues for FastPencil to consider in each area.

11. Imagine you invented a new type of car seat for children, which is lighter and safer than the car seats currently on the market. You have a business plan and have won two business plan contests based on your idea. You also have a working prototype. You'd like to find an angel investor to fund the launch of your firm. Describe how you'd go about finding an angel investor in the area in which you live. Make a list of the specific steps you'd take, and the specific people you'd talk to, to try to locate an appropriate angel investor.

12. In May 2011, LinkedIn (www.linkedin.com) launched a very successful initial public offering (IPO). Study LinkedIn and determine why it was a good candidate for launching a public offering. Do you think LinkedIn could launch an equally successful initial public offering today?

13. Ed Sayers just returned from a meeting with his banker with a frustrated look on his face. He tosses his keys on the kitchen counter and tells his wife, "I just can't understand where my banker is coming from. I have a great idea for a new firm, but the bank isn't interested in helping me with a loan. Tomorrow, I'm going to visit a couple of other banks to see if I have better luck." Do you think Ed will have any better luck with the second and third banks he visits? Why or why not?

14. Joshua Sherman, who lives near Vancouver, Canada, is preparing to pitch an idea for a social gaming Web site to a group of angel investors. The site has some new and novel aspects to it. He made a practice presentation in front of his advisory board, and one question that an adviser urged him to prepare for is "If you're successful, what's to prevent Facebook from launching a similar product?" Joshua frowned, and said he thinks it's unlikely he'll be asked that question. What do you think? If you were Joshua, how would you prepare to answer that question?

15. Alex Gondolas is in the early stages of developing a new laser optics technology that may be of interest to the U.S. Department of Defense. Alex recently attended a seminar for start-ups and was advised to apply for a Small Business Innovation Research grant to fund his project. Alex thought about applying for the grant but decided it was too much hassle and paperwork. If you were advising Alex, would you tell him to rethink his decision? Why or why not?

YOU BE THE VC 10.1

Company: **Joby Energy**

Web: www.jobyenergy.com
Twitter: jobyenergy

Business Idea: Develop airborne wind turbines to harness the immense and consistent power in high-altitude winds, with the objective of producing reliable, sustainable, and low-cost renewable energy.

Pitch: Winds at higher altitudes are faster, are more consistent, and contain three times the power as winds near the earth's surface. As a result, Joby Energy is developing airborne wind turbines that will operate at high altitudes and generate electricity that can be transferred to the ground via a reinforced composite tether.

Here's how it works. The wind-generating apparatus looks like a large series of propellers tethered together via a multiwing structure (pictures of the device are available on Joby Energy's Web site). For launch, the turbines or propellers are supplied with power to enable vertical takeoff. Upon reaching operating altitude, the system uses the wind's power to fly crosswind in a circular path. The high crosswind speed results in the turbines spinning onboard generators at high speeds, which in turn produces electricity. The electricity is transferred to the ground through the electrical tether. Orientation in flight is maintained by an advanced computer system that drives aerodynamic surfaces on the winds and differentially controls rotor speeds. During occasional periods of low wind, bad weather, or electrical storms, the apparatus can be powered to safely land on the ground.

Multiple prototypes of the Joby Energy apparatus have been produced, and the company is progressing with an advanced prototype to validate extended endurance flights and generate rated power. A lease on a permanent test site has been obtained near South Point, Hawaii, and the company is working with state and federal regulators to obtain clearances for testing. The Hawaii location was selected because it offers excellent wind resources, limited precipitation, a good climate, and is relatively unpopulated. In parallel to building prototypes of its wind-generating apparatus, Joby Energy has modeled tropospheric wind data spanning 29 years (1979–2008) to develop global maps of wind speed and wind power.

This work has been undertaken to quantify the potential of high-altitude wind power and to identify the best locations in the world in which to deploy the Joby system.

Each element of the Joby system is being optimized for scalability, manufacturing, and transport. A direct comparison between the energy output of a 2 MW conventional turbine (windmill) operating at 400 feet and a 2 MW Joby Energy turbine operating at 2,000 feet shows a significant improvement in wind-generated power. A Joby Energy turbine yields a capacity factor of nearly double that of a conventional turbine.

Q&A: Based on the material covered in this chapter, what questions would you ask the firm's founders before making your funding decision? What answers would satisfy you?

Decision: If you had to make your decision on just the information provided in the pitch and on the company's Web site, would you fund this company? Why or why not?

YOU BE THE VC 10.2

Company: PledgeMusic

Web: www.pledgemusic.com
Twitter: PledgeMusic
Facebook: PledgeMusic

Business Idea: Provide musicians a platform to reach out to their fan base to financially contribute to upcoming recordings or other musical projects.

Pitch: Musicians often have creative ideas for recordings or similar projects but can't raise the money to move forward. When their fans hear that they've passed on an album or a creative new approach to offering their music, they often react by saying or thinking to themselves, "Man—I wish there had been a way that I could have helped."

Now there is. PledgeMusic is a Kickstarter-type Web site that allows musicians to design fund-raising campaigns to raise money for their next projects. Each fund-raising campaign is accompanied by a video pitch from the artist, explaining the project he or she has in mind. The page for the campaign includes a running tally of the amount of money that's been raised and how much is needed to complete the campaign. A campaign must reach its goal before monies are collected. In exchange for their contributions, the artists provide pledgers gifts or amenities rather than any ownership interest in the initiative. Gifts vary based on the amount of the pledge. For example, in early 2011, a campaign was launched by the Monarchs, an alternative-rock and blues-rock band, to produce its first album. The video appeal was made by Celeste Griffin, the band's folksy lead vocalist. The following is a sample of the amenities or prizes the band offered its pledgers, based on the amount of their pledges: $10—project download; $30—signed CD; $100—two backstage passes; $250—your

name in album credits; $750—day in recording studio; $1,000—write a song for you. In the written appeal, Celeste explained that the band planned to record its first album in July 2011 under the supervision of Mike McCarthy, the producer of artists such as Spoon and Patty Griffin. Celeste emphasized how much she's grown as an artist, and how much the ability to cut an album would mean to the band and its future. She also mentioned that the band has committed to donating a percentage of the money raised to Laps for Cystic Fibrosis, a nonprofit organization dedicated to cystic fibrosis research. Donating a portion of the money raised from pledgers to charity is a practice that PledgeMusic strongly encourages.

When the Monarchs' campaign reached its goal, its PledgeMusic page read "Monarchs:—it's a record!!! All pledgers will receive exclusive periodic updates on how the record is made and will be the first to receive a complimentary download of the album."

For its part, PledgeMusic does not take any ownership interest in the projects that are funded through its Web site, charging a flat 15 percent fee on all money collected.

Q&A: Based on the material covered in this chapter, what questions would you ask the firm's founders before making your funding decision? What answers would satisfy you?

Decision: If you had to make your decision on just the information provided in the pitch and on the company's Web site, would you fund this company? Why or why not?

CASE 10.1

Kickstarter: A New Forum for Raising Seed Capital for For-Profit and Nonprofit Organizations

Web: www.kickstarter.com
Twitter: kickstarter

Bruce R. Barringer, *Oklahoma State University*

R. Duane Ireland, *Texas A&M University*

Introduction

Kickstarter is a fund-raising Web site for creative projects. It's a platform referred to as "crowdfunding," in that it helps individuals and organizations raise money from the general public. Kickstarter was started in April 2009 by Perry Chen, Charles Adler, and Yancy Strickler. Since then, it's collected nearly $40 million in pledges to help fund projects as diverse as creating an iPhone 4 tripod and mount to helping an author publish a guide to hidden art galleries and museums in Tokyo. Kickstarter receives between 100 and 200 new project requests per day. Projects are accepted if they follow Kickstarter's guidelines. The primary requirement is that a project must be creativity-oriented. Kickstarter does not fund charity projects or causes.

How It Works

Once accepted, you use tools provided by Kickstarter to set up your fund-raising campaign. The campaign, which is displayed at Kickstarter.com, includes a description of your project, a video pitch (not required but recommended), the minimum amount of funds you need, and a deadline. If the minimum isn't reached by the deadline, pledgers receive their money back. Pledges are tiered ($25, $50, $75, etc.), with each tier earning a certain incentive. The incentives are "thank-you" gifts or tokens that the person initiating the campaign gives to the people who make the pledges.

Kickstarter has taken several steps to govern the integrity of its campaigns. Money pledged by donors is collected using Amazon Payments. Kickstarter claims no ownership over the projects and the work they produce. It makes money by retaining 5 percent of the funds raised.

Kickstarter doesn't allow people to raise money to start a business, per se. It does allow businesses to fund "projects," like the Heidi Ho Organics campaign described later. The funding of arts and music projects are the most popular. If a project exceeds its goal, the project initiator is able to keep the amount in excess of the goal, less Kickstarter's 5 percent.

The highest grossing Kickstarter project was TikTok + LunaTik watch kits, which turn an iPod nano into a multitouch watch. The campaign raised $941,718, which was 6,283 percent of its goal. The second highest grossing project was *Blue Like Jazz*, a movie. That campaign raised $345,992, which was 276 percent of its goal. Kickstarter maintains an active blog at blog.kickstarter.com. The blog is fun to read and highlights Kickstarter's most successful and unusual campaigns.

The investment community has noticed Kickstarter. The response has been mostly positive. Ron Conway, a prominent Silicon Valley angel investor, was quoted in *The Christian Science Monitor* regarding his take on Kickstarter. Mr. Conway remarked:

> Kickstarter is another very creative way for companies to get funded. And in my opinion, the more companies that get funded, the more innovation there is out there and, hence, technology advances and the USA continues to create jobs in technology. I think it could become a category that's a meaningful way for companies to raise money.

As of April 2011, Kickstarter had 787,700 members.

Typical Kickstarter Project

Here's a typical Kickstarter campaign. Heidi Ho Organics is a vegan food company started in 2010 by Heidi Lovig. Working mostly alone, Lovig has created a range of plant-based vegan cheeze products made from natural, organic ingredients without any additives, fillers, or preservatives. Currently, she is limited to making two pounds of cheeze at a time using a home food processer. Her Kickstarter campaign, which was underway when this feature was written, was to raise $12,245 to buy equipment to increase production and distribution of her cheeze products to local food co-ops. Her long-term goal is to help stimulate local economies around the world by building small subproduction facilities, similar to her facility in Portland, Oregon, to make plant-based vegan cheezes from locally sourced ingredients. The day this case was written, Lovig had 66 backers who had pledged $7,650. Her campaign had eight days to go, and needed to raise an additional $4,695 to be successful.

(continued)

Incentives for Heidi Ho Organics Kickstarter Campaign

Pledge Amount	Incentive
$1 or more	Acknowledgment on the company's Web site.
$10 or more	A handmade thank-you card with our Oregon hazelnut stamp.
$25 or more	A coupon for a package of cheeze at the Portland Farmers Market.
$50 or more	Coupons for two packages of cheeze, which can be redeemed at the Portland Farmers Market or mailed to you.
$100 or more	A "Smoke My Gouda" Tee + coupons for four packages of cheeze, which can be mailed to you.
$250 or more	Coupons for eight packages of cheeze + a limited edition print of a professional photograph of our cheezes—autographed by "The Chef."
$500 or more	Four packages of cheeze each month for three months + Kickstarter supporter limited edition of Heidi Ho Organics Vegan Cheeze Cookbook with copies of some secret recipes and autographed by "The Chef" with a personal note written to you inside.
$1,000 or more	Cookbook and all of its glory + Four packages of cheeze each month for the six months.
$2,500 or more	Two "Smoke My Gouda" Tees + Framed Photos + Cookbook + Four packages of cheeze each month for six months + A romantic four-course Vegan Cheeze and Wine Paring dinner for two prepared by "The Chef" in your home! (Anywhere in Oregon or Washington)

Lovig included a heartfelt pitch on her Kickstarter page, describing the equipment she needs and how it will help her initiative take off. She's also offering the incentives noted in the table above.

How to Run a Successful Kickstarter Campaign

There are several things that people who have run successful Kickstarter campaigns learn. First, Kickstarter shouldn't be thought of as a tool for funding one-off projects or events. Instead, it's best to think of it as a mechanism for providing seed capital to help a project or event get up and running, and then grow it from there. Second, it's important that the person or organization that initiates a Kickstarter campaign promote it. Most people who contribute to a specific campaign don't find it by chance. Instead, they go to Kickstarter.com looking for it. In the table shown next, several methods for promoting a Kickstarter campaign are listed.

Third, the majority of donations are made at the beginning and the end of campaigns. As a result, shorter campaigns are typically more effective than longer ones. Four to five weeks seems to be the sweet spot. If a campaign is too long, people lose interest. Fourth, it's important to not set your financial goal too low. If a Kickstarter campaign is successful, it tends to quickly lose momentum once it reaches 100 percent of its goal—even though more money can be collected. Finally, it's imperative that a video pitch be included. It's much easier to donate money to a person or organization's project if you can hear someone talking about it and see the passion in their eyes.

What's Ahead?

Kickstarter has no immediate plans to broaden the scope of its platform. It does have competitors, including RocketHub and IndieGoGo, but those sites pale in comparison to Kickstarter's volume of projects. There are areas in which Kickstarter is becoming more adventurous. For example, in mid-2010, it held its first Kickstarter Film Festival featuring projects that were

Techniques for Promoting a Kickstarter Campaign

Platform	Execution
E-mail	Send an e-mail to your e-mail distribution list, describing the campaign. Kickstarter campaigns aren't funded entirely by strangers. Instead, they're often funded largely by the campaign initiator's friends, family, business associates, and so forth.
Twitter and Facebook	Reach out to both your Twitter and Facebook audiences. Provide frequent updates. Try to find the balance between saturating your Twitter followers and Facebook friends with Kickstarter info, and providing them with timely reminders.
Blogs and media	Reach out to bloggers and news outlets in the industry that your campaign focuses on. Ask that they mention your campaign and offer support. For example, it would have made sense for Heidi Ho Organics to have reached out to bloggers and journalists who write about organic food.

funded via Kickstarter. The festival included a menu of Kickstarter-funded snacks. There was also music from the Zlante Uste Balkan Brass Band, the focus of the Kickstarter-financed documentary *Brasslands*.

Discussion Questions

1. Do you think Kickstarter is a viable alternative to raising equity funding or debt financing? If so, under what circumstances?
2. Kickstarter is not the first crowdfunding platform, yet it is the most successful. List five reasons that you believe account for Kickstarter's success.
3. The city of Portland, Oregon, recently set up an official curate page at Kickstarter. (www.kickstarter.com/pages/portland). Is this a model for other cities to follow? Is it a potentially effective way for cities to promote arts and entrepreneurship? How should cities go about promoting their Kickstarter pages?
4. Do what degree do you believe Kickstarter itself is a successful start-up?

Application Questions

1. Look at Kickstarter, RocketHub, and IndieGoGo. At each site, listen to three of the video pitches. Try to find pitches of business projects. List the three pitches you listened to at each site and which one you found the most compelling. Also, compare and contrast the crowdfunding approaches of Kickstarter, RocketHub, and IndieGoGo.
2. How can Kickstarter's business model be used in other areas? Make at least two suggestions.

Sources: Kickstarter Web site, www.kickstarter.com (accessed April 14, 2011); M. Ryzik, "For Web-Financed Film Projects, a Curtain Rises," *New York Times*, July 8, 2010, C-1; *Economist*, "The Q&A: Perry Chen, Kickstarter; Crowd-Funding Art," www.economist.com/blogs/prospero/2010/10/crowd-funding_art, (accessed April 12, 2011, originally posted on October 22, 2010); J. Turner, "Creative Idea? Kickstarter Connects Artists with Online Funding: Kickstarter.com Points Online Patrons Toward Worthy Projects They Didn't Know Existed," *The Christian Science Monitor*, December 15, 2010.

CASE 10.2

GoNabit.com: Is the Biggest E-Commerce Acquisition in the Middle East a Bargain?

Web: www.gonabit.com
Twitter: GoNabit Dubai
Facebook: GoNabit

Introduction

Group-buying is one of the Internet's fastest-growing global retail phenomena, and UAE-based GoNabit is the first to bring the concept to the Arab world. The idea behind the GoNabit Web site is fairly simple. GoNabit partners with a range of businesses in the region, from owner-operator small businesses to some of the largest names in the area, to offer substantial discounts on their goods or services. The idea works for all parties because GoNabit is using strength in numbers to help buyers and sellers benefit from discovering one another.

For the merchant, the transaction is entirely risk free because there is no up-front cost either financially or in terms of time. Merchants only have to be prepared to offer a discount between 50 to 90 percent of their regular retail price and in return they receive a substantial increase in business. Plus, being featured on GoNabit can considerably raise brand awareness thanks to the buzz and power of social media. If the merchant provides a good service, it may be able to convert the one-time GoNabit voucher user into a loyal, long-term customer.

For GoNabit's buyer group—or nabbers as they are known—the benefits are equally attractive. Nabbers, who are a savvy, media-minded group with sizeable disposable income, are being constantly exposed to some great offers and cool stuff they can do in their city.

Every day, GoNabit features one or two large deals. Once a minimum number of buyers sign up for the deal, the deal "tips" and the buyer's credit card gets charged. GoNabit then sends a voucher to the buyer, who can print the voucher and take it to the local merchant to redeem the discounted offer. If the minimum number of purchasers is not reached before the deal ends, no one gets the deal.

To retain the buzz and an ever-growing crowd of eager followers, GoNabit also runs a referral program, where subscribers are rewarded for spreading the word to their friends to buy the deal. Referrals can earn subscribers a further discount of 37 dirhams ($10).

(continued)

GoNabit's Start-up Story

GoNabit co-founder, Sohrab Jahanbani, had never given the idea of group buying a great deal of thought before he read about it in November 2009, in an article on Gigaom.com, an online magazine for global technology innovators. Jahanbani was immediately compelled by the idea that pooling customers together could bring down the prices of goods and services in what was clearly a win-win situation for both consumers and the merchant. Back then, there were just a couple of group buying firms in the United States, and the idea of setting one up in the Middle East was no easy decision. Jahanbani's biggest fear was that he would launch this cutting-edge Web site and everyone would ignore it. Was it too early to introduce Internet-based group buying to the Middle East?

Coincidently, another Dubai-based entrepreneur, Dan Stuart, was having the same thoughts about the power of group buying at virtually the same time as Jahanbani, although the pair had never met. Stuart was, at that time, the chief opportunity officer at Bayt.com, the largest jobs Web site in the Middle East. Bayt.com had recently launched Intilaq, a business incubator with a focus on Web start-ups, and Stuart, as a director of Intilaq, was spending much of his time looking at new launch opportunities and evaluating investment proposals. He discovered that he was passionate about keeping his finger on the pulse about what might be new and relevant to the region. It also fueled his desire to set up a Web-based business of his own.

Deciding group buying was the way forward, Stuart started to put a business plan together. Within a short space of time, Stuart was committing every spare hour of his day, seven days a week, to setting up the business. He was doing pretty much everything on his own, from the business modeling to marketing plans to deciding who to hire.

Stuart soon realized that he needed a partner, but was wary of getting together with someone who wouldn't see the business through to success. Luckily mutual friends intervened and suggested that Dan meet Jahanbani.

The pair met for the first time in February 2010 and quickly discovered that they had almost identical plans. It became clear that the time had come for them both to put up or shut up. If they wanted to make this happen, they'd have to roll up their sleeves and get on with it.

Stuart and Jahanbani left their jobs and officially started work in March 2010.

First things first though, the pair needed funding in order to set up the e-commerce business, market its services, and staff it appropriately. Both parties had some capital of their own to invest, but it became clear that outside funding was required.

Stuart approached his old boss, Rabea Ataya, the chief executive of Bayt.com. Stuart had already been given an understanding from Ataya that if he wanted to launch an Internet venture of his own, the Bayt.com boss would look closely at it. Indeed, Ataya had indicated that he was inclined to invest in anything his former director felt sufficiently strongly about.

The pair received substantial (as yet undisclosed) funding from Bayt.com, which was sufficient to launch the business at apparently breakneck speed. Having only begun work in March 2010, the site was up and running and offering deals by May 2010. Getting to market this quickly was important for GoNabit. There were already rumors that the U.S. group buying giant Groupon was planning to launch in the Middle East imminently (as it was, Groupon did not open its virtual doors there until March 2011). There was also a homegrown competitor, Cobone, which was part of the Jabbar Internet Group (previously known as the Maktoob Group, which sold Maktoob.com to Yahoo!). Cobone entered the market in August 2010.

Hence, by moving so quickly, GoNabit was an innovator in many areas. It was the first group buying site in all of its markets and the first one with an Arabic interface.

Stuart and Jahanbani decided to further set themselves apart from other global and Middle Eastern–backed buying groups by starting with and staying true to a pure e-commerce model. Instead of adopting the format of other group buying sites, which offer a wide range of options such as cash-on-delivery, GoNabit opted for credit card and PayPal payments only.

The pair felt vindicated when, within eight weeks of starting their business, GoNabit had chalked up an astonishing 1,400 transactions. By January 2011, Jahanbani calculated that GoNabit had saved its customers more than $1.25 million since the Web site's launch in May. Nabbers were snapping up discounts ranging between 50 to 80 percent on a range of experiences from spa massages, dhow cruises (a traditional Arab sailing vessel), beauty treatments, and diving and desert driving courses. The group buying company also manages to offer 50 percent discounts on some big-ticket products or services that originally cost 1,000 dirhams ($275) or more. Many of the deals are negotiated with some significant local businesses including Jumeirah, Emaar, Ferrari World in Abu Dhabi, and Jashanmal Group.

In early 2011, Stuart and Jahanbani realized that further investment would be required to ensure the growth of the business. Expansion in the Middle East is not straightforward and can require extensive resources. Every city is almost like a new country with an entirely different set of obstacles to overcome from local currency differences to varying legal structures.

By this time, GoNabit was already running deals in four countries having set up offices in the UAE, Lebanon, Jordan, and Kuwait, helped in part by the experience and network of its strategic investor Bayt.com. Stuart and Jahanbani were now keen to expand into new and emerging markets in the Middle East. Already on the radar were Saudi Arabia, Egypt, and Bahrain.

GoNabit's founders knew that they had several ways of raising money and with their track record so far, more doors would be open to them.

The three main questions that Stuart and Jahanbani asked themselves when considering what to do next were:

1. What does it mean for our company and its future?
2. What does it mean for the shareholders?
3. What does it mean for the staff?

GoNabit's founders wanted to make the best decision for all involved. They were comforted by the fact that, as far as the end-user was concerned, they wouldn't have to worry about any huge upheaval in the GoNabit experience, because, any option that Stuart and Jahanbani would take would not change the site drastically.

Stuart and Jahanbani began talks with a number of interested parties, including many international firms that were keen to get a foothold in the Middle Eastern group buying market. The potential investor that most impressed them was the U.S.-based Groupon rival LivingSocial. Washington-based LivingSocial, which is ranked number two in the daily deals market in the United States, was on somewhat of an international buying spree, and was also in talks to buy French daily deals company Dealissime.com. (The deal with Dealissime was complete in June 2011.)

In June 2011, LivingSocial acquired GoNabit in a record-breaking deal. The actual financial terms of the multimillion-dollar deal have yet to be disclosed, but the acquisition of the 13-month old company made history in the Middle East as the first ever large-scale acquisition of an e-commerce company. Another first for GoNabit.

Discussion Questions

1. Do you think GoNabit's investors made wise decisions investing in the company? Three to five years from now, do you think that GoNabit will have disappointed or wowed its investors? Why?
2. Look at Table 10.2. At the time that GoNabit raised its initial round of funding, to what extent did it resemble the ideal candidate for start-up funding as stipulated by the materials in the table? How about the second investment?
3. Put yourself in the role of a critic. What would you say if you adopted the view that GoNabit isn't worthy of millions of dollars in funding? Also, comment on the evolution of GoNabit's business model. Explain your answer.
4. What do you think of Stuart and Jahanbani's exit strategy? How do you think GoNabit's investors will monetize their investment?

Application Questions

1. One of the criticisms of GoNabit is that its service is almost identical to other group buying Web sites such as Groupon (www.groupon.com) and Cobone (www.cobone.com). Look at the Web sites of Groupon, Cobone, and GoNabit. What points of differentiation, if any, do you see between them?
2. Spend some time on GoNabit's Web site (you don't have to actually buy any deals). Did you find the site to be easy to navigate and GoNabit's product offering appealing? What is it that you liked about the experience and what did you not like? Did your experience influence your perception of the wisdom of Bayt.com and LivingSocial's investment in GoNabit?

Sources: "Interview with Dan Stuart CEO and Founder of Group Buying StartUp GoNabit.com," Arab Crunch, http://arabcrunch. com/2010/07/interview-with-dan-stuart-ceo-cofounder-of-group-buying-startup-gonabit-com.html (accessed September 5, 2011, originally posted July 20, 2010); S. Tariq, "Enter the Groupon," *Communicate.ae,* www.communicate.ae/node/3561 (accessed September 5, 2011, originally posted April 1, 2011); "Sohrab Jahanbani's Ultimate Nab: A Story of Low Burn Experimentation" *ActivePR,* http://blog.activepr.biz/birthday-girls-at-active-pr (accessed September 5, 2011, originally posted August 3, 2011); N. Messieh, "LivingSocial Acquires Middle Eastern Group Buying Site GoNabit: The Inside Story," *TNW Middle East,* http://thenextweb.com/me/2011/06/27/livingsocial-acquires-middle-eastern-group-buying-site-gonabit-the-inside-story (accessed September 5, 2011, originally posted June 27, 2011).

ENDNOTES

1. J. Zhang, "The Advantage of Experienced Start-Up Founders in Venture Capital Acquisition: Evidence from Serial Entrepreneurs," *Small Business Economics* 36, no. 2 (2010): 187–208.

2. D. M. Sullivan and M. R. Marvel, "Knowledge Acquisition, Network Reliance, and Early-Stage Technology Venture Outcomes," *Journal of Management Studies* 48, no. 6 (2011): 1169–1193.

3. D. P. Forbes, M. A. Korsgaard, and H. J. Sapienza, "Financing Decisions as a Source of Conflict in Venture Boards," *Journal of Business Venturing* 25, no. 6 (2011): 579–92.

4. PharmaTech.com. "How Long Does Drug Development Take," http://pharmtech.findpharma. com/pharmtech/Latest+News/How-long-does-drug-development-take/ArticleStandard/Article/detail/ 574805?contextCategoryId=45298 (accessed June 1, 2011, originally posted on January 15, 2009).

5. S. Shane, *The Illusions of Entrepreneurship* (New Haven, CT: Yale University Press, 2008).

6. J. Ballou, T. Barton, D. DesRoches, F. Potter, E. J. Reedy, A. Robb, S. Shane, and Z. Zhao, *The Kauffman Firm Survey* (Kansas City, MO: The Kauffman Foundation), March 2008.

7. B. Barringer, *The Truths About Starting a Business* (Upper Saddle River, NJ: Financial Times Press, 2009).

8. Lending Karma homepage, www.lendingkarma.com (accessed May 31, 2011).

9. J. K. Smith, R. L. Smith, and R. T. Bliss, *Entrepreneurial Finance: Strategy, Valuation, and Deal Structure* (Stanford, CA; Stanford University Press, 2011).

10. J. Cornwall, *Bootstrapping* (Upper Saddle River, NJ: Prentice Hall, 2009).

11. B. Barringer, *The Truth About Starting a Business* (Upper Saddle River, NJ: Financial Times, 2009).

12. J. C. Leach and R. W. Melicher, *Entrepreneurial Finance*, 4th ed. (Cincinnati: SouthWestern Cengage Learning, 2012).

13. J. H. Chua, J. J. Chrisman, F. Kellermanns, and Z. Wu, "Family Involvement and New Venture Debt Financing," *Journal of Business Venturing* 26, no. 4 (2011): 472–88; M. G. Jacobides and S. G. Winter, "Entrepreneurship and Firm Boundaries: The Theory of a Firm," *Journal of Management Studies* 44, no. 7 (2007): 1213–41.

14. B. Barringer, *Preparing Effective Business Plans* (Upper Saddle River, NJ: Prentice Hall, 2008).

15. A. L. Maxwell, S. A. Jeffrey, and M. Levesque, "Business Angel Early Stage Decision Making," *Journal of Business Venturing* 26, no. 2 (2011): 212–25; D. Politis, "Business Angels and Value Added: What Do We Know and Where Do We Go?" *Venture Capital* 10, no. 2 (2008): 127–47.

16. E. Gimmon, R. Yitshaki, E. Benjamin, and S. Khavul, "Divergent Views of Venture Capitalists and Entrepreneurs on Strategic Change in New Ventures," *Strategic Change* 20, nos. 3 and 4 (2011): 85–99.

17. J. Melloan, "Angels with Angels," *Inc.*, July 2005.

18. G. Thoma, "Striving for a Large Market: Evidence from a General Purpose Technology in Action," *Industrial and Corporate Change* 18 (2009): 107–38; "ASAP," *Forbes*, June 1, 1998, 24.

19. J. Battelle, *The Search* (New York: Portfolio, 2005).

20. J. Sohl, "The Angel Investor Market in 2010: A Market on the Rebound," *Center for Venture Research*, April 12, 2011.

21. Sohl, "The Angel Investor Market in 2010."

22. PricewaterhouseCoopers/National Venture Capital Association, *MoneyTree Report*, Data Provided by Thomson Reuters, www.nvca.org, 2011.

23. Sohl, "The Angel Investor Market in 2010."

24. Sohl, "The Angel Investor Market in 2010."

25. X. Tian, "The Causes and Consequences of Venture Capital Stage Financing," *Journal of Financial Economics* 101, no. 1 (2011): 132–59.

26. PricewaterhouseCoopers/National Venture Capital Association, *MoneyTree Report*.

27. PricewaterhouseCoopers/National Venture Capital Association, *MoneyTree Report*.

28. PricewaterhouseCoopers/National Venture Capital Association, *MoneyTree Report*.

29. Khosla Ventures homepage, www.khoslaventures. com (accessed June 1, 1011).

30. BEV Capital homepage, www.bevcapital.com (accessed June 1, 2011).

31. PricewaterhouseCoopers/National Venture Capital Association, *MoneyTree Report*.

32. PricewaterhouseCoopers/National Venture Capital Association, *MoneyTree Report*.

33. C. Carpentier, J.-F. L'Her, and M.-M. Suret, "Stock Exchange Markets for New Ventures," *Journal of Business Venturing* 25, no. 2, (2010): 403–22.

34. S. Chahine, I. Fliatotchev, and S. A. Zahra, "Building Perceived Quality of Founder-Involved IPO Firms: Founders' Effects on Board Selection and Stock Market Performance," *Entrepreneurship Theory and Practice* 35, no. 2 (2011): 319–35.

35. M. A. Hitt, R. D. Ireland, and R. E. Hoskisson, *Strategic Management: Competitiveness and Globalization*, 10th ed. (Cincinnati: SouthWestern Cengage Publishing, 2012).

36. T. Adrian and H. S. Shin, "Liquidity and Leverage," *Journal of Financial Intermediation* 19, no. 3 (2010): 418–37.

37. T. J. Chemmanur, S. He, and D. K. Nandy, "The Going-Pubic Decision and the Product Market," *Review of Financial Studies* 23, no. 5 (2011): 1855–908.

38. P. J. Adelman and A. M. Marks, *Entrepreneurial Finance*, 5th ed. (Upper Saddle River, NJ: Prentice Hall, 2010).

39. J. C. Carr, K. S. Haggard, K. M. Hmieleski, and S. A. Zahra, "A Study of the Moderating Effects of

Firm Age at Internationalization on Firm Survival and Short-Term Growth," *Strategic Entrepreneurship Journal* 4, no. 3 (2010): 183–92.

40. V. Bruns, D. V. Holland, D. A. Shepherd, and J. Wiklund, "The Role of Human Capital in Loan Officers' Decision Policies," *Entrepreneurship Theory and Practice*, 32 (2008): 485–506.

41. SBA homepage, www.sba.gov (accessed June 1, 2011).

42. M. Eckblad, "Debunking the Myths About SBA Loans," *Wall Street Journal*, May 16, 2011, R2.

43. E. Malthy, "Vendors Can Help Financing," *Wall Street Journal*, February 18, 2010, B5.

44. "The Post-Banking Loan," *Entrepreneur*, May 2010, 72.

45. Count Me In homepage, www.countmein.org (accessed June 2, 2011).

46. ACCION homepage, www.accion.org (accessed June 2, 2011).

47. T. Vanacker, S. Manigart, M. Meuleman, and L. Sels, "A Longitudinal Study on the Relationship Between Financial Bootstrapping and New Venture Growth," *Entrepreneurship & Regional Development: An International Journal* (2011): in press.

48. J. Brinckmann and M. Hoegl, "Effects of Initial Teamwork Capability and Initial Relational Capability on the Development of New Technology-Based Firms," *Strategic Entrepreneurship Journal* 5, no. 1 (2011): 37–57.

49. SBA homepage, www.sba.gov (accessed June 2, 2011).

50. F. Chirico, R. D. Ireland, and D. G. Sirmon, "Franchising and the Family Firm: Creating Unique Sources of Advantage Through Familiness," *Entrepreneurship Theory and Practice* 35, no. 3 (2011): 483–501.

51. R. E. Hoskisson, J. Covin, H. W. Volberda, and R. A. Johnson, "Revitalizing Entrepreneurship: The Search for New Research Opportunities," *Journal of Management Studies* 48, no. 6 (2011): 1141–1168; B. Barringer and J. Harrison, "Walking a Tightrope: Creating Value Through Interorganizational Relationships," *Journal of Management* 26 (2000): 367–403.

PART 4

Managing and Growing an Entrepreneurial Firm

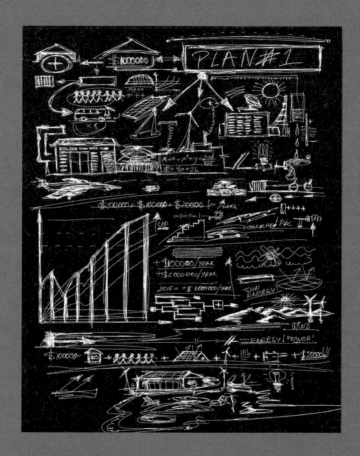

Getting Personal *with* TRUE YOU COSMETICS

Founder:

JESSICA TRUESDALE
BA, Sociology
Spellman College, expected 2011

Dialogue *with*
Jessica Truesdale

CURRENTLY IN MY SMARTPHONE
Last Train to Paris

BEST PART OF BEING A STUDENT
Growing internally and gaining greater knowledge

MY ADVICE FOR NEW ENTREPRENEURS
Always have your own niche.

MY BIGGEST WORRY AS AN ENTREPRENEUR
Ensuring that my team members perform at the highest level

MY BIGGEST SURPRISE AS AN ENTREPRENEUR
Inspiring women of all ages, colors, and creeds

MY FAVORITE SMARTPHONE APP
Evernote and Documents To Go

CHAPTER **11**

Unique *Marketing* Issues

OPENING PROFILE

TRUE YOU COSMETICS
Creating a New Brand in the Cosmetics Industry

Web: www.trueyoucosmetics.net
Twitter: TrueYouBeauty
Facebook: True You Cosmetics

If you asked Jessica Truesdale what she's passionate about, you'd get an answer you don't often hear from college students. She'd most likely say she's passionate about vintage glamour, and in particular how women have used makeup during different periods in U.S. history. If you smiled and asked Jessica, "Where did you get your passion for that?" she'd tell you about her grandmother and mother. Both instilled in her, from a young age, a love and passion for skincare, cosmetics, and American history.

Truesdale, who is majoring in sociology at Spelman College in Atlanta, has converted her love for skincare and cosmetics into a business named True You Cosmetics. The business was launched in October 2010 to sell cosmetics products. True You Cosmetics has positioned itself as a "better for you" cosmetics company with a unique historical twist. Its products are created from cutting-edge formulas including high-grade antioxidants, vitamins, and organic ingredients. They're also true to Truesdale's interest in glamour and American history. True You Cosmetic's Iconic Lip Collection, for example, features a line of lipsticks, each of which is named after a Hollywood icon or someone important to the company's formation. Lipsticks in the line include Emma, named after Emma Truesdale, Jessica's grandmother; Ava, named after Hollywood icon Ava Gardner; and Josephine, named after actress, dancer, and singer Josephine Baker.

True You Cosmetics' base of operations is Atlanta, which allows Truesdale to simultaneously run the company and finish her studies at Spelman. Truesdale works with cosmetics experts to formulate True You Cosmetics' products. Three different manufacturers are involved with creating, producing, and packaging the products. Truesdale has bootstrapped the company to this point, and has four employees. Her long-term strategy is to gain brand recognition and traction through online and direct sales, and then transition to retail sales.

LEARNING OBJECTIVES

After studying this chapter you should be ready to:

1. Explain the purpose of market segmentation.

2. Describe the importance of selecting a target market.

3. Explain why it is important for a start-up to establish a unique position in its target market.

4. Illustrate the two major ways in which a company builds a brand.

5. Identify the four components of the marketing mix.

6. Contrast cost-based pricing and value-based pricing.

7. Explain the difference between advertising and public relations.

8. Explain how firms can use social media to strengthen their brand and promote their products.

9. Weigh the advantages and disadvantages of selling direct versus selling through intermediaries.

10. Describe the seven-step sales process.

A major part of Truesdale's early efforts have been to establish an effective marketing strategy. Her marketing strategy so far has been twofold: to raise awareness of True You Cosmetics and its products and to establish channels through which the products can be sold. In regard to the former, Truesdale makes extensive use of social media, including Twitter, Facebook, and her blog, to connect and engage users with her products. She has found Twitter to be a particularly powerful platform to make product announcements, distribute discounts, run contests, update users on the progress of the company, and in general maintain an upbeat dialogue with customers. In just a few months, the company has garnered over 1,300 followers. She is currently revamping her Facebook page to make it more interactive. Ideas she's kicking around are to include Flash games, allowing people to match their skin tone with particular cosmetics, and online videos depicting how the products are properly used. Truesdale is also working with Ustream to host live demonstrations, broadcast from her Web site and social media platforms, to depict additional information about True You Cosmetics' products. Truesdale has employed a number of additional tactics to get the word out about her products. For example, early on she sent samples of her products to cosmetic industry and beauty bloggers for the purpose of providing them an opportunity to try her products and talk about them in their blogs.

The second major component of Truesdale's marketing strategy has been to establish effective distribution channels for her products. She currently sells online and via direct sales. She has a small but growing number of independent consultants. Called True You Cosmetics Consultants, these individuals buy products at a discount and then resell them at retail price. Her social media strategy is largely geared to driving traffic to her Web site, which has a vintage feel characteristic of her products. She's also been inventive in hosting events where she can demo her products and engage influence makers. For example, she recently hosted a True You Cosmetics "social" for makeup artists in the Atlanta area.

One thing Truesdale has been careful to do, in all of her marketing efforts, is to reinforce the unique story of why True You Cosmetics was formed and to show customers how old beauty trends can be effectively and eloquently used today. These are the central differentiating features of the True You Cosmetics brand.

In this chapter, we'll look at the marketing challenges confronting entrepreneurial firms. Marketing is a broad subject, and there are many books dedicated to marketing and its subfields. However, in this chapter, we zero in on the marketing challenges that are most pressing for young entrepreneurial firms. The reason for doing this is that marketing is an essential component to the success of a start-up firm.[1]

We begin this chapter by discussing how firms define and select their target markets. Next, we discuss how a firm establishes a brand. We then consider the four key aspects of marketing as they relate to young entrepreneurial firms. These four aspects, commonly referred to as the "4Ps" of marketing, are product, price, promotion, and place (or distribution). We conclude the chapter with a discussion of the sales process, which consists of the steps a company goes through to establish relationships with customers and close sales. Many new ventures do a good job of developing products and defining the size of their markets, but do a poor job of dealing with the practicalities of how the products will be sold. It's imperative that a new business have a plan that details how it will sell its product within the confines of a reasonable budget.

SELECTING A MARKET AND ESTABLISHING A POSITION

To succeed a new firm must know who its customers are and how to reach them. A firm uses a three-step process to determine who its customers are. These steps, which are shown in Figure 11.1, include segmenting the market, selecting a target market, and crafting a unique position within the target market.

As noted in Chapter 3, a firm's target market is the limited group of individuals or businesses that it tries to appeal to. It is important that a new venture choose its target market and position itself in its target market quickly because virtually all of its marketing choices hinge on these critical initial choices. For example, GreatCall, a company introduced in Chapter 2, makes cell phones designed specifically for older people. If GreatCall had designed a distribution strategy, for example, prior to determining that it would target older people, it might have designed a strategy that placed its phones in retail outlets not frequented by older people. Its decision to target older people will have a bearing on every element of its marketing plan.

Segmenting the Market

The first step in selecting a target market is to study the industry in which the firm intends to compete and determine the different potential target markets in that industry. This process is called **market segmentation**, as explained in Chapter 4. Market segmentation is important because a new firm typically has only enough resources to target one market segment, at least initially.[2] Markets can be segmented in many ways such as by geography (city, state, country), demographic variables (age, gender, family size, income), psychographic variables (personality, lifestyle, values), behavioral variables (benefits sought, product usage rates, brand loyalty), and product type (varies by product). For example, the computer industry can be segmented by product type (i.e., handheld computers, netbooks, laptops, tablet computers, PCs, minicomputers, and mainframes) or customers served (i.e., individuals, businesses, schools, and government).

Sometimes a firm segments its market on more than one dimension to drill down to a specific market segment that the firm thinks it is uniquely capable of serving. For example, GreatCall probably segmented its market by age and benefits sought. Its ideal customer is someone who is older (age) and is looking for a cell phone that's easy to use (benefits sought).

To test whether you have segmented your market successfully, the requirements for successful market segmentation are as follows:

■ Homogeneity of needs and wants appears within the segment.

■ Heterogeneity of needs and wants exists between the segments.

■ Differences within the segment should be small compared to differences across segments.

LEARNING OBJECTIVE
1. Explain the purpose of market segmentation.

Segmentating the Market	Selecting a Target Market	Crafting a Unique Positioning Strategy
What groups of customers in my market are similar enough that the same product or service will appeal to all of them?	Which specific group of customers have I decided to target?	What position will my firm occupy in the minds of my customers (and potential customers) that will differentiate it from all of my competitors?

FIGURE 11.1
The Process of Selecting a Target Market and Positioning Strategy

- The segment should be distinct enough so that its members can be easily identified.
- It should be possible to determine the size of the segment.
- The segment should be large enough to be profitable.

If an entrepreneur is not familiar with how to segment a particular market, both IBISWorld and Mintel, which are online databases that are often available through large university libraries, provide suggestions. They even show the size of the segments. For example, IBISWorld segments the Gym, Health & Fitness Club Industry (NAICS 71394) by service provided. The $24.8 billion industry is 65 percent gyms and fitness centers, 10 percent other, 7 percent dance centers, 7 percent swimming pools, 6 percent ice and roller rinks, and 5 percent tennis centers.[3]

Despite its importance, market segmentation is a process entrepreneurs commonly overlook. Overlooking this step can result in a faulty assessment of the size of the potential market for a new product or service. If a start-up planned to open a chain of tennis centers, for example, it would be incorrect to say that the total market potential is $24.8 billion. Tennis centers are a segment of the larger Gym, Health & Fitness Club Industry, which is the $24.8 billion market. This doesn't mean that a tennis center business couldn't be profitable or that the new business couldn't expand the market for tennis. It's just that the entrepreneur should enter the business with a realistic assessment of the size of its market.

Selecting a Target Market

Once a firm has segmented the market, the next step is to select a target market. As discussed in previous chapters, the market must be sufficiently attractive, and the firm must be able to serve it well. Typically, a firm (especially a start-up venture) doesn't target an entire segment of a market because many market segments are too large to target successfully. Instead, most firms target a niche market within the segment. For example, within the dance studio market, there are several small niche markets that companies can choose to target. A **niche market** is a place within a market segment that represents a narrow group of customers with similar interests. For example, Broadway Dance Center in New York City targets serious dancers who aspire to earn a living dancing in Broadway plays.[4] That's an entirely different niche than a studio teaching ballroom dancing or a studio teaching ballet to young girls. By focusing on a clearly defined market, a firm can become an expert in that market and then be able to provide its customers with high levels of value and service. Focusing on a clearly defined market requires a firm to know what *not to do* along with what to do. An example of a company that's successfully sorted this out is MailFinch, a company specializing in managing other companies' direct mail campaigns. According to its founder, Paul Singh:

> Looking back at the recent growth of MailFinch, most of the success can be attributed to what the product *can't* do. We do very few things, but we do those things better than anyone else in the game and we make it drop-dead simple to get started (with the MailFinch service).[5]

A firm's choice of target markets must also be in sync with its business model and the backgrounds and skills of its founders and other employees. A firm must also continually monitor the attractiveness of its target market. Societal preferences change, a fact that sometimes causes a target market to lose its attractiveness for a firm and the product or service it has to offer customers.

Establishing a Unique Position

After selecting a target market, the firm's next step is to establish a "position" within it that differentiates it from its competitors. As we discussed in Chapter 5, position is concerned with how the firm is situated relative to competitors. For example, in Pittsburgh, Pennsylvania Art & Style Dance Studio specializes in Latin and Ballroom dancing.[6] That's a different position than the Arthur Murray Dance Studio in Pittsburgh that offers instruction in Fox Trot, Waltz, Tango, Viennese Waltz, Quickstep, and Salsa.[7] A firm's position is defined by its products or services. Determining which position to occupy and compete in is a strategic call on the part of a company based on its mission, its overall approach to the marketplace, and its competitive landscape.

Once a company has identified its position and primary points of differentiation, a helpful technique is to develop a **product attribute map**, which illustrates a firm's positioning strategy relative to its major rivals. A product attribute map for Snap Fitness is shown in Figure 11.2. Snap Fitness, which is the focus of Case 15.1, operates small gyms that are located near residential areas, and are open 24 hours a day. The centers offer weights, treadmills, and exercise machines. They're staffed during the day and are available to members at night by swiping a key card at the main door. The equipment is start-of-the-art, the centers are very clean, and they are secure. They do not offer a wide range of amenities, such as swimming pools, locker rooms, exercise classes, racquetball courts, and massages. The centers offer their members a fast, convenient, and affordable way to develop and maintain fitness. A membership costs around $40 a month for a single membership, $60 for a couple, and $70 for a family.

This firm's product attribute map is based on the two primary attributes that people look for in a fitness center—range of amenities provided and the extent to which the center is both affordable and convenient. The point is to assess Snap Fitness's strengths and/or weaknesses in each of these categories and plot it on the map. The same is done for Snap Fitness's major competitors. The results are shown in Figure 11.2. While Snap Fitness does not rank high in terms of amenities provided, it outranks its competitors by a wide margin in terms of being convenient and affordable. As a result, it stresses its convenience and affordability in its promotions, rather than draw attention to its

LEARNING OBJECTIVE

3. Explain why it is important for a start-up to establish a unique position in its target market.

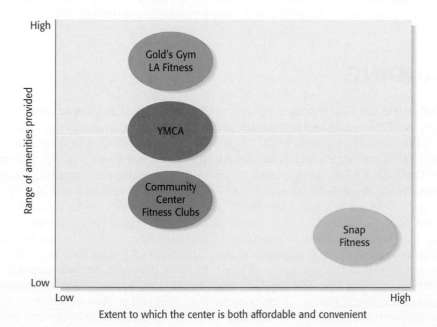

FIGURE 11.2
Product Attribute Map for Snap Fitness

TABLE 11.1   MATCH THE COMPANY TO ITS TAGLINE

Company	Tagline
InstyMeds	A brighter future
Zipcar	A revolution in writing software
XploSafe	Mix it up. Mash it out
Scripped	Learning. Accelerated
SmartyPants	Wheels when you want them
d.light	The total vitamin treat
Kazoo Toys	Technologies for a safer world
Stroome	We make patients better quicker
BenchPrep	Toys with imagination

lack of amenities. Snap Fitness's tagline is "fast convenient affordable."[8] Any firm can develop a similar product attribute map to illustrate its position in an industry and help direct its marketing plan.

To support their positioning strategy, firms often develop a tagline, just like Snap Fitness has done, to reinforce the position they have staked out in the marketplace. A **tagline** is catchy phrase that's used consistently in a company's literature, advertisements, stationery, and even invoices and thus becomes associated with that company—to reinforce the position they have staked out in their market. Table 11.1 is a short matching quiz that asks you to match companies featured in this book with their taglines. A company has created a successful tagline if the message makes you think of its products or services and the position it has established in its market.

As illustrated in the "What Went Wrong?" feature presented next, Ugobe is an example of a firm that did a poor job of selecting a target market and developing a positioning strategy. Ugobe was the creator of Pleo, a small robotic baby dinosaur. Not only did Ugobe fail to identify a target market for Pleo, but the company misunderstood the nature of its early sales, which caused it to focus on growth rather than getting Pleo's marketing strategy right.

BRANDING

LEARNING OBJECTIVE

4. Illustrate the two major ways in which a company builds a brand.

A **brand** is the set of attributes—positive or negative—that people associate with a company. These attributes can be positive, such as trustworthy, innovative, dependable, or easy to deal with. Or they can be negative, such as cheap, unreliable, arrogant, or difficult to deal with. The customer loyalty a company creates through its brand is one of its most valuable assets. Lending support to this sentiment, Russell Hanlin, the CEO of Sunkist Growers, said, "An orange is an orange . . . is an orange. Unless . . . that orange happens to be a Sunkist, a name 80 percent of consumers know and trust."[9] By putting its name on an orange, Sunkist is making a promise to its customers that the orange will be wholesome and fresh. It is important that Sunkist not break this promise. Some companies monitor the integrity of their brands through **brand management**, which is a program used to protect the image and value of an organization's brand in consumers' minds. This means that if Sunkist discovered that some of its oranges weren't fresh, it would take immediate steps to correct the problem.

WHAT WENT WRONG?

How Failing to Establish a Clear Position in the Marketplace Forced an Adorable Robotic Dinosaur to Fall Silent

If you've never met Pleo, log onto YouTube, type "Pleo" into the search box, and then click on one of the video clips that are posted. Pleo is a small robotic baby dinosaur—a Camarasaurus to be exact—that was the creation of Ugobe. Pleo has many lifelike characteristics, and can interact with people through its 38 sensors. Pleo can coo, shake, bark, cry, play tug-of-war, and even act sad if you quit playing with it. The baby dinosaur was first revealed to the world at the DEMO Conference in 2006. It got ample press attention and rave reviews. In 2007, Pleo was offered for sale—at a somewhat hefty price of $350—and sold 100,000 units before the end of the year. Then its sales stalled. In 2008, Ugobe's board removed its CEO and brought in new leadership. Ugobe went to the capital markets later that year to raise additional funding, to keep the company solvent, but no investor would pony up. In April 2009, Ugobe filed bankruptcy and Pleo fell silent. What went wrong?

Several things contributed to Ugobe's demise. First, although Pleo didn't look that complicated, getting a robot to do the things Pleo could do was a major undertaking. John Sosoka, Ugobe's chief technical officer (CTO), in a presentation about Pleo to a class at Stanford University, said Ugobe spent about $7 million building Pleo before it shipped the first unit. When sales slowed in 2008, Ugobe was in trouble financially, and couldn't raise additional funds. But according to Sosoka, even if Ugobe had risen additional funding, it ultimately would have failed anyway. According to Sosoka and others, Ugobe's real problem wasn't financial. It was a marketing problem that Ugobe never solved.

The core marketing problem had two parts. First, despite all of Pleo's positive attributes, Ugobe never really figured out what Pleo was and to whom it should be sold. Was Pleo a pet? Was it a high-end toy? Was it a companion robot for adults? Was it a really cool product? Was it a platform for research? (Sophisticated users could write software add-ons that would enable Pleo to show more emotion.) Pleo was at the same time all of these things and none of these things. In reality, it was in a category that didn't really have a name or a market. Because Ugobe remained as puzzled about what Pleo was and to whom it should be sold as its potential buyers, it never figured out Pleo's positioning strategy or developed a coherent marketing message.

The second part of Ugobe's marketing problem is that the firm may have mistakenly interpreted the meaning of Pleo's early sales. Ugobe clearly believed that the initial interest in Pleo—the 100,000 units that sold in 2007—was validation that Pleo had broad market appeal. It didn't.

In his insightful book, *Crossing the Chasm,* Geoffrey A. Moore explains the nature of this phenomenon. In a nutshell, what Moore said is that there is a chasm between the early adopters of a technologically sophisticated product and mainstream consumers. Early adopters are enthusiasts—they are the visionaries who seek out new products and try them before anyone else. A company doesn't have to have a coherent marketing strategy to find early adopters—the early adopters find them. That's who the 100,000 people who bought Pleo in 2007 likely were, early adopters. According to Moore, a "chasm" needs to be crossed before a product grows beyond early adopters and mainstream consumers join in. If a firm can create a bandwagon effect among its early adopters, and a product becomes a de facto standard, the chasm can be crossed. This never happened in Pleo's case, a reality Ugobe realized too late. By thinking that Pleo had broad market appeal, the company focused on growth rather than its basic marketing problem. Eventually, Pleo's early adopters moved on to the next technological marvel and sales died. Absent accelerating sales, Ugobe was not financially sustainable.

Interestingly, Ugobe's failure wasn't the end of Pleo. At the bankruptcy sale, Innvo Labs, a subsidiary of Jetta Company, Ltd., acquired all the intellectual property related to Pleo and has relaunched the robotic baby dinosaur under the Innvo Labs corporate name.

Questions for Critical Thinking

1. Who do you think should have been identified initially as the target customer for a small robotic baby dinosaur? Should children wanting to play with a unique toy have been the target market? If not, what about adults with a strong interest in technology?
2. What steps could Ugobe have taken to better understand the meaning of its initial sales?
3. Why do you think Ugobe was unsuccessful in its efforts to secure additional funding in 2008? What "red flags" did these investors see when they evaluated the possibility of financially supporting Pleo and the company producing the product?
4. What do you think the odds are that Innvo Labs' relaunching of Pleo will be successful? To increase the likelihood of success, what steps would you recommend that Innvo Labs take?

Sources: J. Sosoka, "The Rise and Fall of Pleo, a Farewell Lecture by John Sosoka, Former CTO of Ugobe," Robotshop.com blog, www.robotshop.com/gorobotics/the-news/latest-news/the-rise-and-fall-of-pleo-a-fairwell-lecture-by-john-sosoka-former-cto-of-ugobe (accessed February 28, 2011, originally posted on May 29, 2009); "Turning Out the Lights: Ugobe, Maker of Robotic Dinosaur," *Wall Street Journal,* April 28, 2009, B1.

This young entrepreneur just opened a skateboard business. He plans to sell skateboards and skateboard accessories through a retail storefront and online. An important task he has ahead of him is building a brand for his company. A brand is the set of attributes that people associate with a company.

© Radius./SuperStock

Table 11.2 lists the different ways people think about the meaning of a brand. All the sentiments expressed in the table are similar, but they illustrate the multifaceted nature of a company's brand.

Start-ups must build a brand from scratch; this process begins with selecting the company's name, as described in Chapter 7's Appendix. One of the keys to effective branding is to create a strong personality for a firm, designed to appeal to the chosen target market.[10] Southwest Airlines, for example, has created a brand that denotes fun. This is a good fit for its historical and still primary target market: people traveling for pleasure rather than business. Similarly, Starbucks and Panera Bread have each created a brand that denotes an experience framed around warmth and hospitality, encouraging people to linger and buy additional products. A company ultimately wants its customers to strongly identify with it—to see themselves as "Southwest Airlines

TABLE 11.2   WHAT'S A BRAND? DIFFERENT WAYS OF THINKING ABOUT THE MEANING OF A BRAND

- A brand is a promise to serve stakeholders' interests.
- A brand is a firm's guarantee of a level of performance.
- A brand indicates the promises a firm makes to those it serves.
- A brand expresses a firm's reputation.
- A brand presents a firm's credentials.
- A brand is an indicator of trust and reduced risk.
- A brand describes a company's nature.
- A brand serves as a handshake between a firm and its customers.

Source: Adapted from *Emotional Branding* by Daryl Travis, copyright © 2000 by Daryl Travis. Used by permission of Pima Publishing, a division of Random House, Inc.

flyers" or as "Panera Bread diners." People won't do this, however, unless they see a company as being different from competitors in ways that create value for them.

So how does a new firm develop a brand? On a philosophical level, a firm must have meaning in its customers' lives. It must create value—something for which customers are willing to pay. Imagine a father shopping for airline tickets so that he can take his three children to see their grandparents for Christmas. If Southwest Airlines can get his family to their destination for $75 per ticket cheaper than its competitors, Southwest has real meaning in the father's life. Similarly, if a young couple invites neighbors to play Morphology, the board game introduced at the beginning of Chapter 3, and playing the game results in lasting friendships, Morphology will have a special place in their hearts.

On a more practical level, brands are built through a number of techniques, including advertising, public relations, sponsorships, support of social causes, social media and good performance. A firm's name, logo, Web site design, Facebook page, and even its letterhead are part of its brand. It's important for start-ups, particularly if they plan to sell to other businesses, to have a polished image immediately so that they have credibility when they approach their potential customers.

Most experts warn against placing an overreliance on advertising to build a firm's brand. A more affordable approach is to rely on word of mouth, the media, and ingenuity to create positive buzz about a company. Creating **buzz** means creating awareness and a sense of anticipation about a company and its offerings.[11] This process can start during feasibility analysis, when a company shows its concept statement or product prototype to prospective buyers or industry experts. Unless a company wants what it is doing to be kept secret (to preserve its proprietary technology or its first-mover advantage), it hopes that people start talking about it and its exciting new product or service. This is certainly the case for movie production studios as they hope that people talking about a movie they enjoyed watching will encourage others to visit their local theaters.[12] In addition, newspapers, magazines, blogs, and trade journals are always looking for stories about interesting companies. In fact, receiving a favorable review of its products or services in a magazine, trade journal, or highly respected blog lends a sense of legitimacy to a firm that would be hard to duplicate through advertisements. Focusing too much on the features and benefits of their products is a common mistake entrepreneurs make when trying to gain attention from the media. Journalists are typically skeptical when entrepreneurs start talking about how great their products are relative to those of their competitors. What journalists usually prefer is a human interest story about why a firm was started or a story focused on something that's distinctly unique about the start-up. The "Savvy Entrepreneurial Firm" feature in this chapter affirms these points. The feature focuses on how Airbnb, which is a marketplace for people to list, discover, and book unique spaces (typically in people's homes or apartments) used blogs as a stepping-stone to generate substantial buzz about its service.

Ultimately, a strong brand can be a very powerful asset for a firm. Over 50 percent of consumers say that a known and trusted brand is a reason to buy a product.[13] As a result, a brand allows a company to charge a price for its products that is consistent with its image. A successful brand can also increase the market value of a company by 50 to 75 percent.[14] This increased valuation can be very important to a firm if it is acquired, merges with another firm, or launches an initial public offering. **Brand equity** is the term that denotes the set of assets and liabilities that are linked to a brand and enable it to raise a firm's valuation.[15] It is important for firms to understand brand equity and how to use it to create value.

SAVVY ENTREPRENEURIAL FIRM

How Airbnb Used Blogs as a Stepping-Stone to Generate Substantial Buzz About Its Service

Web: www.airbnb.com
Twitter: airbnb
Facebook: Airbnb

It's important for entrepreneurial firms to generate press as effectively and inexpensively as possible. One start-up, Airbnb, generated substantial press during its start-up phase at very little cost. Its formula was novel, but is instructive for any start-up trying to generate buzz and positive PR.

Airbnb (the subject of Case 6.1) is a marketplace for people to list, discover, and book unique spaces (typically in people's homes or apartments) while traveling. It's also useful for people who have space to rent to generate extra income. Founded in late 2007, the firm initially targeted people traveling to conferences and events in the United States. However, Airbnb now offers its services worldwide and has grown to allow people to rent space while traveling for any purpose (instead of business only, which was the initial focus).

Early on, observers were struck by the amount of press that Airbnb generated. In its first two years, the company was featured in *Time* magazine, the *New York Times*, the *Washington Post*, CNN, and a variety of other places. There wasn't any obvious reason Airbnb (called Air Bed & Breakfast at the time) was getting so much attention. It didn't have celebrity founders, wasn't backed by a venture capital firm, and didn't spend a ton of money. In fact, it was started by three previously unknown entrepreneurs and was bootstrapped until late 2010. So how did they do it? It all started with blogs.

Shortly after the company launched, the firm's founders e-mailed as many design bloggers as they could, explaining the Airbnb concept. The founders were designers, and the site was first used to help people attending design conferences find rooms in local designers' homes for the duration of the conference. Several of the prominent design blogs, including Core77.com, picked up the story and ran articles about the new service. This initial effort prompted a small mention in Mashable, a widely read social media blog. In an interview about how they generated so much press early on, Brian Chesky and Joe Gebbia, two of Airbnb's founders, characterized getting mentions in blogs as a progressive process. If you get mentioned by small blogs, it's easier to get the attention of larger blogs, and a company sort of

moves up the ladder. The process wasn't totally efficient. They often had to reach out to several blogs to get a single mention, but overall the strategy worked.

Next, they reached out to newspapers and magazines, which was also a successful effort. Airbnb seemed to resonate with journalists because of the unique aspect of its service. But the blogs played an important role here too. One thing the founders of Airbnb learned is that the first thing a newspaper or magazine writer does, when pitched by a new company, is type the firm's name into Google to see if anyone else has written about them. Fair or unfair, a journalist is much more willing to write about a company if others are writing about it too. That's one of the advantages of being covered by blogs—their stories will show up in Google searches. Even mentions in small blogs, which generally appreciate being reached out to, show up in search engine searches.

Even though Airbnb is much more proven today, its founders still reach out to bloggers. They circle back to the blogs that have already written about them and ask them to write additional stories when there is something exciting to write about.

Questions for Critical Thinking

1. How does an entrepreneur establish a "relationship" with an influential blogger?
2. What's the right way and what's the wrong way to approach a blogger about writing a post about a particular company?
3. How important is generating press and PR for a start-up firm? Is it more important for some types of businesses than others? Explain your answer.
4. Case 11.1 focuses on ModCloth, an online retailer that sells independent designer women's fashion. Make a list of the blogs (minimum of five) that ModCloth's founder could have potentially reached out to when the company was launched.

Source: A. Warner, B. Chesky, and J. Gebbia, "Airbnb," Mixergy, www. mixergy.com (accessed March 28, 2011, posted on January 28, 2010).

Although the assets and liabilities that make up a firm's brand equity will vary from context to context, they usually are grouped into the following five categories:

- Brand loyalty
- Name recognition

- Perceived quality (of a firm's products and services)
- Brand associations in addition to quality (e.g., good service)
- Other proprietary assets, such as patents, trademarks, and high-quality partnerships

THE 4Ps OF MARKETING FOR NEW VENTURES

Once a company decides on its target market, establishes a position within that market, and establishes a brand, it is ready to begin planning the details of its marketing mix. A firm's **marketing mix** is the set of controllable, tactical marketing tools that it uses to produce the response it wants in the target market.[16] Most marketers organize their marketing mix into four categories: product, price, promotion, and place (or distribution). For an obvious reason, these categories are commonly referred to as the 4Ps.

LEARNING OBJECTIVE
5. Identify the four components of the marketing mix.

The way a firm sells and distributes its product dramatically affects a company's marketing program. This effect means that the first decision a firm has to make is its overall approach to selling its product or service. Even for similar firms, the marketing mix can vary significantly, depending on the way the firms do business. For example, a software firm can sell directly through its Web site or through retail stores, or it can license its product to another company to be sold under that company's brand name. A start-up that plans to sell directly to the public would set up its promotions program in a much different way than a firm planning to license its products to other firms. A firm's marketing program should be consistent with its business model and its overall business plan.

Let's look more closely at the 4Ps. Again, these are broad topics on which entire books have been written. In this section, we focus on the aspects of the 4Ps that are most relevant to entrepreneurial ventures.

Product

A firm's **product**, in the context of its marketing mix, is the good or service it offers to its target market. Technically, a product is something that takes on physical form, such as an Apple iPhone, an electronic game, or a solar panel. A **service** is an activity or benefit that is intangible and does not take on a physical form, such as an airplane trip or advice from an attorney. But when discussing a firm's marketing mix, both products and services are lumped together under the label "product."

Determining the product or products to be sold is central to the firm's entire marketing effort. As stressed throughout this book, the most important attribute of a product is that it adds value in the minds of its target customers. Let's think about this by comparing vitamins with pain pills, as articulated by Henry W. Chesbrough, a professor at Harvard University:

> We all know that vitamins are good for us and that we should take them. Most of us, though, do not take vitamins on a regular basis, and whatever benefits vitamins provide do not seem to be greatly missed in the short term. People therefore pay relatively very little for vitamins. In contrast, people know when they need a pain killer. And they know they need it now, not later. They can also tell quite readily whether the reliever is working. People will be willing to pay a great deal more for a pain reliever than they pay for a vitamin. In this context, the pain reliever provides a much stronger value proposition than does a vitamin—because the need is felt more acutely, the benefit is greater and is perceived much more quickly.[17]

This example illustrates at least in part why investors prefer to fund firms that potentially have breakthrough products, such as a software firm that is working on a product to eliminate e-mail spam or a biotech firm that is working on a cure for a disease. These products are pain pills rather than vitamins because their benefits would be felt intensely and quickly. In contrast, a new restaurant start-up or a new retail store may be exciting, but these types of firms are more akin to a vitamin than a pain pill. The benefits of these businesses would not be felt as intensely.

As the firm prepares to sell its product, an important distinction should be made between the core product and the actual product. While the core product may be a CD that contains a tax preparation program, the actual product, which is what the customer buys, may have as many as five characteristics: a quality level, features, design, a brand name, and packaging.[18] For example, TurboTax is an actual product. Its name, features, warranty, ability to upgrade, packaging, and other attributes have all been carefully combined to deliver the benefits of the product: helping people prepare their federal and state tax returns while getting the biggest refund possible. When first introducing a product to the market, an entrepreneur needs to make sure that more than the core product is right. Attention also needs to be paid to the actual product—the features, design, packaging, and so on that constitute the collection of benefits that the customer ultimately buys. Anyone who has ever tried to remove a product from a frustratingly rigid plastic container knows that the way a product is packaged is part of the product itself. The quality of the product should not be compromised by missteps in other areas.

The initial rollout is one of the most critical times in the marketing of a new product. All new firms face the challenge that they are unknown and that it takes a leap of faith for their first customers to buy their products. Some start-ups meet this challenge by using reference accounts. A **reference account** is an early user of a firm's product who is willing to give a testimonial regarding his or her experience with the product. For example, imagine the effect of a spokesperson for Apple Inc. saying that Apple used a new computer hardware firm's products and was pleased with their performance. A testimonial such as this would pave the way for the sales force of this new firm's hardware, and the new firm could use it to reduce fears that it was selling an untested and perhaps ineffective product.

To obtain reference accounts, new firms must often offer their product to an initial group of customers for free or at a reduced price in exchange for their willingness to try the product and for their feedback. There is nothing improper about this process as long as everything is kept aboveboard and the entrepreneur is not indirectly "paying" someone to offer a positive endorsement. Still, many entrepreneurs are reluctant to give away products, even in exchange for a potential endorsement. But there are several advantages to getting a strong set of endorsements: credibility with peers, non-company advocates who are willing to talk to the press, and quotes or examples to use in company brochures and advertisements.

Price

Price is the amount of money consumers pay to buy a product. It is the only element in the marketing mix that produces revenue; all other elements represent costs.[19] Price is an extremely important element of the marketing mix because it ultimately determines how much money a company can earn. The price a company charges for its products also sends a clear message to its target market. For example, Oakley positions its sunglasses as innovative, state-of-the art products that are both high quality and visually appealing. This position in the market suggests the premium price that Oakley charges.

If Oakley tried to establish the position described previously and charged a low price for its products, it would send confusing signals to its customers. Its customers would wonder, "Are Oakley sunglasses high quality or aren't they?" In addition, the lower price wouldn't generate the sales revenue Oakley requires to continuously differentiate its sunglasses from competitors' products in ways that create value for customers.

Most entrepreneurs use one of two methods to set the price for their products: cost-based pricing or value-based pricing.

Cost-Based Pricing In **cost-based pricing**, the list price is determined by adding a markup percentage to a product's cost. The markup percentage may be standard for the industry or may be arbitrarily determined by the entrepreneur. The advantage of this method is that it is straightforward, and it is relatively easy to justify the price of a good or service. The disadvantage is that it is not always easy to estimate what the costs of a product will be. Once a price is set, it is difficult to raise it, even if a company's costs increase in an unpredicted manner. In addition, cost-based pricing is based on what a company thinks it should receive rather than on what the market thinks a good or service is worth. It is becoming increasingly difficult for companies to dictate prices to their customers, given customers' ability to comparison shop on the Internet to find what they believe is the best bargain for them.[20]

LEARNING OBJECTIVE
6. Contrast cost-based pricing and value-based pricing.

Value-Based Pricing In **value-based pricing**, the list price is determined by estimating what consumers are willing to pay for a product and then backing off a bit to provide a cushion. What a customer is willing to pay is determined by the perceived value of the product and by the number of choices available in the marketplace. Sometimes, to make this determination, a company has to work backwards by testing to see what its target market is willing to pay. A firm influences its customers' perception of the value through positioning, branding, and the other elements of the marketing mix. Most experts recommend value-based pricing because it hinges on the perceived value of a product or service rather than cost-plus markup, which, as stated previously, is a formula that ignores the customer.[21] A gross margin (a company's net sales minus its costs of goods sold) of 60 to 80 percent is not uncommon in high-tech industries. An Intel chip that sells for $300 may cost $50 to $60 to produce. This type of markup reflects the perceived value of the chip. If Intel used a cost-based pricing method instead of a value-based approach, it would probably charge much less for its chips and earn less profit.

Most experts also warn entrepreneurs to resist the temptation to charge a low price for their products in the hopes of capturing market share. This approach can win a sale but generates little profit. In addition, most consumers make a **price-quality attribution** when looking at the price of a product. This means that consumers naturally assume that the higher-priced product is also the better-quality product.[22] If a firm charges a low price for its products, it sends a signal to its customers that the product is low quality regardless of whether it really is.

A vivid example of the association between price and quality is provided by SmugMug, an online photo-sharing site that charges a $40-per-year base subscription fee. SmugMug, which is growing rapidly, has 300,000 paying customers and more than 1.3 billion photos stored. What's interesting about the company is that most of its competitors, including Shutterfly and Flickr, offer a similar service for free. Ostensibly, the reason SmugMug is able to charge a fee is that it offers higher levels of customer service and has a more user-friendly interface (in terms of how you view your photos online) than its competitors. But the owners of SmugMug feel that its ability to charge goes beyond these obvious points. Some of the free sites have closed abruptly, and their users have lost photos. SmugMug, because it charges, is seen as more reliable and dependable for the long term. (Who wants to lose their photos?) In addition, the owners believe that when people pay for something, they innately assign a higher value to it. As a result, SmugMug users tend to treat the site with respect, by posting attractive, high-quality photos that are in good taste. SmugMug's users appreciate this facet of the site, compared to the free sites, where unseemly photos often creep in.[23]

The overarching point of this example is that the price a company is able to charge is largely a function of (1) the objective quality of a product or service and (2) the perception of value that you create in the minds of your customers relative to competing products in the marketplace. These are issues a firm should consider when developing its positioning and branding strategies.

Promotion

Promotion refers to the activities the firm takes to communicate the merits of its product to its target market. Ultimately, the goal of these activities is to persuade people to buy the product. There are a number of these activities, but most start-ups have limited resources, meaning that they must carefully study promotion activities before choosing the one or ones they'll use. Let's look at the most common activities entrepreneurs use to promote their products.

LEARNING OBJECTIVE

7. Explain the difference between advertising and public relations.

Advertising   **Advertising** is making people aware of a product in hopes of persuading them to buy it. Advertising's major goals are to do the following:

■ Raise customer awareness of a product

■ Explain a product's comparative features and benefits

■ Create associations between a product and a certain lifestyle

These goals can be accomplished through a number of media including direct mail, magazines, newspapers, radio, the Internet, television, and billboard advertising. The most effective ads tend to be those that are memorable and support a product's brand. However, advertising has some major weaknesses, including the following:

■ Low credibility

■ The possibility that a high percentage of the people who see the ad will not be interested

■ Message clutter (meaning that after hearing or reading so many ads, people simply tune out)

■ Relative costliness compared to other forms of promotions

■ The perception that advertising is intrusive[24]

Because of these weaknesses, most start-ups do not advertise their products broadly. Instead, they tend to be very frugal and selective in their advertising efforts or engage in hybrid promotional campaigns that aren't advertising per se but are designed to promote a product or service.

Along with engaging in hybrid promotional campaigns, many start-ups advertise in trade journals or utilize highly focused pay-per-click advertising provided by Google, Bing, or another online firm to economize the advertising dollars. Pay-per-click advertising represents a major innovation in advertising and has been embraced by firms of all sizes. Google has two pay-per-click programs—AdWords and AdSense. AdWords allows an advertiser to buy keywords on Google's homepage (www.google.com), which triggers text-based ads to the side (and sometimes above) the search results when the keyword is used. So, if you type "soccer ball" into the Google search bar, you will see ads that have been paid for by companies that have soccer balls to sell. Many advertisers report impressive results utilizing this approach, presumably because they are able to place their ads in front of people who are already searching for information about their product. Google's other pay-per-click program is called AdSense. It is similar to AdWords, except the advertiser's ads appear on other Web sites instead of Google's homepage. For example, an organization that promotes soccer might allow Google to place some of its client's ads on its Web site. The advertiser pays on a pay-for-click basis when its ad is clicked on the soccer organization's site, just like it does with AdWords. Google shares the revenue generated by the advertisers with the sponsoring site. Table 11.3 provides a summary of the Google AdWords and Google AdSense programs. Yahoo! and Microsoft's programs, which are very similar to Google's, are called Yahoo! Search Marketing and Microsoft adCenter (showing ads on Bing), respectively.

As an aside, the Google AdSense program allows people who know a lot about a particular topic to launch a Web site, populate it with articles, tips, videos, and other useful information and make money online by essentially selling access to the people attracted to the Web site. For example, Tim Carter, a well-known columnist on home repair, has a Web site named Ask the Builder (www.askthebuilder.com). Information and instructions on all types of home building projects and repair are available on this Web site, as are links to areas that focus on specific topics, like air conditioning, cabinets, deck construction, and plumbing. Clicking any one of these areas brings up AdSense ads that deal with that specific area. All together, the site has hundreds of AdSense ads. Carter is able to do this and still attract large numbers of visitors because the information he provides is good and helpful. He might also believe that his ads,

TABLE 11.3 **DESCRIPTION OF GOOGLE ADWORDS AND ADSENSE PROGRAMS FOR ADVERTISERS AND WEB SITE OWNERS**

AdWords	AdSense
Allows advertisers to buy keywords on the Google homepage.	Allows advertisers to buy ads that will be shown on other Web sites instead of Google's homepage.
Triggers text-based ads to the side (and sometimes above) search results when the keyword is used.	Google selects sites of interest for the advertiser's customers.
Advertisers are charged on a pay-per-click basis.	Advertisers are charged on a pay-per-click or per-thousand-impression basis.
The program includes local, national, and international distribution.	Advertisers are not restricted to text-based ads. Choices include text, image, and video advertisements.
Advertisers specify the maximum amount they are willing to pay per click. The ordering of the paid listings on the search results depends on other advertisers' bids and the historical click-through rates of all ads shown for a given search.	Advertisers benefit because their ads are seen as less intrusive than most banner ads, because the content of the ad is often relevant to the Web site.
Advertisers have the option of enabling their ads to be displayed on Google's partner network. This network includes AOL, Ask.com, and Netscape.	Web site owners benefit by using the service to monetize their Web sites.
Advertisers benefit because they are able to place their ads in front of people who are already searching for information about their product.	A companion to the regular AdSense program, AdSense for Search lets Web site owners place the Google search box on their Web site. Google shares any ad revenues it makes from those searches.

in a certain respect, add valuable content to the site. If someone is looking at the portion of his site that deals with how to construct a deck, he or she might actually appreciate seeing ads that point to Web sites where books and blueprints for building decks are available.

Another medium for advertising, which is growing in popularity, is to advertise through social media sites, like Facebook. The advantage of Facebook, in particular, is that it allows companies to deliver highly targeted ads, based on where people live and how they describe themselves on their Facebook profiles. For example, a company that sells licensed sports apparel for the Boston Red Sox can deliver a highly targeted ad to the people most likely to buy its products. The company could deliver ads exclusively to men who live in Massachusetts and cite the "Red Sox" in their Facebook profiles. Any company can identify its ideal potential customer and deliver targeted Facebook ads in the same manner.

The steps involved in putting together an advertisement are shown in Figure 11.3. Typically, for start-up firms, advertisements are the most effective if they're part of a coordinated marketing campaign.[25] For example, a print ad might feature a product's benefits and direct the reader to a Web site or Facebook page for more information. The Web site or Facebook page might offer access to coupons or other incentives if the visitor fills out an information request form (which asks for name, address, and phone number). The names collected from the information request form could then be used to make sales calls.

Public Relations   One of the most cost-effective ways to increase the awareness of the products a company sells is through public relations. **Public relations** refer to efforts to establish and maintain a company's image with the public. The major difference between public relations and advertising is that public relations is not paid for—directly. The cost of public relations to a firm is the effort it makes to network with journalists, blog authors, and other people to try to interest them in saying or writing good things about the company and its products. Several techniques fit the definition of public relations, as shown in Table 11.4. Airbnb's campaign to reach out to bloggers, chronicled in the "Savvy Entrepreneurial Firm" feature earlier in the chapter, is an example of a public relations campaign.

Many start-ups emphasize public relations over advertising primarily because it's cheaper and helps build the firm's credibility. In slightly different words, it may be better to start with public relations than advertising because people view advertising as the self-serving voice of a company that's anxious to

FIGURE 11.3
Steps Involved in
Putting Together
an Advertisement

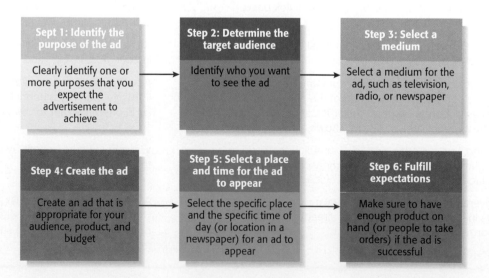

Sept 1: Identify the purpose of the ad
Clearly identify one or more purposes that you expect the advertisement to achieve

Step 2: Determine the target audience
Identify who you want to see the ad

Step 3: Select a medium
Select a medium for the ad, such as television, radio, or newspaper

Step 4: Create the ad
Create an ad that is appropriate for your audience, product, and budget

Step 5: Select a place and time for the ad to appear
Select the specific place and the specific time of day (or location in a newspaper) for an ad to appear

Step 6: Fulfill expectations
Make sure to have enough product on hand (or people to take orders) if the ad is successful

TABLE 11.4 PUBLIC RELATIONS TECHNIQUES

Technique	Description
Press release	An announcement made by a firm that is circulated to the press. Start-ups typically circulate a press release when something positive happens, such as the launch of a new product or the hiring of a new executive.
Traditional media coverage	Any coverage in print or broadcast media. In most cases, start-ups try to cultivate media coverage, as long as it is positive.
Social media coverage	Start-ups use social media (Facebook, Twitter) as a way of communicating and building rapport with customers, and also covet positive mentions in the social media efforts of others. For example, a positive mention by someone who posts on Twitter and has a large number of followers can positively impact a start-up.
Articles in industry press and periodicals	Articles in industry press and periodicals are particularly coveted because they are read by people already interested in the industry in which the start-up is participating.
Blogging	Companies benefit from blogging in three ways: First, by writing their own blog, as a way of building rapport with customers and the general public. Second, by commenting on entries contained in other companies' or people's blogs. Third, by contacting bloggers and asking them to comment on a company's product or service. The general rule of thumb in blogging is that thoughtful and substantive contributions are fine. Outwardly talking about the merits of a company's products is inappropriate, unless it's on the company's own blog.
Monthly newsletter	Many companies stay in touch with their potential target audience by producing and distributing a monthly or quarterly newsletter. Along with containing updates on a firm's products and services, the newsletter should contain more general information of interest to the reader. Companies should avoid sending out newsletters that simply brag about their products. These types of newsletters are often seen as too self-serving.
Civic, social, and community involvement	Start-ups often try to create a positive image of their organization by sponsoring local events or asking their employees to be involved in civic clubs such as the Chamber of Commerce or the Rotary Club.

make a sale.[26] A firm's public relations' effort can be oriented to telling the company's story through a third party, such as a magazine or a newspaper. If a magazine along the lines of *Inc.*, *Entrepreneur* or *Business Week* publishes a positive review of a new company's products, or a company is profiled in a prominent blog, consumers are likely to believe that those products are at least worth a try. They think that because these magazines and blogs have no vested interest in the company, they have no reason to stretch the truth or lie about the usefulness or value of a company's products. Technology companies, for example, that are featured on TechCrunch or Mashable, two popular technology blogs, typically see an immediate spike in their Web traffic and sales as a result of the mention.

There are many ways in which a start-up can enhance its chances of getting noticed by the press, a blogger, or someone who is influential in social media. One technique is to prepare a **press kit**, which is a folder that contains background information about the company and includes a list of its most recent accomplishments. The kit is normally distributed to journalists and made available online. Another technique is to be present at industry trade shows and other events. A **trade show** is an event at which the goods or services in a specific industry are exhibited and demonstrated. Members of the media often attend trade shows to get the latest industry news. For example, the largest trade show for consumer electronics is International CES, which is held in Las Vegas every January. Many companies wait until this show to announce their most exciting new products. They do this in part because they

LEARNING OBJECTIVE

8. Explain how firms can use social media to strengthen their brand and promote their products.

have a captive media audience that is eager to find interesting stories to write about. A recent International CES show is pictured in Chapter 5.

Social Media   Social media consists primarily of blogging and establishing a presence and connecting with customers and others through social networking sites like Facebook or Twitter. Many of the new ventures featured in this book are active users of social media. A good example is ModCloth, the focus of Case 11.1. ModCloth maintains an active blog, has three separate Twitter accounts (one for general product information, one that is more fashion oriented, and one for recruiting), and maintains an energetic Facebook page.

The idea behind blogs is that they familiarize people with a business and help build an emotional bond between a business and its customers. ModCloth's blog (http://blog.modcloth.com), for example, draws attention to the company's products, but also posts fun, entertaining, and informative articles, features, and photos of interest to ModCloth's target market—18- to 32-year-old women. The blog also features contests that provide cash prizes, posts photos of customers wearing ModCloth products, and provides behind-the-scenes glimpses of what it's like to work at ModCloth. For example, employees are allowed to bring dogs to work, which are called ModDogs. Periodically, one of the dogs is featured on the blog.

The key to maintaining a successful blog is to keep it fresh and make it informative and fun. It should also engage its readers in the "industry" and "lifestyle" that a company promotes as much as a company's products. For example, on May 23, 2011, ModCloth posted the following on its blog:

> You are cordially invited to a week of wedding glamour now through Friday, May 27, right here on the ModCloth blog. In honor of our new Wedding stylebook, we're devoting this week to coverage of all the parties, projects, and styles that go into a wedding![27]

This is the type of feature that ModCloth customers probably enjoy seeing.

Many start-ups also benefit from establishing a presence on social networking sites like Facebook and Twitter. Facebook's numbers are huge, which makes it particularly attractive. As of May 2011, Facebook had more than 500 million active users, 50 percent of which log onto Facebook in any given day. The company has also made itself more attractive to businesses since launching a family of social plugins in April 2010. **Social plugins** are tools that Web sites can use to provide its users with personalized and social experiences. Facebook's most popular social plugins, which a Web site can install, include the Like button, the Share button, and the Comment box. These social plugins allow people to share their experiences off Facebook with their friends on Facebook. The Share button, for example, lets users share pages from a company's Web site on their Facebook page with one click.[28] As a result, a young woman who just bought a dress from ModCloth's Web site, because ModCloth has placed the Facebook Share plugin on its site, can immediately post a picture and description of the dress on her Facebook page and write a comment about the purchase. She might say, "Hey everyone, look at the cool dress I just bought at www.modcloth.com." This is tantamount to free advertising for ModCloth.

Along with taking advantage of social plugins, businesses establish a presence on Facebook and Twitter to build a community around their products and services. The benefits include brand building, engaging customers, and getting lead generation and online sales. In regard to branding, a Facebook page or Twitter account can allow a firm to post or tweet material that's consistent with its brand. For example, SafetyWeb, the Web-based service that helps parents keep their kids safe online frequently posts material on Twitter that pertains to child safety. By doing this, SafetyWeb further establishes itself as an expert on child safety issues.

In regard to engagement, many companies use social networks to strengthen their relationships with customers by soliciting feedback, running contests, or posting fun games that pertain to a company's product. For example, every week ModCloth runs a contest called Spy Thursday on Twitter. At 4:00 P.M. each Thursday, the company tweets a fuzzy, abstract, or distorted photo of one of its products. The fifth tweet with the name of the product wins a $25 gift certificate. This type of activity creates a fun way for ModCloth to engage and interact with a certain number of its customers every Thursday. In terms of generating leads, Zappos's Facebook page, for example, is very focused on lead generation. The page directs guests to sign up for a mailing list, fill out forms, visit the company's Web site, etc. These types of activities help Zappos build a prospect list. Some companies are using Facebook to actually generate sales. A growing number of restaurants, for example, are booking reservations through their Facebook pages.

A particularly interesting example of a company that's using both partnerships and social media to promote its products is Moxsie, which is profiled in the "Partnership for Success" feature.

There is a potpourri of additional social media outlets from which firms can benefit. For example, many businesses post videos on YouTube. YouTube now offers heavy users the ability to create a YouTube channel to archive its videos and to create its own YouTube site. An example is ModCloth's YouTube channel at www.youtube.com/modcloth. Businesses can also establish a presence on niche social networking sites that are consistent with their mission and product offerings. An example is Care2 (www.care2.com), which is an online community that promotes a healthy and green lifestyle and takes action on social causes.

Other Promotion-Related Activities   There are many other activities that help a firm promote and sell its products. Some firms, for example, give away free samples of their products. This technique is used by pharmaceutical companies that give physicians free samples to distribute to their patients as appropriate. A similar technique is to offer free trials such as a three-month subscription to a magazine or a two-week membership to a fitness club to try to hook potential customers by exposing them directly to the product or service.

A fairly new technique that has received quite a bit of attention is **viral marketing**, which facilitates and encourages people to pass along a marketing message about a particular product. The most well-known example of viral

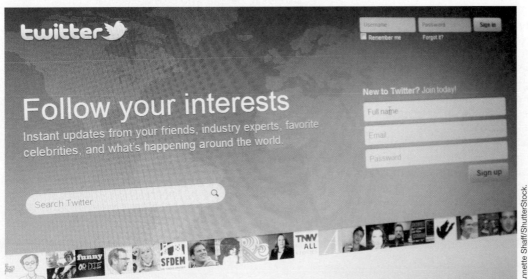

Twitter is becoming an increasingly popular social media tool for businesses. Jessica Truesdale, the founder of True You Cosmetics, uses Twitter to make product announcements, distribute discounts, run contests, and update users on the progress of her company. In just the few months since she launched her company, she has over 2,600 followers.

Annette Shaff/ShutterStock.

PARTNERING FOR SUCCESS

How Landing a Partnership with an Influential Web Site and Soliciting Feedback from Customers Can Accelerate a Start-Up's Visibility and Growth

Web: www.moxsie.com
Twitter: moxsie
Facebook: moxsie

Moxsie is an online retailer that sells fashion items made by independent designers. The site features clothing, accessories, and footwear from new, up-and-coming fashion start-ups and freelancers. Every designer showcased on Moxsie is handpicked by the Moxsie team, and must promote a worthy cause, such as sustainability or eliminating sweatshop labor. Moxsie donates a portion of its sales revenue to charity. During the checkout process on its site, users can pick the charity that they'd like Moxsie to donate a portion of the proceeds from their purchase to. Charities range from the American Red Cross to Soles4Souls, which is a charity that donates shoes to children and adults in need.

One thing that's a challenge for a company like Moxsie, which launched in 2009, is to gain visibility and customers. To that end, in early 2011 Moxsie entered into a partnership with Beyond the Rack, a "private" shopping site with 3 million members that sells fashion items via flash sales. Flash sales, popularized by online retailers like Gilt Groupe and Groupon, are sales that occur for a limited time, like one day or 36 hours. Through its partnership with Beyond the Rack, each month several of Beyond the Rack's flash sales will feature apparel designed by Moxsie designers. This approach is a potential big plus for Moxsie. It will get its name in front of Beyond the Rack's 3 million members, many of whom are fashion-savvy shoppers. The hope is that a portion of these people will not only start shopping on Moxsie's site, but will encourage others to do so as well.

Moxsie is utilizing another unique approach to partnering to gain visibility for its site. It is essentially partnering with its users to figure out which items to offer for sale. It does this via two approaches. First, when meeting with independent fashion designers, Moxsie personnel take photos of the pieces the designers are pitching, post the photos on the firm's Twitter site, and ask followers for feedback on which fabrics, colors, and designs they like or dislike. This approach helps Moxsie determine which items to offer for sale, and the feedback can be invaluable to the designers. Second, sometimes Moxsie broadcasts the meeting themselves on Ustream. Ustream is a service that allows any business or individual to stream an event live over the Internet. Anyone can view the Moxsie meetings and provide feedback to the designers. The most insightful contributors earn Moxsie discounts, points, and virtual badges. Offering badges as a reward may sound a little lame, but Foursquare and others have made it work. At Moxsie, if you view one of the Ustream buyer meetings, you automatically earn your first badge. From that point forward, the quality and quantity of your feedback earns you badges with higher distinction, such as "Head Buyer" and "Celebrity Buyer." As you earn additional badges, you earn more Moxsie discounts, an internship, or even a paid position with Moxsie.

The upshot of both of these approaches is that Moxsie has greatly expanded the number of people who follow it on Twitter, engage in helping it select fashion items, and actually shop on its site. In early 2010, for example, Moxsie had 800 Twitter followers. It now has over 148,000.

Questions for Critical Thinking

1. What are the pluses and minuses to Moxsie's partnership with Beyond the Rack? The companies have not disclosed the financial arrangement between the two of them. What do you think Beyond the Rack receives from Moxsie as a result of featuring Moxsie designers in a portion of its flash sales?
2. Do you think Moxsie is over-relying on social media to gain visibility for its site, or do you think its social media approach is appropriate? What is it that you like and don't like about Moxsie's social media strategy?
3. Do you think Moxsie's approach to awarding virtual badges to people who provide feedback on its merchandizing sessions will prove to be an effective approach in terms of engaging users and obtaining valuable feedback?
4. Gap is a fashion retailer that sells both online and through brick-and-mortar stores. Study the way that Gap uses social media to increase its visibility and gain customers, and briefly describe Gap's approach. Is there anything that Gap is doing that Moxsie could learn from?

Sources: J. Kincaid, "Indie Fashion Store Moxie Lands a Partnership with 'Beyond the Rack,'" TechCrunch, http://techcrunch.com/2011/01/05/indie-fashion-store-moxsie-lands-a-partnership-with-beyond-the-rack (accessed March 20, 2011, originally posted on January 5, 2011); M. Lev-Ram, "Clothes Site Moxsie Lures Future Employees with Foursquare-Style System," *Fast Company*, www.fastcompany.com/node/1709937/print (accessed March 19, 2011, originally posted on December 15, 2010).

marketing is Hotmail. When Hotmail first started distributing free e-mail accounts, it put a tagline on every message sent out by Hotmail users that read "Get free e-mail with Hotmail." Within less than a year, the company had several million users. Every e-mail message that passed through the Hotmail system was essentially an advertisement for Hotmail. The success of viral marketing depends on the pass-along rate from person to person. Very few companies have come close to matching Hotmail's success with viral marketing. However, the idea of designing a promotional campaign that encourages a firm's current customers to recommend its product to future customers is well worth considering.

A technique related to both viral marketing and creating buzz, which was referred to earlier in the chapter, is guerrilla marketing. **Guerrilla marketing** is a low-budget approach to marketing that relies on ingenuity, cleverness, and surprise rather than traditional techniques. The point is to create awareness of a firm and its products, often in unconventional and memorable ways. The term was first coined and defined by Jay Conrad Levinson in the 1984 book *Guerrilla Marketing*. Guerrilla marketing is particularly suitable for entrepreneurial firms, which are often on a tight budget but have creativity, enthusiasm, and passion to draw from.

Place (or Distribution)

Place, or distribution, encompasses all the activities that move a firm's product from its place of origin to the consumer. A **distribution channel** is the route a product takes from the place it is made to the customer who is the end user.

The first choice a firm has to make regarding distribution is whether to sell its products directly to consumers or through intermediaries such as wholesalers or distributors. Within most industries, both choices are available, so the decision typically depends on how a firm believes its target market wants to buy its product. For example, it would make sense for a music studio that is targeting the teen market to produce digital recordings and sell the recordings directly over the Web. Most teens have access to a computer or smartphone and know how to download music. In contrast, it wouldn't make nearly as much sense for a recording company targeting retirees to use the same distribution channel to sell its music offerings. A much smaller percentage of the retiree market knows how to download music from the Web. In this instance, it would make more sense to produce CDs and partner with wholesalers or distributors to place them in retail outlets where retirees shop.

Figure 11.4 shows the difference between selling direct and selling through an intermediary. Let's look at the strengths and weaknesses of each approach.

Selling Direct   Many firms sell direct to customers. Being able to control the process of moving their products from their place of origin to the end user instead of relying on third parties is a major advantage of direct selling. Examples of companies that sell direct are Abercrombie & Fitch, which sells its clothing through company-owned stores, and Fitbit, which sells its exercise and sleep monitoring device through its Web site.

LEARNING OBJECTIVE

9. Weigh the advantages and disadvantages of selling direct versus selling through intermediaries.

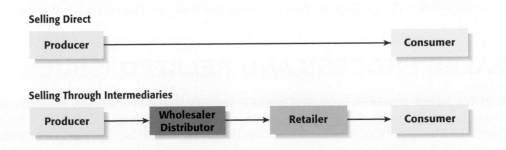

FIGURE 11.4
Selling Direct Versus Selling Through Intermediaries

The disadvantage of selling direct is that a firm has more of its capital tied up in fixed assets because it must own or rent retail outlets, must maintain a sales force, or must support an e-commerce Web site. It must also find its own buyers rather than have distributors that are constantly looking for new outlets for the firm's products.

The advent of the Internet has changed how many companies sell their products. Many firms that once sold their products exclusively through retail stores are now also selling directly online. The process of eliminating layers of middlemen, such as distributors and wholesalers, to sell directly to customers is called **disintermediation**.

Selling Through Intermediaries   Firms selling through intermediaries typically pass off their products to wholesalers or distributors who place them in retail outlets to be sold. An advantage of this approach is that the firm does not need to own as much of the distribution channel. For example, if a company makes MP3 players and the players are sold through retail outlets such as Best Buy and Walmart, the company avoids the cost of building and maintaining retail outlets. It can also rely on its wholesalers to manage its relationship with Best Buy and Walmart and to find other retail outlets to sell its products. The trick to utilizing this approach is to find wholesalers and distributors that will represent a firm's products. A start-up must often pitch wholesalers and distributors much like it pitches an investor for money to win their support and cooperation.

The disadvantage of selling through intermediaries is that a firm loses a certain amount of control of its product. Even if a wholesaler or distributor places a firm's products with a top-notch retailer like Best Buy or Walmart, there is no guarantee that Best Buy or Walmart's employees will talk up the firm's products as much as it would if it had its own stores. Selling via distributors and wholesalers can also be expensive, so it is best to carefully weigh all options. For example, a firm that sells an item for $100 on its Web site and makes $50 (after expenses) may only make $10 if the exact same item is placed by a distributor into a retail store. The $40 difference represents the profits taken by the distributor and the retailer.

Some firms enter into exclusive distribution arrangements with channel partners. **Exclusive distribution arrangements** give a retailer or other intermediary the exclusive rights to sell a company's products. The advantage to giving out an exclusive distribution agreement is to motivate a retailer or other intermediary to make a concerted effort to sell a firm's products without having to worry about direct competitors. For example, if Nokia granted AT&T the exclusive rights to sell a new type of cell phone, AT&T would be more motivated to advertise and push the phone than if many or all cell phone companies had access to the same phone.

One choice that entrepreneurs are confronted with when selling through intermediaries is how many channels to sell through. The more channels a firm sells through, the faster it can grow. But there are problems associated with selling through multiple channels, particularly early in the life of a firm. A firm can lose control of how its products are being sold. For example, the more retailers through which Ralph Lauren sells its clothing, the more likely it is that one or more retailers will not display the clothes in the manner the company wants.

SALES PROCESS AND RELATED ISSUES

A firm's **sales process** (or sales funnel) depicts the steps it goes through to identify prospects and close sales. It doesn't matter whether a firm is selling direct to customers or through intermediaries, it still has a process through

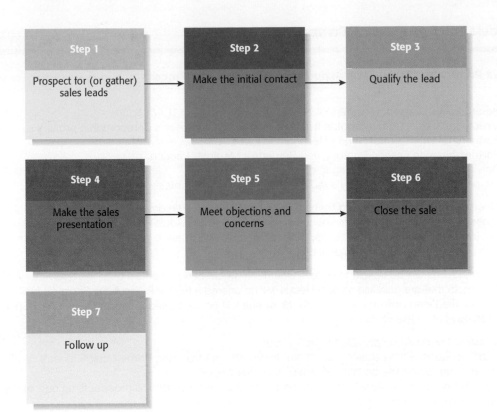

FIGURE 11.5
Sales Process

which it makes sales. If it's selling through an intermediary, like a distributor, it has to convince the distributor to carry its products, and has to offer the distributor varying levels of support.

Some companies simply wing it when it comes to sales, which isn't recommended. It's much better to have a well-thought-out approach to prospecting customers and closing sales. A formal sales process involves a number of identifiable steps. Although the process varies by firm (and industry), it generally includes seven steps, as shown in Figure 11.5. Following a formal or structured process to generate and close sales benefits a firm in two ways. First, it enables a firm to fine-tune its approach to sales and build uniformity into the process. Second, it helps a firm qualify leads, so the firm can spend its time and money pursuing the most likely buyers of its products or services. The most frustrating thing a salesperson encounters is spending time and effort working with a potential buyer, only to find that the buyer doesn't have the money or the authority to make a purchase. A well-thought-out sales process has triggers in it that help a salesperson discern whether spending time with a particular prospect is a good use of his or her time.

Some firms implement their sales strategy by listing the seven steps in the process, and then writing procedures for how each step will be implemented. In fact, some new ventures include this material in their business plan, to provide the reader confidence that they've thought through how they'll close sales. An example of a sales process, with accompanying action steps, for a fictitious business named Prime Adult Fitness is shown in Table 11.5. The example comes from the book *Preparing Effective Business Plans* by Bruce R. Barringer (coauthor of this book). Prime Adult Fitness is a fitness center for people 50 years old or older. Its mission is to make exercise and fitness a vibrant and satisfying part of the lives of people who are 50 years old and older. The company will start with a single fitness center located in Oviedo, Florida, a suburb of Orlando. The steps shown in Table 11.5 is the process the company will use to recruit members and is the method that the in-house staff will follow when people walk into the center and inquire about membership. At times, the

LEARNING OBJECTIVE
10. Describe the seven-step sales process.

TABLE 11.5   SALES PROCESS FOR PRIME ADULT FITNESS

Stage in Process	Ways Prime Adult Fitness Will Support Each Phase of the Process
1. Prospecting (or sales lead)	■ Referrals from current members. ■ Direct mail (targeting households that meet Prime Adult Fitness's demographic profile). ■ Partnership with Central Florida Health Food. ■ Partnership with Oviedo Doctor's and Surgeon's Medical Practice. ■ Downloads from company Web site. ■ Responses from the company's radio and print advertisements.
2. The initial contact	■ All employees will be provided training in building rapport with prospects. ■ Prospects are provided an information packet about Prime Adult Fitness. ■ Radio and print ads will direct prospects to Prime Adult Fitness's Web site, which contains a short video and other promotional material.
3. Qualifying the lead	■ All employees will be trained to assess whether a prospect represents a qualified lead. Prospects that are qualified as good leads will be offered a tour of Prime Adult Fitness's facilities. ■ If a qualified lead does not join initially, he or she will be contacted by phone as a follow-up three days after the visit.
4. Sales presentation	■ Qualified leads will be provided a facility tour. ■ Qualified leads will be shown a short film (nine minutes) featuring Prime Adult Fitness's facility and programs and the benefits of fitness for older people. ■ A packet of testimonials will be developed over time and provided to prospects as part of the sales presentation process.
5. Meeting objections and concerns	■ Employees will be trained on how to meet the most common and obvious objections and concerns. ■ In regard to price objections, a brochure has been prepared that compares (1) Prime Adult Fitness's initial (one-time) enrollment fee and monthly membership fee to other fitness centers and (2) the cost of joining and belonging to a fitness center as opposed to other forms of recreation and entertainment (i.e., boating, golfing). ■ A similar brochure has been prepared to compare Prime Adult Fitness's amenities to the amenities of other fitness centers.
6. Closing the sale	■ All employees will be trained to ask qualified prospects to join.
7. Follow up	■ Each new member will be contacted by phone 30 days after joining as a courtesy to see how things are going. After that, each new member will be contacted by phone once a year. Each phone call will also be used to ask for names of referrals. ■ Prime Adult Fitness will produce a monthly newsletter that will be mailed to each member. ■ Prime Adult Fitness's staff and employees will be trained to engage members and to thank them for their membership and solicit suggestions for improvement on a continual basis.

Source: Bruce R. Barringer, *Preparing Effective Business Plans: An Entrepreneurial Approach* 1e, © 2009. Reprinted by permission of Pearson Education, Inc., Upper Saddle River NJ. (Upper Saddle River, NJ: Pearson Prentice-Hall, 2009.)

process will take weeks to unfold, if Prime Adult Fitness employees have multiple contacts with a prospect, and at times the process will take only a few minutes, as an employee provides a prospect a tour of the facility and answers specific questions. Prime Adult's sales process is offered only as an example. Individual firms can use this example as a template for developing a sales process that fits their individual products and circumstances.

Mapping the sales process in the manner shown in Table 11.5 provides a standard method for a firm's employees to use, and provides a starting point for careful analysis and continuous improvement. Often, when companies lose an important sale and reflect on what went wrong they'll find that an important step in the sales process was missed or mishandled. This is where having a well-thought-out sales process, with accompanying action steps and appropriate employee training, can dramatically improve a company's sales performance.

CHAPTER SUMMARY

1. The first step in selecting a target market is to study the industry in which the firm intends to compete and determine the different potential target markets within that industry. This process is called market segmentation. Markets can be segmented in a number of ways, including product type, price point, distribution channels used, and customers served.

2. After a firm has selected its target market, the next step is to establish a "position" within it that differentiates it from its competitors. The term *position* was introduced in Chapter 5, where it was emphasized that a firm's position in the marketplace determines how it is situated relative to its competitors. From a marketing perspective, this translates into the image of the way a firm wants to be perceived by its customers. Importantly, position answers the question, "Why should someone in our target market buy our good or service instead of our competitor's?"

3. A product attribute map illustrates a firm's position in its industry relative to its major rivals. It is used as a visual illustration of a firm's positioning strategy and helps a firm develop its marketing plan.

4. A company's brand is the set of attributes people associate with it. On a philosophical level, a firm builds a brand by having it create meaning in customers' lives. It must create value. On a more practical level, brands are built through advertising, public relations, sponsorships, supporting social causes, and good performance.

5. A firm's marketing mix is the set of controllable, tactical marketing tools that it uses to produce the response it wants in its target market. Most marketers organize their marketing mix around the 4Ps: product, price, promotion, and place (or distribution).

6. In cost-based pricing, the list price is determined by adding a markup percentage to the product's cost. In value-based pricing, the list price is determined by estimating what consumers are willing to pay for a product and then backing off a bit to provide a cushion.

7. Advertising is making people aware of a good or service in hopes of persuading them to buy it. Public relations refers to efforts to establish and maintain a company's image with the public. The major difference between the two is that advertising is paid for, and public relations isn't—at least directly. The cost of public relations to a firm is the effort it makes to network with journalists and other people to try to interest them in saying and/or writing good things about the company.

8. Social media consists primarily of blogging and establishing a presence and connecting with people through social networking sites like Facebook and Twitter. Businesses blog and engage in social media to build a community around their products and services. The benefits include brand building, engaging customers, and getting lead generation and online sales.

9. The first choice a firm must make regarding distribution is whether to sell its products directly to consumers or through intermediaries (e.g., wholesalers and retailers). An advantage of selling direct is that it allows a firm to maintain control of its products rather than relying on third parties. The disadvantage is that it ties up more capital in fixed assets because the firm must own (or rent) retail outlets or must field a sales force to sell its products. An advantage of selling through intermediaries is that a firm doesn't have to own much of its distribution channel (e.g., trucks and retail outlets). A disadvantage of this approach is that a firm loses some control of its product in that there is no guarantee that the retailers it sells through will talk up and push its products as much as the manufacturer would if it had its own stores.

10. A firm's sales process depicts the steps it goes through to identify leads and close sales. The seven-step sales process includes the following steps: Step 1: Prospect for (or gather) sales leads; Step 2: Make the initial contact; Step 3: Qualify the lead; Step 4: Make the sales presentation; Step 5: Meet objections and concerns; Step 6: Close the sale; Step 7: Follow up.

KEY TERMS

advertising, **396**
brand, **388**
brand equity, **391**
brand management, **388**
buzz, **391**
cost-based pricing, **395**
disintermediation, **404**
distribution channel, **403**
exclusive distribution
   arrangements, **404**

guerilla marketing, **403**
market segmentation, **385**
marketing mix, **393**
place, **403**
press kit, **399**
price, **394**
price-quality attribution, **395**
product, **393**
product attribute map, **387**
promotion, **396**

public relations, **398**
reference account, **394**
sales process, **404**
service, **393**
social plugins, **400**
tagline, **388**
trade show, **399**
value-based pricing, **395**
viral marketing, **401**

REVIEW QUESTIONS

1. What is a target market? Why is it important for a firm to choose its target market early in the process of launching its venture?

2. Explain the importance of market segmentation. Describe several ways in which markets can be segmented.

3. How should a firm go about constructing a product attribute map?

4. What is a niche market? Provide examples of niche markets in the women's clothing industry.

5. Describe what is meant by a firm's positioning strategy.

6. What is a tagline? What is your favorite tagline? Why?

7. What is a brand? Provide an example of a brand that you buy frequently and describe the mental image that pops into your mind when you hear or see the brand's name.

8. What is the purpose of brand management?

9. What is meant by creating "buzz" for a company? Provide an example of a firm that has created effective buzz for its product or service.

10. What is meant by the term *brand equity*?

11. Identify and briefly describe the four elements of a firm's "marketing mix."

12. Describe the difference between a core product and an actual product.

13. What is a reference account? How can having a reference account help a new firm?

14. Contrast cost-based pricing and value-based pricing.

15. What is meant by the phrase "price-quality attribution"? How does an understanding of this phrase help an entrepreneur know how to price a product?

16. What is meant by the term *guerilla marketing*? Provide an example of guerilla marketing not provided in the chapter.

17. Contrast the roles of advertising and public relations in promoting a firm and its products.

18. What is the purpose of writing a blog and establishing a presence on Facebook and Twitter?

19. Contrast the advantages of selling direct versus the advantages of selling through an intermediary.

20. Describe the purpose of having an organized sales process.

APPLICATION QUESTIONS

1. Reread the Opening Profile. After doing this, make a list of all the things that you think that Jessica Truesdale has done right in building True You Cosmetics' marketing program.

2. If you decided to start a small-business consulting service in Columbus, Ohio, how would you approach the following topics: market segmentation, selecting a target market, and developing a positioning strategy?

3. Define the word *brand* in 10 words or less.

4. Reread the "You Be the VC 1.1" feature, which focuses on Windspire Energy. How do you think Windspire Energy segmented the wind-generated power industry? Describe Windspire Energy's positioning strategy.

5. Imagine you're opening a tutoring service near the college or university you attend. Suggest a comprehensive social media strategy that you can employ to build your brand, engage customers, and generate leads and produce sales.

6. Assume that you just invented a new type of computer printer that can be easily folded up and carried like a laptop computer. You have decided to start a company to produce the printer. Select a name and a tagline for your new company. Describe your rationale for both the name and the tagline.

7. Design a guerilla marketing campaign for WebVet, the subject of the "You Be the VC 11.2" feature.

8. Explain what is meant by a "freemium" pricing model. Provide an example of a company, other than one mentioned in this book, that utilizes a freemium model to price its product or service. Do you believe a freemium pricing model is the best choice for the company you selected? Why or why not?

9. Spend some time looking at Red Bull's Web site (the U.S. site). Comment on each element of Red Bull's marketing mix (product, price, promotion, and place in terms of distribution and sales). If you need additional information, conduct Internet or library research to obtain it. On a scale of 1 to 10 (10 is high), rate the strength of Red Bull's overall marketing plan. Justify your ratings.

10. The "You Be the VC 11.2" feature focuses on WebVet, a website that provides pet owners a one-stop destination for information regarding pet health issues. Consider each of the 4Ps and comment on the most important issues for WebVet to consider in each area.

11. Shannon has developed a new type of space heater that is quieter and safer than previous generations of space heaters and is particularly geared to people who live in small spaces, such as apartments or dorm rooms. Shannon doesn't know how to price this product. Describe to Shannon the two most common methods of pricing, and give her your recommendation for how to price the product.

12. Kelly Andrews has developed a new line of jewelry that has created some positive buzz among friends and some business stores in her local community. When asked by a reporter, "Where do you plan to sell your jewelry?" Kelly said, "Hopefully everywhere—jewelry stores, Target, Walmart, gift shops, online, through catalogs, and a dozen other places." Write a critique of Kelly's approach.

13. Study how Proactiv, the subject of Case 11.2, utilizes social media. Provide a brief analysis of Proactiv's social media strategy. On a scale of 1 to 10 (10 is high), how effective do you think Proactiv's social media strategy is? Explain your thinking.

14. Nate Jones, a friend of yours, is in the early stages of conducting a feasibility analysis for an e-commerce Web site, which will focus on the sale of products for extreme sports, such as snowboarding, rock climbing, mountain biking, and hang gliding. Nate is familiar with the concept of branding, and knows that because his company is new he'll have to build a brand from scratch. Compose a 100- to 200-word e-mail message to Nate providing him suggestions for how to approach this task.

YOU BE THE VC 11.1

Company: Legacy Locker

Web: http://legacylocker.com
Twitter: legacylocker
Facebook: Legacy Locker

Business Idea: Provide a service that stores individuals' log-in information to important online services like e-mail accounts, social networks, PayPal, and eBay, and deliver them to caretakers in the event of the individual's death.

Pitch: Have you ever wondered what would happen to your online accounts if you unexpectedly died? Although it's not a pleasant topic to think about, your family members may face a real challenge getting access to your accounts. There have been reports of people having to hire lawyers, for example, to get access to a deceased family member's e-mail account. In some instances, access has been permanently denied in accordance with a particular site's Terms of Service.

Legacy Locker offers a solution to this problem. The site allows users to input their log-in information for the Web services they use, which are then distributed to family members and friends in the event of their death. Users can select which account information will be distributed to whom. (For example, you could send your PayPal information to your spouse and your LinkedIn information to a coworker or friend.) In addition to storing log-in information, Legacy Locker can also be used to send farewell messages. Users can prepare written letters for friends, loved ones, or colleagues, which will be distributed to them following the user's death.

Once a person enrolls in the service, he or she is provided a card that directs family members or medical personnel

to contact Legacy Locker to report a death. To confirm a person's death, Legacy Locker contacts two verifiers designated by the account holder in addition to requiring a certified copy of the death certificate. Legacy Locker's revenue model is a variant of the "freemium" approach that is common on the Web. The service offers a basic free version that covers three digital assets (accounts) that can be passed on to one beneficiary. Paid plans include unlimited assets and beneficiaries, and cost $29.99 per year or $299.99 for a lifetime.

While Legacy Locker's service is available to anyone, the company's go-to-market strategy will be to reach out to will and estate planning professionals, who will be encouraged to bundle the Legacy Locker service within their offerings. There are 25,000 estate planning professionals in the United States servicing 12.5 million people who have established a will or an estate. Legacy Locker's service will allow the professionals to make a provision for their client's digital assets in their estates and wills.

Q&A: Based on the material covered in this chapter, what questions would you ask the firm's founders before making your funding decision? What answers would satisfy you?

Decision: If you had to make your decision on just the information provided in the pitch and on the company's Web site, would you fund this company? Why or why not?

YOU BE THE VC 11.2

Company: WebVet

Web: www.webvet.com
Twitter: WebVet
Facebook: Webvet

Business Idea: Create a Web site that provides pet owners a one-stop destination for information regarding pet health issues.

Pitch: If you're looking for reliable information about human medical conditions, you can quickly turn to WebMD or a similar Web site, which contains useful and authoritative information about any medical issue. But what if your dog stops eating or your cat starts losing its hair? Or what if you're browsing through a pet supply

store and see vitamins for dogs, and wonder which dogs need vitamins and whether they are really necessary. You'll probably worry and do a Google search, and peck around the Web trying to find relevant information.

WebVet was founded to help pet owners answer just these types of questions. It is the WebMD for pets, and includes a comprehensive collection of articles and information, designed to address both the physical and emotional needs of pets. Ask a Vet, Health, Pet Health

Records, New Pets, Care and Training, and Vstore are the site's main components. Ask a Vet includes a dialogue box that allows anyone to ask a vet a pet-related medical or behavioral question. Health is an archive of articles about animals and pet-related issues. Pet Health Records allows pet owners to profile and manage their pet's health throughout its lifetime, and store the information on WebVet's Web site, where it can be retrieved anywhere there is an Internet connection. New Pets provides useful information regarding various issues associated with a "new pet" including introducing a new animal into a home with one or more existing pets. Care and Training provides an archive of articles that focus on non-health-related care and training issues. An example of an article is "Preparing Your Senior Dog for a New Puppy in the House." Finally, Vstore is an online store for pet-related food, medicines, and related products.

All the information posted on WebVet is written by a qualified staff member and is reviewed annually by a panel of veterinarians. Like WebMD for human health, the site does not diagnose, suggest treatment, or take positions on whether one form of treatment for a pet disease is better than another. Instead, the site provides objective information, access to all points of view, and urges its visitors to consult with their veterinarians on the best course of action for their individual pet. Social interaction is also important. The company has created many ways by which pet owners and enthusiasts can interact with the site and with each other. WebVet makes money by selling sponsorships and advertising on its Web site, and via its online store.

Q&A: Based on the material covered in this chapter, what questions would you ask the firm's founders before making your funding decision? What answers would satisfy you?

Decision: If you had to make your decision on just the information provided in the pitch and on the company's Web site, would you fund this company? Why or why not?

CASE 11.1

ModCloth: The 4Ps of a Successful Online Clothing Retailer

Web: www.modcloth.com
Twitter: ModCloth
Facebook: ModCloth

Bruce R. Barringer, *Oklahoma State University*
R. Duane Ireland, *Texas A&M University*

Introduction

ModCloth founders Susan Koger and Eric Koger met in high school. Susan enjoyed shopping for vintage clothing, and over time accumulated so many outfits that she decided to sell some. Eric, who was her boyfriend at the time, offered to build her a Web site to sell the clothes, so she decided to sell online. Susan saw this as way to help pay for college; this initial experience was the foundation for ModCloth's birth.

Susan and Eric both attended Carnegie Mellon in Pittsburgh. ModCloth was a hobby business the first four years. Susan continued to accumulate women's vintage clothing, sell them on her Web site, and ship orders from her dorm room. The "customer care" number on the Web site and boxes was her cell phone number. After graduating in 2006, Susan decided to focus on ModCloth full-time. Eric remained at Carnegie Mellon an extra year to earn an MBA. To make ModCloth a full-time pursuit, Susan broadened her thinking. Up until this point, the only clothes that ModCloth sold were vintage clothing that Susan picked out. She started attending trade shows to make contact with independent designers who designed and made vintage-inspired clothing, which is a much bigger market than vintage clothing. She knew that to appreciably grow ModCloth she'd have to move beyond the small vintage clothing niche and broaden her product line.

To make sure she was on the right track, Susan surveyed 100 of her customers to ask if they'd buy vintage-inspired clothing from ModCloth, along with the vintage clothing the company carried. A total of 95 out of 100 customers surveyed said they would. Armed with this information, Susan approached two or her uncles and raised $20,000 in seed funding to buy inventory. She could now expand ModCloth's product offerings to include both vintage clothing and vintage-inspired clothing.

Fast-forward to the present. In the six years following Susan's ability to raise equity funding from her uncles, ModCloth has grown to a 200-person company. The firm just experienced four years of back-to-back 600 percent per year annual growth. The company is

(continued)

profitable, and over 2 million unique visitors visit its Web site every month. It's raised two rounds of venture capital funding, including a $19.8 million Series B round in June 2010.

A large part of ModCloth's success is attributed to its marketing program. Although it's strictly an online retailer, the 4Ps—product, promotions, place (distribution), and price—have played an integral role in its success. The following is a discussion of ModCloth's 4Ps. The discussion highlights elements of the 4Ps that have contributed to ModCloth's success and illustrates future challenges for the firm.

Product

ModCloth offers a full range of vintage and vintage-inspired apparel products for women including dresses, tops, bottoms, outerwear, swimwear, shoes, and intimates. It sources its products from both small designers that create vintage clothing to larger companies, like BB Dakota, that make vintage-inspired clothing. As a result, its site is populated by a vast assortment of indie designs and one-of-a-kind items to larger lots of vintage-inspired clothing. Its target market is 18- to 32-year-old women, and its clothing has been featured in fashion magazines like *Cosmopolitan*, *Glamour*, *InStyle,* and *Seventeen*. A quick perusal of ModCloth's Web site is the best way to see the fun and unique nature of its products. Each product comes with a descriptive yet somewhat quirky name, along with a colorful description, which adds to the ModCloth shopping experience. A sample of the names of dresses recently for sale on ModCloth's Web site is shown next. When you look at the dresses and their names, you can

see the connection. This is part of ModCloth's efforts to make its shopping experience interesting, engaging, novel, and fun.

Along with its unique products, ModCloth has a twist to its approach that encourages customer participation in regard to the products that are offered for sale. It's "Be the Buyer" program allows customers to be virtual members of its buying team, and invites them to vote on potential clothing designs. ModCloth showcases prospective clothing designs on its site, under the Be the Buyer tab, and asks customers to either "Pick It" or "Skip It," which indicates whether they think ModCloth should carry that item. If a design gets enough votes, the style will be carried by ModCloth, and those that voted for the item will be notified by e-mail. This approach, which is referred to as crowdsourcing, helps ModCloth build an emotional connection with its customers. It also helps it stay fresh, and feature items that customers want and will buy.

Promotions

ModCloth does not emphasize print and media advertising. Instead, its promotional efforts are geared toward engaging current and prospective customers through its blog, social media, and similar marketing techniques.

ModCloth maintains an active blog, which contains new posts every day. To keep readers coming back, the blog features contests that provide cash prizes and/or features customers wearing ModCloth products. By logging onto the blog (http://blog.modcloth.com) you can get a sense of the types of contests that are run. The blog also provides product updates, along with a behind-the-scenes glimpse of what it's like to work at ModCloth. For example, employees are allowed to bring their dogs (affectionately called ModDogs) to work. Periodically, one of the dogs is prominently featured on the blog.

The company is also active on social networks. It has three Twitter accounts. The name, purpose, and number of followers for each account are shown next.

Sample of the Names of Dresses for Sale on ModCloth's Web Site

Poetry & Rose Dress	Tossed Blossoms Dress
Ya'll Ready for This Dress	Herb & Spices Dress
Honolulu Dress	Bird Calling Dress
Bursting into Bloom Dress	Awards Banquet Dress

ModCloth Twitter Accounts

Name of Account	Number of Followers	Purpose
ModCloth	35,257	Provides product information, fun facts, discount coupons, contest updates, and fashion tips. The company also tweets about its employees' favorite books, recipes, movies, and other everyday items.
ModCloth Buzz	2,066	More fashion oriented, the site comments frequently on ModCloth products and general fashion trends. It also provides a platform for ModCloth fashion specialists to interact directly with customers, to share ideas and answer questions.
ModCloth Careers	1,115	For people interested in pursuing a career with ModCloth.

Items posted on ModCloth's blog are frequently referred to in its tweets. For example, in April 2011, ModCloth ran a contest for customers who write reviews about the ModCloth products they buy. During a specific two-week period, customers were encouraged to accompany their reviews with a picture of themselves wearing the ModCloth product they were reviewing. Three reviews with pictures were chosen at random, and the winners won $100 ModCloth gift certificates. The company also runs regular contests on its Twitter accounts. For example, every week ModCloth runs a contest called Spy Thursday. At 4:00 P.M. EST each Thursday, the company tweets a fuzzy, abstract, or distorted photo of one of its products. The fifth tweet with the name of the product wins a $25 gift certificate. Similarly, each Tuesday ModCloth has a special, themed sale where 12 products are discounted 12 percent. Customers find out which products are discounted by following the ModCloth Twitter account.

ModCloth is also active on Facebook and has over 209,000 Facebook friends. Several times a day, ModCloth and its friends post fashion information, fun facts, and a variety of related information on its Facebook wall. Hundreds of pictures of customers wearing ModCloth clothing are also posted. The ModDogs, referred to previously, have their own Facebook page. Simply go to ModDogs on Facebook and you'll see what they're up to at ModCloth's headquarters.

ModCloth has other techniques for engaging customers. For example, the company employs fashion experts, named ModStylists that customers can engage via e-mail, chat, or phone. The ModStylists give advice, answer questions, and interact with customers regarding fashion-related issues. ModCloth also has a YouTube channel (www.youtube.com/modcloth) and regularly posts new content.

Place (or Distribution)

ModCloth does not utilize drop shipping or outsource any of its distribution. Instead, products that are made for ModCloth are shipped to the firm's distribution centers in Pennsylvania and California. Its Internet orders are fulfilled from these distribution centers.

ModCloth employs buyers who scour the world for the most interesting and cost-competitive vintage-inspired clothing. Once an article of clothing is selected, it's photographed and a description of the article is written by ModCloth's creative staff. The creative staff also maintains the company's blog and social network initiatives. ModCloth's IT infrastructure, which enables it to fulfill orders expediently, was built entirely in-house, and is maintained by ModCloth IT specialists. It's built on a Ruby on Rails platform. Ruby on Rails platforms tend to attract the most progressive IT specialists.

ModCloth's recent $19.8 million Series B funding is being used to scale the firm's operations. It has plans to build a new supply chain operation in Los Angeles. It also recently moved its headquarters from Pittsburgh to San Francisco. Approximately 70 percent of the clothing that ModCloth sells is sourced from companies in California, so the move to San Francisco was motivated to place ModCloth's headquarters closer to its suppliers.

Price

It's not exactly known how ModCloth arrives at the price for its products. Products are priced competitively with brick-and-mortar retailers such as Macy's and Dillards. The company offers frequent discounts and promotions, as mentioned. The discounts and promotions are typically not visible on ModCloth's Web site. Instead, they're offered through the company's blog and social media initiatives.

Challenges Ahead

ModCloth has several challenges. The first is to maintain its momentum. It's not known how large the market is for vintage and vintage-inspired women's clothing. So, while it's succeeded in its niche, at some point ModCloth may have to move beyond its niche to maintain growth. Maintaining the uniqueness of its social media initiatives is a second challenge. The risk here is that while ModCloth is now seen as cutting-edge in regard to social media, its competitors may catch up, and its social media efforts may no longer be seen as "special" as is currently the case.

On the positive front, observers give ModCloth high marks for its distinct positioning and for how it engages its customers. The emotional connection it has created between itself and its customers will make it difficult for copycats to make substantial inroads in its vintage and vintage-inspired clothing niche.

Discussion Questions

1. In a short paragraph, describe ModCloth's brand. Comment on the strengths and weaknesses of the brand.
2. What is the difference between ModCloth's core product and its actual product? Describe its actual product and your assessment of whether the actual product provides an attractive mix of characteristics.
3. In what ways, if any, do you think ModCloth will look different five years from now than it looks today?
4. Follow ModCloth's primary Twitter account (ModCloth) for five days. Write a short summary of how ModCloth uses Twitter to engage its customers and promote its products. One a scale of 1 to 10 (10 is high), rate how effectively ModCloth uses Twitter as a promotional tool.

Application Questions

1. Comment on ModCloth's "Be the Buyer" program. To what degree do you think this program plays an integral role in ModCloth's ability to create an emotional connection with its customers? In addition to the Be

(continued)

the Buyer program, make a list of the ways in which ModCloth engages and creates a connection with its customers.

2. What online retailers, in addition to ModCloth, use crowdsourcing to determine what to sell? Compare ModCloth's approach to crowdsourcing to at least two other companies you identify.

Sources: ModCloth Web site, www.modcloth.com (accessed April 22, 2011); J. Kincaid, "ModCloth Raises $19.8 Million Series B for Indie Fashion," TechCrunch, http://techcrunch.com/2010/06/30/modcloth-funding (accessed April 22, 2011, originally posted on June 30, 2010); S. Chun, "Online Fashion Seller ModCloth Finds Social Commerce Strategy a Good Fit," *Pittsburgh Post-Gazette*, www.post-gazette.com/pg/10216/1077355-51.stm (accessed April 22, 2011, originally posted on August 4, 2010).

CASE 11.2

Proactiv: How Three Critical Marketing Decisions Shaped a New Venture's Future

Web: www.proactiv.com
Twitter: proactiv
Facebook: Proactiv

Bruce R. Barringer, *Oklahoma State University*

R. Duane Ireland, *Texas A&M University*

Introduction

In 1995, two dermatologists, Dr. Katie Rodan and Dr. Kathy Fields, developed what they believed was a medical breakthrough in fighting acne. Their mission: to help millions of people rid themselves of acne and acne-related problems. They named their product Proactiv Solutions. This name was chosen because the product could heal existing blemishes and *proactively* help prevent new ones from forming.

Today, Proactiv is the number one selling acne product in the United States, even though it's not available in most stores. It's sold primarily through infomercials, the company's Web site, a subscription service called the "Proactiv Solution Clear Skin Club," and in select upscale boutiques and kiosks. The way Proactiv reached the point it currently occupies is an interesting story. Early in its life, Proactiv was shaped by three critical marketing decisions, from which the company has not wavered, even to this day. This case recounts these decisions and discusses how the decisions shaped this entrepreneurial venture's future.

How It Started

Katie Rodan and Kathy Fields met while they were working summer jobs at a cardiovascular research lab in Los Angeles. The lab was developing a drug to treat post–heart attack patients. Both Rodan and Fields enjoyed the exciting pace of the work as well as the camaraderie they shared with the lab's researchers and doctors. After earning their college degrees, they both went to medical school and became dermatologists. They stayed in touch and often shared with one another

how surprised they were at the number of acne patients they were seeing. At the time, the medical research said that only 3 percent of the adult population had acne, but Rodan and Fields became convinced that the number was higher. They were each seeing acne patients on a daily basis, and they weren't just seeing teenagers. They were seeing women in their 20s, 30s, 40s, and even in their 50s who were suffering from acne and acne-related problems.

Rodan and Fields decided to form a partnership to investigate the acne issue further. They started by talking to their patients, asking them a wide range of acne-related questions. What they found was that the vast majority of their patients hated the acne products on the market. The most common complaints were that the products were very drying and they were very irritating. Worst of all, patients told Rodan and Fields, the available products did not work. At this point, the two physicians started thinking there might be an opportunity for them to create a better product.

Rodan and Fields spent the next couple of years thoroughly investigating the acne products on the market. After testing many of the products on their patients, they made what they believed was a shocking discovery. All of the products on the market were designed to spot-treat a pimple—none were designed to stop the pimple from forming in the first place. This just didn't make sense to the two dermatologists—from both a practical and a medical standpoint. By the time you see a pimple, whatever treatment you administer, it's too little too late. In their judgment, not taking steps to prevent acne from developing was akin to not brushing your teeth and going to the dentist to fill cavities. Why not brush your teeth and floss and try to prevent the cavities from developing in the first place?

This revelation motivated Rodan and Fields to start working on a product of their own—one that would be more proactive in preventing acne and acne-related problems. They hired a chemist, and the three worked together for another couple of years. Finally, they had a product they were happy with and that seemed to work and to satisfy their patients.

Important Revelations

To get ideas about how to market and develop their product, which didn't have a name yet, Rodan hosted dinner parties at her house and conducted brainstorming sessions with the guests. The guests included business executives, market researchers, marketing consultants, an FDA regulatory attorney, the chief financial officer of a major company, and others. One of the things the participants in these sessions stressed to Rodan and Fields was the importance of marketing research. In particular, the group urged Rodan and Fields to hire an unbiased third party to validate their findings. Rodan and Fields took this advice to heart and hired an outside consultant. In focus groups that the consultant led, Rodan and Fields learned two important things about older women. First, evidence suggests that many women who *do* have acne as a medical condition refuse to believe that such is the case. Second, people don't like to talk about their acne with others. Rodan and Fields also learned that their product still needed work. There were several aspects of the product that needed improvement, a need that Rodan and Fields fully intended to take care of.

Three Critical Marketing Decisions That Shaped the Future of the Firm

Critical Marketing Decision 1: We're a Skin Care Company

After Rodan and Fields reformulated the product again, they hired another marketing consultant to advise them as to how they should proceed to successfully market their product. The first piece of advice they got from the consultant was to think of their product as a skin care rather than as an acne product. At the time, the acne market in the United States was about $250 million a year, a low number by consumer products standards. In contrast, the skin care market was several billion dollars a year, making it much more attractive. The consultant told Rodan and Fields to think of their product as a skin care system that just happens to treat acne, rather than an acne medication alone. This recommendation obviously caused Rodan and Fields to have a much broader vision for the scope of the market for their product.

Critical Marketing Decision 2: Our Name Is Proactiv

After Rodan and Fields started thinking of their product as part of the skin care market, they got advice from a

marketing specialist about what to name their product. The name the specialist recommended was Proactiv (proactive without the e). Looking back, Rodan and Fields admit that initially they didn't get the reason for this recommendation. They were hoping for a more cosmetic-sounding name, like Dermo-Beautiful. The name Proactiv turned out to be perfect. It captured the essence of what Rodan and Fields were trying to accomplish—to create a product that would be *proactive* (rather than *reactive*) in dealing with acne and acne-related issues. In other words, the name Proactiv captured the entrepreneurs' interest in signaling to customers that their product was intended to prevent the occurrence of additional acne-related problems for them.

Critical Marketing Decision 3: Infomercials

To get their product on the market, Rodan and Fields initially tried to raise investment capital. They were repeatedly turned down. The biggest objection they encountered was the sentiment that if their product was so good and so obvious, why hadn't Procter & Gamble or Johnson & Johnson already thought of it? Surely they must have dermatologists on their advisory boards telling them what to do, was the comment repeatedly expressed to Rodan and Fields as they talked to those with investment capital. After giving up on raising capital, Rodan and Fields approached Neutrogena to try to get a licensing deal. Neutrogena passed on the deal but did make a suggestion that resonated with Rodan and Fields. Neutrogena said that the most effective way to sell the product would be via infomercials. Initially, Rodan and Fields were shocked, because they had a fairly low opinion of infomercials. But there was one company, according to the folks at Neutrogena, named Guthy-Renker that made high-quality infomercials for professional products like Proactiv. Rodan and Fields also got to thinking that an infomercial might be the best way to educate people about their product. The following list lays out the points in favor of using infomercials to sell a product in which Rodan and Fields had a great deal of confidence.

Why Infomercials Have Worked for Proactiv (Infomercials Are 30–60 Minute Programs That Are Paid For by an Advertiser)

- People need to be reeducated about how to treat acne.
- The reeducation can't be done in a 30-second or 60-second television commercial, or in a print ad.
- Acne is an embarrassing problem, so people will be most open to learning about it in the privacy of their homes.
- The demographic group that spends the most time watching infomercials, women in their 20s, 30s, and 40s, are Proactiv's market.
- Infomercials provide Proactiv the opportunity to show heartfelt testimonials of people who have

(continued)

used the product. Showing "before" and "after" pictures of people who have used the product and have experienced dramatic results has been a particularly persuasive tactic.

Guthy-Renker

After being turned down by Neutrogena, Rodan and Fields were about ready to throw in the towel when they met, simply by chance, a person who introduced them to Guthy-Renker, the infomercial company that people at Neutrogena recommended highly. After several meetings, Guthy-Renker offered to license Proactiv and to create an infomercial to sell the product. It also put up the money to buy the media time needed for the infomercial to be televised. The initial infomercial was targeted toward women in the age group most ignored by the present providers of acne products. The 30-minute spot carefully explained what acne is, how it can affect older women, and how Proactiv was the only product available that potentially prevented acne from occurring. It also offered a complete money-back guarantee. The first infomercial sold twice as much Proactiv as expected, and Guthy-Renker and Proactiv remain close partners today.

It was also Guthy-Renker's idea to get celebrity endorsements for Proactiv. The first celebrity endorser was Judith Light. Light was followed by Vanessa Williams, and now a number of other celebrities endorse the product.

Proactiv Today

Today, Proactiv is strong. The first Guthy-Renker infomercial ran in 1994, and the product has steadily gained market share since. Proactiv is now being sold in Canada, Europe, Latin America, Australia, and Asia as well as in the United States. Neither the product nor the sales strategy has changed since Proactiv was first introduced. The three marketing decisions described here set the direction for the company, and the company remains fully committed to taking only the actions suggested by these decisions.

Discussion Questions

1. How has Proactiv gone about establishing its brand? To what degree do you believe Proactiv is important in its customers' lives?
2. Discuss the things that Rodan and Fields learned, prior to meeting Guthy-Renker, that persuaded them that infomercials were the best way to sell Proactiv. If Proactiv hadn't developed infomercials in partnership with Guthy-Renker, do you think Proactiv would be in existence today? Describe why infomercials were a better choice than print or media advertising for Proactiv when the company was first being introduced.
3. Describe Proactiv's positioning strategy. To what extent did the three critical marketing decisions discussed in the case shape the evolution of Proactiv's positioning strategy?
4. What is the difference between Proactiv's core product and its actual product? Describe its actual product and your assessment of whether the actual product provides an attractive mix of characteristics.

Application Questions

1. In your judgment, why doesn't Proactiv sell through mainline retail stores, like Target and Nordstrom, along with its Web site, subscription service, kiosks, and upscale boutiques? Make your answer as thoughtful and substantive as possible.
2. Use materials included in Chapter 1 to identify the characteristics of successful entrepreneurs you see in Katie Rodan and Kathy Fields. To what extent do you believe these characteristics have contributed to Proactiv's success?

Sources: Proactiv homepage, www.proactiv.com (accessed May 25, 2011); K. Rodan, Stanford Technology Ventures Entrepreneurial Thought Leaders Podcast, April 2006.

ENDNOTES

1. R. Jones and J. Rowley, "Entrepreneurial Marketing in Small Businesses: A Conceptual Exploration," *International Small Business Journal* 29, no. 1 (2011): 25–36; D. F. Kuratko and J. S. Hornsby, *New Venture Management* (Upper Saddle River: Pearson/Prentice Hall, 2009).
2. J. Dahlqvist and J. Wiklund, "Measuring the Market Newness of New Ventures," *Journal of Business Venturing* (2011): in press.
3. T. Hamilton, "Working Out: Demand from Health-Conscious Consumers Is Growing, Supporting the Industry," *IBISWorld Industry Report 71394 Gym, Health & Fitness Clubs in the US,* www.ibisworld. com, March 2011.
4. Broadway Dance Center homepage, www. broadwaydancecenter.com (accessed May 25, 2011).
5. P. Singh, "Startup Market Positioning: Less Is More," Results Junkie Blog, www.resultsjunkies. com/blog/startup-market-positioning-less-is-more (accessed May 25, 2011, originally posted on May 28, 2010).
6. Art 7 Style Dance Studio homepage, www.artandstyledancestudio.com (accessed May 25, 2011).
7. Arthur Murray Dance Studio (Pittsburgh) homepage, www.arthurmurraypgh.com (accessed May 25, 2011).

8. Snap Fitness homepage, www.snapftness.com (accessed May 25, 2011).

9. P. Kotler, *Marketing Insights from A to Z: 80 Concepts Every Manager Needs to Know* (Hoboken, NJ: John Wiley & Sons, 2009), 65.

10. D. S. Kennedy, *The Ultimate Marketing Plan* (Avon, MA: Adams Business, 2011).

11. R. Z. Szabo, L. Hortovanyi, D. F. Tarody, A. Ferincz, and M. Dobak, "The Role of Knowledge in Entrepreneurial Marketing," *International Journal of Entrepreneurial Venturing* 3, no. 2 (2011): 149–67.

12. S. Fournier and J. Avery, "The Uninvited Brand," *Business Horizons* 54, no. 3 (2011): 193–207; E. Moretti, "Social Learning and Peer Effects in Consumption: Evidence from Movie Sales," *Review of Economic Studies* 78, no. 1 (2010): 356–93; I. Mohr, "Buzz Marketing for Movies," *Business Horizons* 50, no. 5 (2007): 395–403.

13. J. Hess, J. Story, and J. Danes, "A Three-Stage Model of Consumer Relationship Investment," *Journal of Product & Brand Management* 20, no. 1 (2011): 14–26; J. Blasberg, V. Vishwanath (and J. Allen), "Tools for Converting Consumers Into Advocates," *Strategy & Leadership* 36, no. 2 (2008): 16–23.

14. N. J. Hicks, "From Ben Franklin to Branding: The Evolution of Health Services Marketing," in *Branding Health Services*, eds. G. Bashe, N. J. Hicks, and A. Zieegenfuss (Gaithersburg, MD: Aspen Publishers, 2000), 1–18.

15. C. H. C. Hsu, "A Customer-Based Brand Equity Model for Upscale Hotels," *Journal of Travel Research* (2011): in press.

16. L. E. Boone and D. L. Kurtz, *Contemporary Marketing*, 15th ed. (Cincinnati: Cengage Learning, 2012).

17. H. W. Chesbrough, *Open Innovation* (Boston: Harvard Business School Press, 2003).

18. P. Kotler and G. Armstrong, *Principles of Marketing*, 13th ed. (Upper Saddle River, NJ: Prentice Hall, 2010).

19. Kotler and Armstrong, *Principles of Marketing*.

20. B. Rosenbloom, *Marketing Channels*, 8th ed. (Cincinnati: Cengage Learning, 2012).

21. W. M. Pride and O. C. Ferrell, *Marketing*, 16th ed. (Cincinnati: Cengage Learning, 2012).

22. J. C. Anderson, "Purchasing Higher-Value, Higher-Price Offerings in Business Markets," *Journal of Business-to-Business Marketing* 17, no. 1 (2010): 29–61.

23. "Our Story," SmugMug homepage, www.smugmug. com (accessed May 27, 2011); D. MacAskill, CEO of SmugMug, nPost homepage, www.npost.com (accessed December 1, 2008, originally posted on January 16, 2007).

24. C. W. Lamb, J. F. Hair, and C. McDaniel, *Essentials of Marketing*, 7th ed. (Cincinnati: Cengage Learning, 2012).

25. D. Lyus, B. Rogers, and C. Simms, "The Role of Sales and Marketing Integration in Improving Strategic Responsiveness to Market Change," *Journal of Database Marketing & Customer Strategy Management* 18, no. 1 (2011): 39–49; R. Ferguson, "Word of Mouth and Viral Marketing: Taking the Temperature of the Hottest Trends in Marketing," *Journal of Consumer Marketing* 25, no. 3 (2008): 179–82.

26. R. D. Smith, *Strategic Planning for Public Relations*, 3rd ed. (New York: Routledge, 2009).

27. ModCloth blog, http://blog.modcloth.com/2011-05-23-save-the-date (originally posted on May 22, 2011).

28. Facebook, www.facebook.com/press/info.php? statistics (accessed May 25, 2011).

Getting Personal *with* METROLEAP MEDIA, INC.

Founder:

MILUN TESOVIC

BS, College of Business
Simon Fraiser University,
expected fall 2011

Dialogue *with*
Milun Tesovic

MY FAVORITE
SMARTPHONE APP
Google Places

MY BIGGEST WORRY
AS AN ENTREPRENEUR
I think failure is the biggest worry
of all entrepreneurs. But for me,
not being able to do what I love is.

BEST PART OF BEING
A STUDENT
The friends you make and the
opportunities and support you
are afforded

WHAT I DO WHEN I'M NOT
WORKING
Travel, snowboard, mentor other
professionals

CURRENTLY IN MY
SMARTPHONE
Ellie Goulding, James Blake

MY ADVICE FOR NEW
ENTREPRENEURS
Great ideas are nothing without
well articulate and thoughtful
execution. Your plan of action is
your best friend.

CHAPTER 12

The Importance of *Intellectual* Property

OPENING PROFILE

METROLEAP MEDIA, INC.

The Key Role of Intellectual Property in Its Early and Ongoing Success

Web: www.metrolyrics.com
Twitter: MetroLyrics
Facebook: MetroLyrics

Milun Tesovic's story is one that sounds too good to be true. In 2002, when he was just 16 years old, he needed money to buy a car. So he made a quick script with his own code and launched a Web site, called MetroLyrics, to put music lyrics online. After the site was up and running he added banner ads to bring in some money. Within a year the site was generating $6,000 per month in advertising revenue—more than enough to buy a car.

Fast-forward to the present. Tesovic's story is even more compelling. MetroLyrics is now the third most popular music site on the Internet and is attracting 40 million unique visitors per month. It's profitable, has never raised venture capital, and is growing. Tesovic, now in his mid-20s, has taken on a partner but remains in control of MetroLyrics. He is also a business student at Simon Frasier University in Vancouver, Canada, majoring in marketing and entrepreneurship.

What's particularly interesting about MetroLyrics is the role that intellectual property has played in the company's development. The original idea for MetroLyrics came from Tesovic's personal experiences. As a youngster he played the guitar, and would frequently look up music lyrics and tablature (musical notations indicating instrument fingering) on the Internet. He was struck by the poor job the lyrics Web sites were doing. The sites were outdated and incomplete, even though music lyrics are one of the most searched for items on the Internet. Most of the sites were also operating illegally. Music lyrics are almost always protected by a copyright, held by either the composer or the music label the composer writes for. As a result, to legally post music lyrics on a Web site, the owner of the site must obtain a license from the copyright holder for each of the songs posted on the site. Even

LEARNING OBJECTIVES

After studying this chapter you should be ready to:

1. Define the term *intellectual property* and describe its importance.

2. Specify the rules of thumb for determining whether a particular piece of intellectual property is worth the time and expense of protecting.

3. Discuss the four major forms of intellectual property: patents, trademarks, copyrights, and trade secrets.

4. Describe the six-step process for obtaining a patent.

5. Identify the four types of trademarks.

6. Identify the types of material that are eligible for copyright protection.

7. Discuss the legal environment that facilitates trade secret protection.

8. Identify the most common types of trade secret disputes.

9. Describe some of the physical measures that firms take to protect their trade secrets.

10. Explain the two primary reasons for conducting an intellectual property audit.

though Tesovic was young when MetroLyrics launched, he was sensitive to this issue. So he started talking to music industry executives to see how MetroLyrics could build a robust database of music lyrics legally. Tesovic's motivation to do this wasn't strictly tied to a desire to obey the law, although that was part of it. He also knew that to create a Web site that people rely on, and come back to frequently, the site had to be clean, accurate, and up-to-date—everything the competing sites weren't. The route to accomplishing that goal, in Tesovic's estimation, was to properly license lyrics from the music industry so the industry would be incented to cooperate with MetroLyrics rather than resist it.

Interestingly, even though Tesovic started talking to music industry executives shortly after launching MetroLyrics, it took time for the industry to warm to his overtures and for proper licensing agreements to be put in place. During this time, MetroLyrics set money aside from advertising revenue to pay to the music industry if the industry proposed licensing agreements that were retroactive to the time MetroLyrics launched. As it turned out, that's exactly what happened. When a protocol for obtaining licensing agreements from the music industry was eventually worked out in 2006, MetroLyrics paid the industry retroactive royalties to 2002, the year MetroLyrics was launched, at the industry's insistence. In a sense, MetroLyrics was a trendsetter in the music industry. Before MetroLyrics came along, there was no model for musicians or the music industry in general to license song lyrics to the owner of a Web site. The licensing model that MetroLyrics and the music industry worked out has now become a model for the industry.

While a healthy respect for the role of copyrights played an important role in the successful launch and growth of MetroLyrics, patents may play a large role in its future. The company currently has a patent pending process that identifies trends in song lyrics. By tracking how its users interact with songs, by age, gender, and other characteristics, MetroLyrics can identify the types of lyrics that most resonate with certain music lovers—information that is of value to composers and others in the music industry. Music is a very powerful medium, and many people feel deeply connected to the music they love and in particular to the lyrics with which they identify. If a composer is writing a song for a female vocalist that targets teenage girls, for example, having an improved sense of the lyrics that resonate with teenage girls can boost the composer's chances of writing a hit song.

MetroLyrics is now a part of MetroLeap Media Inc., a company Tesovic and his partner, Alan Juristovski, established to house MetroLyrics and several related initiatives. All of Tesovic's initiatives are sensitive to intellectual property issues pertaining to copyrights, trademarks, patents, and trade secrets. Tesovic's savvy in dealing with intellectual property and entrepreneurial issues in general haven't gone unnoticed. In 2008, Tesovic received the Simon Fraser University Entrepreneur of the Year Award. In 2009, Tesovic placed first in the Global Student Entrepreneur Awards competition.[1]

Many entrepreneurial firms have valuable intellectual property. In fact, virtually all businesses, including start-ups, have knowledge, information, and ideas that are critical to their success.

For at least three reasons, it is important for businesses to recognize what intellectual property is and how to protect it. First, the intellectual property of a business often represents its most valuable asset.[2] Think of the value of the Facebook and Google trademarks, the Nike "swoosh" logo, or the design of

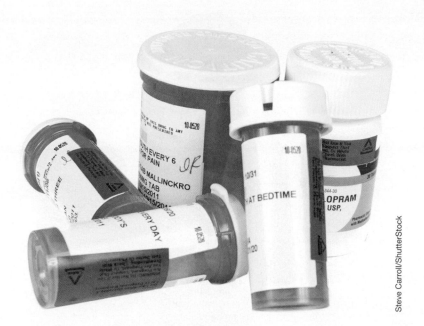

Steve Carroll/ShutterStock

When you purchase prescription medicine, the amount you (and your insurance company) pay is not for the pills themselves. The value you are paying for is the access you now have to the intellectual property that equips the pills to help you get better.

the Apple iPhone. All of these are examples of intellectual property, and because of intellectual property laws, they are the exclusive properties of the firms that own them. Second, it is important to understand what intellectual property is and how to protect it to avoid unintentional violations of intellectual property laws. For example, imagine the hardship facing an entrepreneurial start-up if it selected a name for its business, heavily advertised that name, and was later forced to change the name because it was infringing on a trademark. Finally, intellectual property can be licensed or sold, providing valuable licensing income.

We begin this chapter by defining intellectual property and exploring when intellectual property protection is warranted. There are costs involved with legally protecting intellectual property, and the costs sometimes outweigh the benefits, at least in the short term. We then describe the four key forms of intellectual property. The chapter ends with a discussion of the importance of conducting an intellectual property audit, which is a proactive tool an entrepreneurial firm can use to catalog the intellectual property it owns and determine how its intellectual property should be protected.

THE IMPORTANCE OF INTELLECTUAL PROPERTY

Intellectual property is any product of human intellect that is intangible but has value in the marketplace. It is called "intellectual" property because it is the product of human imagination, creativity, and inventiveness.[3] Traditionally, businesses have thought of their physical assets such as land, buildings, and equipment as their most important assets. Increasingly, however, a company's intellectual assets are the most valuable.[4] In the case of MetroLeap Media, the firm's intellectual property consists of intangible assets such as its process for identifying trends in song lyrics (an invention), its logo, and its Internet domain names. All these assets can provide a business with a competitive advantage in the marketplace, and the loss of such assets can be just as costly (if not more so) to a business as the loss of physical property or equipment.

FIGURE 12.1
Common Mistakes
Firms Make in Regard
to Intellectual Property

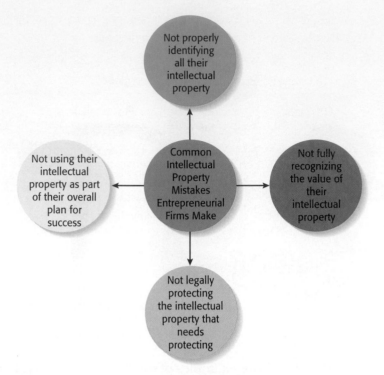

Not all firms are as intellectual property savvy as MetroLeap Media. In fact, common mistakes that entrepreneurial firms make are not properly identifying all their intellectual property, not fully recognizing the value of their intellectual property, not using their intellectual property as part of their overall plan of success, and not taking sufficient steps to protect it. These challenges are presented in Figure 12.1. It can be difficult, however, to determine what qualifies as intellectual property and whether it should be legally protected. Every facet of a company's operations probably owns intellectual property that should be protected. To illustrate this point, Table 12.1 provides examples of the intellectual property that typically resides within the departments of midsize entrepreneurial firms.

The USPTO feels that small businesses are particularly susceptible to not being diligent enough in protecting intellectual property because they frequently lack the resources and expertise available to large firms. As a result, the USPTO has set up a Web site, www.uspto.gov/smallbusiness, to provide small businesses with information about intellectual property protection. If you currently have what you believe may be a patentable idea, go to this Web site to learn more about actions you may take to investigate this possibility.

Intellectual property is also an important part of our nation's economy and its competitive advantage in the world marketplace. "It's a huge issue," former U.S. Commerce Secretary Carlos Gutierrez said. "There is so much of our economy that is linked to branded products, patented products, copyrights. So much of our economy thrives on creativity."[5]

Determining What Intellectual Property to Legally Protect

There are two primary rules of thumb for deciding if intellectual property protection should be pursued for a particular intellectual asset. First, a firm should determine if the intellectual property in question is directly related to

TABLE 12.1　EXAMPLES OF INTELLECTUAL PROPERTY THAT TYPICALLY RESIDE WITHIN A MIDSIZED ENTREPRENEURIAL FIRM'S DEPARTMENTS

Department	Forms of Intellectual Property Typically Present	Usual Methods of Protection
Marketing	Names, slogans, logos, jingles, advertisements, brochures, pamphlets, ad copy under development, customer lists, prospect lists, and similar items	Trademark, copyright, and trade secret
Management	Recruiting brochures, employee handbooks, forms and checklists used by recruiters in qualifying and hiring candidates, written training materials, and company newsletters	Copyright and trade secret
Finance	Contractual forms, PowerPoint slides describing the company's financial performance, written methodologies explaining how the company handles its finances, and employee pay records	Copyright and trade secret
Management information systems	Web site design, Internet domain names, company-specific training manuals for computer equipment and software, original computer code, e-mail lists, name registry	Copyright, trade secret, and Internet domain
Research and development	New and useful inventions and business processes, improvements to existing inventions and processes, and laboratory notes documenting invention discovery dates and charting the progress on various projects	Patent and trade secret

its competitive advantage. For example, Amazon.com has a business method patent on its "one-click" ordering system, which is a nice feature of its Web site and is arguably directly related to its competitive advantage. Similarly, when PatientsLikeMe launched a social networking platform for people with serious diseases, it would have been foolish for the company not to trademark the PatientsLikeMe name. In contrast, if a business develops a product or business method or produces printed material that isn't directly related to its competitive advantage, intellectual property protection may not be warranted.

The second primary criterion for deciding if intellectual property protection should be pursued is to determine whether an item has value in the marketplace. A common mistake that young companies make is to invent a product, spend a considerable amount of money to patent it, and find that the market for the product does not exist or that the existing market is too small to be worthy of pursuit. As discussed in Chapter 3, business ideas should be properly tested before a considerable amount of money is spent developing and legally protecting them. Owning the exclusive right to something no one wants is of little value. Similarly, if a company develops a logo for a special event, it is probably a waste of money to register it with the USPTO if there is a good chance the logo will not be used again.

On other occasions, obtaining intellectual property protection is crucial because if appropriate forms of protection are not obtained, the value of the intellectual property can be lost. This scenario played out for Dippin' Dots, a maker of ice cream treats. Curt Jones, Dippin' Dots' founder, invented a way of flash freezing ice cream mix in a manner that produces small beads of ice cream. The small beads of ice cream, which Dippin' Dots calls "Ice Cream of the Future," are flavorful and fun. Unfortunately, as illustrated in the "What Went Wrong?" feature, Dippin' Dots' patent on its unique way of producing ice cream was recently invalidated, and now the company has two new competitors that are producing ice cream treats in a manner that is very similar to what Dippin' Dots offers. Dippin' Dots' experience is a vivid reminder that a firm must follow the absolute letter of the law in obtaining intellectual property protection or the protection can be lost.

WHAT WENT WRONG?

Dippin' Dots: Why the USPTO Invalidated Its Patent and It Now Has Two New Competitors

Web: www.dippindots.com
Twitter: DippinDots
Facebook: Dippin' Dots

Dippin' Dots is an ice cream snack, sold by Dippin' Dots franchises in the food courts of malls and similar locations. A microbiologist, Curt Jones, founded the company in 1987. Jones pioneered the process of cryogenic encapsulation, which is a fancy way of saying he flash froze ice cream mix in a way that produced small beads of ice cream. The small beads of ice cream, which Dippin' Dots calls "Ice Cream of the Future," are flavorful, light, and fun. Simply buying a Dippin' Dots cup of ice cream is part of the experience. The ice cream beads are literally "poured" into a cup and are often described as "tingly and almost crunchy" when consumed.

Although Dippin' Dots is still going strong (in 2010 for example, the firm had over 3 million Facebook fans, suggesting a strong relationship between it and some of its target customers), the company experienced a major setback in 2007 when its patent was invalidated by the USPTO. Specifically, on February 9, 2007, the Federal Circuit Court ruled that Dippin' Dots' method of making frozen ice cream pellets was invalid because it was obvious. The ruling resulted from a lawsuit that Dippin' Dots filed against Mini Melts, a competitor that started selling a beaded ice cream treat, alleging trade dress infringement on the shape of its multicolored ice cream bits. The suit, *Dippin' Dots, Inc. v. Frosty Bites Distribution, LLL aka Mini Melts,* was unsuccessful. One of the arguments that Mini Melts used in undermining Dippin' Dots was that the company committed patent fraud by not disclosing that it had sold its ice cream product one year prior to applying for its patent. Technically, an inventor of a new product (or process) is required to apply for a patent within one year of inventing the product or the product is considered to be "public art" and the right to file for a patent is forfeited. There is an exception for sales made for testing or experimental purposes (such as in a feasibility test). But the sales must be made for one of these two purposes, and not for commercial purposes.

It turns out that Dippin' Dots and its founder Curt Jones sold novelty ice cream products to over 800 customers using a process very similar to the process that was eventually patented, and the sales took place more than one year before the filing of the patent. Mini Melts argued that the sales invalidated Dippin' Dots' patent, so Dippin' Dots had no right to sue it for trade dress infringement (for making a similar ice cream product). The jury agreed with Mini Melts, and the District

Court for the Northern District of Texas entered a judgment in favor of Mini Melts, finding that Dippin' Dots' patent was invalid. Dippin' Dots appealed to the Federal Circuit Court, which affirmed the lower court's decision. The result was—with a patent no longer protecting the exclusivity of its product—Dippin' Dots had two new competitors, Mini Melts (which in 2011 had become an *Inc.* 500 company) and MolliCoolz. These two firms produced ice cream treats that were very similar to what Dippin' Dots offers. However, MolliCoolz fell on hard times and filed for bankruptcy protection in 2010.

This case is a stark reminder that not only the spirit, but the absolute letter of the law must be followed regarding intellectual property issues. More narrowly, it is a reminder for inventors and entrepreneurs to be particularly aware of the one-year rule for filing a patent application following the invention of a product or process.

Questions for Critical Thinking

1. In what ways could Dippin' Dots be hurt by its patent being invalidated? To what degree was Dippin' Dots' patent an important part of its competitive advantage?
2. How can an entrepreneur be sure that the "letter of the law" is followed when filing a patent application?
3. Do some research on Mini Melts. How similar is this firm's products to what Dippin' Dots introduced to the marketplace? If Dippin' Dots' patent was solid, do you think the company would have solid grounds to sue Mini Melts for infringing on its patent?
4. How can Dippin' Dots differentiate itself from its competitors now that it can't stop its competitors from selling a product that is similar to what it sells?

Source: T. F. Zuber and S. J. Lazaris, "Protecting Your Process Patent: How Dippin' Dots May Make It More Difficult to Secure Process Patents After Prior Sales," www.zuberlaw.com (accessed September 16, 2008). Thomas F. Zuber, Esq. is the Managing Partner of Zuber & Taillieu LLP, practicing intellectual property protection and exploitation from its Los Angeles office. Spyros J. Lazaris, Esq. is a Counsel in the Los Angeles office of Zuber & Taillieu LLP, and the head of its patent and trademark prosecution department. The biographies of both attorneys may be viewed at www.zuberlaw.com.

The Four Key Forms of Intellectual Property

Patents, trademarks, copyrights, and trade secrets are the four key forms of intellectual property. We discuss each form of intellectual property protection in the following sections. Intellectual property laws exist to encourage creativity and innovation by granting individuals who risk their time and money in creative endeavors exclusive rights to the fruits of their labors for a period of time. Intellectual property laws also help individuals make well-informed choices. For example, when a consumer sees a Panera Bread restaurant, she knows exactly what to expect because only Panera Bread is permitted to use the Panera Bread trademark for soups, signature sandwiches, and bakery products.

One special note about intellectual property laws is that it is up to entrepreneurs to take advantage of them and to safeguard their intellectual property once it is legally protected. Police forces and fire departments are available to quickly respond if an entrepreneur's buildings or other physical assets are threatened, but there are no intellectual property police forces or fire departments in existence. The courts prosecute individuals and companies that break intellectual property laws. However, the individual entrepreneur must understand intellectual property laws, safeguard intellectual property assets, and initiate litigation if intellectual property rights are infringed upon or violated.

There is a government-sponsored Web site (www.stopfakes.gov) that provides information about how to file a complaint if a business feels that a "knock off" product is infringing on its intellectual property. Increasingly, counterfeit goods are a problem for firms that have spent considerable resources to brand their products in ways that create value for customers. Counterfeit Callaway golf clubs and "fake" Louis Vuitton purses are examples of goods that counterfeiters target. Check out the blog IP Law For Startups (www.iplawforstartups.com) to keep up to date on all aspects of intellectual property law.

While not one of the four *key* forms of intellectual property, Internet domain names are an important form of intellectual property. Having a short, easy to spell Internet domain name is becoming increasingly important as the Internet becomes an ever more powerful force in business. An Internet domain name is obtained through a domain name registrar like GoDaddy.com, and costs around $10 per year to register. Like other forms of intellectual property, domain names can be bought and sold, and desirable names are valuable. For example, Color.com, a 2011 photo sharing start-up, reportedly paid $350,000 to obtain the Color.com domain name from its previous owner.

PATENTS

A **patent** is a grant from the federal government conferring the rights to exclude others from making, selling, or using an invention for the term of the patent.[6] The owner of the patent is granted a legal monopoly for a limited amount of time. However, a patent does not give its owner the right to make, use, or sell the invention; it gives the owner only the right to exclude others from doing so. This is a confusing issue for many entrepreneurs. If a company is granted a patent for an item, it is natural to assume that it could start making and selling the item immediately. But it cannot. A patent owner can legally make or sell the patented invention only if no other patents are infringed on by doing so.[7] For example, if an inventor obtained a patent on a computer

LEARNING OBJECTIVE

3. Discuss the four major forms of intellectual property: patents, trademarks, copyrights, and trade secrets.

chip and the chip needed technology patented earlier by Intel to work, the inventor would need to obtain permission from Intel to make and sell the chip. Intel may refuse permission or ask for a licensing fee for the use of its patented technology. Although this system may seem odd, it is really the only way the system could work. Many inventions are improvements on existing inventions, and the system allows the improvements to be patented, but only with the permission of the original inventors, who usually benefit by obtaining licensing income in exchange for their consent.[8]

Patent protection has deep roots in U.S. history and is the only form of intellectual property right expressly mentioned in the original articles of the U.S. Constitution. The first patent was granted in 1790 for a process of making potash, an ingredient in fertilizer. The patent was signed by George Washington and was issued to a Vermont inventor named Samuel Hopkins. Patents are important because they grant inventors temporary, exclusive rights to market their inventions. This right gives inventors and their financial backers the opportunity to recoup their costs and earn a profit in exchange for the risks and costs they incur during the invention process. If it weren't for patent laws, inventors would have little incentive to invest time and money in new inventions. "No one would develop a drug if you didn't have a patent," Dr. William Haseltine, former CEO of Human Genome Sciences, a biotech firm, once said.[9]

Since the first patent was granted in 1790, the USPTO has granted over 7 million patents including 233,127 in 2010 alone. The number of patents granted in 2010 was 31 percent more than the number granted in 2009 and 29 percent more than granted in 2007, the next busiest year for the USPTO. These data suggest that entrepreneurship in the United States remains strong. Interestingly, the USPTO, the sole entity responsible for granting patents in the United States, is strained. At the end of 2010, there were 1,245,574 patent applications pending, and it took an average of 35.3 months to get a patent application approved. The USPTO has 6,255 full-time patent examiners to handle its patent caseload.

Some inventors and companies are very prolific and have multiple patents. There is increasing interest in patents, as shown in Table 12.2, as advances in technology spawn new inventions.

It's not only the USPTO office that's strained but other agencies of government deal with intellectual property approval. For example, the U.S. Department of Agriculture must clear genetically modified seeds before they can be placed in use. On average, it takes 1,188 days for the sale of a genetically altered seed to be approved. Observers point out that this delay is slowing the launch of products that could improve crop yields and the global competitiveness of United States farmers.[10]

TABLE 12.2   GROWTH IN PATENT APPLICATIONS IN THE UNITED STATES

	2008	2009	2010
Applications received	496,886	486,499	509,367
Patents issued	182,556	190,122	233,127
Total patents pending	1,208,076	1,279,771	1,245,574
Average time for approval	32.3 months	34.6 months	35.3 months

Source: United States Patent and Trademark Office, *Performance and Accountability Report for Fiscal Year 2010.*

Types of Patents

There are three types of patents: utility patents, design patents, and plant patents. As shown in Figure 12.2, there are three basic requirements for a patent to be granted: The subject of the patent application must be (1) useful, (2) novel in relation to prior arts in the field, and (3) not obvious to a person of ordinary skill in the field.

Utility patents are the most common type of patent and cover what we generally think of as new inventions. Of the 509,367 patent applications filed in 2010, 94 percent were for utility patents.[11] Patents in this category may be granted to anyone who "invents or discovers any new and useful process, machine, manufacture, or composition of matter, or any new and useful improvement thereof."[12] The term of a utility patent is 20 years from the date of the initial application. After 20 years, the patent expires, and the invention falls into the public domain, which means that anyone can produce and sell the invention without paying the prior patent holder. Consider the pharmaceutical industry. Assume a drug produced by a large firm such as Pfizer Inc. is prescribed for you and that, when seeking to fill the prescription, your pharmacist tells you there is no generic equivalent available. The lack of a generic equivalent typically means that a patent owned by Pfizer protects the drug and that the 20-year term of the patent has not expired. If the pharmacist tells you there is a generic version of the drug available, that typically means the 20-year patent has expired and other companies are now making a drug chemically identical to Pfizer's. The price of the generic version of the drug is generally lower because the manufacturer of the generic version of the drug is not trying to recover the costs Pfizer (in this case) incurred to develop the product (the drug) in question.

A utility patent cannot be obtained for an "idea" or a "suggestion" for a new product or process. A complete description of the invention for which a utility patent is sought is required, including drawings and technical details. In addition, a patent must be applied for within one year of when a product or process was first offered for sale, put into public use, or was described in any printed publication, as illustrated in the What Went Wrong? feature dealing with Dippin' Dots, or the right to obtain a patent is forfeited. The requirement that a patent application must be filed within one year of the milestones referred to previously is called the **one year after first use deadline**.

Recently, utility patent law has added business method patents, which have been of particular interest to Internet firms. A **business method patent** is a patent that protects an invention that is or facilitates a method of doing business. Patents for these purposes were not allowed until 1998, when a federal circuit court issued an opinion allowing a patent for a business method, holding that business methods, mathematical algorithms, and software are patentable as long as they produce useful, tangible, and concrete results. This ruling opened a "Pandora's box" and has caused many firms to scramble to try to patent their business methods. Since 1998, the most notable business method patents

The subject of the patent application, whether it is an invention, design, or business method, must be . . .

Useful	Novel	Not Obvious
It must have utility.	It must be different from what has come before (i.e., not in the "prior art").	It must not be obvious to a person of ordinary skill in the field.

FIGURE 12.2

Three Basic Requirements for a Patent

awarded have been Amazon.com's one-click ordering system, Priceline.com's "name-your-price" business model, and Netflix's method for allowing customers to set up a rental list of movies they want mailed to them or that they wish to download for streaming purposes. Activities associated with a business method patent can be an important source of competitive advantage for a firm.

Design patents are the second most common type of patent and cover the invention of new, original, and ornamental designs for manufactured products.[13] Of the 509,367 patent applications filed in 2010, 5.6 percent were for design patents.[14] A design patent is good for 14 years from the grant date. While a utility patent protects the way an invention is used and works, a design patent protects the way it looks. As a result, if an entrepreneur invented a new version of the computer mouse, it would be prudent to apply for a utility patent to cover the way the mouse works and for a design patent to protect the way the mouse looks. Although all computer mice perform essentially the same function, they can be ornamentally designed in an infinite number of ways. As long as each new design is considered by the USPTO to be novel and nonobvious, it is eligible for design patent protection. This is not a trivial issue in that product design is increasingly becoming an important source of competitive advantage for many firms producing many different types of products.

Plant patents protect new varieties of plants that can be reproduced asexually. While less than 1 percent of patent applications filed in 2010 were for plant patents, these patents provide essential protection for companies specializing in plant genetics and related areas. Plants that can be reproduced asexually are reproduced by grafting or crossbreeding rather than by planting seeds. The new variety can be different from previous plants in its resistance to disease or drought or in its scent, appearance, color, or productivity. Thus, a new color for a rose or a new type of hybrid vegetable would be eligible for plant patent protection. The term for plant patent protection is 20 years from the date of the original application.

Table 12.3 provides a summary of the three forms of patent protection, the types of inventions the patents cover, and the duration of the patents.

Who Can Apply for a Patent?

Only the inventor of a product can apply for a patent. If two or more people make an invention jointly, they must apply for the patent together. Someone who simply heard about the design of a product or is trying to patent something that is in the public domain may not apply for a patent.

There are notable exceptions to these rules. First, if an invention is made during the course of the inventor's employment, the employer typically is

TABLE 12.3 SUMMARY OF THE THREE FORMS OF PATENT PROTECTION, THE TYPES OF INVENTIONS THE PATENTS COVER, AND THE DURATION OF THE PATENTS

Type of Patent	Types of Inventions Covered	Duration
Utility	New or useful process, machine, manufacture, or composition of material or any new and useful improvement thereof	20 years from the date of the original application
Design	Invention of new, original, and ornamental designs for manufactured products	14 years from the date of the original application
Plant	Any new varieties of plants that can be reproduced asexually	20 years from the date of the original application

assigned the right to apply for the patent through an **assignment of invention agreement** signed by the employee as part of the employment agreement. A second exception is that the rights to apply for an invention can be sold. This option can be an important source of revenue for entrepreneurial firms. If a firm has an invention that it doesn't want to pursue on its own, the rights to apply for a patent on the invention can be sold to another party.

The Process of Obtaining a Patent

Obtaining a patent is a six-step process, as illustrated in Figure 12.3 and as we discuss here. The costs involved include attorney fees, fees for drawings (which are sometimes lumped together with the attorney fees), and USPTO filing fees. For an individual or business with fewer than 500 employees, it costs about $1,300 in fees, assuming the application is fairly standard and is successful. Attorney fees vary depending on the complexity of the technology involved. An estimate of attorney fees to obtain a patent is provided in Table 12.4.

The majority of inventions independent inventors create range from relatively simple to moderately complex. Businesses are across the board. For a high complex technology, such as a semiconductor product, the costs could substantially exceed $15,000.

LEARNING OBJECTIVE

4. Describe the six-step process for obtaining a patent.

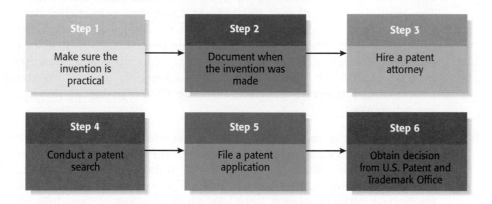

FIGURE 12.3
The Process of Obtaining a Patent

TABLE 12.4   ESTIMATES OF ATTORNEY FEES FOR OBTAINING A PATENT

Invention Type	Examples of Inventions	Fees for an Attorney's Services
Very simple	Coat hanger, a pencil eraser, a bottle opener	$5,000 to $7,000
Relatively simple	Cup holders for automobiles, retractable dog leash, compact flashlight	$7,000 to $9,000
Somewhat complex	Power hand tool, space heater, compact refrigerator	$9,000 to $10,000
Moderately complex	Basic inventory tracking systems, sprinkler systems with several capabilities, simple software with business applications	$10,000 to $12,500
Reasonably complex	Hand-held tracking devices, airport security scanning machines, business methods	$12,500 to $15,000
Very complex	Aviation electronics, fuel-efficient engines for commercial aircraft, Internet-based social media systems	$15,000 and up

Based on Gene Quinn, "The Cost of Obtaining a Patent in the US," IPWatchDog, http://ipwatchdog.com/2011/01/28/the-cost-of-obtainingpatent/id=14668 (accessed April 29, 2011, posted on January 28, 2011).

The six-step process for obtaining a patent is shown next.

Step 1 **Make sure the invention is practical.** As mentioned earlier, there are two rules of thumb for making the decision to patent. Intellectual property that is worth protecting typically is directly related to the competitive advantage of the firm seeking the protection or has independent value in the marketplace.

Step 2 **Document when the invention was made.** Put together a set of documents clearly stating when the invention was first thought of, dates on which experiments were conducted in perfecting it, and the date it was first used and found to operate satisfactorily. Inventors should get in the habit of filling out an "invention logbook" on a daily basis to record their activities. An **invention logbook** documents the dates and activities related to the development of a particular invention. As soon as an inventor has an idea for an invention, a complete description of the invention should be written down, sketches should be made of it, and how it works should be described in detail. The inventor should then sign and date the documents and indicate that he or she is the inventor. If possible, a notary or another party without a financial interest in the invention should witness the inventor's signature. This step is important because if two inventors independently develop essentially the same invention, the right to apply for the patent belongs to the person who came up with it first. The United States adheres to the **first-to-invent rule** rather than the first-to-file rule, meaning that the first person to invent an item or process is given preference over another person who is first to file a patent application. If there is a dispute regarding who was first to invent a product, the dispute is resolved in an administrative proceeding known as an **interference** that a judge at the USPTO presides over.

Step 3 **Hire a patent attorney.** It is highly recommended that an inventor work with a patent attorney. Even though there are "patent-it-yourself" books and Web sites on the market, it is generally naïve for an entrepreneur to think that the patent process can be successfully navigated without expert help. As an indication of the difficulty of writing a patent application, the USPTO requires all attorneys and agents to pass a tough exam before they can interact with the agency on behalf of a client.

Step 4 **Conduct a patent search.** To be patentable, an invention must be novel and different enough from what already exists. A patent attorney typically spends several hours searching the USPTO's database (which is available online at www.uspto.gov) to study similar patents. After the search is completed and the patents that are similar to the invention in question have been carefully studied, the patent attorney renders an opinion regarding the probability of obtaining a patent on the new invention.

Step 5 **File a patent application.** The fifth step, if the inventor decides to proceed, is to file a patent application with the USPTO in Washington, D.C. Applications can be filed electronically or by mail. Unlike copyright and trademark applications, which can be prepared and filed easily by their owners, patent applications are highly technical and almost always require expert assistance. Approximately 80 percent of inventors retain patent attorneys or agents to prepare and file their patent applications.[15]

Step 6 **Obtain a decision from the USPTO.** When the USPTO receives a patent application, it is given a serial number, assigned to an examiner, and then waits to be examined. The patent examiner investigates the application and issues a written report ("Office Action") to the applicant's patent attorney, often asking for modifications to the application. Most of the interactions that applicants have with the USPTO are by mail. Occasionally, an inventor and a lawyer will meet face to face with a patent examiner to discuss the invention and the written report. There is room to negotiate with the patent office to try to make an invention patentable. Eventually, a yes-or-no decision will be rendered. A rejected application can be appealed, but appeals are rare and expensive.

One provision of patent law that is particularly important to entrepreneurs is that the USPTO allows inventors to file a **provisional patent application** for utility patents, pending the preparation and filing of a complete application. A provisional patent application provides the means to establish an early effective filing date for a nonprovisional patent application, and allows the term "Patent Pending" to be applied. There is often confusion regarding what a provisional patent application is. It's not a provisional patent—there is no such thing. It's merely a provisional *application* for a patent, and is used to establish an early filing date for a subsequently filed full utility patent. It can actually give an entrepreneur a false sense of security if not filed correctly. The ins and outs of filing a provisional patent application are explained in this chapter's Savvy Entrepreneurial Firm.

SAVVY ENTREPRENEURIAL FIRM

Knowing the Ins and Outs of Filing a Provisional Patent Application

Web: www.uspto.gov
Twitter: uspto

In start-up circles, it's not uncommon to hear people say that they have a "provisional patent" or that they're protected from someone stealing their invention because a provisional patent has been filed. Neither of these statements can be true, because there is no such thing as a provisional patent. While the people who make those claims are normally well-intentioned, failing to be familiar with the basics of patent law can result in an entrepreneur inadvertently surrendering the patent rights for which he or she has an invention. If this happens, it can cripple a firm that's planning on achieving a sustainable competitive advantage via its exclusive rights on an invention.

Here's an accurate assessment of what takes place for entrepreneurs working in the United States. What's filed with the United States Patent and Trademark Office (USPTO) is a "provisional patent application." It includes specifications (i.e., a description and drawings of an invention), but does not require formal patent claims,

inventors' oaths or declarations, or any information disclosure statement. It's not assigned to a patent examiner, and no judgment is made regarding prior art or the patentability of the invention. Its purpose, in the eyes of the USPTO, is to establish an early filing date for a subsequently filed full utility patent. What's meant by this is that if a provisional patent application is filed on December 1, 2011, and the application is done correctly, this becomes the "priority" filing date for that invention. If someone files a utility patent application for an identical invention a month later, that person is out of luck, as long as the inventor who filed the provisional patent application follows through and files for a full utility patent within one year, and both the provisional patent application and the full utility patent application are deemed to be acceptable. A bonus attached to filing a provisional patent application, which costs $110 to file, is that the inventor can legally use the term "patent pending" in

(continued)

relation to the invention. This designation may provide the inventor a significant marketing advantage, if the invention is already for sale, and signal to prospective inventors that the inventor is taking steps to protect his or her patent rights.

There is a catch, however, to this scenario—the provisional patent application must be completed and filed correctly. All patent applications, including provisional patent applications, are subject to three important statutory requirements:

1. An adequate written description of the invention.
2. Enable one of ordinary skill in the art to make and use the invention.
3. Must set forth the best mode of practicing the invention contemplated by the inventor upon filing.

If any one of these requirements is not met, along with other statutory requirements the USPTO has, it's tantamount to not having filed anything at all. So it's very important that provisional patent applications be sufficiently detailed and filed correctly. Here's what can happen if they're not. Suppose Amy invents a new type of tennis racket. She files a provisional patent application on January 1, 2011, by downloading the application and filing it herself. It's inadequate because it doesn't contain an adequate written description of her invention, but the USPTO doesn't tell Amy it's inadequate because it doesn't examine provisional patent applications until a full utility patent is filed. On July 1, 2011, Amy hires a patent attorney to file for a full utility patent on her invention. After reviewing her file, the USPTO examiner rejects the application, because someone filed a utility patent application for an identical invention a month earlier, on June 1, 2011. The reason for the rejection is that Amy's provisional patent application was deemed to be invalid because the description was inadequate. The fact that Amy filed a provisional patent application on January 1, 2011, five full months before the second party filed for an identical invention, holds no weight because Amy's provisional patent application was deemed to be invalid.

Amy' story illustrates that filing a provisional patent application takes some finesse. Filing a provisional patent application has its place. It's particularly useful for an inventor who invents a new device and wants to lock in a priority filing date while additional prototyping and feasibility analysis are conducted to decide whether it's worth the time and money to file for a full utility patent. It's a balancing act, however. An inventor needs to be far down the road before a provisional patent application makes sense. It may also make sense to hire a patent attorney to file the provisional patent application. Amy's description probably wasn't adequate because she didn't create a prototype of her new tennis racket, and thus was not able to adequately describe it. A patent attorney would have most likely told Amy that her description wasn't adequate, and suggested that more work be completed before the provisional patent application was filed. An idea can't be patented—only the specific expression of an idea, which must contain an adequate description.

The USPTO does allow additional provisional applications for a device to be filed as improvements are made. This protects inventors who are making progress on their device, and want to establish priority dates for improved iterations of an invention as progress is made.

Questions for Critical Thinking

1. Briefly describe the difference between a provisional patent application and a utility patent application. If successful, which of the two applications awards an inventor a patent?
2. Can a provisional patent application be filed for a design patent? Document your research to arrive at the correct answer to this question.
3. Under what circumstances would you (1) suggest to an inventor that he or she could file a provisional patent application without a patent attorney or (2) suggest to an inventor that he or she needs to hire a patent attorney to file the provisional patent application?
4. Spend some time studying the USPTO's Web site, or doing some Internet research on patents. Inventor's Digest (www.inventorsigest.com) is another good resource for learning about patents. Discuss one fact about patents or the application process you find interesting and isn't included in the material in this chapter.

Sources: USPTO, www.uspto.gov (accessed April 1, 2011); Jon H. Muskin, "Pitfalls of Provisional Patent Applications," *Inventors Digest*, www.inventorsdigest.com/archives/4111 (accessed April 1, 2011, posted on July 20, 2010).

In some instances, entrepreneurs license their patents to larger firms, which have nationwide distribution channels to market a product. In fact, consumer product companies like Procter &Gamble (P&G) and General Mills, which at one time relied strictly on their own scientists to develop new products, now have formal programs for inventors and entrepreneurs to submit product ideas, as illustrated in the "Partnering for Success" feature. The arrangements described in the "Partnering for Success" feature represent a win-win for both inventors and larger firms. The inventor receives distribution for his or her product and potential licensing income, and the large firm receives an innovative new product to place in its distribution channels. One requirement most large firms have is that an idea must be patented or a patent must be applied for before they will consider licensing it.

PARTNERING FOR SUCCESS

Individual Inventors and Large Firms: Partnering to Bring New Products to Market

A common problem that inventors and entrepreneurs have is distributing their products. Gary Schwartzberg is a case in point. Schwartzberg, along with a partner, developed a new type of bagel. Dubbed the "Bageler," the bagel was tube-shaped and filled with cream cheese. Schwartzberg was able to get the product into supermarkets and schools in South Florida, where he lived, but couldn't achieve wider distribution. He finally mailed Kraft a box of his cream-cheese-filled bagels with a proposal. He picked Kraft because he wanted to use Philadelphia Cream Cheese (a Kraft product) to fill the bagel.

By coincidence, Kraft had been working on a similar product but couldn't get it right. Schwartzberg had a patented process for "encapsulating" the cream cheese in the center of the bagel without the cream cheese escaping during the baking process. Kraft bit and after some back and forth, Schwartzberg and Kraft hammered out a deal. Schwartzberg told the *Wall Street Journal* that he couldn't discuss the details of the deal because of a confidentiality agreement with Kraft, but says it's structured as a strategic alliance and he "has skin in the game." Schwartzberg's product, which is now called Bagel-fuls, is sold nationwide by Kraft Foods.

Entrepreneurs and inventors are finding that large consumer products companies are increasingly interested in what they have to offer. For example, Lifetime Brands, the United States' leading resource for nationally branded kitchenware, tabletop, and home décor products, is soliciting ideas from outside inventors. A section of its homepage titled "Share your ideas" reads, "Lifetime Brands recognizes that good ideas come from unexpected places. Is there something you've always wanted in your kitchen but just can't find? Is there a tool or gadget that you've been itching to improve? Tell us about it!" Instructions are then provided for how to submit a product idea. In a different industry, GE is looking outside its company for new ideas in a number of areas. It recently sponsored the GE Ecomagination Challenge, which was a $200 million solicitation for energy-related ideas. Phase II of the challenge, which focused on improving the use of energy in homes, solicited 809 new ideas. Although this specific challenge is over, GE will be soliciting ideas in other areas in similar ways. When an *Inventors Digest* reporter asked GE's CEO Jeff Immelt at what stage an inventor needs to be in order to submit an idea to GE, he replied that GE would consider "any protected IP."

Companies vary in terms of what stage an idea needs to be at before it can be submitted for consideration. The best way to find out is to study the portion of a company's Web site that provides instructions for how to submit ideas. Not all companies are open to new ideas, but many are. For example, P&G's idea submission site is titled "P&G Connect + Develop." General Mills' site is titled "General Mills Open Innovation" and Black & Decker's idea site is simply titled "Product Ideas." In fact, Black & Decker has a brochure posted on its site (simply click on the "About" tab and follow the link titled "Submit an Idea") that describes its idea submission and evaluation process. Its process is similar to the process of many firms.

Questions for Critical Thinking

1. Why do you think companies are increasingly open to ideas from outside inventors?
2. For an inventor or entrepreneur, what are the upsides to working with a company like General Mills or GE? What, if any, are the downsides?
3. Find an idea submission site for a company not mentioned in the feature. Describe how to submit an invention to the company. What seems to be the keys to getting an idea accepted by the company?
4. In most cases, do you think inventors and entrepreneurs get a fair shake when they license a product or enter into an alliance with a large firm? What steps should entrepreneurs take to make sure they are getting a fair deal?

Sources: Patrick Raymond, "Jeff Immelt Opens Up: GE's CEO Wants Your IP." *Inventors Digest*, February 8, 2011, www.inventorsdigest.com/archives/5594; *The Wall Street Journal* (Eastern Edition) by S. Coval. Copyright 2005 by Dow Jones & Company.

Patent Infringement

Patent infringement takes place when one party engages in the unauthorized use of another party's patent. A typical example of an infringement claim was that initiated by Alacritech, a start-up firm, which claimed that Microsoft violated two of its patents on technology used to speed the performance of computers connected to networks. According to court documents, Alacritech showed its technology to Microsoft, hoping that Microsoft would license it.

But Microsoft passed on the offer and later announced a surprisingly similar technology, called Chimney. Alacritech again offered to license the technology to Microsoft but was rebuffed. In response, Alacritech filed suit against Microsoft. Microsoft claimed that its technology was developed independently.[16] After hearing the case, the U.S. District Court in San Francisco sided with Alacritech and filed a preliminary injunction against Microsoft, preventing it from shipping products that contained the contested technology. Later, the suit was settled out of court, with Microsoft agreeing to license Alacritech's technology.[17]

The tough part about patent infringement cases is that they are costly to litigate, which puts start-up firms and their entrepreneurs at quite a disadvantage. While there is no way of knowing how much it cost Alacritech to sue Microsoft, a typical patent-infringement suit, according to *Fortune Small Business*, costs each side at least $500,000 to litigate.[18]

TRADEMARKS

A **trademark** is any word, name, symbol, or device used to identify the source or origin of products or services and to distinguish those products or services from others. All businesses want to be recognized by their potential clientele and use their names, logos, and other distinguishing features to enhance their visibility. Trademarks also provide consumers with useful information. For example, consumers know what to expect when they see a Macy's store in a mall. Think of how confusing it would be if any retail store could use the name Macy's.

As is the case with patents, trademarks have a rich history. Archaeologists have found evidence that as far back as 3,500 years ago, potters made distinctive marks on their articles of pottery to distinguish their work from others. But consider a more modern example. The original name that Jerry Yang and David Filo, the cofounders of Yahoo!, selected for their Internet directory service was "Jerry's Guide to the World Wide Web." Not too catchy, is it? The name was later changed to Yahoo!, which caught on with early adopters of the Internet.

The Four Types of Trademarks

There are four types of trademarks: trademarks, service marks, collective marks, and certification marks (see Table 12.5). Trademarks and service marks are of the greatest interest to entrepreneurs.

Trademarks, as described previously, include any word, name, symbol, or device used to identify and distinguish one company's products from another's. Trademarks are used in the advertising and promotion of tangible products, such as Apple for smartphones, Nike for athletic shoes, Ann Taylor for women's clothing, and Zynga for online games.

Service marks are similar to ordinary trademarks, but they are used to identify the services or intangible activities of a business rather than a business's physical product. Service marks include *The Princeton Review* for test prep services, eBay for online auctions, and Verizon for cell phone service.

Collective marks are trademarks or service marks used by the members of a cooperative, association, or other collective group, including marks indicating membership in a union or similar organization. The marks belonging to the American Bar Association, The International Franchise Association, and the Entrepreneurs' Organization are examples of collective marks.

TABLE 12.5 SUMMARY OF THE FOUR FORMS OF TRADEMARK PROTECTION, THE TYPE OF MARKS THE TRADEMARKS COVER, AND THE DURATION OF THE TRADEMARKS

Type of Trademark	Type of Marks Covered	Duration
Trademark	Any word, name, symbol, or device used to identify and distinguish one company's goods from another Examples: *Apple, d.light, Dry Soda, ModCloth, and Zeo*	Renewable every 10 years, as long as the mark remains in use
Service mark	Similar to trademarks; are used to identify the services or intangible activities of a business, rather than a business's physical products Examples: *1-800-FLOWERS, Amazon.com, eBay, Game Truck, Mint.com, and Zipcar*	Renewable every 10 years, as long as the mark remains in use
Collective mark	Trademarks or service marks used by the members of a cooperative, association, or other collective group Examples: *Information Technology Industry Council, International Franchise Association, Rotary International*	Renewable every 10 years, as long as the mark remains in use
Certification mark	Marks, words, names, symbols, or devices used by a person other than its owner to certify a particular quality about a good or service Examples: *100% Napa Valley, Florida Oranges, National Organic Program, Underwriters Laboratories*	Renewable every 10 years, as long as the mark remains in use

Finally, **certification marks** are marks, words, names, symbols, or devices used by a person other than its owner to certify a particular quality about a product or service. The most familiar certification mark is the UL mark, which certifies that a product meets the safety standards established by Underwriters Laboratories. Other examples are the Good Housekeeping Seal of Approval, Stilton Cheese (a product from the Stilton region in England), and 100% Napa Valley (from grapes grown in the Napa Valley of northern California).

What Is Protected Under Trademark Law?

Trademark law, which falls under the **Lanham Act**, passed in 1946, protects the following items:

- **Words:** All combinations of words are eligible for trademark registration, including single words, short phrases, and slogans. YouTern, Pledgemusic, and the National Football League are examples of words and phrases that have been registered as trademarks.
- **Numbers and letters:** Numbers and letters are eligible for registration. Examples include 3M, 4Food, and AT&T. Alphanumeric marks are also registerable, such as 1-800-FREE-411.
- **Designs or logos:** A mark consisting solely of a design, such as the Golden Gate Bridge for Cisco Systems or the Nike swoosh logo, may be eligible for registration. The mark must be distinctive rather than generic. As a result, no one can claim exclusive rights to the image of the Golden Gate Bridge, but Cisco Systems can trademark its unique depiction of the bridge. Composite marks consist of a word or words in conjunction with a design. An example is the trademark for Zephyrhill's bottled water, which includes Zephyrhill's name below a picture of mountain scenery and water.

■ **Sounds:** Distinctive sounds can be trademarked, although this form of trademark protection is rare. Recognizable examples of such sounds include the MGM's lion's roar, the familiar four-tone sound that accompanies "Intel Inside" commercials, and the Yahoo! yodel.

■ **Fragrances:** The fragrance of a product may be registerable as long as the product is not known for the fragrance or the fragrance does not enhance the use of the product. As a result, the fragrance of a perfume or room deodorizer is not eligible for trademark protection, whereas stationery treated with a special fragrance in most cases would be.

■ **Shapes:** The shape of a product, as long as it has no impact on the product's function, can be trademarked. The unique shape of the Apple iPod has received trademark protection.[19] Apple filed a lawsuit against Samsung in April 2011 to protect its patents including those related to product shapes. Specifically, "Apple's lawsuit claims that the look and feel of Samsung's products as well as the packaging that they come in infringe upon Apple's trade dress."[20] The Coca-Cola Company has trademarked its famous curved bottle. The shape of the bottle has no effect on the quality of the bottle or the beverage it holds; therefore, the shape is not functional.

■ **Colors:** A trademark may be obtained for a color as long as the color is not functional. For example, Nexium, a medicine pill that treats acid reflux disease, is purple and is marketed as "the purple pill." The color of the pill has no bearing on its functionality; therefore, it can be protected by trademark protection.

■ **Trade dress:** The manner in which a product is "dressed up" to appeal to customers is protectable. This category includes the overall packaging, design, and configuration of a product. As a result, the overall look of a business is protected as its trade dress. In a famous case in 1992, *Two Pesos, Inc., v. Taco Cabana International Inc.*, the U.S. Supreme Court protected the overall design, colors, and configuration of a chain of Mexican restaurants from a competitor using a similar decor.[21]

Trademark protection is very broad and provides many opportunities for businesses to differentiate themselves from one another. The key for young entrepreneurial firms is to trademark their products and services in ways that draw positive attention to them in a compelling manner.

Exclusions from Trademark Protection

There are notable exclusions from trademark protection that are set forth in the U.S. Trademark Act:

■ **Immoral or scandalous matter:** A company cannot trademark immoral or scandalous matter, including profane words.

■ **Deceptive matter:** Marks that are deceptive cannot be registered. For example, a food company couldn't register the name "Fresh Florida Oranges" if the oranges weren't from Florida.

■ **Descriptive marks:** Marks that are merely descriptive of a product or service cannot be trademarked. For example, an entrepreneur couldn't design a new type of golf ball and try to obtain trademark protection on the words *golf ball*. The words describe a type of product rather than a brand of product, such as Titleist or MaxFli, and are needed by all golf ball manufacturers to be competitive. This issue is a real concern for the manufacturers of very popular products. Recently, Xerox was in danger of losing trademark protection for the Xerox name because of the common use of the word *Xerox* as a verb (e.g., "I am going to Xerox this").

■ **Surnames:** A trademark consisting primarily of a surname, such as Anderson or Smith, is typically not protectable. An exception is a surname combined with other wording that is intended to trademark a distinct product, such as William's Fresh Fish or Smith's Computer Emporium.

The Process of Obtaining a Trademark

As illustrated in Figure 12.4 selecting and registering a trademark is a three-step process. Once a trademark has been used in interstate commerce, it can be registered with the USPTO. It can remain registered forever as long as the trademark stays in use. The first renewal is between the fifth and the sixth year following the year of initial registration. It can be renewed every 10 years thereafter, as long as the trademark stays in use.

Technically, a trademark does not need to be registered to receive protection and to prevent other companies from using confusingly similar marks. Once a mark is used in commerce, such as in an advertisement, it is protected. There are several distinct advantages, however, in registering a trademark with the USPTO: Registered marks are allowed nationwide priority for use of the mark, registered marks may use the federal trademark registration symbol (®), and registered marks carry with them the right to block the importation of infringing goods into the United States. The right to use the trademark registration symbol is particularly important. Attaching the trademark symbol to a product (e.g., My Yahoo!®) provides notice of a trademark owner's registration. This posting allows an owner to recover damages in an infringement action and helps reduce an offender's claim that it didn't know that a particular name or logo was trademarked.

There are three steps in selecting and registering a trademark:

Step 1 **Select an appropriate mark.**   There are several rules of thumb to help business owners and entrepreneurs select appropriate trademarks. First, a mark, whether it is a name, logo, design, or fragrance, should display creativity and strength. Marks that are inherently distinctive, such as the McDonald's Golden Arches; made-up words, such as *Google* and *eBay*; and words that evoke particular images, such as *Double Delight Ice Cream*, are strong trademarks. Second, words that create a favorable impression about a product or service are helpful. A name such as *Safe and Secure Childcare* for a day care center positively resonates with parents.

Step 2 **Perform a trademark search.**   Once a trademark has been selected, a trademark search should be conducted to determine if the trademark is available. If someone else has already established rights to the proposed mark, it cannot be used. There are several ways to conduct a trademark search, from self-help searches to hiring a firm specializing in trademark clearance checks. The search should include both federal and state searches in any states in which business will be conducted. If the trademark will be used overseas, the search should also include the countries where the trademark will be used.

FIGURE 12.4
The Process of Obtaining a Trademark

Although it is not necessary to hire an attorney to conduct a trademark search, it is probably a good idea to do so. Self-searches can also be conducted. A simple-to-use search engine is available at the USPTO's Web site (www.uspto.org). Using this Web site, a person can check the agency's database of registered, abandoned, canceled, and expired marks and pending applications. Adopting a trademark without conducting a trademark search is risky. If a mark is challenged as an infringement, a company may have to destroy all its goods that bear the mark (including products, business cards, stationery, signs, and so on) and then select a new mark. The cost of refamiliarizing customers with an existing product under a new name or logo could be substantial.

Step 3 **Create rights in the trademark.**   The final step in establishing a trademark is to create rights in the mark. In the United States, if the trademark is inherently distinctive (think of Starbucks, iTunes, or Facebook), the first person to use the mark becomes its owner. If the mark is descriptive, such as BUFFERIN for buffered aspirin, using the mark merely begins the process of developing a secondary meaning necessary to create full trademark protection. **Secondary meaning** arises when, over time, consumers start to identify a trademark with a specific product. For example, the name CHAP STICK for lip balm was originally considered to be descriptive, and thus not afforded trademark protection. As people started to think of CHAP STICK as lip balm, it met the threshold of secondary meaning and was able to be trademarked.

There are two ways that the USPTO can offer further protection for firms concerned about maintaining the exclusive rights to their trademarks. First, a person can file an **intent-to-use trademark application**. This is an application based on the applicant's intention to use a trademark. Once this application is filed, the owner obtains the benefits of registration. The benefits are lost, however, if the owner does not use the mark in business within six months of registration. Further protection can be obtained by filing a formal application for a trademark. The application must include a drawing of the trademark and a filing fee (ranging from $275 to $375, depending on how the application is filed). After a trademark application is filed, an examining attorney at the USPTO determines if the trademark can be registered.

COPYRIGHTS

A **copyright** is a form of intellectual property protection that grants to the owner of a work of authorship the legal right to determine how the work is used and to obtain the economic benefits from the work.[22] The work must be in a tangible form, such as a book, operating manual, magazine article, musical score, computer software program, or architectural drawing. If something is not in a tangible form, such as a speech that has never been recorded or saved on a computer disk, copyright law does not protect it.

Businesses typically possess a treasure trove of copyrightable material, as illustrated earlier in Table 12.1. A work does not have to have artistic merit to be eligible for copyright protection. As a result, things such as operating manuals, advertising brochures, and training videos qualify for protection. The Copyright Revision Act of 1976 governs copyright law in the United States. Under the law, an original work is protected automatically from the time it is created and put into a tangible form whether it is published or not. The first copyright in the United States was granted on May 31, 1790, to a Philadelphia educator named John Barry for a spelling book.

What Is Protected by a Copyright?

Copyright laws protect "original works of authorship" that are fixed in a tangible form of expression. The primary categories of material that can be copyrighted follow:

- **Literary works:** Anything written down is a literary work, including books, poetry, reference works, speeches, advertising copy, employee manuals, games, and computer programs. Characters found in literary works are protectable if they possess a high degree of distinctiveness. A character that looks and acts like Garfield, the cartoon cat, would infringe on the copyright that protects Garfield.

- **Musical compositions:** A musical composition, including any accompanying words, that is in a fixed form (e.g., a musical score, cassette tape, CD, or an MP3 file) is protectable. The owner of the copyright is usually the composer and possibly a lyricist. **Derivative works**, which are works that are new renditions of something that is already copyrighted, are also copyrightable. As a result of this provision, a musician who performs a unique rendition of a song written and copyrighted by Miley Cyrus, Lady Gaga, or the Jonas Brothers, for example, can obtain a copyright on his or her effort. Of course, each of these artists would have to consent to the infringement on its copyright of the original song before the new song could be used commercially, which is a common way that composers earn extra income.

- **Computer software:** In 1980, Congress passed the **Computer Software Copyright Act**, which amended previous copyright acts. Now, all forms of computer programs are protected.

- **Dramatic works:** A dramatic work is a theatrical performance, such as a play, comedy routine, newscast, movie, or television show. An entire dramatic work can be protected under a single copyright. As a result, a dramatic work such as a television show doesn't need a separate copyright for the video and audio portions of the show.

- **Pantomimes and choreographic works:** A pantomime is a performance that uses gestures and facial expressions rather than words to communicate a situation. Choreography is the arrangement of dance movements. Copyright laws in these areas protect ballets, dance movements, and mime works.

- **Pictorial, graphic, and sculptural works:** This is a broad category that includes photographs, prints, art reproductions, cartoons, maps, globes, jewelry, fabrics, games, technical drawings, diagrams, posters, toys, sculptures, and charts.

> **LEARNING OBJECTIVE**
> 6. Identify the types of material that are eligible for copyright protection.

Other categories of items covered by copyright law include motion pictures and other audiovisual works, sound recordings, and architectural works.

As can be seen, copyright law provides broad protection for authors and the creators of other types of copyrightable work. The most common mistake entrepreneurs make in this area is not thinking broadly enough about what they should copyright.

Exclusions from Copyright Protection

There are exclusions from copyright protection. The main exclusion is that copyright laws cannot protect ideas. For example, an entrepreneur may have the idea to open a soccer-themed restaurant. The idea itself is not eligible for copyright protection. However, if the entrepreneur writes down specifically what the soccer-themed restaurant will look like and how it would operate, that description is copyrightable. The legal principle describing this concept is called the **idea–expression dichotomy**. An idea is not copyrightable, but the specific expression of an idea is.

Other exclusions from copyright protection include facts (e.g., population statistics), titles (e.g., *Introduction to Entrepreneurship*), and lists of ingredients (e.g., recipes).

How to Obtain a Copyright

As mentioned, copyright law protects any work of authorship the moment it assumes a tangible form. Technically, it is not necessary to provide a copyright notice or register work with the U.S. Copyright Office to be protected by copyright legislation. The following steps can be taken, however, to enhance the protection offered by the copyright statutes.

First, copyright protection can be enhanced for anything written by attaching the copyright notice, or "**copyright bug**" as it is sometimes called. The bug—a "c" inside a circle—typically appears in the following form: © [first year of publication] [author or copyright owner]. Thus, the notice at the bottom of a magazine ad for Dell Inc.'s computers in 2011 would read, "© 2011 Dell Inc." By placing this notice at the bottom of a document, an author (or company) can prevent someone from copying the work without permission and claiming that they did not know that the work was copyrighted. Substitutes for the copyright bug include the word "Copyright" and the abbreviation "Copr."

Second, further protection can be obtained by registering a work with the U.S. Copyright Office. Filing a simple form and depositing one or two samples of the work with the U.S. Copyright Office completes the registration process. The need to supply a sample depends on the nature of the item involved. Obviously, one could not supply one or two samples of an original painting. The current cost of obtaining a copyright is $35 per item. Although the $35 fee seems modest, in many cases it is impractical for a prolific author to register everything he or she creates. In all cases, however, it is recommended that the copyright bug be attached to copyrightable work and that registration be contemplated on a case-by-case basis. A copyright can be registered at any time, but filing promptly is recommended and makes it easier to sue for copyright infringement.

Copyrights last a long time. According to current law, any work created on or after January 1, 1978, is protected for the life of the author plus 70 years. For works made for hire, the duration of the copyright is 95 years from publication or 120 years from creation, whichever is shorter. For works created before 1978, the duration times vary, depending on when the work was created. After a copyright expires, the work goes into the public domain, meaning it becomes available for anyone's use.

Copyright Infringement

Copyright infringement is a growing problem in the United States and in other countries, with estimates of the costs to owners at more than $20 billion per year. For example, less than a week after the film was released in the United

States, bootleg video discs of the original Harry Potter movie were reported to be for sale in at least two Asian countries. **Copyright infringement** occurs when one work derives from another, is an exact copy, or shows substantial similarity to the original work. To prove infringement, a copyright owner is required to show that the alleged infringer had prior access to the copyrighted work and that the work is substantially similar to the owner's.

There are many ways to prevent infringement. For example, a technique frequently used to guard against the illegal copying of software code is to embed and hide in the code useless information, such as the birth dates and addresses of the authors. It's hard for infringers to spot useless information if they are simply cutting and pasting large amounts of code from one program to another. If software code is illegally copied and an infringement suit is filed, it is difficult for the accused party to explain why the (supposedly original) code included the birth dates and addresses of its accusers. Similarly, some publishers of maps, guides, and other reference works will deliberately include bits of phony information in their products, such as fake streets, nonexistent railroad crossings, and so on, to try to catch copiers. Again, it would be pretty hard for someone who copied someone else's copyrighted street guide to explain why the name of a fake street was included.[23]

Current law permits limited infringement of copyrighted material. Consider **fair use**, which is the limited use of copyrighted material for purposes such as criticism, comment, news reporting, teaching, or scholarship. This provision is what allows textbook authors to repeat quotes from magazine articles (as long as the original source is cited), movie critics to show clips from movies, and teachers to distribute portions of newspaper articles. The reasoning behind the law is that the benefit to the public from such uses outweighs any harm to the copyright owner. Other situations in which copyrighted material may be used to a limited degree without fear of infringement include parody, reproduction by libraries, and making a single backup copy of a computer program or a digital music file for personal use. Case 12.2, titled "Protecting Intellectual Property: Elvis's Memory and Intellectual Property Live On," focuses on a copyright infringement case in which the courts ruled that Fair Use was not being employed appropriately.

The rampant illegal downloading and sharing of music—copyright infringement—is a major challenge the music industry continues to struggle with. Hackers are always looking for a new ways to skirt the law.

Edward Bartel/Dreamstime

Copyrights and the Internet

Every day, vast quantities of material are posted on the Internet and can be downloaded or copied by anyone with a computer and an Internet connection. Because the information is stored somewhere on a computer or Internet server, it is in a tangible form and probably qualifies for copyright protection. As a result, anyone who downloads material from the Internet and uses it for personal purposes should be cautious and realize that copyright laws are just as applicable for material on the Internet as they are for material purchased from a bookstore or borrowed from a library.

Copyright laws, particularly as they apply to the Internet, are sometimes difficult to follow, and it is easy for people to dismiss them as contrary to common sense. For example, say that a golf instructor in Phoenix posted a set of "golf tips" on his Web site for his students to use as they prepare for their lessons. Because the notes are on a Web site, anyone can download the notes and use them. As a result, suppose that another golf instructor in a different part of the United States or in a different country ran across the golf tips, downloaded them, and decided to distribute them to his students. Under existing law, the second golf instructor probably violated the intellectual property rights of the first. Arguably, he should have gotten permission from the first golf instructor before using the notes even if the Web site didn't include any information about how to contact the first instructor. To many people, this scenario doesn't make sense. The first golf instructor put his notes on a public Web site, didn't include any information about how to obtain permission to use them, and didn't even include information about how he could be contacted. In addition, he made no attempt to protect the notes, such as posting them on a password-protected Web page. Still, intellectual property rights apply, and the second instructor runs the risk of a copyright infringement suit.

There are a number of techniques available for entrepreneurs and Webmasters to prevent unauthorized material from being copied from a Web site. Password protecting the portion of a site containing sensitive or proprietary information is a common first step. In addition, there are a number of technical protection tools available on the market that limit access to or the use of online information, including selected use of encryption, digital watermarking (hidden copyright messages), and digital fingerprinting (hidden serial numbers or a set of characteristics that tend to distinguish an object from other similar objects).

TRADE SECRETS

Most companies, including start-ups, have a wealth of information that is critical to their success but does not qualify for patent, trademark, or copyright protection. Some of this information is confidential and needs to be kept secret to help a firm maintain its competitive advantage. An example is a company's customer list. A company may have been extremely diligent over time tracking the preferences and buying habits of its customers, helping it fine-tune its marketing message and target past customers for future business. If this list fell into the hands of one or more of the company's competitors, its value would be largely lost, and it would no longer provide the firm a competitive advantage over its competitors.

A **trade secret** is any formula, pattern, physical device, idea, process, or other information that provides the owner of the information with a competitive advantage in the marketplace. Trade secrets include marketing plans, product formulas, financial forecasts, employee rosters, logs of sales calls, and

LEARNING OBJECTIVE

7. Discuss the legal environment that facilitates trade secret protection.

laboratory notebooks. The medium in which information is stored typically has no impact on whether it can be protected as a trade secret. As a result, written documents, computer files, audiotapes, videotapes, financial statements, and even an employee's memory of various items can be protected from unauthorized disclosure.

Unlike patents, trademarks, and copyrights, there is no single government agency that regulates trade secret laws. Instead, trade secrets are governed by a patchwork of various state laws. The federal **Economic Espionage Act**, passed in 1996, does criminalize the theft of trade secrets. The **Uniform Trade Secrets Act**, which a special commission drafted in 1979, attempted to set nationwide standards for trade secret legislation. Although the majority of states have adopted the act, most revised it, resulting in a wide disparity among states in regard to trade secret legislation and enforcement.

What Qualifies for Trade Secret Protection?

Not all information qualifies for trade secret protection. In general, information that is known to the public or that competitors can discover through legal means doesn't qualify for trade secret protection. If a company passes out brochures at a trade show that are available to anyone in attendance, nothing that is in the brochure can typically qualify as a trade secret. Similarly, if a secret is disclosed by mistake, it typically loses its trade secret status. For example, if an employee of a company is talking on a cell phone in a public place and is overheard by a competitor, anything the employee says is generally exempt from trade secret protection. Simply stated, the general philosophy of trade secret legislation is that the law will not protect a trade secret unless its owner protects it first.

Companies can maintain protection for their trade secrets if they take reasonable steps to keep the information confidential. In assessing whether reasonable steps have been taken, courts typically examine how broadly the information is known inside and outside the firm, the value of the information, the extent of measures taken to protect the secrecy of the information, the effort expended in developing the information, and the ease with which other companies could develop the information. On the basis of these criteria, the strongest case for trade secret protection is information that is characterized by the following:

- ■ Is not known outside the company
- ■ Is known only inside the company on a "need-to-know" basis
- ■ Is safeguarded by stringent efforts to keep the information confidential
- ■ Is valuable and provides the company a compelling competitive advantage
- ■ Was developed at great cost, time, and effort
- ■ Cannot be easily duplicated, reverse engineered, or discovered.

Trade Secret Disputes

Trade secret disputes arise most frequently when an employee leaves a firm to join a competitor and is accused of taking confidential information along. For example, a marketing executive for one firm may take a job with a competitor and create a marketing plan for the new employer that is nearly identical to the plan being worked on at the previous job. The original employer could argue that the marketing plan on which the departed employee was working was a company trade secret and that the employee essentially stole the plan and took

LEARNING OBJECTIVE

8. Identify the most common types of trade secret disputes.

it to the new job. The key factor in winning a trade secret dispute is that some type of theft or misappropriation must have taken place. Trade secrets can be lawfully discovered. For example, it's not illegal for one company to buy another company's products and take them apart to see how they are assembled. In fact, this is a relatively common practice, which is another reason companies continuously attempt to innovate as a means of trying to stay at least one step ahead of competitors.

A company damaged by trade secret theft can initiate a civil action for damages in court. The action should be taken as soon after the discovery of the theft as possible. In denying the allegation, the defendant will typically argue that the information in question was independently developed (meaning no theft took place), was obtained by proper means (such as with the permission of the owner), is common knowledge (meaning it is not subject to trade secret protection), or was innocently received (such as through a casual conversation at a business meeting). Memorization is not a defense. As a result, an employee of one firm can't say that "all I took from my old job to my new one was what's in my head" and claim that just because the information conveyed wasn't in written form, it's not subject to trade secret protection. If the courts rule in favor of the firm that feels its trade secret has been stolen, the firm can stop the offender from using the trade secret and obtain financial damages.

Trade Secret Protection Methods

Aggressive protection of trade secrets is necessary to prevent intentional or unintentional disclosure. In addition, one of the key factors in determining whether something constitutes a trade secret is the extent of the efforts to keep it secret. Companies protect trade secrets through physical measures and written agreements.

LEARNING OBJECTIVE

9. Describe some of the physical measures that firms take to protect their trade secrets.

Physical Measures   There are a number of physical measures firms use to protect trade secrets, from security fences around buildings, to providing employees access to file cabinets that lock, to much more elaborate measures. The level of protection depends on the nature of the trade secret. For example, although a retail store may consider its inventory control procedures to be a trade secret, it may not consider this information vital and may take appropriate yet not extreme measures to protect the information. In contrast, a biotech firm may be on the cusp of discovering a cure for a disease and may take extreme measures to protect the confidentiality of the work being conducted in its laboratories.

The following are examples of commonly used physical measures for protecting trade secrets:

■ **Restricting access:** Many companies restrict physical access to confidential material to only the employees who have a "need to know." For example, access to a company's customer list may be restricted to key personnel in the marketing department.

■ **Labeling documents:** Sensitive documents should be stamped or labeled "confidential," "proprietary," "restricted," or "secret." If possible, these documents should be secured when not in use. Such labeling should be restricted to particularly sensitive documents. If everything is labeled "confidential," there is a risk that employees will soon lose their ability to distinguish between slightly and highly confidential material.

■ **Password protecting confidential computer files:** Providing employees with clearance to view confidential information by using secure passwords can restrict information on a company's computer network, Web site, or intranet. Companies can also write-protect documents to ensure that employees can read but not modify certain documents.

■ **Maintaining logbooks for visitors:** Visitors can be denied access to confidential information by asking them to sign in when they arrive at a company facility, wear name badges that identify them as visitors, and always be accompanied by a company employee.

■ **Maintain logbooks for access to sensitive material:** Many companies maintain logbooks for sensitive material and make their employees "check out" and "check in" the material.

■ **Maintaining adequate overall security measures:** Commonsense measures are also helpful. Shredders should be provided to destroy documents as appropriate. Employees who have access to confidential material should have desks and cabinets that can be locked and secured. Alarms, security systems, and security personnel should be used to protect a firm's premises.

Some of these measures may seem extreme. However, unfortunately we live in an imperfect world and because of this, companies need to safeguard their information against both inadvertent disclosure and outright theft. Steps such as shredding documents may seem like overkill at first glance but may be very important in ultimately protecting trade secrets. Believe it or not, there have been a number of cases in which companies have caught competitors literally going through the trash bins behind their buildings looking for confidential information.

Written Agreements It is important for a company's employees to know that it is their duty to keep trade secrets and other forms of confidential information secret. For the best protection, a firm should ask its employees to sign nondisclosure and noncompete agreements, as discussed in Chapter 7.

Intellectual property, and the problems that underlie the need for intellectual property to be created, are important enough that firms have been started strictly for the purpose of helping companies solve problems and obtain the intellectual property that they need.

CONDUCTING AN INTELLECTUAL PROPERTY AUDIT

The first step a firm should take to protect its intellectual property is to complete an intellectual property audit. This is recommended for all firms, regardless of size, from start-ups to mature companies. An **intellectual property audit** is conducted to determine the intellectual property a company owns.

The following sections describe the reasons for conducting an intellectual property audit and the basic steps in the audit process. Some firms hire attorneys to conduct the audit, whereas others conduct the audit on their own. Once an audit is completed, a company can determine the appropriate measures it needs to take to protect the intellectual property that it owns and that is worth the effort and expense of protecting.

Why Conduct an Intellectual Property Audit?

LEARNING OBJECTIVE
10. Explain the two primary reasons for conducting an intellectual property audit.

There are two primary reasons for conducting an intellectual property audit. First, it is prudent for a company to periodically determine whether its intellectual property is being properly protected. As illustrated in Table 12.6, intellectual

TABLE 12.6   TYPES OF QUESTIONS TO ASK WHEN CONDUCTING AN INTELLECTUAL PROPERTY AUDIT

Patents	Copyrights
■ Are products under development that require patent protection? ■ Are current patent maintenance fees up to date? ■ Do we have any business methods that should be patented? ■ Do we own any patents that are no longer consistent with our business plan that could be sold or licensed? ■ Do our scientists properly document key discovery dates?	■ Is there a policy in place regarding what material needs the copyright bug and when the bug is to be put in place? ■ Is there a policy in place regarding when copyrightable material should be registered? ■ Is proper documentation in place to protect the company's rights to use the material it creates or pays to have created? ■ Are we in compliance with the copyright license agreements into which we have entered?

Trademarks	Trade Secrets
■ Are we using any names or slogans that require trademark protection? ■ Do we intend to expand the use of trademarks in other countries? ■ Do we need additional trademarks to cover new products and services? ■ Is anyone infringing on our trademarks?	■ Are internal security arrangements adequate to protect the firm's intellectual property? ■ Are employees who do not have a "need to know" routinely provided access to important trade secrets? ■ Is there a policy in place to govern the use of nondisclosure and noncompete agreements? ■ Are company trade secrets leaking out to competitors?

property resides in every department in a firm, and it is common for firms to simply overlook intellectual property that is eligible for protection.

The second reason for a company to conduct an intellectual property audit is to remain prepared to justify its value in the event of a merger or acquisition. Larger companies purchase many small, entrepreneurial firms primarily because the larger company wants the small firm's intellectual property. When a larger company approaches, the smaller firm should be ready and able to justify its valuation.

The Process of Conducting an Intellectual Property Audit

The first step in conducting an intellectual property audit is to develop an inventory of a firm's existing intellectual property. The inventory should include the firm's present registrations of patents, trademarks, and copyrights. Also included should be any agreements or licenses allowing the company to use someone else's intellectual property rights or allowing someone else to use the focal company's intellectual property.

The second step is to identify works in progress to ensure that they are being documented in a systematic, orderly manner. This is particularly important in research and development. As mentioned earlier, if two inventors independently develop essentially the same invention, the right to apply for the patent belongs to the person who invented the product first. Properly dated and witnessed invention logbooks and other documents help prove the date an invention was made.

The third step of the audit is to specify the firm's key trade secrets and describe how they are being protected. Putting this information in writing helps minimize the chance that if a trade secret is lost, someone can claim that it wasn't really a trade secret because the owner took no specific steps to protect it.

CHAPTER SUMMARY

1. Intellectual property is any product of human intellect that is intangible but has value in the marketplace. It is called intellectual property because it is the product of human imagination, creativity, and inventiveness.

2. Patents, trademarks, copyrights, and trade secrets are the major forms of intellectual property. A common mistake companies make is not thinking broadly enough when identifying their intellectual property assets. Almost all companies, regardless of size or age, have intellectual property worth protecting. But to protect this property, firms must first identify it.

3. There are two rules of thumb for determining whether intellectual property is worth the time and expense of protecting. First, a firm should determine whether the intellectual property in question is directly related to its current competitive advantage or could facilitate developing of future competitive advantages. Second, it's important to know whether the intellectual property has independent value in the marketplace.

4. Obtaining a patent is a painstaking, six-step process that usually requires the help of a patent attorney. A patent can be sold or licensed, which is a common strategy for entrepreneurial firms.

5. Trademarks, service marks, collective marks, and certification marks are the four types of trademarks. Trademark law is far-reaching, helping businesses be creative in drawing attention to their products and services. Examples of marks that can be protected include words, numbers and letters, designs and logos, sounds, fragrances, shapes, and colors. Immoral or scandalous matter, deceptive matter, descriptive marks, and surnames are ineligible for trademark protection.

6. Copyright law protects original works of authorship that are fixed in a tangible form of expression. This is a broad definition and means that almost anything a company produces that can be written down, recorded, or videotaped or that takes a tangible form itself (such as a sculpture) is eligible for copyright protection. Examples of copyrightable material include literary works, musical compositions, dramatic works, and pictorial, graphic, and sculptural works.

7. Unlike patents, trademarks, and copyrights, there is not a single government agency that regulates trade secret laws. Instead, trade secrets are governed by a patchwork of various state laws. The federal Economic Espionage Act does criminalize the theft of trade secrets.

8. Trade secret disputes arise most frequently when an employee leaves a firm to join a competitor and is accused of taking confidential information along. Firms protect their trade secrets through both physical measures and written agreements.

9. Firms use a number of physical measures to protect their trade secrets. These include restricting access, labeling documents, password protecting computer files, maintaining logbooks for visitors, and maintaining adequate overall security measures.

10. There are two primary reasons for conducting an intellectual property audit. First, it is prudent for a company to periodically assess the intellectual property it owns to determine whether it is being properly protected. Second, a firm should conduct a periodic intellectual property audit to remain prepared to justify its value in the event of a merger or acquisition.

KEY TERMS

assignment of invention agreement, **429**
business method patent, **427**
certification marks, **435**
collective marks, **434**
Computer Software Copyright Act, **439**
copyright, **438**
copyright bug, **440**
copyright infringement, **441**
derivative works, **439**
design patents, **428**
Economic Espionage Act, **443**
fair use, **441**
first-to-invent rule, **430**
idea–expression dichotomy, **440**
intellectual property, **421**
intellectual property audit, **445**
intent-to-use trademark application, **438**
interference, **430**
invention logbook, **430**
Lanham Act, **435**
one year after first use deadline, **427**
patent, **425**
patent infringement, **433**

REVIEW QUESTIONS

1. What distinguishes intellectual property from other types of property, such as land, buildings, and inventory? Provide several examples of intellectual property and describe their importance to a firm.

2. What are the two primary rules for determining whether intellectual property protection should be pursued for a particular intellectual asset?

3. Search the USPTO database and find three patents issued to Donald E. Weder of Highland Park, Illinois. Describe the patents. In what areas are most of Mr. Weder's patents?

4. What are the major differences between utility patents and design patents? Provide an example of each.

5. What is a business method patent? Provide an example of a business method patent and explain how having such a patent can provide a firm a competitive advantage in the marketplace.

6. Give an example of a design patent. Explain how having a design patent can provide a firm a competitive advantage in the marketplace.

7. Describe the purpose of an assignment of invention agreement. Is it a good idea for firms to ask their employees to sign assignment of invention agreements?

8. What are the six steps in applying for a patent? Make your answer as thorough as possible.

9. What is a trademark? Provide several examples of trademarks, and describe how they help a firm establish a competitive advantage in the marketplace.

10. What are the three steps involved in selecting and registering a trademark?

11. What is meant by the term *trade dress*?

12. What is a copyright?

13. In the context of copyright law, what is meant by the term *derivative work*? Provide an example of when this concept is important for the creators of copyrightable material.

14. If an entrepreneur has an idea for a themed restaurant based on television game shows, is the idea itself eligible for copyright protection? Why or why not?

15. What is a copyright bug? Where would one expect to find the bug, and how is it used?

16. What is meant by the phrase *copyright infringement*? Would you characterize copyright infringement as a minor or as a major problem in the United States and in other countries? Explain.

17. What is a trade secret? Provide an example of a trade secret, and describe how it helps a firm establish a competitive advantage in the marketplace.

18. What information does not qualify for trade secret protection? Make your answer as thorough as possible.

19. What types of physical measures do firms take to protect their trade secrets?

20. What are the two primary purposes of conducting an intellectual property audit? What risks does a company run if it doesn't periodically conduct an intellectual property audit?

APPLICATION QUESTIONS

1. Imagine you're about to attend a one-day seminar dealing with intellectual property law, and you contact a friend of yours who is in the process of starting a business to urge her to attend the seminar with you. She says to you, "I'm really busy because I'm just about to launch my start-up, so I'll have to pass. If they offer the same seminar next year, I'll go with you then." How would you respond to your friend?

2. Spend some time studying Wakoopa, the subject of the "You Be the VC 12.2" feature. Make a list of the forms of intellectual property protection that Wakoopa should have to properly protect itself. Be as specific as possible in compiling your list.

3. Access the UPSTO Web site and look up U.S. Patent Number 5,443,036. Describe the purpose of the patent. Do you think

this patent describes an invention that has commercial potential? On a scale of 1 to 10 (10 is high), how large do you think the potential is?

4. Tyler Simms just invented a new product that he is convinced is unique and will make him wealthy. The product is a toothbrush with a tube of toothpaste attached to the handle. Tyler is anxious to file a patent application on the product, but when he tells you about the idea, you say—"Whoa, let's do a preliminary patent application search first to see if someone else has already patented this idea." What do you find when you help Tyler with the preliminary search?

5. Reacquaint yourself with Plumgarth's the subject of Case 5.2. Do you think Plumgarth's unique method of connecting the growers of local food products with the buyers of local food products is suitable for a business method patent? If so, if you were the founder of Plumgarths would you spend the money to try to obtain a business method patent? Why or why not?

6. According to the chapter a trademark registered with the USPTO can theoretically remain registered forever as long as it stays in use. Does the owner of a trademark have to take affirmative action to demonstrate to the USPTO office that a trademark is remaining in use? If so, describe the process.

7. Pam Tarver just opened an information technology consulting company and has thought for a long time about what to name it. She finally settled on the fictitious name Infoxx. Search the USPTO database to determine if the name Infoxx is available. Is it? If it is available, describe how Pam would go about obtaining a trademark on Infoxx or any other name.

8. Rick Sanford lives in a small community in northern Minnesota. He is planning to open the only fried chicken restaurant in his area and would like to trademark the words *fried chicken*. Because of his special circumstances, can he do this?

9. Ken and Jackie Smith just purchased a small winery in the Napa Valley of northern California. One thing they noticed when they were investigating the winery is that the owners never placed the "100% Napa Valley" certification mark on their bottles. Now that they own the winery Ken and Jackie are looking into using the mark. Investigate what is required to place the "100% Napa Valley"

certification mark on a bottle of wine. If Ken and Jackie's winery qualifies, should they use the mark?

10. Maggie Simpson has always admired her Grandmother Thompson's cooking and has considered putting together a cookbook titled *Grandma Thompson's Favorite Recipes*. Some of Grandma's recipes are truly original, and before she writes the book, Maggie would like to copyright several of the most original ones. Can she do this?

11. Spend some time looking at the Web site of Inventors Digest (www.inventorsdigest. com), a magazine dedicated to inventors' issues. Look through the past issues archive. Select an article that deals with an intellectual property topic not fully fleshed out in this chapter. Write a short summary of the article and briefly comment on the usefulness of the information.

12. Spend some time studying Kim Levine, the homemaker who created Wuvit, a pillow filled with 100 percent natural grain. Describe how the Wuvit was created and the steps that Levine took to bring it to market. Speculate on the intellectual property issues surrounding this product.

13. Suppose you were asked by the founders of Nila LED, the subject of the "You Be the VC 8.1" feature, to advise them on protecting their trade secrets. Assume the company operates out of a single facility where it manufactures its current products and is in the process of developing new products. Make a list of recommendations for the company.

14. Two years ago, Mike Carini opened a restaurant called Mike's Italian. To his horror, Mike just found out that several disgruntled customers have launched a Web site with the Internet address www.avoidmikesitalian.com. The site contains testimonials by people who have eaten at Mike's and have not been satisfied. Is there anything that Mike can do to shut down the Web site?

15. Refer to Case 9.1, which focused on Dry Soda, the maker of nonalcoholic soda that's paired with fine food. If you were hired to conduct an intellectual property audit for Dry Soda, list 10 specific things you would check (or audit) to make sure that Dry Soda is doing exactly what it should be doing regarding the intellectual property that it owns.

YOU BE THE VC 12.1

Company: Bolt-A-Blok Systems

Web: www.bolt-a-blok.com
Facebook: Bolt A Blok

Business Idea: Alter traditional methods of concrete block construction to enable the assembly of the blocks to be completed in a manner that requires no water, has immediate occupancy (no cure time), is faster than current procedures, and in the end is stronger and more resistant to weather-related disasters such as hurricanes and earthquakes.

Pitch: Globally there is a desperate and immediate need for temporary and permanent housing that can be built quickly onsite. Instances like the January 2010 earthquake in Haiti, which left over 1.5 million people homeless, the 2011 tsunami in Japan, and the tornados that struck Tuscaloosa, Alabama, in April 2011 and Joplin, Missouri, in May 2011 illustrate the need for rapid and sound construction techniques that can be used to provide for immediate shelter. Concrete block construction is a seemingly ideal solution because it's relatively inexpensive, provides good fire protection, insulates against heat and cold, and is strong. Regrettably, conventional construction techniques make concrete blocks impractical for quick construction and occupancy. A concrete block building must be built by an experienced mason, requires water to make fresh concrete mortar to cement the blocks together (to form the desired length and height of a wall), and takes several days to cure before activities to construct a facility can proceed.

Bolt-A-Block provides a solution to these problems. Its patent-pending system uses anti-corrosive steel fasteners and bars to bind concrete blocks together rather than using concrete mortar. The fasteners and bars provide post tensioning that increases the overall capacity and acts as steel to reinforce the wall. As a result, the Bolt-A-Blok system is faster and easier than traditional concrete block construction methods, requires no water, requires no cure time, and results in a structurally stronger building. These attributes make the Bolt-A-Blok system ideal for use in multiple settings, certainly including disaster recovery situations as well as for routine residential and commercial construction.

The Bolt-A-Blok system has undergone extensive efficacy testing. As of March 2009, 80 independent tests had been completed affirming the system's strengths and capabilities. Engineering and design analyses reveal that structures built via Bolt-A-Blok meet or exceed Dade County, Florida (Miami) hurricane specifications and California seismic specifications. Bolt-A-Blok has five U.S. and 43 foreign patents pending and two registered trademarks. Bolt-A-Blok was the 2010 *Wall Street Journal* Technology Innovation Award Winner Runner Up.

Video demonstrations of how the Bolt-A-Blok building is constructed are available on the company's Web site and Vimeo.com.

Q&A: Based on the material covered in this chapter, what questions would you ask the firm's founders before making your funding decision? What answers would satisfy you?

Decision: If you had to make your decision on just the information provided in the pitch and on the company's Web site, would you fund this company? Why or why not?

YOU BE THE VC 12.2

Company: Wakoopa

Web: www.wakoopa.com
Twitter: Wakoopa
Facebook: Wakoopa

Business Idea: To establish a social network for software users to make it easier to track, share, and find software.

Pitch: Buying computer software online or from a store is often a tricky task, and keeping up to date with the latest releases can be confusing. There are thousands of new software programs every year and dozens of different operating systems. It can be difficult to get a completely impartial view. Although there are many online Web sites and magazines offering software reviews, there is no way of knowing how long the reviewer has used the program and what kind of program he or she usually likes.

Wakoopa was founded by two Dutch bloggers, Robert Gaal and Wouter Broekhof, to solve these problems and create a social network for software users.

Wakoopa's sign-up process is very simple: Users provide a user name and password and then are given a page with the download links for the Wakoopa tracking software. They then install a small application on their PC or Mac that works by performing a check every 15 minutes to track what software they use for a range of applications such as music players, office software, and photo editing, and how long they use it for. The information gathered can then be shared with friends, and personal profiles are automatically updated with any news, updates, or reviews on each specific application. It helps people decide whether or not to spend money on a program, because they can check out the statistics beforehand and see if the program is a one-hit wonder, or if it has proved its value to many users in the long term.

The Wakoopa site features a list of the current programs running with user reviews and a list of new versions of software. There is also a "software I might like" section, which provides recommendations based on current software usage.

In the first six months following its launch in April 2007, 17,000 people downloaded the Wakoopa tracking program. In the following year, that sum doubled again, helping to generate some 250 million hours of unique and useful data about software, including lists of the most popular and most used software applications on a year-by-year basis. Early adopters of the site are primarily tech-savvy software developers and gamers, although there is evidence that the service is being used more widely by consumers who are happy to see their own desktop behavior become public. The payback is a lively social network for software and the opportunity to test the pulse of what are the most popular and unpopular new Web applications.

Gaal and Broekhof have ambitious plans for Wakoopa and want the site to become the place for software information and will achieve this by adding in more features and supporting more operating systems.

Q&A: Based on the material covered in this chapter, what questions would you ask the firm's founders before making your funding decision? What answers would satisfy you?

Decision: If you had to make your decision on just the information provided in the pitch and on the company's Web site, would you fund this firm? Why or why not?

CASE 12.1

You Make the Call: Can a Company Patent How It Makes a Peanut Butter and Jelly Sandwich?

www.smuckers.com
www.albies.com

Bruce R. Barringer, *Oklahoma State University*
R. Duane Ireland, *Texas A&M University*

Introduction

Here's a question that a panel of judges recently decided: Can a company patent how it makes a peanut butter and jelly sandwich? More specifically, in this instance, judges considered whether J. M. Smucker's method of making Uncrustables—which is a crustless peanut butter and jelly sandwich sealed inside soft bread—is worthy of legal protection against imitators. While the nature of this case is interesting, the legal rulings resulting from the case have broader implications. At stake is how generous the patent office should be in awarding patents—an issue with solid arguments on both sides.

There were actually two cases leading up to the case that resulted in the final verdict. The three cases are designated Round 1, Round 2, and Round 3 of Smucker's battle to patent the peanut butter and jelly sandwich.

The case involves Smucker's Uncrustables sandwich. Uncrustables are found in the frozen food section of most grocery stores. They are 2-ounce peanut butter and jelly pockets that come in two flavors—grape and strawberry—and are sealed inside soft bread. They come in boxes of 4, 10, or 18 sandwiches per box. To make an Uncrustables ready to eat, the customer simply needs to let it thaw for 30–60 minutes after being taken out of the freezer.

The Uncrustables was developed in 1995 by David Geske, of Fargo, North Dakota, and Len Kretchman, of Fergus Falls, Minnesota. The two started

(continued)

mass-producing them for Midwestern schools. Smucker's took note of their success and bought Geske and Kretchman's company in 1999. The purchase of the company included a general patent on crustless peanut butter and jelly sandwiches (Patent No. 6,004,596) that Geske and Kretchman had obtained.

Round 1: Smucker's Versus Albie's Foods

It wasn't long before Smucker's was defending its turf. In 2001, Smucker's ordered a much smaller firm, Albie's Foods, to stop selling its own crustless peanut butter and jelly sandwich. Albie's was selling the sandwich to a local school district. Albie's fought back, and the case was eventually dismissed. In its arguments, Albie's contended that the "pasty"—a meat pie with crimped edges, which the company saw its crustless peanut butter and jelly sandwich as a variation of—had been a popular food in northern Michigan since the immigration of copper and iron miners from England in the 1800s.

Round 2: Smucker's and the Patent Office

Stung by its experience with the case it brought against Albie's, Smucker's returned to the USPTO to try to get its general patent on crustless peanut butter and jelly sandwiches broadened as a means of being able to better defend the Uncrustables. The patent office rejected the application. The gist of Smucker's argument was that its sandwich's sealed edge is unique and its layering approach, which keeps the jelly in the middle of the sandwich, is one-of-a-kind, and as such, should be protected by law. The patent office disagreed with this view. It said that the crimped edge, which was one of the things Smucker's argued was unique about its sandwich, is similar to the crimped edges in ravioli and pie crusts. In addition, the patent office determined that putting jelly in the middle of a peanut butter and jelly sandwich is hardly unique, and as evidence cited a 1994 *Wichita* (Kansas) *Eagle* newspaper article on back-to-school tips that suggested just this approach.

Round 3: Smucker's Appeals

Smucker's appealed the patent office's decision to the U.S. Court of Appeals. During the court hearings the attorney representing Smucker's argued that the method for making the Uncrustables is unique because the two slices of bread are sealed by compression but are not "smashed" as they are in tarts or ravioli. (Recall, the patent office's original decision compared the process of making Uncrustables to that of making ravioli.) Smucker's further argued that it wouldn't be fair to let other companies simply copy the Uncrustables and benefit from the hard work of Smucker's scientists and the money that the company had invested to produce what it believed was a unique product. The Uncrustables is also a big seller for Smucker's. According to a *Wall Street Journal* article, the product generated sales of $27.5 million in 2004.

Broader Issues Involved

The Smucker's case was watched closely because of the broader issues involved. Critics of the U.S. patent process contend that the USPTO is too generous when awarding patents—a generosity that they say stifles innovation and drives up the cost for consumers. Close to 500,000 patents are filed each year, and nearly 65 percent of them are granted. In the Smucker's case, the critics would argue that Smucker's shouldn't get the patent, because it will deter other food companies from making their own versions of peanut butter and jelly sandwiches, which will keep the price of the Uncrustables high. Advocates of the U.S. patent process argue the opposite—that patents motivate a company like Smucker's to invest in new-product innovation, and that absent patent protection, a company like Smucker's would have no incentive to develop a product like the Uncrustables.

The Court's Ruling

In mid-April 2005, after listening to all the arguments, the U.S. Court of Appeals ruled on whether Smucker's should get the patent it was requesting. Which way do you think the court ruled?

Discussion Questions

1. Go to the USPTO's Web site (www.uspto.gov) to look up Patent No. 6,004,596. Read the patent. After reading the patent, are you more inclined or less inclined to side with the Smucker's point of view?
2. Type "Uncrustables" into the Google search engine and look at the Uncrustables sandwich. Spend a little time reading about the Uncrustables on Smucker's Web site. Again, after looking over the Web site, are you more inclined or less inclined to side with the Smucker's point of view?
3. In regard to the arguments espoused by the "critics" of the U.S. patent system and the "advocates" of the U.S. patent system, which of the points of view do you agree with? Thinking as an entrepreneur, use your own words to state why you think the critics or the advocates have a stronger point of view.
4. So what do you think happened? Do you think Smucker's did or didn't get the patent it was requesting?

Application Questions

1. What would be the impact, if any, on the entrepreneurial sector of the U.S. economy if patents became increasingly hard to get? Would it help or hurt the majority of entrepreneurial companies? Why?
2. Based on the material in the chapter, are there facets of the U.S. patent system and, in particular, the operations of the USPTO that you think need to be improved or changed? What are these facets? Using the perspective of an entrepreneur, what changes do you believe should be made?

Source: *Wall Street Journal* (Eastern Edition) by S. Munzo. Copyright 2005 by Dow Jones & Company, Inc.

CASE 12.2

Protecting Intellectual Property: Elvis's Memory and Intellectual Property Live On

Web: www.elvis.com
Facebook: Elvis Presley
Twitter: ElvisPresley

Bruce R. Barringer, *Oklahoma State University*
R. Duane Ireland, *Texas A&M University*

Introduction

Savvy owners of intellectual property are always on the lookout for people who infringe on their intellectual property and take legal action when necessary. From 2002 to 2005, this scenario played out in a dispute involving a company named Passport Video and the copyright holders of music and videos produced by the late Elvis Presley.

Alleged Copyright Violation

Elvis, affectionately known as "The King" of rock and roll, was a musical icon for more than 20 years until his death on August 16, 1977. During his career Elvis was very prolific, and a wide variety of people own the copyrights to his music, videos, and films. In 2002, Passport Video, a video production company, produced a video documentary of Elvis's life titled *The Definitive Elvis*. The documentary, which included eight DVDs and 16 hours of video, focused on every aspect of Elvis's life and was priced at $99.00. Each episode contained shots of Elvis performing—many of which were taken from sources that are copyrighted and owned by Elvis Presley Enterprises or others. The shots included Presley home movies (owned by Elvis Presley Enterprises), material from *The Ed Sullivan Show*, and portions of *Ed Sullivan Rock & Roll Classics—Elvis Presley* (owned by SOFA Entertainment). Other material included shots from *The Elvis 1968 Comeback Special*, *Aloha from Hawaii*, and *Elvis in Concert*, which included songs written by Jerry Leiber and Mike Stoller. Passport did not get permission to use the material. As a result, the copyright holders, who caught wind of the production of the video, informed Passport Video that they objected to the production of the videos. Passport Video persisted, and in August 2003 the copyright holders sued Passport Video for unauthorized use of footage and copyright violations. They also asked for a preliminary injunction stopping Passport Video from selling any more copies of the documentary, which a U.S. District Court granted.

Passport's Defense

Passport mounted a defense, claiming that its use of the copyrighted material was fair use and that it had spent over $2 million producing and marketing the documentary. Fair use is a doctrine in U.S. copyright law that allows limited use of copyrighted material without requiring permission from the copyright holder. In general, the following uses are protected under this doctrine:

- Quotation of the copyrighted work for review or criticism or in a scholarly or technical work
- Use in a parody or satire
- Brief quotation in a news report
- Reproduction by a teacher or a student of a small part of the work to illustrate a lesson
- Incidental reproduction of a work in a newsreel or broadcast of an event being reported
- Reproduction of a work in a legislative or judicial proceeding

Passport Video also asserted that it interviewed more than 200 people to make the documentary and that only 5 to 10 percent of the length of the videos contained copyright material.

The Initial Decision, the Appeal, and the Final Decision

After listening to both sides, the U.S. District Court ruled in favor of the plaintiffs, saying that fair use didn't apply and Passport Video should have obtained the appropriate copyright permissions. The court stated that Passport Video released the videos with full knowledge that the plaintiffs did not consent to their production, and that Passport Video's documentary would mislead consumers (regarding its legal production) and damage the plaintiffs.

Passport persisted, appealing the decision to the Ninth Circuit Court of Appeals, arguing that its documentary of Elvis's life constituted scholarly research and should therefore be protected under fair use. In a 2005 ruling, the Ninth Circuit Court of Appeals disagreed and affirmed the ruling of the lower court. In its ruling, the court said, "The King is dead. His legacy,

(continued)

and those that wish to profit from it, remain very much alive." The court found that Passport's documentary was for commercial use rather than scholarly research, although the commercial nature of the project was not the deciding factor. Instead, the extent to which the copyrighted material was used tipped the decision for the court, which referred to the lower court's original assessment in its ruling. In its decision, the Ninth Circuit Court of Appeals, quoting from the decision of the lower court, said:

> Passport's use of clips from television appearances, although in most cases of short duration, were repeated numerous times throughout the tapes. While using a small number of clips to reference an event for biographical purposes seems fair, using a clip over and over will likely no longer serve a biographical purpose. Additionally, some of the clips were not short in length. Passport's use of Elvis' appearance on The Steve Allen Show plays for over a minute and many more clips play for more than just a few seconds.

The ruling barred Passport from selling any additional copies of *The Definitive Elvis*. It also outlined the limits of the fair use defense.

Subsequent to the ruling, the United States District Court in Los Angeles awarded plaintiffs Elvis Presley Enterprises, SOFA Entertainment, and songwriters Leiber and Stoller $2.8 million in monetary damages and attorneys' fees to be paid by Passport Entertainment and its owner, Dante Pugliese. Leiber and Stroller wrote "Hound Dog" and other Elvis hits. The ruling was considered to be a significant monetary judgment for a copyright infringement case.

Takeaways

In this case, the copyright law did exactly what it is designed to do: protect the legal owners of Elvis's material from copyright infringement. It also put publishers on notice that claiming fair use has limits and is not a blanket escape from paying copyright holders appropriate licensing fees. The ruling suggested that arguing fair use is more likely to hold water when used in conjunction with scholarly work or historical analysis than commercial projects.

Discussion Questions

1. Do you agree with the Ninth Circuit Court ruling? Why or why not?
2. Why do you think the copyright holders of Elvis's work objected to Passport's video series? How were they "harmed" by the production and sale of the videos?
3. Do you think Passport Video acted ethically and honestly and believed that its production was protected by fair use, or do you think the firm was simply using fair use as a way of avoiding paying royalties for the copyrighted material it was using?
4. What can entrepreneurs who are interested in trademark law learn from this case?

Application Questions

1. Do some Internet research and find another case of copyright infringement. Write a brief summary of the case. Indicate whether the case has been decided, and whether you sympathize with the defendants or the plaintiffs in the case. If the case has been decided, indicated whether you agree with the ruling.
2. The "You Be the VC 12.1" feature in this chapter focuses on Bolt-A-Blok, a company that has developed a new approach to concrete block production that requires no water, has immediate occupancy (no cure time), is faster than current procedures, and is stronger and more resistant to weather-related disasters such as hurricanes and earthquakes. Write a short intellectual property plan for Bolt-A-Blok. Include in the plan all facts of Bolt-A-Blok that should be protected, and the form of intellectual property protection that should be used in each instance.

Sources: H. R. Cheeseman, *The Legal Environment of Business and Online Commerce*, 5th ed. (Upper Saddle River, NJ: Prentice Hall, 2007); Ruling by the United States District Court for the Central District of California in the case of *Elvis Presley Enterprises v. Passport Video*, November 6, 2004.

ENDNOTES

1. Personal Conversation with Milun Tesovic, March 19, 2011.
2. H. R. Cheesman, *The Legal Environment of Business and Online Commerce*, 6th ed. (Upper Saddle River, NJ: Prentice Hall, 2010).
3. A. I. Poltorak and P. J. Lerner, *Essentials of Intellectual Property: Law, Economics, and Strategy* (New York: Wiley & Sons, 2011).
4. N. Kamukama, A. Ahiauzu, and J. M. Ntayi, "Competitive Advantage: Mediator of Intellectual Capital and Performance," *Journal of Intellectual Capital* 12, no. 1 (2011): 152–64; G. Martin-de-Castro, M. Delgado-Verge, P. Lopez-Saez, and J. E. Navas-Lopez, "Towards An Intellectual Capital-Based View of the Firm: Origins and Nature," *Journal of Business Ethics* 98, no. 4 (2010): 649–62.
5. A. Murray, "Protecting Ideas Is Crucial for U.S. Businesses," *Wall Street Journal*, November 9, 2005, A2.
6. U.S. Patent and Trademark Office, "What Are Patents, Trademarks, Servicemarks, and

Copyrights?" www.uspto.gov (accessed April 1, 2011); J. Pila, *The Requirement for an Invention in Patent Law* (Oxford: Oxford University Press, 2010).

7. D. J. Bjornstad, R. Santore, and M. McKee, "Selling Complementary Patents: Experimental Investigation," *Journal of Law and Economics* 53, no. 1 (2010): 167–83.

8. T. Rayna and L. Striukova, "Large-Scale Open Innovation: Open Source vs. Patent Pools," *International Journal of Technology Management* 52, no. 3-4 (2010): 477–96.

9. G. Wolff, *The Biotech Investor's Bible* (New York: John Wiley & Sons, 2001).

10. S. Kilman, "Biotech Firms Seek Speedier Review of Seeds," *Wall Street Journal*, April 28, 2010, A8.

11. United States Patent and Trademark Office, *Performance and Accountability Report for Fiscal Year 2010.*

12. U.S. Patent and Trademark Office, www.uspto.gov (accessed April 10, 2011).

13. D. Bouchoux, *Intellectual Property: The Law of Trademarks, Copyrights, Patents, and Trade Secrets for the Paralegal*, 3rd ed. (Cincinnati: Cengage Learning, 2009).

14. United States Patent and Trademark Office, *Performance and Accountability Report for Fiscal Year 2010.*

15. Bouchoux, *Intellectual Property.*

16. P. Thurrott, "Start-Up Cleans Microsoft's Chimney in Court," *WindowsITPro*, April 14, 2005.

17. A. Gilbert, "Microsoft Settles Infringement Suit," *ZDNet*, July 14, 2005.

18. "Protection Money," *Fortune Small Business*, October 2005.

19. D. Orozco and J. Conley, "Shape of Things to Come," *Wall Street Journal*, May 12, 2008, R6.

20. D. Diskin, "Apple's Samsung Lawsuit: The Trademark Issues." *Copyright and Trademark Blog*, http://copymarkblog.com/2011/04/22/apples-samsung-lawsuit-the-trademark-issues (accessed April 28, 2011, posted on April 22, 2011).

21. G. Gelb and B. Gelb, "When Appearances Are Deceiving," *Wall Street Journal*, December 1, 2007, B1.

22. InvestorWords.com, "Definition of Copyright," www.investorwords.com (accessed March 23, 2011); C. E. Bagley and C. E. Dauchy, *The Entrepreneur's Guide to Business Law*, 4th ed. (Cincinnati: Cengage Learning, 2012).

23. L. G. Bryer, S. J. Lebson, and M. D. Asbell, *Intellectual Property Strategies for the 21st Century Corporation: A Shift in Strategic and Financial Management* (New York: Wiley & Sons, 2011).

Getting Personal *with* PURBLU BEVERAGES, INC.

Founder:

BEN LEWIS
BS, Business Administration,
Wharton School of Business,
expected fall 2011

Dialogue *with*
Ben Lewis

BEST ADVICE I'VE RECEIVED
Be generous

**MY FAVORITE
SMARTPHONE APP**
OpenTable or E*trade

**MY BIGGEST SURPRISE
AS AN ENTREPRENEUR**
The time commitment

**BEST PART OF BEING
A STUDENT**
The opportunity to experiment with
new ideas with no consequence

**FIRST ENTREPRENEURIAL
EXPERIENCE**
Lemonade stand

**MY BIGGEST WORRY
AS AN ENTREPRENEUR**
Running out of money

CHAPTER 13

Preparing for and *Evaluating* the Challenges of Growth

OPENING PROFILE

PURBLU BEVERAGES, INC.
Growing in a Cautious, Yet Deliberate Manner

Web: www.drinkgive.com
Twitter: drinkgive
Facebook: drink give. do good.

Ben Lewis wasn't like most high school students. While still a student at Shady Side Academy in Pittsburgh, he and three classmates conceived a business. Their business was GIVE, a bottled water company, with not one but two unusual twists. First, 10 cents of every bottle sold would be donated to charity. And second, the bottles would come in four colors, allowing the buyer to choose which charity his or her donation would go to. Blue bottles would direct money toward children in need, pink bottles toward breast cancer research, orange bottles toward muscular disorders, and green bottles toward environmental causes.

GIVE was formally launched in the summer of 2007, following Lewis's high school graduation. The three classmates went their separate ways, leaving Lewis in charge of GIVE and its future. Early on, Lewis borrowed warehouse space at a friend's dad's office and started selling from the trunk of his car. He had to drive four hours from Pittsburgh to find a bottler who would take a chance on him and agree to make small production runs. Lewis's early customers were delis and grocery stores in the Pittsburgh area who bought into his enthusiasm and vision. The novelty of his age, the philanthropic nature of his business, and the way GIVE water was bottled generated media attention and heightened Lewis's visibility. By the end of the summer. GIVE water was in a local Whole Foods Market, and the company was gaining momentum.

In the fall of 2007, Lewis entered the Wharton School of Business at the University of Pennsylvania, but didn't give up on GIVE. He juggled a full course load and his business. GIVE sold well at its initial Whole Foods Market location, and proved that it could outsell some national brands. By mid-2008, GIVE was in Whole Foods stores across the company's Mid-Atlantic region, and was moving into additional retail outlets. From the beginning, Lewis's conviction was to build GIVE into a brand rather than a bottled water company. While bottled water was a tough entry point, it

LEARNING OBJECTIVES

After studying this chapter you should be ready to:

1. Explain the term *sustained growth*.
2. Describe how firms can properly prepare for growth.
3. Discuss the six most common reasons firms pursue growth.
4. Explain the importance of knowing the stages of growth.
5. Describe the most important factors for firms to focus on during each stage of growth.
6. Describe the managerial capacity problem and how it inhibits firm growth.
7. Discuss the challenges for firm growth imposed by adverse selection and moral hazard.
8. Discuss the day-to-day challenges of growing a firm.
9. Explain why "cash flow management" is a challenge for growing a firm.
10. Explain how "quality control" can become a challenge for growing a firm.

forced Lewis to think carefully about how to differentiate GIVE from its competitors. Lewis's philosophy behind GIVE's philanthropy, which was the company's principle form of differentiation, was motivated by two factors. First, it was consistent with Lewis's personal beliefs and upbringing. And second, it was a way of building interest and passion around his brand. Lewis believed that when people bought GIVE water, their sense of giving transcended the 10 cents per bottle that their purchase would send to a charity. He believed that the act of giving would create a culture of passion and enthusiasm around his brand, which would motivate people to seek out his products and want to get more involved. Consistent with this philosophy, GIVE adopted the tagline "drink give. do good." The story Lewis wove around GIVE is that by performing an everyday act, like buying bottled water, a person helps make his or her community a better place to live. GIVE's model was to find local and regional charities to donate the 10 cents per bottle to rather than support national organizations. It also helped consumers feel good about its products by using biodegradable bottles and by bottling on both coasts to reduce the amount of energy it takes for GIVE water to travel from its point of origin to retail outlets.

GIVE was now operating under a corporate name PurBlu Beverages. In the summer of 2009, Lewis's company upped the ante by introducing GIVE Energy, an all-natural energy drink that supports grassroots sustainable energy initiatives such as wind, solar, and biofuel projects. GIVE Energy's presence quickly grew to several thousand stores across the United States and became one of the best-selling energy drinks in Whole Foods Market. In March 2010, the company introduced GIVE Energy Lite to complement its line of energy drinks with only 10 calories per serving using organic Agave and Stevia sweeteners. The company also launched Tonic Health Shot, an all-natural functional health shot made of natural ingredients to address a range of health needs including Detox, Focus, Energy, Calm, and Immunity.

In November 2010, PurBlu Beverages entered into a strategic partnership with Green Shoots Distribution, a national distributor for natural food and beverage brands. Green Shoots will assume the distribution function for PurBlu products, which will allow Lewis and his management team to focus on product development, branding, and the strategic direction of the firm. As for Lewis, he remains at the helm of PurBlu Beverages and hopes to finish his degree at The Wharton School of Business in fall 2011.

The PurBlu Beverages case is encouraging in that the company has gotten off to a good start and has achieved growth in a well-executed manner. Its true test will be whether it is able to achieve **sustained growth**, which is growth in both revenues and profits over a sustained period of time. Evidence shows that relatively few firms generate sustained and outstanding, profitable growth.[1] As evidence of this, consider the fact that since the first *Inc.* 500 list of the fastest growing companies was published in 1982, "18,630 unique companies have made the *Inc.* 500 or *Inc.* 5000. Just 119 businesses have made the list six or more times; 35 have made it seven or more times; and 14 have made it eight or nine times."[2] In addition, a study sponsored by the SBA Office of Advocacy found that only 3 percent of all firms are "gazelles" or rapid growth firms at any given time. Small firms also tend to follow the economy in terms of job growth (or loss) and growth prospects. Although small businesses with fewer than 500 employees create the most jobs in the United States, in a recessionary period they lose the most jobs too. In 2009, during the depths of the U.S. recession, small businesses accounted for 60 percent of the job losses.[3]

Although challenging, most entrepreneurial ventures try to grow and see it as an important part of their ability to remain successful.[4] This sentiment was expressed by Hewlett-Packard (HP) cofounder David Packard, who wrote that while HP was being built, he and cofounder Bill Hewlett had "speculated many times about the optimum size of a company." The pair "did not believe that growth was important for its own sake" but eventually concluded that "continuous growth was essential" for the company to remain competitive.[5] When HP published a formal list of its objectives in 1996, one of the seven objectives was growth.[6] For HP, acquiring Compaq Computer Corporation contributed to the firm's continuing commitment to growth. Although a controversial strategic decision, acquiring Compaq seems to have provided HP with the breadth and depth it needed to improve its ability to compete against strong computer competitors such as Dell Inc. In fact, HP now holds the largest percentage of the global market for personal computers.

The first part of the chapter focuses on preparing for growth, including a discussion of three specific areas that a firm can focus on to equip itself for growth. The second part of the chapter focuses on reasons for growth. Although sustained growth is almost always the result of deliberate intentions, a firm can't always choose its pace of growth. This section lists the seven primary reasons that motivate and stimulate business growth. The chapter's third section focuses on managing growth, which centers on knowing and managing the stages of growth. We examine the challenges of growth, including the managerial capacity problem and the day-to-day challenges of growing a firm, in the chapter's final section.

PREPARING FOR GROWTH

Most entrepreneurial firms want to grow. Especially in the short term, growth in sales revenue is an important indicator of an entrepreneurial venture's potential to survive today and be successful tomorrow. Growth is exciting, and for most businesses, is an indication of success. Many entrepreneurial firms have grown quickly, producing impressive results for their employees and owners as a result of doing so: consider Google, Zappos, and Zipcar, among others, as examples of this.

While there is some trial and error involved in starting and growing any business, the degree to which a firm prepares for its future growth has a direct bearing on its level of success.[7] This section focuses on three important things a business can do to prepare for growth.

> **LEARNING OBJECTIVE**
> **2.** Describe how firms can properly prepare for growth.

Appreciating the Nature of Business Growth

The first thing that a business can do to prepare for growth is to appreciate the nature of business growth. Growing a business successfully takes preparation, good management, and an appreciation of the issues involved. In many cases, it also takes a strong economy, as indicated in the 2009 job loss statistics provided previously. The following are issues about business growth that entrepreneurs should appreciate.

Not All Businesses Have the Potential to Be Aggressive Growth Firms   The businesses that have the potential to grow the fastest over a sustained period of time are ones that solve a significant problem or have a major impact on their customers' productivity or lives. This is why the lists of fast-growing firms are often dominated by health care, technology, social media, and entertainment companies. These companies can potentially have the most significant impact on their customers' businesses or lives. This point is affirmed by contrasting the men's clothing store industry with the biotechnology industry. From 2009 to 2010, the average men's clothing store in the United States grew by 1.3 percent while the average biotechnology company grew by 7.8 percent.[8] While there is nothing wrong with starting and owning a men's clothing store, it's important to have a realistic outlook of how fast the business will likely grow. Even though an individual men's clothing store might get off to a fast start, as its gets larger, its annual growth will normally start to reflect its industry norm.

A Business Can Grow Too Fast   Many businesses start fast and never let up, which stresses a business financially and can leave its owners emotionally drained. This sentiment is affirmed by Vipin Jain, the CEO of Retrevo, a consumer electronics company. Jain has started several companies. When asked what lessons he's learned as a serial entrepreneur, Jain replied:

> I think one thing (I've) learned is to not get carried away. Building a startup not only takes a good vision and a good market that you want to go after, but it also requires systematic execution. You can only run at a certain pace. Don't try to overrun yourself. Be conservative in your spending. Don't burn all the cash you have, because you need that. You need to be very, very conscientious about how your business grows and what kind of expenses you have to support your growth.[9]

Sometimes businesses grow at a measured pace and then experience a sudden upswing in orders and have difficulty keeping up. This scenario can transform a business with satisfied customers and employees into a chaotic workplace with people scrambling to push the business's product out the door as quickly as possible. The way to prevent this from happening is to recognize when to put the brakes on and have the courage to do it. This set of circumstances played out early in the life of The Pampered Chef, a company that sells kitchen utensils through home parties. Just about the time the company was gaining serious momentum, it realized that it didn't have a sufficient quantity of products in its inventory to serve the busy Christmas season. This reality posed a serious dilemma. The Pampered Chef couldn't instantly increase its inventory (its vendors were all low and the company was small, so it couldn't make extraordinary demands), yet it didn't want to discourage its home consultants from making sales or signing up new consultants. One option was to institute a recruiting freeze (on new home consultants), which would slow the rate of sales. Doris Christopher, the company's founder, remembers asking others for advice. Most advised against instituting a recruiting freeze, arguing that the lifeblood of any direct sales organization is to sign up new recruits. In the end, the company decided to institute the freeze and slowed its sales enough to fill all orders on time during the holiday season. The freeze was lifted the following January, and the number of The Pampered Chef recruits soared. Reflecting on the decision, Doris Christopher later wrote:

> Looking back, the recruiting freeze augmented our reputation with our sales force, customers, and vendors. People saw us as an honest company that was trying to do the right thing and not overestimating our capabilities.[10]

Other businesses have faced similar dilemmas and have sometimes made the right call, and other times haven't. The overarching point is that growth must be handled carefully. A business can only grow as fast as its infrastructure allows, as will be emphasized throughout this chapter. Table 13.1 provides a list of 10 warning signs that a business is growing too fast.

TABLE 13.1   10 WARNING SIGNS THAT A BUSINESS IS GROWING TOO FAST

- Borrowing money to pay for routine operating expenses
- Extremely tight profit margins
- Over-stretched staff
- Declining product quality
- E-mail starts going unanswered
- Customer complaints are up
- Employees dread coming to work
- Productivity is falling
- Operating in a "crisis" mode becomes the norm rather than the exception
- Those working with the business's financial structure are starting to worry

One company that almost succumbed to the challenges of rapid growth is Threadless, as chronicled in the "Partnering for Success" feature shown next. At one point early in its life, Threadless was growing so quickly that it's back-end operations couldn't keep up, and it was experiencing multiple problems. Fortunately, the company brought on a strategic partner at just the right time to help correct the problems. The feature is a vivid illustration of how vulnerable even the most seemingly successful firms are to the rigors of rapid growth.

Business Success Doesn't Always Scale   Unfortunately, the very thing that makes a business successful might suffer as the result of growth. This is what business experts often mean when they say growth is a "two edged sword." For example, businesses that are based on providing high levels of individualized service often don't grow or scale well. For example, an investment brokerage service that initially provided high levels of personalized attention can quickly evolve into providing standard or even substandard service as it adds customers and starts automating its services. Its initial customers might find it harder to get individualized service than it once was and start viewing the company as just another ordinary business.

There is also a category of businesses that sell high-end or specialty products that earn high margins. These businesses typically sell their products through venues where customers prioritize quality over price. These businesses can grow, but only at a measured pace. If they grow too quickly, they can lose the "exclusivity" they are trying to project, or can damage their special appeal. Fashion clothing boutiques often limit the number of garments they sell in a certain size or color for a similar reason. Even though they know they could sell more of a particular blouse or dress, they deliberately limit their sales so their customers don't see each other wearing identical items.

Staying Committed to a Core Strategy

The second thing that a business can do to prepare for growth is to stay committed to a core strategy. As discussed in Chapter 6, an important part of a firm's business model is its core strategy, which defines how it competes relative to its rivals. A firm's core strategy is largely determined by its core competencies, or what it does particularly well. While this insight might seem self-evident, it's important that a business not lose sight of its core strategy as it prepares for growth. If a business becomes distracted or starts pursuing every opportunity for growth that it's presented, it can easily stray into areas where it finds itself at a competitive disadvantage. For example, eBags, an online merchant that specializes in selling handbags, luggage, and backpacks,

PARTNERING FOR SUCCESS

How Threadless Averted Collapse by Bringing on a Partner with Back-End Operational Expertise

Web: www.threadless.com
Twitter: threadless
Facebook: Threadless

Threadless is a community-centered T-shirt design site started in 2000 by Jack Nickell and Jacob DeHart. It's called "Threadless" because it started as a thread on the Dreamlist message board. Dreamlist was a place where designers could exchange information, and in November 2000, Nickell hosted a T-shirt design contest and let fellow designers pick the winner. The contest was such a hit that Nickell and DeHart decided to move it off the Dreamlist message board for the purpose of creating a Web site where future contests could be hosted.

Threadless was run as a hobby for most of 2001 through 2003, until Nickell and DeHart quit their jobs to start a Web consultancy firm and focus more intently on Threadless. The income they earned from Threadless quickly overshadowed what they were earning from the consultancy business, so in January 2004, they started focusing on Threadless full time. The way Threadless works is that designers submit T-shirt designs to Threadless, and members of the community score them on a scale of 0 to 5. The Threadless staff then picks the 5 to 10 best designs, and the shirts are printed and offered for sale. The designers who are chosen receive a cash prize and store credit. Threadless makes money from the T-shirt sales.

Threadless grew quickly. In 2005, it sold over one million T-shirts—all designed by the Threadless community. Nickell and DeHart were experiencing difficulties managing the growth. The firm's back-end operations were the main problem. Orders weren't going out on time, the Threadless Web site was down intermittently, and some months the company would max out the amount it could process through its merchant account and would have to stop taking orders. Worst of all, in 2005, T-shirts that were ordered in anticipation of Christmas weren't delivered until the following January.

Rather than collapsing under the weight of these problems, Nickell and DeHart took bold action. They sold a minority interest in Threadless to Insight Partners, a venture capital firm. They could have hired a consulting firm with operational expertise, but wanted a partner that would have a long-term interest in Threadless's success. Insight Partners turned out to be an ideal choice. At that time, Insight had a program called Insight Onsight, where it would send personnel to evaluate its portfolio companies' operations. Insight sent personnel to evaluate Threadless's back-end operations and make recommendations. It moved Threadless's Web site to a new host, which was better equipped to help Threadless scale its Web site traffic and sales. It also helped Threadless improve the functioning of its warehouse and fulfillment operations. Threadless's problems were smoothed out and it moved forward. It hasn't experienced significant technical or order fulfillment glitches since.

Today, Threadless is receiving about 1,500 T-shirt designs per week, and its staff picks the top 10 T-shirts to sell. Each designer selected receives $2,000 in cash, a $500 gift certificate, and an additional $500 for each reprint. The success of Threadless's business model and growth strategy has led to several spin-offs, which advertise themselves as the "Threadless" of their industry.

Questions for Critical Thinking

1. Do you think Threadless would exist today if Nickell and DeHart hadn't taken decisive action in 2005 and brought Insight Partners into the company as a strategic investor? Why or why not?
2. Why do you think Nickell and DeHart wanted a strategic investor to help Threadless work through its operational problems rather than hire a consulting firm? Hiring a consulting firm wouldn't have required Threadless to surrender any equity.
3. Name at least two companies that are using crowdsourcing business models, similar to the model that Threadless pioneered in the early 2000s. How are the business models and the companies behind them performing?
4. Look at the "You Be the VC" features at the end of Chapters 13 and 14. Which company do you think has the highest likelihood of experiencing rapid growth? What can the company do to avoid the problems that Threadless experienced?

Sources: Threadless, www.threadless.com (accessed April 15, 2011); Andrew Warner and Jack Nickell, "Threadless: Growing a Design Community. Selling Millions of T-Shirts with Jack Nickell," Mixergy Podcast, www.mixergy.com (accessed April 15, 2011).

at one point acquired a Web site that sells shoes. After three years, it sold the site (Shoedini.com) to Zappos after concluding that the shoe business was too far of a stretch from the company's core strategy and its core competencies.

The way most businesses typically evolve is to start by selling a product or service that is consistent with their core strategy and increase sales by incrementally moving into areas that are different from, but are related to, their core strengths and capabilities. This is what Zappos, the subject of Case 9.2, is doing. The company started by selling shoes and has gradually expanded into clothing, bags, housewares, and beauty products. The success of its new product lines will be determined largely by whether the company's existing core competencies are sufficient to profitably sell these items. If they aren't, then Zappos will have to develop or acquire additional core competencies, or it is likely to struggle to effectively manage its growth.

A parable that helps affirm why sticking to a core strategy is so important is provided by Jim Collins in his book *Good to Great.* In the book, Collins retells the fable of the fox and the hedgehog, which was originally told by Isaiah Berlin. According to the fable, because he is sly, cunning, and strong, everyone thinks the fox is better than the hedgehog. All the lowly hedgehog knows how to do is one thing—curl up in a ball, with its spikes out, to deter intruders. The ironic thing is that whatever the fox does, and no matter how many of its 100 tricks it tries to use, the hedgehog always wins, because it knows how to do one thing well—roll up and stick its spikes out. In *Good to Great,* Collins says businesses that are successful over the long haul are more like hedgehogs than foxes. Rather than moving swiftly in all directions, like foxes, successful businesses keep their heads down and do one thing particularly well. Like the hedgehog, they see what is essential and ignore the rest.[11]

Planning for Growth

The third thing that a firm can do to prepare for growth is to establish growth-related plans.[12] This task involves a firm thinking ahead and anticipating the type and amount of growth it wants to achieve.

It is important that a business establish growth-related plans and objectives. Here, the three founders of a young entrepreneurial firm are charting their growth plans for several years in the future.

nyul/Fotolia

The process of writing a business plan, covered in Chapter 4, greatly assists in developing growth-related plans. A business plan normally includes a detailed forecast of a firm's first three to five years of sales, along with an operations plan that describes the resources the business will need to meet its projections. Even though a business will undoubtedly change during its first three to five years, it's still good to have a plan. Many businesses periodically revise their business plans as a foundation for helping them guide their growth-related decisions.

It's also important for a business to determine, as early as possible, the strategies it will choose to employ as a means of pursuing growth. For example, Proactiv, the acne medicine company and focus of Case 11.2, is a single-product company and has grown by steadily increasing its domestic sales, introducing its products into foreign countries, and by encouraging nontraditional users of acne medicine, like adult males, to use its product. Proactiv's decision to stick with one product and to avoid growing through initiatives like acquisitions and licensing has allowed the company to focus on marketing and building its brand. Zipcar, on the other hand, has engaged in a number of strategic acquisitions to consolidate its leadership position in the car sharing industry. It's also expanded beyond car sharing into several related areas. In 2009, for example, it launched a service called FastFleet to help cities more efficiently use the cars they own.

On a more personal level, a business owner should step back and measure the company's growth plans against his or her personal goals and aspirations. The old adage, "Be careful what you wish for," is as true in business as it is in other areas of life. For example, if a business has the potential to grow rapidly, the owner should know what to expect if the fast-growth route is chosen. Fast-growth normally implies a quick pace of activity, a rapidly rising overhead, and a total commitment in terms of time and attention on the part of the business owners. The upside is that if the business is successful, the owner will normally do very well financially. The trade-offs implied by this scenario are acceptable to some business owners and aren't to others.

Entrepreneurs also benefit from employing commonsense strategies for growing their firms. For example, as illustrated in the "Savvy Entrepreneurial Firm" feature shown next, during the early formative years of the L'Aroma Gourmet business, its founders gained the loyalty of local consumers by asking them to test their coffee and comment on various flavors and styles. While a simple gesture, this action generated valuable research and awareness of the business ahead of its launch.

REASONS FOR GROWTH

Although sustained, profitable growth is almost always the result of deliberate intentions and careful planning in that firms cannot always choose their pace of growth. A firm's **pace of growth** is the rate at which it is growing on an annual basis. Sometimes firms are forced into a high-growth mode sooner than they would like. For example, when a firm develops a product or service that satisfies a need for many customers such that orders roll in very quickly, it must adjust quickly or risk faltering. In other instances, a firm experiences unexpected competition and must grow to maintain its market share.

This section examines the six primary reasons firms try to grow to increase their profitability and valuation, as depicted in Figure 13.1.

SAVVY ENTREPRENEURIAL FIRM

L'Aroma Gourmet: How a Simple Initiative Can Contribute to a Start-up's Early Growth

There are an increasing number of coffeehouses around the Egyptian capital of Cairo and deciding where to get a decent cup of coffee to share with friends is a tough choice. In 2002, Ahmed Gaafar, Nader Montasser, and Yehia El Ghamrawy—three friends with backgrounds in IT, fast-moving consumer goods, and advertising respectively—agreed that the coffee sold in the city was not good enough to drink. They believed that a store with high-quality drinks coupled with a good atmosphere would be a success—and they were the people to open one.

But with little experience in the field, where would they start? To begin with, the trio flirted with the idea of opening a franchise of an international brand because a big name would clearly add a lot of value to their business. Yet, after meeting with many chains and even being shortlisted by some, they thought it might be more interesting to create their own concept instead of following a standard franchise model.

Unfortunately, they knew very little about making coffee, so they hired an expert from the United States to teach them. The process took an exhausting six months but, even after all that time, the three would-be coffee shop entrepreneurs felt they were knowledgeable about the theory behind making good coffee, but were lacking in practical experience.

Gaafar, Montasser, and El Ghamrawy turned to their friends around the city for help. For three months, whenever they heard of a party, event, or competition, the entrepreneurs went along to serve coffee. Soon, word of the strange marketing initiative spread and demand grew. It enabled the three to test various flavors, tastes, and styles of coffee as well as their price structure. At the end of the pilot period, they had a far greater understanding of how the Egyptian coffee consumer thinks, and they took all of this feedback into consideration when they opened their first shop.

One of the important factors that emerged from this feedback was how important the quality of the coffee ingredients was to consumers. Although the three found local importers wary of doing business with a start-up with no track record and no stores, they managed to find a supplier in Italy and signed an exclusive agreement.

They also discovered that their pilot group was more attracted by a relaxed atmosphere in a coffee shop, where they felt like they were in their living room. Many of their friends saw the multinational coffee giants as too impersonal, wanting to get the consumer and the coffee out the door quickly.

When Gaafar, Montasser, and El Ghamrawy opened their first L'Aroma Gourmet outlet at the El Gezira Club in Zamalek, they already had a customer base of keen locals who had taken part in the lengthy pilot. They were eager to sample more of the entrepreneurs' fine coffee.

Within five years, that first coffeehouse has expanded to a chain of 12 stores, with sales increasing at 65 percent a year. This is at a time when multinationals, such as Starbucks, have also arrived in Cairo, yet L'Aroma Gourmet has experienced such success that there are plans for dozens more coffeehouses in the future.

Questions for Critical Thinking

1. Do you think the same type of initiative, asking friends and friends of friends to sample a product and then give constructive feedback, would work if these entrepreneurs were opening a coffeehouse in Cairo today? Explain your answer.
2. If you had to guess, without looking, if L'Aroma Gourmet is an active user of Twitter and Facebook, what would your guess be? Explain your thought process. How is their actual use different from your original guess?
3. How can establishing early relationships with consumers help a firm spur and sustain its own growth?
4. Ahmed Gaafar says Egyptians prefer local products and businesses when they can offer international quality. What have these entrepreneurs done to prove this theory and what else could they do to maintain their growth as more multinationals encroach on their market?

Sources: Ministry of Finance, "The Path to Growth: Experiences of Egyptian Entrepreneurs," www.sme.gov.eg/Jan_publications/Growth_?EN.pdf (accessed September 4, 2011, originally posted January 2008); "L'Aroma: Home of Egyptian Baristas," www.masress.com.

FIGURE 13.1
Appropriate Reasons
for Firm Growth

- Economies of scale
- Economies of scope
- Market leadership
- Influence, power, and survivability
- Need to accommodate the growth of key customers
- Ability to attract and retain talented employees

Capturing Economies of Scale **Economies of scale** are generated when increasing production lowers the average cost of each unit produced. This phenomenon occurs for two reasons. First, if a company can get a discount by buying component parts in bulk, it can lower its variable costs per unit as it grows larger. **Variable costs** are the costs a company incurs as it generates sales. Second, by increasing production, a company can spread its fixed costs over a greater number of units. **Fixed costs** are costs that a company incurs whether it sells something or not. For example, it may cost a company $10,000 per month to air-condition its factory. The air-conditioning cost is fixed; cooling the factory will cost the same whether the company produces 10 or 10,000 units per month.

A related reason firms grow is to make use of unused resources such as labor capacity and a host of others. For example, a firm may need exactly 2.5 full-time salespeople to fully cover its trade area. Because a firm obviously can't hire 2.5 full-time salespeople, it may hire 3 salespeople and expand its trade area.[13]

Capturing Economies of Scope Economies of scope are similar to economies of scale, except the advantage comes through the scope (or range) of a firm's operations rather than from its scale of production. For example, a company's sales force may be able to sell 10 items more efficiently than 5 because the cost of travel and the salesperson's salary is spread out over 10 products rather than 5. Similarly, a company such as PurBlu Beverages (the focus of this chapter's "Opening Profile") captures economies of scope in its advertising when the same feature is used to advertise water drinks as well as the firm's new energy drink and energy lite drink.

Market Leadership **Market leadership** occurs when a firm holds the number one or the number two position in an industry or niche market in terms of sales volume. Many firms work hard to achieve market leadership, to realize economies of scale and economies of scope, and to be recognized as the brand leader. Being the market leader also permits a firm to use slogans such as "Number 1 App in the iTunes store" in its promotions, helping it win customers and attract talented employees as well as business partners.

Influence, Power, and Survivability Larger businesses usually have more influence and power than smaller firms in regard to setting standards for an industry, getting a "foot in the door" with major customers and suppliers, and garnering prestige. In addition, larger businesses can typically make a mistake yet survive more easily than entrepreneurial ventures. Commenting on this issue, Jack Welch, GE's former CEO, once said, "Size gives us another big advantage; our reach and resources enable us to go to bat more frequently, to take more swings, to experiment more, and unlike a small company, we can miss on occasion and get to swing again."[14]

A firm's capacity for growth affects its survival in additional ways. For example, a firm that stays small and relies on the efforts and motivation of its founder or a small group of people is vulnerable if those people leave the firm or lose their passion for the business. This reason was partly to blame for the failure of YouCaster, as profiled in Chapter 1. YouCaster failed in part because its founders lost interest in the business and decided to move on to other things. As a firm grows and adds employees, it's normally not as vulnerable to the loss of a single person or a small group of people's participation or passion for the business.

Need to Accommodate the Growth of Key Customers   Sometimes firms are compelled to grow to accommodate the growth of a key customer. For example, if Intel has a major account with an electronics firm buying a large number of its semiconductor chips and the electronics firm is growing at a rate of 20 percent per year, Intel may have to add capacity each year to accommodate the growth of its customer or else risk losing some or all of its business.

Ability to Attract and Retain Talented Employees   The final reason that firms grow is to attract and retain high-quality personnel. It is natural for talented employees to want to work for a firm that can offer opportunities for promotion, higher salaries, and increased levels of responsibility. Growth is a firm's primary mechanism to generate promotional opportunities for employees, while failing to retain key employees can be very damaging to a firm's growth efforts. High turnover is expensive, and in knowledge-based industries in particular, such as biotechnology and film production, a company's number one asset is the combined talent, training, and experience of its employees. In less knowledge-intensive settings, turnover may not be as critical, but it is still costly. The American Management Association estimates that the cost of hiring and training a person earning $8 per hour varies from 25 percent to 200 percent of annual compensation.[15] Entrepreneurial ventures rarely have the excess financial capital needed to support the unfavorable relationship between employee hiring and turnover. However, when talented individuals leave a large company either voluntarily or through layoffs, entrepreneurial ventures have opportunities to hire people with skills the venture did not pay for them to develop.

MANAGING GROWTH

Many businesses are caught off guard by the challenges involved with growing their companies. One would think that if a business got off to a good start, steadily increased its sales, and started making money, it would get progressively easier to manage the growth of a firm. In many instances, just the opposite happens. As a business increases its sales, its pace of activity quickens, its resource needs increase, and the founders often find that they're busier than ever. Major challenges can also occur. For example, a business might project its next year's sales and realize it will need more people and additional equipment to handle the increased workload. The new equipment might need to be purchased and the new people hired and trained before the increased business generates additional income. It's easy to imagine serious discussions among the members of a new venture's management team trying to figure out how that will all work out.

   The reality is that a company must actively and carefully manage its growth for it to expand in a healthy and profitable manner. As a business grows and becomes better known, there are normally more opportunities that present themselves, but there are more things that can go wrong too. Many potential problems and heartaches can be avoided by prudently managing the growth process. This section focuses on knowing and managing the stages of growth. The final section in this chapter focuses on a related topic—the challenges of growth.

Knowing and Managing the Stages of Growth

The majority of businesses go through a discernable set of stages referred to as the organizational life cycle.[16] The stages, pictured in Figure 13.2, include introduction, early growth, continuous growth, maturity, and decline. Each stage must be managed differently. It's important for an entrepreneur to be familiar with these stages, along with the unique opportunities and challenges that each stage entails.

Introduction Stage   This is the start-up phase where a business determines what its core strengths and capabilities are and starts selling its initial product or service. It's a very "hands-on" phase for the founder or founders who are normally involved in every aspect of the day-to-day life of the business. The business is typically very nonbureaucratic with no (or few) written rules or procedures. The main goal of the business is to get off to a good start and to try to gain momentum in the marketplace.

The main challenges for a business in the introduction stage are to make sure the initial product or service is right and to start laying the groundwork for building a larger organization. It's important to not rush things. This sentiment is affirmed by April Singer, the founder of Rufus Shirts, a company that makes high-end shirts for men. Before growing her business beyond the introduction stage, Singer made sure that her unique approach for making men's shirts worked and that it resonated in the marketplace:

> Before growing too much too fast, I wanted to spend two seasons making sure that the concept worked, that I shipped well, and that consumers liked the product. They did.[17]

This affirmation gave Singer the confidence to expand her business and move into a more aggressive growth mode. In regard to laying the groundwork to build a larger organization, many businesses use the introduction stage to try different concepts to see what works and what doesn't, recognizing that trial and error gets harder as a business grows. It's important to document what works and start thinking about how the company's success can be replicated when the owner isn't present or when the business expands beyond its original location.

Early Growth Stage   A business's early growth stage is generally characterized by increasing sales and heightened complexity. The business is normally still focused on its initial product or service but is trying to increase its market share and might have related products in the works. The initial

FIGURE 13.2
Organizational Life Cycle

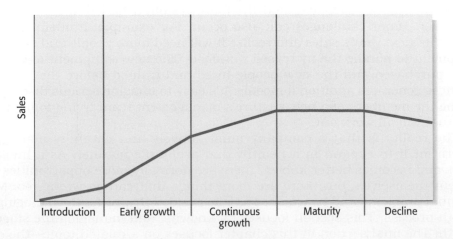

formation of policies and procedures takes place, and the process of running the business will start to consume more of the founder's or founders' time and attention.

For a business to be successful in this stage, two important things must take place. First, the founder or owner of the business must start transitioning from his or her role as the hands-on supervisor of every aspect of the business to a more managerial role. As articulated by Michael E. Gerber in his excellent book *The E-Myth Revisited*, the owner must start working "on the business" rather than "in the business."[18] The basic idea is that early in the life of a business, the owner typically is directly involved in building the product or delivering the service that the business provides. As the business moves into the early growth stage, the owner must let go of that role and spend more time learning how to manage and build the business. If the owner isn't willing to make this transition or doesn't know it needs to be made, the business will never grow beyond the owner's ability to directly supervise everything that takes place, and the business's growth will eventually stall.

The second thing that must take place for a business to be successful in the early growth stage is that increased formalization must take place. The business has to start developing policies and procedures that tell employees how to run it when the founders or other top managers aren't present. This is how franchise restaurants run so well when they're staffed by what appears to be a group of teenagers. The employees are simply following well-documented policies and procedures. This task was clearly on the mind of Emily Levy, the founder of EBL Coaching, a tutoring service for children who are struggling in school or trying to overcome disabilities, when she was asked by Ladies Who Launch (a support network for female entrepreneurs) early in the life of her business about her growth plans:

> My future goals include continuing to spread EBL Coaching's programs nationally, using our proprietary materials and self-contained multisensory methods. I have already developed a series of workbooks, called "Strategies for Success," addressing specific study skills strategies, that are being used in a number of schools across the country. The real challenge will be figuring out how to replicate our programs while maintaining our high quality of teaching and personalized approach.[19]

Continuous Growth Stage The need for structure and more formal relationships increases as a business moves beyond its early growth stage and its pace of growth accelerates. The resource requirements of the business are usually a major concern, along with the ability of the owner and manager to take the firm to the next level. Often the business will start developing new products and services and will expand to new markets. Smaller firms may be acquired, and the business might start more aggressively partnering with other firms. When handled correctly, the business's expansion will be in areas that are related to its core strengths and capabilities, or it will develop new strengths and capabilities to complement its activities.

The toughest decisions are typically made in the continuous growth stage. One tough decision is whether the owner of the business and the current management team have the experience and ability to take the firm any further. This scenario played out for Rachel Ashwell, the founder of Shabby Chic, a home furnishing business. Ashwell expanded her company to five separate locations, inked a licensing deal with Target, wrote five how-to books related to her business, and hosted her own television show on the Style Network before concluding that her business had stalled. Her choice was to continue running the business or find more experienced management to grow it further. She opted for the latter, and Shabby Chic is growing again.[20]

LEARNING OBJECTIVE
5. Describe the most important factors for firms to focus on during each stage of growth.

The importance of developing policies and procedures increases during the continuous growth stage. It's also important for a business to develop a formal organizational structure and determine clear lines of delegation throughout the business. Well-developed policies and procedures lead to order, which typically makes the process of growing a business more organized and successful.

Maturity   A business enters the maturity stage when its growth slows. At this point, the firm typically focuses more intently on efficiently managing the products and services it has rather than expanding in new areas. Innovation slows. Formal policies and procedures, although important, can become an impediment if they are too rigid and strict.[21] It's important that the firm continues to adapt and that the founders, managers, and employees remain passionate about the products and services that are being sold. If this doesn't happen, a firm can easily slip into a no-growth situation.

A well-managed firm that finds its products and services are mature often looks for partnering or acquisition opportunities to breathe new life into the firm. For example, PepsiCo and Coca-Cola, two firms in the maturity stage of their life cycles, are aggressively acquiring small beverage companies. They're doing this to combine fresh new products with their staple products to maintain some upward momentum, even though their staple products are mature. For example, in 2007 Coca-Cola acquired FUZE Beverages, a maker of noncarbonated fruit drinks, and in 2010 Pepsi purchased Wimm-Bill-Dann, a Russian dairy products and fruit juice company.

If a company does grow organically while in the maturity stage, it normally focuses on the "next generation" of products it already sells rather than invest in new or related products or services.

Decline   It is not inevitable that a business enter the decline stage and either deteriorate or die. Many American businesses have long histories and have thrived by adapting to environmental change and by selling products that remain important to customers. Eventually all business's products or services will be threatened by more relevant and innovative products. When this happens, a business's ability to avoid decline depends on the strength of its leadership and its ability to appropriately respond.

A firm can also enter the decline stage if it loses its sense of purpose or spreads itself so thin that it no longer has a competitive advantage in any of its markets. A firm's management team should be aware of these potential pitfalls and guard against allowing them to happen.

CHALLENGES OF GROWTH

There is a consistent set of challenges that affect all stages of a firm's growth. The challenges typically become more acute as a business grows, but a business's founder or founders and managers also become more savvy and experienced with the passage of time. The challenges illustrate that no firm grows in a competitive vacuum. As a business grows and takes market share away from rival firms, there will be a certain amount of retaliation that takes place. This is an aspect of competition that a business owner needs to be aware of and plan for. Competitive retaliation normally increases as a business grows and becomes a larger threat to its rivals.

This section is divided into two parts. The first part focuses on the managerial capacity problem, which is a framework for thinking about the overall challenge of growing a firm. The second part focuses on the four most common day-to-day challenges of growing a business.

Managerial Capacity

In her thoughtful and seminal book *The Theory of the Growth of the Firm*, Edith T. Penrose argues that firms are collections of productive resources that are organized in an administrative framework.[22] As an administrative framework, the primary purpose of a firm is to package its resources together with resources acquired outside the firm for the production of products and services at a profit. As a firm goes about its routine activities, the management team becomes better acquainted with the firm's resources and its markets. This knowledge leads to the expansion of a firm's **productive opportunity set**, which is the set of opportunities the firm feels it's capable of pursuing. The opportunities might include the introduction of new products, geographic expansion, licensing products to other firms, exporting, and so on. The pursuit of these new opportunities causes a firm to grow.

LEARNING OBJECTIVE

6. Describe the managerial capacity problem and how it inhibits firm growth.

Penrose points out, however, that there is a problem with the execution of this simple logic. The firm's administrative framework consists of two kinds of services that are important to a firm's growth—entrepreneurial services and managerial services. **Entrepreneurial services** generate new market, product, and service ideas, while **managerial services** administer the routine functions of the firm and facilitate the profitable execution of new opportunities. However, the introduction of new product and service ideas requires substantial managerial services (or managerial "capacity") to be properly implemented and supervised. This is a complex problem because if a firm has insufficient managerial services to properly implement its entrepreneurial ideas, it can't quickly hire new managers to remedy the shortfall. It is expensive to hire new employees, and it takes time for new managers to be socialized into the firm's culture, acquire firm-specific skills and knowledge, and establish trusting relationships with other members of their firms.[23] When a firm's managerial resources are insufficient to take advantage of its new product and services opportunities, the subsequent bottleneck is referred to as the **managerial capacity problem**.

As the entrepreneurial venture grows, it encounters the dual challenges of adverse selection and moral hazard. **Adverse selection** means that as the number of employees a firm needs increases, it becomes increasingly difficult for it to find the right employees, place them in appropriate positions, and provide adequate supervision.[24] The faster a firm grows, the less time managers have to evaluate the suitability of job candidates and the higher the chances are that an unsuitable candidate will be chosen. Selecting "ineffective" or "unsuitable" employees increases the venture's costs. **Moral hazard** means that as a firm grows and adds personnel, the new hires typically do not have the same ownership incentives as the original founders, so the new hires may not be as motivated as the founders to put in long hours or may even try to avoid hard work. To make sure the new hires are doing what they are employed to do, the firm will typically hire monitors (i.e., managers) to supervise the employees. This practice creates a hierarchy that is costly and isolates the top management team from its rank-and-file employees.

LEARNING OBJECTIVE

7. Discuss the challenges for firm growth imposed by adverse selection and moral hazard.

The basic model of firm growth articulated by Penrose is shown in Figure 13.3, and Figure 13.4 shows the essence of the growth-limiting

FIGURE 13.3
Basic Model of Firm Growth

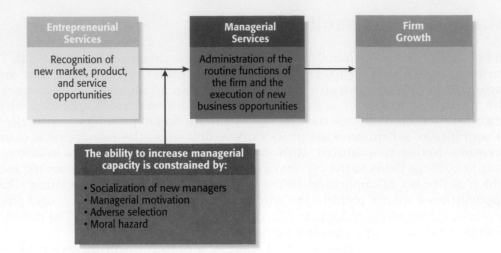

managerial capacity problem.[25] Figure 13.4 indicates that the ability to increase managerial services is not friction free. It is constrained or limited by (1) the time required to socialize new managers, (2) how motivated entrepreneurs and/or managers are to grow their firms, (3) adverse selection, and (4) moral hazard.

Wesabe, the focus of this chapter's "What Went Wrong?" feature, suffered as a result of trying to build out its own capabilities or managerial capacity in a key area rather than partnering with a company that was willing to license it the capability. A competitor licensed the technology and sped ahead of Wesabe. Wesabe's own attempt to build out the capability took longer than it thought it would, and it never recovered.

The reality of the managerial capacity problem is one of the main reasons that entrepreneurs and managers worry so much about growth. Growth is a generally positive thing, but it is easy for a firm to overshoot its capacity to manage growth in ways that will diminish the venture's sales revenues and profits.

Day-to-Day Challenges of Growing a Firm

Along with the overarching challenges imposed by the managerial capacity problem, there are a number of day-to-day challenges involved with growing a firm. The following is a discussion of the four most common challenges.

Cash Flow Management   As discussed in Chapters 8 and 10, as a firm grows, it requires an increasing amount of cash to service its customers. In addition, a firm must carefully manage its cash on hand to make sure it maintains sufficient liquidity to meet its payroll and cover its other short-term obligations. There are many colorful anecdotes about business founders who have had to rush to a bank and get a second mortgage on their houses to cover their business's payroll. This usually occurs when a business takes on too much work, and its customers are slow to pay. A business can literally have $1 million in accounts receivable but not be able to meet a $25,000 payroll. This is why almost any book you pick up about growing a business stresses the importance of properly managing your cash flow.

Growth usually increases rather than decreases the challenges involved with cash flow management because an increase in sales means that more cash will be flowing into and out of the firm. Some firms deal with potential cash flow shortfalls by establishing a line of credit at a bank or by raising investment capital. Other firms deliberately restrict the pace of their growth to

How Trying to Build Out Its Own Capabilities in a Key Area Contributed to the Failure of a Promising Firm

In November 2006, Wesabe launched a site to help people manage their personal finances. While it wasn't the first personal finance site on the Web, it was the first to use a Web 2.0 approach. The site automatically aggregated and stored all of its users' financial accounts and, most especially, was able to "learn" from the accumulated data its users uploaded to make recommendations for better financial decisions. Because of its helpful functionality, Wesabe got off to a good start and, until September 2007, was considered the leader in online personal finance. Then Mint.com launched, and from that point forward, Wesabe was in second place at best. Two years later, Mint was acquired by Intuit for $170 million—one of the fastest and most successful exits in software history. In contrast, just short of a year later, Wesabe shut down.

What Went Wrong?

Marc Hedlund, one of Wesabe's cofounders, wrote a thoughtful blog post about Wesabe's failure. While he attributes Wesabe's failure to several factors, two are prominent in Hedlund's opinion. The first speaks to the importance of allowing partners to build some of a firm's capabilities or managerial capacity, while the second focuses on the importance of a first mover remaining sharp and competitive in light of inevitable competition.

The first mistake Wesabe made is that it chose not to partner with Yodlee. Yodlee is a company that provides account aggregation services, which is a highly technical business. If a user is willing to provide his or her account-access information (account numbers, user IDs, and passwords) for bank accounts, credit cards, and investment accounts, Yodlee can "scrape" the appropriate sites and compile all the information in one place. Yodlee was a tough negotiator so Wesabe decided not to tie itself to Yodlee, even though Yodlee could deliver to Wesabe a huge capability it needed. Mint.com partnered with Yodlee out of the gates, and, as a result, it was easy for its users to populate their Mint.com accounts with their financial information. Wesabe built its own data acquisition system, which took longer and wasn't as elegant. Wesabe eventually launched a Yodlee-like Web interface, but it didn't come online until six months after Mint.com went live. In retrospect, Hedlund believes that passing on Yodlee was probably enough to kill Wesabe. It should have known that if it didn't use Yodlee, a competitor would come along that would. That would have been okay if

Wesabe had had a solution as capable as Yodlee. But it didn't, and the minute users looked at side-by-side comparisons of Wesabe versus Mint.com, Wesabe was at a disadvantage in that its product's functionality wasn't as solid as what was available from a competitor.

The second mistake Wesabe made was misunderstanding its users. Wesabe deliberately forced people to do some of the data entry and other work on the site themselves, thinking that forcing users to get close to their data would change their financial behavior—for the better. Mint.com did just the opposite. It focused on making the user do almost no work at all, by automating all key processes and giving them instant gratification. As a result, Wesabe's site was perceived as "harder to use" than Mint.com's. While Wesabe's intentions may have been noble, it misread its users. As hard as it is to admit, users were more interested in expediency and an elegant interface than performing the hard work of getting close to their financial data.

The combination of Mint's better data aggregation method (via Yodlee) and the higher amount of work that Wesabe made the user do gave users a better experience on Mint versus Wesabe. Although Wesabe had the first-mover advantage, Mint simply outcompeted Wesabe and gained the upper hand.

Questions for Critical Thinking

1. Why do you think Wesabe opted not to use Yodlee and build its own account aggregation services? Similarly, why do you think Mint.com jumped at the chance to partner with Yodlee?
2. How does an entrepreneurial firm find the right balance between not "overestimating" its capabilities (i.e., Wesabe thought it could build an account aggregation service faster than it did) and still be willing to do much of the work that needs to be done without paying others to do it?
3. How could Wesabe have avoided misunderstanding its users and allowing Mint.com to obtain the perceived usability advantage it obtained?
4. What can entrepreneurial firms learn about the management capacity problem from Wesabe's experience?

Source: Marc Hedlund, "Why Wesabe Lost to Mint." *Marc Hedlund's blog*, http://blog.precipice.org/wey-wesabe-lost-to-mint (accessed March 10, 2011).

Two female entrepreneurs just launched a casual dining restaurant. Their ability to grow their business successful will hinge largely on how they manage the day-to-day challenges associated with growth.

Mangostock/Dreamstime

avoid cash flow challenges. The latter option is preferred by Dave Schwartz, the founder of Rent-A-Wreck, a discount car rental company, who grew his firm through earnings rather than debt or investment capital. Commenting on this issue, Schwartz said:

> One of the main things I tell people starting out is not to grow too quickly. Often it's better to grow slowly, and when you do expand, try to grow with cash flow.[26]

Price Stability   If firm growth comes at the expense of a competitor's market share, price competition can set in. For example, if an entrepreneur opened a fast-casual restaurant near a Panera Bread that started eroding the Panera Bread's market share, Panera Bread will probably fight back by running promotions or lowering prices. This type of scenario places a new firm in a difficult predicament and illustrates why it's important to start a business by selling a differentiated product to a clearly defined target market. There is no good way for a small firm to compete head-to-head against a much larger rival on price. The best thing for a small firm to do is to avoid price competition by serving a different market and by serving that market particularly well.

LEARNING OBJECTIVE

10. Explain how "quality control" can become a challenge for growing a firm.

Quality Control   One of the most difficult challenges that businesses encounter as they grow is maintaining high levels of quality and customer service. As a firm grows, it handles more service requests and paperwork and contends with an increasing number of prospects, customers, vendors, and other stakeholders. If a business can't build its infrastructure fast enough to handle the increased activity, quality and customer service will usually suffer. What happens to many businesses is that they run into the classic chicken-or-egg quandary. It's hard to justify hiring additional employees or leasing more office space until the need is present, but if the business waits until the need is present, it usually won't have enough employees or office space to properly service new customers.

There is no easy way to resolve this type of quandary other than to recognize that it may take place and to plan for it in the best way possible. Many businesses find innovative ways to expand their capacity to try to avoid shortfalls in quality control or customer service.

Capital Constraints Although many businesses are started fairly inexpensively, the need for capital is typically the most prevalent in the early growth and continuous growth stages of the organizational life cycle. The amount of capital required varies widely among businesses. Some businesses, like restaurant chains, might need considerable capital to hire employees, construct buildings, and purchase equipment. If they can't raise the capital they need, their growth will be stymied.

Most businesses, regardless of their industry, need capital from time to time to invest in growth-enabling projects. Their ability to raise capital, whether it's through internally generated funds, through a bank, or from investors, will determine in part whether their growth plans proceed.

CHAPTER SUMMARY

1. Sustained growth is defined as growth in both revenues and profits over an extended period of time.

2. Growing a business successfully takes preparation, good management, and an appreciation of the issues involved. The three primary things that a business can do to prepare for growth are appreciating the nature of business growth, staying committed to a core strategy, and planning for growth.

3. Growth is not a random or chance event. It is something firms pursue deliberately. The six most common reasons that firms grow in an effort to increase their profitability and valuation are as follows: to capture economies of scale; to capture economies of scope; to achieve market leadership; to maintain influence, power, and survivability; to accommodate the growth of key customers; and to maintain an ability to attract and retain talented employees.

4. Many businesses are caught off guard by the challenges involved with growing their companies. As a business increases its sales, its pace of activity quickens, its resource needs increase, and the founders often find that they're busier than ever.

5. The majority of businesses go through a discernable set of stages referred to as the organizational life cycle. The stages include introduction, early growth, continuous growth, maturity, and decline.

6. The introduction phase is where a business determines what its core strengths and capabilities are and starts selling its initial product or service. The business is typically very nonbureaucratic with no (or few) written rules or procedures. The main goal of the business is to get off to a good start and try to gain momentum in the marketplace.

7. A business's early growth stage is characterized by increasing sales and heightened complexity. For a business to succeed in this stage (1) the founder or owner of the business must start transforming from his or her role as the hands-on supervisor of every aspect of the business to a more managerial role, and (2) increased formalization must take place.

8. The toughest decisions are typically made in the continuous growth stage. One tough decision is whether the owner of the business and the current management team have the experience and ability to take the firm any further.

9. The managerial capacity problem suggests that firm growth is limited by the managerial capacity (i.e., personnel, expertise, and intellectual resources) that firms have available to implement new business ideas. The basic idea is that it does a firm little good to have exciting ideas about growth when it lacks the managerial capacity to implement its ideas.

10. The day-to-day challenges of managing growth include cash flow management, price stability, quality control, and capital constraints.

KEY TERMS

adverse selection, **471**
economies of scale, **466**
entrepreneurial
    services, **471**
fixed costs, **466**

managerial capacity problem,
    471
managerial services, **471**
market leadership, **466**
moral hazard, **471**

pace of growth, **464**
productive opportunity set,
    471
sustained growth, **458**
variable costs, **466**

REVIEW QUESTIONS

1. What is sustained growth? Why is it important?

2. Can most firms be classified as rapid-growth firms? Explain your answer.

3. What are the potential downsides to firm growth?

4. Explain why not all businesses have the potential to be aggressive-growth firms.

5. Is it possible for a firm to grow too fast? If so, what are the potential downsides?

6. Why is it difficult for some firms to grow or scale their operations?

7. What are the benefits of planning for growth?

8. Describe economies of scale and economies of scope as rationales for firm growth.

9. List three reasons firms work hard to achieve market leadership.

10. How does a firm's growth rate affect its ability to attract and retain talented employees?

11. Briefly describe each of the five stages in the organizational life cycle.

12. Give a brief overview of the managerial capacity problem.

13. Explain what is meant by adverse selection.

14. Explain what is meant by moral hazard.

15. What is meant by the statement in the chapter that reads, "The reality of the managerial capacity problem is one of the main reasons that entrepreneurs and managers worry so much about growth"?

16. Explain why cash flow management is an important issue for a firm entering a period of rapid growth.

17. How do rapid growth firms deal with potential cash flow shortfalls?

18. Explain why price stability is an important issue for a firm entering a period of rapid growth.

19. According to the chapter, one of the most difficult challenges involved with rapid growth is quality control. Why is this so?

20. In what stage or stages of the organizational life cycle are capital constraints most prevalent?

APPLICATION QUESTIONS

1. Pete Martin just purchased a copy of *Inc.* magazine's annual issue that ranks the top 500 fastest-growing privately owned companies in America. Pete was amazed by some of the stories in the article and is more encouraged than ever to start his own art restoration firm. Pete believes his firm can grow 100 percent or more per year. He is ready to cash out his savings and get started. Is Pete starting this venture with realistic expectations? If not, what should his expectations be?

2. Seven months ago, Sam Peters launched a chain of kiosks that are located in malls and sell smartphone accessories. His first kiosk was in a mall in Washington, DC., and he is now expanding into Maryland, Virginia, and Pennsylvania. Sam's

company has grown quickly from 1 kiosk to 142, and he hopes to add 200 kiosks per year over the next five years. Recently, a Virginia business periodical ran an article on Sam's business, focused primarily on whether the business was growing too fast. Sam was upset when he read the article, and called you to vent his irritation. After he calmed down he said to you, "Tell me the truth. Is there something to what these guys are saying? I'm opening new kiosks as fast as I can. Isn't that a good thing?" What would you say in response to Sam's questions?

3. Patty Stone owns an industrial equipment company named Get Smart Industrial that sells three products in the oil services industry. Get Smart's products are sold via a direct sales force. Patty wants to grow the firm by adding new products but has run into resistance from her chief financial officer (CFO), who argues that adding new products will increase inventory costs and place a strain on the company's cash flow. While Patty is sensitive to her CFO's concerns, what arguments can she make in favor of adding new products as a way of effectively growing her firm?

4. Brian Willard, who lives in Denver, just read a lengthy article about Redbeacon, the subject of Case 13.1. He's thinking about launching a Web-based service similar to Redbeacon's. Brian just inherited a substantial sum of money and is willing to put it into the business. One thing that Brian plans to do is roll out his business on a nationwide basis, rather than on a region-to-region basis like Redbeacon is doing. Brian feels that by doing this, he'll be able to leapfrog Redbeacon and become the preferred provider for people using the Internet to find local service providers. Comment on the wisdom of Brian's strategy.

5. Three years ago, Chris Dees launched a medical products company that specializes in providing products for people with diabetes. His company is number one in its industry. Recently, a couple of competitors have entered the picture, and Chris is wondering if it is worth the fight to remain number one. In terms of firm growth, what advantages are there to being the market leader?

6. Kyle Simms just succeeded his father as the CEO of a consumer products firm in Mission Viejo, California. Prior to returning to the family business, Kyle had spent 11 years at Procter & Gamble in Cincinnati. Kyle's dad built a solid company, but over the past five years, its growth was flat. Kyle wants to grow the company, but at the same time, doesn't want to disturb its healthy culture or overshoot its ability to manage its growth. Kyle's question to you is, "How do I manage this careful balance?" What would you tell him?

7. Sarah Jeffers lives in Austin, Texas, where she has owned a graphics design company for 3 years. She spends 12 hours a day at work micromanaging every aspect of her business, yet she still can't get the business to grow. Talk to Sarah about what needs to take place for her business to move from the early growth stage to

the continuous growth stage of its organizational life cycle.

8. Take a second look at Windspire, the subject of the "You Be the VC 1.1" feature. Imagine you just read an article that said that the founders of Windspire have decided to expand beyond wind-powered energy, and will add full solar energy products to its limited product line. Comment on the wisdom of this strategy.

9. Meredith Colella is a food products engineer who has developed an innovative approach for the packaging of meat. Her approach will extend the shelf life of most meat products by about 30 percent. Meredith is getting ready to try to sell the idea to investors. What could Meredith tell the investors that would give them confidence that she is prepared to cope with the challenges of rapid growth?

10. Spend some time studying PurBlu Beverages, the subject of the student-initiated business profiled at the beginning of the chapter. In what ways have PurBlu Beverages' business practices and its strategic decisions helped limit the impact of the managerial capacity problem?

11. Tracy Gibbons owns a sports apparel company in Columbia, South Carolina. She just attended a seminar where one of the speakers said, "Participating in business partnerships can help firms lessen the impact of the managerial capacity problem." Tracy's not sure what the speaker meant by that statement. Can you help Tracy understand how participating in business partnerships can help firms lessen the impact of the managerial capacity problem?

12. Collin Ryan owns an electronics firm in central Michigan. As a result of some innovative new products that his company plans to roll out over the next two to three years, he expects a substantial increase in sales. To gear up for the increase in sales, Collin needs to hire 35 to 50 new employees. What hazards does a company like Collin's run into when it needs to hire a large number of new employees quickly? What alternatives, if any, would Collin have to hiring a large number of new employees?

13. Imagine you have a friend who has created a new board game. A prototyping lab in the College of Engineering where your friend goes to college made him a prototype of the game, which he took to a trade

show and got an enthusiastic response. He even obtained orders for 2,000 copies of the game. When you asked your friend how he plans to pay for the initial production run of the game, he said that he plans to bootstrap his company and will pay for everything from his profits. Does your friend have a good sense of the financial implications of launching a new product into the marketplace? What scenario is more likely to play out for your friend?

14. Spend some time familiarizing yourself with Driptech, the subject of the "You Be the VC 13.1" feature. Reacquaint yourself with the four specific "Day-to-Day

Challenges of Growing a Firm" outlined in the chapter. Comment on how each of these challenges may test Driptech's ability to successfully experience growth.

15. Look at the Web site of Scuba Toys (www.scubatoys.com). As you'll see, this firm makes a wide range of products for all types of water sports. Spend some time familiarizing yourself with Scuba Toys' products and its business model. Scuba Toys is about to launch an aggressive growth strategy. Write a one-page set of recommendations for Scuba Toys that outlines some of the issues it should be aware of as it launches its growth initiative.

YOU BE THE VC 13.1

Company: **Driptech**

Web: www.driptech.com
Twitter: Driptech
Facebook: Driptech

Business Idea: Manufacture and sell affordable, water efficient irrigation systems for small-plot farmers in developing nations.

Pitch: In many developing countries, farmers have no means to grow crops during periods of low rainfall or drought. Often, a farmer gets a crop during a season of good rainfall, but that season may be followed by several seasons of low rainfall or drought. The drip-irrigation systems that are sold locally are typically too expensive for subsistence farmers to buy. As a result, when rains come sporadically, food irrigation is often used, which is an inefficient way to irrigate crops and wastes water.

Driptech, which is a for-profit social venture, was founded to address this global problem. Its founder, Peter Frykman, developed Driptech's core solution as part of a graduate class at Stanford University—Entrepreneurial Design for Extreme Affordability. Following a trip to Ethiopia, Frykman realized small farms need cheap, low-maintenance, drip irrigation systems to reduce effort and to conserve water. To achieve this goal, Frykman and his team developed a drip irrigation system that consists of low-cost laser-punched plastic tubes linked to a water tank. Gravity drives water through the tubing and to the plants' roots from the holes. Simple tap valves control the flow of water. The entire system can be installed and maintained by an individual farmer.

The Driptech system is about one-fourth the cost of a traditional drip irrigation system, which Driptech hopes will spur widespread adoption. The secret sauce that allows Driptech to provide such a low price-point is in the innovative way the system is designed and manufactured. Its proprietary technology uses the same machines that make plastic carry bags to punch precision holes in plastic tubing (which is the heart of Driptech's system). There are thousands of these machines across the world. This allows Driptech's systems to be manufactured near the point of sale, rather than from a central location, which economizes on labor and transportation costs. Traditional drip-irrigation systems are made in specialized factories and need skilled technicians. In addition, the Driptech system is made from fewer parts than traditional drip-irrigation systems and takes less effort to install.

There are vast worldwide markets for the Driptech system, which is most appropriate for small farms. In India alone, 86 percent of farmers farm less than two hectares (1 hectare is about 2.5 acres). The relationship between farmers and the size of their farms is similar in China. Driptech asserts that by investing $20 in its drip-irrigation system, a farmer could recover five times that much in increased crop production in a single year. Driptech's systems will be sold by the company and through NGOs working to improve agricultural practices in developing countries.

Q&A: Based on the material covered in this chapter, what questions would you ask the firm's founders before making your funding decision? What answers would satisfy you?

Decision: If you had to make your decision on just the information provided in the pitch and on the company's Web site, would you fund this company? Why or why not?

YOU BE THE VC 13.2

Company: CleanFish

Web: www.cleanfish.com
Twitter: CleanFishInc
Facebook: Clean Fish Alliance

Business Idea: Identify the best seafood fishermen and farmers, help them brand their products, and match their brands with discerning chefs, restaurant managers, and consumers who are looking for sustainable and healthy seafood products.

Pitch: Increasingly consumers, whether dining at a restaurant or shopping at a store, are asking if the seafood they're buying is safe and where it comes from. This growing sentiment is causing restaurants, hotels, and grocery stores to sharpen their focus on obtaining seafood from certified sustainable, responsible fisheries and aquaculture farms. Marriott International, for example, recently launched a sustainable seafood program called "Future Fish," making it the first large global hotel chain to adopt such a policy. The program will influence how chefs in the company's 780 full-service hotels purchase their seafood, what types of seafood they buy, and how they'll market their seafood to their customers. Guests may also notice new types of seafood on hotel menus—or a certain type of fish that's missing because it's not deemed sustainable.

CleanFish, which is working with Marriot on its efforts, was founded to help facilitate just this type of initiative. The company advised ecoconscious fishermen, fish farms, and wild fisheries on ways to better manage their fishing operations, so their product can be certified as sustainable and will be more appealing to chefs,

consumers, and companies like Marriott. CleanFish helps the best producers brand their fish, so their fish will be clearly identifiable, and then find markets for the fish under the umbrella of the CleanFish brand and reputation. This approach allows CleanFish to add value at both ends of the value chain for fish. At the producer end, the company provides training and branding assistance. At the consumer end, the company provides assurance that only the best quality sustainable seafood will carry the CleanFish designation.

As part of what it does, CleanFish chronicles the stories of the origins of great-tasting sustainable fish and the fishermen and others who are part of the story. It carries those stories to the chefs and consumers of fish in a celebration of the wonderful taste and nutritional benefit of artisan-grown fish. Through these stories, a chef can tell a patron the history of a particular fish that's on his or her menu (assuming the fish carries the CleanFish certification), where the fish comes from, and the circumstances surrounding how the fish is raised and brought to market.

Q&A: Based on the material covered in this chapter, what questions would you ask the firm's founders before making your funding decision? What answers would satisfy you?

Decision: If you had to make your decision on just the information provided in the pitch and on the company's Web site, would you fund this company? Why or why not?

CASE 13.1

Redbeacon: Pursuing a Measured, Yet Promising Path to Growth

Web: www.redbeacon.com
Twitter: Redbeacon
Facebook: Redbeacon

Bruce R. Barringer, *Oklahoma State University*
R. Duane Ireland, *Texas A&M University*

Introduction

Need to get a faucet fixed? Need to find a personal trainer? Need to hire a carpenter for a home repair? Think about how people normally find service providers to meet these and similar needs. They

either ask or friend or go straight to a search engine to start sorting through possibilities. Once they've jotted down several potential choices, they start calling around to see who's available and how much it will cost.

(continued)

Redbeacon, which launched in September 2009, was founded to make this process more efficient. You can log onto Redbeacon's Web site, describe a job you need done, and Redbeacon will search its massive database of service providers to find three to five companies in your area to bid on your job. You'll look at the quotes, the ratings and reviews from others who have used the provider, the background checks provided by Redbeacon, and make a selection. You then click on one button that says "Book It" and the appointment is set. Redbeacon is free to the user. It makes money by taking a 10 percent commission on the jobs it books for service providers.

Redbeacon is now a fast-growing company that's raised $7.4 million in funding and is expanding its most popular services to the top 50 cities in the United States. But rather than coming out of the gates fast, Redbeacon deliberately got off to a fairly slow start. And while it's now expanding rapidly in certain areas, part of the company is still growing slowly as it continues to get to know its users and tests and retests the usability of its site.

2009 TechCrunch50

Redbeacon's approach is distinctive in the local service provider space. For people who need a plumber or electrician, and want to browse through multiple choices, Redbeacon isn't for them. Instead, it's aimed at customers who want a more streamlined approach. By providing its customers only four to five bids, it solves for them the paradox of choice. The customer who makes the request will also know that the four to five bidders are interested in the job and what they'll charge. In contrast, when calling names from a Google or yellowpages.com search, it may take several tries and considerable time before a customer is able to find a good match with a service provider.

Redbeacon's launch coincided with the TechCrunch50 business plan competition in September 2009. TechCrunch was a prestigious business plan competition that ran from 2007 to 2009. It started as TechCrunch40, with the idea of finding the best Web 2.0 companies to place in front of the industry's most influential investors, companies, and press. Out of the hundreds of companies that applied and 50 that were chosen to present at the 2009 conference, Redbeacon came out on top. Winning the competition catapulted Redbeacon's stature and attracted the attention of a number of prominent investors. Interestingly, rather than jumping at the chance to get funding, Redbeacon's cofounders Ethan Anderson and Aaron Lee resisted. They listened politely and made numerous contacts, but did not pursue funding. Their growth plans hinged on proving their concept and finding the right product market fit before pursuing investment capital.

Early Growth Strategy

Immediately after TechCrunch50, in September 2009, Redbeacon signed up 1,000 service providers in the San Francisco Bay Area and launched its service. Even though they were a Web-based firm, they confined their launch to San Francisco, so they could closely monitor how their users were using the site and solicit feedback from local service providers. The initial response was very positive, and the service seemed to be working. One hundred percent of its users were getting quotes for jobs that they submitted in the top 100 categories. Most quotes were received within one day.

In late 2009 and early 2010, Redbeacon added Seattle and Washington, DC, as locations for its services. It picked San Francisco and Seattle as its west coast points of entry because they are tech-savvy communities. It picked Washington, DC, because it's a transient city with people coming and going, which translates into individuals and families needing home repair and related jobs done. They also wanted to test their service in an entirely different part of the country. All this time, Redbeacon persistently collected data on what its users liked and didn't like, and continued to test and retest the usability of its site.

Financially, Redbeacon was totally self-funded at this point, which covered the September 2009 to mid-2010 period. It's only funding, other than revenues, was $200,000—$150,000 from the founders and $50,000 from winning the TechCrunch50 competition. The company also maintained a low burn rate, even though it was growing. Its staff was small and it operated on a shoestring.

Redbeacon learned several things about its service and its users as a result of its careful attention to detail. First, the ideal number of bids to pass along is four. Beyond that, its bookings did not go up. Apparently, having a smaller number rather than a larger number of choices actually helps people make a decision to proceed. Second, on average, its customers saved 40 percent on jobs by using Redbeacon. Service providers are more competitive when they know they're bidding against others. Third, legitimacy helps service providers win jobs. As a result, Redbeacon implemented a badge system to allow service providers to display specific badges on their profiles once they met certain requirements. A service provider can display a safety badge, for example, by passing a full background check. Similarly, if a service provider is in good standing with a nationally recognized business group, like the Better Business Bureau, it can display a different badge. Finally, Redbeacon found that the three most requested services through its site were maids (or housekeepers), handymen, and personal trainers.

Redbeacon's Approach

Step 1	Step 2	Step 3
Request a local search	Compare prices from qualified professionals	Schedule the job online

First Funding

In late summer 2010, Redbeacon felt it had sufficient data to validate that its concept was sound. At this point it sought venture capital funding to scale the business at a national level. It's solicitation for capital attracted substantial interest, and it eventually raised $7.4 million from Mayfield Fund and Venrock, two top-tier venture capital firms. In an interview focused on Redbeacon's early growth phase and initial funding, cofounder Ethan Anderson said Redbeacon chose MayField Fund and Venrock because the two firms "showed a lot of interest and passion for its space, its opportunity, and its team."

Current Growth Strategy

Currently, Redbeacon has a two-pronged growth strategy. First, it's rolling out its most popular services, such as maid, handyman, and personal trainer services, in the top 50 cities in the United States. Second, it's holding back on lesser demanded services and is rolling them out on a city-by-city basis. The reason it's holding back on lesser demanded service, like DJ and wedding planner services, is to collect more data and to build its database. Redbeacon has an interesting way of attracting new service providers. It's building a database of service providers, like wedding planners, in cities where it isn't currently active in anticipation of future growth. When it gets a request from someone who doesn't know that Redbeacon isn't active in his or her community, it queries its database to see if it has identified anyone in that area that can do the job. If it has, it makes a cold call to the service provider, explains what Redbeacon is, and says, "This one's on us. If you'd like to bid on the job, we'll handle the bidding process, and if the customer bites, we'll hook the two of you up." Redbeacon doesn't collect a dime. The only stipulation it makes is that the next time it directs work to the same service provider it will require the service provider to enroll in its program.

Redbeacon is also adding more social components to its service. It now allows users to show the bids they receive to their Facebook friends, and allows their Facebook friends to give a thumbs up or a thumbs down on bidders. For example, someone could show their Facebook friends bids from five wedding photographers. Their friends could then look at the photographers' profiles, which usually include examples of their work. They could then help the person who requested the bids pick the wedding photographer to hire.

Future Initiatives

Redbeacon has been reluctant to enter the space currently occupied by Groupon and LivingSocial, which offer daily deals. It sees itself as having a different clientele. Groupon and LivingSocial offer daily deals from service providers, such as restaurants, massage therapists, and hair salons, which can handle multiple customers generated through the deal. Redbeacon sees itself as a platform for matching users and service providers on a one-on-one basis. Its providers tend to be smaller companies that couldn't handle a sudden avalanche of work. As a result, it doesn't see itself anytime soon offering daily deals, such as 50 percent off of a specific plumber's services.

An initiative Redbeacon is actively pursuing is establishing partnerships with the three major search engines. This is a somewhat surprising approach, since most observers see the search engines as Redbeacon's chief rivals. The most common way that people find local service providers is through search engines like Google, Yahoo!, and Bing. Rather than view these companies as competitors, Redbeacon is trying to partner with them. The pitch it's making to Google, Yahoo!, and Bing is that when a person is searching for a local service provider, like a plumber or electrician, rather than just serving them up a list of names and paid ads, it should include a tab that will direct the searcher to Redbeacon to get actual bids for a job. Redbeacon would, of course, then share the revenues generated from those referrals with the appropriate search engine.

Redbeacon currently has several partnerships with moms' groups established through Big Tent. Big Tent (www.bigtent.com) is a service that helps people organize groups. Moms are big users of Redbeacon because they usually oversee their families' homes, and, as a result, deal with their service-related problems. Redbeacon has established co-branding relationships with several moms' groups. Its service is displayed on their respective Web sites, and the site receives an affiliate fee for each Redbeacon job that originates through the site. Redbeacon is looking for similar strategic relationships.

Discussion Questions

1. Look at the material in this chapter under the heading "Preparing for Growth." Evaluate the degree to which Redbeacon has been sensitive to the three issues under this heading.

2. Look at Figure 13.2, which depicts the organizational life cycle. Which stage of the organizational life cycle is Redbeacon currently in? What issues will the founders of Redbeacon have to be sensitive to during this particular stage? What issues, if any, do you think will be problematic for Redbeacon?

3. The section of the chapter labeled "Day-to-Day Challenges of Growing a Firm" lists four primary challenges: cash flow management, price stability, quality control, and capital constraints. Briefly comment on how Redbeacon has dealt with each of these challenges. Which of the four challenges do you think will pose the greatest challenge for the founders of Redbeacon moving forward?

4. Evaluate Redbeacon's future initiatives. Do you think Redbeacon should be more open to developing a parallel Groupon or LivingSocial type of strategy and offer daily deals featuring local service providers? Do you agree with its overtures to Google, Yahoo!, and Bing? How likely is it that one of these companies will partner with Redbeacon? Finally, do you think it's a good strategy for Redbeacon to develop co-branding strategies with organizations such as the moms' groups as mentioned in the case?

(continued)

Application Questions

1. Many observers have noted that Thumbtack.com, a Redbeacon rival, is rolling out its nationwide service more quickly than Redbeacon is. Do you think Redbeacon has been too timid in terms of the pace of its growth? Does Redbeacon risk falling behind if it doesn't expand as rapidly as Thumbtack.com?

2. Make a list of five things that start-ups can learn from Redbeacon regarding how to manage the early growth of an entrepreneurial firm.

Sources: Redbeacon, www.redbeacon.com (accessed April 8, 2011); Ethan Anderson and Jason Calacanis, This Week in Startups pod cast, Episode 130 (accessed April 8, 2011, originally posted on April 8, 2011).

CASE 13.2

What Entrepreneurs Can Learn from Chamillionaire

Web: www.chamillionaire.com
Twitter: Chamillionaire
Facebook: Chamillionaire

Bruce R. Barringer, *Oklahoma State University*

R. Duane Ireland, *Texas A&M University*

Introduction

There are many similarities between music and entrepreneurship. To be successful, musicians must have talent, establish a brand, build a following, find distribution for their product, and handle their money properly. Entrepreneurs must also do these things. If they don't, they won't grow their firms and reach their full potential.

Hakeem Seriki, better known as Chamillionaire, is a Grammy Award–winning rap artist. He's also interested in technology and entrepreneurship, and frequently attends tech-related business events. He's open about his interest in business, and asks questions and shares his thoughts at the events he attends. He's also given several interviews about how he built his career and his interest in entrepreneurship. The interviews are riveting. Chamillionaire comes across as an authentic, inquisitive, hard-working person whose success is anything other than accidental. In fact, the way he built his music career provides lessons not only for other musicians, but for entrepreneurs.

Chamillionaire began his career in the late 1990s selling CDs from the trunk of his car. As an independent artist, he built a following of hundreds of thousands of devoted fans. He signed with Universal Records in 2005. In 2007, he won a Grammy Award for Best Rap Performance by a Duo or Group for "Ridin." He is currently a rapper, singer, record executive, and entrepreneur.

The following are 10 takeaways from a synthesis of Chamillionaire's public comments. A table at the end of this feature provides the URLs for two of Chamillionaire's best interviews. If you listen to the interviews, you'll hear the sincerity in Chamillionaire's voice. Of course, you may not agree with everything he says; but, we believe you'll be struck by his business and entrepreneurial savvy and the heartfelt way in which he expresses his views.

1. Authenticity

Chamillionaire has a strong sense of who he is and the type of person he wants to be. These convictions govern the things he does and doesn't do. For example, he interacts frequently with his fans and finds tangible ways to show his appreciation. He also believes that his most devoted fans are interested in him first. If he can establish a rapport with them, their interest in buying his music will follow.

Chamillionaire leaves money on the table at times. He's been asked several times to appear in reality television shows; to date, he has declined each of these opportunities. He says that not every dollar is a good dollar. He believes that appearing in reality television shows would hurt his brand, so he doesn't do it. At times, he's had to guard his authenticity. For example, at one point a Web site he was involved with started signing his name to blog posts. He said "no—my fans will know that's not coming from me. No matter how busy I am, if something needs to go out, contact me and I'll write it."

2. Failure, Trial and Error, and Confidence

As a young musician, Chamillionaire describes himself as the silent kid who sat in the corner and watched things. He'd watch the mistakes rap stars made, and think, "If I'm ever at that level, I'm not going to do that." He'd also listened to all kinds of music, and says his style is bits and pieces of others. He started by selling mixed tapes. He put up a Web site and did creative things to drive traffic to his site. He kept a list of music stores with addresses and phone numbers and would periodically call the stores and ask how many of his CDs they needed. He knew that their answer would hinge solely on how many people had come into the stores and asked for the CDs.

Not everything he did led to the outcomes Chamillionaire desired. He relied primarily on feedback from fans to discern what was working and what wasn't. He jumped on new technologies. Early on, he used a Web-based service called SHOUTcast, which was an online radio that allowed him to play his songs, interrupt a song, do a commercial break, and connect with fans. He believes that confidence comes from trial and error. "All the failures that people get so scared of is what I did. It made me confident about what would work. Confidence doesn't come from being a 'know-it-all,' it's because I've done this 10 times already."

3. Learning

Chamillionaire is a sponge. As a kid, he says he got upset because he wanted to learn faster. When performing, he focuses on connecting with his audience, looking into people's eyes to see how they're reacting. He says little things he learns from his audience form his future marketing campaigns. Early in his career, he read every single e-mail message he received, and says he was constantly amazed at the insights he gleaned from fans. Someone would write, "Hey Chamillionaire, the quality of your latest CD wasn't so good," so he'd work hard to bring the next one up.

When listening to feedback, Chamillionaire learned to focus on not necessarily what people thought was good—he says there are a million opinions about what's good—but what people wanted from him. Chamillionaire still does this today. You can get a good sense of how he interacts with his fans and solicits feedback by following him on Twitter.

Chamillionaire

Donna Ward/Abacausa.com/Newscom

4. Marketing Innovation

Early in his career, Chamillionaire did everything he could to capture his fans' e-mail addresses. This was before Facebook and Twitter, so e-mail was the primary method for communicating. Creating his own domain and giving out a @chamillionaire.com e-mail address to anyone who wanted it are creative actions Chamillionaire took. These actions were ways of creating buzz. People saw their friends with a @chamillionaire e-mail address, causing them to want one as well. They'd have to go to Chamillionaire's Web site to get it.

One time Chamillionaire announced that a new CD was going to "drop" at New Year's and put a counter on his Web site counting down the minutes. His fans started calling stores to try to reserve the CD. He'd then get calls from stores asking how they could meet the demand. Sometimes he didn't even have a product when he did things like this but the hype would focus him on what to make.

Periodically, Chamillionaire drops free tracks on Twitter to maintain fan interest. He believes that marketing entails leaps of faith. His first mixed tape was a triple disk. No one was selling triple disks at the time. He had to come up with $30,000 of his own money to do it. The CDs flew off the shelf, allowing him to more than make his money back.

5. Social Media

Chamillionaire is active on the most popular social media platforms. He says "Wherever the masses go, you have to have some kind of presence there." He also wants to be where his audience is. Many of the kids who listen to his music are now on Ustream, a platform that allows people to stream events live on the Internet. So Chamillionaire has become a prolific Ustream user.

The day this case was written (April 2011), Chamillionaire had 828,924 Twitter followers and 325,569 Facebook fans. That's a lot. He often posts everyday things on Twitter and Facebook, in part to let his fans know that it's really him. For instance, he might say something like "Kobe is better than Michael Jordan ever was." These kinds of comments stir the pot and elicit an avalanche of comments from followers. It's mostly good natured and allows Chamillionaire to interact with his fans in an authentic manner. He believes that some artists err by trying to sell their fans at every opportunity.

6. Importance of Good Content

Although Chamillionaire is good at marketing and social media, he is quick to say that the quality of what you're doing—the content—is what ultimately carries the day. He believes people forget that. He says, "You can say all you want about marketing—how many dollars you put behind it, how many people you have on staff—but people ultimately have to like it."

7. Landing a Deal with a Major Record Label

For a musician, landing a deal with a major record label is the equivalent of raising venture capital for an

(continued)

entrepreneur. Chamillionaire didn't approach a major label until he had 3.5 million hits on his Web site and hundreds of thousands of fans. That put him in the driver's seat, rather than the other way around.

He was a little edgy when he approached Universal—the label he eventually signed with. He wore tags from other labels, to show he was in high demand, and said he was perfectly comfortable leaving the negotiations without a deal. It was a risky approach but it worked. His lawyer called him later in the day and asked "What did you say to those guys, this is the best first time deal I've ever seen."

8. Money

Chamillionaire thinks chasing every deal is a mistake. He thinks long term—about the integrity of his brand—in every financial decision. He's also true to his values. For example, he says that he could have made a lot more money over the years on merchandizing, but just couldn't bring himself to do it at times. For example, one company wanted to launch worldwide distribution of T-shirts with his face on the front. He said that he wouldn't want to wear a T-shirt with his face on it. So he didn't take the deal.

He's also learned from watching what he believes are mistakes of others. For example, at one point he was being mentored by an older rapper who bought a $20,000 pinkie ring. He lost it at a club and replaced it with another $20,000 pinkie ring. He said to the guy, "Really—you're going to spend $20,000 on a pinkie ring?"

A problem Chamillionaire sees with money is that "everyone wants to win the lottery." What he means by this is that people search for the big score, the big hit that will make them rich. He says "Sometimes it's about the long tail. You can make a lot of money if you make a small amount of money from lots of people." He says you do this by selling people what they want.

9. Partners

Chamillionaire has had mixed success with partners. He's had public disagreements with Universal, and other partners, such as MySpace. He's partnered with start-ups that are helping musicians get on iTunes and find distribution for their products apart from the major labels. One company he's worked with is TuneCore, a Digital Music platform that allows artists to sell their music online. He believes that all young artists should be familiar with these types of options.

One thing in particular that has frustrated Chamillionaire in working with partners is their tendency to tell him things can't be done. As is the case with most successful entrepreneurs, he says you have to have the self-confidence to push through that and allow your own creativity to come through.

10. The Future

Chamillionaire says he thinks about his future every day. He admires Zynga, the maker of online games like Farmville and Texas Hold'Em Poker. He says the way Zynga is able to engage people and draw them in—in almost an addictive manner—is something that fascinates him. He's looking for ways to use the psychology behind Zynga's approach in the music industry.

Not everything goes smoothly for Chamillionaire. He's open about his desire to split with Universal. He has found that the bureaucracy of working with a large firm has limited his creativity rather than spurred it. He may be better suited to working as an independent artist.

Chamillionaire believes that people who are creating technologies "hold the future of the world in their hands" and he's eager to learn what's next. He attends entrepreneurship and tech events to keep up to date. He says that "for a rapper it's not a cool thing to do." "But I don't want people to see me as just a rapper."

Podcast Interviews with Chamillionaire

Title	Date	URL
This Week in Venture Capital	10/20/10	http://www.youtube.com/watch?v=4x0FPhjl1Kw&list=SL
Stanford Technology Ventures Podcast	11/4/09	http://ecorner.stanford.edu/authorMaterialInfo.html?mid=2278

Discussion Questions

1. For each of the 10 takeaways discussed in this feature, write a short "lesson learned" for entrepreneurs.
2. If you could ask Chamillionaire a series of five follow-up questions, what would the questions be? Briefly describe why you'd ask each question.
3. Which of the 10 takeaways struck you as the most compelling? Explain your answer.
4. Are you surprised that a rap artist is so interested in entrepreneurship and technology? To what degree do you think other musicians might benefit from following Chamillionaire's lead? How about entrepreneurs? Do you think there are things that entrepreneurs can learn from musicians? If so, what do you think those things might be?

Application Questions

1. Why do you think Chamillionaire is speaking out about the importance of technology and entrepreneurship?
2. Listen to one of the interviews with Chamillionaire included in the table. Comment on the interview. List at least three takeaways from the interview not mentioned in this feature.

Sources: Mark Suster and Chamillionaire, This Week in Venture Capital, Episode 26, http://www.youtube.com/watch?v=4x0 FPhjl1Kw&list=SL (accessed April 10, 2011, originally posted on October 20, 2010); Quincy Jones III and Chamillionaire, Stanford Technology Ventures Podcast, http://ecorner.stanford.edu/ authorMaterialInfo.html?mid=2278 (accessed April 10, 2011, originally posted on November 4, 2009).

ENDNOTES

1. P. Stenholm, "Innovative Behavior as a Moderator of Growth Intentions," *Journal of Small Business Management* 49, no. 2 (2011): 233–51; S. Shane, *The Illusions of Entrepreneurship* (New Haven, CT: Yale University, 2008)

2. "*Inc.* 500/5000," *Inc.*, www.inc.com, December 2010.

3. SBA, *The Small Business Economy* (Washington: D.C.: U.S. Government Printing Office, 2010), www.sba.gov/sites/default/files/sb_econ2010.pdf.

4. N. Malchow-Moller, B. Schjerning, and A. Sorensen, "Entrepreneurship, Job Creation and Wage Growth," *Small Business Economics* 36, no 1. (2010): 15–32; W. J. Baumol and R. J. Strom, "Entrepreneurship and Economic Growth," *Strategic Entrepreneurship Journal* 1, nos. 3–4 (2007): 233–38.

5. D. Packard, *The HP Way: How Bill Hewlett and I Built Our Company*, ed. D. Kirby with Karen Lewis (New York: HarperBusiness, 1996).

6. Packard, *The HP Way*.

7. C. Keen and H. Etemad, "The Impact of Entrepreneurial Capital and Rapidly Growing Firms: The Canadian Example," *International Journal of Entrepreneurship and Small Business* 12, no. 3 (2011): 273–89.

8. IBISWorld homepage, www.ibisworld.com (accessed April 29, 2011).

9. nPost homepage, www.npost.com (accessed November 19, 2008).

10. D. Christopher, *The Pampered Chef* (New York: Doubleday, 2005).

11. J. Collins, *Good to Great* (New York: Collins Books, 2001).

12. F. G. Alberti, S. Sciascia, C. Tripodi, and F. Visconti, "The Entrepreneurial Growth of Firms Located in Clusters: A Cross-Case Study," *International Journal of Technology Management* 54, no. 1 (2011): 53–79.

13. M. Hughes, R. E. Morgan, R. D. Ireland, and P. Hughes, "Network Behaviors, Social Capital, and Organisational Learning in High-Growth Entrepreneurial Firms," *International Journal of Entrepreneurship and Small Business* 12, no. 3. (2011): 257–72; A. Macpherson and R. Holt, "Knowledge, Learning and Small Firm Growth:

A Systematic Review of the Evidence," *Research Policy* 36, no. 2 (2007): 172–92.

14. J. Welch, "Growth Initiatives," *Executive Excellence* 16, no. 6 (1999): 8–9.

15. "Compilation of Turnover Cost Studies," Sasha Corporation, www.sashacorp.com (accessed May 2, 2011).

16. J. M. Shulman, R. A. K. Cox, and T. T. Stallkamp, "The Strategic Entrepreneurial Growth Model," *Competitiveness Review* 21, no. 1 (2011): 29–46.

17. Ladies Who Launch, http://applications.ladies wholaunch.com/featuredlady.cfm/featureid/76 (accessed November 17, 2008).

18. M. Gerber, *The E-Myth Revisited* (New York: HarperCollins, 2004).

19. Ladies Who Launch.

20. Entrepreneur, "When Success Isn't Enough," www. entrepreneur.com/magazine/entrepreneur/2007/november/185574.html (accessed November 19, 2008, originally posted on November 2007).

21. C. C. Julian, "Product Adaptation in International Joint Ventures: An Empirical Investigation," *International Journal of Trade and Global Markets* 4, no. 2 (2011): 50–65; A. Nair and W. R. Boulton, "Innovation-Oriented Operations Strategy Typology and Stage-Based Model," *International Journal of Operations and Production Management* 28, no. 8 (2008): 748–71.

22. E. T. Penrose, *The Theory of the Growth of the Firm*, 3rd ed. (Oxford: Oxford University Press, 1995).

23. E. T. Penrose, *The Theory of the Growth of the Firm* (New York: John Wiley & Sons, 1959).

24. C. A. Un and A. Montoro-Sanchez, "R&D Investment and Entrepreneurial Technological Capabilities: Existing Capabilities as Determinants of New Capabilities," *International Journal of Technology Management* 54, no. 1 (2011): 29–52; J. J. Reuer and R. Ragozzino, "Adverse Selection and M&A Design: The Roles of Alliances and IPOs," *Journal of Economic Behavior and Organization* 66, no. 2 (2008): 195–212.

25. Penrose, *The Theory of the Growth of the Firm* (1959).

26. D. Bartholomew, "The Perfect Pitch," *Priority*, December/January, 2004.

Getting Personal *with* PHONE HALO

Cofounders:

CHRIS HERBERT
BS, College of Engineering,
University of California, Santa Barbara,
spring 2007

CHRISTIAN SMITH
BS, College of Engineering,
University of California, Santa Barbara,
spring 2007

Dialogue *with*
Chris Herbert

CURRENTLY IN MY SMARTPHONE
A State of Trance with Armin van Buuren

MY ADVICE FOR NEW ENTREPRENEURS
Make sure your team can build and ship the product without outside investment.

WHAT I DO WHEN I'M NOT WORKING
Surfing, kitesurfing, studying Japanese, and hanging out with friends

FIRST ENTREPRENEURIAL EXPERIENCE
Building a haunted house

MY BIGGEST SURPRISE AS AN ENTREPRENEUR
If you're on the brink of failure, you're also on the brink of success.

BEST ADVICE I'VE RECEIVED
Know what you don't know.

CHAPTER 14

Strategies for *Firm Growth*

PHONE HALO
Pivoting to Pursue New Strategies for Growth

Web: www.phonehalo.com
Twitter: PhoneHalo
Facebook: Phone Halo

In 2008, Chris Herbert wanted to enter the business plan competition at the University of California, Santa Barbara (UCSB). He and several friends were brainstorming business ideas in the Carrillo Dining Commons and were about to give up when a friend walked in, dejected because he had lost his mobile phone. Herbert thought, "That's it. Let's develop a device that prevents people from losing their mobile phones."

Herbert partnered with two friends, Christian Smith and Tyler Crain, to flesh out the idea. All three were engineering students at UCSB. They entered their preliminary idea, of a bi-directional keychain sensor that sends an alert when you've moved a certain distance from your mobile phone, into their college's business plan competition. They lost. Undeterred, the three continued to work on the idea. The following year they entered the same competition, which is hosted by USCB's College of Engineering, and took first place. All three team members graduated in May 2009, and rejected job offers to work on the idea full time, which is now named Phone Halo. They literally worked out of a garage in downtown Santa Barbara, building the initial prototype of their device. To develop the Phone Halo system, the three founders had to learn on the fly in regard to the technical aspects of building an iPhone app and a hardware device that would communicate seamlessly with each other. Herbert's training was in optical fibers, but he refocused on Bluetooth and the wireless elements of the Phone Halo system. Crain's training was in computer algorithms, and he refocused on software and application development. Smith's training was in manufacturing engineering, and he refocused on industrial design.

The first full prototype of the Phone Halo system was ready in October 2009. The three founders took Phone Halo to the International Consumer Electronics Show in January 2010, and received a big boost. Their app and device were written up in the *Wall Street Journal* and in several blogs. The thing that intrigued the

LEARNING OBJECTIVES

After studying this chapter you should be ready to:

1. Explain the difference between internal growth strategies and external growth strategies.

2. Identify the keys to effective new product development.

3. Explain the common reasons new products fail.

4. Discuss a market penetration strategy.

5. Explain what an "international new venture" is and describe its importance to entrepreneurial ventures.

6. Discuss the objectives a company can achieve by acquiring another business.

7. Identify a promising acquisition candidate's characteristics.

8. Explain "licensing" and how it can be used as a growth strategy.

9. Explain "strategic alliances" and describe the difference between technological alliances and marketing alliances.

10. Explain "joint ventures" and describe the difference between a scale joint venture and a link joint venture.

press and the bloggers the most is how the system works. The app is available through the BlackBerry and Android online markets, and the hardware device is available at Amazon.com. Once the app is downloaded, it uses Bluetooth to wirelessly connect to the Phone Halo hardware device. The device can be attached to anything—your keychain, wallet, purse, or even to your wrist. If you're carrying the device and it gets about 30 feet from your phone, both the device and your phone will make a sound, to alert you that they've been separated. Your phone will then text you its GPS coordinates allowing you to find it if following the sound doesn't work. You can even have your phone's GPS coordinates e-mailed to your friends or posted on one of your social networking sites. The app is free and the hardware device costs about $60.

Phone Halo received another boost when the cofounders presented their product at Demo Spring 2011. Demo is a technology conference that focuses on showcasing new products from both start-ups and established companies. The Phone Halo system was a hit, and even won one of the conference's prestigious awards. It also won the *Popular Mechanics* Editor's Choice Award in 2011. In the photo, Hubert is on the left and Smith is on the right, holding memorabilia acknowledging the award.

Although Phone Halo's cofounders were buoyed by the publicity they generated at the 2010 International Consumer Electronics Show and Demo Spring 2010, 2010 was a tough year for the company. One of the three cofounders, Tyler Crain, left the company to take a fellowship in France. That was a blow because Crain was Phone Halo's main software engineer. Jacques Habra, a businessperson the Phone Halo team met the second year they entered the UCSB business plan competition, had been helping with business development but was moving on. The funding environment was also tough. It was particularly difficult to get Phone Halo's hardware device into big-box stores, like Best Buy, where they'd have visibility and shelf space. Big-box stores are very demanding in terms of the requirements they place on suppliers. For example, to have its product in Best Buy, Phone Halo would have to maintain inventory and build out its own supply chain, so it could deliver product to Best Buy in an expedient manner. Phone Halo didn't have the financial resources to go this route.

In late 2010, Phone Halo, now led by Herbert and Smith, pivoted and adopted a licensing model to move the firm forward. Instead of producing the Phone Halo mobile phone app and hardware device themselves, they would license their technology to third parties. Right out of the gates, they landed a licensing deal with Cobra Electronics, a leading manufacturer of electronics products. Cobra is now producing the Cobra Phone Tag, a Bluetooth-enabled tracking system for mobile phones and other valuables, powered by Phone Halo's technology. In early 2011, *Popular Mechanics* awarded Cobra Electronics one of its Editor's Choice Awards for the Cobra Phone Tag. Phone Halo is now seeking additional licensing opportunities to accelerate its growth.[1]

Phone Halo's experience is not unusual. While many young entrepreneurial firms are able to build on their initial strategy for growth, others, like Phone Halo, pivot when their initial strategy isn't working and pursue one or more new avenues for growth. In this chapter, we discuss the most common strategies firms use to grow. The growth strategies are divided into internal strategies for growth and external strategies for growth, as shown in Figure 14.1.

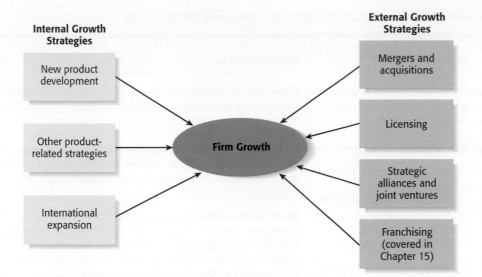

FIGURE 14.1
Internal and External
Growth Strategies

INTERNAL GROWTH STRATEGIES

Internal growth strategies involve efforts taken within the firm itself, such as new product development, other product-related strategies, and international expansion, with the purpose of increasing sales revenue and profitability. Many businesses, such as ModCloth, Zipcar, and Zappos, are growing through internal growth strategies. The distinctive attribute of internally generated growth is that a business relies on its own competencies, expertise, business practices, and employees. Internally generated growth is often called **organic growth** because it does not rely on outside intervention. Almost all companies grow organically during the early stages of their organizational life cycles.

Effective though it can be, there are limits to internal growth. As a company enters the middle and later stages of its life cycle, sustaining growth strictly through internal means becomes more challenging. Because of this, the fear is that a company will "hit the wall" in terms of growth and will experience flat or even declining sales. This can happen when a company has the same product or service that it's trying to sell to the same list of potential buyers. Companies in this predicament need to either expand their client list, add new products or services to complement their existing ones, or find new avenues to growth. Sometimes companies face this challenge through no fault of their own. For example in 2009 Wing Zone, a restaurant franchise, was experiencing flat sales in that prospective franchisees couldn't get financing because of the credit crunch. To work around this challenge, the company decided to expand internationally. In November 2010 it opened its first international franchise in Panama City, Panama. Several other franchise organizations, including Massage Heights, Molly Maids, and fire and water cleanup companies PuroClean and Servpro, have recently expanded internationally for the same reason.[2]

Some start-ups, to avoid quickly hitting the wall in terms of growth, configure their initial products or services in ways that have built in growth potential. This tactic is illustrated in the "Savvy Entrepreneurial Firm" feature shown on p. 491. SwitchFlops is an example of a company that has "built-in" avenues for future growth as a result of the unique nature of its product and how it's configured.

We list the distinct advantages and disadvantages of internal growth strategies in Table 14.1.

> **LEARNING OBJECTIVE**
> 1. Explain the difference between internal growth strategies and external growth strategies.

TABLE 14.1   ADVANTAGES AND DISADVANTAGES OF INTERNAL GROWTH STRATEGIES

Advantages	Disadvantages
Incremental, even-paced growth. A firm that grows at an even pace can continually adjust to changing environmental conditions to fine-tune its strategies over time. In contrast, a firm that doubles its size overnight through a merger or acquisition is making a much larger commitment at a single point in time.	**Slow form of growth.** In some industries, an incremental, even-paced approach toward growth does not permit a firm to develop competitive economies of scale fast enough. In addition, in some industries, it may not be possible for a firm to develop sufficient resources to remain competitive. A high level of merger and acquisition activity typically characterizes these industries.
Provides maximum control. Internal growth strategies allow a firm to maintain control over the quality of its products and services during the growth process. In contrast, firms that grow through collaborative forms of growth, such as alliances or joint ventures, must share the oversight function with their business partners.	**Need to develop new resources.** Some internal growth strategies, such as new product development, require a firm to be innovative and develop new resources. While internal innovation has many positive attributes, it is typically a slow, expensive, and risky strategy.
Preserves organizational culture. Firms emphasizing internal growth are not required to blend their organizational culture with another organization. As a result, the venture can grow under the auspices of a clearly understood, unified corporate culture.	**Investment in a failed internal effort can be difficult to recoup.** Internal growth strategies, such as new product development, run the risk that a new product or service idea may not sell, making it difficult to recoup the development cost the firm incurred.
Encourages internal entrepreneurship. Firms that grow via internal growth strategies are looking for new ideas from within the business rather than from outside stakeholders. This approach encourages a climate of internal entrepreneurship and innovation.	**Adds to industry capacity.** Some internal growth strategies add to industry capacity, and this can ultimately help force industry profitability down. For example, a restaurant chain that grows through geographic expansion may ultimately force industry profitability down by continuing to open new restaurants in an already crowded market.
Allows firms to promote from within. Firms emphasizing internal growth strategies have the advantage of being able to promote within their own organizations. The availability of promotional opportunities within a firm is a powerful tool for employee motivation.	

New Product Development

New product development involves designing, producing, and selling new products (or services) as a means of increasing firm revenues and profitability. In many fast-paced industries, new product development is a competitive necessity. For example, the average product life cycle in the computer software industry is 14 to 16 months, at the most. Just thinking of how quickly we are introduced to new computers, new iPads, and related products quickly highlights for us how rapidly products change in this industry! Because of these rapid changes, to remain competitive, software companies must always have new products in their pipelines. For some companies, continually developing new products is the essence of their existence.

Although developing new products can result in substantial rewards, it is a high-risk strategy. The key is developing innovative new products that aren't simply "me-too" products that are entering already crowded markets. When properly executed though, there is tremendous upside potential to developing new products and/or services. Many biotech and pharmaceutical companies, for example, have developed products that not only improve the quality of life for their customers but also provide reliable revenue streams. In many cases, the products are patented, meaning that no one else can make them, at least until the patents expire. Successful new products can also provide sufficient cash flow to fund a company's operations and provide resources to support developing additional new products. For example, Amgen, a large and historically profitable biotech company, has two stellar pharmaceutical products,

SwitchFlops: How to Create Built-In Avenues for Future Growth

Web: www.lindsay-phillips.com
Twitter: SwitchFlops
Facebook: SwitchFlops

One thing that savvy growth-minded start-ups do is configure their products or services in ways that have built-in growth potential. Producing "one-off" products or services leads to limited growth potential. Instead, it's best to produce products and services that if successful provide natural segues to complementary products and services that can be added later.

SwitchFlops are sandals with interchangeable straps. Lindsay Phillips developed the original idea for these products when enrolled in high school, as part of an art project when she was 16. Amazed by the response, Phillips continued with the project. She started designing functional flops with colorful straps, each adorned by a unique button. She realized that by using a hook and loop fastener on each flop, she could create a shoe that accommodated interchangeable straps. This was the birth of SwitchFlops. A shopper buys one pair of SwitchFlops sandals, and can then purchase interchangeable straps.

During her college years, Phillips fine-tuned her design, merchandising, and manufacturing skills working summers at Polo Ralph Lauren's leather goods division in New York City. She also traveled to Europe for classes and enrolled in the Semester at Sea program. These later two experiences exposed her to a variety of colors, cultures, and patterns that helped her fashion unique strap designs. A patent on her unique approach was granted in 2004. SwitchFlops made its retail debut in January 2007 at the Surf Expo Trade Show in Orlando, Florida, where it was showcased as a new, creative product.

SwitchFlops started with several basic sandal designs and 10 straps. Most customers bought more than one pair of sandals and several straps allowing them to "customize" their look by trading out sandals and straps. Most customers seemed to enjoy this experience. SwitchFlops' value proposition was both versatility and value.

Today, SwitchFlops sandals cost $49 and the straps cost between $12 and $15 each. To make it fun, the sandals and straps all have names. Sandals include Lilly, Missy Wedge Heel, and Emma. Straps include Annan

Strap, Rowan, Mary Lee, and Casey Strap. There are now multiple SwitchFlops sandals and straps to choose from. Today, SwitchFlops sandals and straps are sold in more than 4,000 stores around the world. Phillips has evolved her footwear line and currently sells ballet flats, wedges, and espadrilles along with sandals and has added shopping bags, scarves, and sandals for children to her firm's product lines.

SwitchFlops sandals benefit from being both fashion-conscious and economical. Instead of owning 10 pairs of sandals, a customer can own two or three, and have multiple "looks" by changing out straps. By making a product (sandals) that is based on buying add-ons (straps), the strategy has also benefited SwitchFlops and helped fuel its growth.

Questions for Critical Thinking

1. As an up-and-coming entrepreneur, what things did Lindsay Phillips do to equip herself to lead a growth-oriented firm?
2. Think of a company that sells a product or service that's similar to SwitchFlops, in that the product or service provides a natural segue to add-on products or services. Briefly explain the product and its built-in avenues for future growth.
3. Of the companies featured in the "You Be the VC" features in the book, which company has a product or service that is best positioned for natural segues for future growth? Explain your answer.
4. Why do you think SwitchFlops has been so successful? Draw lessons from several chapters of the book to formulate your answer.

Sources: Lindsay Phillips Web site, www.lindsay-phillips.com (accessed April 14, 2011); Business Pundit Blog, "SwitchFlops: A Smart, Successful Fashion Startup," www.businesspundit.com/switchflops-a-smart-successful-fashion-startup (accessed April 13, 2011, originally posted on September 8, 2010).

Enbrel and Neupogen. Enbrel is a tumor necrosis factor (TNF) blocker that is used to treat rheumatoid arthritis as well as some related conditions, and Neupogen helps prevent infection in cancer patients undergoing certain types of chemotherapy. These products have provided the company sufficient revenue to cover its overhead, fund new product development, and generate profits for an extended period of time.[3]

The keys to effective new product and service development, which are consistent with the material on opportunity recognition (Chapter 2) and feasibility analysis (Chapter 3), follow:

■ **Find a need and fill it:** Most successful new products fill a need that is presently unfilled. "Saturated" markets should be avoided. For example, in the United States as well as in most developed countries, consumers have a more-than-adequate selection of appliances, tires, credit cards, and cell phone plans. These are crowded markets with low profit margins. The challenge for entrepreneurs is to find unfilled needs in attractive markets and then find a way to fill those needs.

■ **Develop products that add value:** In addition to finding a need and filling it, the most successful products are those that "add value" for customers in some meaningful way.

■ **Get quality and pricing right:** Every product represents a balance between quality and pricing. If the quality of a product and its price are not compatible, the product may fail and have little chance for recovery. To put this in slightly different terms, customers are willing to pay higher prices for higher-quality products and are willing to accept lower quality when they pay lower prices.

■ **Focus on a specific target market:** Every new product and service should have a specific target market in mind, as we have highlighted throughout this book. This degree of specificity gives the innovating entrepreneurial venture the opportunity to conduct a focused promotional campaign and select the appropriate distributors. The notion that "it's a good product, so somebody will by it" is a naïve way to do business and often contributes to failure.

■ **Conduct ongoing feasibility analysis:** Once a product or service is launched, the feasibility analysis and marketing research should not end. The initial market response should be tested in focus groups and surveys, and incremental adjustments should be made when appropriate.

LEARNING OBJECTIVE

3. Explain the common reasons new products fail.

There is also a common set of reasons that new products fail, as articulated by EcoStrategy Group and shown in Table 14.2.[4] It behooves entrepreneurs to be aware of these reasons and to work hard to prevent new product failures as a result of poor execution in these areas.

TABLE 14.2   THE TOP 10 REASONS NEW PRODUCTS FAIL

1. Target market is not defined correctly.
2. Product is not positioned effectively.
3. Product's benefits are not understood by the target customer.
4. Product doesn't address important customer needs.
5. Product is seen as incomplete, or it requires too many ancillary services or other prerequisites.
6. Product costs too much or the total cost of ownership is out of line with perceived benefits.
7. Sales and marketing efforts are not focused and aligned.
8. Sales cycles are longer than expected.
9. The company is under-investing in marketing and sales efforts.
10. The target market is smaller than originally projected or the product is too far ahead of the market.

This discussion is a reminder that achieving healthy growth, whether via the development of new products or another means, a firm must sell a product or service that legitimately creates value and has the potential to generate profits along with sales.

Other Product-Related Strategies

Along with developing new products, firms grow by improving existing products or services, increasing the market penetration of an existing product or service, or pursuing a product extension strategy.

Improving an Existing Product or Service A business can often increase its revenue by **improving an existing product or service**—enhancing quality, making it larger or smaller, making it more convenient to use, improving its durability, or making it more up-to-date. Improving an item means increasing its value and price potential from the customer's perspective. For example, software firms routinely increase revenues by coming out with "updated" versions of an existing software product.

A mistake many businesses make is not remaining vigilant enough regarding opportunities to improve existing products and services. It is typically much less expensive for a firm to modify an existing product or service and extend its life than to develop a new product or service from scratch. For example, many women have set aside the flat irons that they've used for years to do their hair and have bought a ceramic flat iron because they're safer and do a better job. Selling "improved" flat irons is a much less expensive way for curling iron manufacturers to grow sales than to develop a completely new product.

Increasing the Market Penetration of an Existing Product or Service A **market penetration strategy** involves actions taken to increase the sales of a product or service through greater marketing efforts or through increased production capacity and efficiency. An increase in a product's market share is typically accomplished by increasing advertising expenditures, offering sales promotions, lowering the price, increasing the size of the sales force, or increasing a company's social media efforts. Consider Proactiv, the skin-care company that is the focus of Case 11.2. Since its inception in 1994, Proactiv has relied on celebrity endorsers to demonstrate and promote its product. Judith Light and Vanessa Williams were the firm's first celebrity endorsers. Over the years, the company has added additional celebrity endorsers, including Anthony Robbins, Jessica Simpson, and Jane Seymour to appeal to a broader and more diverse clientele. Avril Lavigne, Katy Perry, Julianne Hough, Jenna Fischer, and Justin Bieber are celebrities recently added to Proactiv's list of well-known endorsers of the firm's products. Adding Justin Bieber exposes Proactiv to a new market—teenage boys. Dr. Katie Rodan, a cofounder of Proactiv, points to the celebrity endorser program as one of the savviest actions the company has taken to build market share.[5]

Another example is the prepaid card, like the Starbucks Card, that almost all restaurants and retailers now offer. By making it more convenient for customers to purchase its products, restaurants and retailers boost their revenues. Prepaid cards also make it easier to give a restaurant's or retailer's offering as a gift. Think of how many people buy Target, Macy's, or Pottery Barn prepaid (gift) cards as birthday or holiday gifts. A benefit to those receiving these cards is the opportunity to use them to buy a product that fulfills a true need.

Increased market penetration can also occur through increased capacity or efficiency, which permits a firm to have a greater volume of product or service

> **LEARNING OBJECTIVE**
> 4. Discuss a market penetration strategy.

Proactiv is a one product company that has grown by increasing its market penetration over time. Proactiv just added Justin Bieber as a celebrity endorser in an attempt to open a new market for its product—teenage boys. Here, Bieber is holding a bottle of Proactiv acne treatment.

Proactive/Splash News/Newscom

to sell. In a manufacturing context, an increase in product capacity can occur by expanding plant and equipment or by outsourcing a portion of the production process to another company. **Outsourcing** is work that is done for a company by people other than the company's full-time employees. For example, a firm that previously manufactured and packaged its product may outsource the packaging function to another company, and as a result free up factory space to increase production of the basic product. Additionally, a firm might outsource its information technology function to free up resources that could be invested in product development efforts.

Extending Product Lines   A **product line extension strategy** involves making additional versions of a product so that it will appeal to different clientele or making related products to sell to the same clientele. For example, a company may make another version of a low-end product that is a little better and then make another version of it that represents the top of the line to appeal to different clientele. This is a strategy that allows a firm to take one product and extend it into several products without incurring significant additional development expense. Computer manufacturers provide a good example of how to execute a product line extension strategy. Each manufacturer sells several versions of its desktop and laptop computers. The different versions of the same computer typically represent good, better, and best alternatives based on processor speed, memory capacity, monitor size, graphic capabilities, and other features. In regard to making related products to sell to the same clientele, many firms start by offering one product or service and then expand into related areas. For example, Ben Lewis, the student/entrepreneur profiled at the beginning of Chapter 13, started PurBlu Beverages in 2007 by selling GIVE bottled water—a basic bottled water. In 2008 he added GIVE Strength, an electrolyte-infused bottled water. In 2009, PurBlu added GIVE Energy, an all-natural energy drink. In 2010, GIVE Energy Lite, a lower-calorie version of its GIVE Energy drinks, was added to the firm's portfolio of products.

Firms also pursue product extension strategies as a way of leveraging their core competencies into related areas. For example, Zipcar has applied the expertise it developed through its consumer car sharing service to launch Zipcar for business, an initiative that allows businesses to use Zipcar's services in the same way that individuals do. Similarly, it recently launched FastFleet, a service to help cities more efficiently use cars in their fleet. An account of the history of Oracle, a computer database software company, provides a particularly interesting example of the potential payoff of a product extension strategy. The example demonstrates that product extension strategies can take time and patience to pay off but can lead to breakthrough growth strategies:

> As Ellison [Oracle's CEO] recognized that he had sold a database to almost every one of the biggest companies in the world, he knew he would need new products to sell. That is how he came up with the idea of applications. Oracle applications would sit on top of and use Oracle databases to perform functions such as inventory management, personnel record keeping, and sales tracking. The proof of his thinking took almost seven years, but by 1995, the company generated nearly $300 million in license revenues from application products and an additional $400 million in applications-related services.[6]

Geographic Expansion **Geographic expansion** is another internal growth strategy. Many entrepreneurial businesses grow by simply expanding from their original location to additional geographic sites. This type of expansion is most common in retail settings. For example, a small business that has a successful retail store in one location may expand by opening a second location in a nearby community. Gap Inc., Walgreens, and Panera Bread are examples of firms that have grown through geographic expansion. Of course, McDonald's, which now has over 32,000 worldwide locations, is the classic example of incredibly successful growth through geographic expansion. Interestingly, Subway, another firm achieving a significant level of success through geographic expansion, now has more locations worldwide than does McDonald's. The keys to successful geographic expansion follow:

■ **Perform successfully in the initial location:** Additional locations can learn from the initial location's success.

■ **Establish the legitimacy of the business concept in the expansion locations:** For example, a particular type of fitness center may be well accepted in its original location because it has been there a long time and has a loyal clientele. However, potential clientele in a neighboring community may be completely unfamiliar with its unique products and services. A common mistake an entrepreneurial venture makes when it expands from one community to another is to assume that if something works in one community, it will automatically work in another.

■ **Don't isolate the expansion location:** Sometimes the employees in an expansion location feel isolated and that they are not receiving adequate training and oversight from the headquarters location. It is a mistake to believe that an expansion location can excel without the same amount of attention and nurturing that it took to build the business in the original location.

International Expansion

International expansion is another common form of growth for entrepreneurial firms.[7] According to a PricewaterhouseCoopers's survey of rapid-growth entrepreneurial firms, 46 percent of the 350 firms surveyed sell in international markets.[8] A look at the world's population and purchasing power statistics affirms the importance of international markets for growth-oriented firms. Approximately 95 percent of the world's population and two-thirds of its total purchasing power are located outside the United States. Influenced by these data, an increasing number of the new firms launched in the United States today are international new ventures.

LEARNING OBJECTIVE

5. Explain what an "international new venture" is and describe its importance to entrepreneurial ventures.

International new ventures are businesses that, from inception, seek to derive competitive advantage by using their resources to sell products or services in multiple countries.[9] From the time they are started, these firms, which are sometimes called "global start-ups," view the world as their marketplace rather than confine themselves to a single country. ASOS, for example, which is a fashion Web site, was an international firm from its inception. It now generates over 35 percent of its revenues from overseas sales.[10] Other new firms are not international from the start, but choose to enter international markets shortly after they gain product acceptance in the United States. For example, Slingbox, which makes a product that lets people watch TV on their computers while they are away from home, was founded in 2004. Having gained favorable reaction to its product in the United States, the company started testing a beta version of its product in Europe in 2006. Slingbox now sells its product in the United States, 26 European countries, five Asian countries, and Canada.[11]

Although there is vast potential associated with selling overseas, it is a fairly complex form of firm growth. Of course, alert entrepreneurs should carefully observe any changes in purchasing power among the world's societies that may result from a financial crisis like the one the world experienced in 2008 and 2009. Let's look at the most important issues that entrepreneurial firms should consider in pursuing growth via international expansion.

Assessing a Firm's Suitability for Growth Through International Markets   Table 14.3 provides a review of the issues that should be considered, including management/organizational issues, product and distribution issues,

---

TABLE 14.3   EVALUATING A FIRM'S OVERALL SUITABILITY FOR GROWTH THROUGH INTERNATIONAL MARKETS

Management/Organizational Issues

Depth of management commitment. A firm's first consideration is to test the depth of its management commitment to entering international markets. Although a firm can "test the waters" by exporting with minimal risk, other forms of internationalization involve a far more significant commitment. A properly funded and executed international strategy requires top management support.

Depth of international experience. A firm should also assess its depth of experience in international markets. Many entrepreneurial firms have no experience in this area. As a result, to be successful, an inexperienced entrepreneurial firm may have to hire an export management company to familiarize itself with export documentation and other subtleties of the export process. Many entrepreneurial firms err by believing that selling and servicing a product or service overseas is not that much different than doing so at home. It is.

Interference with other firm initiatives. Learning how to sell in foreign markets can consume a great deal of entrepreneurs' or managers' time. Overseas travel is often required, and selling to buyers who speak a different language and live in a different time zone can be a painstaking process. Overall, efforts must be devoted to understanding the culture of the international markets the venture is considering. Thus, a firm should weigh the advantages of involvement in international markets against the time commitment involved and the potential interference with other firm initiatives.

TABLE 14.3   CONTINUED

Product and Distribution Issues

Product issues. A firm must first determine if its products or services are suitable for overseas markets. Many pertinent questions need to be answered to make this determination. For example, are a firm's products subject to national health or product safety regulations? Do the products require local service, supplies, or spare parts distribution capability? Will the products need to be redesigned to meet the specifications of customers in foreign markets? Will foreign customers find the products desirable? All these questions must have suitable answers before entering a foreign market. A firm can't simply "assume" that its products are salable and easily serviceable in foreign countries.

Distribution issues. How will the product be transported from the United States to a foreign country? Alternatively, how would an entrepreneurial firm transport a product produced in Sweden to a market in the United States? Is the transportation reliable and affordable? Can the product be exported from the venture's home operation, or will it have to be manufactured in the country of sale?

Financial and Risk Management Issues

Financing export operations. Can the foreign initiative be funded from internal operations, or will additional funding be needed? How will foreign customers pay the firm? How will the firm collect bad debts in a foreign country? Informed answers to these questions must be obtained before the firm initiates overseas sales.

Foreign currency risk. How will the firm manage fluctuations in exchange rates? If the entrepreneurial firm is located in America and it sells to a buyer in Japan, will the American firm be paid in U.S. dollars or in Japanese yen?

and financial and risk management issues, when a venture considers expanding into international markets. If these issues can be addressed successfully, growth through international markets may be an excellent choice for an entrepreneurial firm. The major impediment in this area is not fully appreciating the challenges involved.

Foreign Market Entry Strategies   The majority of entrepreneurial firms first enter foreign markets as exporters, but firms also use licensing, joint ventures, franchising, turnkey projects, and wholly owned subsidiaries to start international expansion.[12] These strategies, along with their primary advantages and disadvantages, are explained in Table 14.4.

Selling Overseas   Many entrepreneurial firms first start selling overseas by responding to an unsolicited inquiry from a foreign buyer. It is important to handle the inquiry appropriately and to observe protocols when trying to serve the needs of customers in foreign markets. Following are several rules of thumb for selling products in foreign markets:

■ Answer requests promptly and clearly. Do not ignore a request just because it lacks grammatical clarity and elegance. Individuals using a nonnative language to contact a business located outside their home nation often are inexperienced with a second language.

■ Replies to foreign inquires, other than e-mail or fax, should be communicated through some form of airmail or overnight delivery. Ground delivery is slow in some areas of the world.

■ A file should be set up to retain copies of all foreign inquiries. Even if an inquiry does not lead to an immediate sale, the names of firms that have made inquiries will be valuable for future prospecting.

■ Keep promises. The biggest complaint from foreign buyers about U.S. businesses is failure to ship on time (or as promised). The first order is the most important in that it sets the tone for the ongoing relationship.

■ All correspondence should be personally signed. Form letters are offensive in some cultures.

TABLE 14.4 PRIMARY ADVANTAGES AND DISADVANTAGES OF VARIOUS FOREIGN-MARKET ENTRY STRATEGIES

Foreign-Market Entry Strategy	Primary Advantage	Primary Disadvantage
Exporting. Exporting is the process of producing a product at home and shipping it to a foreign market. Most entrepreneurial firms begin their international involvement as exporters.	Exporting is a relatively inexpensive way for a firm to become involved in foreign markets.	High transportation costs can make exporting uneconomical, particularly for bulky products.
Licensing. A licensing agreement is an arrangement whereby a firm with the proprietary rights to a product grants permission to another firm to manufacture that product for specified royalties or other payments. Proprietary services and processes can also be licensed.	The licensee puts up most of the capital needed to establish the overseas operation.	A firm in effect "teaches" a foreign company how to produce its proprietary product. Eventually, the foreign company will probably break away and start producing a variation of the product on its own.
Joint ventures. A joint venture involves the establishment of a firm that is jointly owned by two or more otherwise independent firms. Fuji-Xerox, founded in 1962, for example, is a joint venture between an American and a Japanese firm.	Gaining access to the foreign partner's knowledge of local customs and market preferences.	A firm loses partial control of its business operations.
Franchising. A franchise is an agreement between a franchisor (the parent company that has a proprietary product, service, or business method) and a franchisee (an individual or firm that is willing to pay the franchisor a fee for the right to sell its product, service, and/or business method). U.S. firms can sell franchises in foreign markets, with the reverse being true as well.	The franchisee puts up the majority of capital needed to operate in the foreign market.	Quality control.
Turnkey projects. In a turnkey project, a contractor from one country builds a facility in another country, trains the personnel that will operate the facility, and *turns* over the *keys* to the project when it is completed and ready to operate.	Ability to generate revenue.	It is usually a one-time activity, and the relationships that are established in a foreign market may not be valuable to facilitate future projects.
Wholly owned subsidiary. A firm that establishes a wholly owned subsidiary in a foreign country has typically made the decision to manufacture in the foreign country and establish a permanent presence.	Provides a firm total control over its foreign operations.	The cost of setting up and maintaining a manufacturing facility and permanent presence in a foreign country can be high.

■ Be polite, courteous, friendly, and respectful. This is simple common sense, but politeness is particularly important in some Asian cultures. In addition, avoid the use of business slang that is indigenous to the United States, in that the slang terms lack meaning in many other cultures. Stated simply, be sensitive to cultural norms and expectations.

■ For a personal meeting, always make sure to send an individual who is of equal rank to the person with whom he or she will be meeting. In some cultures, it would be seen as inappropriate for a salesperson from a U.S. company to meet with the vice president or president of a foreign firm.

EXTERNAL GROWTH STRATEGIES

External growth strategies rely on establishing relationships with third parties, such as mergers, acquisitions, strategic alliances, joint ventures, licensing, and franchising. Thus, joint ventures, licensing, and franchising are strategic options entrepreneurial firms use to both enter foreign markets (as explained previously) and accomplish external growth. Each of these strategic options is discussed in the following sections, with the exception of franchising, which we consider separately in Chapter 15.

An emphasis on external growth strategies typically results in a more fast-paced, collaborative approach toward growth than the slower-paced internal strategies, such as new product development and expanding to foreign markets. External growth strategies level the playing field between smaller firms and larger companies.[13] For example, Pixar, the small animation studio that produced the animated hits *Toy Story*, *Finding Nemo*, and *Up*, had a number of key strategic alliances with Disney, before Disney acquired Pixar in 2006. By partnering with Disney, Pixar effectively co-opted a portion of Disney's management savvy, technical expertise, and access to distribution channels. The relationship with Disney helped Pixar grow and enhance its ability to effectively compete in the marketplace, to the point where it became an attractive acquisition target. Similarly, by acquiring other companies, relatively young firms such as Pixar can gain access to patents and proprietary techniques that take larger firms years to develop on their own.

There are distinct advantages and disadvantages to emphasizing external growth strategies, as shown in Table 14.5.

TABLE 14.5 ADVANTAGES AND DISADVANTAGES OF EMPHASIZING EXTERNAL GROWTH STRATEGIES

Advantages	Disadvantages
Reducing competition. Competition is lessened when a firm acquires a competitor. This step often helps a firm establish price stability by eliminating the possibility of getting in a price war with at least one competitor. By turning potential competitors into partners and through alliances and franchises, the firm can also reduce the amount of competition it experiences.	**Incompatibility of top management.** The top managers of the firms involved in an acquisition, an alliance, a licensing agreement, or a franchise organization may clash, making the implementation of the initiative difficult.
Getting access to proprietary products or services. Acquisitions or alliances are often motivated by a desire on the part of one firm to gain legitimate access to the proprietary property of another.	**Clash of corporate cultures.** Because external forms of growth require the combined effort of two or more firms, corporate cultures often clash, resulting in frustration and subpar performance.
Gaining access to new products and markets. Growth through acquisition, alliances, or franchising is a quick way for a firm to gain access to new products and markets. Licensing can also provide a firm an initial entry into a market.	**Operational problems.** Another problem that firms encounter when they acquire or collaborate with another company is that their equipment and business processes may lack full compatibility.
Obtaining access to technical expertise. Sometimes, businesses acquire or partner with other businesses to gain access to technical expertise. In franchise organizations, franchisors often receive useful tips and suggestions from their franchisees.	**Increased business complexity.** Although the vast majority of acquisitions and alliances involve companies that are in the same or closely related industries, some entrepreneurial firms acquire or partner with firms in unrelated industries. This approach vastly increases the complexity of the combined business. The firm acquiring a brand or partnership with another company to gain access to its brand may subsequently fail to further develop its own brand and trademarks. This failure can lead to an increased dependency on acquired or partnered brands, reducing the firm's ability to establish and maintain a unique identity in the marketplace.
Gaining access to an established brand name. A growing company that has good products or services may acquire or partner with an older, more established company to gain access to its trademark and name recognition.	
Economies of scale. Combining two or more previously separate firms, whether through acquisition, partnering, or franchising, often leads to greater economies of scale for the combined firms.	**Loss of organizational flexibility.** Acquiring or establishing a partnership with one firm may foreclose the possibility of acquiring or establishing a partnership with another one.
Diversification of business risk. One of the principal driving forces behind all forms of collaboration or shared ownership is to diversify business risk.	**Antitrust implications.** Acquisitions and alliances are subject to antitrust review. In addition, some countries have strict antitrust laws prohibiting certain business relationships between firms.

Mergers and Acquisitions

LEARNING OBJECTIVE

6. Discuss the objectives a company can achieve by acquiring another business.

Many entrepreneurial firms grow through mergers and acquisitions. A **merger** is the pooling of interests to combine two or more firms into one. An **acquisition** is the outright purchase of one firm by another. In an acquisition, the surviving firm is called the **acquirer**, and the firm that is acquired is called the **target**. This section focuses on acquisitions rather than mergers because entrepreneurial firms are more commonly involved with acquisitions than mergers.

Acquiring another business can fulfill several of a company's needs, such as expanding its product line, gaining access to distribution channels, achieving economies of scale, gaining access to technology that will enhance its current offerings, or gaining access to talented employees. In most cases, a firm acquires a competitor or a company that has a product line or distinctive competency that it needs. For example, in 2010 Facebook acquired photo site Divvyshot as a way of enhancing its existing photo sharing site. Similarly, in 2008 Twitter acquired a company called Summize to bring search into Twitter. Summize also had a highly talented engineering team that Twitter was anxious to get its hands on.[14]

Although it can be advantageous, the decision to grow the entrepreneurial firm through acquisitions should be approached with caution.[15] Many firms have found that the process of assimilating another company into their current operation is not easy and can stretch finances to the brink.

Finding an Appropriate Acquisition Candidate If a firm decides to grow through acquisition, it is extremely important for it to exercise extreme care in finding acquisition candidates. Many acquisitions fail not because the companies involved lack resolve, but because they were a poor match to begin with. There are typically two steps involved in finding an appropriate target firm. The first step is to survey the marketplace and make a "short list" of promising candidates. The second is to carefully screen each candidate to determine its suitability for acquisition. The key areas to focus on in accomplishing these two steps are as follows:

LEARNING OBJECTIVE

7. Identify a promising acquisition candidate's characteristics.

- The target firm's openness to the idea of being acquired and its ability to receive consent for its acquisition from key third parties. The third parties from whom consent may be required include bankers, investors, suppliers, employees, and key customers.
- The strength of the target firm's management team, its industry, and its physical proximity to the acquiring firm's headquarters.
- The perceived compatibility of the target company's top management team and its corporate culture with the acquiring firm's top management team and corporate culture.
- The target firm's past and projected financial performance.
- The likelihood the target firm will retain its key employees and customers if acquired.
- The identification of any legal complications that might impede the purchase of the target firm and the extent to which patents, trademarks, and copyrights protect the firm's intellectual property.
- The extent to which the acquiring firm understands the business and industry of the target firm.

The screening should be as comprehensive as possible to provide the acquiring firm sufficient data to determine realistic offering prices for the firms under consideration. A common mistake among acquiring firms is to pay too much for the businesses they purchase. Firms can avoid this mistake by basing their bids on hard data rather than on guesses or intuition.

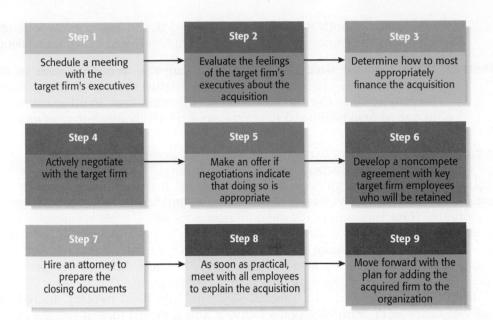

FIGURE 14.2
The Process of Completing the Acquisition of Another Firm

Based on *Wall Street Journal* (Eastern Edition) by C. DeBaise. Copyright 2007 by Dow Jones & Company Inc.

Steps Involved in an Acquisition   Completing an acquisition is a nine-step process, as illustrated in Figure 14.2:

Step 1   **Schedule a meeting with the target firm's executives:**   The acquiring firm should have legal representation at this point to help structure the initial negotiations and help settle any legal issues. The acquiring firm should also have a good idea of what it thinks the acquisition target is worth.

Step 2   **Evaluate the feelings of the target firm's executives about the acquisition:**   If the target is in a "hurry to sell," it works to the acquiring firm's advantage. If the target starts to get cold feet, the negotiations may become more difficult.

Step 3   **Determine how to most appropriately finance the acquisition:** The acquiring firm should be financially prepared to complete the transaction if the terms are favorable.

Step 4   **Actively negotiate with the target firm:**   If a purchase is imminent, obtain all necessary shareholder and third-party consents and approvals.

Step 5   **Make an offer if negotiations indicate that doing so is appropriate:** Both parties should have the offer reviewed by attorneys and certified public accountants that represent their interests. Determine how payment will be structured.

Step 6   **Develop a noncompete agreement with key target firm employees who will be retained:**   This agreement, as explained in Chapter 7, limits the rights of the key employees of the acquired firm to start the same type of business in the acquiring firm's trade area for a specific amount of time.

Step 7   **Hire an attorney to prepare the closing documents:**   Complete the transaction.

Step 8   **As soon as practical, meet with all employees to explain the acquisition:**   A meeting should be held as soon as possible with the employees of both the acquiring firm and the target firm. Articulate a vision for the combined firm and ease employee anxiety where possible.

Step 9   Move forward with the plan for adding the acquired firm to the organization: In some cases, the acquired firm is immediately assimilated into the operations of the acquiring firm. In other cases, the acquired firm is allowed to operate in a relatively autonomous manner.

Along with acquiring other firms to accelerate their growth, entrepreneurial firms are often the targets of larger firms that are looking to enter a new market or acquire proprietary technology. Selling to a large firm is often the goal of an investor-backed company, as a way of creating a liquidity event to allow investors to monetize their investment. Some entrepreneurs allow their companies to be bought by larger firms as a way of accelerating their growth. For example, in 2008 Honest Tea sold a large stake of itself to Coca-Cola, primarily as a means of integrating itself into Coke's worldwide distribution channels. Coke is now providing Honest Tea access to markets it could have never penetrated on its own.

In 2007 StumbleUpon, an Internet start-up, sold itself to eBay. Incredibly, just two years later StumbleUpon's founder and a group took it private again. The reasons for the abrupt turnaround are chronicled in the "What Went Wrong?" feature that follows. The feature is a reminder that acquisitions are complex and don't always work out as envisioned.

WHAT WENT WRONG?

Be Careful What You Wish For: How StumbleUpon's Founder Sold His Company to eBay and Two Years Later Bought It Back Again

Web: www.stumbleupon.com
Twitter: StumbleUpon
Facebook: StumbleUpon

For two main reasons, many entrepreneurial firms aspire to be bought by larger companies. First, by selling to a large firm, an entrepreneurial venture is able to create a liquidity event for its investors. Second, being acquired by a large company often allows a small firm to accelerate its growth and make good progress toward achieving its mission. Typically, a small firm often doesn't have the marketing and distribution muscle to get wide market exposure. By selling to a large firm, a small firm's products can take off by being integrated into the larger firm's marketing program and distribution channels.

In 2007 StumbleUpon, an Internet start-up, sold itself to eBay for $75 million. StumbleUpon is a discovery engine (a form of Web search engine) that finds and recommends Web sites to its users. It was founded in 2001 by Garrett Camp and three friends while Camp was pursuing a masters' degree at the University of Calgary. StumbleUpon's service grew in popularity over time and attracted $1.2 million in investment capital. The setup of its service allows users to "stumble upon" Web sites that they normally wouldn't have known about. People who are passionate about StumbleUpon's site say they like it because of the surprise factor of what they see next. StumbleUpon makes money via targeted advertising. The sites a user stumbles upon are not entirely random. Advertisers can buy placements from StumbleUpon that ensure a certain number of page views from StumbleUpon users each day.

Unlike the rationale for a larger firm buying a small firm provided previously, it was never entirely clear why eBay bought StumbleUpon. The most likely scenario is that eBay felt it could grow StumbleUpon and benefit from its increased ad revenue. It was also thought that eBay might use StumbleUpon's functionality to help eBay customers stumble through eBay's listings, and potentially buy things they wouldn't have thought to buy through the fun of discovering them via the "stumble across" format. Incredibly, just two years after eBay bought StumbleUpon, its founder, Garret Camp, and a group of investors bought it back, meaning that StumbleUpon is again a private company. What went wrong?

In a very transparent interview with the *Wall Street Journal*, Garrett Camp chronicled the reasons the eBay acquisition didn't work out. Camp and the majority of his team stuck with StumbleUpon during the two years it was owned by eBay, working on StumbleUpon as eBay employees. StumbleUpon was able to operate fairly autonomously, although it was part of eBay and subject to eBay's oversight and administrative rules.

There were two categories of problems that prompted Camp to repurchase StumbleUpon from eBay. First, by being part of a large company, Camp and his team lost lots of flexibility and control—in making decisions, troubleshooting problems, and hiring employees. In short, they felt StumbleUpon's entrepreneurial fire was being smothered. Little things were also troublesome. For example, when they sent an offer letter to a job candidate it went out on eBay letterhead. They asked if they could put StumbleUpon's logo on the letter, but there wasn't a procedure to allow that to happen.

The second category of problems dealt with recruiting and hiring high-potential employees. First, the process of hiring was slower inside eBay than it was when StumbleUpon was an independent firm. That put StumbleUpon at a disadvantage when job candidates it was competing for were getting instant offers from private firms. Second, the stock price for a large company like eBay is fairly stable. That made it difficult for StumbleUpon to compete for top engineering talent. By going to work for a start-up or growing private firm, an engineer's stock options are likely to accelerate in value much more quickly than working for a large firm like eBay.

Fortunately, this "What Went Wrong?" feature has a happy ending, at least from StumbleUpon's perspective. In late 2010, the firm announced that it had signed up its 10 millionth user, and said its number of advertisers climbed by 20 percent and its headcount by over 50 percent in 2010. StumbleUpon recently launched an iPhone and Android app as well.

Questions for Critical Thinking

1. Of the issues that were problematic for Camp and his team, in regard to growing StumbleUpon as an eBay subsidiary rather than as an independent firm, what single issue do you think was the most problematic?
2. Why do you think eBay allowed Camp and his investors to take StumbleUpon private again? Do you think there were frustrations on eBay's part in working with Camp and his team?
3. What lessons does this feature teach the founders of rapidly growing entrepreneurial firms that are likely acquisition targets?
4. The "You Be the VC 14.2" feature focuses on thredUP, an online platform for the parents of growing children to exchange the clothes their children grow out of for clothes their children need. Identify a large company that might purchase thredUP if thredUP does well. From thredUP's point of view, make of list of the advantages and disadvantage of being acquired by that company.

Sources: Jeanette Borzo, "The Perils of Being the Little Fish," *Wall Street Journal*, November 15, 2010, p. B2; Mathew Ingram, "Update: StumbleUpon—Not Much Attention, but Big Traffic." *GigaOM blog*, http://gigaom.com/2010/09/03/stumbleupon-and-fark-not-much-attention-but-big-traffic (accessed March 15, 2011, originally posted on September 3, 2010).

Licensing

Licensing is the granting of permission by one company to another company to use a specific form of its intellectual property under clearly defined conditions. Virtually any intellectual property a company owns that is protected by a patent, trademark or copyright can be licensed to a third party. Licensing also works well for firms that create novel products but do not have the resources to build manufacturing capabilities or distribution networks, which other firms may already have in place. For example, Phone Halo, the business profiled at the beginning of the chapter, has adopted a licensing model. Instead of producing the Phone Halo mobile app and hardware device itself, the company is licensing the products to third parties that already have manufacturing capabilities and distribution networks available.

LEARNING OBJECTIVE
8. Explain "licensing" and how it can be used as a growth strategy.

Entrepreneurial firms can also benefit by licensing technology from larger companies. For example Mint.com, the subject of Case 14.1, licenses technology from Yodlee, a larger firm. Yodlee's technology enables Mint.com to access its members' account information, like credit card balances and payment due dates. Recall Wesabe, the subject of the "Went Went Wrong" feature in Chapter 13, tried to build a personal financial management Web site similar to Mint.com and decided to build its own capabilities for scrapping bank Web sites rather than license the technology from Yodlee. Marc Hedlund, one of Wesabe's cofounders, attributes this decision to one of the reasons Wesabe failed.

The terms of a license are spelled out through a **licensing agreement**, which is a formal contract between a licensor and a licensee. The **licensor** is the company that owns the intellectual property; the **licensee** is the company purchasing the right to use it. A license can be exclusive, nonexclusive, for a specific purpose, and for a specific geographic area.[16] In almost all cases, the licensee pays the licensor an initial payment plus an ongoing royalty for the right to use the intellectual property. There is no set formula for determining the amount of the initial payment or the royalties—these are issues that are part of the process of negotiating a licensing agreement.[17] Entrepreneurial firms often press for a relatively large initial payment as a way of generating immediate cash to fund their operations.

There are two principal types of licensing: technology licensing and merchandise and character licensing.

Technology Licensing   **Technology licensing** is the licensing of proprietary technology that the licensor typically controls by virtue of a utility patent. This type of licensing agreement commonly involves one of two scenarios. First, firms develop technologies to enhance their own products and then find noncompetitors to license the technology to spread out the costs and risks involved. Second, companies that are tightly focused on developing new products pass on their new products through licensing agreements to companies that are more marketing oriented and that have the resources to bring the products to market.

Striking a licensing agreement with a large firm can involve tough negotiations. An entrepreneur should carefully investigate potential licensees to make sure they have a track record of paying licensing fees on time and are easy to work with. To obtain this information, it is appropriate to ask a potential licensee for references. It is also important that an entrepreneur not give away too much in regard to the nature of the proprietary technology in an initial meeting with a potential licensee. This challenge means finding the right balance of piquing a potential licensee's interest without revealing too much. Nondisclosure agreements, described in Chapter 7, should be used in discussing proprietary technologies with a potential licensee.

Merchandise and Character Licensing   **Merchandise and character licensing** is the licensing of a recognized trademark or brand that the licensor typically controls through a registered trademark or copyright. For example, Harley-Davidson licenses its trademark to multiple companies that place the Harley trademark on T-shirts, jackets, collectibles, gift items, jewelry, watches, bike accessories, and so on. By doing this, Harley not only generates licensing income but also promotes the sale of Harley-Davidson motorcycles. Similarly, entrepreneurial firms such as eBay and Starbucks license their trademarks not only to earn licensing income but also to promote their products or services to a host of current and potential customers.

The key to merchandise and character licensing is to resist the temptation to license a trademark too widely and to restrict licensing to product categories that have relevance and that appeal to a company's customers. If a company licenses its trademark too broadly, it can lose control of the quality of the products with which its trademark is identified. This outcome can diminish the strength of a company's brand. For example, a company such as ModCloth might license its trademark to a watch manufacturer that is interested in producing a line of ModCloth women's watches. ModCloth would want to make sure that the watches bearing its trademark were fashionable, were of similar quality to its clothing, and were appealing to its clientele. ModCloth can enforce these standards through the terms of its licensing agreements.

Character licensing represents a major source of income and growth for a film company like Pixar, which is now a division of Walt Disney Corporation. Familiar characters from the film *Finding Nemo*, including Marlin (left) and Dory (right), now adorn products as varied as T-shirts, dinner plates, lunch bags, and children's bedspreads.

Strategic Alliances and Joint Ventures

The increase in the popularity of strategic alliances and joint ventures has been driven largely by a growing awareness that firms can't "go it alone" and succeed.[18] As with all forms of firm growth, strategic alliances and joint ventures have advantages and disadvantages. We present these points in Table 14.6.

Strategic Alliances   A **strategic alliance** is a partnership between two or more firms that is developed to achieve a specific goal. Various studies show that participation in alliances can boost a firm's rate of patenting,[19] product innovation,[20] and foreign sales.[21] Alliances tend to be informal and do not involve the creation of a new entity (such as in a joint venture). Although engaging in alliances can be tremendously helpful for an entrepreneurial firm, setting up an alliances and making it work can be tricky. This dimension of alliances is highlighted in the Partnering for Success feature shown on the next page.

Technological alliances and marketing alliances are two of the most common forms of alliances.[22] **Technological alliances** feature cooperation in research and development, engineering, and manufacturing. Research-and-development alliances often bring together entrepreneurial firms with specific technical skills and larger, more mature firms with experience in development and marketing. By pooling their complementary assets, these firms can typically produce a product and bring it to market faster and cheaper than either firm could alone.[23] Pfizer's blockbuster drug Celebrex, for example, was created via a technological alliance. Celebrex is a prescription arthritis medicine. **Marketing alliances** typically match a company with a distribution system with a company that has a product to sell in order to increase sales of a product or service. For example, an American food company may initiate an alliance with Nestlé (a Swiss food company) to gain access to Nestlé's distribution channels in Europe. The strategic logic of this type of alliance for both partners is simple. By finding more outlets for its products, the partner that is supplying the product can increase economies of scale and reduce per unit cost. The partner that supplies the distribution channel benefits by adding products to its product line, increasing its attractiveness to those wanting to purchase a wide array of products from a single supplier.

Both technological and marketing alliances allow firms to focus on their specific area of expertise and partner with others to fill their expertise gaps. This

> **LEARNING OBJECTIVE**
>
> 9. Explain "strategic alliances" and describe the difference between technological alliances and marketing alliances.

TABLE 14.6   ADVANTAGES AND DISADVANTAGES OF PARTICIPATING IN STRATEGIC ALLIANCES AND JOINT VENTURES

Advantages	Disadvantages
Gain access to a particular resource. Firms engage in strategic alliances and joint ventures to gain access to a particular resource, such as capital, employees with specialized skills, or modern production facilities.	**Loss of proprietary information.** Proprietary information can be lost to a partner who is already a competitor or will eventually become one. This is a common worry.
Economies of scale. In many industries, high fixed costs require firms to find partners to expand production volume as a means of developing economies of scale.	**Management complexities.** Because strategic alliances and joint ventures require the combined effort of two or more firms, managing them can be challenging. Frustrations and costly delays often occur as a result.
Risk and cost sharing. Strategic alliances and joint ventures allow two or more firms to share the risk and cost of a particular business endeavor.	**Financial and organizational risks.** The failure rate for strategic alliances and joint ventures is high.
Gain access to a foreign market. Partnering with a local company is often the only practical way to gain access to a foreign market.	**Risk becoming dependent on a partner.** A power imbalance arises if one partner becomes overly dependent on the other. This situation increases the potential for opportunism on the part of the stronger partner. Opportunistic behavior takes advantage of a partner.
Learning. Strategic alliances and joint ventures often provide the participants the opportunity to "learn" from their partners.	**Partial loss of decision autonomy.** Joint planning and decision making may result in a loss of decision autonomy.
Speed to market. Firms with complementary skills, such as one firm being technologically strong and another having strong market access, partner to increase speed to market in hopes of capturing first-mover advantages.	**Partners' cultures may clash.** The corporate cultures of alliance partners may clash, making the implementation and management of the alliance difficult.
Neutralizing or blocking competitors. Through strategic alliances and joint ventures, firms can gain competencies and market power that can be used to neutralize or block a competitor's actions.	**Loss of organizational flexibility.** Establishing a partnership with one firm may foreclose the possibility of establishing a partnership with another firm.

Based on B. R. Barringer and J. S. Harrison, "Walking a Tightrope: Creating Value Through Interorganizational Relationships," *Journal of Management* 26, no. 3 (2002): 367–403.

PARTNERING FOR SUCCESS

Three Steps to Alliance Success

Although strategic alliances are an increasingly popular way for entrepreneurial firms to accelerate growth, they should be approached strategically and carefully. A failed alliance can cause a firm to lose money and can be very time consuming and frustrating to exit from. Alliances are often compared to marriages and other close relationships: easy to get into but very hard to get out of—at least gracefully.

There are three key steps in setting up and executing a successful alliance relationship. The following are the three steps, along with words of advice on how to handle each one.

Selecting a Partner

Any company or group of companies that has something a firm needs is a potential alliance partner. For example, small food companies often partner with large food companies to gain access to their distribution channels. But a company should remember that a potential partner is looking for a leg up too in the form of some type of advantage while competing in the marketplace. If the small food company has to give the large food company "exclusive" distribution rights to its best products to get the deal, it may not be worth it. Entering into an alliance should improve a company's situation—it's shouldn't be a jump ball. Alliances take a great deal of effort to manage and certainly to manage successfully. If each company in an alliance breaks even in terms of outcomes, the alliance is not usually worth it, because of the time and effort it takes from other activities.

Also, a firm should always investigate the reputation of the companies it is thinking about partnering with. Asking for references of other businesses the company is partnering with is appropriate, even if the company is well known. If a company is reluctant or unwilling to provide references, look elsewhere.

According to Guy Kawasaki, a respected Silicon Valley entrepreneur and venture capitalist, most companies form alliances for the wrong reason: to make the press and analysts happy. Kawasaki says this is foolish. Alliances should be formed for one of two reasons in Kawasaki's opinion: to either increase revenues or decrease costs.

Cutting the Deal

Negotiating an alliance can take multiple meetings, conference calls, and e-mail messages. So it's best to cut to the chase, as early as possible, to discern if a deal is possible. It's easy for a small firm to get sucked into months of negotiations with a large company like Microsoft or Google, only to have the deal fall through. It probably won't hurt Microsoft or Google if a handful of its employees lose time failing to negotiate an alliance agreement with a small firm. The lost time on the part of the small firm may be much more damaging.

The most important consideration in cutting a deal is to make sure the potential partners truly have synergies (i.e., 2 + 2 = 5), and that the synergies are sustainable. Otherwise, experts agree, "no contract will hold them together." Also, firms should be leery of entering into an alliance if there is any hint that the people who will actually implement the alliance aren't totally on board. The worst-case scenario is two CEOs who meet at a conference and start talking about their two firms "working together." If they start kicking around alliance ideas that don't make sense, the midlevel people in an organization need to be empowered to hold their ground. The people who have to implement the alliance, for both organizations, should be heard. If they're less than enthused about an alliance proposal, it should be scrapped.

If an alliance agreement is struck, it should be accompanied by a set of operating principles that guide its day-to-day operation. It's also smart to include an "out" clause, which allows each party in the alliance to terminate its involvement relatively easily.

Making It Work

The biggest obstacle to making an alliance work is that the corporate cultures of organizations often vary in substantially important ways. As a result, the first thing that should be determined when deciding how to manage an alliance is how decisions are made. A start-up may be use to making decisions on the fly, while a large company partner may route decisions through several committees before a final decision is made. Unless the partners know what to expect, frustrations can result.

Each alliance partner should also appoint an internal "champion" who has direct responsibility for the alliance's health and progress. "A bunch of people helping out when they can" doesn't cut it. An alliance should have a boss inside each involved organization, just like employees have bosses.

The individuals who will make the alliance work for all the parties involved should also meet face to face. It's normally easier for people to trust one another and work together across distances if they've met at least one time and have had an opportunity to get to know one another as individuals.

Questions for Critical Thinking

1. In what ways is it easy for the founder of a firm to get caught up in the potential advantages of participating in alliances without remaining equally focused on the potential disadvantages?
2. Think about the partnership arrangements you've been involved with, even if your experience has been limited to working with other students in team settings in classes. What are some of the challenges in making alliances work that are not mentioned in the feature?
3. Do some Internet research and find an example of an alliance between a small firm and a large firm that seems to be working well. Briefly describe the nature of the alliance and explain its success.
4. The "You Be the VC 14.1" feature focuses on Cityscape Farms, a start-up that's creating urban greenhouse systems for year-round production of sustainable local fresh foods. Brainstorm three to five likely alliance partners for Cityscape Farms. Explain how each partner can help Cityscape either increase its revenue or decrease its costs.

Sources: "Inc. Guidebook, Build Business Alliances," *Inc*, June 1, 2010; Guy Kawasaki, "The Art of Partnering," How to Change the World, http://blog.guykawasaki.com/2006/02/the_art_of_part.html#axzz1IOLXJ1Sv (accessed April 1, 2011, originally posted on February 6, 2006).

approach is particularly attractive to entrepreneurial firms, which often don't have the financial resources or time to develop all the competencies they need to bring final products to market quickly. Michael Dell describes the early years of Dell Inc.:

As a small start-up, we didn't have the money to build the components [used to make up a PC] ourselves. But we also asked, "Why should we want to?" Unlike many of our competitors, we actually had an option: to buy components from the specialists, leveraging the investments they had already made and allowing us to focus on what we did best—designing and delivering solutions and systems directly to customers. In forging these early alliances with suppliers, we created exactly the right strategy for a fast-growing company.[24]

Joint Ventures   A **joint venture** is an entity created when two or more firms pool a portion of their resources to create a separate, jointly owned organization.[25] An example is Beverage Partners Worldwide, which is a joint venture between Coca-Cola and Nestlé. The joint venture markets ready-to-drink chilled teas based on green tea and black tea in more than 40 countries worldwide.

Gaining access to a foreign market is a common reason to form a joint venture.[26] In these cases, the joint venture typically consists of the firm trying to reach a foreign market and one or more local partners. Joint ventures created for reasons other than foreign market entry are typically described as either scale or link joint ventures.[27] In a **scale joint venture**, the partners collaborate at a single point in the value chain to gain economies of scale in production or distribution. This type of joint venture can be a good vehicle for developing new products or services. In a **link joint venture**, the position of the parties is not symmetrical, and the objectives of the partners may diverge. For example, many of the joint ventures between American and Canadian food companies provide the American partner with access to Canadian markets and distribution channels and the Canadian partner with the opportunity to add to its product line.

A hybrid form of joint venture that some larger firms utilize is to take small equity stakes in promising young companies. In these instances, the large companies act in the role of corporate venture capitalists, as explained in Chapter 10. Intel officially established a venture capital program in the early 1990s, named Intel Capital. Investing in private companies, this program seeks to help start-up ventures grow from their initial stages to a point of either issuing an initial public offering or being acquired. Notable investments, many of which deal with companies outside the United States, include Actions Semiconductor (a Chinese firm), MySQL (a Swedish firm), Research In Motion (a Canadian firm that makes the popular BlackBerry), and WebMD.[28] Firms typically make investments of this nature in companies with the potential to be either suppliers or customers in the future. The equity stake provides the large company a "say" in the development of the smaller firm. On occasion, the larger firm that has a small equity stake will acquire the smaller firm. These transactions are called **spin-ins**. The opposite of a spin-in is a **spin-out**, which occurs when a larger company divests itself of one of its smaller divisions and the division becomes an independent company. Hewlett-Packard, for example, spun off its test-and-measurement equipment division, as Agilent Technologies, which advertises itself as the "world's premiere measurement company."

CHAPTER SUMMARY

1. Internal growth strategies rely on efforts generated within the firm itself, such as new product development, other product-related strategies, international expansion, and Internet-driven strategies. External growth strategies rely on establishing relationships with third parties, such as mergers, licensing, strategic alliances, joint ventures, and franchising.

2. The keys to effective new product development are as follows: find a need and fill it, develop products that add value, get quality and pricing right, focus on a specific target market, and conduct an ongoing feasibility analysis.

3. The reasons that new products fail include an inadequate feasibility analysis, overestimation of market potential, bad timing (i.e., introducing a product at the wrong time), inadequate advertising and promotion, and poor service.

4. A market penetration strategy seeks to increase the sales of a product or service through greater marketing efforts or through increased production capacity and efficiency.

5. International new ventures are businesses that, from inception, seek to derive significant competitive advantage from the use of resources and the sale of outputs in multiple countries.

6. Acquiring another business can fulfill several of a company's needs, such as expanding its product line, gaining access to distribution channels, achieving competitive economies of scale, or expanding the company's geographic reach.

7. A promising acquisition candidate has the following characteristics: operates in a growing industry, has proprietary products and/or processes, has a well-defined and established market position, has a good reputation, is involved in very little, if any, litigation, is open to the idea of being acquired by another firm, is positioned to readily obtain key third-party consent to an acquisition, and is located in a geographic area that is easily accessible from the acquiring firm's headquarters location.

8. Licensing is the granting of permission by one company to another company to use a specific form of its intellectual property under clearly defined conditions. Virtually any intellectual property a company owns can be licensed to a third party. Licensing can be a very effective way of earning income, particularly for intellectual property-rich firms, such as software and biotech companies.

9. A strategic alliance is a partnership between two or more firms that is developed to achieve a specific objective or goal. Technological alliances involve cooperating in areas such as research and development, engineering, and manufacturing. Marketing alliances typically match one firm with a partner's distribution system that is attractive to the company trying to increase sales of its products or services.

10. A joint venture is an entity that is created when two or more firms pool a portion of their resources to create a separate, jointly owned organization. In a scale joint venture, the partners collaborate at a single point in the value chain to gain economies of scale in production or distribution by combining their expertise. In a link joint venture, the position of the parties is not symmetrical and the objectives of the partners may diverge.

KEY TERMS

acquirer, **500**
acquisition, **500**
external growth strategies, **498**
geographic expansion, **495**
improving an existing product
    or service, **493**
internal growth strategies, **489**
international new
    ventures, **496**
joint venture, **508**
licensee, **504**

licensing, **503**
licensing agreement, **504**
licensor, **504**
link joint venture, **508**
marketing alliances, **505**
market penetration
    strategy, **493**
merchandise and character
    licensing, **504**
merger, **500**
new product development, **490**

organic growth, **489**
outsourcing, **494**
product line extension
    strategy, **494**
scale joint venture, **508**
spin-ins, **508**
spin-outs, **508**
strategic alliance, **505**
target, **500**
technological alliances, **505**
technology licensing, **504**

REVIEW QUESTIONS

1. Describe the difference between an internal and an external growth strategy. Provide examples of each strategy and how each one contributes to firm growth.

2. Describe the keys to effective new product and service development.

3. Describe some of the common reasons new products fail.

4. What is a market penetration strategy? Provide an example of a market penetration strategy, and describe how using it effectively might increase a firm's sales.

5. What is a product line extension strategy? Provide an example of a product line extension strategy, and describe how its effective use might increase a firm's sales.

6. What is a geographic expansion strategy, and what are the keys to implementing a successful geographic expansion strategy for an entrepreneurial firm?

7. What is an international new venture? Explain why it might be to the benefit of an entrepreneurial start-up to position itself as an international new venture from the outset.

8. What are the six foreign-market entry strategies? Briefly describe each strategy.
9. What are several rules of thumb to follow for selling products overseas?
10. Describe the difference between a merger and an acquisition. In what ways can acquisitions help firms fill their needs?
11. What are the characteristics of a promising acquisition candidate?
12. What is the difference between a licensor and a licensee?
13. What does the term *licensing* mean? How can licensing be used to increase a firm's revenues?
14. Describe the purpose of a licensing agreement. In a licensing agreement, which party is the licensor, and which is the licensee?
15. Describe the difference between technology licensing and merchandise and character

licensing. Provide examples of both types of licensing and how they can increase a firm's sales.
16. Over the past several years, why have strategic alliances and joint ventures become increasingly prevalent growth strategies? Make your answer as thoughtful and as thorough as possible.
17. Describe the difference between techno-logical alliances and market alliances. Provide examples of both types of alliances and how they can increase a firm's sales.
18. What is a joint venture?
19. How does a joint venture differ from a strategic alliance?
20. Describe the difference between a scale joint venture and a link joint venture. Provide examples of both types of joint ventures and how their effective use can increase a firm's sales.

APPLICATION QUESTIONS

1. Spend some time studying thredUP, the focus of the "You Be the VC 14.2" feature. Is it more likely that thredUP will grow through internal or external growth strategies? Provide suggestions of internal growth strategies and external growth strategies that make sense for thredUP.
2. Reacquaint yourself with Proactiv, the subject of Case 11.2. Proactiv has relied almost exclusively on internal or organic growth since it launched in the late 1990s. Do you think Proactiv's approach to growth has been appropriate? Has the company erred by not being more adventurous in its use of the various growth strategies?
3. Jessica Martin, a classmate of yours, just returned from an entrepreneurship boot camp, which was sponsored by her university's technology incubator and consisted of three days of intense focus on how to successfully launch a firm. You overheard Jessica telling another classmate that the boot camp was extremely helpful and she's already signed up for another three-day boot camp that will focus on how to successfully grow a firm. The classmate looked at Jessica and said, "How in the world can you spend three days taking about how to successfully grow a firm?" Jessica opened her notebook and showed the classmate the 10-item agenda for the upcoming three-day boot camp. What do you think the 10 items consist of?

(Consider the material in Chapter 13 and this chapter in formulating your answer.)
4. Think of a company that you're familiar with that has grown via a product line extension strategy. Provide an overview of the company and how it rolled out its product line extension strategy.
5. Spend some time studying Chipotle, the popular Mexican food restaurant chain. Identify the growth strategies Chipotle has utilized. Comment on Chipotle's overall approach to growth and any growth-related challenges that you think Chipotle has today.
6. Zynga is a social network game developer that develops browser-based games that work both stand-alone and as application widgets on social networking sites like Facebook and MySpace. What are the pluses and minuses of Zynga's approach to launching games that rely on another company's platform (i.e., Facebook and MySpace) to reach its intended audience? Is Zynga growing via internal, external, or hybrid forms of growth?
7. Refer to Joby Energy, the subject of the "You Be the VC 10.1" feature. Which of the foreign market entry strategies described in Table 14.4 make sense for Joby Energy? If you were the founder of Joby Energy, which strategy would you pursue first if you decided to grow via international expansion?
8. Cisco Systems, Microsoft, and IBM are consistently the largest acquirers of small,

technology-based entrepreneurial firms. Why would Cisco Systems, Microsoft, and IBM, which each employ hundreds of product development specialists and engineers, buy other firms to acquire technology and add to their product lines, rather than developing the technology and new products in-house?

9. Google reportedly offered to buy Groupon for $5 billion to $6 billion in November 2010—an offer that Groupon turned down. Why do you think Google wanted to acquire Groupon, and why do you think Groupon turned Google down?

10. Brian Brunner is an entrepreneur who has invented several devices that are used in the telecommunications industry. He has patented the devices and manufactures them in a job shop in Oklahoma City. Brian sells the devices directly to AT&T and Verizon. Last week, Brian got a certified letter in the mail from Nokia, indicating that firm's interest in licensing the technology that is represented in one of his devices. Brian doesn't know anything about licensing and has turned to you for help. What would you tell Brian about licensing, and how would you suggest that he respond to Nokia's letter?

11. A friend of yours owns a chain of 25 fitness centers in Florida and Georgia. The fitness centers cater primarily to young professionals, ages 21 to 40. Your friend is worried because his centers have declined in terms of overall membership. Your friend told you that he's interested in pursuing strategic alliances to rev up the growth of his centers but is having trouble thinking about the types of companies he can partner with. Provide your friend with some suggestions.

12. Review the "You Be the VC" features for Chapters 10 through 14. Which of the companies featured is most likely to own intellectual property that other companies will want to license? Explain your answer.

13. Reacquaint yourself with Dry Soda, the focus of Case 9.1. Suppose the company hired you to investigate how licensing, strategic alliances, and joint ventures could spur its growth. How would you approach the investigation? Are the licensing, strategic alliances, and joint venture opportunities limited or plentiful? What types of deals do you think would be appropriate for Dry Soda?

14. Study the popular social networking site LinkedIn. What growth strategies has the company employed? Make recommendations for appropriate growth strategies for the future.

15. Which of the growth strategies discussed in the chapter are the most risky? Which are the least risky? What role should risk play in a company's decision to pursue a particular growth strategy?

YOU BE THE VC 14.1

Company: Cityscape Farms

Web: www.cityscapefarms.com
Twitter: CityscapeFarms
Facebook: Cityscape Farms

Business Idea: Create urban greenhouse systems for year-round production of sustainable and local fresh food.

Pitch: Food travels 1,500 miles on average in the United States to get to consumers. At the same time, global demand for food is increasing. By 2050, the earth's population will grow to nine billion people (compared to roughly seven billion today). That steep increase in population requires the development of new methods of farming in order to feed our planet's inhabitants. Concurrently, traditional methods of farming, which rely largely on petroleum to fuel farm vehicles and for fertilizers and pesticides, are coming under increased scrutiny. Petroleum is a nonrenewable resource. In addition, a growing number of people prefer organic food, which is largely grown without the use of petroleum-based chemicals. Modern agriculture also uses 70 percent of the world's fresh water withdrawals, is the largest source of water pollution, and is the largest consumer of land.

Cityscape Farms offers an alternative. Instead of focusing on the countryside, where food must be trucked to processers and ultimately consumers, the company is focused on cities, and is building greenhouses on rooftops and in vacant lots. Cityscape's approach utilizes aquaponics, which is a combination of aquaculture (fish cultivation) and hydroponics (soil-less farming), where fish and plants are grown in a symbiotic system. Each greenhouse includes a fish tank. Water from the tank, which is enriched by the fish waste, flows through a filter and a pump, and is then distributed into growing trays, where fruits and vegetables are grown. The water is then returned to the tank. It's a closed-loop organic and pesticide-free system. It also requires a relatively low water usage. Fruits and vegetables can normally be grown via aquaponics for one-tenth the amount of water required of traditional farming. Once the system is operable, the only new water entered into the system is to replace that lost by evaporation. No chemical fertilizers are used. Instead, as part of the filtering process, a bacterium is introduced, which turns the fish waste in the water into nitrates that in turn fertilize the plants. The plants filter out the nitrates and return clean water to the tank. As an added benefit, there are advantages to integrating a farm into a building. It reduces the need for supplemental lighting and lowers the cost of cooling a structure. All of these benefits are available with extant technology.

The reason Cityscape Farms is focusing its efforts on cities is because that's where the people are. Presently, just less than 50 percent of the world's population (3.3 billion people) lives in cities, a trend that is expected to accelerate. By producing food in cities, Cityscape Farms not only reduces the need to transport food long distances to reach consumers, but can deliver to consumers safer, fresher, and tastier food products.

Cityscape Farms is currently preparing to go to market with its solution. According to Wikipedia, a sprinkling of rooftop hydroponic greenhouse can be found around the world, including at academic centers in the United States (Washington University and Barnard College, among others), on a hospital (Changi) in Singapore, in Holland, in India, and in parts of the developing world. Individuals having mind-sets that place high value on environmentally friendly actions such as those promoted by Cityscape will be critical to the firm's success.

Q&A: Based on the material covered in this chapter, what questions would you ask the firm's founders before making your funding decision? What answers would satisfy you?

Decision: If you had to make your decision on just the information provided in the pitch and on the company's Web site, would you fund this company? Why or why not?

YOU BE THE VC 14.2

Company: thredUP

Web: www.thredup.com
Twitter: thredUP
Facebook: thredUP

Business Idea: Provide a convenient online platform for the parents of growing children to exchange the clothes their children grow out of for clothes their children need.

Pitch: The average kid grows out of a set of clothes every three to six months. In the United States, evidence suggests that by the age of 17, kids have outgrown over 1,300 items and parents have spent nearly $20,000 on their clothes. There are existing ways for parents to sell or exchange outgrown clothes, including swap parties, eBay, and consignment shops. But these are inconvenient solutions, and often yield very little money or results for the effort involved. The problem is particularly acute for the parents of babies and young children. As adorable as kids' clothes are there's no escaping the fact that healthy young children grow out of clothing quickly.

If you're a parent with a baby or young child, or know someone who is, you're probably nodding your head in agreement. There's just not a good solution for selling or exchanging used clothing to acquire new clothing—until now. thredUP is a Web site that allows parents to exchange boxes of lightly worn clothes that no longer fit their kids for similar clothes from like-minded families. Here's how it works. Users can browse thredUP for boxes of 10 to 18 tops, bottoms, or a mix of both, and search by gender, size, and season. Once a selection is made, the user pays $5 plus shipping, and the box is on its way.

The user is then obligated to assemble a similar quantity of clothing to put into a box and inform thredUP of what's in the box. thredUP will then list that box on its Web site. When someone chooses their box, the user will be sent a link to the USPS Web site, where they'll be provided access to a free shipping box, a printable mailing label, and schedule a pick up for the box. This process can be repeated over and over again, as a user's child grows and needs new clothing. Added benefits to the service are that it helps families save time and money and is environmentally friendly in that, currently, over 20 billion pounds of clothing and textiles enter U.S. landfills every year. By helping families share rather than prematurely discard used clothes, thredUP can help reduce that number.

thredUP makes money in two ways: (1) the $5 transaction fee for each swap and (2) via premium memberships, which sell for $4.99 per month or $29.99 per year. A premium membership provides subscribers specific information about what's in the boxes they're considering.

Q&A: Based on the material covered in this chapter, what questions would you ask the firm's founders before making your funding decision? What answers would satisfy you?

Decision: If you had to make your decision on just the information provided in the pitch and on the company's Web site, would you fund this company? Why or why not?

CASE 14.1

How Mint.com Went from Launch to a $170 Million Acquisition in 24 Months

Web: www.mint.com

Twitter: mint.com

Facebook: Mint.com

Bruce R. Barringer, *Oklahoma State University*

R. Duane Ireland, *Texas A&M University*

Introduction

How did Mint.com go from launch to a $170 million acquisition in 24 months? The answer isn't as spectacular as you might think. Using a football metaphor, Mint.com did it more through blocking and tackling than through big plays. Mint.com's story is one of how a start-up that solves a real problem, and executes very well, can overcome obstacles and win the support of others. It's also a story of how a small company can take on a big rival, and by positioning itself for the future rather than the past, can motivate the rival to acquire it rather than trying to put it out of business through aggressive competition. Let's see how all of this took place.

Aaron Patzer

Aaron Patzer started Mint.com when he was just 25. After earning degrees from Duke and Princeton, he took a job with Nascentric, a Silicon Valley start-up. During this time, he was managing his personal finances with Quicken and Microsoft Money, and became increasingly frustrated with his experiences. He asked around and found others who were aggravated with these products and personal finance in general. He started thinking about how to build a product that would not only be an improvement to Quicken and Microsoft Money, but would make the entire process of managing money more efficient and potentially rewarding.

   Patzer struggled with whether to act on his instincts and eventually decided to move forward. His thought process during this period is best illustrated through his own words. In an interview with Carson McComas, the creator of WorkHappy.net, a popular blog, Patzer reflected on how he made the decision to quit his job and focus on Mint.com full-time:

> I began to think about the business nights and weekends. But it's hard to find time when you've got a full time (and very demanding job). One day I said to myself, "If you give it 100% and fail, I can live with that. But I can't live with going half-way,

part-time." So on March 1, [2006], I quit my job and began working on Mint. The first few months were tough, and I basically oscillated day to day between thinking "This is the greatest idea ever" and "This will never work." Who am I to take on Intuit (the maker of Quicken) and Microsoft? If this was a good idea, someone would have done it before.

Patzer went on to say that the thing that gave him the most inner confidence was that he knew he was exceptionally good at one thing: algorithms—the key to computer programming. He also knew he was persistent and extremely passionate about his idea.

Prelaunch Stage—March 2006 until September 2007

Patzer worked 14 to 16 hours a day, 6½ days a week, from March 2006 to the fall of the same year banging out the early prototype of Mint.com. Needing money to make key hires, improve on Mint.com's consumer interface, and buy servers, Patzer approached several investors. None bit. The problem was the way Mint.com was set up. Quicken and Microsoft Money were software products that people bought and then installed on their computers. Mint.com was an online dashboard. When you signed up for a Mint.com account, it asked you to provide all of your bank, credit card, and investment account information, user IDs, and passwords. Mint.com, through a partnership with a financial services firm, could then "scrape" the sites of your bank and credit card companies, and provide a real-time update of your financial information. It could also e-mail you due date reminders, low-balance alerts, unusual activity alerts, and the like. A user could log onto his or her Mint.com account at any time and see all of his or her account information on a single screen. This is the better experience that Patzer was looking for. The average American has 11 separate bank, credit card, loan, and investment accounts. Patzer's idea was that having a single place where all the account information is displayed and updated on a consistent basis would be a superior customer experience.

(continued)

The investors all said the same thing. People will not trust a start-up with their account information—let alone their user IDs and passwords. Patzer persisted. In September 2006 he found an investor that believed in his vision and was able to persuade a venture capital firm to go along. Mint.com's first round of funding was $750,000, $325,000 from First Round Capital and $425,000 from other investors.

Two things helped Mint.com raise more money. The first was carefully explaining the security aspects of its service, not only to potential investors but to literally anyone who would listen. Mint.com is a read-only system. What this means is that even if someone broke into its system, they couldn't steal someone's money or even move it around. They could just look at account balances and how people spent their money. In addition, Mint.com had bank-level security in place from the outset. It had the same level of encryption and bank-end protections that a bank did. Mint.com also did something very smart. It turned the security issue on its head. It argued that rather than putting people at risk, it actually protected people's finances. By allowing its customers to view all of their financial information at a single site, customers could quickly log on to their account and scan their financial information to see if anything seemed out of place. In addition, it sent its customers low-balance and unusual activity alerts.

The second thing that helped Mint.com raise additional money is that it won TechCrunch40, a high-profile business plan competition, in fall 2007. TechCrunch40, which was later named TechCrunch50, was a prestigious business plan competition that ran from 2007 to 2009. Looking back, Patzer says that the seven minutes he had to pitch Mint.com at the competition was the seven most important minutes of his life. The conference was an enormous platform. It was well attended by press, investors, and large companies looking for strategic partners. Over 700 companies applied for the 2007 competition. The top 40 were chosen to present. Winning gave Mint.com the outside validation it needed to move beyond the small group of investors that believed in it to a larger group that was now willing to give it a second look. It also explains Mint.com's fast start with users. The enormous press generated by the TechCrunch40 win placed Mint.com's name in front of an untold number of people in a very positive manner.

During this time, Mint.com was intently focused on execution. One of the rules of TechCrunch40 was that the competitors had to be at the prelaunch stage, so Mint.com was still in a testing mode. Patzer made his first key hires. His first hire was Jason Putorti, the designer who had built apple.com, to plan and design Mint.com's customer interface. According to Patzer, Putori cared about every pixel, and it showed in the beauty and functionality of the site. Putori brought people into Mint.com offices, literally right off the street, to test the site and see where the rough spots were. He brought in young people, old people, men, women—as diverse of a group as he could find. Patzer's third hire was David Michaels, VP of Engineering. Michaels had 15 years' experience in security, including financial Web services.

Two Years as an Independent Company—September 2007 until September 2009

Mint.com formally launched in September 2007, just after TechCrunch40. The skeptics were wrong. In its first four months it signed up 100,000 people, all of whom entered their financial information, including account numbers, user IDs, and passwords, into Mint.com. Mint.com didn't have a single security breach. Its numbers accelerated through the end of 2007 and into 2008. Mint.com is free to the user. Its revenue model is to make referrals to its users, and then collect affiliate fees when its users follow through. For example, if Mint.com sees that a specific user is paying 16.9 percent interest on a credit card, and the user is financially sound, it will suggest a lower-interest rate credit card. If the user takes the offer, Mint.com makes a small commission.

Buoyed by its TechCrunch40 win and steady growth, Mint.com raised $31 million through several venture capital rounds from September 2007 until mid-2009. The purpose of the capital was to build out the company's infrastructure to accommodate its growth. During this period, Patzer remained Mint.com's primary spokesperson and evangelist. He would accept almost any opportunity to talk about Mint.com and its story. As a result, Mint.com's growth was paralleled by persistent public relations efforts on the part of the company to keep itself in the news and on the minds of journalists and bloggers.

In late 2009, just prior to the Intuit acquisition, Mint.com had 1.5 million users tracking nearly $50 billion in assets. It was also widely considered to be one of the up-and-coming Web 2.0 companies.

The Intuit Acquisition—September 2009

Intuit acquired Mint.com in September 2009, just 24 months after Mint.com launched. That's a quick run-up to an acquisition. Venture capitalists, for example, typically have a three- to five-year investment horizon, meaning they'd like to see the companies they invest in get acquired or launch an IPO sometime during that period. Most of Mint.com investors monetized their investment in 24 months or less.

For its part, Intuit was a strong company in 2009, with over $1.1 billion in sales and several marquee products, including Quicken, Quick Books, and TurboTax. But it was also a boxed software company, struggling to gain a footing on the Web. Its fear was that Web-based services like Mint.com represented the future, while boxed software products like Quicken represented the past. In June 2009, Microsoft contributed to this fear by discontinuing sales of Microsoft Money, its boxed financial software product. In the end, many analysts believe it was a no-brainer for Intuit to buy Mint.com. It gave Intuit a quick entry into the Web-based side of personal financial management.

The acquisition was also good timing for Mint.com. Patzer and his team were interested in continuing to accelerate Mint.com's growth. Intuit had the financial resources to do that, and by being part of a large company, Patzer could focus solely on product development rather than raising funds. One of the conditions of the deal was that Patzer was able to continue to operate Mint.com in an autonomous manner. He was also named general manager of Intuit's personal finance division. As an added bonus for Intuit, Patzer's charge was not only to continue to build Mint.com, but to instill some of its Web savvy into other Intuit products.

Discussion Questions

1. If you had been a venture capitalist at the time Patzer was originally pitching Mint.com, would you have had the same concerns as the venture capitalists at that time did? Why do you think the venture capitalists weren't more forward thinking? Why do you think Patzer didn't see the initial reaction to Mint.com as reason to either give up or to significantly modify his service?

2. Evaluate how effectively Mint.com prepared for its launch and early growth. What specific steps did the company take to prepare for and stimulate its early growth?

3. Do you think Intuit's acquisition of Mint.com was a win for both Intuit and Mint.com? In what ways does an acquisition by a large firm potentially accelerate the growth of a small firm, beyond what the small firm could have accomplished on its own?

4. Why do you think Intuit didn't create an online site similar to Mint.com, rather than spending $170 million to acquire Mint.com?

Application Questions

1. What are the inherent challenges involved when a large firm acquires a small firm, particularly if the core management team from the small firm joins the large firm? Which of these challenges do you think will be particularly difficult for Patzer and his team?

2. Do some research on Intuit's acquisition of Mint.com, and report on the current status of the acquisition, in terms of successes and disappointments. In your opinion, has the acquisition been a good thing for Mint.com and its users? Explain your answer.

Sources: Mint.com Web site, www.mint.com (accessed April 8, 2011); Carson McComas, "Interview with Aaron Patzer, founder of Mint.com," Workhappy.net, www.workhappy.net/2008/02/interview-wit-1.html (accessed April 8, 2011, originally posted on February 19, 2008) Used with permission of Mint.com and Aaron Patzer; Olaf De Senerpont Domis, "Intuit to Buy Mint.com," LexisNexis Academic, www.lexisnexis.com/hottopics/lnacademic/ (accessed April 8, 2011, originally posted on September 14, 2009).

CASE 14.2

Will Groupon Maintain Its Sizzling Pace of Growth?

Web: www.groupon.com
Twitter: www.grouponOKO (varies by city)
Facebook: Groupon

Bruce R. Barringer, *Oklahoma State University*
R. Duane Ireland, *Texas A&M University*

Introduction

Groupon is a deal-of-the-day Web site that is located in major geographic markets across the world. Launched in October 2008 by Andrew Mason, Groupon has been characterized as one of the fastest-growing companies of all time. It was first offered in Chicago, followed soon thereafter by Boston, New York City, and Toronto. Since then its growth has been spectacular. It is now in over 550 cities, has 44 million subscribers and 3,100 employees. According to an August 2010 feature in *Forbes*, Groupon topped $500 million in revenues in 2010 and is on pace to become the fastest company in history to reach $1 billion in sales.

Groupon's name is a combination of the words *group* and *coupon*. Most subscribers see Groupon as a fun way to shop and learn about businesses that

previously were unknown to them. For businesses, Groupon is largely a customer acquisition tool. It's becoming increasingly difficult for brick-and-mortar stores and organizations to drive traffic to their locations. As a result, they're looking for ways to increase foot traffic and jump-start their sales.

How It Works

Groupon offers one deal a day in each of the markets it serves. If a certain number of people sign up within a specified time, the deal is "on." If not enough people sign up, the deal is "off" and no one is charged. The day this case was written the Groupon deal in Oklahoma City, Oklahoma, was $5 for $10 worth of breakfast and lunch fare at Ground Floor Café, a restaurant in downtown Oklahoma City. A total of

(continued)

50 people needed to take the deal for it to be "on." By 7:55 A.M. the day the deal was posted, the 50 person minimum had been met. By noon, 229 people had taken the deal and by 5:00 P.M. the number was 337. To participate, an individual must be a Groupon subscriber, which is free. Once a subscriber takes a deal, a reservation is made in his or her name, and the subscriber's credit card is charged once the deal is "on." A voucher is then delivered via e-mail to confirm the purchase. The voucher is taken to the merchant offering the deal to redeem the purchase. There is usually an expiration date on the voucher—6 to 12 months is common. A 6- to 12-month time frame gives the purchaser a comfortable amount of time to use the voucher, and spreads out the number of people coming into a business to redeem the voucher.

Once you become a Groupon subscriber, you sign up for one or more cities, and then receive the daily deal for each city via e-mail, Twitter, or Facebook. Groupon makes money by keeping approximately half the money the customer pays for a deal. So, if an $80 massage is offered for $40, then Groupon and the retailer spit the $40. Groupon's primary target market is 18- to 34-year-old urban females.

A visual depiction of Groupon's business model, from both the business side and subscriber side, is shown below.

Groupon's Pitch to Merchants

Groupon's pitch to merchants is that it's a customer acquisition tool. The hope is that the people who take the deal will not only redeem their coupon, but will spend more money when they're in the store and will become repeat customers. Groupon works best for service-based businesses that have high fixed costs and low variable costs, making the cost of offering a deep discount palatable. Groupon's five most common groups of offerings include restaurants and cafés, food, salon, makeup and spa, and tickets.

Groupon is particularly attractive to small businesses that have trouble getting the word out about their offerings and don't have a large advertising budget. A small yoga studio is an example of such a business. Prior to Groupon, the studio's options for increasing awareness would have been newspaper, radio, online, and via social networks. The disadvantage of these forms of advertising, with the exception of social networks, is that they must be paid for up front. Groupon is free. The yoga studio doesn't pay Groupon to set up the campaign. It simply splits with Group on the revenue that's generated. Typically, a business like a yoga studio can take on additional customers without increasing its fixed costs. The only additional costs incurred to service the business brought in by Groupon may be to hire additional instructors to offer more classes.

Not all Groupon campaigns have worked out, and the company has come under increasing criticism. For example, a successful deal could temporarily swamp a small business with too many customers, risking the possibility that customers won't be satisfied or that the business will not be able to satisfy the demand. For example, one coffee shop in Portland, Oregon, signed up with Groupon in mid-2010, and offered $13 worth of products for $6. Nearly 1,000 people bought the deal the day it was advertised, swamping the small shop for three months. In a blog post, the owner said that the volume of sales coupled with the deep discount threatened the survival of the business. Similarly, U.S. Toy Company's store in Kansas City offered $20 worth of merchandise for $10 in July 2010, hoping to spur sales and acquire new customers. About 2,800 people took the deal. The campaign was a disappointment. According to the company, about 90 percent of the Groupon takers were already customers, and the

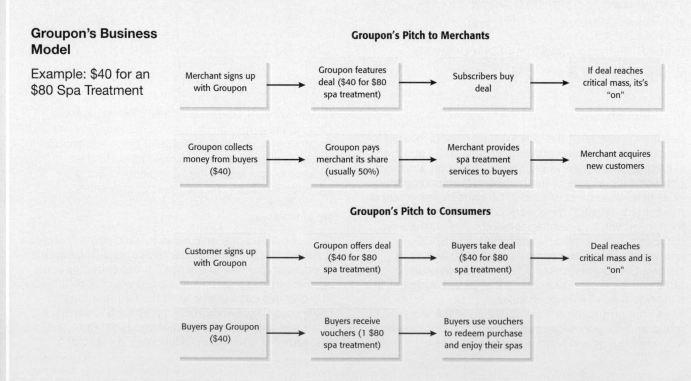

majority of them came into the store only to redeem their $20 coupon. The company says it lost money on about three-quarters of its Groupon-related sales. For its part, Groupon says that its overall satisfaction level is high, and 97 percent of businesses that run Groupon campaigns ask to be featured again.

Groupon's Growth Strategy

Groupon has grown organically and via acquisitions. Its organic growth has been generated largely by signing up new subscribers and expanding to new cities. It's also been a busy acquirer. Groupon made at least 10 acquisitions in 2010 and early 2011, including European deal-of-the day site MyCityDeal, Indian deal-of-the day site SoSasta.com, mobile technology company Mob.ly, and Pelago, the parent company of check-in-service site Whrrl.

Groupon has fueled its growth through several rounds of substantial funding. In early 2011, it raised $950 million from a group of investors. In early 2010, it raised $135 million. Observers speculate that Groupon has used the money to expand its sales force, scale its back-end operations, make acquisitions, and prepare for future growth. It's rumored to be anticipating an IPO in the foreseeable future.

Future Growth Prospects and Challenges Ahead

Looking forward, Groupon has both possibilities for additional growth and challenges that it must deal with. Likely possibilities for future growth are shown next.

Groupon's Future Growth Possibilities

Internal Growth Possibilities

1. Enroll new subscribers via viral marketing, paid advertising, and social media.
2. Expand to new domestic cities.
3. Expand to new international markets.
4. Develop new products, such as a separate Groupon-owned site that isn't tied to specific geographic areas, but focused on products, such as high-end luxury goods.
5. Increase participation of current subscribers and enroll new subscribers by making it more convenient to interact with Groupon via mobile platforms.

External Growth Possibilities

1. Acquire deal-of-the-day sites in the United States and abroad, and re-brand them with the Groupon brand.
2. Acquire deal-of-the-day sites in the United States and abroad and allow them to operate autonomously.
3. Enter into strategic alliances with major retailers to provide back-end functionality for deal-of-the-day offerings they make to their customers. For example, a retailer like Best Buy could offer daily deals, which must be redeemed at a Best Buy store. The idea would be to drive foot traffic to stores.

The viability of each of these possibilities for growth hinges on two factors: (1) whether they're in Groupon's best-interest to pursue and (2) whether they're within Groupon's capabilities. For instance, in regard to the former, Groupon has resisted deal-of-the-day initiatives that focus on products rather than services, and are national rather than local in scope. There were multiple deal-of-the-day sites that focused on products, such as electronics and jewelry, that preceded Groupon and failed. Groupon has built its success on offering local deals for service providers. In regard to the later, observers wonder how large Groupon can grow before it needs to pause to allow its leadership capacity to catch up with its growth.

Groupon also faces challenges with the primary one being the number of copycat sites that are being launched and are trying to erode the firm's market share. Its most direct competitor is LivingSocial, which has a business model that's very similar to Groupon's. Other sites are springing up, both domestically and internationally. In China, for example, there are now more than 50 Groupon-type daily deal sites. It's unclear how Groupon will deal with increasing competition.

Groupon also runs the risk that negative publicity will deter business participation. Reports about merchants who have lost money running Groupon campaigns may cause some prospects to pause. In addition, it runs the risk of subscriber fatigue. By appearing in its subscribers e-mail boxes every day, some subscribers may tire of the drumbeat of Groupon deals and eventually drop the service.

Discussion Questions

1. Evaluate Groupon's strategies for growth. Do you think Groupon has done a good job in terms of identifying the most fruitful avenues for growth, or do you think Groupon should have been more creative in its growth strategies? Make a list of things that Groupon *hasn't done* that you think have indirectly contributed to its growth.
2. How does a company go about getting its business featured on Groupon?
3. Of the current challenges facing Groupon, which one do you think is the most threatening? If you were

(continued)

the CEO of Groupon, how would you address this challenge?

4. Refer to the table shown in this case that lists Groupon's internal growth possibilities and its external growth possibilities. Of the eight growth possibilities, rank them 1 to 8 in terms of the order of likelihood that Groupon will utilize that possibility as part of its future growth strategy. Explain the rationale for your rankings.

Application Questions

1. Some observers have questioned whether Groupon's pace of growth is sustainable. Briefly make the argument for and the argument against the sustainability of Groupon's growth.

2. Sign up for Groupon in a city of your choice (it's free). Follow the Groupon deals for at least a week. Record your observations. Do you think Groupon's business model and its basic approach are sound? What is it that you liked and didn't like during the week that you followed Groupon? Do you think Groupon will remain attractive to businesses and consumers?

Sources: Groupon Web site, www.groupon.com (accessed April 17, 2011); Shira Ovide, "Groupon Merchant: 'There's a Flaw in Their Business,'" *Wall Street Journal*, January 7, 2011, B3; Bari Weiss, "Groupon's $6 Billion Gambler," *Wall Street Journal*, December 20, 2010; Ylan Q. Mui, "Some Businesses Are Victims of Social-Couponing (Groupon, LivingSocial) Success," *Washington Post*, September 17, 2010; Christopher Steiner, "Meet the Fastest Growing Company Ever," *Forbes*, August 30, 2010.

ENDNOTES

1. Personal conversation with Chris Herbert, March 20, 2011.
2. J. Daley, "Many American Franchises Are Not Only Surviving the Recession but Thriving In It by Expanding Their Operations Globally," *Entrepreneur*, May 2011, 100–103.
3. Amgen Home Page, www.amgen.com (accessed April 26, 2011).
4. K. Janowski, "Top 10 Reasons New Products Fail," *EcoStrategy Group*, www.ecostrategygroup. com/top10reasons.pdf, 2008, p. 2 (accessed April 28, 2011).
5. K. Rodan, "Stanford Technology Ventures," Entrepreneurial Thought Leaders Podcast, April 20, 2006.
6. F. M. Stone, *The Oracle of Oracle* (New York: AMACOM Books, 2002), 125.
7. S. Prashantham and C. Dhanaraj, "The Dynamic Influence of Social Capital on the International Growth of New Ventures," *Journal of Management Studies* 47, no. 6 (2010): 967–94; Y. Yamakawa, M. W. Peng, and D. L. Deeds, "What Drives New Ventures to Internalize from Emerging to Developed Economies?" *Entrepreneurship Theory and Practice* 32, no. 1 (2008): 59–82.
8. PricewaterhouseCoopers, "Fast-Growth CEOs Set Revenue Target and Investment Plans Higher, PricewaterhouseCoopers's Finds," *Trendsetter Barometer*, August 23, 2005.
9. S. Prashantham and S. Young, "Post-Entry Speed of International New Ventures," *Entrepreneurship Theory and Practice* 35, no. 2 (2011): 275–92; B. M. Oviatt and P. P. McDougall, "Defining International Entrepreneurship and Modeling the Speed of Internationalization," *Entrepreneurship Theory and Practice* 29 (2005): 537–53.
10. C. Rigby, "International Sales Now More Than a Third of Asos' Business," *InternetRetailing* www.internetretailing.net/2010/07/international-

sales-now-more-than-a-third-of-asos-business (accessed April 28, 2011, originally posted on July 15, 2010).
11. Slingbox Web site, www.slingbox.com (accessed April 28, 2011).
12. C. N. Pitelis and D. J. Teece, "Cross-Border Market Co-Creation, Dynamic Capabilities and the Entrepreneurial Theory of the Multinational Enterprise," *Industrial and Corporate Change* 19, no. 4 (2010): 1247–70.
13. D. Bonardo, S. Paleari, and S. Vismara, "The M&A Dynamics of European Science-Based Entrepreneurial Firms," *Journal of Technology Transfer* 35, no. 1 (2010): 141–80.
14. F. Wilson, "A Look Back at Summize," A VC Blog, www.avc.com/a_vc/2010/04/a-look-back-at-summize.html (accessed April 28, 2011, originally posted on April 20, 2010).
15. V. I. Ivaov and F. Xie, "Do Corporate Venture Capitalists Add Value to Start-Up Firms? Evidence from IPOs and Acquisitions of VC-Backed Companies," *Financial Management* 39, no. 1 (2010): 129–52.
16. A. Gambardella and A. M. McGahan, "Business-Model Innovation: General Purpose Technologies and Their Implications for Industry Structure," *Long Range Planning* 43, no. 2–3 (2010): 262–71.
17. I. M. Cockburn, M. J. MacGarvie, and E. Muller, "Patent Thickets, Licensing and Innovative Performance," *Industrial and Corporate Change* 19, no. 1 (2010): 899–925.
18. T. K. Das and N. Rahman, "Determinants of Partner Opportunism in Strategic Alliances: A Conceptual Framework," *Journal of Business and Psychology* 25, no. 1 (2010): 55–74; J. Wiklund and D. A. Shepherd, "The Effectiveness of Alliances and Acquisitions: The Role of Resource Combination Activities," *Entrepreneurship Theory and Practice* 33, no. 1 (2009): 193–212.

19. S. X. Zeng, X. M. Xie, and C. M. Tam, "Relations Between Cooperation Networks and Innovation Performance of SMEs," *Technovation* 30, no. 3. (2010): 181–94. S. A. Moskalev and R. B. Swensen, "Joint Ventures Around the Globe from 1990–2000: Forms, Types, Industries, Countries and Ownership 'Patterns,'" *Review of Financial Economics* 16, no. 1 (2007): 29–67.

20. N. Rosenbusch, J. Brinckmann, and A. Bausch, "Is Innovation Always Beneficial? A Meta-Analysis of the Relationship Between Innovation and Performance in SMEs," *Journal of Business Venturing* (2010): 441–57.

21. N. Evers, "Exploring Market Orientation in New Export Ventures," *International Journal of Entrepreneurship and Innovation Management* 13, nos. 3–4 (2010): 357–76; M. J. Leiblein and J. J. Reuer, "Building a Foreign Sales Base: The Roles of Capabilities and Alliances for Entrepreneurial Firms," *Journal of Business Venturing* 19, (2004): 285–307.

22. R. E. Hoskisson, J. Covin, H. W. Volberda, and R. A. Johnson, "Revitalizing Entrepreneurship: The Search for New Research Opportunities," *Journal of Management Studies* 48, no. 6 (2011): 1141–1168.

23. U. Wassmer, "Alliance Portfollios: A Review and Research Agenda," *Journal of Management* 38, no. 6 (2010): 141–71.

24. M. Dell, *Direct from Dell* (New York: HarperBusiness, 1999), 50.

25. E. Rasmussen, S. Mosey, and M. Wrights, "The Evolution of Entrepreneurial Competencies: A Longitudinal Study of University Spin-Off Venture Emergence," *Journal of Management Studies* 48, no. 6 (2011): 1314–1345; Y. Luo, "Are Joint Ventures Partners More Opportunistic in a More Volatile Environment?" *Strategic Management Journal* 28, no. 1 (2007): 39–60.

26. J. W. Webb, G. M. Kistruck, R. D. Ireland, and D. J. Ketchen, Jr., "The Entrepreneurship Process in Base of the Pyramid Markets: The Case of Multinational Enterprise/Nongovernment Organization Alliances," *Entrepreneurship Theory and Practice* 34, no. 3 (2010), 555–81.

27. T. W. Tong and J. J. Reuer, "Competitive Consequences of Interfirm Collaboration: How Joint Ventures Shape Industry Profitability," *Journal of International Business Studies* 41, no. 8 (2010): 1056–73.

28. Intel Capital homepage, www.intel.com/capital (accessed April 27, 2011).

Getting Personal *with* COLLEGE NANNIES & TUTORS

Founder:

JOSEPH KEELEY
BS, Entrepreneurship,
St. Thomas University, 2003

Dialogue *with*
Joseph Keeley

CURRENTLY IN MY
SMARTPHONE
Darius Rucker

BEST PART OF BEING
A STUDENT
Having the unsaid permission
to explore

MY ADVICE FOR NEW
ENTREPRENEURS
Ask for help early and often.

WHAT I DO WHEN I'M NOT
WORKING
Chase my 2 kids or golf

MY BIGGEST SURPRISE
AS AN ENTREPRENEUR
How good employees help your
business and how much bad
employees hurt the business

MY BIGGEST WORRY
AS AN ENTREPRENEUR
Not getting there fast enough

CHAPTER 15

Franchising

COLLEGE NANNIES & TUTORS

Franchising as a Form of Business Ownership and Growth

Web: www.collegenannies.com
Facebook: College Nannies & Tutors

Joseph Keeley grew up in a small town in North Dakota. After graduating from high school in 2000, he moved to St. Paul, Minnesota, to attend St. Thomas University. One of Keeley's passions was hockey, which he fulfilled as a member of St. Thomas's varsity hockey team. While playing hockey, he became acquainted with a couple who had two young boys and a girl. As the summer following his freshman year approached, the couple asked him if he'd be interested in watching their kids as a full-time summer job. Keeley jumped at the chance. While his two roommates spent the summer digging pools for a local contractor, Keeley engaged in fun activities with the children while acting as their nanny and role model.

The summer job got Keeley to thinking about how young kids could benefit from being around positive role models and how college students are uniquely capable of filling that role. The idea was so compelling that during his sophomore year he launched a company called Summer College Nannies. Matching college students with families that needed part-time or full-time nanny services was the firm's core service. Early on he viewed himself more as a matchmaker than as a potential franchisor and thought of his business primarily as a way to earn extra cash. But as time went on, two things struck Keeley. First, rather than just a means of earning extra money, he started to see real potential in the college nanny idea. For many parents, a service wasn't available to help them find a safe and reliable nanny. He also liked the idea of making a positive difference in the lives of families and young children. Second, he found that working on a "real" business enhanced his classroom experiences. "I feel I had 10 times the education that anyone else did because I had a working, living project everyday," Keeley said, reflecting on this point.[1]

As the business picked up steam, St. Thomas provided Keeley with office space, and he turned Summer College Nannies into a self-made internship. To get advice, he started dropping in on St. Thomas entrepreneurship professors, who urged him to enroll in

LEARNING OBJECTIVES

After studying this chapter you should be ready to:

1. Explain franchising and how it differs from other forms of business ownership.

2. Describe the differences between a product and trademark franchise and a business format franchise.

3. Explain the differences among an individual franchise agreement, an area franchise agreement, and a master franchise agreement.

4. Describe the advantages of establishing a franchise system as a means of firm growth.

5. Identify the rules of thumb for determining when franchising is an appropriate form of growth for a particular business.

6. Discuss the factors to consider in determining if owning a franchise is a good fit for a particular person.

7. Identify the costs associated with buying a franchise.

8. Discuss the advantages and disadvantages of buying a franchise.

9. Identify the common mistakes franchise buyers make.

10. Describe the purpose of the Franchise Disclosure Document.

the entrepreneurship program—which he did. As time went on, Keeley entered and won several business plan competitions with the Summer College Nannies business idea. He also won the 2003 Global Student Entrepreneurship Award, which is presented by the Entrepreneurs' Organization and included a $20,000 prize. At the awards ceremony, Keeley met Peter Lytle, an angel investor and well-known Minneapolis entrepreneur. Although he had interviewed for traditional jobs, by this time Keeley had decided that he would devote his time and energy to his own business venture after graduating with his college degree. Lytle was so impressed with Keeley and his business idea that he offered to invest, and Keeley accepted the offer. At this point, Lytle helped Keeley expand his vision for the business to include tutors, and College Nannies & Tutors was born. Lytle has since passed away, but was instrumental in the most formative years of the business.

Following graduation, the money Lytle invested provided Keeley the time and resources to more fully develop the College Nannies & Tutors business idea. The company started generating some buzz, primarily through media coverage and word of mouth. One of the things that interested the media was the fact the Keeley, a male and a recent college graduate, was starting a company in an industry—childcare—that traditionally females dominated. The first College Nannies & Tutors center was opened in Wayzata, a suburb of Minneapolis. In college, Keeley took a class in franchising and learned about the potential of this form of business. As Keeley fine-tuned his business idea over two long years of testing and planning, it became clear that College Nannies & Tutors could be a viable franchise. Interestingly, part of the firm's franchising process included proprietary ways for screening nannies through background checks, interviews, and psychological assessments and matching them with families. Commenting on the suitability of College Nannies & Tutors for franchising, Keeley remarked, "[And] there's value there as a franchise because we've figured it out. You (a potential franchisee) don't have to go through the learning curve."[2]

Currently, College Nannies & Tutors has approximately 79 franchise locations across several states, and its franchisees had combined sales of $18 million in 2010. The company's goal is to boost systemwide sales to $100 million in five to seven years. As for Keeley, he remains as passionate about College Nannies & Tutors as he was in 2003 when the company started. His success as an entrepreneur hasn't gone unrecognized. In 2010, he was named Ernst & Young Entrepreneur of the Year for the Upper Midwest Region.[3]

As with College Nannies & Tutors, many retail and service organizations find franchising to be an attractive form of business ownership and growth. In some industries, such as automotive and retail food, franchising is a dominant business ownership. Franchising is less common in other industries, although it is used in industries as diverse as Internet service providers, furniture restoration, personnel staffing, and senior care.

There are instances in which franchising is not appropriate. For example, new technologies are typically not introduced through franchise systems, particularly if the technology is proprietary or complex. Why? Because by its nature, franchising involves sharing of knowledge between a franchisor and its franchisees; in large franchise organizations, thousands of people may be involved in doing this. The inventors of new technologies typically involve as few people as possible in the process of rolling out their new products or services because they want to keep their trade secrets secret. They typically reserve their new technologies for their own use or license them to a relatively small number of companies, with strict confidentiality agreements in place.[4]

Still, franchising is a common method of business expansion and is growing in popularity. In 2007 (the most recent year reliable statistics are available), 765,723 individual franchise outlets were operating in the United States. These operations accounted for 7.6 million jobs and a combined economic output of $654.2 billion. Each of these numbers is expected to be stronger for 2011 and beyond, as the U.S. economy appears to be making progress with its efforts to pull out of the recent global recession.[5] You can even go to a Web site (www.franchising.com) to examine the array of franchises available for potential entrepreneurs to consider. This Web site groups franchising opportunities by industry, location, type, eco-friendly, women based, and several other criteria. These categorizations highlight the breadth of franchising opportunities now available for consideration.[6]

Unfortunately, not all the news about franchising is positive. Because many franchise systems operate in competitive industries and grow quickly, the failure rate is relatively high. In one highly regarded study, 45 percent of all retail franchises included in the study failed in their first four to seven years.[7] Plus, despite its proliferation, franchising is a relatively poorly understood form of business ownership and growth. While most students and entrepreneurs generally know what franchising is and what it entails, the many subtle aspects of franchising can be learned only through experience or careful study.

We begin this chapter, which is dedicated to franchising as an important potential path to entrepreneurship and subsequent venture growth, with a description of franchising and when to use it. We then explore setting up a franchise system from the franchisor's perspective and buying a franchise from the franchisee's point of view. Next, we look at the legal aspects of franchising. We close this chapter by considering a few additional topics related to the successful use of franchising.

WHAT IS FRANCHISING AND HOW DOES IT WORK?

Franchising is a form of business organization in which a firm that already has a successful product or service (**franchisor**) licenses its trademark and method of doing businesses to other businesses (**franchisees**) in exchange for an initial franchise fee and an ongoing royalty.[8] Some franchisors are established firms; others are first-time enterprises that entrepreneurs are launching. This section explores the origins of franchising and how franchising works.

> **LEARNING OBJECTIVE**
> 1. Explain franchising and how it differs from other forms of business ownership.

What Is Franchising?

The word *franchise* comes from an old dialect of French and means "privilege" or "freedom." Franchising has a long history. In the Middle Ages kings and lords granted franchises to specific individuals or groups to hunt on their land or to conduct certain forms of commerce. In the 1840s, breweries in Germany granted franchises to certain taverns to be the exclusive distributors of their beer for the region. Shortly after the U.S. Civil War, the Singer Sewing Machine Company began granting distribution franchises for its sewing machines and pioneered the use of written franchise agreements. Many of the most familiar franchises in the United States, including Kentucky Fried Chicken (1952), McDonald's (1955), Burger King (1955), Midas Muffler (1956), and H&R Block (1958), started in the post–World War II era of the 1940s and 1950s.

The franchise organization Comfort Keepers demonstrates how franchises are started. A year before the company was founded, Kristina Clum, a registered nurse, noticed that her parents were having trouble with ordinary daily chores. She wanted someone to come into their home to help them but was unable to find people willing to do so. So Kristina and her husband Jerry founded a business dedicated to helping seniors cope with everyday nonmedical tasks, such as meal preparation, light housekeeping, grocery shopping, laundry, and errands. The first Comfort Keepers office was opened in Springfield, Ohio, in March 1998, and the second was opened in Dayton a year later.

Comfort Keepers is a timely idea that addresses a need for a particular target market. As we've discussed in earlier chapters, having a solid business idea is critical to achieving firm growth. In 2011, it's estimated there will be over 41 million people in the United States over the age of 65.[9] That number is expected to steadily increase. Comfort Keepers' services may provide some seniors the option of staying in their homes as opposed to entering more costly assisted living centers. In August 1999, the company began franchising and by 2011 had over 660 franchise outlets throughout the United States, Canada, Ireland, Australia, New Zealand, and Singapore.[10]

The Comfort Keepers business idea lends itself to franchising because the company has a good trademark and a good business method. Moreover, because the nature of the business keeps the cost of starting a Comfort Keepers franchise relatively low, there is a substantial pool of people available to purchase the franchise. For Comfort Keepers and its franchisees, franchising is a win-win proposition. Comfort Keepers wins because it is able to use its franchisees' money to quickly grow its business and strengthen its brand. The franchisees win because they are able to start a business in a growing industry relatively inexpensively and benefit by adopting the Comfort Keepers trademark and method of doing business.

How Does Franchising Work?

There is nothing magical about franchising. It is a form of growth that allows a business to get its products or services to market through the efforts of business partners or "franchisees." As described previously, a franchise is an agreement between a franchisor (the parent company, such as College Nannies & Tutors or Comfort Keepers) and a franchisee (an individual or firm that is willing to pay the franchisor a fee for the right to sell its product, service, and/or business method).[11] Planet Smoothie, for example, is a very successful franchise system. The franchisor (Planet Smoothie, Inc.) provides the rights to individual businesspersons (the local franchisees) to use the Planet Smoothie trademark and business methods. In turn, the franchisees pay Planet Smoothie a franchise fee and an ongoing royalty for these privileges and agree to operate their Planet Smoothie restaurants according to Planet Smoothie Inc.'s standards.

There are two distinctly different types of franchise systems: the product and trademark franchise and the business format franchise. A **product and trademark franchise** is an arrangement under which the franchisor grants to the franchisee the right to buy its products and use its trade name. This approach typically connects a single manufacturer with a network of dealers or distributors. For example, General Motors has established a network of dealers that sell GM cars and use the GM trademark in their advertising and promotions. Similarly, ExxonMobil has established a network of franchisee-owned gasoline stations to distribute its gasoline. Product and trademark franchisees are typically permitted to operate in a fairly autonomous manner. The parent company, such as GM or ExxonMobil, is generally concerned more with maintaining the integrity of its products than with monitoring the day-to-day activities of its dealers or station owners. Other examples of product and trademark franchise systems include agricultural machinery dealers, soft-drink

LEARNING OBJECTIVE

2. Describe the differences between a product and trademark franchise and a business format franchise.

bottlers, and beer distributorships. Rather than obtaining a royalty or franchise fee, the product and trademark franchisor obtains the majority of its income from selling its products to its dealers or distributors at a markup.

The second type of franchise, the **business format franchise**, is by far the more popular approach to franchising and is more commonly used by entrepreneurs and entrepreneurial ventures. In a business format franchise, the franchisor provides a formula for doing business to the franchisee along with training, advertising, and other forms of assistance. We show the top 10 business lines in which business format franchises operate in Table 15.1. While a business format franchise provides a franchisee a formula for conducting business, it can also be very rigid and demanding. For example, fast-food restaurants such as McDonald's and Burger King teach their franchisees every detail of how to run their restaurants, from how many seconds to cook french fries to the exact words their employees should use when they greet customers (such as "Will this be dining in or carry out?"). Business format franchisors obtain the majority of their revenues from their franchisees in the form of royalties and franchise fees.

For both product and trademark franchises and business format franchises, the franchisor–franchisee relationship takes one of three forms of a franchise agreement (see Figure 15.1). The most common type of franchise arrangement is an individual franchise agreement. An **individual franchise agreement** involves the sale of a single franchise for a specific location. For example, an individual may purchase a Play It Again Sports franchise to be constructed and operated at 901 Pearl Street in Boulder, Colorado. An **area franchise agreement** allows a franchisee to own and operate a specific number of outlets in a particular geographic area. For example, a franchisee may purchase the rights to open five Play It Again Sports franchises within the city limits of Sioux Falls, South Dakota. This is a very popular franchise arrangement, because in most cases it gives the franchisee exclusive rights for a given area. Finally, a **master franchise agreement** is similar to an area franchise agreement, with one major difference. A master franchisee, in addition to having the right to open and operate a specific number of locations in a particular area, also has the right to offer and sell the franchise to other people in its area. For example, ProntoWash is a mobile car washing service that uses environmentally friendly soaps, waxes, and other products. The company sells master franchise agreements that provide a master franchisee the right to open a certain number of ProntoWash outlets in a defined geographic area. After its own outlets have been opened, the master franchisee

LEARNING OBJECTIVE

3. Explain the differences among an individual franchise agreement, an area franchise agreement, and a master franchise agreement.

TABLE 15.1   TOP 10 BUSINESS LINES IN WHICH BUSINESS FORMAT FRANCHISES OPERATE

- Automotive
- Commercial and Residential Services
- Quick Service Restaurants
- Table/Full-Service Restaurants
- Retail Food
- Lodging
- Real Estate
- Retail Products and Services
- Business Services
- Personal Services

Based on International Franchise Organization, "Highlights of the 2011 Franchise Business Economic Outlook," www.franchise.org (accessed May 19, 2011, originally posted on January 2011).

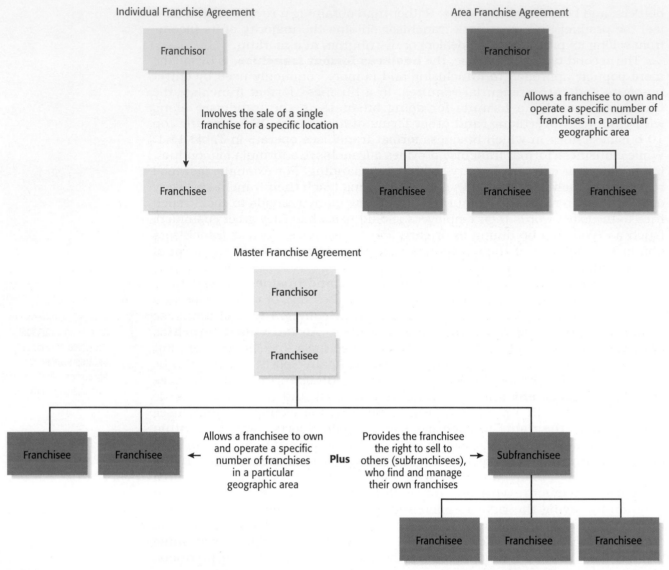

FIGURE 15.1
Different Types of Franchise Systems

can then sell the rights to open additional ProntoWash locations in the same area to other individuals.[12] The people who buy franchises from master franchisees are typically called **subfranchisees**.

A person who owns and operates more than one outlet of the same franchisor, whether through an area or a master franchise agreement, is called a **multiple-unit franchisee**. According to FRANdata, a research firm in Arlington, Virginia, 53 percent of all U.S. franchise units are controlled by multiunit franchisees.[13] For the franchisee, there are advantages and disadvantages to multiple-unit franchising. By owning more than one unit, a multiple-unit franchisee can capture economies of scale and reduce its administrative overhead per unit of sale. The disadvantages of multiple-unit franchising are that the franchisor takes more risk and makes a deeper commitment to a single franchisor. In general, franchisors encourage multiple-unit franchising. By selling an additional franchise to an existing franchisee, a franchisor can grow its business without adding to the total number of franchisees with whom it must maintain a relationship to conduct its business.

ESTABLISHING A FRANCHISE SYSTEM

Establishing a franchise system should be approached carefully and deliberately. While the process is a familiar one to a company such as McDonald's, which as of May 2011 had over 32,500 franchised units worldwide and generated $76.7 billion in sales revenue in 2010, franchising is an unfamiliar process to a new franchise organization. Franchising is a complicated business endeavor, which means that an entrepreneur must look closely at all of its aspects before deciding to franchise. Indeed, franchising often involves the managerially demanding tasks of training, supporting, supervising, and nurturing franchisees.

An entrepreneur should also be aware that over the years a number of fraudulent franchise organizations have come and gone and left financially ruined franchisees in their wake. Because of this, franchising is a fairly heavily regulated form of business expansion. Even with this regulation, though, caution is in order for those pursuing franchising as a business opportunity.

Despite the challenges, franchising is a popular form of growth. It is particularly attractive to new firms in retailing and services because it helps firms grow and alleviates the challenge of raising substantial amounts of money. There is some anecdotal evidence, however, that many companies are hasty in putting together their franchise programs and as a result do a poorer job than they might have were they to take their time.[14] Although franchising is often touted as an easy way to rapidly expand a business, an effective franchise system needs to be as consciously initiated, managed, and supported as any other form of business expansion.[15] An example of a franchise organization that has been consciously managed and has grown in a sensible manner is Wahoo's Fish Taco, as illustrated in the "Savvy Entrepreneurial Firm" feature.

Now let's look more closely at the issues to consider when an entrepreneur is trying to decide if franchising is an appropriate approach to growing a business.

> **LEARNING OBJECTIVE**
> 4. Describe the advantages of establishing a franchise system as a means of firm growth.

When to Franchise

Retail firms grow when two things happen: first, when the attractiveness of a firm's products or services become well known, whether it is a new restaurant or a fitness center, and, second, when a firm has the financial capability to build the outlets needed to satisfy the demand for its products or services.

There are at least two options firms have as a means to grow. Building company-owned outlets is one of these options. However, this choice presents a company with the challenge of raising the money to fund its expansion. As discussed in Chapter 10, this option is typically pursued through debt, investment capital, or earnings, none of which is easy to achieve for a start-up venture.

Franchising is a second growth alternative available to firms. Franchising is perhaps especially attractive to young firms in that the majority of the money needed for expansion comes from the franchisees. Franchising is appropriate when a firm has a strong or potentially strong trademark, a well-designed business model, and a desire to grow. A franchise system will ultimately fail if the franchisee's brand doesn't create value for customers and its business model is flawed or poorly developed.

In some instances, franchising is simply not appropriate. For example, franchising works for Burger King but would not work for Walmart. While Burger King has a large number of franchise outlets, each individual outlet is relatively small and has a limited menu, and policies and procedures can be written to cover almost any contingency. In contrast, although Walmart is

> **LEARNING OBJECTIVE**
> 5. Identify the rules of thumb for determining when franchising is an appropriate form of growth for a particular business.

Wahoo's Fish Taco: A Moderate-Growth Yet Highly Successful Franchise Organization

Web: www.wahoos.com
Twitter: WahoosFish Taco
Facebook: Wahoo's Fish Tacos

Wahoo's Fish Taco is a franchise organization that offers Mexican food mixed with Brazilian and Asian flavors. It is a "fast-casual" restaurant that was founded in Costa Mesa, California, in 1988 by Chinese-Brazilian brothers Edurado Lee, Mingo Lee, and Wing Lam, who mixed traditional Chinese and Brazilian flavors with dishes they encountered traveling in Mexico. The first Wahoo's Fish Taco restaurant was started to combine the brothers' love for surfing and food.

Wahoo's is now just over 20 years old and has about 50 locations, primarily in California, Texas, Colorado, and Hawaii. Although it's been very successful, it couldn't be characterized as a "rapid growth" franchise system. Instead, the founders have elected to make Wahoo's Fish Taco a relatively slow growth system, focusing on branding and service quality rather than rapid growth. This philosophy has been an entrenched part of the way Wahoo's Fish Taco has done business since the beginning. It started with a single restaurant in 1988; the second unit was added only when the founders had saved enough money to build it debt free. This pattern has characterized the company's growth. Early on, it only added one new restaurant a year, then two, then three, and so on. Despite its success, it has averaged only about 2.5 restaurants per year since its founding. For many years, the company only sold franchises to people the founders personally knew and trusted.

Wahoo's Fish Taco has now adopted a somewhat more aggressive philosophy toward growth, although its core values remain the same. In 2009, the company hired Tom Orbe, a business professional, to accelerate its growth plans. It plans to add 100 locations in the next five years. The expansion is motivated by the company's strong financial position and also by the increased availability of prime locations at reasonable prices, which is fallout of the recent recession. The company anticipates receiving a large number of inquiries for the additional 100 locations. It plans to apply four criteria to selecting franchises: passion for the brand, community involvement, restaurant experience, and financial capacity. Consistent with Wahoo's Fish Taco's history, locations will only be offered in select areas, and no international expansion is immediately planned.

Along with its staple dishes, which include fish tacos, enchiladas, burritos, and salads, Wahoo's Fish Taco's offers many vegetarian and vegan options, such as tofu, banzai veggies, and brown rice.

Questions for Critical Thinking

1. What are the advantages and disadvantages of Wahoo's Fish Taco's slow growth philosophy of franchise expansion?
2. Spend some time looking at Wahoo's Fish Taco's Web site, focusing particularly on its menu and its store layout. Do you think the business is well-positioned or poorly positioned to take advantage of current trends in the types of restaurants that are doing well and food preferences? Explain your answer.
3. Wahoo's Fish Taco anticipates a large degree of interest in the 100 franchises that it plans to award over the next five years. Does the company risk "leaving money on the table" by placing an arbitrary 100 on the number of franchises it plans to add? If you were advising Wahoo's Fish Taco, and the company received applications from 200 rather than 100 highly qualified candidates to open Wahoo's Fish Taco franchises, would you advise the company to stick to 100 or to allow 200 new franchise locations to open?
4. Evaluate Wahoo's Fish Taco's four criteria for selecting franchises. Do you think these are appropriate criteria? If you were asked to suggest a fifth and a sixth criteria, what would they be?

Sources: Wahoo's Fish Taco's Web site, www.wahoos.com (accessed March 31, 2011); April Forristall, "Q&A: Tom Orbe, Wahoo's Fish Taco," SeafoodSource.com, www.seafoodsource.com/newsarticledetail.aspx?id=4294968230 (accessed March 31, 2011).

similar to Burger King in that it, too, has a strong trademark and thousands of outlets, Walmart stores are much larger, more expensive to build, and more complex to run compared to the complexity of running a Burger King restaurant. It would be nearly impossible for Walmart to find an adequate number of qualified people who would have the financial capital and expertise to open and successfully operate a Walmart store.

Steps to Franchising a Business

Let's assume that as an entrepreneur you have decided to use franchising as a means of growing your venture. What steps should you take to develop a franchise system? As illustrated in Figure 15.2, you, as an entrepreneur, should take nine steps in order to successfully set up a franchise system.

Step 1   **Develop a franchise business plan:**   The franchise business plan should follow the format of a conventional business plan that we discussed in Chapter 4 and should fully describe the rationale for franchising the business and act as a blueprint for rolling out the franchise operation. Particular attention should be paid to the location of the proposed franchise outlet. For example, a Baskin-Robbins franchise that is successful in the food court of a mall in an upscale area doesn't mean that it will be successful in a less heavily trafficked strip mall in an average-income neighborhood.

Step 2   **Get professional advice:**   Before going too far, a potential franchisor should seek advice from a qualified franchise attorney, consultant, or certified public accountant. If the business cannot be realistically turned into a franchise, then a qualified professional can save a potential franchisor a lot of time, money, and frustration by urging that the process be stopped. If the business can be turned into a franchise, then it is advisable to get professional advice to help direct the entire process.

Step 3   **Conduct an intellectual property audit:**   As we discussed in Chapter 12, this step is necessary to determine the intellectual property a company owns and to ensure that the property is properly registered and protected. All original written, audio, and visual material, including operating manuals, training videos, advertising brochures, and similar matter, should be afforded copyright protection. If a firm has a unique business model that includes a unique business method, it should consider obtaining a patent for its business method. These protective measures are vital because once a company begins franchising, its trademarks and business model and any unique

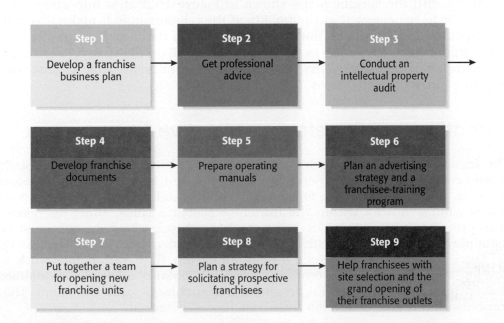

FIGURE 15.2
Nine Steps in Setting
Up a Franchise System

business methods are disseminated, making them more visible to customers and competitors. In addition, a franchisor should make sure that its trademark is not infringing on the trademark of any other firm.

Step 4 **Develop franchise documents:** Later in the chapter, we discuss the documents that are required to franchise a business. Here, we can note that at the beginning of the franchise evaluation process, a prospective franchisor should prepare the Franchise Disclosure Document (formally called the Uniform Franchise Offering Circular) and the franchise agreement. A franchise attorney can provide specific information regarding the content and format of these documents.

Step 5 **Prepare operating manuals:** Businesses that are suitable for franchising typically have a polished business system that can be fairly easily taught to qualified franchisees. The franchisor should prepare manuals that document all aspects of its business model.

Step 6 **Plan an advertising strategy and a franchisee-training program:** Prospective franchisees will want to see an advertising strategy and a franchisee-training program in place. The scope of each program should match the speed at which the franchisor wants to grow its business.

Step 7 **Put together a team for opening new franchise units:** A team should be developed and prepared to help new franchisees open their franchise units. The team should be well trained and equipped to provide the franchisee a broad range of training and guidance.

Step 8 **Plan a strategy for soliciting prospective franchisees:** There are many channels available to franchisors to solicit and attract potential franchisees. Franchise trade fairs, newspaper ads, franchise publications, social media platforms, and Internet advertising are examples of these channels.

Step 9 **Help franchisees with site selection and the grand opening of their franchise outlets:** Location is very important to most retail businesses, so a franchisor should be heavily involved in the site selection of its franchisees' outlets. The franchisor should also help the franchisee with the grand opening of the franchise outlet.

Along with the specific steps shown in Figure 15.2, it is important for a franchisor to remember that the quality of the relationships it maintains with its franchisees often defines the ultimate success of the franchise system. It is to the franchisor's advantage to follow through on all promises and to establish an exemplary reputation. This is an ongoing commitment that a franchisor should make to its franchisees.

Selecting and Developing Effective Franchisees

The franchisor's ability to select and develop effective franchisees strongly influences the degree to which a franchise system is successful. For most systems, the ideal franchisee is someone who has solid ideas and suggestions but is willing to work within the franchise system's rules. Bold, aggressive entrepreneurs typically do not make good franchisees. Franchisees must be team players to properly fit within the context of a successful franchise system.

Once franchisees are selected, it is important that franchisors work to develop their franchisees' potential. Table 15.2 contains a list of the qualities that franchisors look for in prospective franchisees and the steps that franchisors can take to develop their franchisees' potential.

TABLE 15.2 **SELECTING AND DEVELOPING EFFECTIVE FRANCHISEES**

Qualities to Look for in Prospective Franchisees

- Good work ethic
- Ability to follow instructions
- Ability to operate with minimal supervision
- Team oriented
- Experience in the industry in which the franchise competes
- Adequate financial resources and a good credit history
- Ability to make suggestions without becoming confrontational or upset if the suggestions are not adopted
- Represents the franchisor in a positive manner

Ways Franchisors Can Develop the Potential of Their Franchisees

- Provide mentoring that supersedes routine training
- Keep operating manuals up-to-date
- Keep product, services, and business systems up-to-date
- Solicit input from franchisees to reinforce their importance in the larger system
- Encourage franchisees to develop a franchise association
- Maintain the franchise system's integrity

Advantages and Disadvantages of Establishing a Franchise System

There are two primary advantages to franchising. First, early in the life of an organization, capital is typically scarce, and rapid growth is needed to achieve brand recognition and economies of scale. Franchising helps a venture grow quickly because franchisees provide the majority of the capital.[16] For example, if Comfort Keepers were growing via company-owned outlets rather than franchising, it would probably have only a handful of outlets rather than the more than 660 it has today. Many franchisors even admit that they would have rather grown through company-owned stores but that the capital requirements needed to grow their firms dictated franchising. This sentiment is affirmed by an executive at Hardee's, who wrote the following about the growth of this fast-food chain:

> Hardee's would have preferred not to have franchised a single location. We prefer company-owned locations. But due to the heavy capital investment required, we could only expand company-owned locations to a certain degree—from there we had to stop. Each operation represents an investment in excess of $100,000; therefore, we entered the franchise business.[17]

Second, a management concept called **agency theory** argues that for organizations with multiple units (such as restaurant chains), it is more effective for the units to be run by franchisees than by managers who run company-owned stores. The theory is that managers, because they are usually paid a salary, may not be as committed to the success of their individual units as franchisees, who are in effect the owners of the units they manage.[18]

The primary disadvantage of franchising is that an organization allows others to profit from its trademark and business model. For example, each time Comfort Keepers sells a franchise it gets a $38,500 franchise fee and an ongoing royalty, which is 3 to 5 percent of gross sales. However, if Comfort Keepers had provided its service itself in the same location, it would be getting 100 percent of the gross sales and net profits from the location. This is the main reason some organizations that are perfectly suitable for franchising grow through company-owned stores rather than franchising. An example is Darden Restaurants Inc., the parent company of Red Lobster, Olive Garden, Bahama Breeze, LongHorn Steakhouse, The Capital Grill, and Seasons 52. With over 1,800 locations, this firm is the largest publicly held casual dining restaurant chain in the world.[19] All of Darden's units are company owned. Starbucks is another company that is suitable for franchising but has only a small number of franchise outlets. We provide a more complete list of the advantages and disadvantages of franchising as a means of business expansion in Table 15.3.

TABLE 15.3 ADVANTAGES AND DISADVANTAGES OF FRANCHISING AS A METHOD OF BUSINESS EXPANSION

Advantages	Disadvantages
Rapid, low-cost market expansion. Because franchisees provide most of the cost of expansion, the franchisor can expand the size of its business fairly rapidly.	**Profit sharing.** By selling franchises instead of operating company-owned stores, franchisors share the profits derived from their proprietary products or services with their franchisees. For example, before being acquired by FedEx, Kinko's did not sell franchises, allowing it to retain all its profits.
Income from franchise fees and royalties. By collecting franchise fees, the franchisor gets a fairly quick return on the proprietary nature of its products/services and business model. The franchisor also receives ongoing royalties from its franchisees without incurring substantial risk.	**Loss of control.** It is typically more difficult for a franchisor to control its franchisees than it is for a company to control its employees. Franchisees, despite the rules governing the franchise system, still often view themselves as independent businesspeople.
Franchisee motivation. Because franchisees put their personal capital at risk, they are highly motivated to make their franchise outlets successful. In contrast, the managers of company-owned outlets typically do not have their own capital at risk. As a result, these managers may not be prone to work as hard as franchisees or be as attentive to cost savings.	**Friction with franchisees.** A common complaint of franchisors is dealing with the friction that often develops between franchisors and franchisees. Friction can develop over issues such as the payment of fees, hours of operation, caveats in the franchise agreement, and surprise inspections.
Access to ideas and suggestions. Franchisees represent a source of intellectual capital and often make suggestions to their franchisors. By incorporating these ideas into their business model, franchisors can in effect leverage the ideas and suggestions of their individual franchisees.	**Managing growth.** Franchisors that are in growing industries and have a strong trademark often grow quickly. Although this might seem like an advantage, rapid growth can be difficult to manage. A franchisor provides each of its franchisees a number of services, such as site selection and employee training. If a franchise system is growing rapidly, the franchisor will have to continually add personnel to its own staff to properly support its growing number of franchisees.
Cost savings. Franchisees share many of the franchisors' expenses, such as the cost of regional and national advertising.	**Differences in required business skills.** The business skills that made a franchisor successful in the original business are typically not the same skills needed to manage a franchise system. For example, Sam Jones may be a very effective owner/manager of a seafood restaurant. That does not necessarily mean, however, that he will be an effective manager of a franchise system if he decided to franchise his seafood restaurant concept.
Increased buying power. Franchisees provide franchisors increased buying power by enlarging the size of their business, allowing them to purchase larger quantities of products and services when buying those items.	**Legal expenses.** Many states have specific laws pertaining to franchising. As a result, if a franchisor sells franchises in multiple states, legal expenses can be high to properly interpret and comply with each state's laws. Unfortunately, from the franchisor's point of view, some of the toughest laws are in the most populated states.

When a company decides to investigate franchising as a means of growth, it should ensure that it and its product or service meet several criteria. Businesses that fail to satisfy these criteria are less likely to make effective franchise systems. Before deciding to franchise, a firm should consider the following:

LEARNING OBJECTIVE
6. Discuss the factors to consider in determining if owning a franchise is a good fit for a particular person.

- **The uniqueness of its product or service:** The business's product or service should be unique along some dimension that creates value for customers. Businesses with a unique product or service typically have the best potential to expand.

- **The consistent profitability of the firm:** The business should be consistently profitable, and the future profitability of the business should be fairly easy to predict. When developing a franchise system, a company should have several prototype outlets up and running to test and ensure the viability of the business idea. Remember, a franchisee is supposed to be buying a way of doing business (in the form of a business model) that is "proven"—at least to a certain extent. Franchisors that learn how to run their businesses through the trial and error of their franchisees have typically franchised their businesses prematurely (especially from the franchisees' point of view).

- **The firm's year-round profitability:** The business should be profitable year-round, not only during specific seasons. For example, a lawn and garden care franchise in North Dakota should be set up to provide the franchisee supplemental products and services to sell during off-peak seasons. Otherwise, owning the franchise may not be an attractive form of business ownership. This issue is particularly problematic for some ice cream and smoothie franchises in northern states, which experience a significant decline in sales during winter months.

- **The degree of refinement of the firm's business systems:** The systems and procedures for operating the business should be polished and the procedures documented in written form. The systems and procedures should also be fairly easy to teach to qualified candidates.

- **The clarity of the business proposition:** The business proposition should be crystal clear so that prospective franchisees fully understand the business proposition to which they are committing. The relationship between the franchisor and the franchisee should be completely open, and communication between them should be candid.

After determining that the firm satisfies these criteria, the entrepreneur should step back and review all the alternatives for business expansion. No single form of business expansion is the best under all circumstances. For any entrepreneurial venture, the best form of expansion is the one that increases the likelihood that the venture will reach its objectives.

One franchise organization that started fast but is now faltering is Curves International, as depicted in this chapter's "What Went Wrong?" feature.

BUYING A FRANCHISE

Now let's look at franchising from the franchisee's perspective. Purchasing a franchise is an important business decision involving a substantial financial commitment. Potential franchise owners should strive to be as well informed as possible before purchasing a franchise and should be well aware that it is often legally and financially difficult to exit a franchise relationship. Indeed, an individual franchise opportunity should be meticulously scrutinized. Close scrutiny of a potential franchise opportunity includes activities such as meeting with the

WHAT WENT WRONG?

Trouble at Curves International

Web: www.curves.com
Twitter: CurvesNews
Facebook: Curves

Curves International, whose 30-minute workout and singular focus on women made it among the world's fastest-growing franchise organizations, seems to be losing at least a bit of steam.

Over the past three years, nearly one-third of Curve's 7,700 franchises have closed, according to a recent franchise disclosure the company filed. In 2009, more than 1,000 Curves franchises closed while only 35 new ones opened.

While opinions vary about what went wrong with Curves, experts agree on four points: (1) the company failed to keep up with changing trends, including more flexible hours for busy working women, (2) cheaper competition, (3) the poor economy, and (4) the company sold too many franchises that are located too close together.

Founded in 1992, Curves was an instant hit, largely because it targeted an underserved part of the market: busy and unfit women. Curves' founders believed that many women 30 years old and older cared deeply about their health and appearance but didn't want to join a fitness center full of people who were already fit. So they created a fitness center "just for them" that was convenient, affordable, and restricted to females. The Curves "concept" was structured on a stripped-down version of the traditional fitness center, based on a tightly structured 30-minute workout using 8 to 12 exercise machines. Curves fitness centers do not have locker rooms, showers, aerobic classes, or juice bars. Instead they're designed to be convenient and quick. Monthly dues vary, but range from about $29 to $49 per month.

Curves disagrees with its critics' assessments. Mike Raymond, Curve's president, says that the majority of the franchises that have closed are due to a "pruning of the system," and that many of its franchisees bought into Curves for the wrong reasons. He says failed franchisees were motivated primarily as investors rather than owners.

Of the four reasons cited for Curves' troubles, an inability to keep up with changing trends may be the biggest culprit. Some Curves locations aren't open over the noon hour, causing some patrons to look elsewhere for their workouts. Also, 24-hour fitness centers, including Snap Fitness and Anytime Fitness, have opened in many areas, providing busy women even more flexibility than Curves. Some members may have also tired of Curves' bare-bones approach and gravitated to fitness centers that offer aerobics classes, Yoga, Pilates, and dressing rooms with showers.

According to a July 2010 article in the *Wall Street Journal*, Curves also gained a reputation in the fitness industry for a lack of flexibility. In fact, some Curves franchisees say they began asking headquarters for changes in their format so they could retain members, but found that their requests were largely ignored.

Curves was one of the world's premier franchise organizations throughout the 1990s and early 2000s, boasting nearly 4 million members worldwide at the end of 2008. Its membership number is now sharply lower.

Questions for Critical Thinking

1. Why do you think Curves has remained inflexible to change? To what degree do you think this single factor contributes to Curves' recent troubles? Do you believe that Curves will continue losing franchises, or do you think the company will recover and start growing again?

2. To what degree do you believe that Curves' headquarters (the franchisor) is culpable in the failure of so many Curves' franchise locations? Do you buy Mike Raymond's explanation for why so many Curves' franchises are going out of business?

3. If you were thinking about buying a franchise, write three questions that you'd ask a franchise organization you were thinking about buying into as a direct result of reading this feature.

4. The "You Be the VC 15.1" feature focuses on Smartwash2U, a franchise organization that focuses on providing self-service laundry with minimum price and quality service. If you were the CEO of Smartwash2U, how would you attract your customers and convince them to stay with you?

Source: R. Gibson, "Curves Loses Stamina, Closing Fitness Clubs," Wall Street Journal, July 7, 2010.

franchisor and reading the Franchise Disclosure Document, soliciting legal and financial advice, and talking to former franchisees that have dropped out of the system one is considering. In particularly heavily franchised industries, such as fast food and automobile repair, a prospective franchisee may have 20 or more franchisors from which to make a selection. It is well worth franchisees' time to carefully select the franchisor that best meets their individual needs.[20]

Some franchise organizations are designed to provide their franchisees a part-time rather than a full-time income, which is attractive to some people. An example is Stroller Strides, a company that gathers new mothers together to do 45-minute power walks with their babies in strollers. The initial franchise fee ranges between $3,700 and $6,050. Owning a Stroller Strides franchise is ideal for a woman who wants to work two to three hours a day rather than eight and is passionate about fitness.

Franchising may be a particularly good choice for someone who wants to start a business but has no prior business experience. Along with offering a refined business system, well-run franchise organizations provide their franchisees training, technical expertise, and other forms of ongoing support.

Is Franchising Right for You?

Entrepreneurs should weigh the possibility of purchasing a franchise against the alternatives of buying an existing business or launching their own venture from scratch. Answering the following questions will help determine whether franchising is a good fit for people thinking about starting their own entrepreneurial venture:

- Are you willing to take orders? Franchisors are typically very particular about how their outlets operate. For example, McDonald's and other successful fast-food chains are very strict in terms of their restaurants' appearance and how the unit's food is prepared. Franchising is typically not a good fit for people who like to experiment with their own ideas or are independent minded.
- Are you willing to be part of a franchise "system" rather than an independent businessperson? For example, as a franchisee you may be required to pay into an advertising fund that covers the costs of advertising aimed at regional or national markets rather than the market for your individual outlet. Will it bother you to have someone use your money to develop ads that benefit the "system" rather than only your outlet or store? Are you willing to lose creative control over how your business is promoted?
- How will you react if you make a suggestion to your franchisor and your suggestion is rejected? How will you feel if you are told that your suggestion might work for you but can be put in place only if it works in all parts of the system?
- What are you looking for in a business? How hard do you want to work?
- How willing are you to put your money at risk? How will you feel if your business is operating at a net loss but you still have to pay royalties on your gross income?

None of these questions is meant to suggest that franchising is not an attractive method of business ownership for entrepreneurs. It is important, however, that a potential franchisee be fully aware of the subtleties involved with franchising before purchasing a franchise outlet.

The Cost of a Franchise

The initial cost of a business format franchise varies, depending on the franchise fee, the capital needed to start the business, and the strength of the franchisor. For example, some franchisors, like McDonald's, own the land and buildings that their franchisees use, and lease the property to the franchisees.

> **LEARNING OBJECTIVE**
> **7.** Identify the costs associated with buying a franchise.

Buying a franchise is a big step and specific franchise opportunity should be thoroughly investigated before a decision is made. This couple purchased a Wild Birds Unlimited franchise in 2007 and has experienced good success.

s44/Zuma Press/Newscom

In contrast, other organizations require their franchisees to purchase the land, buildings, and equipment needed to run their franchise outlets. Table 15.4 shows the total costs of buying into several franchise organizations. As you can see, the total initial cost varies from a low of $58,400 for a Comfort Keepers franchise to more than $2.4 million for a KFC franchise.

Also shown in Table 15.4 is a breakdown of the number of company-owned units and the number of franchise units maintained by different organizations. Company-owned units are managed and operated by company personnel, and there is no franchisee involved. Franchise organizations vary in their philosophies regarding company-owned versus franchised units. As we noted earlier in this chapter, some companies (e.g., Subway) are strictly franchisors and

TABLE 15.4   INITIAL COSTS TO THE FRANCHISEE OF A SAMPLE OF FRANCHISE ORGANIZATIONS

Franchise Organization	Year Started Franchising	Company-Owned Units	Franchised Units	Franchise Fee	Ongoing Royalty Fee	Total Initial Investment
Bark Busters	1994	4	364	$37,500	8%	$69,100–$97,100
Comfort Keepers	1999	0	660	$38,500	3%–5%	$58,410–$85,280
Game Truck	2008	1	25	varies	7%	$115,250–$320,500
Huntington Learning Centers	1985	33	318	$43,000	8%	$162,000–$257,600
KFC	1952	4,281	11,983	$45,000	5%	$1.3 million–$2.4 million
McDonald's	1955	6,399	26,338	$45,000	varies	$1 million–$1.9 million
Papa John's Pizza	1986	620	2,909	$25,000	5%	$98,823–$528,123
School of Rock	2005	21	36	$49,500	8%	$115,650–$400,400
Subway	1974	0	34,134	$15,000	8%	$84,300–$258,300
Wild Birds Unlimited	1983	0	274	$18,000	4%	$92,157–$140,736

Based on Entrepreneur.com, www.entrepreneur.com (accessed May 19, 2011).

have no company-owned units. Other companies, such as Papa John's Pizza, maintain large numbers of both company-owned and franchised units. In addition, some U.S.-based franchise systems have more foreign franchises than domestic franchises. For example, of the 11,983 franchises in KFC's system, 4,307 are in the United States and 7,676 are in foreign countries.

When evaluating the cost of a franchise, prospective franchisees should consider all the costs involved. Franchisors are required by law to disclose all their costs in a document called the Franchise Disclosure Document and send it to the franchisee. (We'll talk about this document in more detail later in this chapter.) To avoid making a hasty judgment, a franchisee may not purchase a franchise for 14 days from the time the circular is received. The following costs are typically associated with buying a business format franchise:[21]

- **Initial franchise fee:** The initial franchise fee varies, depending on the franchisor, as shown in Table 15.4. High overhead brick-and-mortar franchises charge less (4 to 5 percent of gross sales) while low overhead home-based and service business charge more (8 to 10 percent of gross sales).

- **Capital requirements:** These costs vary, depending on the franchisor, but may include the cost of buying real estate, the cost of constructing a building, the purchase of initial inventory, and the cost of obtaining a business license. Some franchisors also require a new franchisee to pay a "grand opening" fee for its assistance in opening the business.

- **Continuing royalty payment:** In the majority of cases, a franchisee pays a royalty based on a percentage of weekly or monthly gross income. Note that because the fee is typically assessed on gross income rather than net income, a franchisee may have to pay a monthly royalty even if the business is losing money. Royalty fees are usually around 5 percent of gross income.[22]

- **Advertising fees:** Franchisees are often required to pay into a national or regional advertising fund, even if the advertisements are directed at goals other than promoting the franchisor's product or service. (For example, advertising could focus on the franchisor's attempt at attracting new franchisees.) Advertising fees are typically less than 3 percent of gross income.

- **Other fees:** Other fees may be charged for various activities, including training additional staff, providing management expertise when needed, providing computer assistance, or providing a host of other items or support services.

Although not technically a fee, many franchise organizations sell their franchisee products that they use in their businesses, such as restaurant supplies for a restaurant franchise. The products are often sold at a markup and may be more expensive than those the franchisee could obtain on the open market.

There are some franchise organizations that use a more hybrid fee structure than the pricing formula shown here. An example is Stroller Strides, which charges an initial franchise fee based on the population density of the territory encompassed by the franchise. At a cost of $3,700, Plan A is for a population of 30,000 to 100,000 that is within a 4-mile radius of the franchisee. Costing $4,775, Plan B is for a population of 100,001 to 200,000 that is within a 7-mile radius of the franchisee. Plan C, which cost $6,050, is for a population of 200,001 to 300,000 that is within a 10-mile radius of the franchisee. There are no ongoing royalties. Franchisees are changed a monthly fee of $170 for Plan A, $280 for Plan B, and $390 for Plan C.[23]

The most important question a prospective franchisee should consider is whether the fees and royalties charged by a franchisor are consistent with the franchise's value or worth. If they are, then the pricing structure may be fair and equitable. If they are not, then the terms should be renegotiated or the prospective franchisee should look elsewhere.

An increasingly common way that franchise organizations decrease costs, and increase sales, is by partnering with one another through co-branding relationships. This practice is discussed in this chapter's "Partnering for Success" feature.

PARTNERING FOR SUCCESS

Using Co-Branding to Reduce Costs and Boost Sales

Have you ever stopped at a gas station and caught a quick lunch at an Arby's or a Blimpie sub sandwich inside? Or have you ever noticed that Baskin-Robbins and Dunkin' Donuts often share the same building? If either of these two scenarios applies to you, then you have witnessed co-branding firsthand.

Co-branding takes place when two or more businesses are grouped together. Co-branding is becoming increasingly common among franchise organizations that are looking for new ways to increase sales and reduce expenses. As we describe next, there are two primary types of co-branding arrangements that apply to franchise organizations.

Two Franchises Operating Side by Side

The first type of co-branding arrangement involves two or more franchises operating side by side in the same building or leased space. This type of arrangement typically involves a franchise like a donut shop that is busiest in the morning and a taco restaurant that is busiest at lunch and dinner. By locating side by side, these businesses can increase their sales by picking up some business from the traffic generated by their co-branding partner and can cut costs by sharing rent and other expenses.

Side-by-side co-branding arrangements are not restricted to restaurants. Sometimes the benefit arises from the complementary nature of the products involved, rather than time of day. For example, a franchise that sells exercise equipment could operate side by side with a business that sells vitamins. By locating side by side, these two businesses could realize the same types of benefits as the donut shop and the taco restaurant.

Two Franchises Occupying the Exact Same Space

The second type of co-branding arrangement involves two franchises occupying essentially the same space. For example, it is increasingly common to see sub shops inside gasoline stations and other retail outlets. The relationship is meant to benefit both parties. The sub shop benefits by opening another location without incurring the cost of constructing a freestanding building or leasing expensive shopping mall space. The gasoline station benefits by having a quality branded food partner to help it attract road traffic and by collecting lease income. Having a sub shop inside its store also helps a gasoline station become a "destination stop" for regular customers rather than simply another gas station serving passing cars.

Important Considerations

Although co-branding can be an excellent way for franchise organizations to partner for success, a firm should consider three questions before entering into a co-branding relationship:

- Will the co-branding arrangement maintain or strengthen my brand image?
- Do I have adequate control over how my partner will display or use my brand?
- Are there tangible benefits associated with attaching my brand to my partner's brand? For example, will my partner's brand have a positive effect on my brand and actually increase my sales?

If the answer to each of these questions is yes, than a co-branding arrangement may be a very effective way for a franchise organization to boosts sales and reduce expenses.

Questions for Critical Thinking

1. Do you think co-branding will continue to gain momentum, or do you think it is a fad that will wane in terms of its popularity? Explain your answer.
2. What are the potential downsides of co-branding? What might make a franchise hesitant to enter into a co-branding relationship with another franchise organization?
3. Consider the College Nannies & Tutor's Opening Profile. Suggest some co-branding relationships that College Nannies & Tutors might consider forming.
4. Make a list of the types of businesses that might work well together in a co-branding relationship. Several initial examples include (a) a quick oil change and a tire store, (b) a bakery and a coffeehouse, and (c) a florist and a candy store.

Finding a Franchise

There are thousands of franchise opportunities available to prospective franchisees. The most critical step in the early stages of investigating franchise opportunities is for the entrepreneur to determine the type of franchise that is the best fit. For example, it is typically unrealistic for someone who is not a mechanic to consider buying a muffler repair franchise. A franchisor teaches a franchisee how to use the contents of a business model, not a trade. Before buying a franchise, a potential franchisee should imagine operating the prospective franchise or, better yet, should spend a period of time working in one of the franchisor's outlets. After working in a print shop for a week, for example, someone who thought she might enjoy running a print shop might find out that she hates it. This type of experience could help avoid making a mistake that is costly both to the franchisee and to the franchisor.

There are many periodicals, Web sites, and associations that provide information about franchise opportunities. Every Thursday, for example, ads for franchise opportunities appear in special sections of the the *Wall Street Journal* and *USA Today*. Periodicals featuring franchise opportunities include *Inc.* and *Entrepreneur* and franchise-specific magazines such as *The Franchise Handbook* and *Franchise Times*. Prospective franchisees should also consider attending franchise opportunity shows that are held periodically in major U.S. cities and the International Franchise Expo, which is held annually in different cities across the United States. The U.S. Small Business Administration is another good source of franchise information. There are also several excellent franchise-focused individuals and organizations that post frequently on Twitter. Examples include FranchiseBiz, Franchising411, and FranchiseTwit. Because of the risks involved in franchising, the selection of a franchisor should be a careful, deliberate process. One of the smartest moves a potential franchise owner can make is to talk to current franchisees and inquire if they are making money and if they are satisfied with their franchisor. Reflecting on how this approach helped ease her inhibitions about buying a franchise, Carleen Peaper, the owner of a Cruise Planner franchise, said:

> I was really apprehensive about making an investment of my time and money into a franchise, so I e-mailed 50 Cruise Planner agents with a set of questions, asking for honest feedback. Everyone responded. That was a big thing and helped me determine that I wanted to join them.[24]

Table 15.5 contains a list of sample questions to ask a franchisor and some of its current franchisees before investing. Potential entrepreneurs can expect to learn a great deal by studying the answers they receive in response to these questions.

Advantages and Disadvantages of Buying a Franchise

There are two primary advantages to buying a franchise over other forms of business ownership. First, franchising provides an entrepreneur the opportunity to own a business using a tested and refined business model. This attribute lessens the probability of business failure. In addition, the trademark that comes with the franchise often provides instant legitimacy for a business.[25] For example, an entrepreneur opening a new Gold's Gym would likely attract more customers than an entrepreneur opening a new, independently owned fitness center because many people who are a part of the target market of Gold's Gym have already heard of the firm and have a positive impression of it. Second, when an individual purchases a franchise, the franchisor typically

TABLE 15.5 QUESTIONS TO ASK BEFORE BUYING A FRANCHISE

Questions to Ask a Franchisor

■ What is the background of the company and its performance record?
■ What is the company's current financial status?
■ What are the names, addresses, and phone numbers of existing franchisees in my trade area?
■ Describe how you train and mentor your franchisees.
■ If at some point I decide to exit the franchise relationship, how does the exit process work?
■ In what ways do you work with a franchisee who is struggling?

Questions to Ask Current Franchisees

■ How much does your franchise gross per year? How much does it net? Are the procedures followed to make royalty payments to the franchisee burdensome?
■ Are the financial projections of revenues, expenses, and profits that the franchisor provided me accurate in your judgment?
■ Does the franchisor give you enough assistance in operating your business?
■ How many hours, on average, do you work a week?
■ How often do you get a vacation?
■ Have you been caught off-guard by any unexpected costs or expectations?
■ Does your franchisor provide ongoing training and support to you?
■ If you had to do it all over again, would you purchase a franchise in this system? Why or why not?

provides training, technical expertise, and other forms of support. For example, many franchise organizations provide their franchisees periodic training both at their headquarters location and in their individual franchise outlets.

The cost involved is the main disadvantage of buying and operating a franchise. As mentioned earlier, the franchisee must pay an initial franchise fee. The franchisee must also pay the franchisor an ongoing royalty as well as pay into a variety of funds, depending on the franchise organization. Thus, franchisees have both immediate (i.e., the initial franchise fee) and long-term (i.e., continuing royalty payments) costs. By opening an independent business, an entrepreneur can keep 100 percent of the profits if it is successful.

Table 15.6 contains a list of the advantages and disadvantages of buying a franchise.

Steps in Purchasing a Franchise

Purchasing a franchise system is a seven-step process, as illustrated in Figure 15.3. The first rule of buying a franchise is to avoid making a hasty decision. Again, owning a franchise is typically costly and labor-intensive, and the purchase of a franchise should be a careful, deliberate decision. Once the decision to purchase a franchise has been nearly made, however, the following steps should be taken. If at any time prior to signing the franchise agreement the prospective franchisee has second thoughts, the process should be stopped until the prospective franchisee's concerns are adequately addressed.

Step 1 **Visit several of the franchisor's outlets:** Prior to meeting with the franchisor, the prospective franchisee should visit several of the franchisor's outlets and talk with their owners and employees. During the visits, the prospective franchisee should continually ask, "Is this the type of business I would enjoy owning and operating or managing?"

Step 2 **Meet with a franchise attorney:** Prospective franchisees should have an attorney who represents their interests, not the franchisor's.

TABLE 15.6 ADVANTAGES AND DISADVANTAGES OF BUYING A FRANCHISE

Advantages	Disadvantages
A proven product or service within an established market. The most compelling advantage to buying a franchise is that the franchise offers a proven product or service within an established market.	**Cost of the franchise.** The initial cost of purchasing and setting up a franchise operation can be quite high, as illustrated in Table 15.4.
An established trademark or business system. The purchase of a franchise with an established trademark provides franchisees with considerable market power. For example, the purchaser of a McDonald's franchise has a trademark with proven market power.	**Restrictions on creativity.** Many franchise systems are very rigid and leave little opportunity for individual franchisees to exercise their creativity. This is an often-cited frustration of franchisees.
Franchisor's training, technical expertise, and managerial experience. Another important attribute of franchising is the training, technical expertise, and managerial experience that the franchisor provides the franchisee.	**Duration and nature of the commitment.** For a variety of reasons, many franchise agreements are difficult to exit. In addition, virtually every franchise agreement contains a noncompete clause. These clauses vary in terms of severity, but a typical clause prevents a former franchisee from competing with the franchisor for a period of two years or more.
An established marketing network. Franchisees who buy into a powerful franchise system are part of a system that has tremendous buying power and substantial advertising power and marketing prowess.	**Risk of fraud, misunderstandings, or lack of franchisor commitment.** Along with the many encouraging stories of franchise success, there are also many stories of individuals who purchase a franchise only to be disappointed by the franchisor's broken promises.
Franchisor ongoing support. One of the most attractive advantages of purchasing a franchise rather than owning a store outright is the notion that the franchisor provides the franchisee ongoing support in terms of training, product updates, management assistance, and advertising. A popular slogan in franchising is that people buy franchises to "be in business for themselves but not by themselves."	**Problems of termination or transfer**. Some franchise agreements are very difficult and expensive to terminate or transfer. Often, a franchisee cannot terminate a franchise agreement without paying the franchisor substantial monetary damages.
Availability of financing. Some franchisors offer financing to their franchisees, although these cases are the exception rather than the rule. This information is available in section 10 of the Franchise Disclosure Document.	**Poor performance on the part of other franchisees.** If some of the franchisees in a franchise system start performing poorly and make an ineffective impression on the public, that poor performance can affect the reputation and eventually the sales of a well-run franchise in the same system.
Potential for business growth. If a franchisee is successful in the original location, the franchisee is often provided the opportunity to buy additional franchises from the same franchisor. For many franchisees, this prospect offers a powerful incentive to work hard to be as successful as possible.	**Potential for failure.** Some franchise systems simply fail to reach their objectives. When this happens, franchisees' wealth can be negatively affected. Indeed, when a franchise system fails, it commonly brings its franchisees down with it.

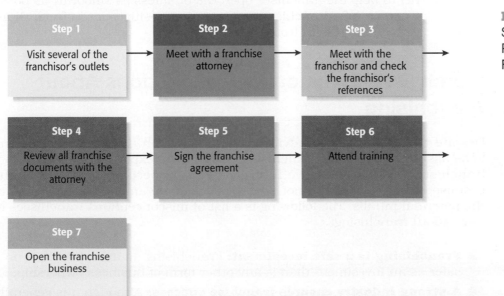

FIGURE 15.3
Seven Steps in Purchasing a Franchise

The attorney should prepare the prospective franchisee for meeting with the franchisor and should review all franchise documents before they are signed. If the franchisor tries to discourage the prospective franchisee from retaining an attorney, this is a red flag.

Step 3   **Meet with the franchisor and check the franchisor's references:** The prospective franchisee should meet with the franchisor, preferably at the franchisor's headquarters. During the meeting, the prospective franchisee should compare what was observed firsthand in the franchised outlets with what the franchisor is saying. Additional references should also be checked. The Franchise Disclosure Document is a good source for references. In section 20 of this document, there is a list of all the franchisees that have dropped out of the system in the past three years along with their contact information. Several of these should be called. Although it may seem to be overkill, the mantra for prospective franchisees is to check, double-check, and triple-check a franchisor's references.

Step 4   **Review all franchise documents with the attorney:** The franchise attorney should review all the franchise documents, including the Franchise Disclosure Document and the franchise agreement.

Step 5   **Sign the franchise agreement:** If everything is a go at this point, the franchise agreement can be signed. The franchise agreement is the document in which the provisions of the franchisor–franchisee relationship are outlined. We discuss this agreement in greater detail later in this chapter.

Step 6   **Attend training:** Almost all franchise organizations provide their franchisees training. For example, Comfort Keepers requires each of its new franchisees to attend an intensive eight-day training program at its corporate headquarters, and ongoing opportunities for training are made available.

Step 7   **Open the franchise business:** For many franchises, particularly restaurants, the first two to three weeks after the business is opened may be its busiest period, as prospective customers "try it out." This is why many franchise organizations send experienced personnel to help the franchisee open the business as smoothly as possible. One goal of a franchisee is generating positive word of mouth about the business right from the start.

Watch Out! Common Misconceptions About Franchising

LEARNING OBJECTIVE
9. Identify the common mistakes franchise buyers make.

Despite the abundance of advice available to them, many franchisees make false assumptions about franchising. Part of the explanation for this is that franchising has an attractive lure. It is easy to become enthralled with the promise of franchising and not spend an adequate amount of time examining the potential pitfalls. The following is a list of misconceptions franchisees often have about franchising:

■ **Franchising is a safe investment:** Franchising, in and of itself, is no safer as an investment than is any other form of business ownership.

■ **A strong industry ensures franchise success:** Although it is generally important to operate in a growing industry, the strength of an industry does not make up for a poor product, a poor business model, poor management, or inappropriate advertising. There are many firms that fail in growing industries just as there are firms that succeed in unattractive ones.

■ **A franchise is a "proven" business system:** A franchisor sells a franchisee the right to use a particular business model. Whether the model is proven or not is subject to the test of time. Obviously, companies such as Subway, Papa John's Pizza, and H&R Block are using models that are polished and that have worked well over time. Most prospective franchisees, however, cannot afford a Papa John's Pizza or a Subway unit and will be considering a lesser-known franchise. All too frequently, companies start selling franchises before their systems are anywhere close to being proven—a fact that should cause entrepreneurs to be wary.

■ **There is no need to hire a franchise attorney or an accountant:** Professional advice is almost always needed to guide a prospective franchisee through the franchise purchase process. A prospective franchisee should never give in to the temptation to save money by relying solely on the franchisor's advice.

■ **The best systems grow rapidly, and it is best to be a part of a rapid-growth system:** While some franchise systems grow rapidly because they have a good trademark and a polished business model, other franchise systems grow quickly because their major emphasis is on selling franchises. It is to a franchisee's benefit to be part of a system that has a solid trademark and business system—as that trademark and system will attract more customers—but some franchise systems grow so quickly that they outrun their ability to provide their franchisees adequate support.

■ **I can operate my franchise outlet for less than the franchisor predicts:** The operation of a franchise outlet usually costs just as much as the franchisor predicts.

■ **The franchisor is a nice person—he'll help me out if I need it:** Although it may be human nature to rely on the goodwill of others, don't expect anything from your franchisor that isn't spelled out in the franchise agreement.

Because these misconceptions are often hard to detect, some prospective franchisees attend seminars or franchise "boot camps" that teach them the ins and outs of franchising, including the things to watch out for when they talk to prospective franchisors. These types of seminars and boot camps are regularly offered by organizations such as Women in Franchising, the United States Hispanic Chamber of Commerce, and the International Franchising Organization.

LEGAL ASPECTS OF THE FRANCHISE RELATIONSHIP

According to the Federal Trade Commission (FTC), a franchise exists any time that the sale of a business involves (1) the sale of goods or services that bear a trademark, (2) the retention of significant control or assistance by the holder of the trademark on the operation of the business, and (3) royalty payments by the purchaser of the business to the owner of the trademark for the right to use the trademark in the business.

The legal and regulatory environment surrounding franchising is based on the premise that the public interest is served if prospective franchisees are as informed as possible regarding the characteristics of a particular franchisor.

The offer and sale of a franchise is regulated at both the state and the federal level. The legal aspects of the franchise relationship are unique enough that some attorneys specialize in franchise law.

Federal Rules and Regulations

Except for the automobile and petroleum industries, federal laws do not directly address the franchisor–franchisee relationship. Instead, franchise disputes are matters of contract law and are litigated at the state level. During the 1990s, Congress considered several proposals for federal legislation to govern franchise relationships, but none became law.

However, the offer and sale of a franchise is regulated at the federal level. Under the Franchise Rule, which is enforced by the Federal Trade Commission (FTC), franchisors must furnish potential franchisees with written disclosures that provide information about the franchisor, the franchised business, and the franchise relationship. The disclosures must be supplied at least 14 business days before a franchise agreement can be signed or the franchisee pays the franchisor any money.[26] In most cases, the disclosures are made through a lengthy document referred to as the Franchise Disclosure Document, which is accepted in all 50 states and parts of Canada. The **Franchise Disclosure Document (FDD)** contains 23 categories of information that give a prospective franchisee a broad base of information about the background and financial health of the franchisor. A summary of the information contained in the FDD is provided in Table 15.7. A prospective franchisee should fully understand all the information contained in the FDD before a franchise agreement is signed.

LEARNING OBJECTIVE

10. Describe the purpose of the Franchise Disclosure Document.

The FDD requires the franchisor to attach a copy of the franchise agreement and any other related contractual documents to the circular. The **franchise agreement**, or contract, is the document that consummates the sale of a franchise. Franchise agreements vary, but each agreement typically contains two sections: the purchase agreement and the franchise or license agreement. The purchase agreement typically spells out the price, the services to be provided by the franchisor to the franchisee, and the "franchise package," which refers to all the items the franchisee has been told to expect. The franchise or license agreement typically stipulates the rights granted to the franchisee (including the right to use the franchisor's trademark), the obligations and duties of the franchisor, the obligations and duties of the franchisee, trade restrictions, rights and limitations regarding the transfer or termination of the franchise agreement, and who is responsible for attorney fees if disputes arise. Most states have enacted a statute of frauds that requires franchise agreements to be in writing.

The federal government does not require franchisors to register with the FTC. The offer of a franchise for sale does not imply that the FTC has examined the franchisor and has determined that the information contained in the franchisor's FDD is accurate. The franchisor is responsible for voluntarily complying with the law, and it is the responsibility of prospective franchisees to exercise due diligence in investigating franchise opportunities. Although most franchisor–franchisee relationships are conducted in an entirely ethical manner, it is a mistake to assume that a franchisor has a fiduciary obligation to its franchisees. What this means is that if a franchisor had a **fiduciary obligation** to its franchisees, it would always act in their best interest, or be on the franchisees' "side." Commenting on this issue, Robert Purvin, an experienced franchise attorney, wrote:

> While the conventional wisdom talks about the proactive relationship of the franchisor to its franchisees, virtually every court case decided in the U.S. has ruled that a franchisor has no fiduciary obligation to its franchisees. Instead, U.S. courts have agreed with franchisors that franchise agreements are "arms length" business transactions.[27]

TABLE 15.7 INFORMATION CONTAINED IN THE FRANCHISE DISCLOSURE DOCUMENT (FDD) ALONG WITH EXPLANATIONS OF THEIR MEANINGS

Section and Item	Explanation
1. The franchisor, its predecessors, and affiliates 2. Business experience of the franchisor 3. Litigation experience of the franchisor 4. Bankruptcy on the part of the franchisor	These items provide information about the franchisor's operating history, business affiliations, and past litigation and bankruptcy experience, if any. It is not uncommon for a large company to have experienced some litigation. It would be a red flag, however, if a disproportionate percentage of the litigation involved suits with current or former franchisees.
5. Initial franchise fee 6. Other fees 7. Initial investment	These items specify the fees that the franchisee is subject to along with the franchisees' initial investment, which can be quite substantial. The "other fees" section should be carefully studied to avoid any surprises.
8. Restrictions on sources of products and services 9. Franchisee's obligations	These items stipulate the franchisee's obligations, along with restrictions pertaining to where the franchisee is permitted to purchase supplies and services. Some franchise agreements require the franchisee to purchase supplies from the franchisor.
10. Financing available 11. Franchisor's obligations	These items spell out the franchisor's obligations, along with a description of the financing (if any) that the franchisor offers to the franchisee. The franchisor's obligations typically include providing assistance in opening the franchise's unit, ongoing training, and advertising.
12. Territory 13. Trademarks 14. Patents, copyrights, and proprietary information	These items describe the territorial rights granted the franchisee (if any) and the franchisor's right to grant other franchises and open company-owned outlets. In addition, items 13 and 14 specify the principal trademarks, patents, and copyrights and other proprietary information owned by the franchisor and the extent to which these items can be used by the franchisee.
15. Obligation to participate in the actual operation of the franchise business	This section addresses the franchisee's obligation to participate personally in the operation of the franchise. Franchisors typically do not want absentee franchisees.
16. Restrictions on what the franchisee may sell 17. Renewal, termination, transfer, and dispute resolution	These sections deal with what the franchisee may sell and how the franchisor resolves disputes with its franchisees. Item 17 also contains important information about the manner in which franchisees can renew, terminate, and/or transfer their franchise.
18. Public figures	This section lists public figures affiliated with the franchise through advertising and other means.
19. Earnings claim	If a franchisor makes an earnings claim in connection with an offer of a franchise, then certain past and projected earnings information must be provided.
20. List of outlets	This section is quite exhaustive and contains (1) the number of franchises sold by the franchisor, (2) the number of company-owned outlets, (3) the names of all franchisees and the addresses and telephone numbers of all their outlets (within certain limitations), (4) an estimate of the number of franchises to be sold in the next year, and (5) a list of all franchisees (covering the past three years) who have dropped out of the system, including their last-known home addresses and telephone numbers.
21. Financial statements	This section contains the franchisor's previous two years of independently audited financial statements.
22. Contracts	These last two sections contain copies of the documents that franchisees have to sign.
23. Receipt **Attachments:** Franchise Agreement (or contract) Equipment Lease Lease for Premises Loan Agreement	These are the common exhibits attached to the FDD.

Purvin's statement suggests that a potential franchisee should not rely solely on the goodwill of a franchisor when negotiating a franchise agreement. A potential franchisee should have a lawyer who is fully acquainted with franchise law and should closely scrutinize all franchise-related legal documents.

State Rules and Regulations

In addition to the FTC disclosure requirements, 15 states have franchise investment laws that provide additional protection to potential franchisees.[28] The states are California, Hawaii, Illinois, Indiana, Maryland, Michigan, Minnesota, New York, North Dakota, Oregon, Rhode Island, South Dakota, Virginia, Washington, and Wisconsin. The franchise investment laws require franchisors to provide presale disclosures, known as "offering circulars," to potential franchisees. Thirteen of the states have laws that treat the sale of a franchise like the sale of a security. These states require that a franchisor's FDD be filed with a designated state agency and be placed into public record.

These state laws give franchise purchasers important legal rights, including the right to bring private lawsuits against franchisors for violation of state disclosure requirements.

By requiring franchisors to file their FDDs with a state agency, these states provide franchise purchasers important legal protection, including the right to sue a franchisor for violation of state disclosure requirements (if the franchise purchaser feels that full disclosure in the offering circular was not made). For example, if someone purchased a franchise in one of the states fitting the profile described previously and six months later discovered that the franchisor did not disclose an issue required by the FDD (and, as a result, felt that he or she had been damaged), that person could seek relief by suing the franchisor in state court. All 15 states providing additional measures of protection for franchisees also regulate some aspect of the termination process. Although the provisions vary by state, they typically restrict a franchisor from terminating the franchise before the expiration of the franchise agreement, unless the franchisor has "good cause" for its action.

MORE ABOUT FRANCHISING

There are a number of additional issues pertaining to the franchisor–franchisee relationship. Three important topics, for both franchisors and franchisees, are franchise ethics, international franchising, and the future of franchising as a method of business ownership and growth.

Franchise Ethics

The majority of franchisors and franchisees are highly ethical individuals who are interested only in making a fair return on their investment. In fact, instances of problems between franchisors and their franchisees tend to be isolated occurrences rather than prevalent practices.[29] There are certain features of franchising, however, that make it subject to ethical abuse. An understanding of these features can help franchisors and franchisees guard against making ethical mistakes. These features are the following:

■ **The get-rich-quick mentality:** Some franchisors see franchising as a get-rich-quick scheme and become more interested in selling franchises than in using franchising as a legitimate means of distributing their product or service. These franchisors have a tendency to either oversell the potential of their franchise or overpromise the support they will offer to their franchisees.

■ **The false assumption that buying a franchise is a guarantee of business success:** Buying a franchise, as is the case with all other business investments, involves risk. Any statement to the contrary is typically misleading or unethical. A franchisor must steer clear of claims that it has the "key" to business success, and a franchisee needs to be wary of all such claims.

■ **Conflicts of interest between franchisors and their franchisees:** The structure of the franchise relationship can create conflicts of interest between franchisors and their franchisees. For example, franchisees benefit from the profits of a unit, while franchisors benefit from increased revenues (recall that a franchisor's royalty is typically paid on a percentage of gross profits rather than net profits). This anomaly in the franchise arrangement can motivate franchisors to take steps that boost revenues for the entire system but hurt profits for individual franchisees. For example, a franchisor might insist that a franchisee sell a product that has high revenue but low margins (or net income). Similarly, a franchisor might sell several franchises in a given geographic area to maximize the revenue potential of the area regardless of the effect on each individual franchisee's net income. These actions can at times be ethically questionable and can often lead to contentious conflicts of interest in franchise systems.

Despite the protection of law and the advocacy of franchise associations, individual franchisors and franchisees must practice due diligence in their relationships. "Buyer beware" is a good motto for franchisors selecting franchisees and prospective franchisees selecting franchisors. Entering into a franchise relationship is a major step for both parties and should be treated accordingly. The metaphor used frequently to describe the franchisor–franchisee relationship is marriage. Similar to marriage, the franchisor–franchisee relationship is typically close, long-term, and painful to terminate. Each side of the franchise partnership should scrutinize the past ethical behavior of the other before a franchise agreement is executed.

International Franchising

International opportunities for franchising are becoming more prevalent as the markets for certain franchised products in the United States have become saturated.[30] Indeed, heavily franchised companies, such as McDonald's, KFC, and Century 21 Real Estate, are experiencing much of their growth in international markets. For example, McDonald's opened 286 units abroad in 2009, compared to 53 domestic openings.[31] The trend toward globalization in many industries is also hastening the trend toward international franchising, and the growing middle classes in many countries are creating large populations of consumers eager for American-style goods. In fact, to illustrate how global many familiar franchise systems have become, there is a Papa John's pizzeria in Karachi, Pakistan, a Denny's in Christchurch, New Zealand, and a Chili's Grill and Bar on a riverboat on the Egyptian Nile.

A U.S. citizen who is thinking about buying a franchise abroad may be confronted with the choice of buying from an American company or a foreign company regardless of the location in the world. For U.S.

The restaurant industry remains one of the most rapidly growing areas of franchising because it caters to all ages and demographics. Here, a Chinese girl is enjoying KFC in Shanghai, China. KFC has over 7,600 franchises in foreign countries.

©TAO Images/SuperStock

citizens, these are some of the steps to take before buying a franchise in a foreign country:

■ **Consider the value of the franchisor's name in the foreign country:** There are very few franchise systems whose names are known worldwide. Beyond a select few—McDonald's, Coca-Cola, and KFC come to mind—the majority of trademarks well known to Americans may be known to only a small percentage of the population of a foreign country. When considering the purchase of a U.S.-based franchise in a foreign country, carefully evaluate the value of the trademark in that country.

■ **Work with a knowledgeable lawyer:** Many of the legal protections afforded to prospective franchisees in the United States are unavailable in foreign countries, highlighting the need for the purchaser of a franchise in a foreign country to obtain excellent legal advice. All the hazards involved with purchasing a domestic franchise are magnified when purchasing a franchise in a foreign country.

■ **Determine whether the product or service is salable in a foreign country:** Just because a product or service is desirable to Americans is no guarantee of success in a foreign culture. Before buying a franchise in a foreign country, determine if sufficient marketing research has been conducted to ensure that the product or service will have a sufficient market in the foreign country.

■ **Uncover whether the franchisor has experience in international markets:** It is typically not a good idea to be a franchisor's "test case" to see if the franchisor wants to operate in foreign markets. Be leery of franchisors with aggressive expansion plans but little international experience.

■ **Find out how much training and support you will receive from the franchisor:** If your franchise unit will be in a foreign country and the franchisor remains headquartered in the United States, make sure you fully understand the amount of training and support you can expect. Will the franchisor have an area representative in your country? If not, do you have to make an international phone call each time you want to talk to your franchisor? Will your franchisor be willing to travel to the foreign country to offer you training and support? Who pays for the international travel of the franchisor's training staff? Who is responsible for advertising in the foreign country, the franchisor or the franchisee?

■ **Evaluate currency restrictions:** Evaluate any restrictions that the foreign country places on the convertibility of its currency into U.S. dollars.

To avoid some of the potential problems alluded to here, U.S. franchisors typically structure their expansion into a foreign country through the following:

■ **Direct franchising arrangement:** Under a direct franchise arrangement, the U.S. franchisor grants the rights to an individual or a company (the developer) to develop multiple franchised businesses within a country or territory. For example, if Play It Again Sports decided to sell franchises for the first time in Spain, Play It Again Sports may grant the rights to a Spanish company to develop multiple Play It Again Sports franchises there.

■ **Master franchise agreement:** Under a master franchise arrangement, the U.S. firm grants the right to an individual or company (the master franchisee) to develop one or more franchise businesses and to license others to develop one or more franchise businesses within the country or territory.

■ **Other agreements:** Combinations of other arrangements are also employed by franchisors expanding to foreign markets. Examples include joint-venture arrangements, direct-sales arrangements, or straight franchising agreements.

The Future of Franchising

The future of franchising appears bright. According to PricewaterhouseCoopers' *2010 Franchise Business Economic Outlook* report, some 900,000 franchise businesses employ over 9.5 million people in the United States and generate roughly $850 billion in direct economic output.[32] Franchising represents a large and growing segment of the retail and service sectors of U.S. businesses and is in some cases replacing more traditional forms of business ownership. More and more college graduates are choosing careers in industries that are heavily dominated by franchising. Franchising is also becoming more popular among seniors.[33]

There are also innovations taking place in franchising. For example, a growing number of restaurant franchises, including Cousins Submarines, Tasti D-Lite, and Toppers Pizza, have taken their businesses mobile by creating food trucks. The trucks are parked in high-traffic areas and attract pedestrians and people from nearby office buildings and neighborhoods.[34]

CHAPTER SUMMARY

1. A franchise is an agreement between a franchisor (the parent company, such as McDonald's) and a franchisee (an individual or firm that is willing to pay the franchisor a fee for the right to sell its product or service).

2. There are two distinctly different types of franchise systems: the product trademark franchise and the business format franchise. A product trademark franchise is an arrangement under which the franchisor grants to the franchisee the right to buy its products and use its trade name. Automobile dealerships and soft-drink distributorships are examples of product trademark franchises. In a business format franchise, the franchisor provides a formula for doing business to the franchisee along with training, advertising, and other forms of assistance. Curves, Comfort Keepers, and College Nannies & Tutors are examples of this type of franchise system.

3. An individual franchise agreement involves the sale of a single franchise for a specific location. An area franchise agreement allows a franchisee to own and operate a specific number of outlets in a particular geographic area. A master franchise agreement is similar to an area franchise agreement with one major exception. In addition to having the right to operate a specific number of locations in a particular area, the franchisee also has the right to offer and sell the franchise to other people in the area.

4. The advantages of setting up a franchise system include rapid, low-cost market expansion; income from franchise fees and royalties; franchisee motivation; access to ideas and suggestions; cost savings; and increased buying power. The disadvantages of setting up a franchise system include sharing profits with franchisees, loss of control, friction with franchisees, managing growth, differences in required business skills, and legal expenses.

5. The rules of thumb for determining whether franchising is a good choice for growing a business are as follows: The product or service the business sells should be unique; the business should be consistently profitable; the business should be profitable year-round, not only during a specific season; the business system and procedures should be polished; and the business proposition should be clear so that prospective franchisees fully understand the relationship to which they are committing.

6. Preparing answers to the following questions helps the entrepreneur determine if franchising is a good fit as a way to launch a venture: Are you willing to take orders? Are you willing to be part of a franchise system? How will you react if you make a suggestion to your franchisor and your suggestion is rejected? What are you looking for in a business? How willing are you to put your money at risk?

7. The following costs are typically associated with buying a business format franchise: initial franchise fee, capital requirements (such as land, buildings, and equipment), continuing royalty payment, advertising fee, and other fees (depending on the franchise system).

8. The advantages of buying a franchise include a proven product or service within an established market; an established trademark or business system; the franchisor's training, technical expertise, and managerial experience; an established marketing network; ongoing franchisor support; availability of financing; and potential for business growth. The disadvantages of buying a franchise include cost of the franchise; restrictions on creativity; duration and nature of commitment; risk of fraud, misunderstanding, or lack of franchisor commitment; problems of termination or transfer; and the possibility of poor performance on the part of other franchisees.

9. The common mistakes made by franchise buyers include believing that franchising is a completely safe investment, believing that a great industry ensures franchise success, putting too much faith in the idea that a franchise is a "proven" business system, believing that there is no need to hire a franchise attorney or accountant, being overly optimistic about how fast the franchise outlet will grow, believing that "I can operate my franchise outlet for less than the franchisor predicts," and believing that just because the franchisor is a nice person, he or she will always be there to help out when needed.

10. The Franchise Disclosure Document (FDD) is a document with 23 categories of information. This document provides a prospective franchisee a broad base of information about a franchisor's background and financial health. The FDD must be provided by the franchisor to a prospective franchisee at least 10 business days before a franchise contract can be signed or the franchisee pays the franchisor any money.

KEY TERMS

agency theory, **531**
area franchise agreement, **525**
business format franchise, **525**
fiduciary obligation, **544**
franchise agreement, **544**
Franchise Disclosure
   Document (FDD), **544**

franchisees, **523**
franchising, **523**
franchisor, **523**
individual franchise agreement,
   525
master franchise agreement,
   525

multiple-unit franchisee,
   526
product and trademark
   franchise, **524**
subfranchisees, **526**

REVIEW QUESTIONS

1. What is franchising? How does it differ from other forms of business ownership?

2. Describe the differences between a product and trademark franchise and a business format franchise. Provide at least two examples of both types of franchise arrangements.

3. What is the difference among an individual franchise agreement, an area franchise agreement, and a master franchise agreement? If you wanted to open a large number of 1901 franchises (see "You Be the VC 15.2"), which type of franchise arrangement would be best for you and why?

4. Why is it important for a franchisor to develop detailed and thorough operating manuals?

5. What are the advantages and disadvantages of establishing a franchise system?

6. What are the rules of thumb for determining whether franchising is a good choice for a particular business? Provide an example of a business that wouldn't be suitable for franchising.

7. What are some of the issues an entrepreneur should consider when answering the question "Is franchising a good choice for me?" Briefly describe the profile of someone who isn't suitable for franchising.

8. What are the costs involved in purchasing a business format franchise? Are these costs similar across franchise systems, or do they vary widely? Which costs are one-time costs and which costs continue indefinitely?

9. If an individual Planet Smoothie franchise is losing money, does it still have to pay a monthly royalty? Explain how this is possible.

10. Describe some of the resources available to prospective franchisees to identify franchise opportunities.

11. What are the principal advantages and disadvantages of buying a franchise?

12. Why is it important for a prospective franchisee to retain his or her own franchise attorney?

13. "Franchising is a safe investment." What would you think if you saw this statement in a book or magazine?

14. What is the purpose of the Franchise Disclosure Document (FDD)? Are there any regulations regarding when the FDD must be provided to a prospective franchisee? If so, what are they?

15. What is the purpose of a franchise agreement? Identify the two sections of the franchise agreement and describe the purpose of each one.

16. To date, every court case that has been adjudicated in the United States indicates that franchisors do not have a fiduciary responsibility to their franchisees. What do these rulings suggest to entrepreneurs considering the possibility of buying into a franchise system? Why?

17. What are some of the aspects of franchising that make it subject to ethical abuses? What steps can a prospective franchisee take to ensure that a specific franchisor is reliable and ethical?

18. For U.S. citizens, what are the main issues that should be considered before buying a franchise in a foreign country?

19. What are the main reasons that many U.S. franchise systems are expanding into global markets? Do you think this expansion will continue to gain momentum or will decline over time? Provide an example of a franchise organization, other than one referred to in the chapter, that is expanding rapidly oversees.

20. Does franchising have a bright or a dim future in the United States? Make your answer as substantive and thoughtful as possible.

APPLICATION QUESTIONS

1. Reread the Opening Profile, which focuses on Joseph Keeley and the franchise organization that he founded—College Nannies & Tutors. Think of an activity, other than nanny and tutoring services, that you believe college students might be particularly good at, has a defined need, and can be turned into a franchise. Describe how that activity could be turned into a franchise organization.

2. Think of the current point that you're at in your career or educational process. Do you think you'd be capable of owning and operating a franchise today or shortly after you graduate? If so, what type of franchise do you think you'd be most capable of successfully leading?

3. Pick a franchise organization that you admire. Spend some time looking at the company's Web site. Describe how the company is set up. Is it a product and trademark franchise or a business format franchise? Does it sell individual franchise agreements, area franchise agreements, master franchise agreements, or some combination of the three? How many company-owned stores and how many franchise outlets are in the system? Report any particularly interesting or unusual things you learned about the system.

4. Identify a franchise location near where you live and ask to talk to the owner. Show the owner one of the two "You Be the VC" features at the end of this chapter and ask the person whether he or she thinks the company will be successful. Write a brief summary of the owner's response.

5. Select a franchise organization that is located on your campus or near your campus that isn't involved in any co-branding arrangements. Suggest several co-branding relationships that would make sense for this company.

6. Bill Watts has decided to buy a sub shop franchise called Super Subs. He lives in Cedar Falls, Iowa, and will be the first Super Subs franchisee in the state. Along with buying a Super Subs franchise, Bill would also like to purchase the rights to offer and sell Super Subs franchises to other people in the Cedar Falls area. What type of franchise agreement should Bill negotiate with Super Subs? For Bill, what are the advantages and disadvantages of this type of arrangement?

7. Make a list of five large franchise organizations. Do some Internet research to see if you can determine if these organizations are offering programs to help potential franchisees gain access to financing.

8. A growing number of franchise organizations, including Wings Over, Great Harvest Bread Company, and Beef O' Brady's, are allowing their franchisees to tweak their menus and change the appearances of their facilities to better compete with local businesses. Do you think this is a good idea? What are the upsides and downsides of this approach?

9. Look at Table 15.4. If you were offered the opportunity to buy into any one of the franchise organizations listed in Table 15.4, which one would it be? Explain the rationale for your selection.

10. A friend of yours owns a carpet installation and cleaning business, which is a full-time job. To increase his income, he's thinking about buying a 1-800-Water Damage franchise, which is a franchise that helps home owners and businesses restore property that has been damaged by a flood or water leak. His thinking is that he already has most of the equipment he needs to perform this type of service and has an experienced crew. Is your friend a good candidate for a 1-800-Water Damage franchise? If not, what type of franchise could he buy that would be a good fit with his current business?

11. Suppose you ran into an old friend who is just about to buy into a replacement batteries retail franchise. He tells you that he is excited about the opportunity because the system he is about to buy into (1) is in an industry that virtually guarantees its success, (2) has a "proven" business model, and (3) is operated by people who are so honest that he can skip the expense of hiring a franchise attorney to review the documents he has to sign. If your friend asked you, "What do you think? Am I approaching this opportunity correctly?" how would you respond?

12. Suppose you became interested in opening a School of Rock franchise. You fly to Philadelphia and visit the company's headquarters. After learning more about the opportunity, you tell the School of Rock representatives that you're really interested and would like to move forward. If School of Rock follows the procedures it's supposed to in negotiating with you as a prospective franchisee, what should you expect from this point forward?

13. Recently, a good friend of yours gave a talk to a community group about franchising. Three of the people in the audience approached your friend after the talk to ask if their businesses are suitable for franchising. The first person owns a dance studio, the second a veterinary practice, and the third a business that produces smartphone apps. Your friend has turned to you for advice. What would you say?

14. Do you think Starbucks could have benefited from placing a greater reliance on franchising over the years? What are the benefits to Starbucks as a result of the decision to avoid going the franchise route?

15. Suppose you are an American citizen living in Japan. You just lost your job with an electronics company that merged with a firm in Singapore. You would like to stay in Japan and are thinking about buying an American business services franchise that is expanding to Japan. What are some of the issues you should evaluate before buying an outlet in an American franchise system that is selling franchises in Japan?

YOU BE THE VC 15.1

Company: Smart Wash

Web: www.smartwash2u.com

Business Idea: Launch a laundry franchise system that provides effective bio-friendly wash as an alternative to traditional laundry care practices.

Pitch: Many people these days, with their busy schedules, opt to send their laundry to external parties. People particularly do not have time to do their laundry and hence place their expensive and precious clothes in the hands and mercy of conventional dry cleaners or launderettes. However, the main disadvantage of conventional dry cleaning is that the solvent is recycled for up to 50 washes, and the process does not get rid sweat odor from the clothes. The laundry service industry is all about giving the best quality care to the fabric, so Smart Wash decided to do this and also to revolutionize the conventional laundry system.

In view of the problem faced by many launderettes, Smart Wash had decided to adopt the "Lagoon System." What exactly is the "Lagoon System"? The system is an integrated wet cleaning system. It is known as a bio-friendly system as it uses water as the basis for all laundry activities including washing, drying, and ironing. The "Lagoon System" was developed by Electrolux Laundry System and Hohenstein Institute in Krefel, Germany with the "green" concept at the forefront of their minds. Smart Wash, in an alliance with Electrolux Products Sdn Bhd, has integrated the self-service laundry concept into the hearts of many Malaysians, especially those who are living in the city center. It certainly provides quality service at an affordable price.

In fact, Smart Wash is able to reduce its costs as a result of the self-service concept as each outlet only requires

three workers at a time. The decreased cost enables Smart Wash to offer discounted prices to customers which in return helps them save money. The Smart Wash concept also offers flexible opening hours depending on the location of each outlet.

Currently, the concept introduced by Smart Wash is so popular and efficacious that Smart Wash has more than 48 outlets in various residential towns, condominiums, and university campuses all over Malaysia. This self-service concept was in fact introduced way back in August 1997 when the Malaysian government realized that the concept of drying clothes in front of houses and condominiums was an eyesore. However, customers wanted a better service at an affordable price in order to change their routines. This is where Smart Wash steps in. The concept has gained trust from millions of users all over Malaysia, and it hopes to open more outlets locally and internationally.

Q&A: Based on the material covered in this chapter, what questions would you ask the firm's founders before making your funding decision? What answers would satisfy you?

Decision: If you had to make your decision on just the information provided in the pitch and on the company's Web site, would you fund this company? Why or why not?

Source: Anushia Chelvarayan, Multimedia University, Malaysia.

YOU BE THE VC 15.2

Company: **1901**

Web: www.1901.com
Twitter: 1901HotDogs
Facebook: 1901

Business Idea: Create a food business franchise that has unique outlets and provides an array of choices to serve people on the go.

Pitch: The fast-food industry has become very competitive lately, having to accommodate modern lifestyle changes. More and more people all over the world have less time and less resources, turning to fast food. 1901 is a Malaysian home-grown quick serve franchise business famous for its hot dogs. The hot dogs are "Halal" certified and they cater to all walks of life. The name refers to the year the term *hot dog* was born in St. Louis, Missouri, United States. 1901, established in 1997, believed that many Malaysians would like to run their own business. Therefore, the founders decided to set up a franchise and made it affordable to all. By doing this, those who aspire to run their own business but do not have the knowledge and experience may still be able to pursue their dreams. The "pushcart" and "snack café" concept introduced by 1901 were reminiscent of American hot dog stores. In fact, to this day due to their unique concept store, many people still believe that 1901 is an American hot dog chain. However, this is definitely not true. Possessing a true entrepreneurial spirit, the Malaysian founders have propelled the company from its humble beginning of a single pushcart in one of the leading shopping malls in the country to a total of more than 80 outlets today.

To be competitive among its rivals, 1901 has well positioned itself as a lighter, healthier food at a low price. This is an added advantage as consumers are becoming more aware of nutritional concerns. Since organizations that show social responsibility will also receive increased attention, 1901 took advantage of the opportunity to be charitable and introduced the Food for the Homeless Program. The program is conducted every Wednesday on certain streets in Kuala Lumpur's city center whereby food packets are dropped off for the homeless. According to the founders, providing food is one of the ways to give these homeless people hope and a will to live. The program has been included as one of their social responsibilities, and 1901 believes that by helping people who are less privileged, it is also meeting and achieving its company goals as well.

1901 was awarded the Most Promising Franchisor of the Year award for 2000/2001 by the Malaysian Franchise Association. The award recognizes the achievements of upcoming, enterprising franchisors that are well positioned for the future. With a vision to build a world where everyone is a friend, 1901 will certainly achieve its success by emphasizing high standards, understanding, and generosity among management and franchisees as well as staff, customers, and vendors.

Q&A: Based on the material covered in this chapter, what questions would you ask the firm's founders before making your funding decision? What answers would satisfy you?

Decision: If you had to make your decision on just the information provided in the pitch and on the company's Web site, would you fund this company? Why or why not?

Source: Anushia Chelvarayan, Multimedia University, Malaysia.

CASE 15.1

Snap Fitness: Fast, Convenient, and Intriguing Options for Growth

Web: www.snapfitness.com
Twitter: snapfitness247
Facebook: Snap Fitness

Bruce R. Barringer, *Oklahoma State University*

R. Duane Ireland, *Texas A&M University*

Imagine you're a police officer who works the evening shift. You go to work at 3:30 P.M. and complete your shift at midnight. You've always enjoyed working out late in the day but don't have room for a home gym in your apartment. You've checked out the Gold's Gym and the Bally Total Fitness Center near where you live. They both close at 11:00 P.M., so going to a fitness center isn't an option—until now! Snap Fitness is a rapidly growing franchise organization that features gyms that are open 24 hours a day, seven days a week. The state-of-the-art fitness concept began franchising in 2004 and already has over 2,200 franchise locations in the United States, Canada, India, Mexico, Australia, and New Zealand, and is in the process of opening centers in the United Kingdom. Snap Fitness is currently opening about 20 to 30 new centers a month.

Beginnings

Snap Fitness was founded by Pete Taunton. For most of his career, Taunton ran big-box fitness centers that offered all the amenities. By the time he opened his fifth center, he was burned out. He recalls seeing his kids twice a day—when they woke up in the morning and when they went to bed at night. He left the fitness industry, but a year later a group of former employees approached him about opening a new business. He was tired of 75-hour workweeks and didn't want to make a large investment. So he took a piece of paper and a pen and listed all the amenities that his former gyms had on the left-hand side of the paper and a smaller number of "must haves" on the right side. Taunton had learned long ago that rock-climbing walls, racquetball courts, and swimming pools were nice to have but most people never used them. The "must haves" list became the blueprint for Snap Fitness.

Business Concept

Snap Fitness's centers are small gyms that are located near residential areas. The centers, which offer weights, treadmills, and exercise machines to customers, are staffed during the day and are available to members at night by swiping a key card at the main door. The equipment is state-of-the art, the centers are very clean, and they are secure. At night, security cameras monitor activities and members wear electronic devices around their necks that when pushed summon paramedics or police.

The centers offer their members a fast, convenient, and affordable way to stay fit. A membership costs around $40 a month for a single membership, $60 for a couple, and $70 for a family (rates vary by location), which is well below big-box fitness center rates. There are no contracts—members pay month by month—and membership in one Snap Fitness permits the member to use any Snap Fitness center in North America. Because the centers are small—the average Snap Fitness center is 2,500 to 3,500 square feet compared to more than 20,000 square feet for a Gold's Gym or a Bally's Fitness Center—they can be located near where people live. In fact, the company claims that the majority of its members don't have more than a two-mile drive to the Snap Fitness center to which they belong. As a result, the members quickly learn each other's names and have things in common, such as kids that go to the same schools or they live in the same neighborhoods.

Snap Fitness supports an online platform at www.mysnapfitness.com on which members can build their own Web pages. The Web pages allow members to construct their own wellness plan, tailor their meals to fit their weight loss goals, talk confidentially to health and wellness coaches by phone (for an extra fee), and build customized workout plans that can be tracked and are supported with video tutorials using 3-D animation. Members can also sign up for a program called easyFit, which is a three-step program. Step 1: You receive a tiny monitor that you attach near your hip that monitors your activity and calories burned, whether you're at a Snap Fitness center or anywhere else; Step 2: The activity is recorded on your mysnapfitness Web page; Step 3: You get points for exercise and other positive behaviors as a

(continued)

motivation tool. The point system makes it easy to set and track goals, compare progress over time, and compete with others. Points also help members win discounts and prizes.

Snap Fitness Centers are limited in the amenities they offer so they don't appeal to everyone. There are no locker rooms, child care, juice bars, aerobic classes, racquetball courts, or swimming pools. A Snap Fitness membership is a strict trade-off between cost and convenience versus a larger array of amenities. In addition, the small gym franchise concept is unproven, despite the early success of Curves International and others. A number of small aerobics studios opened a number of years ago, and the vast majority of them failed.

Franchise Operations

Snap Fitness is actively selling franchises. To qualify, a prospective franchisee needs a minimum net worth of $250,000 and $500,000 in liquid assets. The initial franchise fee is $15,000 and the royalty is a flat $499 per month (rather than a percentage of gross income). It costs between $79,400 to $195,800 to get a Snap Fitness Center up and running. The buildings are leased so there is no real estate purchase involved. A franchisee signs a five year commitment with the company, which is renewable.

The leanness of the company's business model makes it attractive to many franchisees. The franchisor handles all billing and collecting processes. Because the centers are not manned at night, a person can own and operate a Snap Fitness franchise and keep normal hours. Most franchisees own more than one location and have only one to two employees per location. A total of 70 percent of Snap Fitness locations are owned by absentee owners. Many of the owners are semiretirees or have other jobs. The simplicity of Snap Fitness's approach has also attracted young owners. In fact, Snap Fitness was recently named one of the "Top 21 Franchises for Young Entrepreneurs" by Under30CEO.com. In November 2010, Samantha and Oliver Beltran opened a Snap Fitness franchise in Palestine, Texas. Both Samantha and Oliver were 22 years old at the time.

Looking Ahead

Snap Fitness has gotten off to a strong start. It's the fastest growing franchise in the 24/7 category and was recently named one of the top 500 franchises in the United States by *Entrepreneur* magazine, ranking number 33 in *Entrepreneur*'s Franchise 500.

For its part, Snap Fitness attributes its success to the uniqueness of its approach, for both its franchisees and its members. In a press release commenting on its recent recognition by *Entrepreneur*, Snap Fitness founder and CEO Peter Taunton remarked, "Our ability to present our franchise owners with an easy to manage franchise opportunity and members with an affordable and convenient work out option is a testament to what (sets us) apart from the competition."

Snap Fitness's challenge now will be to maintain its momentum and properly manage its growth. The fitness industry is an $18.5 billion industry. Snap Fitness anticipates continued rapid expansion.

Discussion Questions

1. Snap Fitness has positioned itself as a "neighborhood" chain of fitness centers and claims that the majority of its members are within a two-mile drive of the center to which they belong. How big of a competitive advantage do you think this positioning strategy provides Snap Fitness?
2. Look at Figure 15.1 in the chapter. What type of franchise system makes the most sense for Snap Fitness?
3. What types of characteristics do you think Snap Fitness looks for in its franchisees?
4. What do you think lies ahead for Snap Fitness? What are some of the things that can go right and what are some of the things that can go wrong as this firm continues to sell franchises and grows?

Application Questions

1. What similarities do you see between Snap Fitness and Curves International? What can Snap Fitness learn from Curves' successes and its recent troubles?
2. Analyze easyFit, one of the tracking and motivational components of Snap Fitness's offering. How important of a component of Snap Fitness's business model do you think easyFit will become? If easyFit is successful, do you think Snap Fitness's competitors will have a hard time or an easy time imitating it?

Sources: Snap Fitness homepage, www.snapfitness.com (accessed May 20, 2011); Entrepreneur.com, www.entrepreneur.com/franchises/snapfitnessinc/328995-0.htmleur.com (accessed May 20, 2011); P. Strait, "Snap Fitness Named Among Top Franchisors for Young Entrepreneurs," Snap Fitness Press Release, www.snapfitness.com (accessed May 20, 2011, originally posted on April 2011); P. Strait, "Snap Fitness Raises the Bar with New Personal Wellness Program," Snap Fitness Press Release, www.snapfitness.com (accessed May 20, 2011, originally posted on April 2011); P. Taunton, "Trimming the Fat," *Fortune Small Business*, February, 2008, 61; J. Gustafson, "Small Gyms Proliferate Here," *Journal of Business* (September 11, 2008): A1.

CASE 15.2

Game Truck: Bringing Multiplayer Gaming to Its Customer's Homes

Web: www.gametruck.org
Facebook: Game Truck

Bruce R. Barringer, *Oklahoma State University*

R. Duane Ireland, *Texas A&M University*

Introduction

The idea for Game Truck first came to Scott Novis at his son's fourth birthday party. They were at a pizza arcade and the noise, expense, and frustration caused him to think about a better alternative. What's more, he knew that the electronic games he was working on at his job were better than anything in the arcade. That experience led to an epiphany. Instead of taking kids to an arcade for birthday parties or similar events, why not bring the arcade to their homes? And what if, instead of making something "kiddy," the arcade featured the best video games available on the latest consoles? And what if it was something that people of all ages could enjoy?

These thoughts were the foundation for the launching of Game Truck, Novis's entrepreneurial venture. Game Truck is the world's first mobile video game theater. The basic idea was to create a mobile arcade or truck that contained the latest video games, video game consoles, and large screens for people to play multiplayer video games. By making the arcade mobile, it could be taken anywhere for people to enjoy.

There are several different models of the mobile arcade or truck, from a tow-behind trailer to a "top of the line" all-in-one unit that looks like a large bus. The mobile theater will travel to any location that has a large enough parking area for it to set up. Once it arrives, it is entirely self-sufficient and provides its own power. It can accommodate up to 16 players, who can engage in multiplayer video games aided by ultra-modern consoles and 54-inch screens. Instructors are available to help participants learn new games or troubleshoot any problems that occur. Along with providing a venue for a fun birthday party or another occasion, a staple concept of the Game Truck experience is to encourage people to play electronic games with one another. A common complaint that parents have is that computer games isolate their children, and cause them to focus on playing against their computer rather than socializing with other kids. The Game Truck experience is designed to bring kids, their friends, and their families together to participate in multiplayer games in a fun and highly engaging environment. Founded in 2006, Game Truck now has over 40 franchisees that are making Game Truck parties available on a weekly basis in cities across the United States.

Sound simple enough? It is, but as straightforward as the Game Truck concept is, it took a great deal of effort and hard work to get off the ground. And there are also questions regarding how Game Truck will continue to grow and evolve its offering.

Scott Novis

Game Truck's founder, Scott Novis, is no stranger to electronic games. He has nearly a decade of video game development experience, working for several companies. His two stops prior to Game Truck were particularly instrumental. At one point, he was the VP for Development for Rainbow Studios, which is one of the largest video game development studios in the Southwestern United States. During Novis's tenure, Rainbow Studios was responsible for some of the most successful games of the PS2 era. His stop just prior to Game Truck was with Walt Disney Corporation, where he developed a new kind of video game studio, dubbed the Walt Disney Nintendo Center for Excellence.

Novis's vision for Game Truck was to create a physical, mobile space where people could play the best video games on the latest consoles with their friends in an effortless, affordable, and fun atmosphere. It also had to be operable by virtually anyone with a passion for video games and a desire to work with kids and their families.

Fortunate Convergence of Technologies and Early Testing

Novis and Game Truck benefited from a fortunate convergence of technologies, which took place at about the time Novis's ideas for Game Truck came together. The three technologies, each of which is instrumental to Game Truck's offering, are shown next.

The first Game Truck prototype was built in Novis's garage in Tempe, Arizona, and the basic concept is currently patent-pending. To see how the prototype would perform, Novis and his brother Chris threw the first Game Truck party for a friend and neighbor.

(continued)

Technologies Instrumental
to Game Truck's Founding

Inexpensive portable power	Cost efficient flat screen TVs	Arrival of high definition video game consoles

Along with its mobile capabilities and the highly engaging nature of the experience it offers, Game Truck is also a mission-driven organization. Its tagline is "We are redefining the way people play." Its mission is built on four principles: (1) Respect the Games, (2) Respect the Video Game Lifestyle, (3) Respect Mom, and (4) Respect Education. Collectively, these principles promote the philosophy that rather than separating children from their parents, electronic games can bring children and their parents together via the interactive nature of multiplayer games. In addition, Game Truck's principles promote the ideals that games should involve physical activity, should be tools that parents can use to set limits and instill discipline, and through instruction regarding how electronic games are made should spur interest among kids in fields like computer programming, mathematics, and graphic design. In fact, as an ancillary offering, Game Truck has taken these principles and formed them into an educational program named P3.

Franchise Setup and Game Truck Offering

Game Truck is selling area franchise agreements. Depending on the circumstances, the initial franchise fee has ranged from a low of $19,500 to a high of $89,500. Other expenses include the Game Truck trailer(s), along with the equipment that goes inside it, monthly royalties, and other marketing and operational support fees.

Game Truck offers its franchisees multiple levels of assistance and support. The size of a franchisee's territory is determined by taking into consideration factors such as number of schools in a particular area, the average family income level of the area, and other demographic factors. Each Game Truck franchisee is provided training in regard to how to book parties, how to operate the Game Truck trailer, and how to set up a local marketing plan. Because the training program is so comprehensive, no prior experience is necessary to own and operate a Game Truck franchise. Once a franchise agreement is in place, a Game Truck franchisee can be up-and-running within six to eight weeks.

A Game Truck party costs $299 for the first two hours, and $100 for each additional weekday hour and $125 for each additional weekend hour. Parents choose the games that will be played. For example, M (mature) rated games can be removed from parties for younger children. Currently, the Game Truck has 62 games for parents to choose from. One unique aspect of Game Truck's offering to its franchisees is that because most parties are held on weekends, a Game Truck franchisee can be owned and operated by someone who has another job.

One aspect of its business Game Truck points to as a positive indicator for continued success is that its Phoenix, Arizona, headquarters serves as a base for ongoing refinement of the Game Truck experience. The company remains laser focused on bringing people together in a multiplayer gaming context in the most innovative, cutting-edge, and cost-effective manner possible.

Challenges Ahead

As Game Truck evaluates future growth and the ongoing viability of its basic concept, several questions will need to be answered. First, is there a market for its mobile game studios beyond the staple kid's party market? Some Game Truck franchisees have booked corporate events. There may be other possibilities. Second, although many observers see the electronic games market as recession-proof, there is always the possibility that downturns in the economy may deter parents and other potential users from booking a Game Truck party, which costs a minimum of $299 for two hours. What can Game Truck do to minimize that possibility? Finally, is Game Truck's business model scalable utilizing the franchise concept? Will Game Truck be successful in its efforts to find a sufficient number of future franchisees who are passionate about gaming, have the financial ability to own and operate a Game Truck franchise, and are able to either operate the franchise successfully on a part-time basis or book sufficient parties to make it a full-time pursuit? There is a possibility that some Game Truck franchisees may find themselves caught in the middle—it's too much work to operate as a part-time business but it doesn't provide enough income to justify doing it full-time. How Game Truck resolves these challenges will be instrumental to its future success.

Discussion Questions

1. What do you think of Game Truck's basic concept?
2. Would you characterize Game Truck's potential nationwide market as small, medium, or large? Would the concept work in the town where your college or university is located? Explain your answer.
3. What qualities do you think Game Truck looks for in prospective franchisees? If you were a prospective franchisee, what questions would you ask the company as part of your due diligence process?
4. Address each of the rhetorical questions posed at the end of the case. Add two challenges that Game Truck may face that are not mentioned in the case. Comment

on how problematic each of the challenges are, and whether you think the company will be able to successfully meet its challenges.

Application Questions

1. If you had the choice to open a Game Truck franchise or a video arcade in a popular mall, which would you choose? Why?

2. Game Truck's overarching mission is to bring families together via multiplayer video games. To what degree do you think this portion of Game Truck's offering is an important draw?

Sources: Game Truck homepage, www.gametruck.com (accessed January 22, 2011); Franchise Genius, "Game Truck," www.franchisegenius.com/The-Game-Truck-Franchise (accessed January 22, 2011).

ENDNOTES

1. L. Wolf, "Learning Curve," *Upsizemag.com*, www.upsizemag.com (accessed June 1, 2006).
2. Wolf, "Learning Curve."
3. Personal Conversation with Joseph Keeley, May 19, 2011.
4. M. Bianchi, D. Chiaroni, V. Chiesa, and F. Frattini, "Organizing for External Technology Commercialization: Evidence from a Multiple Case Study in the Pharmaceutical Industry," *R&D Management* 41, no. 1 (2011): 120–37.
5. International Franchise Organization, "Highlights of the 2011 Franchise Business Economic Outlook," www.franchise.org (accessed May 19, 2011, originally posted January 2011).
6. Franchising.com homepage, www.franchising.com (accessed May 19, 2011).
7. T. Bates, "Analysis of Survival Rates Among Franchise and Independent Small Business Startups," *Journal of Small Business Management* 33, no. 2 (1995): 26–36.
8. J. G. Combs, D. J. Ketchen, Jr., C. L. Shook, and J. C. Short, "Antecedents and Consequences of Franchising: Past Accomplishments and Future Challenges," *Journal of Management* 37, no. 1 (2011): 99–126.
9. *CIA World Factbook*, www.cia.gov/library/publications/the-world-factbook/geos/us.html (accessed May 19, 2011).
10. Entrepreneur.com, www.entrepreneur.com/franchises/comfortkeepers/282228-0.html (accessed May 19, 2011).
11. R. E. Kidwell and A. Nygaard, "A Strategic Deviance Perspective on the Franchise Form of Organizing," *Entrepreneurship Theory and Practice* 35, no. 3 (2011): 467–82.
12. ProntoWash, www.prontowash.com/franchising_master_faq.php#2 (accessed May 19, 2011).
13. FRANdata, www.frandata.com (accessed May 19, 2011).
14. E. Croonen, "Trust and Fairness During Strategic Change Processes in Franchise Systems," *Journal of Business Ethics* 95, no. 2 (2010): 191–209.
15. A. Watson and R. Johnson, "Managing the Franchisor-Franchisee Relationship: A Relationship Marketing Perspective," *Journal of Marketing Channels* 17, no. 1 (2010): 51–68.
16. F. Chirico, R. D. Ireland, and D. G. Sirmon, "Franchising and the Family Firm: Creating Unique Sources of Advantage Through Familiness," *Entrepreneurship Theory and Practice* 35, no. 3 (2011): 483–501.
17. R. Bennett, "To Franchise or Not: How to Decide," in *Franchising Today: 1966–1967*, eds. C. L. Vaughn and D. B. Slater (New York: Matthew Bender and Company, 1967), 20.
18. W. E. Gillis, E. McEwan, T. R. Crook, and S. C. Michael, "Using Tournaments to Reduce Agency Problems: The Case of Franchising," *Entrepreneurship Theory and Practice* 35, no. 3 (2011): 427–47.
19. "Darden Restaurants, Inc.," *Standard & Poor's Stock Report*, www.standardandpoors.com (accessed May 20, 2011); Darden Restaurants, "Our Brands," www.dardens.com (accessed May 20, 2011).
20. D. Grewal, G. R. Iyer, R. G. Javalgi, and L. Radulovich, "Franchise Partnership and International Expansion: A Conceptual Framework and Research Propositions," *Entrepreneurship Theory and Practice* 35, no. 3 (2011): 533–57.
21. Federal Trade Commission, *Consumers Guide to Buying a Franchise* (Washington, DC: U.S. Government Printing Office, 2011).
22. I. Kotliarov, "Royalty Rate Structure in Case of Franchising," *Annals of Economics and Finance* 12, no. 1 (2011): 139–56.
23. Stroller Strides homepage, www.strollerstrides.com (accessed May 19, 2011).
24. J. Bennett, "Cruise Franchisee Says It's Been Smooth Sailing," *StartupJournal.com*, www.startupjournal.com (accessed May 30, 2006).
25. J. G. Combs, D. J. Ketchen, Jr., and J. C. Short, "Franchising Research: Major Milestones, New Directions, and Its Future Within Entrepreneurship," *Entrepreneurship Theory and Practice* 35, no. 3 (2011): 413–25.
26. Bureau of Consumer Protection, "Buying a Franchise: A Consumer Guide," http://business.ftc.gov/documents/inv05-buying-franchise-consumer-guide#2 (accessed May 19, 2011).

27. R. L. Purvin, *The Franchise Fraud* (New York: John Wiley & Sons, 1994), 7.

28. Federal Trade Commission, www.ftc.gov/bcp/franchise/netdiscl.shtm (accessed May 19, 2011).

29. Federal Trade Commission, "Buying a Franchise: A Consumer Guide"; T. Mellewigt, T. Ehrmann, and C. Decker, "How Does the Franchisor's Choice of Different Control Mechanisms Affect Franchisees' and Employee-Managers' Satisfaction?" *Journal of Retailing* (2011): in press.

30. R. Gibson, "U.S. Franchises Find Opportunities to Grow Abroad," *Wall Street Journal*, August 11, 2009, B5.

31. Ibid

32. PricewaterhouseCoopers, *2010 Franchise Business Economic Outlook*, www.franchise.org/uploadedFiles/Franchise_Industry/Resources/Education_Foundation/2010%20Franchise%20Business%20Outlook%20Report_Final%202009.12.21.pdf (posted on December 21, 2009).

33. All Business, "Hot Trend: Seniors Buying Franchises," www.allbusiness.com/franchises/buying-a-franchise/14572171-1.html (accessed May 19, 2011).

34. S. Needleman, "Restaurant Franchises Try Truckin' as a Way to Grow," *Wall Street Journal*, October 28, 2010, B1.

GLOSSARY

7(A) loan guaranty program. The main Small Business Administration (SBA) program available to small businesses operating through private sector lenders providing loans that are guaranteed by the SBA; loan guarantees reserved for small businesses that are unable to secure financing through normal lending channels. (364)

10-K. A report that is similar to the annual report, except that it contains more detailed information about the company's business. (285)

accounts receivable. The money owed to a firm by its customers. (282)

acquirer. The surviving firm in an acquisition. (500)

acquisition. The outright purchase of one firm by another. (500)

adverse selection. The challenge a firm must face as it grows such that as the number of employees a firm needs increases, it becomes more difficult to find the right employees, place them in appropriate positions, and provide adequate supervision. (471)

advertising. Making people aware of a product or service in hopes of persuading them to buy it. (396)

advisory board. A panel of experts who are asked by a firm's managers to provide counsel and advice on an ongoing basis; unlike a board of directors, an advisory board possesses no legal responsibilities for the firm and gives nonbinding advice. (328)

agency theory. A management concept that argues that managers, because they are paid a salary, may not be as committed to the success of the businesses they manage as the owners, who capture the business's profits. This theory supports the notion of franchising, because franchisees are in effect the owners of the units they manage. (531)

area franchise agreement. Agreement that allows a franchisee to own and operate a specific number of outlets in a particular geographic area. (525)

articles of incorporation. Documents forming a legal corporation that are filed with the secretary of state's office in the state of incorporation. (260)

assignment of invention agreement. A document signed by an employee as part of the employment agreement that assigns the employer the right to apply for the patent of an invention made by the employee during the course of his or her employment. (429)

assumptions sheet. An explanation in a new firm's business plan of the sources of the numbers for its financial forecast and the assumptions used to generate them. (157, 293)

balance sheet. A snapshot of a company's assets, liabilities, and owner's equity at a specific point in time. (287)

barriers to entry. Conditions that create disincentives for a new firm to enter an industry. (179)

board of advisers. A panel of experts asked by a firm's management to provide counsel and advice on an ongoing basis. (156)

board of directors. A panel of individuals who are elected by a corporation's shareholders to oversee the management of the firm. (156, 326)

bootstrapping. Using creativity, ingenuity, or any means possible to obtain resources other than borrowing money or raising capital from traditional sources. (350)

brainstorming. A technique used to quickly generate a large number of ideas and solutions to problems; conducted to generate ideas that might represent product or business opportunities. (85)

brand. The set of attributes—positive or negative—that people associate with a company. (388)

brand equity. The set of assets and liabilities that is linked to a brand and enables it to raise a firm's valuation. (391)

brand management. A program that protects the image and value of an organization's brand in consumers' minds. (388)

break-even point. The point where total revenue received equals total costs associated with the output. (295)

budgets. Itemized forecasts of a company's income, expenses, and capital needs that are also important tools for financial planning and control. (283)

burn rate. The rate at which a company is spending its capital until it reaches profitability. (347)

business angels. Individuals who invest their personal capital directly in new ventures. (355)

business concept blind spot. An overly narrow focus that prevents a firm from seeing an opportunity that might fit its business model. (217)

business format franchise. By far the most popular approach to franchising in which the franchisor provides a formula for doing business to the franchisee along with training, advertising, and other forms of assistance. (525)

business license. A legal authorization to operate a business in a city, county, or state. (254)

business method patent. A patent that protects an invention that is or facilitates a method of doing business. (427)

business model. A company's plan for how it competes, uses its resources, structures its relationships, interfaces with customers, and creates value to sustain itself on the basis of the profits it generates. (51, 206)

business model innovation. Initiative that revolutionizes how products are sold in an industry. (217)

business plan. A written document describing all the aspects of a business venture, which is usually necessary to raise money and attract high quality business partners. (51, 138)

buyback clause. A clause found in most founders' agreements that legally obligates the departing founder to sell to the remaining founders his or her interest in the firm if the remaining founders are interested. (247)

buying intentions survey. An instrument that is used to gauge customers' interest in a product or service. (110)

buzz. An awareness and sense of anticipation about a company and its offerings. (391)

C corporation. A legal entity that in the eyes of the law is separate from its owners. (259)

carry. The percentage of profits that the venture capitalist gets from a specific venture capital fund. (357)

certification marks. Marks, words, names, symbols, or devices used by a person other than its owner to certify a particular quality about a product or service. (435)

closely held corporation. A corporation in which the voting stock is held by a small number of individuals and is very thinly or infrequently traded. (260)

code of conduct. A formal statement of an organization's values on certain ethical and social issues. (243)

collective marks. Trademarks or service marks used by the members of a cooperative, association, or other collective group, including marks indicating membership in a union or similar organization. (434)

common stock. Stock that is issued more broadly than preferred stock and that gives the stockholders voting rights to elect the firm's board of directors. (260)

competitive analysis grid. A tool for organizing the information a firm collects about its competitors to see how it stacks up against its competitors, provide ideas for markets to pursue, and identify its primary sources of competitive advantage. (193)

competitive intelligence. The information that is gathered by a firm to learn about its competitors. (192)

competitor analysis. A detailed evaluation of a firm's direct, indirect, and future competitors. (150, 175)

Computer Software Copyright Act. In 1980, Congress passed this act, which amended previous copyright acts; now, all forms of computer programs are protected. (439)

concept statement. A preliminary description of a business that includes descriptions of the product or service being offered, the intended target market, the benefits of the product or service, the product's position in the market, and how the product or service will be sold and distributed. (108)

concept test. A representation of the product or service to prospective users to gauge customer interest, desirability, and purchase intent. (108)

constant ratio method of forecasting. A forecasting approach using the percent of sales method in which expense items on a firm's income statement are expected to grow at the same rate as sales. (295)

consultant. An individual who gives professional or expert advice. Consultants fall into two categories: paid consultants and consultants who are made available for free or at a reduced rate through a nonprofit or governmental agency. (332)

contribution margin. The amount per unit of sale that is left over and is available to "contribute" to covering the firm's fixed costs and producing a profit. (152)

copyright. A form of intellectual property protection that grants to the owner of a work of authorship the legal right to determine how the work is used and to obtain the economic benefits of the work. (438)

copyright bug. The letter c inside a circle with the first year of publication and the author copyright owner (e.g., © 2007 Dell Inc). (440)

copyright infringement. Violation of another's copyright that occurs when one work derives from another work or is an exact copy or shows substantial similarity to the original copyrighted work. (441)

core competency. A unique skill or capability that transcends products or markets, makes a significant contribution to the customer's perceived benefit, is difficult to imitate, and serves as a source of a firm's competitive advantage over its rivals. (218)

core strategy. The overall manner in which a firm competes relative to its rivals. (215)

corporate entrepreneurship. Behavior orientation exhibited by established firms with an entrepreneurial emphasis that is proactive, innovative, and risk taking. (32)

corporate venture capital. A type of capital similar to traditional venture capital, except that the money comes from corporations that invest in new ventures related to their areas of interest. (359)

corporation. A separate legal entity organized under the authority of a state. (259)

corridor principle. States that once an entrepreneur starts a firm and becomes immersed in an industry, "corridors" leading to new venture opportunities become more apparent to the entrepreneur than to someone looking in from the outside. (81)

cost-based pricing. A pricing method in which the list price is determined by adding a markup percentage to the product's cost. (395)

cost leadership strategy. Generic strategy in which firms strive to have the lowest costs in the industry relative to competitors' costs and typically attract customers on the basis of price. (218)

cost of goods sold. The materials and direct labor needed to produce firm's revenue. (152)

cost of sales. All of the direct costs associated with producing or delivering a product or service, including the material costs and direct labor costs (also cost of goods sold). (287)

cost reduction strategy. A marketing strategy that is accomplished through achieving lower costs than industry incumbents through process improvements. (189)

creative destruction. The process by which new products and technologies developed by entrepreneurs over time make current products and technologies obsolete; stimulus of economic activity. (47)

creativity. The process of generating a novel or useful idea. (83)

crowd funding. A method of funding in which people pool their money and other resources, usually via the Internet, to support efforts initiated by other people or organizations. (364)

current assets. Cash plus items that are readily convertible to cash, such as accounts receivable, inventories, and marketable securities. (289)

current liabilities. Obligations that are payable within a year, including accounts payable, accrued expenses, and the current portion of long-term debt. (289)

current ratio. A ratio that equals the firm's current assets divided by its current liabilities. (289)

customer advisory boards. A panel of individuals set up by some companies to meet regularly to discuss needs, wants, and problems that may lead to new product, service, or customer service ideas. (87)

customer interface. The way in which a firm interacts with its customers. (223)

day-in-the-life research. A form of anthropological research used by companies to make sure customers are satisfied and to probe for new product ideas by sending researchers to the customers' homes or business. (87)

debt financing. Getting a loan; most common sources of debt financing are commercial banks and the Small Business Administration's (SBA's) guaranteed loan program. (351)

debt-to-equity ratio. A ratio calculated by dividing the firm's long-term debt by its shareholders' equity. (282)

declining industry. An industry that is experiencing a reduction in demand. (187)

derivative works. Works that are new renditions of something that is already copyrighted, which are also copyrightable. (439)

design patents. The second most common type of patent covering the invention of new, original, and ornamental designs for manufactured products. (428)

differentiation strategy. A strategy that firms use to provide unique or different products to customers.

Firms using this strategy typically compete on the basis of quality, service, timeliness, or some other dimension that creates unique value for customers. (218)

disintermediation. The process of eliminating layers of intermediaries, such as distributors and retailers, to sell directly to customers. (404)

distribution channel. The route a product takes from the place it is made to the customer who is the end user. (403)

double taxation. Form of taxation in which a corporation is taxed on its net income. When the same income is distributed to shareholders in the form of dividends, it is taxed again on shareholders' personal income tax returns. (260)

due diligence. The process of investigating the merits of a potential venture and verifying the key claims made in the business plan. (359)

Economic Espionage Act. Passed in 1996, an act that makes the theft of trade secrets a crime. (443)

economies of scale. A phenomenon that occurs when mass producing a product results in lower average costs. (179, 466)

efficiency. How productively a firm utilizes its assets relative to its rate of return. (282)

elevator speech (or pitch). A brief, carefully constructed statement that outlines the merits of a business opportunity. (352)

emerging industry. A new industry in which standard operating procedures have yet to be developed. (187)

employer identification number (EIN). A tax identification number; is used when filing various tax returns. (254)

entrepreneurial alertness. The ability to notice things without engaging in deliberate search. (81)

entrepreneurial firms. Companies that bring new products and services to market by creating and seizing opportunities. (44)

entrepreneurial intensity. The position of a firm on a conceptual continuum that ranges from highly conservative to highly entrepreneurial. (32)

entrepreneurial services. Those services that generate new market, product, and service ideas. (471)

entrepreneurship. The process by which individuals pursue opportunities without regard to resources they currently control. (32)

equity financing. A means of raising money by exchanging partial ownership in a firm, usually in the form of stock, for funding. (351)

ethical dilemma. A situation that involves doing something that is beneficial to oneself or the organization, but may be unethical. (245)

ethics training programs. Programs designed to teach employees how to respond to the types of ethical dilemmas that might arise on their jobs. (244)

exclusive distribution arrangements. An agreement that gives a retailer or other intermediary the exclusive rights to sell a company's products in a specific area for a specific period of time. (404)

execution intelligence. The ability to fashion a solid business idea into a viable business is a key characteristic of successful entrepreneurs. (39)

executive summary. A quick overview of the entire business plan that provides a busy reader everything that he or she needs to know about the distinctive nature of the new venture. (148)

external growth strategies. Growth strategies that rely on establishing relationships with third parties, such as mergers, acquisitions, strategic alliances, joint ventures, licensing, and franchising. (498)

factoring. A financial transaction whereby a business sells its accounts receivable to a third party, called a factor, at a discount in exchange for cash. (364)

fair use. The limited use of copyright material for purposes such as criticism, comment, news reporting, teaching, or scholarship. (441)

fast-track program. A provision in the SBIR Program in which some applicants can simultaneously submit Phase I and Phase II grant applications. (366)

feasibility analysis. A preliminary evaluation of a business idea to determine if it is worth pursuing. (105)

fictitious business name permit. A permit that's required for businesses that plan to use a fictitious name, which is any name other than the business owner's name (also called dba or doing business as). (255)

fiduciary obligation. The obligation to always act in another's best interest; it is a mistake to assume that a franchisor has a fiduciary obligation to its franchisees. (544)

final prospectus. Documents issued by the investment bank after the Securities and Exchange Commission (SEC) has approved the offering that sets a date and issuing price for the offering. (361)

financial feasibility analysis. A preliminary financial assessment of a new venture that considers the total start up cash needed, financial performance of similar businesses, and the overall financial attractiveness of the proposed venture. (119)

financial management. The process of raising money and managing a company's finances in a way that achieves the highest rate of return. (281)

financial ratios. Ratios showing the relationships between items on a firm's financial statements that are used to discern whether a firm is meeting its financial objectives and how it stacks up against industry peers. (283)

financial statements. Written reports that quantitatively describe a firm's financial health. (283)

financing activities. Activities that raise cash during a certain period by borrowing money or selling stock, and/or use cash during a certain period by paying dividends, buying back outstanding stock, or buying back outstanding bonds. (291)

first-mover advantage. A sometimes significant advantage, created by the opportunity to establish brand recognition and/or market power, gained by the first company to produce a product or service or the first company to move into a market. (187)

first-to-invent rule. States that first person to invent an item or process is given preference over another person who is first to file a patent application. (430)

fixed assets. Assets used over a longer time frame, such as real estate, buildings, equipment, and furniture. (289)

fixed costs. The costs that a company incurs in operating a business whether it sells something or not (e.g., overhead). (153, 466)

focus group. A gathering of five to ten people who have been selected based on their common characteristics relative to the issue being discussed; conducted to generate ideas that might represent product or business opportunities. (86)

follow-on funding. Additional funding for a firm following the initial investment made by investors. (359)

forecasts. Estimates of a firm's future income and expenses, based on its past performance, its current circumstances, and its future plans. (293)

founders' agreement. A written document that deals with issues such as the relative split of the equity among the founders of a firm, how individual founders will be compensated for the cash or the "sweat equity" they put into the firm, and how long the founders will have to remain with the firm for their shares to fully vest (also shareholders' agreement). (247)

founding team. A team of individuals chosen to start a new venture; has an advantage over firms started by an individual because a team brings more talent, resources, ideas, and professional contacts to a new venture than does a sole entrepreneur. (318)

fragmented industry. An industry characterized by a large number of firms approximately equal in size. (187)

franchise agreement. The document that consummates the sale of a franchise, which typically contains two sections: (1) the purchase agreement and (2) the franchise or license agreement. (544)

Franchise Disclosure Document (FDD). Accepted in all 50 states and part of Canada, a lengthy document that contains 23 categories of information that give a prospective franchisee a broad base of information about the background and financial health of the franchisor. (544)

franchisee. An individual or firm that enters into a franchise agreement and pays an initial fee and an ongoing royalty to an franchisor in exchange for using the franchisor's trademark and method of doing business. (523)

franchising. A form of business organization in which a firm that already has a successful product or service (franchisor) licenses its trademark and method of doing businesses to other businesses (franchisees) in exchange for an initial franchise fee and an ongoing royalty. (523)

franchisor. A firm with a successful product or service that enters into a franchising agreement to license its trademark and method of doing business to other businesses in exchange for fee and royalty payments. (523)

fulfillment and support. The way a firm's product or service "goes to market" or how it reaches its customers; also, the channels a company uses and the level of customer support it provides. (224)

full business plan. A document that spells out a company's operations and plans in much more detail than a summary business plan; the format that is usually used to prepare a business plan for an investor. (144)

general partner. The venture capitalists who manage a venture capital fund. (357)

general partnership. A form of business organization in which two or more people pool their skills, abilities, and resources to run a business. (258)

geographic expansion. An internal growth strategy in which an entrepreneurial business grows by simply expanding from its original location to additional geographical sites. (495)

geographic roll-up strategy. When one firm starts acquiring similar firms that are located in different geographic areas. (187)

global industry. An industry that is experiencing significant international sales. (189)

global strategy. An international expansion strategy in which firms compete for market share by using the same basic approach in all foreign markets. (189)

guerilla marketing. A low budget approach to marketing that relies on ingenuity, cleverness, and surprise rather than traditional techniques. (403)

heterogeneous team. A team whose individual members are diverse in terms of their abilities and experiences. (320)

historical financial statements. Reflect past performance and are usually prepared on a quarterly and annual basis. (285)

homogenous team. A team whose individual members' experiences and areas of expertise are very similar to one another. (320)

idea. A thought, impression, or notion. (70)

idea bank. A physical or digital repository for storing ideas. (89)

idea–expression dichotomy. The legal principle describing the concept that although an idea is not able to be copyrighted, the specific expression of an idea is. (440)

illiquid. Describes stock in both closely held and private corporations, meaning that it typically isn't easy to find a buyer for the stock. (260)

improving an existing product or service. Enhancing a product or service's quality by making it larger or smaller, making it easier to use, or making it more up-to-date, thereby increasing its value and price potential. (493)

income statement. A financial statement that reflects the results of the operations of a firm over a specified period of time: prepared on a monthly, quarterly, or annual basis. (286)

individual franchise agreement. The most common type of franchise agreement, which involves the sale of a single franchise for a specific location. (525)

industry. A group of firms producing a similar product or service, such as airlines, fitness drinks, or electronic games. (114, 174)

industry analysis. Business research that focuses on the potential of an industry. (174)

industry/market feasibility. An assessment of the overall appeal of the industry and target market for the product or service being proposed. (114, 525)

initial public offering (IPO). The first sale of a company's stock to the public and an important milestone for a firm for four reasons: it is a way to raise equity capital; it raises a firm's public profile; it is a liquidity event; and it creates another form of currency (company stock) that can be used to grow the company. (361)

innovation. The process of creating something new, which is central to the entrepreneurial process. (47)

inside director. A person on a firm's board of directors who is also an officer of the firm. (326)

insourcing. An approach that takes place when a service provider comes inside a partner's facilities and helps the partner design and manage its supply chain. (221)

intellectual property. Any product of human intellect, imagination, creativity, or inventiveness that is intangible but has value in the marketplace and can be protected through tools such as patents, trademarks, copyrights, and trade secrets. (90, 421)

intellectual property audit. A firm's assessment of the intellectual property it owns. (445)

intent-to-use trademark application. An application based on the applicant's intention to register and use a trademark. (438)

interference. An administrative proceeding overseen by a judge, which takes place when there is a dispute regarding who was the first person to invent a product. (430)

internal growth strategies. Growth strategies that rely on efforts generated within the firm itself, such as new product development, other product related strategies, or international expansion. (489)

international new ventures. Businesses that, from inception, seek to derive significant competitive advantage by using their resources to sell products or services in multiple countries. (496)

intranet. A privately maintained Internet site that can be accessed only by authorized users. (89)

invention logbook. Documentation of the dates and activities related to the development of a particular invention. (430)

inventory. A company's merchandise, raw materials, and products waiting to be sold. (282)

investing activities. Activities that include the purchase, sale, or investment in fixed assets, such as real estate and buildings. (291)

investment bank. A financial institution that acts as an underwriter or agent for a firm issuing securities. (361)

joint venture. An entity created when two or more firms pool a portion of their resources to create a separate, jointly owned organization. (508)

Lanham Act. An act of Congress, passed in 1946, that spells out what is protected under trademark law. (435)

leadership strategy. A competitive strategy in which the firm tries to become the dominant player in the industry. (189)

lease. A written agreement in which the owner of a piece of property allows an individual or business to use the property for a specified period of time in exchange for regular payments. (365)

liability of newness. Situation that often causes new firms to falter because the people who start the firms can't adjust quickly enough to their new roles, and because the firm lacks a "track record" with customers and suppliers. (317)

licensee. A company that purchases the right to use another company's intellectual property. (504)

licensing. The granting of permission by one company to another company to use a specific form of its intellectual property under clearly defined conditions. (503)

licensing agreement. The formal contract between a licensor and licensee. (504)

licensor. The company that owns the intellectual property in a licensing agreement. (504)

lifestyle firms. Businesses that provide their owners the opportunity to pursue a particular lifestyle and earn a living while doing so (e.g., ski instructors, golf pros, and tour guides). (44)

limited liability company (LLC). A form of business organization that combines the limited liability advantage of the corporation with the tax advantages of the partnership. (262)

limited partners. Participants in a partnership, such as a venture capital fund, which have limited liability, meaning that they are only liable up to the amount of their investment and have no management authority. (357)

limited partnership. A modified form of a general partnership that includes two classes of owners: general partners and limited partners. The general partners are liable for the debts and obligations of the partnership, but the limited partners are liable only up to the amount of their investment. The limited partners may not exercise any significant control over the organization without jeopardizing their limited liability status. (259)

limited partnership agreement. Sets forth the rights and duties of the general and limited partners, along with the details of how the partnership will be managed and eventually dissolved. (259)

line of credit. A borrowing "cap" is established and borrowers can use the credit at their discretion; requires periodic interest payments. (362)

link joint venture. A joint venture in which the position of the parties is not symmetrical and the objectives of the partners may diverge. (508)

liquid market. A market in which stock can be bought and sold fairly easily through an organized exchange. (260)

liquidity. The ability to sell a business or other asset quickly at a price that is close to its market value; also, a company's ability to meet its short-term financial obligations. (256, 282)

liquidity event. An occurrence such as a new venture going public, finding a buyer, or being acquired by another company that converts some or all of a company's stock into cash. (351)

long-term liabilities. Notes or loans that are repayable beyond one year, including liabilities associated with purchasing real estate, buildings, and equipment. (289)

managerial capacity problem. The problem that arises when the growth of a firm is limited by the managerial capacity (i.e., personnel, expertise, and intellectual resources) that a firm has available to investigate and implement new business ideas. (471)

managerial services. The routine functions of the firm that facilitate the profitable execution of new opportunities. (471)

market analysis. An analysis that breaks the industry into segments and zeros in on the specific segment (or target market) to which the firm will try to appeal. (150)

market leadership. The position of a firm when it is the number one or the number two firm in an industry or niche market in terms of sales volume. (466)

market penetration strategy. A strategy designed to increase the sales of a product or service through greater marketing efforts or through increased production capacity and efficiency. (493)

market segmentation. The process of studying the industry in which a firm intends to compete to determine the different potential target markets in that industry. (150, 385)

marketing alliance. Typically matches a company with a distribution system with a company with a product to sell in order to increase sales of a product or service. (505)

marketing mix. The set of controllable, tactical marketing tools that a firm uses to produce the response it wants in the target market; typically organized around the four Ps—product, price, promotion, and place (or distribution). (393)

marketing strategy. A firm's overall approach for marketing its products and services. (153)

master franchise agreement. Similar to an area franchise agreement, but in addition to having the right to operate a specific number of locations in a particular area, the franchisee also has the right to offer and sell the franchise to other people in the area. (525)

mature industry. An industry that is experiencing slow or no increase in demand, has numerous (rather than new) customers, and has limited product innovation. (187)

mediation. A process in which an impartial third party (usually a professional mediator) helps those involved in a dispute reach an agreement. (252)

merchandise and character licensing. The licensing of a recognized trademark or brand, which the licensor typically controls through a registered trademark or copyright. (504)

merger. The pooling of interests to combine two or more firms into one. (500)

milestone. In a business plan context, a noteworthy event in the past or future development of a business. (150)

mission statement. A statement that describes why a firm exists and what its business model is supposed to accomplish. (149, 216)

moderate risk takers. Entrepreneurs who are often characterized as willing to assume a moderate amount of risk in business, being neither overly conservative nor likely to gamble. (42)

moral hazard. A problem a firm faces as it grows and adds personnel; the assumption is that new hires will not have the same ownership incentives or be as motivated to work as hard as the original founders. (471)

multidomestic strategy. An international expansion strategy in which firms compete for market share on a country by country basis and vary their product or services offerings to meet the demands of the local market. (189)

multiple-unit franchisee. An individual who owns and operates more than one outlet of the same franchisor, whether through an area or a master franchise agreement. (526)

net sales. Total sales minus allowances for returned goods and discounts. (287)

network entrepreneurs. Entrepreneurs who identified their idea through social contacts. (83)

networking. Building and maintaining relationships with people whose interests are similar or whose relationship could bring advantages to a firm. (322)

new product development. The creation and sale of new products (or services) as a means of increasing a firm's revenues. (490)

new-venture team. The group of founders, key employees, and advisors that move a new venture from an idea to a fully functioning firm. (117, 316)

niche market. A place within a large market segment that represents a narrow group of customers with similar interests. (386)

niche strategy. A marketing strategy that focuses on a narrow segment of the industry. (189)

noncompete agreement. An agreement that prevents an individual from competing against a former employer for a specific period of time. (251)

nondisclosure agreement. A promise made by an employee or another party (such as a supplier) to not disclose a company's trade secrets. (251)

one year after first use deadline. Requirement that a patent must be filed within one year of when a product or process was first offered for sale, put into public use, or was described in any printed publication. If this requirement is violated, the right to apply for a patent is forfeited. (427)

operating activities. Activities that affect net income (or loss), depreciation, and changes in current assets and current liabilities other than cash and short-term debt. (291)

operating expenses. Marketing, administrative costs, and other expenses not directly related to producing a product or service. (287)

operating leverage. An analysis of the firm's fixed costs versus its variable costs. (153)

operational business plan. A blueprint for a company's operations; primarily meant for an internal audience. (144)

opportunity. A favorable set of circumstances that creates a need for a new product, service, or business. (69)

opportunity gap. An entrepreneur recognizes a problem and creates a business to fill it. (69)

opportunity recognition. The process of perceiving the possibility of a profitable new business or a new product or service. (81)

organic growth. Internally generated growth within a firm that does not rely on outside intervention. (489)

organizational chart. A graphic representation of how authority and responsibility are distributed within a company. (156)

organizational feasibility analysis. A study conducted to determine whether a proposed business has sufficient management expertise, organizational competence, and resources to be successful. (117)

other assets. Miscellaneous assets including accumulated goodwill. (289)

outside director. Someone on a firm's board of directors who is not employed by the firm. (326)

outsourcing. Work that is done for a company by people other than the company's full-time employees. (494)

owner's equity. The equity invested in the business by its owner(s) plus the accumulated earnings retained by the business after paying dividends. (289)

pace of growth. The rate at which a firm is growing on an annual basis. (464)

partnership agreement. A document that details the responsibility and the ownership shares of the partners involved with an organization. (258)

passion for their business. An entrepreneur's belief that his or her business will positively influence people's lives; one of the characteristics of successful entrepreneurs. (35)

patent. A grant from the federal government conferring the rights to exclude others from making, selling, or using an invention for the term of the patent. (425)

patent infringement. This is when one party engages in the unauthorized use of another's patent. (433)

peer-to-peer lending. A category of financial transactions which occur directly between individuals or "peers." (364)

percent of sales method. A method for expressing each expense item as a percent of sales. (295)

piercing the corporate veil. The chain of effects that occurs if the owners of a corporation don't file their yearly payments, neglect to pay their annual fees, or commit fraud, which may result in the court ignoring the fact that a corporation has been established, and the owners could be held personally liable for actions for the corporation. (260)

place. The marketing mix category that encompasses all of the activities that move a firm's product from its place of origin to the consumer (also distribution). (403)

plant patents. Patents that protect new varieties of plants that can be reproduced asexually by grafting or cross-breeding rather than by planting seeds. (428)

position. How the entire company is situated relative to its competitors. (150, 175)

preferred stock. Stock that is typically issued to conservative investors, who have preferential rights over common stockholders in regard to dividends and to the assets of the corporation in the event of liquidation. (259)

preliminary prospectus. A document issued by an investment bank that describes the potential offering to the general public while the SEC is conducting an investigation of the offering (also red-herring). (361)

press kit. A folder typically distributed to journalists and made available online that contains background information about a company and includes a list of the company's most recent accomplishments. (399)

price. The amount of money consumers pay to buy a product; one of the four Ps in a company's marketing mix. (394)

price/earnings (P/E) ratio. A simple ratio that measures the price of a company's stock against its earnings. (287)

price-quality attribution. The assumption consumers naturally make that the higher priced product is also the better quality product. (395)

primary research. Research that is original and is collected firsthand by the entrepreneur by, for example, talking to potential customers and key industry participants. (105)

prior entrepreneurial experience. Prior start up experience; this experience has been found to be one of the most consistent predictors of future entrepreneurial performance. (321)

private corporation. A corporation in which all of the shares are held by a few shareholders, such as management or family members, and the stock is not publicly traded. (260)

private placement. A variation of the IPO in which there is a direct sale of an issue of securities to a large institutional investor. (362)

product. The element of the marketing mix that is the good or service a company offers to its target market; often thought of as something having physical form. (393)

product and trademark franchise. An arrangement under which the franchisor grants to the franchisee the right to buy its product and use its trade name. (524)

product attribute map. A map that illustrates a firm's positioning strategy relative to it's major rivals. (387)

product/customer focus. A defining characteristic of successful entrepreneurs that emphasizes producing good products with the capability to satisfy customers. (37)

product line extension strategy. A strategy that involves making additional versions of a product so they will appeal to different clientele. (494)

product/market scope. A range that defines the products and markets on which a firm will concentrate. (217)

product prototype. The first physical manifestation of a new product, often in a crude or preliminary form. (154)

product/service feasibility analysis. An assessment of the overall appeal of the product or service being proposed. (107)

productive opportunity set. The set of opportunities the firm feels it is capable of pursuing. (471)

pro forma balance sheet. Financial statements that show a projected snapshot of a company's assets, liabilities, and owner's equity at a specific point in time. (299)

pro forma financial statements. Projections for future periods, based on a firm's forecasts, and typically completed for two to three years in the future. (157, 285)

pro forma income statement. A financial statement that shows the projected results of the operations of a firm over a specific period. (299)

pro forma statement of cash flows. A financial statement that shows the projected flow of cash into and out of a company for a specific period. (301)

profit margin. A measure of a firm's return on sales that is computed by dividing net income by average net sales. (287)

profitability. The ability to earn a profit. (282)

promotion. The marketing mix category that includes the activities planned by a company to communicate the merits of its product to its target market with the goal of persuading people to buy the product. (396)

provisional patent application. A part of patent law that grants "provisional rights" to an inventor for up to one year, pending the filing of a complete and final application. (431)

public corporation. A corporation that is listed on a major stock exchange, such as the New York Stock Exchange or the NASDAQ, in which owners can sell their shares at almost a moment's notice. (260)

public relations. The efforts a company makes to establish and maintain a certain image with the public through networking with journalists and others to try to interest them in saying or writing good things about the company and its products. (398)

ratio analysis. Ratios showing the relationships between items on a firm's financial statements that are used to discern whether a firm is meeting its financial objectives and how it stacks up against industry peers. (157)

reference account. An early user of a firm's product who is willing to give a testimonial regarding his or her experience with the product. (394)

regression analysis. A statistical technique used to find relationships between variables for the purpose of predicting future values. (294)

relevant industry experience. Experience in the same industry as an entrepreneur's current venture that includes a network of industry contacts and an understanding of the subtleties of the industry. (321)

resource leverage. The process of adapting a company's core competencies to exploit new opportunities. (219)

road show. A whirlwind tour taken by the top management team of a firm wanting to go public; consists of meetings in key cities where the firm presents its business plan to groups of investors. (361)

rounds. Stages of subsequent investments made in a firm by investors. (359)

salary-substitute firms. Small firms that yield a level of income for their owner or owners that is similar to what they would earn when working for an employer (e.g., dry cleaners, convenience stores, restaurants, accounting firms, retail stores, and hairstyling salons). (44)

sales forecast. A projection of a firm's sales for a specified period (such as a year); most firms though forecast their sales for two to five years into the future. (294)

sales process. The systematic process a business engages in to identify prospects and close sales. (404)

Sarbanes-Oxley Act. A federal law that was passed in response to corporate accounting scandals involving prominent corporations, like Enron and WorldCom. (361)

SBA Guaranteed Loan Program. An important source of funding for small businesses in general in which approximately 50 percent of the 9,000 banks in the United States participate. (364)

SBIR Program. Small Business Innovation Research (SBIR) competitive grant program that provides over $1 billion per year to small businesses for early stage and development projects. (366)

scale joint venture. A joint venture in which the partners collaborate at a single point in the value chain to gain economies of scale in production or distribution. (508)

secondary market offering. Any later public issuance of shares after the initial public offering. (361)

secondary meaning. This arises when, over time, consumers start to identify a trademark with a specific product. For example, the name CHAP STICK for lip balm was originally considered to be descriptive, and thus not afforded trademark protection. (438)

secondary research. Data collected previously by someone else for a different purpose. (107)

service. An activity or benefit that is intangible and does not take on a physical form, such as an airplane trip or advice from an attorney. (393)

service marks. Similar to ordinary trademarks but used to identify the services or intangible activities of a business rather than a business's physical product. (434)

service prototype. A representation of what the service will be like and how the customer will experience it. (154)

shareholders. Owners of a corporation who are shielded from personal liability for the debts and obligations of the corporation. (259)

signaling. The act of a high-quality individual agreeing to serve on a company's board of directors, which indicates that the individual believes that the company has the potential to be successful. (327)

single-purpose loan. One common type of loan in which a specific amount of money is borrowed that must be repaid in a fixed amount of time with interest. (362)

skills profile. A chart that depicts the most important skills that are needed and where skills gaps exist. (322)

social plugins. Tools that Web sites use to provide its users with personalized and social experiences. (400)

sole entrepreneurs. Entrepreneurs who identified their business idea on their own. (83)

sole proprietorship. The simplest form of business organization involving one person, in which the owner maintains complete control over the business and business losses can be deducted against the owner's personal tax return. (256)

sources and uses of funds statement. A document, usually included in the financial section of a business plan, that lays out specifically how much money a firm needs, where the money will come from, and what the money will be used for. (157)

spin-in. A transaction that takes place when a large firm that has a small equity stake in a small firm, decided to acquire a 100% interest in the firm. (508)

spin-out. The opposite of a spin-in that occurs when a larger company divests itself of one of its smaller divisions. (508)

stability. The strength and vigor of the firm's overall financial posture. (282)

statement of cash flows. A financial statement summarizing the changes in a firm's cash position for a specified period of time and detailing why the changes occurred. Similar to a month end bank statement, it reveals how much cash is on hand at the end of the month as well as how the cash was acquired and spent during the month. (291)

stock options. Special form of incentive compensation providing employees the option or right to buy a certain number of shares of their company's stock at a stated price over a certain period of time. (260)

strategic alliance. A partnership between two or more firms that is developed to achieve a specific goal. (505)

strategic assets. Anything rare and valuable that a firm owns, including plant and equipment, location, brands, patents, customer data, a highly qualified staff, and distinctive partnerships. (219)

strong-tie relationships. Relationships characterized by frequent interaction that form between like-minded individuals such as coworkers, friends, and spouses; these relationships tend to reinforce insights and ideas the individuals already have and, therefore, are not likely to introduce new ideas. (83)

STTR Program. A government grant program, similar to the SBIR program, which requires the participation of a research organization, such as a research university or a federal laboratory. (367)

subchapter S corporation. A form of business organization that combines the advantages of a partnership and C corporation; similar to a partnership, in that the profits and losses of the business are not subject to double taxation, and similar to a corporation, in that the owners are not subject to personal liability for the behavior of the business. (261)

subfranchisees. The people who buy franchises from master franchisees. (526)

summary business plan. A business plan 10 to 15 pages long that works best for companies very early in their development that are not prepared to write a full plan. (144)

supplier. A company or vendor that provides parts or services to another company. (220)

supply chain. A network of all the companies that participate in the production of a firm's a product, from the acquisition of raw materials to the final sale. (220)

supply chain management. The coordination of the flow of all information, money, and material that moves through a product's supply chain. (220)

sustainable competitive advantage. A competitive advantage that is sustainable normally as the result of the unique combination of a firm's core competencies and strategic assets. (219)

sustained growth. Growth in both revenues and profits over an extended period of time. (458)

sweat equity. The value of the time and effort that a founder puts into a new firm. (349)

tagline. A phrase that is used consistently in a company's literature, advertisements, promotions, stationery, and even invoices to develop and to reinforce the position the company has staked out in its market. (149)

target. In an acquisition, the firm that is acquired. (500)

target market. The limited group of individuals or businesses that a firm goes after or tries to appeal to at a certain point in time. (223)

technological alliances. Business alliances that cooperate in R&D, engineering, and manufacturing. (505)

technology licensing. The licensing of proprietary technology, which the licensor typically controls by virtue of a utility patent. (504)

trademark. Any work, name, symbol, or device used to identify the sources or origin of products or services and to distinguish those products and services from others. (434)

trade secret. Any formula, pattern, physical device, idea, process, or other information that provides the owner of the information with a competitive advantage in the marketplace. (442)

trade show. An event at which the goods or services in a specific industry are exhibited and demonstrated. (399)

triggering event. The event that prompts an individual to become an entrepreneur (e.g., losing a job, inheriting money, accommodating a certain lifestyle). (50)

Uniform Trade Secrets Act. Drafted in 1979 by a special commission in an attempt to set nationwide standards for trade secret legislation; although the majority of states have adopted the act, most revised it, resulting in a wide disparity among states in regard to trade secret legislation and enforcement. (443)

utility patents. The most common type of patent covering what we generally think of as new inventions that must be useful, must be novel in relation to prior arts in the field, and must not be obvious to a person of ordinary skill in the field. (427)

value. Relative worth, importance, or utility. (44)

value-based pricing. A pricing method in which the list price is determined by estimating what consumers are willing to pay for a product and then backing off a bit to provide a cushion. (395)

value chain. The string of activities that moves a product from the raw material stage, through manufacturing and distribution, and ultimately to the end user. (212)

variable costs. The costs that are not fixed that a company incurs as it generates sales. (153, 466)

vendor credit. A form of credit in which a vendor extends credit to a business in order to allow the business to buy its products and/or services upfront but defer payment until later. (364)

venture capital. The money that is invested by venture capital firms in start ups and small businesses with exceptional growth potential. (356)

venture-leasing firms. Firms that act as brokers, bringing the parties involved in a lease together (e.g., firms acquainted with the producers of specialized equipment match these producers with new ventures that are in need of the equipment). (365)

viral marketing. A new marketing technique that facilitates and encourages people to pass along a marketing message about a particular product or service. (401)

virtual prototype. A computer generated 3-D image of an idea. (154)

weak tie relationships. Relationships characterized by infrequent interaction that form between casual acquaintances who do not have a lot in common and, therefore, may be the source of completely new ideas. (83)

window of opportunity. The time period in which a firm or an entrepreneur can realistically enter a new market. (69)

working capital. A firm's current assets minus its current liabilities. (289)

NAME INDEX

COMPANY INDEX

SUBJECT INDEX

Chapter	Recommended Cases	HBS # / Other Sources	Description
1. Introduction to Entrepreneurship	Icedelights (Roberts)	898196	Three college students decide to buy a company. The case focuses on their thoughts about an entrepreneurial career, their search process, and the evaluation of a business opportunity.
	Corporate Entrepreneurship for Dummies (Perkins & Thornberry)	BAB114	Chronicles the evolution of the "Dummies" series of books within IDG Books, offering insights into what it takes to foster an entrepreneurial culture in an established organization.
2. Recognizing Opportunities and Generating Ideas	Entrepreneurs at Twitter: Building a Brand, a Social Tool or a Tech Powerhouse (Mark)	910M28	Twitter has become an increasingly popular micro-blogging service, yet it remains unclear how Twitter will make money. The case focuses on the all-important distinction between a "bright idea" and a "business opportunity."
3. Feasibility Analysis	The Piercer (Sharen & Nolan)	908M57	Two students have developed an innovative product for an entrepreneurship class assignment. The case emphasizes how to use secondary research to investigate the merits of a business idea.
	PANELpro (Richard Ivey School of Business)	909A03	PANELPro is a startup company and presently a subcontract assembler of control panels. The case illustrates the differences between consumer and B2B marketing research.
4. Writing a Business Plan	Heather Evans (HBS Premier Case Collection)	384079	Focuses on the efforts of Heather Evans and her attempts to start her own dress business. Examines the business plan and the process of acquiring control over resources necessary to implement the plan.
	ZenG Business Plan (Applegate)	808146	This business plan enables students to decide whether to invite an entrepreneur to present to potential angel investors.
5. Industry and Competitor Analysis	LeapFrog Enterprises (Applegate & Collins)	808109	Explores the success factors leading to the company's rise to the number three ranking in the aggressively competitive toy industry.
	Howard Schultz and Starbucks Coffee Company	801361	Case examines how, in the midst of widespread competition and socioeconomic change, Schultz and his company influenced millions of consumers' tastes and came to lead the coffee industry.
6. Developing an Effective Business Model	Creating Successful Business Models: Lessons from Social Entrepreneurship (Elkington & Hartigan)	8028BC	The case explores several compelling examples of business models from the world of social and environmental enterprise.
	Zipcar: Refining the Business Model	803096	Provides students an understanding of the notion of a business model.
7. Preparing the Proper Ethical and Legal Foundation	Legal Aspects of Entrepreneurship: A Conceptual Framework (Bagley)	802161	An article. Identifies many of the legal issues likely to arise in the course of starting and growing a company.
	NanoGene Technologies, Inc. (Roberts & Cry)	803117	Describes a company during the start-up phase and focuses on the founders' decisions regarding splitting the equity and compensation.
8. Assessing a New Venture's Financial Strength and Viability	Caribbean Internet Café (Bryant & Theobalds)	99B02	An entrepreneur is hoping to open Caribbean Internet Café in Kingston, Jamaica. The case introduces a number of financial-planning related issues such as capital budgeting, contribution margin, and break-even analysis.

Chapter	Recommended Cases	HBS # / Other Sources	Description
	Dog Concierges, LLC: Transaction Analysis and Statement of Cash Flows Preparation	UV1770	An effective case for exploring the preparation of the three basic financial statements (balance sheet, income statement, and statement of cash flows).
9. Building a New-Venture Team	Taking the Plunge: New Luxury Ventures (Sarasvathy)	UV2014	Case explores the psychology of entrepreneurship as a young IBM executive decides whether to become an entrepreneur.
	Leigh Rawdon (Han, Gruenfeld, & Sweeney)	E389	Case provides students' a woman's life story and journey to entrepreneurship to study and evaluate, particularly around finding the right partner and taking a career leap.
10. Getting Financing or Funding	Amazon.com Going Public (Sherman & Katz)	899003	Amazon.com, an early pioneer in e-commerce, prepares its IPO in the face of turbulent market conditions.
	How Venture Capitalists Evaluate Potential Venture Opportunities (Roberts & Barley)	805019	Four venture capitalists from leading Silicon Valley firms are interviewed about the frameworks they use to evaluate potential venture opportunities.
11. Unique Marketing Issues	Clocky: The Runaway Alarm Clock (Ofek & Sherman)	507016	Clocky is an innovative alarm clock that, in addition to ringing, rolls around the room in order to force its owner to get out of bed. The challenge is how to position Clocky in its market.
	Nuway Software (Neufeld & Chandrasekhar)	909E05	The founder and president of Nuway Software must determine the pricing strategy for their new internally-developed software product.
	Homeless World Cup: Social Entrepreneurship, Cause Marketing, and Partnership With Nike (Foster, Hornblower, & O'Reilly)	E376	The case guides students through the many challenges that accompany building and marketing a social entrepreneurial venture.
12. The Importance of Intellectual Property	The Wright Brothers and Their Flying Machines	811034	To explore entrepreneurship in an emerging industry and the role of patents.
13. Preparing for and Evaluating the Challenges of Growth	Rubbish Boys (Wasserman & Galper)	808101	Introduces students to the challenges of growth for the company that became 1-800-GOT-JUNK?
	Swagruha Foods (Ramakrishna, Kaushik, Jhawar, Narasimhan, Pal, Sidhu, & Srivastava)	909M68	Highlights a firm that has successfully overcome the initial survival challenge and has a stable base of customers, but is unable to grow beyond a certain point.
14. Strategies for Firm Growth	Sirtis Pharmaceuticals: Living Healthier, Longer (Stuart & Kiron)	808112	Describes a set of growth-related issues confronting an early stage bio-pharmaceutical company. Should it establish alliances, add to its product line, enter into licensing agreements?
	International Expansion at Infusion (Williams & Davis)	W11026	Explores the nature of international expansion in a fast-growing professional services business.
15. Franchising	San Francisco Coffee House: An American Style Franchise in Croatia	908A13	Provides a practical example of when and how to use franchising.
	Marble Slab Creamery: A Grand Occasion	909A34	The franchise owner of a Marble Slab Creamery must submit a grand opening proposal to franchise headquarters. The proposal is to include the chosen target market, the franchise location, and decisions regarding product variety and pricing.